PHILOSOPHY
In Action

WAYNE SPROULE

D1065732

Fitzhenry & Whiteside

National Library of Canada Cataloguing in Publication
        Sproule, Wayne, 1944-
Philosophy in action / Wayne Sproule.
Includes bibliographical references and index.
ISBN 1-55041-109-8 (pbk.) ISBN 1-55041-841-6 Hardcover
        1. Philosophy--Introductions. I. Title.
BD31.S64 2002   100   C2002-903707-7

All inquires should be addressed to:
Fitzhenry & Whiteside Limited
195 Allstate Parkway,
Markham, Ontario L3R 4T8

In the United States:
311 Washington Street
Brighton, Massachusetts 02135

www.fitzhenry.ca   *godwit@fitzhenry.ca*

2 3 4 5 6 7 8 9 10

Fitzhenry & Whiteside acknowledges with thanks the Canada Council for the Arts, the Government of Canada through its Book Publishing Industry Development Program, and the Ontario Arts Council for their support in our publishing program.

Cover and Interior Design: Wycliffe Smith
Electronic page make-up: Wycliffe Smith Design Inc.

Printed and bound in Canada

CONTENTS

Unit 2 ETHICS

Unit 3 HUMAN NATURE

U n i t 5   POLITICAL AND SOCIAL PHILOSOPHY

KNOWING AND THINKING

The word "philosophy" conjures up various images for many people. One image in particular is of ancient Greeks, such as Socrates and Plato, who used discourse in an attempt to make sense of the world they lived in and the universe in general. The early philosophers asked questions no less different than the ones we ask today. What is the material world made of? How do we acquire knowledge? How can we be certain of what we know? Are some reasoning processes more reliable than others? What is the origin of the universe? How should we live our lives?

The early philosophers used logic and critical thinking to answer these questions. Both of these are forms of reasoning that still apply in our modern world. Scientists use reasoning to determine if their theories are correct; psychologists use reasoning when they make general predictions of behaviour based on detailed studies; detectives use reasoning to determine who is guilty when a crime is committed. Similarly, each of us, in one way or another, is a philosopher when we use reasoning to deal with situations and concerns in our daily lives.

Philosophy provides us with ways to look at and think through questions and problems. It also provides techniques for determining if the arguments that we or others present are faulty in reasoning. It is important to note that mathematics and science began as philosophy because the reasoning processes lay the groundwork for acquiring new knowledge.

In this unit, we will explore our understanding of knowledge and thinking. We will look at classical ideas, and then we will investigate several modern developments in the area of knowledge, particularly in science. Throughout this unit, we will apply logic and critical thinking to analyze contemporary issues.

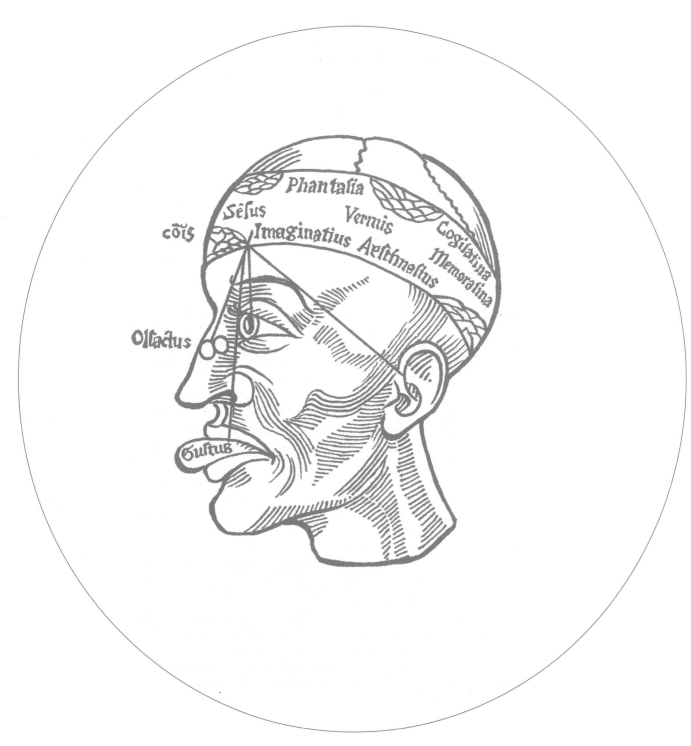

What is your perception of the reasoning process? Can you relate to the picture shown here?

Introducing Philosophy

We use the term "philosophy" in a number of ways. We may say we are being philosophical about a situation, or that we take a philosophic view of life. We may say that we are searching for the philosophic basis of a topic, or that some person is more philosophical than practical. In fact, each of these uses of the term describes some aspect of philosophy.

Philosophy is the use of reason and argument to search for truth and knowledge about reality. This can be the reality of human life and society or the reality of nature and the universe. The root of all philosophic inquiry lies in a question, a puzzle, or a riddle from which the inquirer proceeds to use thoughtful reflection and logical processes to investigate the truth. Although the inquirer will encounter and digest similar questions and solutions along the route of his or her quest, in the long run, the philosophic question can only be answered by the inquirer's own thoughtful reasoning.

Each of us thinks philosophically at some time in our lives. Most of us have wondered, as we stare at the night sky, what is the meaning of life or the origin of the universe. At crucial times in our lives, each of us may ask ourselves what decisions we should make or how we should live our lives. We ask ourselves why we are here or what the meaning of truth or justice might be. To the extent that we pursue such questions with thoughtful reasoning, and seek to find answers, we are practising philosophy.

Rodin's *The Thinker*

What separates philosophic inquiry from other types of investigation?

History of Philosophy and Its Various Branches

What do philosophers study? Put another way, how do we know when we are studying a philosophic topic? In general, a topic falls within the range of the philosopher's gaze when it requires thoughtful reasoning. Almost any topic, or area of study, is potentially open to philosophic inquiry, provided that thoughtful reasoning can be applied. In fact, some topics today lend themselves more than others to philosophic inquiry.

Topics for philosophic investigation can be found in everyday life, and are as wide as the imagination. Any aspect of one's life can be the subject for philosophic investigation. Any issue or problem can serve as the starting point. The important matter is that the inquirer is concerned about it, and that it is the type of question that can benefit from reasoning. Some areas of everyday life that could be topics for philosophic investigation are: education, family, business, work, play, sports, medicine, health, aging, happiness, friendship, law, ethics, punishment, rewards, social class, euthanasia, abortion, religion, death, war, technology, science, art, gender, hatred, and prejudice. These topics and many others are but starting points from which questions can be raised.

What Philosophers Study: Past and Present

There have always been philosophers in the sense that there have always been people who thought carefully about the universe and about the human condition. In ancient times, philosophic ideas and methods were usually passed from generation to generation by word of mouth, from teacher to student. Because these earliest thoughts and philosophies were oral rather than written, most of them have been lost over the centuries.

About three to four thousand years ago, ideas began to be recorded in writing by philosophers and students in the early civilizations of China, India, the Middle East, Africa, and the small city-states around the Mediterranean. Here especially, at the crossroads between three continents and many civilizations, a rich array of ideas came together from all over the known world, and were recorded. From this time, about 2500 years ago, philosophy as we know it developed.

Athens, the Greek city-state, was strategically located at the crossroads between the continents of Asia, Africa, and Europe. By

Ptolemy's ancient map of the Mediterranean and Middle East

Why was the Mediterranean an area of the world rich in ideas?

the fifth century BCE, Athens had developed a culture rich in ideas which encouraged thoughtful investigation of knowledge in many areas, including medicine, astronomy, civics, and philosophy. It was here that Western philosophy was to have its first known chapter.

In ancient Greek, the word "philosophy" meant "love of knowledge," and originally the word was used to describe the quest for knowledge. Philosophy began with the search for answers to puzzling questions in many areas of study. The people who investigated those questions were called philosophers. They studied such widely diverse topics as ethics, social organization, the sciences, and the nature of the universe. In fact, what we now call the natural sciences (physics, chemistry, and biology) were once known as "natural philosophy."

Time Line

Early Philosophers

SOCRATES
(469 BCE–399 BCE)
uses discourse as a
method of reasoning

PLATO
(428 BCE–347 BCE)

ARISTOTLE
(384 BCE–322 BCE)

Socrates

Master of Discourse and Reasoning

Socrates (469 BCE-399 BCE) was one of the earliest Athenian philosophers. The ideas he suggested and the way he lived his life as a philosopher remain important to us today. As a young man, Socrates spent time in the army, serving with bravery. He took his turn in government, as was expected of all Athenian citizens. He also studied the ideas of earlier thinkers in the sciences and in the study of the human condition. It was the human condition that fascinated him most.

Socrates spent a good deal of time in the public squares and meeting places of Athens, engaging his fellow citizens in discussions about human affairs and the question of how one should live life. Socrates' method was to ask apparently innocent questions that forced his companions to analyze their deepest beliefs and ideas. Those he spoke with often realized that they had not thought their ideas through carefully. Sometimes these people were important community leaders who were not very happy at being made to look foolish. Sometimes, Socrates' philosophic opponents were professional philosophers such as the Sophists, who argued any point of view that would earn them money.

Gradually, a small group of young thinkers became Socrates' students. He taught them how to investigate ideas and to apply reasoning to problems. Plato, one of these students, eventually became a major philosopher himself. In fact, it is primarily because of Plato that we know anything at all about Socrates, for as far as we know, Socrates never wrote down any of his own ideas. Socrates believed philosophy was to be discussed and argued verbally. Because of Plato, Socrates became a transitional figure between the old oral tradition of ideas and the developing written tradition.

As time passed and Socrates' influence grew, Athenian leaders grew increasingly annoyed at this "gadfly." They decided he had questioned established ideas for too long, and that he was a threat to their position and to the state. Socrates was charged with corrupting the youth of Athens with his ideas. He was put on trial, found guilty, and sentenced to death. Although the law of the time granted Socrates the right to go into exile if he would recant his ideas, Socrates refused to do so. Right up until the day of his execution, Socrates' friends were eager to help their teacher escape. In fact, Athenian authorities assumed he would do so. But Socrates insisted he had done nothing wrong and refused to compromise in this way.

"If you put me to death, you will not easily find anyone to take my place, God has specially appointed me to this city, as though it were a large thoroughbred horse which because of its great size, is inclined to be lazy and needs the stimulation of some stinging fly. It seems to me that God has attached me to this city to perform the office of such a fly, and all day long I never cease to settle here, there, and everywhere, rousing, persuading, reproving every one of you. You will not easily find another like me, gentlemen, and if you take my advice you will spare my life. I suspect, however, that before long you will awake from your drowsing, and in your annoyance you will take Anytus' advice and finish me off with a single slap, and then you will go on sleeping till the end of your days, unless God in his care for you sends someone to take my place....

"I tell you ... to let no day pass without discussing goodness and all the other subjects about which you hear me talking and examining both myself and others....[It] is really the very best thing that a man can do, and ... life without this sort of examination is not worth living."

[Plato, *Apology*. In *Plato: The Collected Dialogues*, trans. by Hugh Tredennick, ed. by Edith Hamilton and Huntington Cairns. New York: Pantheon Books, 1961.]

The authorities finally ordered Socrates' execution. He was given a cup of poisonous hemlock to drink. After spending time with his friends and students, Socrates drank the poison. While his colleagues wept all around him, Socrates faced death bravely. He took his belief that the "unexamined life was not worth living" to the grave, refusing to save himself by recanting. Socrates' ideas were more important to him than life itself. His ideas, the way he lived his life, and the manner of his death have become one of the great symbols of the philosophic quest.

Socrates considered the search for truth, and the willingness to live by truth, so important that he was willing to accept death rather than betray his principles. Are there ideas in the world today that are important enough for great effort and sacrifice?

For man, the unexamined life is not worth living.
          Socrates

Think wrongly, if you please, but in all cases think for yourself.
          Doris Lessing

**Subject Specialities
in Philosophy**
- - - - - - - - - -

PYTHAGORAS
(c. 571 BCE–500 BCE)
sets up a mystic
following for
mathematics

**ANTOINE-LAURENT
LAVOISIER**
(1743–1794)
founds chemistry
as separate from
alchemy

GREGOR MENDEL
(1822–1884)
experiments with
heredity before the
advent of genetics

ISAAC NEWTON
(1642–1727)
distinguishes physics
from natural
philosophy

Over time, however, the quest for knowledge was divided into areas of specialty. Some topics remained within the realm of philosophy while others moved into new disciplines. This divergence occurred because the knowledge available in any given subject area exploded to become more than one person could master. New methods of research and inquiry were also developed in each discipline. Up until the seventeenth century, it was possible for one person to master most of the existing knowledge at that time. One notable example was Leonardo da Vinci (1452–1519). He was an artist, a scientist, an inventor, and a student of anatomy, to name but a few of his areas of accomplishment.

Today, our collective knowledge has increased to the point where it is necessary for an individual to specialize in order to master a subject area. Some people study science, specializing in physics, chemistry, biology, zoology, aeronautics, math, or aspects of each of these. Others study human life and society, specializing in psychology, sociology, archeology, or anthropology. Still others study the arts, law, history, speech, or some other subject.

Philosophers have always investigated important questions that could not be readily answered by other methods. Today, philosophers continue their inquiries in

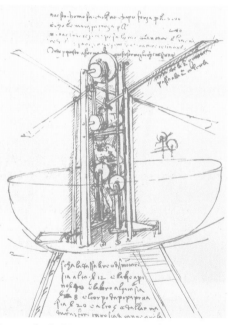

Leonardo da Vinci was very much a Renaissance man, dabbling in subjects as diverse as art and science. Among his great inventions were drawings for a flying machine.

those areas of learning where thoughtful reasoning and argument is important. They continue to study the nature of the universe and the place of human beings in it. They study how we live our lives as individuals, and how we interact with other human beings as a society. Philosophers study what is possible for us to know and to understand, and why. Observation alone cannot provide answers in such areas of investigation.

Philosophy is an important component of all subject areas. Each subject and every aspect of life contains philosophic questions to be asked and answered through reasoning. In law, for example, we can determine through observation how a society interacts with its criminals, but how do we determine what the concept of justice means, or what justice should be? In medicine, scientific analysis can identify the nature of disease, but how do we determine what attitudes and ethics a doctor should have towards the patient? There are philosophic questions in education, business, economics, and all other subject areas. Such questions call for thoughtful reasoning. Different people may arrive at different answers to such issues. How participants should pursue answers to these questions, and how they should act during the course of their pursuit, requires philosophic inquiry, thought, and argument.

Branches of Philosophy

Philosophers have fields of interest to which they channel most of their energies. Examples of these fields are the purpose and nature of the universe, ethics, social institutions, the nature of knowledge, the type of knowledge that we can have, the way we should live our lives, and the way we should treat others. Philosophy and philosophic reasoning help us determine the foundation or basic assumptions of different fields of study, and the best way to proceed when exploring a particular field.

Philosophy has several major branches or areas of specialization, each of which addresses unique and specific questions and concerns. The following brief descriptions provide a general overview of these major branches.

Logic

Logic is the study of effective reasoning and solid argument. Many rules of logic were developed centuries ago by Greek philosopher Aristotle. He was primarily responsible for developing the rules of logical deduction, the processes by which conclusions can be reached with certainty. More recently, inductive reasoning, how we reach probable conclusions, was incorporated into the study of logic. A third area called informal logic describes the thought processes we use in a number of areas of everyday life.

A knowledge of logic is valuable in many areas of life. Logic helps us determine the strength or weakness of an idea, an argument, or a proposed course of action. Logic becomes a valuable asset when someone, such as a salesperson or politician, is trying to convince us to believe or act in a certain way. A knowledge of logic can also help us make more effective arguments, or critically analyze problems we face.

Metaphysics

Metaphysics is the branch of philosophy which attempts to determine what exists, that is, the basic structure of reality. Philosophers of metaphysics ask such questions as: What is the material world made of? What causes things to occur? What brings about change? Is everything permanent? What is time and space? What is God?

From earliest times, philosophers have grappled with metaphysical questions. In ancient Greece, philosopher Thales suggested that water was the building block of the universe. Some of his contemporaries believed that all things were made of earth, air, or fire. Although we no longer accept many of these ideas, the curiosity and theories of those early metaphysical philosophers paved the way for others to investigate reality. Today, philosophers and scientists continue to search for the ultimate basis of reality.

What causes anything to occur? Why do some things happen while others do not? In modern times, causation became an important topic in metaphysics and in everyday life. Modern philosophers, like their ancient counterparts, grapple with the issue of whether we are free to make decisions, or whether our actions are determined by outside forces. They also strive to determine why people behave as they do and to what degree they are responsible for their own actions. Are criminals responsible for their actions, or are they shaped by early experiences beyond their control?

Questions about the nature of time and space are important in today's world.

What we need is not the will to believe but the wish to find out, which is exactly the opposite.
Bertrand Russell

Science is what you know, philosophy is what you don't know.
Bertrand Russell

Renowned physicist Stephen Hawking uses science to gain knowledge about the universe. Using theoretical physics as his methodology, Hawking tries to answer such questions as: Is the universe finite or infinite, Does it have a beginning, and How was it created?

Increasingly powerful telescopes peer into space and the distant past of the universe. Such scientific investigations raise new questions about what time and space are. Scientific philosophers such as Albert Einstein, Stephen Hawking, Carl Sagan, Freeman Dyson, and others have contributed to our thoughts and ideas on this topic.

What of the existence and nature of God? Are questions about God suitable for philosophic inquiry or can they be answered through faith alone? What is faith? How should we look at the existence of evil in the world if there is an all-powerful, all-knowing, and all-beneficial God? Is there more than one god? Should we regulate our lives in ways that a god or gods would wish?

Ethics

Ethics is the study of how we should live our lives and how we should treat other people. We use ethics in our search for rules of behaviour in specific situations, and to develop general rules by which to guide behaviour. Ethical questions have perplexed us since the beginning of civilization, when human beings began to live in groups.

Many theories have been developed to provide guidance to help us resolve ethical issues. Several early philosophers, including Socrates and Confucius, focussed their attention on how we should live our lives and treat others. Others have continued the search. Immanuel Kant, for example, believed that right action should be judged by good motives. John Stuart Mill believed that an action should be based on the greatest good for the greatest number of people.

Some philosophers believe it is possible to find universal ethical principles that all people should follow. Others believe that ethical rules and behaviour vary from one social group to another.

Ethics concerns us all because each of us must decide how to live our own life and how to treat others. Each of us has developed a philosophy of ethical behaviour which we constantly refine during the course of our lives.

Epistemology

Epistemology is the study of what it is possible to know, and how certain we can be of that knowledge. Epistemology is often considered the basis upon which other branches of philosophy are built because it is the bedrock which we use to determine what can be known and verified in any subject. Observation and logical reasoning are crucial in science; eyewitness reports and physical evidence are used in law; primary source documents are critical

Statue of Justice holding scales and sword.

This alone I know, that I know nothing.
Socrates

When a man knows he is to be hanged in a fortnight, it concentrates his mind wonderfully.
Samuel Johnson

How is information evaluated in a court of law?

for historical studies. Each subject has a philosophy of knowledge upon which it builds new information.

There are several major theories of what we can know, and how we can be most certain of our knowledge. Many philosophers of epistemology are in one of two major groups: rationalists, who believe in the power of the mind to develop knowledge; and empiricists, who rely upon information obtained through the senses. In modern times, the necessity for accurate scientific methods and critical analysis of the quality of scientific information has drawn both rationalists and empiricists to the study of knowledge.

Recent developments in computer tech-nology have increased the need for sound epistemological theories. Efforts to develop artificial intelligence, or AI, through "think-ing computers" has generated increased interest in epistemology, as scientists wonder if it is possible to build a computer that thinks like a human being.

In our own personal lives, we are con-stantly determining better ways to acquire information and to judge its validity. Under-standing how philosophers have studied knowledge can help us to develop our own theories of knowledge and increase our insight into the workings of our own minds, allowing us to think more effectively and make better decisions.

Social and Political Philosophy

Social and political philosophy is the study of the fundamental principles of society and of the state. This branch of philosophy searches for the best forms of society and government. Plato's ideal society, which he described in *The Republic*, is one governed by kings who thought like philosophers.

Social and political philosophers are interested in justice, that is, in how valued goods and services should be distributed to people, and in how wrongdoers should be treated. Greek philosopher Socrates spent his life determining the best forms of social justice, and was executed for his trouble.

Today, political and social philosophies

Political philosophy is interested in such questions as: How much authority should the state possess? How much freedom should individuals have?

cover a very broad range of topics. Political philosophers analyze how democratic and other forms of government function and how they might be improved. Social philosophers study many aspects of society, from family life to economics, and discuss how each should function. Feminist philosophers study the changing social roles of women and men.

Philosophy of the Arts, Sciences, and other Disciplines

Some philosophers study a specific subject or academic discipline such as the arts, sciences, history, law, education, or economics. In each case, philosophers explore the basic principles and goals upon which the discipline is based. They provide insight into the inquiry process in that field, the conclusions that are drawn, and alternative ways to consider the subject.

For example, there are various views of what constitutes a good education. Some people believe that the primary purpose of education is to prepare young people for the working world. Others believe that education should provide a broad base of knowledge, increase understanding of one's culture, and improve the ability to think and to make decisions. Philosophy provides methods by which such issues can be investigated.

Scientists and people in the arts ask similar questions. However, the method of inquiry that scientists use differs from that used in the arts.

Understand Concepts

1. Describe the difference between each pair of items.
   (a) a philosophic and a non-philosophic question
   (b) a philosophic and a non-philosophic topic
2. (a) How has the scope of philosophy changed over time?
   (b) In what ways does philosophy continue to be involved in our modern-day lives?
3. (a) Define the major branches of philosophy.
   (b) For each branch in part (a), identify two central questions.

Apply and Develop

4. Why is the death of Socrates considered to be significant in the history of ideas?
5. Philosophic reflection begins with philosophic questions. From the list below, determine those questions you believe would benefit from philosophic reflection and those that can be dealt with primarily through observation. In some cases, both observation and reflection may be needed.
   (a) What colour is grass?
   (b) Does everyone perceive colours in the same way?
   (c) Does God exist?
   (d) Should life imprisonment be the penalty for murder?
   (e) What is the penalty for theft?
   (f) Are people primarily generous or selfish?
   (g) What is the best way to live your life?
   (h) Will people work harder for fame or fortune?
   (i) Should you seek fame or fortune in life?
   (j) When is it acceptable to break rules?
   (k) Should you help the homeless whenever possible?
   (l) How many homeless are there in Canada today?
6. What branch of philosophy deals with each of the questions below? Explain your choice.
   (a) Does God exist?
   (b) If you perform this experiment, what conclusions will you be able to draw?
   (c) Which political party should you vote for in the next election?
   (d) Even though that is a pretty picture, is it really a work of art?
   (e) Should you lie to your best friend in order to make that friend happy?
   (f) Is it possible to really know what someone else is thinking?
   (g) Can you hold someone responsible for committing a crime, if that person had a deprived childhood and terrible life experiences?

Communicate Ideas

7. Comment on the reasons Socrates gave for accepting his death sentence. Do you agree with his reasons and with his decision?

The Process of Philosophic Inquiry

We think philosophically in everyday life, although we may not always be aware of doing so. We must choose how to act, and what paths we wish to take in life. Perhaps we must choose what courses we will take next semester, or even what school to attend. Filling in course codes and sending in applications are practical matters that we learn through demonstration, example, and practice. However, deciding which courses to take and which subjects will benefit us raises philosophic questions. We must know ourselves, determine what provides us with satisfaction, and know where we want to be in ten or twenty years. To answer those questions, we must use reasoning and think philosophically.

The same philosophic inquiry applies in many social situations. Often, we must understand and judge the words and actions of others in order to develop our own opinions. We may hear a speaker on a TV talk show express strong views on an important social issue, such as euthanasia or capital punishment. We may hear a political candidate present an argument urging support for his or her party in the next election. How do we understand and judge such positions and arguments? How do we make up our own minds on these issues? In order to formulate our own views and make our own decisions, we must judge the strength of the positions being put forward and the arguments that are made. We must determine what is important to us in life, and the type of society in which we want to live. These are philosophic issues that require philosophic inquiry.

Who practises philosophic inquiry? Certainly, professional philosophers do. These scholars are often found in universities, where they read, write, and teach philosophy. Other people trained in philosophic methods use their skills in their occupations, such as journalism, law, politics, and religion. People practising philosophy can be identified not only by the topics they study, but also by the methods they use to investigate questions. They search for truth using reflective thought, and can defend their conclusions using logical argument.

Philosophic inquiry involves several key components: asking questions, gathering information, reasoning, forming a conclusion, and defending a conclusion. These steps can be applied to all philosophic investigations whether we are asking what career we want to pursue or how poverty affects society.

> Knowledge is a process of piling up facts; wisdom lies in their simplification.
> *Martin H. Fisher*

> Wisdom and power follow endurance and patience.
> *Mohammed*

Asking Questions

All philosophic inquiry begins with a question, the goal of which is to determine truth and knowledge. Without the guiding parameters of the question, philosophic inquiry remains purposeless and wanders aimlessly. The question does not need to be profound, or even important to other people. However, it should be meaningful and arouse curiosity in the inquirer. We can ask philosophic questions about any topic or aspect of reality: human life, social circumstances, nature, or the universe.

QUESTIONS ARE THE BEGINNING

What types of questions are asked in philosophic investigations in everyday life? It is important to stress that philosophic questions can be asked on almost any topic. The following list may help you think in a philosophic mode.

- What is the situation or condition you are observing or thinking about?
- How do you and others think about the situation or condition?
- Why is the situation or condition the way it is?
- What problems, issues, or decisions arise from the situation or condition?
- Are there better ways to perform the activity, or to think about it?
- Why is the situation or condition significant for you and for others?

What is the situation … ?

Philosophy, like the other social and physical sciences, asks what something is. The difference is that philosophers often try to bring a new perspective to their investigation, or to find an underlying reality about it, which may not have been noticed before. When the philosopher describes what something is, he or she is trying to do more than make an observation, although that is obviously a starting point. In addition to observing a situation with new and keen eyes, which will discern what may not have been noticed before, a philosopher also attempts to compare and contrast the situation with something else.

How do you and others think about the situation … ?

Philosophers often want to know how people view a specific situation or condition. What do they see? What do they think about it? Why? What do we think about our friends, our family, or another group important to us? How do we view them?

Why is the situation the way it is … ?

Sometimes philosophers examine how a social or personal situation occurred historically. They investigate underlying reasons, such as human motives or even human nature, which may have precipitated the condition under study. For example, why do we believe that children should go to school until they are at least sixteen? Where did this idea come from? Are there other methods of education that might apply? Philosophers seek alternate points of view and actions for any given situation.

What problems, issues, or decisions arise … ?

A common starting point for philosophic investigation occurs when a controversial problem or issue arises in our society or in our personal lives. People disagree over what should be done, and have difficulty in reaching a consensus. Philosophers are trained to investigate issues or problems by using reason and logic to analyze specific situations, and to investigate possible solutions.

Are there better ways … ?

Philosophers are not restricted to describing and explaining the world. They also explore more productive methods of living in the world. Throughout history, thinkers like Plato and Confucius have examined the societies around them and proposed alternatives. How does this process differ from daydreaming and imagining? Philosophy can incorporate both these processes, but the essence of philosophic alternatives, or utopias, is that they are based on a clear understanding of an existing situation and that they provide convincing reasons for an alternative.

Why is the situation significant … ?

We often accept ideas or make assumptions without really thinking about them. Philosophers are trained to point out to us why some ideas or assumptions are important, for either good or bad reasons. Feminist philosophers, for example, have showed us the unconscious assumptions that guide our views of how men and women live their lives and how these assumptions shape who we are.

Gathering Information

Before we can answer a question, we need to gather information and ideas about the topic. The first source of information is our own experience, examining our own thoughts about the subject and the question. A second source is our observation of the situation with a clear and steady gaze. What does it look like? How do people act and think? What do those people involved in that life situation have to say? A third source is comments from people who have already investigated the problem or situation. These people may be philosophers, observers, or thinkers concerned with the topic.

Reasoning

Once information about a philosophic inquiry has been collected, it must be organized, analyzed, and judged. What information seems to make most sense and seems to be most convincing? What points of view are presented and with what reasons? With which ideas do you tend to agree? Understanding what others have said or written about an issue or topic is a key element of practising philosophic inquiry. When you read or listen to a philosophic point of view or argument, it is necessary to understand and analyze as fully as possible what the argument is, and why it is

being made. It is important to analyze the argument critically. What are its strengths and weaknesses? What arguments have been left out? What rebuttals could be made against the argument being presented?

Philosophic inquiry relies heavily on the use of reflection and reasoning. What does this mean? Philosophic questions are not investigated solely through observation, although careful observation is often an essential element. Investigation requires reasoning, which is the logical progression of thought processes that move the inquirer from one idea to another.

Reasoning is different from other types of thinking we know about, such as daydreaming or random thought processes. Reasoning requires that evidence, or reasons, be used to support ideas. These reasons may be based on observation or on important values, but reasons *must* be given.

Using this approach allows us to practise philosophic inquiry, rather than simply learn about it. As you study philosophy further by reading this book, by taking courses, or by dealing with important questions in your life, you can practise philosophic inquiry by analyzing the ideas of others with a critical eye, formulating your response to those points of view by using your own.

Analyzing and judging information are important steps when undertaking a philosophic inquiry.

Forming A Conclusion

The end of a philosophic investigation is to determine your own point of view or conclusion. These may be firm and convincing or less so. It is very important that you know and understand the reasons that support your position. Just because someone else, such as a famous philosopher, said something does not mean that you should accept it. Reasons must be critically analyzed, and should be accepted or rejected based on their own merits.

Defending A Conclusion

At some point, you may be required to express your point of view, and the reasons that support it. For example, you may do this orally in a discussion, presentation, or debate. You may communicate your conclusion in a paper. In either case, the essence of philosophic explanation is to state a point of view or conclusion clearly, and give the reasons that support it as strongly and logically as possible.

All education is
self-discovery.
Ray Bradbury

Practising Philosophic Inquiry in Everyday Life

Philosophic inquiry is not restricted to professionals, although we can learn much from them. Philosophy is, in many ways, a part of our everyday lives. Imagine walking down the street and finding a wallet lying on the ground. The wallet contains a name, an address, and money. While you know you should return the wallet to its owner, your own finances are pretty lean. How do you decide what to do? Perhaps you consider what you have been taught by society, your family, friends, or religion. Maybe you think about how the other person must feel, having lost the wallet. Maybe you think about your own needs and those of your family. Finally, after mulling over these various points of view, you make a decision based on the reasons that seem most important to you. *Et voilà!* You have just worked through a problem in ethical philosophy. You have made a personal decision based on reasoning.

We also practise philosophy when we consider the public and social matters that confront us daily. You may be discussing a social issue, the problem of the homeless perhaps, with your peers. Someone suggests that everyone, rich or poor, secure or homeless, is responsible for himself or herself. You argue that not everyone begins with equal life opportunities, so those who are more fortunate have a responsibility to help the less fortunate. Such discussions usually involve several points of view, each supported by reasons and arguments. Several courses of action are usually suggested. Discussions like this deal with several branches of philosophy, as people try to determine what is human nature and what type of society we want to live in.

We usually practise philosophic inquiry in our professional lives, in our chosen fields of work. Among other things, this includes what we believe our work involves, what its purpose is, and how that purpose can best be achieved. Sometimes we acquire these points of view, this philosophy or work ethic, from our co-workers. We also develop and expand our own philosophies as we continue to work in the field. Suppose you have decided to enter the teaching profession. At the faculty of education where you acquire

For there was never
yet philosopher
That could endure
the toothache
patiently.
*Shakespeare,
"Much Ado About
Nothing"*

your teacher training, you will hear how others view the profession. As you consider these views for yourself, and as you begin to teach, you will probably refine or change these accepted views. As you remain in the teaching profession over time, your personal philosophy may continue to change based on your experiences. You are developing your own philosophy of teaching, one which suits your values and life goals and fits with your ideas of children, society, and education. You probably will defend your point of view with reasons and arguments.

Does that mean that all people approach life with a philosophy? Does it mean that we deal with every aspect of our own lives philosophically? The answer to both questions is no. There are some ideas that are accepted without thinking or because others believe them to be true. Although some of our points of view are formed philosophically, many of our opinions are developed in other ways. The philosopher believes that the thoughtful, reasoned approach is usually superior.

Understand Concepts

1. What are the major aspects of philosophic inquiry?
2. Who practises philosophy and for what purposes?

Apply and Develop

3. Develop philosophic and non-philosophic ways to deal with each of the situations below.
   (a) buying a CD you have been thinking about
   (b) taking a philosophy course next year in college or university
   (c) telling your parents that you want to do something, such as accepting a part-time job, of which they may disapprove
   (d) cheating on a test or copying someone's essay
4. Choose one aspect of your own life where philosophic inquiry would be useful. Explain how you might proceed.
5. Consider a situation or condition of importance to you in your own life, for example, your family, school, possible careers, or a social problem. Apply the generic philosophic questions to one of these important areas of your life, developing specific questions for consideration. This is the beginning of developing a philosophic inquiry of importance to you personally.

Think Critically

6. Describe your perception of the philosophic process at this point in your studies. How does this differ from your ideas of philosophy before you began your studies in the discipline? Discuss your answers with a classmate and with the whole class.

Communicate Ideas

7. Debate this issue: "The unexamined life is not worth living." (Socrates)
8. Interview a friend or family member about his or her philosophy of life, ethical philosophy, philosophy of family, philosophy of education, and philosophy of work in a particular occupation. Use the questions presented in this section to guide your interview. Write a summary of your interview in three to four pages.

The Value of Philosophy

Why should we study philosophy? There are many good ways to spend our time and efforts. We could be studying economics, cooking, mathematics, or science. We could be watching TV or hanging out with our friends. These are all good things to do on occasion. There are, however, a number of good reasons to spend some of our time studying philosophy.

Philosophy provides an opportunity to study interesting and important topics that cannot be studied readily elsewhere. Philosophy encourages us to explore the nature of the universe and of reality. It provides a procedure through which we can understand things and with which we can question how we might live life. Philosophy can provide us with insights into how we should live within our society, and why we make the choices we do in our social environment. Philosophy is an invitation to study topics that are important to human existence.

Digital Art, *Thinking Ahead*

For most people, philosophy becomes the opportunity to think about a facet of life that is personally rewarding or intriguing. People interested in sports, woodworking, or drama may want to read about and ponder the philosophy of sport, carpentry, or theatre. They may want to understand the goals, the basic principles, or even the differing opinions about their particular fields of interest. All subject areas and all aspects of life are based on some philosophic points of view. Involvement in one particular field or aspect of life leads most people to ponder the philosophic groundwork—the goals, principles, and assumptions—that supports it.

Will the study of philosophy help us to earn a living? In some cases, yes! You may choose to continue your study of philosophy, and make it your life's work. Philosophy can be a genuine wage-earning profession. Professors of philosophy earn a living by writing and teaching. In other cases, the study of philosophy provides insight into other work that we do. It will provide us with a larger perspective of the field to which we choose to devote our energies. Philosophy can help us think and make decisions more rationally and effectively. Studying the philosophy of science broadens the vision of the scientist. Studying the philosophy of law, or of medicine is necessary for the lawyer or the doctor.

Developing Thinking Skills and Attitudes

Philosophy teaches us the processes and procedures for thinking about problems and issues. Philosophy provides us with methods to ask questions, develop and test ideas, and make decisions. Philosophy outlines rules for judging the validity of the conclusions we draw. It suggests ways we can apply ideas and methods to understand new problems and situations. Philosophy provides experience and practice in thoughtful reflection, in creating and supporting ideas, and in analyzing the ideas of others.

Studying philosophy can help us make better decisions in our everyday lives. When we use logic and social or political philosophical principles we can become very effective at investigating questions that are important to us. We learn how to use information to form sound conclusions in many facets of our lives. Philosophy brings a practical value to most people in their everyday thoughts and actions.

Philosophy teaches us useful and valuable attitudes towards knowledge. It helps us question ideas and actions rather than accept, without critical analysis, what has been thought or done. A philosophic attitude may encourage us to question our own stereotyped views, or views that we may hold without good reason. Such questioning can lead to new ideas and procedures that are sometimes an improvement over old traditions. Philosophic attitudes can lead us to develop creative new approaches to challenges. They teach us to have a more open mind to the ideas of others, and to reserve judgement until we have carefully digested the new ideas and concepts presented to us.

[Calvin and Hobbes. Copyright 1993 Watterson. Reprinted with permission. All rights reserved. Dist. by Universal Press Syndicate.]

The Value of Philosophy

Bertrand Russell

Doubt is not a very
agreeable state,
but certainty is a
ridiculous one.
Voltaire

It will be well to consider … the value of philosophy and why it ought to be studied…. [M]any men, under the influence of science or of practical affairs, are inclined to doubt whether philosophy is anything better than innocent but useless trifling, hair-splitting distinctions, and controversies on matters concerning which knowledge is impossible.

This view of philosophy appears to result, partly from a wrong conception of the ends of life, partly from a wrong conception of the kind of goods which philosophy strives to achieve. Physical science, through the medium of inventions, is useful to innumerable people who are wholly ignorant of it…. This utility does not belong to philosophy. If the study of philosophy has any value at all for others than students of philosophy, it must be only indirectly, through its effects upon the lives of those who study it….

But … to determine the value of philosophy, we must first free our minds from the prejudices of what are wrongly called "practical" men. The "practical" man, as this word is often used, is one who recognizes only material needs, who realizes that men must have food for the body, but is oblivious of the necessity of providing food for the mind. If all men were well off, if poverty and disease had been reduced to their lowest possible point, there would still remain much to be done to produce a valuable society; and even in the existing world, the goods of the mind are at least as important as the goods of the body. It is exclusively among the goods of the mind that the value of philosophy is to be found….

Philosophy, like all other studies, aims primarily at knowledge. The knowledge it aims at is the kind of knowledge which gives unity and system to the body of the sciences, and the kind which results from a critical examination of the grounds of our convictions, prejudices, and beliefs. But it cannot be maintained that philosophy has had any very great measure of success in its attempts to provide definite answers to its questions…. It is true that this is partly accounted for by the fact that, as soon as definite knowledge concerning any subject becomes possible, this subject ceases to be called philosophy, and becomes a separate science. The whole study of the heavens, which now belongs to astronomy, was once included in philosophy; Newton's great work was called "the mathematical principles of natural philosophy." Similarly, the study of the human mind, which was, until very lately, a part of philosophy, has now been separated from philosophy and has become the science of psychology. Thus, to a great extent, the uncertainty of philosophy is more apparent than real: those questions which are already capable of definite answers are placed in the sciences, while those only to which, at present, no definite answer can be given, remain to form the residue which is called philosophy.

Profundity of thought
belongs to youth,
clarity of thought
to old age.
Friedrich Nietzsche

This is, however, only a part of the truth concerning the uncertainty of philosophy. There are many questions … of the profoundest interest to our spiritual life—which, so far as we can see, must remain insoluble to the human intellect unless its powers become of quite a different order from what they are now. Has the universe any unity of plan or purpose … ? Is consciousness a permanent part of the universe, giving hope of indefinite growth in wisdom, or is it a transitory accident on a small planet on which life must ultimately become impossible? Are good and evil of importance to the universe or only to man? Such questions are asked by philosophy, and variously answered by various philosophers…. [T]he answers suggested by philosophy are none of them demonstrably true. Yet, however slight may be the hope of discovering an answer, it is part of the business of philosophy to continue the consideration of such questions, to make us aware of their importance, to examine all the approaches to them, and to keep alive that speculative interest in the universe which is apt to be killed by confining ourselves to definitely ascertainable knowledge….

The value of philosophy is, in fact, to be sought largely in its very uncertainty. The man who has no tincture of philosophy goes through life imprisoned in the prejudices derived from common sense, from the habitual beliefs of his age or his nation, and from convictions which have grown up in his mind without the cooperation or consent of his deliberate reason. To such a man the world tends to become definite, finite, obvious; common objects rouse no questions, and unfamiliar possibilities are contemptuously rejected. As soon as we begin to philosophize, on the contrary, we find … that even the most everyday things lead to problems to which only very incomplete answers can be given. Philosophy, though unable to tell us with certainty what is the true answer to the

PEANUTS® Charles M. Schulz

[Copyright 1965 by United Features Syndicate Inc. Reprinted with permission.]

doubts which it raises, is able to suggest many possibilities which enlarge our thoughts and free them from the tyranny of custom. Thus, while diminishing our feeling of certainty as to what things are, it greatly increases our knowledge as to what they may be … and it keeps alive our sense of wonder by showing familiar things in an unfamiliar aspect.

Apart from its utility in showing unsuspected possibilities, philosophy has a value … through the greatness of the objects which it contemplates, and the freedom from narrow and personal aims resulting from this contemplation. The life of the instinctive man is shut up within the circle of his private interests…. The private world of instinctive interests is a small one, set in the midst of a great and powerful world which must, sooner or later, lay our private world in ruins. Unless we can so enlarge our interests as to include the whole outer world, we remain like a garrison in a beleaguered fortress, knowing that the enemy prevents escape and that ultimate surrender is inevitable. In such a life there is no peace, but a constant strife between the insistence of desire and the powerlessness of will. In one way or another, if our life is to be great and free, we must escape this prison and this strife.

One way of escape is by philosophic contemplation. Philosophic contemplation does not, in its widest survey, divide the universe into two hostile camps—friends and foes, helpful and hostile, good and bad—it views the whole impartially....

The true philosophic contemplation ... finds its satisfaction in every enlargement of the not-Self, in everything that magnifies the objects contemplated, and thereby the subject contemplating ... The free intellect will see as God might see, with a here and now, without hopes and fears, without the trammels of customary beliefs and traditional prejudices, calmly, dispassionately, in the sole and exclusive desire of knowledge....

The mind which has become accustomed to the freedom and impartiality of philosophic contemplation will preserve something of the same freedom and impartiality in the world of action and emotion. It will view its purposes and desires as parts of the whole.... Thus contemplation enlarges not only the objects of our thoughts, but also the objects of our actions and our affections: it makes us citizens of the universe, not only of one walled city at war with all the rest. In this citizenship of the universe consists man's true freedom, and his liberation from ... narrow hopes and fears.

Thus, to sum up our discussion of the value of philosophy: Philosophy is to be studied, not for the sake of any definite answers to its questions, since no definite answers can, as a rule, be known to be true, but rather for the sake of the questions themselves, because these questions enlarge our conception of what is possible, enrich our intellectual imagination, and diminish the dogmatic assurance which closes the mind against speculation; but above all because, through the greatness of the universe which philosophy contemplates, the mind is rendered great, and becomes capable of that union with the universe which constitutes its highest good.

[Bertrand Russell, *The Problems of Philosophy* (1912). Oxford: Oxford University Press, 1969, 153–61.]

IDEAS AND ISSUES

Understand Concepts

1. What are some of the reasons that are given for studying philosophy?
2. Provide arguments that you could make against these reasons.

Apply and Develop

3. Identify the major question raised in Russell's essay.
4. Describe a situation in your life where philosophy can be useful.

Communicate Ideas

5. In one to two pages, present the position or point of view identified by Russell.
6. What are the major arguments made in support of Russell's position?
7. Discuss arguments that oppose one or more of Russell's with your classmates. How convincing are your arguments to the other students?

Review and Reflect

Philosophy began as the study of all things through the use of reason. Philosophic investigation can be applied to all aspects of everyday life, and it attempts to search for truth through the use of reflective thought. The process of philosophic inquiry involves a process of asking questions, gathering information, reasoning, forming a conclusion, and defending it with sound reasons.

Today, philosophy has specific areas of study. The major branches include logic; metaphysics; ethics; epistemology; social and political philosophy; and the philosophy of the arts, sciences, and other disciplines.

The value in philosophy lies in its methods: the use of reason to investigate important issues and problems, and the acquisition of new knowledge and answers, as a result. It allows us to broaden our scope of thought by making us question attitudes and ideas that we may have previously accepted as our own without critical analysis. Many philosophers, such as Socrates, felt that their work was so important that they risked all for its sake.

Formal Logic and Critical Thinking

Humans are the only creatures on Earth that can reflect and reason. No other organism on our planet has this capability, although the possibility exists that other organisms in the universe unknown to us do. Every day we find ourselves in situations where people have opposing points of view and must apply reasoning to determine which argument is most logical. Although one person may present a very convincing argument about a particular subject, we must analyze that point of view carefully, using a well-defined process.

Logic is the study of how we reason. Understanding the reasoning process is important not only in philosophy, but in most areas of life. For example, sometimes we know there is something wrong with an idea that is being presented but are not sure why. Other times, we may sense a fallacy in an argument or thought process, but cannot pinpoint what it is. Forceful and persuasive communication of ideas to others, either verbally or through the use of the written word, requires the application of logic, because logic helps us identify problems, weaknesses, and pitfalls in our reasoning. Applying logic enables us to make clear and powerful arguments.

There are two major categories of logic: formal and informal. Formal logic is the study of those principles that differentiate correct or good reasoning from incorrect or bad reasoning. Formal logic studies how arguments are made and the strength of conclusions based on reasons. Informal logic, also known as critical thinking, focusses on reasoning used in everyday life, such as in social situations, and in the workplace. It also includes judging the reasons that salespeople or politicians present to us. Informal logic or critical thinking encompasses formal logic but also includes rhetoric, the use of emotional and other non-logical techniques to convince and persuade others.

Detectives use formal logic to investigate crime. This involves both deductive and inductive reasoning.

The Building Blocks of Formal Logic

When we reason, several processes take place in a very specific order. Suppose a political candidate is presenting a case that supports funding for affordable housing projects. You will likely hear that candidate present reasons to justify his or her position on that issue. Those reasons will then allow you to make an inference. You will in turn form a conclusion based on the reasons presented. In the study of logic, the processes that you use to form your conclusion are important. These processes include reasoning, argument, and inference.

Reasoning

We use several different types of thought processes every day. We imagine, hope, remember, plan, and decide. Reasoning, a specific type of thinking, is another one of these processes and is central to philosophy, logic, and daily life. In simple terms, reasoning means the process of providing reasons in support of an idea or an action.

We give reasons in almost every aspect of our lives. Sometimes these reasons are sound, sometimes not; sometimes our reasons are convincing, sometimes not. We expect other people to give reasons for their ideas and interactions with us. They in turn expect that we will provide reasons for why we do what we do. A reason is a statement or action that justifies or supports a belief or action. For example, perhaps you missed philosophy class yesterday. When you enter the classroom today your teacher asks, "Well?" You answer, "I was away yesterday." The teacher responds, "I know that, but I want to know the reason." Later in the day,

Understanding how to reason helps us make sense of world events.

you may fill out a university application form. One question asks, "Why do you want to attend this university?" You know it is important to provide a convincing answer, for your future may depend on the reason you give. Reasons are asked for and given all the time. To the child who asks why he should eat his carrots, the parent provides a reason by saying that they are good for him. To the employee who asks why she should go to work today, the employer provides a reason saying that she wants to get paid. Reasoning takes place in most life situations.

Reasoning is extremely important in philosophy because it is the primary method by which philosophers support their ideas. One of the most important aspects of philosophy is understanding and judging the validity of reasons provided for ideas. As you continue to study philosophy, you will find yourself giving and judging reasons consistently. As you live your life outside the classroom, you may find yourself becoming more aware of the validity of reasons given for ideas and actions.

Argument

We often use the word argument to refer to a disagreement between people. However, argument has another meaning. In philosophy, an argument is the use of one or more reasons to support an idea or action. A lawyer may present an argument in support of a client; a political leader may argue in support of government policy. You may use an argument when you try to convince your parents that you should have the car on Saturday night. Your friends may use an argument to persuade you to go out with them to a show.

Consider these statements: "Darn, I just missed the bus. There won't be another one for 20 minutes. I'm going to be late for school." In this case, the first two sentences are reasons, or premises. The third sentence is a conclusion. Both the premises and the conclusion are statements, or propositions. In many arguments, especially those that occur in everyday discussion, a conclusion does not necessarily follow the reasons or premises. For example, consider these statements: "I don't think I will mow the lawn today. For one thing the grass is wet. Also, it isn't really that tall." In this case, the conclusion, the action to be taken, is the first sentence.

How can we identify premises and conclusions? First, we must determine which statement is supported by other statements. That statement is the conclusion. A conclusion may be a general idea or an action and is based on premises or reasons. Sometimes specific words such as "so," "therefore," or "consequently" indicate that a sentence is a conclusion. There are other words, such as "since" and "because," that indicate reasons or premises. Since such indicators are not always present, we may have to insert them mentally. For example, consider these statements: "Kevin cannot run in the cross-country race. He has not been training regularly. He has a pulled muscle as well." Which are the premises and which is the conclusion? If you are having trouble deciding, rearrange the statements like this: "Since Kevin has not been training regularly, and since he has a pulled muscle, therefore he cannot run in the cross-country race."

Arguments are used for several purposes. Sometimes they determine the truth about something. For example, we may present an argument that life could exist on Mars. Sometimes arguments are used to convince us that something is good or valuable, rather than bad or of little value.

We might, for example, present an argument to say that Canada is the best country to live in. Sometimes arguments are provided in recommendation of a policy or course of action. For example, we may argue that Canadians should give more aid to poorer nations than we already do.

Inference

Inferring is the mental process that occurs when we move from premises or reasons to a conclusion. Inferring, in fact, is the process of using existing information to develop new information. Consider the statement: If I drink that hot coffee quickly, I will probably burn my mouth. Based on past experience, the inference that you will burn your mouth seems reasonable. Here is another example: I studied for the last philosophy test and received an 'A.' So if I study for the next test, I will probably get a good grade. Again, based on existing infor-mation, the consequences of the last test, you infer new information about a future test. Here is one more inference of a slightly different nature: I am either in this room, or I am somewhere else. I am not somewhere else, so I must be in this room. It seems pretty clear that "I must be in this room" can be inferred from the information given.

You may notice from the previous examples that an inference can sometimes lead to certain conclusions, and sometimes to probable conclusions. Having studied for the last test and receiving an 'A' does not guarantee the same outcome for the next test. However, in the case of whether you are in this room or somewhere else, there is little doubt and a lot of certainty. Some conclusions and the inferences they involve bring certainty; others bring mere probability. This difference is important when we examine the two types of reasoning, deductive and inductive, in the next two sections.

[Calvin and Hobbes. Copyright 1991 Universal Press Syndicate. Reprinted with permission.]

Understand Concepts

1. Define and explain briefly the meanings of each of these terms: logic, reasoning, argument, and inference.

Apply and Develop

2. Reasoning is not merely thinking of one thing after another. Reasoning depends on one statement being supported by another. For each sentence below, determine which statement is an example of reasoning and which is not.
   (a) I enjoy the weekends and I spend time with my friends.
   (b) On the weekends I spend time with my friends because I have more free time.
   (c) Philosophy teaches logical thinking; it is also a way to learn to analyze arguments.
   (d) Logical thinking in philosophy helps us think critically.

3. In each of the arguments below, determine which propositions are premises and which are conclusions. You may want to place the words "since" and "therefore" in front of each sentence.
   (a) Sabina must have left home already. She doesn't answer the phone. I know she was intending to leave early for school.
   (b) Success in my philosophy course requires that homework be done regularly. I have completed every homework assignment. I should get a good mark.
   (c) All human beings have rights. Children are human beings. Children have rights.
   (d) Fewer people smoke cigarettes now. Anti-smoking campaigns have convinced people that smoking is unhealthy. Warnings on cigarette packages have influenced smoking trends. Smoking is no longer considered to be as cool as it used to be.

4. What is the purpose of each argument in exercise 3?

5. Does each statement below illustrate an argument? Justify your answers.
   (a) Alana has no money and she is unhappy.
   (b) Jacob has no money, therefore he is unhappy.
   (c) This triangle has equal sides and equal angles.
   (d) This triangle has equal sides; hence it has equal angles.

6. Choose the premises and the conclusion in each argument below. Give reasons for your choices.
   (a) Jim has no stamina. He ought to exercise more often. He does not have as much energy as he should.
   (b) Mario must have left home already. He doesn't answer the phone. I know he was intending to go downtown.
   (c) There are more homeless people in major Canadian cities than ever before. Many of these people suffer from a mental illness. Others may be alcoholic or dependent on drugs. In some cases, these people have lost their jobs and find themselves unable to pay rent. In any case, more should be done to help them find a place to stay. In a climate such as Canada's, being homeless is a life-threatening condition.

Deductive Reasoning

We divide arguments and the reasoning they involve into two major categories: deduction and induction. Both these forms of reasoning and argument are important in philosophy. Both forms contain premises and conclusions. However, there are significant differences between them. In this section, we will consider deduction or deductive reasoning, and in the next we will examine induction or inductive reasoning.

In deductive reasoning, if the premises are accepted, the conclusion is logically guaranteed. Here is a classic example of an argument that uses deductive reasoning.

All humans are mortal.

Socrates is a human.

Therefore Socrates is mortal.

If the first two statements, the premises, are accepted, then the third statement, the conclusion, must also be accepted. Once an argument is identified as a valid deductive argument, you can be certain of the conclusion. Several forms of deductive argument have been identified, most of these by Greek philosopher Aristotle (384 BCE–322 BCE).

Valid Forms of Deductive Reasoning

Here are some forms of deductive reasoning which philosophers regard as valid. That is, we recognize the argument as an accepted and correct form of reasoning. In these forms of deduction, once the premises are accepted, then the conclusion must logically also be accepted.

Indicating the validity of an argument, however, does not mean that the propositions which make up the argument are necessarily true. In fact, valid arguments can be, and often are, presented even though each proposition is clearly not true in the real world. Testing for truth is another process altogether. For example, none of the following propositions is true, so far as can be known. Yet here is a valid deductive argument.

If my name is Wendy, then I am
a squirrel.

My name is Wendy.

Therefore I am a squirrel.

The first proposition is a conditional statement because it is in the form "if … , then …." The first part of this statement, "if … ," is called the antecedent because it comes before. The second part, "then … ," is called the consequent because it comes after the antecedent and is a consequence.

There are several categories of valid deductive arguments. Once you have identified an argument as one of the examples listed in the table on the next page, you will know that it is logically valid. Each of these arguments is stated as a syllogism, a form of reasoning in which a conclusion is drawn from two reasons or premises. Although we do not usually present arguments this way in everyday life, syllogisms help us see the forms of reasoning clearly and simply. Turn-

Valid Deductive Forms	Examples
Affirming the Antecedent *(agreeing that the antecedent is true)* If *p*, then *q* *p* Therefore *q*	If the butler was asleep, he did not hear the door open. The butler was asleep. Therefore he did not hear the door open. If Thelma was home all night, she was not at the scene of the crime. Thelma was home all night. Therefore she was not at the scene of the crime.
Denying the Consequent *(denying that the consequent is true)* If *p*, then *q* Not-*q* Therefore not-*p*	If the jewellery box is missing, the ring has been stolen. The ring has not been stolen. Therefore the jewellery box is not missing. If Sanjeet's car has a blood stain, he is a suspect. Sanjeet is not a suspect. Therefore his car does not have a blood stain.
Chain Argument If *p*, then *q* If *q*, then *r* Therefore if *p*, then *r*	If Chie was upset, she left the party early. If Chie left the party early, she may have gone home. Therefore if Chie was upset, she may have gone home. If Thelma was in Sanjeet's car, Thelma went to the party. If Thelma went to the party, she was not home all night. Therefore if Thelma was in Sanjeet's car, Thelma was not home all night.
Disjunctive Syllogism *(referring to two alternatives)* Either *p* or *q* Not-*p* Therefore *q*	The thief came from either the door or the window. The thief did not come from the door. Therefore the thief came from the window. Thelma is telling either the truth or a lie. Thelma is not telling the truth. Therefore Thelma is telling a lie. All men are either detectives or criminals. Sanjeet is not a detective. Therefore Sanjeet is a criminal.

ing an everyday argument into a syllogism can help us judge its validity.

The last example in the table on page 35 is a reminder that argument forms are not necessarily statements of truth. It is not true that all men are detectives or criminals. The argument itself, however, is a valid one. For any argument to be a valid deductive argument, we must accept, for its sake, its premises although we do not necessarily need to believe them. The question to ask is: If you accept the premises, do you have to accept the conclusion? If the answer is yes, then it is a valid deductive argument.

Invalid Forms of Deductive Reasoning

Time Line

History of Reasoning

SOCRATES
(469 BCE–399 BCE)
uses discourse as a method of reasoning

PLATO
(428 BCE–347 BCE)

ARISTOTLE
(384 BCE–322 BCE)
identifies many deductive forms

There are several forms of invalid deduction of which we need to be aware. Some invalid deductive arguments appear on the surface to be valid; they are sometimes very convincing indeed. In fact, once you become aware of invalid arguments, you begin to notice how often they are used, and how those individuals who present these arguments manage to get away with them. For example, a TV commercial may claim, "If you buy our dishwasher detergent, your dishes will be spotless. Without it, your dishes will have those ugly water spots." What is not stated, but what is clear to you as the consumer, is the fact that you have other alternatives. So, in fact, the argument presented here by the advertiser is invalid. Here is how we would analyze its form:

Where have you seen invalid forms of deduction used in your own experiences?

If our dishwasher detergent makes dishes spotless
And you do not use our dishwasher detergent
Therefore your dishes will have ugly water spots

What is wrong with this argument? The conclusion does not follow necessarily from the premises. You, the consumer, have the option of purchasing another product; you also have the option of drying your dishes carefully, or doing any number of other things to prevent water spots. This form of invalid deduction is called the fallacy of denying the antecedent because the antecedent is denied as being true.

There are several other invalid deductive forms. If you can identify an argument as one of the examples listed in the table you will know that it is

INVALID DEDUCTIVE FORMS	EXAMPLES
Fallacy of Denying the Antecedent If p, then q Not-p Therefore not-q	If the sun shines, the house will be bright. The sun is not shining. Therefore the house is dark. If it rains, the flowers will grow. It did not rain. Therefore the flowers will not grow.
Fallacy of Affirming the Consequent If p, then q q Therefore p	If you jog every day, you will be fit. You are fit. You must jog every day. If you exceed the speed limit, you will crash. You crashed. Therefore you exceeded the speed limit.

logically invalid. In each case, determine why the conclusions drawn do not necessarily follow from the premises stated.

We use deductive reasoning regularly in everyday life, although we are often not aware of it. If Beverly is in the room with us, we deduce that she is not in another room. We use deduction to categorize things. We may say to ourselves that all oranges are round, orange, and sweet. So when we bite into a round, orange-coloured, sweet-tasting object, we deduce that it is an orange. Of course, if all oranges did not have those characteristics, then we would be mistaken. But if we accept the premises, then the conclusion follows.

There are two ways to be fooled. One is to believe what isn't true; the other is to refuse to believe what is true.

Sören Kierkegaard

Deductive reasoning can be likened to puzzles and brain teasers, each statement must fit the other perfectly in order to make a valid deduction.

Understand Concepts

1. What are the characteristics of deductive reasoning?
2. (a) Differentiate between valid and invalid deduction.
   (b) How do valid and invalid deduction differ from truth and falsehood?

Apply and Develop

3. What type of deduction is illustrated by each set of statements below? Determine if it is a valid or invalid form. Note that the premises do not necessarily have to be true.
   (a) All mammals have four legs.
       My cat is a mammal.
       Therefore my cat has four legs.
   (b) All mammals have four legs.
       My cat has four legs.
       Therefore my cat is a mammal.
   (c) If it is Monday, I should be at school.
       It is Monday.
       Therefore I should be at school.
   (d) All cats are dogs.
       All dogs are fish.
       Therefore all cats are fish.
   (e) All cats are dogs.
       All dogs purr.
       Therefore all cats purr.
   (f) Some cats eat mice.
       All mice are mammals.
       Therefore some cats eat mammals.
4. Create your own examples to illustrate each form of valid and invalid deductive reasoning.

Communicate Ideas

5. Write a persuasive paragraph on any topic you choose and include one of the forms of deduction in this section. Trade paragraphs with a classmate and have them identify the elements of your deduction. Share your paragraphs with the rest of the class.
6. Read a newspaper editorial or column and search for examples of valid and invalid forms of deduction. Justify your choices to the rest of the class.
7. Look for examples of deductive arguments used in everyday life—in TV commercials, by public speakers, and by your friends and family. Change these arguments into "if … , then …" syllogistic form to see if they are valid or invalid, and determine what type they are.

Inductive Reasoning

In the previous section, we examined deductive reasoning in detail. Here, we will consider a second major type of reasoning, inductive reasoning. By observing specific objects and experiencing specific situations in this world, we learn and draw general conclusions. We look for patterns in the world, and develop mental categories for the objects and experiences we find. Inductive reasoning, the process of moving from specific cases to general conclusions, is important because it is reasoning based on what we learn from our experiences.

Conclusions Based on Observations

Philosophers in the ancient world, such as Aristotle, believed that all of us need to learn from experience, drawing conclusions from the observation of specific objects and the experience of specific events in the world around us. The search to understand inductive reasoning proceeded further during the sixteenth century, when philosophers turned their attention to the rapid changes and discoveries being made in the world of science.

Central to this new consciousness of science was the establishment of a method of experimentation, which involved the observation and comparison of objects and movements. Francis Bacon (1561–1626) called this process "putting nature to the test." Experimentation was a powerful new method because it relied on careful observation of real events rather than the blanket acceptance of traditional ideas or those dictated by authority.

This new method also raised several questions, for example, How does one move from a single observation, or a single experiment, to the establishment of general ideas or scientific laws? In other words, How does one draw valid general conclusions from specific instances?

Such questions led to the development of the theory of inductive reasoning and argument. Scientific philosophers, such as Francis Bacon, were determined to understand how this form of reasoning, which was becoming of increasing importance to scientific inquiry, takes place.

Central to the idea of inductive reasoning is the belief that a number of observations of specific objects or events are used to develop a more general conclusion or generalization. For example, in botany, several leaves can be examined and a generalization about leaves can be formed. In order to reach a generalization or conclusion, an experiment must be performed repeatedly.

Inductive reasoning became a powerful tool for scientists, past and present. Galileo Galilei (1564–1642), for example, observed and made careful records of the movements of the planets. He was able to confirm Nicolaus Copernicus' (1473–1543) theory that the Earth and other planets circled the sun, rather than the other way around. Medical researchers, such as William Harvey (1578–1657), observed the human body and arrived at general conclusions about the circulation of the blood. Philosophers, such as Francis Bacon, provided the theory of how inductive reasoning should be practised.

We learn much about the world using inductive reasoning. Young children observe the activities around them and draw conclusions. While still in the crib, babies attempt a never-ending series of methods to gain attention. Some of these attempts succeed, others do not, but all babies soon draw conclusions about the best attention-getting activity. As we grow older, we observe the behaviours of others around us, and our observations help us develop general ideas about the people we meet and interact with, and their idiosyncrasies. Perhaps we encounter a number of people from Scotland, and conclude that Scots speak with a distinctive accent. Perhaps we play a musical instrument with specific fingering and come to the conclusion that, as long as we employ the same fingering, the music will always sound the same. We watch the sun rise in the east and conclude that the sun will always rise in the east. Many of the assumptions and arguments we make are based on specific examples from which we have drawn general conclusions. You may say, "I know that Johannes regularly shops at the Home Handy Depot." If someone asks you, "How do you know that?" you reply, "I saw him there two Saturdays in a row." Inductive reasoning is an essential and powerful way to develop new ideas and knowledge.

Inductive reasoning does not provide us with certainty in the same way that deductive reasoning does. With inductive reasoning, we only know that our conclusions are valid to varying degrees of probability. Review the examples provided in the previous paragraph. Note that an element of doubt is always possible. Subsequent observations may change our general conclusions. Perhaps we may meet people from Scotland who do not speak in the manner we expect. Standing on the North Pole, we will observe that the sun does not rise in the east during the summer, but remains above the horizon all day. In the case of Johannes, perhaps he was working on a special project, which required materials only available from Home Handy Depot, and he never frequents the store in his normal course of practice.

The great power of induction is that it can lead to new knowledge. Specific observations can be used to formulate general rules or laws about the universe. Specific examples from our own lives lead us to think about how general these instances might be. Consider the following three arguments. Are the conclusions certain or not?

Premise:	In my experience, the weather becomes colder starting in September.
Premise:	Others I have spoken to have observed the same thing.
Conclusion:	It is likely that the weather will get colder after this September.
Premise:	Many smokers are short of breath when they run.
Premise:	Barb is a smoker.
Conclusion:	Barb will be short of breath when she runs.
Premise:	Since Selda began her part-time evening job, her grades have dropped from "A" to "B."
Premise:	Since Joshua began partying with his friends every evening, his grades have gone from "B" to "C."
Premise:	Antoine spends most of his evenings on the phone or watching TV. He may fail algebra.
Conclusion:	Students who do not study consistently in the evening will not do their best academically.

Time Line

Early Inductive Reasoning
- - - - - - - - - - -

FRANCIS BACON
(1561–1626)
establishes a type of scientific reasoning

NICOLAUS COPERNICUS
(1473–1543)
proposes that the Earth orbits the sun

GALILEO GALILEI
(1564–1642)
uses inductive reasoning to determine planetary motion

WILLIAM HARVEY
(1578–1657)
makes observations about human blood circulation

In the first argument, if you were to travel to the southern hemisphere in September, the weather would become warmer. The conclusion given is probable, with certain limitations. In the second argument, we should warn Barb that smoking is bad for her health. Barb, however, may have just begun to smoke; therefore she would not necessarily be noticeably short of breath when she runs. Here, as in the first argument, the chances are probable, but not guaranteed. How much certainty do you think you could place in the argument about studying in the evening? Can you base this conclusion on three people? If not, then how many people do you need to observe?

Inductive reasoning allows general conclusions to be reached as the result of several examples of observation of an occurrence. Conclusions reached as a result of inductive reasoning are probable to a greater or lesser degree. What generalizations can you draw about all mammals from observing only the five shown below?

EXAMPLE OF INDUCTIVE REASONING

Case 1	Case 2	Case 3	Case 4	Case 5
Cat	Dog	Giraffe	Elephant	Human
has a backbone	has a backbone	has a backbone	has a backbone	has a backbone
has four legs	has four legs	has four legs	has four legs	has two legs
reproduces sexually	reproduces sexually	reproduces sexually	reproduces sexually	reproduces sexually
has many offspring at a time	has many offspring at a time	usually has one offspring at a time	usually has one offspring at a time	usually has one offspring at a time
is warm-blooded	is warm-blooded	is warm-blooded	is warm-blooded	is warm-blooded
has fur	has fur	has hair on skin	has hair on skin	has hair on skin
has a diaphragm	has a diaphragm	has a diaphragm	has a diaphragm	has a diaphragm

Based on this limited observation of several mammals, identify what appear to be characteristics of mammals generally. What other characteristics would you suggest from your observations of other mammals?

The Major Forms of Inductive Reasoning

Although inductive reasoning in many cases, but not always, involves using the observation of specific objects or the experience of specific events to form general conclusions, there are different ways that this can occur. In fact, there are three major forms of inductive reasoning: inductive generalization, statistical generalization, and induction by confirmation. With each of these forms of inductive reasoning, there is a difference in the way the conclusions are drawn.

Inductive Generalization

Inductive generalization uses specific examples to draw general conclusions. People use inductive generalizations to observe situational patterns which they project on new cases. What pattern do you see in the following premises?

Premise: In the 1950s, one out of five households in North Bay had a television set.

Premise: In the 1970s, four out of five households in North Bay had a television set.

Premise: In the 1990s, there were 1.5 television sets for every household in North Bay.

What conclusions do you think would be most acceptable inductively? Looking at the conclusions below, which of them is most probable or most likely to be drawn from this information? Which of these conclusions is least justified, based on the premises?

Conclusion: The ratio of television sets to households has increased over time.

Conclusion: The ratio of television sets to households will increase in the future.

Conclusion: People in North Bay like watching television.

INDUCTIVE GENERALIZATION	EXAMPLE
When p occurs, the most observed result is q p occurred q will probably occur	When I tidy my room, my parents are often happy. I tidied my room this morning. My parents will probably be happy.

Statistical Induction

Another form of inductive reasoning is statistical induction. This is similar to inductive generalization since it moves from specific cases to draw a general conclusion. The specific cases, however, are based on statistical information. Statistical induction predicts that something will happen with a numerical probability.

Statistical Induction	Examples
A is the population of careful eaters. *B* is the population of careful eaters with heart disease.	
Some percentage of all *A*'s will become *B*'s.	70% of careful eaters avoid heart disease.
A has *x*% chance of being a *B*.	Bill is a careful eater. Bill has a 70% chance of avoiding heart disease.

[Calvin and Hobbes. Copyright © Universal Press Syndicate. Reprinted with permission.]

Induction by Confirmation

Induction by confirmation is a common form of scientific reasoning. Here, a hypothesis is suggested. Certain observations must be made if the hypothesis is to be considered acceptable. When using this form of inductive reasoning, you must determine if these observations *can* be made. The hypothesis is tested by observing if evidence exists to support it.

Induction by confirmation is often used in social science research. Sociologists, anthropologists, and historians develop hypotheses about society, culture, and history. Then they gather data to support their hypotheses. The same is true in philosophy: as philosophers suggest theories about ethics, society, and the universe, they then look for arguments and reasons to support or deny their hypotheses.

The legal system relies heavily on induction by confirmation. A police detective hypothesizes that a suspect has committed a crime. The detective looks for evidence to support or deny that hypothesis. Should the case go to trial, the court will also employ this form of reasoning. If a witness testifies or a smoking gun is found, deductive reasoning can be used to find a person guilty. Many times, however, there is no witness or smoking gun, so inductive reasoning must be used to settle the case. Here is an example:

Hypothesis:	Jim robbed the corner store.
Observations expected:	Whoever robbed the store will have a motive, opportunity, and means.
Observations noted:	Jim needed money, was in the area, and was found with a replica of a gun.
Conclusion:	There is evidence supporting the hypothesis that Jim robbed the corner store.

We use induction by confirmation regularly in our everyday lives. Suppose you arrive home in the evening. The lights and TV are turned on in the house. A kettle is steaming on the stove. What reasonable or probable inductive conclusion can you draw? Probably that someone is home and has started making tea. You do not know this for certain, but your conclusion is highly probable. This is induction by confirmation.

Induction by confirmation is used in many other areas. Perhaps you watch TV mystery shows and follow the detectives as they seek to discover the culprit. Often, the detectives will use induction by confirmation to point suspicion towards a suspect. Then, towards the end of the show, they may use deduction to pin the suspect into a corner from which there is no escape. Consider the case below from nineteenth century detective Sherlock Holmes, who was often described as using deduction in solving mysteries. He actually used induction by confirmation more often than deduction, as the next excerpt illustrates.

> To be uncertain is to be uncomfortable, but to be certain is to be ridiculous.
> *Chinese proverb*

The Hound of the Baskervilles

Arthur Conan Doyle

"So far as I can follow you, then, Mr. Holmes," said Sir Henry Baskerville, "someone cut out this message with a scissors—"

"Nail-scissors," said Holmes. "You can see that it was a very short-bladed scissors, since the cutter had to take two snips over 'keep away'."

"That is so. Someone, then, cut out the message with a pair of short-bladed scissors .... But I want to know why the word 'moor' should have been written?"

"Because he could not find it in print. The other words were all simple and might be found in any issue, but 'moor' would be less common."

"Why, of course, that would explain it. Have you read anything else in this message, Mr. Holmes?"

"There are one or two indications, and yet the utmost pains have been taken to remove all clues. The address, you observe, is printed in rough characters. But the *Times* is a paper which is seldom found in any hands but those of the highly educated. We may take it, therefore, that the letter was composed by an educated man who wished to pose as an uneducated one, and his effort to conceal his own writing suggests that that writing might be known, or come to be known, by you. Again, you will observe that the words are not gummed on in an accurate line, but that some are much higher than others. 'Life', for example, is quite out of its proper place. That may point to carelessness or it may point to agitation and hurry upon the part of the cutter. On the whole I incline to the latter view, since the matter was evidently important, and it is unlikely that the composer of such a letter would be careless. If he were in a hurry it opens up the interesting question why he should be in a hurry, since any letter posted up to early morning would reach Sir Henry before he would leave his hotel. Did the composer fear an interruption—and from whom?"

"We are coming now rather into the region of guesswork," said Dr. Mortimer.

"Say, rather, into the region where we balance probabilities and choose the most likely. It is the scientific use of the imagination, but we have always some material basis on which to start our speculations."

[Arthur Conan Doyle, *The Hound of the Baskervilles*. New York: McClure, Phillips & Co., 1902, 46–8.]

Much detective work is inductive, looking for evidence that suggests, rather than proves conclusively, who the criminal might be.

Understand Concepts

1. Define the terms: inductive reasoning, inductive generalization, statistical induction, and induction by confirmation.
2. How does inductive reasoning differ from deductive reasoning?

Apply and Develop

3. Using the excerpt from *The Hound of the Baskervilles*, create a chart with these headings: conclusions Holmes reached, evidence for the conclusion, and the likelihood that he was correct.
4. What type of inductive argument is used in each of the cases below? Assess the strengths and weaknesses of each argument.
   (a) A questionnaire was used to determine if the people of Collingsville were satisfied with the recreational facilities in the city. Approximately 2000 of the 15 000 questionnaires were returned. Of these, eighty percent were satisfied. The city council concluded that four-fifths of the people were satisfied with the facilities.
   (b) Records show that in the past, ninety percent of this college's graduates found a job within three months. My roommate will be relieved to know that even with a 'D' average he still has a ninety percent chance of getting a job.
   (c) The graduating class of Central High School was surveyed. They were asked if they expected a university education to improve their communication skills. Eighty-eight percent answered yes. We can conclude that eighty-eight percent of all Central High students think that a university education will improve communication skills.
   (d) A recent survey showed that over sixty percent of Canadian students do not know important dates in Canadian history. That would mean that over sixty percent of students in my Canadian history class would probably not do well on a test of these dates.
   (e) Last year, Miranda and Kwan spent six hours a day training with coach Elio. Both made Canada's national swim team. This year, I plan to train just as hard with the same coach. I bet I'll make the team.
   (f) Although the defendant denies intending to shoot his wife, the only conclusion that fits the facts is that he did intend to kill her. If he intended to do it, then he would have purchased the gun ahead of time, which he did. He would have taken her to a secluded spot, which he did. He would have set up an alibi, which he did. He would have had a motive, which he does. All the evidence you have heard supports the conclusion that he intended to kill his wife. You should, therefore, find him guilty of first-degree murder.

Informal Logic, or Critical Thinking

We began this chapter by discussing how reasoning takes place in everyday situations. We give reasons to others and to ourselves for what we believe and what we do. Our reasons may not always be good ones, but we do expect reasons to be given for things that affect us.

Reasoning may be used in relatively minor affairs, such as deciding what movie to watch, as well as in more important areas, such as determining what college or career to choose. We give reasons for a variety of purposes, including:
- explaining our behaviour
- objecting to an idea or action
- getting a job
- convincing others of the merits of a movie
- deciding between competitive products
- presenting a new idea
- persuading others of a fact or a course of action.

We have already looked at how reasoning is analyzed through formal logic, particularly through deduction and induction. In this section, we will consider how reasoning may occur in everyday situations and how we can analyze these events. The study of everyday reasoning, the type we do regularly when we listen to a political candidate, when we write an argumentative essay, or when we decide how to spend our vacation, is called informal logic or critical thinking.

Informal logic or critical thinking includes the type of argument analysis we find in formal logic, combined with the types of arguments and persuasive forms we use in everyday life. These forms usually involve rhetorical devices, words or arguments used to convince through choice of language or emotional statements. For example, when we are trying to convince somebody of something, we use both deductive and inductive reasoning, as well as other persuasive techniques. We may use an emotional appeal to convince someone of the value of our ideas; we may imply an idea, rather than state it outright. When we write a research paper that argues a specific point of view or thesis, we use language to convince the reader of our position. Politicians and advertisers use a variety of techniques to persuade us to agree with their ideas or to buy their product. Informal logic studies these techniques. Informal logic is also an important tool that should be used in reading a philosophic argument. You will use informal logic as you discuss or write your own arguments, and as you defend your own position against the opposing views of others.

Criteria for Judging Arguments Using Critical Thinking

Critical thinking involves two major tasks: judging the value of information and judging the strength of arguments. We decide what to believe or do based on making such judgements.

We have discovered that one way to judge information and arguments is to determine if they are based on valid deductive or inductive reasoning. Informal logic includes judging the value of other aspects of persuasion. We need to judge whether information is relevant, whether it is empirical or factual, what its biases are, and how reliable the source of information is.

Relevance

Judging relevance means determining whether the information or arguments presented have any bearing on the matters at hand. Relevant information or arguments must be considered; irrelevant information or arguments should be discounted or rejected. A charge of irrelevance when upheld by a judge in a court of law, for example, immediately places the information presented off the record. In a doctor's office, symptoms are only relevant if they help determine the illness and its possible remedies. In philosophy, relevance is determined by whether the information provides knowledge about the topic, or whether the argument presented supports or negates a point of view. Irrelevance can become a major weakness when one writes an essay, or participates in a debate.

There are several steps involved in determining relevance. First, determine the topic or issue under discussion. Second, identify criteria to judge whether information presented relates to the topic. Third, sort the information into two categories marked "relevant" and "irrelevant."

> Our intellect and other gifts have been given to be used for God's greater glory, but sometimes they become the very god for us. That is the saddest part: we are losing our balance when this happens.
>
> *Mother Teresa*

Judging relevance is particularly important when forming a strong argument.

Empirical Value

Some information is empirical and some is not. Empirical information can be verified, or obtained through the senses. Non-empirical or affective statements express beliefs, opinions, or values that cannot be verified through observation. "Roses are red" is an empirical statement because it can be verified by looking at some examples of roses. "I like red roses" is a non-empirical statement because it expresses a value that cannot be verified by further observation. Identifying whether a statement is empirical or non-empirical is an important step in determining the value of a statement.

Determining whether information is empirical or not is not always easy. People rarely announce whether what they are saying is empirical or not. Moreover, people also often make statements that purport to be empirical but are not. For example, someone may tell you, "That is an excellent movie." Is that person making an empirical statement that can be tested by further observation, or is that person expressing his or her own values and preferences? Here, one needs to determine the basis for the judgement, and whether such a conclusion can be verified by further observation, or whether it is a preference without observable evidence.

Bias

Bias is the tendency to view objects, people, or events from a particular point of view. We all have biases of one type or another. We may tend to favour one way of life over another, one product over another, perhaps for reasons of which we are only partly aware. Awareness of one's own or another person's biases enables us to understand ideas more accurately and fully.

The sources of bias are many. Bias can result from the way we were brought up, the culture we live in, the experiences we have

had, or our emotional and mental nature. Since we acquire biases from many varied sources in our environment, or from our own psychological nature, we may not even be aware that the views we hold may contain biases. We may accept them as fact, as truth. As an anthropologist once said, "A fish is the last one to be aware that the environment is made of water; a member of a culture may be equally unaware that what one holds as truth is acquired uncritically from the culture."

The impact of bias on points of view, arguments, and selection of information can be significant. Bias may result from ignoring some information and giving heightened importance to other information. Bias may be as a result of limited information or of attitudes that limit how one takes in information. Bias may result in the distortion or weakening of an argument.

Everyone uses mental shortcuts to make sense of a complex world. Often, such shortcuts are employed as we make judgements about groups of people. Generally, however, as people acquire more information about a group or a topic, they are open to revising their judgements. When someone is resistant to new information and strives to maintain an old point of view despite new, and often contradictory information, that person is said to possess a stereotype, a simple idea of reality that is resistant to change. When a person refuses to abandon these old views, especially with regard to other groups of people, that person is said to be prejudiced.

It is important to look for bias as we judge information, arguments, or points of view. If we detect biases and point them out, then the argument wherein it is being used is weakened. Awareness and honesty about our own biases are ways to prevent others from using them against our arguments and points of view. Such self-awareness also

> Fortunately for serious minds, a bias recognized is a bias sterilized.
>
> *A. Eustace Haydon*

> Prejudice is the child of ignorance.
>
> *William Hazlitt*

leads to the development of stronger, more accurate, and more inclusive ways of viewing the world and its people.

Reliability

We say that information and its source is reliable when it can be trusted. Of course, if philosophy, science, and other forms of inquiry teach anything, it is to judge and keep a critical eye open to all information. This suggests that there are degrees or levels of reliability. Some information, along with its source, has more credibility than other information.

There are many occasions in life when we judge the reliability of information and its source. We may put more trust in what our friends and family say to us, because they have our best interests at heart. We may judge what a salesperson tells us as less reliable, just as we might regard someone who is trying to convince us of something for other self-interested motives as less reliable. In work and business situations, we must learn which are our most reliable sources of information before we can act effectively. The credibility of a source is often paramount when we read editorial comments, or

How can we judge the reliability of information presented during election campaigns or on the news?

assess a talk-show commentary. The reliability of a source is also important in academic subjects such as history, science, and sociology.

In philosophy, the ideas of well-known philosophers are respected, but these ideas are also subject to criticism by any thoughtful person. Philosophic ideas suggested by people we do not know, or those that are broadcast on the Internet, for example, must be subjected to greater scrutiny, and judged as less reliable until proven otherwise.

There are a number of ways to judge reliability. We may examine the credentials of the person offering us information. Information from someone who has a great deal of experience in a subject may be more reliable than information from someone with less or no experience. Information from someone who has often provided accurate information in the past may be trusted more than if it came from a new or unknown source. Someone who has a solid reputation may be considered a better source than someone whose reputation is questionable. In the long run, each person must make his or her own judgement about the reliability of information he or she receives and about its sources.

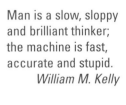

Man is a slow, sloppy and brilliant thinker; the machine is fast, accurate and stupid.
William M. Kelly

Understand Concepts

1. How does informal logic or critical thinking differ from formal logic?
2. Define and give an example of each term.
   (a) relevance
   (b) empirical value
   (c) bias
   (d) reliability

Apply and Develop

3. In each argument below, a reason is given to support an idea or an action. Determine how convincing you think the reason is in each case. Indicate any weaknesses that you detect in the reasoning.
   (a) A manufacturer said, "Cars built in this country are better because they provide jobs for Canadians."
   (b) A political candidate said, "Voters should support me because when I was in office the economy grew steadily."
   (c) "Study your family's medical history," said the physician. "Some diseases run in families and your chances of acquiring them may be increased as a result."
4. Identify which information is most relevant to understanding Canadian geography. Justify your choices.
   (a) the Rocky Mountains
   (b) the capital city of Manitoba
   (c) Washington, D.C.
   (d) the equator
   (e) the southern hemisphere
   (f) grain production on the prairies
5. Which empirical statements below can be supported by observable evidence? Give reasons for your choices.
   (a) Most prison inmates are men.
   (b) A dollar is worth 100 cents.
   (c) Warm climates are better than cold.
   (d) I prefer working outdoors.
   (e) Exercise is beneficial to one's health.
   (f) It is wrong to cheat on your income tax.
   (g) It is illegal to cheat on your income tax.
6. Choose an article from a newspaper—a news report or an editorial. Identify statements that are empirical and those that are not.

7. The statements below have been identified as conditions that increase the reliability of observations.
   - Observer is alert to the situation.
   - Observer has expertise in the area under consideration.
   - Observer has a reputation as a good source.
   - Observer provides good reasons for observations.
   - Observer has no conflict of interest.
   - Observer is skilled in the technique being used.
   - There is sufficient time for observations to be made.
   - There is minimal inferring.
   - A short time elapses between observing and reporting.
   - Reporting is performed by observer rather than through hearsay.
   - Other observers corroborate observations.
   - There are conditions of clear access to observed situation.
   - There is competent use of technology, if appropriate.
   - A statement is not a response to a leading question.

   Apply these criteria to reports in a newspaper, to a witnesses in a court case, or to witnesses to an event. Determine how reliable the report is.

8. Use the criteria in exercise 7 to judge who would provide the most reliable information in this situation. Justify your choices.

   There has been an accident in which a truck smashed into the rear of a passenger bus. As an investigator of the crash, you must determine which informants would provide the most reliable information. You must also give your reasons.

   Informants
   (a) driver of the truck
   (b) passenger who was reading her paper in the bus
   (c) manufacturer of the braking system of the truck
   (d) widow of a man killed in the crash
   (e) police investigator
   (f) farmer in his field who witnessed the crash
   (g) amateur videotape taken by a witness on a nearby highway

Logical Fallacies

Logical fallacies are methods of argument that contain flaws in how the conclusions are drawn. There are several types of logical fallacies, each having a particular flaw. Once a logical fallacy is identified, the argument it makes is immediately weakened or negated.

Logical fallacies are caused by one of several factors. Sometimes the premises of an argument are irrelevant, or not related to the conclusion. Sometimes the premises are too weak. Determine the weakness in each of the following logical fallacies. How would you respond if this logical fallacy were used in an argument against you?

Personal Attack (ad hominem, against the person)

This logical fallacy attacks the person making the argument, rather than the argument or issue involved. It is an attempt to discredit the spokesperson rather than what that person is saying. An example of this logical fallacy is: How can you possibly believe what Dahlia says? She has a reputation for being a hot-head and never doing her research.

Guilt by Association

Guilt by association presumes that a person has a characteristic because of his or her relationship with people or objects with like characteristics. For example, consider the statement: I wouldn't believe him because his father was convicted of fraud. Another example is: Do you really want to go out with a person who hangs around that crowd?

Straw Person

This fallacy occurs when someone attacks a minor or irrelevant part of an opponent's position and concludes that the opponent's real position has been refuted. For example, when Juan is punished by his parents for cheating on an exam, he replies, "You're picking on me. You didn't punish Kiki when she talked back." Another example is: I may have robbed the store, but I certainly didn't double park while I was there.

Post Hoc

Because one event follows another, a false conclusion is sometimes drawn that one event causes the other. Consider the statement: I had bad luck because a black cat crossed my path. Another example is: Every time I try to do something important in my life, I seem to get a bad cold.

Begging the Question

An argument begs the question when its premises assume the truth of the conclusion. Begging the question is an argument based on circular reasoning. For example: Anand must be telling the truth. Why? Because Anand always tells the truth. Another example is: It is important to be aware of style and fashion. Why is that? Because style and fashion are valuable in life.

Hasty Conclusion

This fallacy is also known as jumping to a conclusion. It occurs when one tries to draw a firm conclusion, inductively, based on insufficient evidence. For example, consider this situation: Gina returns to class to get her book. Seeing the teacher's purse on the floor, she puts the purse back on the desk. At that moment the teacher walks in, and accuses Gina of theft.

Inconsistency

An inconsistency arises when an argument contains a contradiction. Consider this situation: The witness stated that the defendant was at the scene of the crime that afternoon. However, the previous witness accompanied the defendant on a tour of the countryside from early morning until late in the evening.

False Dichotomy

A false dichotomy occurs when we are offered only two alternatives to an argument which in reality has more than two. Consider the statement: Since we will never eliminate poverty, it is a waste of time trying to help the poor. Another example is: I can either go to college full-time or be a drop-out.

It is much easier to bury a problem than to solve it.
Ludwig Wittgenstein

It is surprisingly easy to be deceived by logical fallacy.

Glittering Generalities

This fallacy provides no details whatsoever about an argument, but only general statements surrounded by emotional or glittering words. An example of this fallacy is: Bill is a brilliant candidate who constantly battles for truth, justice, and freedom. Another example is: It's wonderful and marvellous that you belong to me!

Appeal to Authority

This fallacy relies on the use of an important or well-known person or source instead of evidence to support a position or product. Celebrity salespeople are a classic example of this technique at work. Another example is: It must be true since my teacher said so, or I saw a medical doctor on TV saying how wonderful this new product was for curing backache.

Card-Stacking

Card-stacking, also known as stacking the deck, presents only facts which favour one point of view, while ignoring those facts which support an opposing opinion or belief. We often see advertisements declaring things like, "This brand of cola provides more taste than the others," and no evidence is provided from those people who might prefer a competitive product.

Bandwagon

The bandwagon fallacy uses popularity or public opinion as a reason for believing or doing something. Consider the statement: Buy new Neekee running shoes. Everybody's doing it. Another example is: Nine out of ten people vote for Marietta. You should too.

Understand Concepts

1. Prepare a three-column chart to organize your knowledge of logical fallacies. Organize the chart using the headings: name of fallacy, description, and two examples for each (one of which you make up yourself).

Apply and Develop

2. What is the logical fallacy in each argument below?
   (a) If you want to believe the testimony of a known criminal, go ahead.
   (b) It must be true. I read it in a philosophy book.
   (c) There are only two types of people in the world; stingy people and generous ones.
   (d) "I must be causing the sun to rise," said the rooster, "because it comes up after I begin to crow."
   (e) A recent study revealed that students who cram get lower grades than those who do not, so I won't open a book during the exam period.
   (f) You can either achieve good grades or have fun. Since Lesia has fun, her grades will drop.
   (g) He was right to lie for his country, because every good citizen tells lies to protect his country.
   (h) Buy this car and get the best in excellent quality and transportation.
   (i) Since Nirmala is a friend of Troy, who is in trouble with the law, Nirmala must also be a troublemaker.
   (j) Those shoes are used by professional athletes, so they are good enough for me.
   (k) My father says that all reasonable people vote for that candidate, and my dad knows what he is talking about.
   (l) Nine out of ten doctors surveyed use NoPain headache tablets.
   (m) "Did you know that automobiles from Turin are safer and more economical?"
   "What about their expensive repairs?"
   "That isn't worth considering."

Communicate Ideas

3. Analyze magazine advertisements or TV commercials for their use of logical fallacies. Briefly describe the ad or TV commercial on the left half of a page. Explain how it uses logical fallacies on the right half. Share your analysis with others in your class.
4. Write a short paragraph that deliberately includes a logical fallacy. Exchange paragraphs with a classmate, identify and explain the fallacy in question. You may choose to write on one of these topics: Why Philosophy Should Be a Compulsory Course in Schools, Why Logical People Make Better Friends, or Why People Should Buy…(supply your own product here).

Review and Reflect

Logic is the study of how we reason, in philosophy and in other areas of inquiry. It is largely concerned with how arguments are made and analyzed. Most philosophic explanations are, in fact, extended arguments, the purpose of which is to establish a thesis or draw a conclusion.

There are two major categories of logic: formal, which includes deduction and induction; and informal or critical thinking, which includes formal logic and rhetoric. Critical thinking focusses on reasoning used in everyday life. In deductive reasoning, the conclusion follows necessarily if the premises are accepted. In inductive reasoning, the conclusion is only probable to some degree. Deductive reasoning helps clarify the meaning and relationships between existing pieces of knowledge. Inductive reasoning helps determine new knowledge from existing knowledge. There are several forms of both deduction and induction.

Informal logic, or critical thinking, deals with the types of reasons that we use regularly in everyday life. This type of reasoning considers how people try to convince others using language and rhetoric, in addition to logic and argument. In analyzing reasoning in everyday or informal situations, and in philosophic writing, several elements are important to consider: relevance, empirical and non-empirical information, bias, and reliability. Logical fallacies are one way to identify a weakness in an argument.

In philosophy, there are times when we need to understand, analyze, and assess the arguments made by others. At other times, the philosopher strives to make his or her own arguments effective, or convincing.

Analyzing and making arguments in philosophy is a skill developed through practice. It is also an extremely valuable skill that is transferable to almost every aspect of our everyday lives. We make arguments on a regular basis: with friends and acquaintances; when purchasing or selling items; in our financial affairs; in the workplace; and when discussing politics and social issues. Understanding how to make and analyze arguments is an invaluable tool for all of us.

What We Can Know

What can we know? How certain can we be of our knowledge? We are aware that our opinions differ from others in many ways, such as in our judgement of a movie we saw with a friend, in our political and social views of the world, in our assessment of someone's character, and in our views of the purpose of life. If opinions vary widely about so many things, what can we really know with certainty?

The philosophical study of knowledge and of how we know anything is called epistemology. Epistemologists try to determine how much certainty we can place on different types of knowledge. If our knowledge can be shown to have a solid grounding, then we can trust it and act upon it. However, if the basis for believing something is less firm, it may be unwise to act on that knowledge. A clear idea of what we can know, and know with some certainty, is an important basis for any investigation and for most activities.

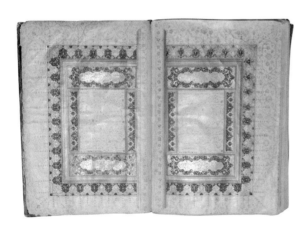

In this chapter, we will raise and discuss several epistemological questions. What can we know? How do we acquire information and ideas? Is certainty possible? To what degree is doubt important? Throughout the ages, different answers to these questions have been proposed by pre-Socratic philosophers, Plato, Aristotle, and Tao. Although these questions were posed long ago and theories have been suggested, we still ask them today.

Originally, most of our knowledge about life was passed down through various religious traditions. Today, science has become the authority for knowledge for many people. How certain can we be that the information from science and religion is the truth?

Questioning What We Know

Unsettling though it may be, epistemology encourages us to question what we know and to consider the sources of our knowledge. We may need to reassess some of our pet beliefs. Such questioning may also bring us greater understanding and more certainty of those ideas we decide to keep. Let us begin this process with the following exercise. For each item under the first heading, write down how you know this knowledge and how certain you are that it is true.

Some Things You May Know	How Do You Know This?	How Certain Are You?
• The earth is round. • Cats have four legs. • God exists. • Two plus two equals four. • Falling from great heights causes injury. • Canada is a democratic country. • There are students in the next room. • Your teacher stands before you now. • Plants produce oxygen. • Love conquers all. • Grass is green. • Stealing is wrong. • Columbus discovered America. • The Earth orbits around the sun.		

You may have indicated several different ways of knowing, in the examples listed in the table. Moreover, your level of certainty probably varied from one statement to another. You may feel quite sure of the truth of some beliefs, but you are less sure about others. Why is this? Compile a new list of beliefs that are important to you, and analyze them in the same way.

This type of questioning is an important

first step in epistemology, just as it is in most branches of philosophy. Philosophy demands that we question what we know, that we do not simply accept ideas as they are presented to us. In philosophy, we should be willing to provide reasons for what we know, or for what we think we know. We should also be willing to doubt ideas until good reasons are given for us to accept them. Epistemology provides us with the tools to investigate truth and certainty.

Knowledge and Authority

In the previous exercise, you may have referred to an authority on the subject to indicate how you know something is true. In epistemology, the word authority indicates a source of knowledge that recommends, justifies, or accepts an idea as true.

There are several types of epistemological authority. If, for example, you said the grass is green because you see it with your own eyes, you are accepting your senses as an authority. Do you believe that stealing is wrong because your parents say that is so? Or your religious leaders? Or your teachers? Parents, religious leaders, and teachers are traditional sources of authority. Consider the statement: The Earth orbits around the sun. Did this statement come from a science textbook, and, thus, originally from a scientist? If so, you have accepted an expert in the field as your authority. When you examine carefully all our knowledge, a great deal of it is accepted on the basis of some authority.

Reasoning is an important method that philosophers provide to support a point of view or idea. Consider the statement: Two plus two equals four. Why do you believe this to be true? Do you accept it because your grade one teacher told you so? Or did you figure it out by yourself, counting out two apples and two apples? Probably both. Which proof is most convincing? If you are most convinced by puzzling over the problem by yourself, then perhaps you accept reasoning as a major authority in your life.

Let us examine a few more examples. To what authorities is each individual appealing in his or her statements: observation, commonly accepted knowledge, reasoning, expert authority, or tradition?

Allan: My dog always knows when I am coming home. She sits in the window waiting for me every day after school.

Uli : That's ridiculous! Everyone knows that dogs can't tell time!

Carlos: Since I lost all my money at the casino, I should be in for a string of good luck in the future.

Danielle: Statistics show that you have an equally good chance of losing your money in the future as well.

Usha: Since my husband and I have great personalities, our children will inherit these.

Chie: Research shows that early experiences are more important than heredity in shaping personality.

Gemma: My family believes I will be happier if I marry someone from my own culture.

Jacques: I think you should both check your horoscopes to ensure compatibility.

Certainty and Doubt

Do you hold ideas about which you have no doubts, ideas you accept absolutely, and that are so basic to you that you require no proof of their validity? When anyone feels this way about something, it is described as dogmatism, the acceptance of an idea without question. Each of us holds basic areas of life about which we are certain, ideas that we hold without question. Think about the ideas you hold as absolute in your own life, perhaps your own existence, the value of others, how your society is organized, or the value of your religion.

Doubt is another quite different approach to knowledge; it is the questioning of whether something is true or not. Doubt is an important part of everyday life and of

We need to really trust our own selves and our own thinking, and not allow others to convince us that our thoughts, ideas and plans and visions aren't valid.
Wilma Mankiller

Every great advance in natural knowledge has involved the absolute rejection of authority.
Thomas Huxley

philosophy. If we accepted everything we heard or saw in this world at face value, we would be very gullible people. None of us believes every advertising message we hear or even everything our friends tell us. We filter information through our own ideas to judge its certainty.

Calling knowledge into doubt is called scepticism, and it is an important part of practising philosophy. Philosophical scepticism comes in more than one form. Sceptical relativists, for example, believe there is more than one truth for any issue. Absolute sceptics suggest that we can know very little about this world with certainty.

It is possible to be sceptical in some areas of life and not in others. We may be sceptical about government or about science, for example, and dogmatic about religion. How dogmatic and how sceptical are you? Test yourself in the questionnaire below by responding to each statement in each of the three categories as indicated: (1) do not know, (2) tend to agree or disagree, and (3) strongly agree or strongly disagree.

Add up your total score in each category. A higher score for any category suggests increased dogmatism or certainty; a lower score suggests increased scepticism or uncertainty. In what areas of life are you most dogmatic? In what areas are you sceptical? How do your scores compare with others in your class?

It is important for us to be aware of the sources of our knowledge and of how much faith we place in that knowledge. This advice is an undisputed truth both in everyday life and in philosophy. Of course, we cannot go through life questioning everything. Some things we must likely accept on faith, or on authority. However, in areas of importance, we may wish to adopt a questioning, even a sceptical, point of view in order to judge and use information wisely.

	1	2	3
Religion • God exists. • There is an afterlife. • My religion is important to me.			
Science • Doctors cure most diseases. • Scientists make life better for everyone. • No one knows how the universe began.			
Morality • There is a right and a wrong way to live. • Men and women should have equal opportunities. • Children should not be spanked.			

IDEAS AND ISSUES

Understand Concepts

1. Define each term based on your understanding: epistemology, knowledge, authority, certainty, and doubt.
2. Describe some of the sources from which we acquire knowledge.
3. Identify several authorities for knowledge. For each of these authorities, list what you think might be typical strengths and weaknesses.

Apply and Develop

4. (a) Identify five things about which you are certain in life. For each of these, indicate why you feel certain.
   (b) Identify five things you think might be true but of which you are not certain. Explain why you feel uncertain.
5. (a) In your view, what makes something certain?
   (b) What makes you question some things in life?

Think Critically

6. (a) Refer to the table on the previous page. Identify the statements that you believe may be true.
   (b) For each item in part (a), determine upon what authority you hold that item to be true.
7. Do you think it is possible to find more certainty when inquiring into the natural world, as opposed to inquiring into the human social world?

Communicate Ideas

8. Prepare a convincing argument for any one of the propositions that follow, and present this to the class. The class is to cast doubt on your arguments and your proposition. Try to defend your position using logic and rhetoric.
   (a) There is nothing outside of my mind about which I can be sure. It is likely that there is no reality beyond my consciousness.
   (b) I know, without doubt, that I exist as a material being.
   (c) It is not possible for change to occur, for if it did an object would become something else and that is impossible.
   (d) All things constantly change, therefore there is nothing that is permanent in the universe.
   (e) Since my senses constantly fool me into believing things that are not true, I should rely instead on the thoughts in my head alone.
   (f) Seeing is believing.

The Questions of the Natural Philosophers

The natural philosophers, also called the pre-Socratic philosophers, lived in the Mediterranean region before the time of Socrates and Plato. They were primarily concerned with questions about the universe, the natural world and its processes. Two major questions interested these thinkers: Of what is the natural world made? To what degree do things remain the same over time and to what degree do all things change?

The study of the natural world and of the universe is called cosmology, from the Greek word *kosmos* meaning world or universe. Cosmology is a branch of metaphysics, the study of determining what exists. The questions raised by the natural philosophers were important ones, for they initiated the study of philosophy by others. While some conclusions formulated by the natural philosophers about the universe had lasting value, many have been discarded as human knowledge has progressed. Nevertheless, it is interesting to see how these thinkers initiated the study of cosmology so long ago.

The natural philosophers are also important because of the manner in which they sought to gain knowledge, a manner that utilized reason and observation as important tools in the search for truth. The natural philosophers lived during a time when most people accepted things to be true by tradition, by myth, or by the authority of others. This is why their contributions are important to the study of epistemology. Later philosophers such as Socrates, Plato, and Aristotle built on the methods and ideas of these early natural philosophers.

> One cannot step twice into the same river, for the water into which you first step has flowed on.
> *Heraclitus*

> If a thing moves, then it must move either in the place where it is or in a place where it is not. But it cannot move where it is nor can it move where it is not; so it cannot move.
> *Zeno*

The Substance of All Things

Thales of Miletus (624 BCE–546 BCE) lived in a Greek colony in Asia Minor. He wanted to know: Of what are all things composed? Looking around, Thales observed that most objects in the world were composed more or less of water. He concluded, therefore, that water was the basic substance from which all things were made. While we may not accept this conclusion today, it is interesting to note that Thales searched for and accepted the overall concept of an integral, connected universe, one owing its existence to the links provided by one substance. Philosophers who came many years after him would continue this inquiry.

Thales did not possess modern microscopes or the other technologies available to us today to help him in his observations of the world. He did, however, ask a fundamental question, and proceeded by using his senses and his rational mind to attempt to answer it. Asking provocative questions, observing the world, and using thoughtful rational methods to develop ideas are the basic, underlying processes in philosophy, science, and all other serious investigative processes.

Anaximander (611 BCE–547 BCE), a student of Thales, was interested in many things: the development of living organisms, geography, astronomy, and almost every aspect of human concern. Anaximander suggested that all life came from the sea and that all living things, including humans, evolved from sea creatures. Only fragments of his writings remain, as with most of the natural philosophers, but we do know that Anaximander was also searching for the basis of all things, although he came up with a different conclusion from that of his teacher. Anaximander suggested that everything in the world, including water, developed from a more elementary substance, which he called *apeiron*. Anaximander claimed that apeiron was something without boundary, limit, or definition—in short, a mysterious concept.

A third Miletian philosopher, Anaximenes (585 BCE–528 BCE), was a young associate of Anaximander. Anaximenes considered air to be the basis of all creation. Anaximenes stated that when air became finer, it became fire. When it was made thicker, air became wind, then clouds, water, earth, and stones. Not only was Anaximenes' theory suggesting a less mysterious and more observable idea of a universal building-block substance than that of Anaximander, it also provided an explanation of how one basic substance can become many things.

Pythagoras (571 BCE–496 BCE) was born on the island of Samos, across the Aegean sea from Miletus. He moved to southern Italy and settled in the Greek city of Croton where he headed a school of philosophy from 525 BCE to 500 BCE It is said that Pythagoras' followers were more like disciples than students. They attended his school devotedly and were inspired by his ideas. They were also sworn to secrecy; there was a strong mystical element to the Pythagorean community. In spite of this, most of our information about the Pythagorean community comes from Pythagoras' students.

Pythagoras approached the question of the nature of the universe quite differently from the Miletians. While they searched for the basic substance out of which all things are made, Pythagoras looked to establish the basic or universal forms or shapes of life. Both substance and form would become important in philosophers' future attempts to define the nature of the world and all things within it.

Pythagoras developed the theory that numbers, rather than elements like air and water, were the basic principles of everything. He suggested that numbers determined the shape of all things, and he became one of the first people to recognize the importance of mathematics in understanding the natural world. For example, he indicated that number one represents a point, two a line, three a surface, and four a solid. The Pythagoreans also saw music as a major example of mathematics in the universe when they discovered the relationship between the length, tautness, and pitch of a string.

Pythagoras included both mysticism and mathematics in his philosophy. He believed that numbers could be assigned to all things

Time Line

Study of Matter

- - - - - - - - - - -

THALES OF MILETUS
(624 BCE–546 BCE)
concludes that water is the basic substance of matter

ANAXIMANDER
(611 BCE–547 BCE)
suggests that all life originated from the sea

ANAXIMENES
(585 BCE–528 BCE)
suggests air can be transformed into fire, wind, clouds, water, earth, and stones

PYTHAGORAS
(571 BCE–496 BCE)
suggests that numbers are the basic element of all things

in life, that numbers were sublime (an exalted form of thought and expression) and should be used to dictate religious ritual as well as the purification of the soul. Legend has it that a Pythagorean follower was taken to the sea and drowned because he divulged to some non-Pythagoreans the fact that some geometric quantities could not be expressed as whole numbers.

Pythagoras transformed existing arithmetic and geometric information into an orderly logical system. His concepts would later be used by the famous Greek mathematician Euclid, and his focus on mathematics would influence the philosophic teachings of Plato, more than one hundred years later.

All of these early philosophers speculated about the nature of the universe. They did not, however, follow up their theories with what we would call a modern investigation or experiment. One historian noted that these early philosophers thought in "adventurous, innocent and primitive ways, as most of us do in childhood, about the origins and essential nature of the cosmos." This judgement seems a little harsh, considering that these thinkers were at the beginning of a long investigative process.

Permanence and Change

How can something retain its identity over time, and yet undergo change? An acorn becomes an oak tree. A person is thought of as the same person over time, yet looks, acts, and thinks differently from childhood through to old age. Imagine you bought a car, kept it for many years, but were forced to replace one part after another to keep it running. Eventually, you have replaced every single part, and nothing of the original car remains. Is your car now the same car you bought many years ago? Natural philosophers of the fourth century B.C. turned their attention to questions like these, without, of course, using the car analogy. These philosophers puzzled over how something could appear to

This woman is holding a picture of herself at a younger age. What is most real, change or permanence?

be permanent, yet undergo change. This question would eventually have long-term effects on the history of philosophy.

Heraclitus (540 BCE–480 BCE) was born in Ephesus in Asia Minor. He had a reputation for haughtiness, and was disliked for most of his life. Eventually, he moved to the mountains and became a recluse. Heraclitus and Socrates would have made poor philosophical partners. However, we remember Heraclitus today as one of the first philosophers to consider the problem of permanence and change. He suggested that all things are in a state of constant change. In his famous illustration of this idea, Heraclitus pointed out that it is impossible to step into the same river twice.

Heraclitus reasoned that fire was the prime example of change because it is constantly changing shape, needs constant tending, and continually gives off heat, smoke, and ashes. Heraclitus thought the world was like a constant fire because all things eventually become something else. Even water becomes fire, and fire changes to earth and water.

Heraclitus did not believe in a universe of chaos, however. On the contrary, he believed that a rational, intelligible structure or order underlay the world's impermanence, although the nature of this order (which he called *logos*) may not be understood by human consciousness. Heraclitus theorized that everything in existence is fundamentally connected in a unity that exists beyond the temporary nature of our apparently ever-changing world. This contrast between apparent change and underlying structure would become a major part of future philosophic thought.

Parmenides (510 BCE–480 BCE) was a citizen of Elea in southern Italy. He took quite a different view of permanence and change. Parmenides believed that everything which exists has always existed. He reasoned that nothing can ever become anything other than what is already is. Therefore change can never occur.

Parmenides admitted that change seems to occur, especially when we use our senses to gain knowledge and understanding. He called using our senses "the way of seeming," and stated that our senses fool us. On the other hand, when we use our reason, or "the way of truth," as he called it, it is clear that nothing was ever created and nothing changes. A triangle is always a triangle, and the moon is always the moon. As American writer Gertrude Stein put it, "A rose is a rose is a rose."

Empedocles (490 BCE– 430 BCE) tried to reconcile the problems of change raised by Heraclitus and Parmenides. He claimed that things do change, yet one thing cannot become another. Why do things appear to change then? His answer was that everything is made up of four elements: earth, air, fire, and water. He reasoned that these elements change in proportion, combining and separating into objects that appear different, like the mixture of colours on an artist's palette.

Empedocles asked himself why the elements even change at all. Love and strife was his answer. Love keeps things together; strife separates them. While the terminology may seem naive, Empedocles' idea bears looking at. Ask a physicist today what makes things move in the world of nature, and you will hear about positive and negative forces.

Yin and Yang in Far Eastern Philosophy

In Eastern philosophy, there is also an idea that the universe is composed of opposites, *yin* and *yang*, our active and passive natures.

Everything in the universe is in a continual state of change, moving from *yin* to *yang* and from *yang* to *yin*. The states of *yin* and *yang* are relative, not absolute. All things exist in complementary opposition with other things; there must be cold in order to have hot. Opposition is needed to create movement, or change. Without it things would remain the same.

If the tendency of any change is contraction, then the dominant force is *yang*. Some characteristics of contraction are density, heat, weight, speed, and activity, among others. If the tendency of any change is

Study of
Permanence
- - - - - - - - - - -

HERACLITUS
(540 BCE–480 BCE)
suggests that all things are in a state of change

PARMENIDES
(510 BCE–480 BCE)
believes change can never occur

EMPEDOCLES
(490 BCE–430 BCE)
suggests that earth, fire, water, and air are the basic elements of all things; only their proportions change

The classic symbol for **yin** *and* **yang**. *Some things such as salt are predominantly* **yang** *and other things such as fruits are predominantly* **yin**. *How does the concept of* **yin** *and* **yang** *differ from the ideas of the natural philosophers?*

Everything flows; nothing remains.
Heraclitus

There is a coherent plan in the universe, though I don't know what it's a plan for.
Fred Hoyle

expansion, then the dominant force is *yin*. Less density, coolness, lightness, slower speed, and less activity are among some of the characteristics of expansion. This movement from *yin* to *yang* and back again governs all things, from the annual pattern of the planets around the sun to the way plants grow.

Everything in the universe involves polarity. Nothing is neutral, or only *yin*, or only *yang*. All things have both *yin* and *yang* but one of these forces exists in excess. All physical forms, including humans, are *yang* at the centre and *yin* at the surface. Eastern tradition says that in order for us to remain healthy we must balance the *yin* and *yang* forces present in our lives. Our diet, activity, spiritual attitude, and environment—the biological, psychological, and spiritual—are all seen as being related to the whole person; no aspect of these is considered separate from another.

The Contradiction Between Reason and the Senses

As they searched for truth about the universe, the pre-Socratic philosophers used their senses to perceive, and their reason to understand. Some thinkers concentrated on the former method, while others focussed on the latter. They initiated a search to determine the best method of finding out about the universe; that search continues today.

Zeno (489 BCE–? BCE) was a follower of Parmenides. He continued to investigate the contradictions that seemed to exist between knowledge gained from the senses and that gained from reason. Zeno believed the senses appear to show us that all things are changeable, while reasoning suggests that all ideas and objects must be permanent. Zeno concluded that Parmenides' theory was right on two counts: reason is the way to knowledge, while permanence is the true reality.

As an example, Zeno used the relationship between a seed and the sound it creates. He stated that when a single seed drops to the ground, it appears to make no sound at all. When a whole bushel of seeds is dropped, or overturned, the sound is clear to all. Zeno concluded that our senses must have deceived us in the case of the single seed, because a sound must certainly have been produced, although we could not detect it.

Zeno is famous for the paradoxes or puzzles he developed to illustrate contradictions between knowledge gained through the senses, and that gained through reasoning. One of these puzzles involved a hundred metre race between the fleet Greek hero, Achilles, and a tortoise, where the tortoise is given a 50 metre head start. Our senses tell us that Achilles will probably overtake the tortoise. Our reason tells us that by the time Achilles reaches the place where the tortoise started, the tortoise has already moved farther ahead to a new location. When Achilles reaches that spot, the tortoise has moved yet again, and so on until the end of the race.

Anaxagoras (500 BCE–428 BCE) was the first Athenian philosopher about whom we have some historical record. He also devoted himself to the ongoing problems of reality, and how we understand it. Anaxagoras distinguished between mind and matter, a distinction which would have far-reaching effects in the world of philosophy. Anaxagoras theorized that it is through the mind that we bring order to the world of matter. Without mind, matter would be a confusing, ever-changing panorama. In addition, according to Anaxagoras, our human minds organize sensory information into categories or concepts. Our minds, for example, separate matter into that which is warm, light, and dry, from that which is cold, dark, and moist.

Democritus (460 BCE–370 BCE) struggled with the two major questions of his predecessors: What is matter? How, if at all, do things change? Democritus developed the idea that everything is made up of indestructible and eternal atoms that move about in the vacuum of space. He suggested that as they move, these atoms interlock to form clusters, creating material objects. Democritus concluded that atoms are therefore the basic elements of matter, not earth, air, fire, and water as his predecessors had thought. Democritus' theory was eons ahead of his time, and indeed almost sounds modern. Moreover, it was developed purely through reason, without the benefit of microscopes or other sophisticated scientific equipment. Democritus' theory did not pass muster, however, with major movers and shakers of philosophic thought, and it faded out of the picture for over two thousand years, as Empedocles' four-elements theory reigned supreme.

The natural or pre-Socratic philosophers made important attempts to understand our natural world. While the answers they developed may sometimes seem naive to us today, the questions they asked were important for the philosophers and scientists who followed after them. The questions these early thinkers asked prompted other philosophers and scientists to explore alternative solutions. The issues the natural philosophers raised about how to find true knowledge, the study of epistemology, still remains a recurring theme in philosophy to this day.

The learned is happy, nature to explore, The fool is happy, that he knows no more.
Alexander Pope

Truth is not discovered by proofs but by exploration. It is always experimental.
Simone Weil

It both is and is not;
neither is, nor is not.
The Buddha

As objects move away from us they appear to grow smaller. What would Zeno have said about this?

Pythagoras

The Pythagorean Society

Pythagoras of Samos (571 BCE–496 BCE) was both an important and mysterious figure, as relatively few documented details of his life are known.

Pythagoras' father, Mnesarchus, was a merchant from Tyre and his mother, Pythias, a native of Samos. Pythagoras spent his childhood in Samos but he also travelled extensively with his father. Well educated and well-travelled, Pythagoras was greatly influenced by the philosophers Pherekydes, Thales, and Anaximinder.

In his late twenties or early thirties, Pythagoras travelled to Egypt where, it is suggested, he adopted many of the beliefs he would later impose on the society that he formed in Italy. Some of these customs included the secrecy of the Egyptian priests, their refusal to eat beans, their refusal to wear clothes made from animal skins, and their striving for purity.

After returning to Samos, Pythagoras founded a school, called the semicircle, in which local Samians held political meetings. It is speculated that the Samians were not happy with Pythagoras' teaching methods and this, in part, led to his decision to leave Samos and form a philosophical and religious school in Croton.

Pythagoras was the head of the school, or Society, and the inner circle of followers were called mathematikoi. The mathematikoi lived permanently with the Society, had no personal possesions and were strict vegetarians. Pythagoras taught the mathematikoi himself and instructed his Society members in observing strict rules, or beliefs:

Pythagoras of Samos

1. that at its deepest level, reality is mathematical in nature
2. that philosophy can be used for spiritual purification
3. that the soul can rise to union with the divine
4. that certain symbols have a mystical significance, and
5. that all brothers of the order should observe strict loyalty and secrecy.

There was also an outer circle, whose members were known as akousmatics. They were permitted personal possessions, not required to be vegetarians and joined the Society only during the day for teachings.

Pythagoras' school practised secrecy and communalism; therefore, his actual work is unknown and difficult to distinguish from the work of his followers. It is known that the Pythagoreans studied mathematics—not problem-solving but the principles of mathematics—the concept of number, the concept of triangle (or other mathematical figure), and the abstract idea of a proof.

While studying the properties of numbers, Pythagoras believed that all relations could be reduced to number relations and that all numbers had personalities. It is important to note that the famous geometry theorem, Pythagoras' Theorem, was probably known many years earlier, but it was Pythagoras who was the first to prove it.

But Pythagoras was also a philosopher, living by philosophic and ethical teachings. Very little of what Pythagoras taught his followers was known as he preferred oral instruction and therefore, there are no actual documented writings of his work.

Equally mysterious are the theories surrounding his death. One idea argues that the Pythagorean Society at Croton was attacked around 508 BCE by Cylon, a Croton noble. Following the attack, some claim Pythagoras escaped to Metapontiun where he later died. Some historians believe he committed suicide in Metapontium because of the attack on his Society.

However, it is known that the Pythagorean Society thrived for many years after Cylon's attack, in fact, the Society spread to many other cities across Italy. Based on this theory, it is suggested that Pythagoras returned to Croton and, as some speculate, was almost 100 years old at the time of his death.

Understand Concepts

1. Identify three major issues raised by the natural philosophers.
2. Summarize the ideas of each of the natural philosophers in a chart with these headings:
   • Questions they asked
   • Positions they took
   • Arguments they used
   • Your view of their ideas

Think Critically

3. Survey the contributions made to philosophy by the pre-Socratic, or natural, philosophers. Determine which of these contributions you think are of more importance, and which are less. Defend your choices.
4. Develop your own theories in response to the major questions asked by the natural philosophers. Explain how you would defend your theories.

Communicate Ideas

5. Take the positions of one of the natural philosophers. Use argument, rhetoric, and logic to convince the class of the validity of your beliefs.

Inquire and Research

6. Find out more about *yin* and *yang* in Far Eastern philosophy. Explain how Eastern medicine uses this knowledge in diagnosing and treating health conditions.
7. Find out more about the natural philosophers by reading *A History of Western Philosophy*, Book 1, Part 1, by Bertrand Russell. Describe the judgements that Russell makes about these philosophers individually and in general. State if you agree with Russell, or if you think his judgement is fair. Write a response paper that discusses and critiques Russell's points of view.

The Ideas of Plato

Many philosophers have pondered the questions: What can we know? How certain can we be about our knowledge? One of the first and most influential of these was Plato, an Athenian of the fifth century BCE So powerful has Plato's influence been on succeeding thinkers, that it has been said, perhaps with little exaggeration, that all Western philosophy since Plato's era has become merely a footnote to his ideas.

Plato was born into a noble Athenian family in 428 BCE Athens at that time was a very intellectually oriented city-state, where many ideas in philosophy and in other fields were being developed. All Athenian citizens were required by law to participate in the government of their society. As a youth, Plato studied civics with Socrates, who instilled in his pupil a passion for philosophy. In 399 BCE, Socrates was sentenced to death for allegedly corrupting the morals of Athenian youth. Socrates drank poison in the presence of his students, after explaining to them why he was ending his life in this way. Plato was devastated; he became disillusioned with politics and left Athens in disgust, travelling to Egypt, Italy, and Sicily in search of greater truths.

Plato conversing with students. Discourse and questioning were central to Plato's approach in developing knowledge. Why would that approach have been perceived as threatening to authority figures at that time? Would that same threat be perceived today?

He did not find them, and returned to Athens two years later to set up his Academy just outside the city. Plato invited young Athenians to join him in his research into the mysteries of science, mathematics, astronomy, and philosophy. In many ways, Plato's Academy became one of the first recorded universities. Plato would lecture to his students and discuss his ideas with them, just as teachers and professors do today. Like his mentor Socrates, Plato believed that knowledge developed, and was refined through the processes of discourse and questioning.

Unlike Socrates, Plato documented his ideas, and a thorough record of his thoughts and philosophy remains to this day. Plato's early writings contain dialogues with Socrates and Socrates' peers outlining certain philosophic principles. Often, we are not sure which ideas are those of Socrates and which are those of Plato. Plato's later work was more expressive of his own ideas, some of which differed substantially from those of his beloved teacher Socrates. Plato was never satisfied that he had found the true way, and he continued to learn, teach, and write until his death in 347 BCE.

How did Plato answer the two questions with which we began this chapter: What can we know, and how certain can we be about our knowledge? One place to begin is with Plato's allegory of the cave. An allegory is a fictional representation that is used to illustrate an idea. Plato proved very creative in his allegories.

The Cave

Plato

Imagine men living in an underground cave equipped with an entrance open to the light and a long passage traversing the entire cavern. These men have been confined since childhood, chained by the leg and by the neck. They cannot move and can see only what is in front of them, because the neck restraint will not let them turn their heads. Some distance higher up is the reflection of a fire's light upon the wall in front of them. The actual fire burns behind them; between the prisoners and the fire is a track with a parapet—built like the screen at a puppet show, which hides the performers while they manipulate their puppets over the top....

Behind this parapet, imagine persons carrying various artificial objects, including wooden or stone representations of people and animals. These figures are large and project above the parapet. It is a strange picture, but one on which the prisoners concentrate, because they have nothing else to do. It is an unnatural situation, but Plato created the scene because he wanted to illustrate the following points.

In the first place, the prisoners see nothing of themselves or of one another, except for the shadows [cast] by the firelight on the wall of the cave facing them; likewise, they do not actually see the objects being carried along the parapet; but only their shadows cast upon the wall in front of them. Thus the prisoners recognize reality as nothing more than shadows.

Consider what would happen if one prisoner was set free, and suddenly forced to stand up, turn his head, and walk with eyes lifted to the light. These movements would all be extremely painful, and the prisoner would be too dazzled by the light to identify those real objects whose shadows he had been accustomed to seeing. What do you think the prisoner would say if someone told him what he had seen earlier, when he was chained and unable to move, was a meaningless illusion, and that now, because he was free and able to look at the actual artificial objects themselves, he was getting a truer view? Suppose, in addition, the prisoner was shown each of the objects being carried along the parapet, and asked to identify it. Would the prisoner not be perplexed, and believe the objects now in view were not so real as what he saw earlier, reflected by the light of the fire in front of him?...

What if the prisoner was forced to look at the firelight itself, would his eyes not ache; would it not seem natural that he would try to escape and turn back to the shadows that he could see distinctly, convinced that they really were more real than the artificial recreations being shown to him?...

Suppose someone dragged the prisoner forcibly up the steep and rugged passageway, out of the cave and into the sunlight. Wouldn't the prisoner again be blinded by the light, and [be] unable to make out a single object from those around him—objects that he is informed are the most real objects of all?

The prisoner would need to acclimatize his eyes and senses before he could begin to perceive the things which surrounded him in that upper world. It would be easiest, at first, to discern the shadows, then the images of men and objects reflected in water, and ultimately, the objects themselves. Finally, the prisoner would be able to watch the heavenly bodies and the sky itself by night, looking at the light of the moon and stars rather than the Sun and the Sun's light during the daytime....

Perhaps, the prisoner might remember his fellow prisoners in the cave, remember too what passed for wisdom in his former dwelling-place; certainly, the prisoner would rejoice in his change and be sorry for the others....

What would happen if the prisoner returned to the cave, to his former shackles, and, once again, be unable to move? Coming suddenly out of the sunlight, his eyes would be filled with darkness, which would take some time to adjust. The prisoner might be asked his opinion about the shadows before him, but be unable to see them because his eyes would still be dazzled by sunlight. His fellow prisoners might laugh at him, as a result, saying that he had gone up into the light only to come back with his sight ruined, that it was worth no one's while even to attempt the ascent....

Every feature in this [allegory] has meaning. The cave corresponds to the region revealed to humans through our sense of sight; the firelight within the cave corresponds to the power of the Sun. The ascent to view objects in the upper world represents the upward journey of the human soul into the region of what we can know.

[Plato, *The Republic*. Trans. by Francis MacDonald Cornford. New York: Oxford University Press, 1945, 227–31.]

Plato's Theory of True Knowledge

Of what things are you most and least certain? Rank the statements below from most to least certain. Give your reasons.

- All triangles have three sides and three angles.
- Two plus two equals four.
- You are reading this book.
- You believe that there are people in the next room.
- We live in the twenty-first century.

Plato believed that most people have only partial and unclear knowledge. Like the prisoners in his cave, they are surrounded by shadows and misleading ideas. But Plato was also hopeful that human beings could attain true knowledge, that people can move from the intellectual darkness of the cave into the world of light, from a world of mere appearance to the world of reality.

The Sophists were another group of teachers active in Athens during Plato's era. They believed there was no true or single form of knowledge, and they taught their students that truth was whatever someone could make you believe through argument and rhetoric. Plato, like his teacher Socrates before him, was opposed to the Sophist doctrine. Socrates believed in the existence of a single moral truth, if one could but find it. Plato extended this idea by postulating the existence of a single connected truth about everything in the universe.

Plato believed that knowledge was divided into two major categories. First, there was knowledge of the visible world, achieved through the senses. Plato believed that this knowledge was subject to change, that it was based on opinion, and was therefore of less value. Second, there was knowledge gained through rational thought. This knowledge was permanent and consisted of the greater truth. The prisoners of Plato's cave only had knowledge of their visible world, knowledge that was clearly limited and of less value. The escaped prisoner in Plato's allegory fled the world of illusion to find greater truth outside the cave of visual experience.

Plato believed that each of these categories of knowledge contained two subcategories. The world of experience, our visible world, also includes things that we imagine or *believe* might be true. This type of knowledge, according to Plato, was of lower truth value. Plato was not impressed with

Levels of Knowing	Objects	Modes of Thinking
Intelligible world of knowledge	The Good Forms Mathematics	Knowing Thinking
World of Appearances	**Visible Things**	**Believing**
Opinion	Images	Imagining

the fact that we might imagine a unicorn someplace in the world, or picture in our mind people sitting in the next classroom or even a character in a book. Nor did Plato believe there was much to be said for the truth value in art.

The world of visible truth is also the world of things we observe: the chair we sit on, the cat on the table, the snow on the ground, or the lamp lighting our book. While most people accept these things as truth, Plato believed that observations were still just opinions, and only slightly more credible than our imagination.

Real knowledge, Plato maintained, lies only in the intelligible, within the reasoning mind. This truth, too, is divided into two categories. The lower form of knowledge coming to us from the reasoning mind, Plato believed, is the world of thinking: the type of thinking that scientists do when they view an experiment and draw conclusions, or the type of thinking that mathematicians do when they examine the angles of one triangle to make judgements

Plato believed that all objects in the universe were visible copies of eternal ideas of these objects.

about triangles in general. This level of knowledge requires thinkers to use concrete visible objects as springboards from which to launch further thought. Thinkers realize there is more to know and more to find out than what they have on hand.

The optimum level of knowledge, according to Plato, the highest knowledge possible, is knowledge of what he called "The Good." A person who knows The Good understands totally how all triangles are similar, and how all things in the universe are connected. A person who knows The Good no longer needs to rely on the imperfect visible world as a source of information. Instead, all knowledge is cerebral, comprehended solely through the workings of the mind.

Plato was a rationalist; he believed that it is through reasoning, and not through the senses, that the highest knowledge and wisdom can be achieved. Refer to the ranking you did on the previous page. How would Plato rank these statements? Would he have agreed with your ranking?

> I am not young enough to know everything.
> *Oscar Wilde*

Plato's Theory of Form and Change

Like the pre-Socratic philosophers before him, Plato sought to discover the essential nature of things. Like other philosophers, before and after him, Plato wanted knowledge that was eternal and changeless. But everything he saw in the real world was changeable and impermanent. The triangle you draw on paper is destroyed when you burn the paper. The dog that walks past you on the lawn is gone from view in a moment and will be gone forever someday. Your perception of beauty in a painting or in a person is changeable and may well be different from the idea of beauty that someone else may have. We are like the prisoners in the cave, said Plato, because we have only a fleeting and limited knowledge of these things.

Still, he noted, no matter how many triangles, dogs, or objects of beauty we perceive temporarily, we do have a general concept of a triangle, a dog, or beauty. If asked to think about any of these objects, or to draw them, we could do so. Plato wondered how it was possible to have an idea of a dog, triangle, or anything else for that matter, not tied to a specific example. What was Plato's answer? He reasoned that each example of an object in the universe was a visible, if imperfect, copy of the more eternal idea, or "form" (as he put it) of a triangle, a dog, or beauty. The goal of learning, he wrote, was to comprehend the idea or form of things, rather than stick to the specific example of it in the visible world.

Plato was trying to solve the question of how things can be different from all other things, yet share similar important characteristics. How can a person be an individual yet still be like the billions of other people in the world? How are we able to recognize the common characteristics of all people, all tables, all cups, and everything else that exists in the universe? We can do this, Plato concluded, because we are working towards understanding the idea or form of objects. When we understand the idea or form of a person, a table, or a cup we have complete knowledge of it.

Where does this idea or form exist? If

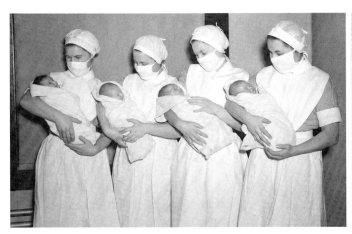

How can babies or bicycles be different from all other things yet share similar characteristics?

this question causes you some problems, you are in good company, for it has perplexed philosophers for thousands of years. Plato seemed to suggest that forms or ideas have an independent existence beyond their specific examples in the everyday world. Plato's student Aristotle had a great deal more to contribute to this topic, as we shall see in the next section.

Plato's Theory of Acquiring Knowledge

Plato agreed with Socrates that the surest way to acquire knowledge was by using the dialectic method. A dialectic, or dialectic investigation, means discussing an idea critically, questioning it, and subjecting it to counter argument and opposing ideas. Many people, philosophers and non-philosophers alike, argue that we can learn a great deal by observing and gathering information from the material objects in the world around us. Plato believed, however, that such knowledge was imperfect and impermanent, and that it led to false beliefs and errors. The best knowledge, according to Plato, came only from the reasoning mind.

Teachers that use the Socratic method of questioning help students to discover knowledge themselves.

If observation is an imperfect method of gaining knowledge, then where do we get the information that we use to build knowledge? Plato believed all ideas are innate, within the mind at birth, but unrecognized. We are all unaware of this existing knowledge, Plato said, and the purpose of dialectic is to reveal it to our conscious awareness. Through rational thought, critical examination, and dialectic discussion with others, we may uncover the eternal innate ideas that already exist in our minds.

In the "Meno dialogue," Plato describes Socrates talking to a slave boy who has never learned mathematics. By questioning the young slave, and by subjecting his answers to further questioning, Socrates leads him to solve a complex problem in geometry. Socrates never provides the boy with solutions or clues, yet the boy eventually solves the problem using dialectic. What was Plato's conclusion? The slave possessed an innate knowledge of geometry that merely needed to be transferred to his conscious thought.

Plato's views on learning and on knowledge had a profound impact on philosophy. Although the specific ideas he developed about learning may be open to question, Plato left a powerful legacy. Belief in the extraordinary capability of the rational mind to gain understanding was an idea that shaped the future development of Western philosophy.

IDEAS AND ISSUES

Understand Concepts
1. (a) Summarize Plato's allegory of the cave.
   (b) In a brief paragraph, explain the meaning of this allegory.
2. (a) Outline Plato's idea of what knowledge is, generally, and in its various levels.
   (b) Summarize Plato's idea of how knowledge is acquired.

Think Critically
3. (a) To what degree do you believe that Plato's views of knowledge and its acquisition are useful?
   (b) How would you be critical of Plato's epistemology, his ideas of knowledge and its acquisition? Justify your answer.
4. Plato, like Socrates, argued that one can draw existing, but unconscious, knowledge to the surface by asking the right questions. Suggest another possible explanation.
5. Explain how you think we develop general concepts of anything—chairs, food, beauty, or people. How did Plato believe that we arrive at general concepts, or ideas, of things?

Communicate Ideas
6. Debate this issue: The world of imagination can provide greater truths than the world of things or of rational ideas.

Inquire and Research
7. Research the sources of Plato's ideas by considering the work of the pre-Socratic philosophers. Which of these ideas does he agree or disagree with most? Organize your comparisons in a way to illustrate them clearly, such as in chart form. Explain your comparison to the rest of the class.
8. Find out more about Plato's views of knowledge by reading *The Republic*, Part 3, Chapters 23–25. Choose one major area of Plato's ideas to analyze and critique. Do this in a persuasive essay.

The Ideas of Aristotle

Aristotle was born in northern Greece in 384 BCE At age seventeen, he went to study at Plato's academy in Athens, where he remained until Plato's death twenty years later.

"All men possess by nature the desire to know," Aristotle wrote at the beginning of his book *Metaphysics*. Whether this statement is true or not, it certainly describes Aristotle's view of himself and of other people. Aristotle believed that the universe was there to learn from, and was open to investigation by any person who cared to search its secrets.

Aristotle was descended from a long line of doctors, and perhaps shared the physician's desire to know the workings of all living organisms. He loved to investigate the specific events of his world, and he was in many ways a predecessor of modern scientific investigation. In the following account, he describes a chick being born:

"About the twentieth day, if you open the egg and touch the chick, it moves inside and chirps, and it is already coming to be covered with down, when, after the twentieth day is past, the chick begins to break the shell...."

Aristotle's achievements were great but they could not have taken place without the contributions of other philosophers before him. To which of the pre-Socratic philosophers do you think Aristotle owes an intellectual debt?

As a young man, Aristotle was influenced powerfully by Plato's ideas. As time went on, however, he developed his own views, and often disagreed with his teacher.

Aristotle remained in Athens until the time of Plato's death. There is some reason to believe that he hoped to become the president of the Academy. However, the presidency fell to Plato's nephew, and Aristotle left when King Philip of Macedon invited Aristotle to tutor his son Alexander. By all accounts, Alexander was not a very attentive student, although eventually the young prince-turned-king would lead conquering armies as far east as India. Perhaps philosophy was not Alexander's main interest at the time.

Aristotle did not return to Athens until twelve years later, when he set up a school in a grove sacred to Apollo and the Muses. He called his school the Lyceum, named after the gardens where Socrates used to go to think. The Lyceum contained several lecture rooms, a library, a map room, an altar, and a building called the "Temple of the Muses." A grant from Alexander the Great provided for the purchase of books and maps.

In the Lyceum's peripatus, a covered pathway, Aristotle would walk and talk with his students. He also gave lectures to students, and occasionally, when a popular topic warranted it, for larger audiences. In the mornings, Aristotle would lecture on logic and first principles to a small group of students. In the afternoons, he spoke to the public on rhetoric, politics, ethics, and other subjects. In many ways, Aristotle's Lyceum resembled a modern university because it had a complex curriculum and a program of post-graduate studies.

When Alexander the Great died in 323 BCE, Athenians reacted against all things Macedonian. Because Aristotle had strong connections with Alexander and with Macedonia, he rapidly became unpopular in Athens, and was charged with "impiety." Unlike Socrates, Aristotle decided to flee "lest the Athenians should sin twice against philosophy," he claimed.

Aristotle died one year later, at age sixty-two, from a stomach ailment aggravated by overwork, or so it was rumoured. He left a considerable inheritance to his daughter. His will asked that the bones of his wife be dug up and buried beside him.

Aristotle's ideas, teachings, and writings sowed the seeds for the development and study of Western philosophy. For over two thousand years, his name was so eminent in European thought that he was called "the philosopher," as though there were no others.

Aristotle's Theory of True Knowledge

Aristotle agreed with Socrates and Plato that it was possible to know what is real in the universe that surrounds us. He also agreed that real truth is unchanging. As time went on, however, Aristotle came to disagree with Plato's concept of form or idea. Plato believed that eternal and perfect forms or ideas existed for all things: tables, chairs, dogs, cats, chipmunks, trees, and so on. But Aristotle could not accept the concept that forms or ideas existed separately from the things themselves.

Aristotle observed that we use our senses to experience specific objects around us. From specific objects, he noted, we develop universal concepts of objects. When we observe many different dogs (basset hounds, collies, shepherds, bulldogs, poodles, grey-hounds, retrievers, or terriers), we develop a concept of what a dog is. We do not need to move beyond the things themselves in order to develop general, universal ideas. In fact, Aristotle believed Plato's universal forms or ideas reside within the particular entities that they embodied. He believed that we develop the idea of a human being by observing many human beings, the idea of a sunny day by living through many sunny days, the idea of a school classroom by sitting in many school classrooms. It is not necessary, he wrote, to separate these ideas from their physical representations.

Aristotle also disagreed with Plato's belief that information provided by the senses was of lesser quality, changeable, and thus suspect. Aristotle, in fact, encouraged people to use their senses to understand the world around them. By using our senses of seeing, hearing, touching, tasting, and smelling, he stated, we build up our general knowledge and develop universal concepts and principles. He also disputed Plato's suggestion that human beings enter life with innate ideas. Aristotle had a healthy respect for the information we acquire through our senses. In fact, he believed that what we see, hear, touch, taste, and smell is an accurate image of the world around us, as he describes in this passage:

"… from sense-perception there arises memory; and when there is repeated memory of the same thing, there arises *experience* (for though there are many memories, they make up a single experience). And from experience—the whole universe now established in the mind (the one distinct from the many, whatever is *one and the same* in all the many instances)—there arises the starting point of a skill, or of scientific knowledge (skill if it concerns what merely comes to be, scientific knowledge if it concerns what is).

"Thus these dispositions are neither innate in a determinate form nor on the other hand do they arise from other higher states of knowledge, but they come about from sense-perception."
[Aristotle, *Posterior Analytics*, Books 1 and 2. In *Western Philosophy*, Trans. and ed. by John Cottingham. Oxford: Blackwell Publishers Ltd., 1996, 21.]

Plato's and Aristotle's contrasting views of the world and how we understand knowledge became the foundations of epistemology. Plato's rationalism and Aristotle's use of the senses gave birth to many of our modern philosophic and everyday views of how we understand our world.

The World of Classical Greece

Why did so much of Western philosophy begin in ancient Greece, especially in the city-state of Athens during the fifth and fourth centuries B.C.? It was from Athens that the great philosophers Socrates, Plato, and Aristotle emerged. Many philosophic questions were raised at that time that are still being asked today. Why was this not-so-large city-state such a hotbed of philosophic ideas and creativity?

Several explanations have been suggested. Geographically, Athens was at the crossroads of three continents: Asia, Africa, and Europe. This placed Athenian citizens in a strategic location to intercept and interpret the philosophies emerging from the great civilizations of China, India, the Middle East, and Africa. Another theory suggests that, for a time, Athenian society was particularly open to new ideas and thinkers in the arts, sciences, literature, and philosophy. This acceptance of divergent ideas may have been influenced by Athenian democracy, which encouraged all citizens to take part in public debate.

When Athens ended its war with Persia in 479 BCe and the city was rebuilt, the "golden age" of Athens began. The Acropolis, the "citadel or city on the hill," was constructed as a sacred shrine. The Parthenon was erected in honour of its patron goddess, Athena. The Dionysus Theatre was rebuilt to host the great tragedies of Aeschylus, Sophocles, and Euripedes. Even the comedies of Aristophanes were presented there, one of them portraying Socrates as the Athenian buffoon. This ancient city became a wellspring of many new ideas in politics, economics, history, biology, physics, mathematics, logic, theology, philosophy, ethics, and psychology.

It was from this environment that Socrates, who spent much of his time in the old city square, speaking with those who passed by, whether they wanted to talk or not, emerged. Athens also fostered the Sophists, who argued that there was no absolute right or wrong, only what could be defended with argument. It was in Athens that Plato and Aristotle wrote their great works.

The Athens of ancient Greece, however, had limitations. None of its slaves, who made up eighty percent of the population, and none of its women, participated in the life or government of the city-state. These restrictions seriously limited the potential of ancient Athenians to consider the nature and rights of humanity. Nevertheless, it is true that during that time in Athens many ideas made their way into the world for others to consider.

He who influences the thought of his times, influences all the times that follow. He has made his impress on eternity.
Hypatia

Hypatia

The Philosopher in Alexandria

Hypatia (370 BCE–415 BCE) was born in Alexandria, Egypt, the daughter of well-known mathematician, teacher, and philosopher Theon. Alexandria, at that time, was a city of 600 000 inhabitants, and comprised some 4700 hectares. The city possessed an outstanding library of thousands of volumes, all of which were inscribed on papyrus. From an early age, Hypatia dedicated herself to philosophy and the pursuit of knowledge. She persuaded her father to send her to Athens for further study in philosophic matters, mathematics, and astronomy.

Painting of Hypatia

Upon her return to Alexandria, Hypatia began to teach and write. She was regarded as the head of Alexandria's Neo-Platonist philosophical school. She is believed to have written several commentaries and a treatise entitled *The Astronomical Canon.*

Her fame and popularity grew. She enjoyed walking the streets of Alexandria interpreting the works of Plato, Artistotle, and others to any who wished to hear. Hypatia carried on a wide correspondence; letters addressed to "the Philosopher in Alexandria" were delivered to her without delay.

Hypatia was also a successful inventor, credited with the creation of an astrolabe (an instrument used to observe the movements of celestial bodies), a water-distillation device, a mechanism for measuring the specific gravity of water, and a planisphere. Eventually Hypatia's public popularity angered political officials who became jealous of her power. One day in 415 BCE, she was dragged from her classroom and stoned to death by an angry mob. She was only forty-five-years-old.

Hypatia's legacy has long proved to be fascinating to both historians and philosophers. Here is how one lecturer communicated to his students his mental image of her.

"Approaching the academy, she dismounts, ascends the white marble steps and enters by the door, on either side of which sit two silent sphinxes. As we follow her into the hall, we see that it is lighted by numerous swinging lamps filled with perfumed oil; the rotunda of the ceiling has been embellished by a Greek artist, with figures of Jupiter and his divine companions, who appear to be rapt in the words which fall from his lips.

"The walls have been decorated by Egyptian artists, with pictures of the sacred animals, the crocodile, the cat, the cow, and the dog; and with sacred vegetables, the onion, the lotus, and the laurel…. On an elevated platform is a divan in purple velvet, and upon a little table is placed the silver statue of Minerva, goddess of wisdom and patron of Hypatia. Behind the table sits the philosophic young woman dressed in a robe of white, fastened about her throat and waist by a band of pearls, and carrying upon her brow the laurel crown which Athens had decreed to her…."

Little is left us today of Hypatia's legacy. Some of her letters survive, as well as her commentaries. Two of her most often quoted aphorisms are:

"Reserve your right to think, for even to think wrongly is better than not to think at all."

"To teach superstitions as truth is a most terrible thing."

IDEAS AND ISSUES

Understand Concepts

1. Make a comparison chart that indicates how Plato and Aristotle agreed and disagreed about what knowledge was and how knowledge can be acquired.
2. (a) Describe the elements that may have contributed to the importance of Athens as an intellectually dynamic society.
   (b) What were some of the weaknesses that you also see in this society?

Apply and Develop

3. Describe how Plato and Aristotle would explain learning in each of the situations listed below. Who do you think would have the better explanation?
   (a) deciding what career is best for you
   (b) learning to distinguish between different plants
   (c) learning a new language
   (d) deciding on the beauty of a work of art

Think Critically

4. Assess Aristotle's epistemology, that is, his views of what knowledge is and how it can be attained. Determine to what degree you agree or disagree with his views. Justify your answer.
5. (a) Outline the general characteristics that you think would contribute to a social environment where ideas can flourish, such as in a classroom, in a business, or in a nation.
   (b) To what degree do you believe that such an environment exists in Canada today?

Communicate Ideas

6. Debate this issue: Plato's theory of knowledge is superior to Aristotle's.
7. Write a short persuasive essay that responds to the question: In what ways are the theories of knowledge of both Plato and Aristotle important to us today?

Inquire and Research

8. Find out more about fifth century BCE Athens. Choose one aspect to describe and analyze, such as the political system, social system, science, arts, philosophy, or other. Describe in what ways this aspect of Athenian society was significant for the future.
9. Socrates' trial, including the charges against him and his defence, is described in Plato's *Apology*. Summarize the arguments and make your own judgement about Socrates' innocence or guilt.

The Ideas of Chuang Tzu

Philosophers in China were also pondering philosophic questions at the same time that Plato and Aristotle were teaching. One school of philosophic thought in the Far East was Taoism. Tao means "the way," the deep and mysterious process from which all things arise and which shapes all of life. The Taoist way is to live and exist as a part of that natural process. One of the most influential Taoists was Chuang Tzu.

Chuang Tzu's Theory of True Knowledge

Not much is known with certainty about the life of Chuang Tzu (365 BCE –290 BCE). What we do know often comes from his writings because he often wrote himself into the cast of characters. We know that Chuang Tzu lived during the time when the ruling Chou Dynasty had split into

several constantly warring states. China's old social order had collapsed and people were struggling to create a new one. It was a period of social chaos.

This was also a golden age for Chinese philosophy. A "Hundred Schools of Thought" tried to imagine and plan what

Symbols of Taoist religion

the new social order should be. Confucianism was one such school which, like its successors, was founded by thinkers who wandered through the countryside with their followers, instructing all they came in contact with, and trying to convince Chinese rulers to follow their teachings. Chuang Tzu was one of these wandering philosophers.

Chuang Tzu wondered about what it was possible to know and of what we could be certain. He asked many questions: Could the rational mind understand the world? How do we know that what we believe to be real and actual is not merely an illusion?

Chuang Tzu's philosophy of knowledge has been described as a sort of scepticism about what can be known because he doubted that we can ever really know truthfully about the world. He believed that there was no really solid ground for judging between two opposing views held by people with different perspectives. As a result, he said, one should attach less importance to social institutions and social behaviour, for there is no way to distinguish between those views that are better or worse.

Chuang Tzu's philosophy, and Taoism generally, has also been described as a form of relativism, that is, a belief that there may be more than one truth. Chuang Tzu believed that there may be a number of ways to consider what is right and wrong. Even things that seem certain, the distinction between the self and others or between life and death, may not be as certain as we think. Because of this, he said, we should not hold specific social ways of doing things to be so important, since they are open to the judgement of different people from different perspectives.

What was the impact of this view of knowledge on human action? How does one know the right way to act or the type of social order to set up? According to Taoists, the human world should conform to the natural world. Individuals, social groups, and institutions should certainly not force their own views and thoughts on others, but try to search for the right way as indicated by the natural order. Sometimes this means allowing things to follow their natural course, rather than interfering or imposing one's will on others or on nature.

The Butterfly

Chuang Tzu

When we dream we do not know that we are dreaming. In our dreams we may even interpret our dreams. Only after we are awake do we know we have dreamed. Finally there comes a great awakening, and then we know life is a great dream. But the stupid think they are awake all the time, and believe they know it distinctly. Are we … rulers? Are we … shepherds?… When I say you were dreaming, I am also dreaming. This way of talking may be called perfectly strange. If after ten thousand generations we could meet one great sage who can explain this, it would be like meeting him in as short a time as in a single morning or evening.

Suppose you and I argue. If you beat me instead of me beating you, are you really right and am I really wrong? If I beat you instead of you beating me, am I really right and are you really wrong? Or are we both partly right and partly wrong? Or are we both wholly right and wholly wrong?...

We say this is right or is wrong, and is so or is not so. If the right is really right, then the fact that it is different from the wrong leaves no room for argument. If what is so is really so, then the fact that it is different from what is not so leaves no room for argument. Forget the passage of time (life and death) and forget the distinction of right and wrong.

Once I, Chuang Chou [Tzu], dreamed that I was a butterfly and was happy as a butterfly. I was conscious that I was quite pleased with myself, but I did not know that I was Chou. Suddenly I awoke, and there I was, visibly Chou. I do not know whether it was Chou dreaming that he was a butterfly or the butterfly dreaming that it was Chou. Between Chou and the butterfly there must be some distinction. [But one may be the other.] This is called the transformation of things.

[Wing-tsit Chan, comp. and trans. In *A Source Book in Chinese Philosophy* Chuang Tzu, *Zhuangzi*. Princeton: Princeton University Press, 1963.]

Understand Concepts

1. Explain what Chuang Tzu says in the first and last paragraph of "The Butterfly."
2. (a) According to Chuang Tzu, what is wrong with the usual ways of settling arguments?
   (b) What does he recommend? Suggest any advantages and problems that you see with this.

Think Critically

3. (a) Explain how you could prove that you are awake right now. Convince someone that you are.
   (b) What arguments can be used against your position?
4. What do you think Plato or Aristotle would say to Chuang Tzu about his philosophy? Provide reasons in your answer.

Communicate Ideas

5. (a) Compare Chuang Tzu's points of view about knowledge and certainty with those of Plato, particularly with Plato's allegory of the cave.
   (b) Role-play a discussion taking place between Plato, Aristotle, and Chuang Tzu around these questions:
   (i) What is knowledge?
   (ii) How certain can you be of what you know?
   (iii) Is there one truth about any given topic, or are several possible?
6. Develop your own epistemology using the questions in exercise 5 as a starting point. Write your answer in one to two pages. You may decide to accept some of the ideas of the philosophers discussed in this chapter or you may develop some of your own. In any case, you must clearly state your position and provide reasons for it. Convince others of the worth of your epistemology.

Review and Reflect

Epistemology is the study of what we can know, and how certain we can be of our knowledge. Questions about knowledge are fundamental because without a concept of what we can know, and with what certainty, all other ideas can potentially be built on weak premises. Questions of epistemology arose in the ancient world in several places around the Mediterranean and in China.

The pre-Socratic natural philosophers pondered the questions: Of what is the natural world made? To what degree do things remain the same over time and to what degree do all things change? They questioned whether knowledge acquired through reason is truer than that acquired through the senses.

Both Socrates and Plato maintained that knowledge developed through the process of discourse and questioning. Plato believed that the highest knowledge can be achieved through reasoning, not through the senses. Aristotle, on the other hand, believed that information acquired through the senses was equal to that acquired through reasoning; in fact, he maintained that it was necessary to use the senses in order to gain knowledge. Chuang Tzu was sceptical that absolute knowledge could ever be acquired.

Questions of knowledge and truth are important to us in everyday life. We form judgements of the world and about others based on what we learn. We act on information provided to us, from within and from without. We make judgements about truth and certainty in all areas of life. Without a view of what knowledge is in everyday life and how certain we can be of it, all information is suspect.

CHAPTER 4

The Philosophy of Science

Philosophers of the ancient world, such as Plato, Aristotle, and Chuang Tzu, sought to determine what it was possible to know, and how certain one could be of that knowledge. Their ideas were accepted, often without question, for many hundreds of years, until the sixteenth and seventeenth centuries, when a renewed quest was initiated for more direct answers to the same questions.

There were practical reasons for this new search. With the increasing importance of scientific experimentation, scientists needed to know more about the knowledge they were discovering, as well as how to develop new knowledge. Francis Bacon, René Descartes, John Locke, and other scientific philosophers sought answers to the age-old questions: What is truth? How certain can we be that we have the truth?

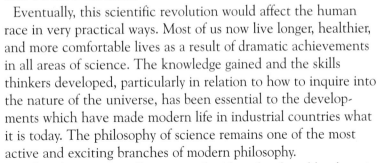

Eventually, this scientific revolution would affect the human race in very practical ways. Most of us now live longer, healthier, and more comfortable lives as a result of dramatic achievements in all areas of science. The knowledge gained and the skills thinkers developed, particularly in relation to how to inquire into the nature of the universe, has been essential to the developments which have made modern life in industrial countries what it is today. The philosophy of science remains one of the most active and exciting branches of modern philosophy.

In this chapter, we will examine the ideas developed by the scientific philosophers, and the questions they asked, including:
- What are the characteristics of a good scientific method?
- How do we know if knowledge is supported by data?
- What is a "cause"?
- What role does observation and reason play in science and in everyday life?
- Is science purely rational and logical, or does it reflect the society in which it operates?
- Can there be more than one truth about any one phenomenon?
- How does science progress?
- What advantage does science have over other types of knowledge?

The questions about our origins are still being examined in many fields of science. How do we know that we have found the truth?

The Development of Science and the Philosophy of Science

What is a scientist? How do scientists do their work? Which of our beliefs are based on science; which of these beliefs may be true but have not yet been tested scientifically; and which will likely never be tested scientifically? Despite the importance of science in our world today, many non-scientists have a difficult time answering these questions. We tend to take for granted the advances that science has achieved. Moreover, many of our everyday beliefs are not very scientific. For example, how would you respond to the statements below?

- It is bad luck to walk under a ladder.
- My horoscope said I would have a good day and meet some great new people.
- Bad things happen in threes. So I must soon be in for a run of good luck.
- If a coin lands heads several times, the odds are greater that it will land tails the next time.
- The fortune teller read my tea leaves and said I would inherit a lot of money.
- I believe in the power of the mind to communicate telepathically.
  For example, when the phone rings I often know it is my friend calling before I pick it up.
- I know someone who recovered from a cold in ten days by eating raw vegetables. I think I will do that too.

While there is little or no hard scientific evidence to support these statements, many people base their ideas and actions on them. Perhaps you or someone you know believes in one or more of them. Will any of these be proven scientifically in the future?

The Middle Ages, the Renaissance, and the Scientific Revolution

For about two thousand years, philosophers of the ancient world such as Plato, Aristotle, and Chuang Tzu held sway over the ideas of those who were curious about the natural world. This was partly because the intellectual climate of the time did not encourage development of new ideas. Instead, people were encouraged to rely on accepted tradition and authority for any knowledge about natural science they required. There were also few new methods of acquiring knowledge.

After the fall of the Western Roman empire in the fifth century, political, cultural, and intellectual development in the Western world declined, and would continue to decline until the tenth century. Pirates roamed the Mediterranean Sea, which was once controlled by the Romans. Ancient cities and centres of learning fell into ruin. Europe became local, rural, and basic as its people struggled to survive. Conditions no longer suited the philosophic life.

There was little time for intellectual pursuits, and very few people had opportunities to learn. Scholarly work was devoted to the preservation of the old, rather than the development of new ideas. Venerated texts were labouriously copied by hand in the monasteries of medieval Europe. The quest for new knowledge virtually ceased during this period of European history.

All was not so grim in other parts of the world, however. Philosophy and science continued to develop in the Islamic nations of the Persian Gulf, the Middle East, and North Africa, as well as in China. In Central and South America, there were thriving intellectual and scientific communities, a fact we are only recently beginning to discover. But for many centuries, the ideas of these civilizations were unknown to each other.

By the eleventh century, European civilization began to revive, a result, some historians have suggested, of increased prosperity. Another contributing factor was the wealth of new ideas crusaders brought back from the Middle East. The new kingdoms and principalities established during this period provided a measure of peace and stability, both of which fostered the exploration of intellectual pursuits. New universities in England, France, and Italy provided havens for philosophers and other scholars. Here, ideas were developed and critically analyzed in ways that had not occurred for centuries.

The fifteenth and sixteenth centuries saw an explosive intellectual awakening in Europe, the social and cultural rebirth that we know today as the Renaissance. New ideas from the East, coupled with the establishment of recognized institutes of learning, and improved social conditions, encouraged many people to devote their lives to education and the pursuit of knowledge.

Historians suggest that the Renaissance was driven by several philosophies. One was humanism, the belief that the starting point for acquiring and judging knowledge was humanity and the world around us, as opposed to some source beyond this world. Secondly, unlike medieval scholars, Renaissance thinkers renewed the belief that it was possible to develop new knowledge rather than simply preserve it from the past. Thirdly, Renaissance intellectuals also stressed the importance of the individual both in life in general, and in the discovery of new knowledge.

Time Line

Early Scientific Thought

- - - - - - - - - - -

SOCRATES
(469 BCE–399 BCE)

PLATO
(428 BCE–347 BCE)

ARISTOTLE
(384 BCE–322 BCE)

CHUANG TZU
(365 BCE–290 BCE)

FALL OF WESTERN ROMAN EMPIRE
(476 CE)

MIDDLE AGES
(476–C. LATE 15TH CENTURY)
affects Europe

GOLDEN AGE OF BAGDHAD
(8TH AND 9TH CENTURIES)
allows thinkers to develop science, art, and philosophy

RENAISSANCE
(C. 14TH CENTURY)
begins in ITALY

The Renaissance encouraged creative exploration in the sciences, the arts, philosophy, and in other areas of thought. Michelangelo and Leonardo da Vinci studied, painted, and sculpted. Copernicus, Galileo, and other scientists developed radical new scientific ideas that were often diametrically opposed to the accepted theories of ancient times. Bacon, Descartes, Locke, and others explored new methods to identify the discovery of more certain knowledge in philosophy and in science.

Although this major intellectual rebirth occurred initially in the sciences of astronomy and physics, it soon spread to medicine and chemistry. Copernicus (1473– 1543) was one of the first people to question the ancient view that the sun, planets, and stars revolved around the Earth. Galileo (1564–1642) studied the stars with a telescope, and was put under house arrest for supporting Copernicus' ideas. These thinkers challenged accepted views, traditions, and authority and often paid a steep personal price for doing so. Such was the Scientific Revolution.

Other philosophers of science studied how scientific truths could be achieved and with what certainty. Bacon, Descartes, and Locke provided a philosophic framework within which scientists could study the universe and humanity's place in it. These thinkers often returned to the questions raised by the ancient philosophers: Should we trust the workings of our mind more than the information from our senses? This provoked a debate Plato and Aristotle would have enjoyed.

If I have seen farther it is by standing on the shoulders of giants.

Isaac Newton

The Renaissance was a time of renewal and exploration in many areas of life. How do each of these figures of the time represent Renaissance ideals of humanism and individualism?

Understand Concepts

1. (a) What were three questions of interest to philosophers of science?
   (b) For each of these, why might non-scientists also be interested?
2. (a) Describe the view of knowledge that was widespread in Europe during the Middle Ages.
   (b) Explain how this affected philosophical thinking.
3. Describe the conditions that encouraged philosophic thought during the Renaissance.
4. (a) What were the central elements of Renaissance thought?
   (b) Explain how each element in part (a) influenced philosophy.
5. What different areas of endeavour did the Renaissance have an impact on?

Think Critically

6. (a) What do you think makes some knowledge scientific and other knowledge non-scientific?
   (b) How does this affect the degree of certainty that you would place in a piece of knowledge? That is, would you automatically accept it if it can be shown to have scientific support, or would you have less acceptance if it was based on something other than scientific evidence?
7. (a) Identify five beliefs you have that you think are supported by scientific evidence. Describe what that evidence is.
   (b) Identify five beliefs you hold that are likely not supported by scientific evidence. Explain why you accept these beliefs.

Inquire and Research

8. Find out more about the time period of the Middle Ages or the Renaissance. In particular, determine:
   (a) conditions that contributed to, or hindered, the development of ideas, and
   (b) the types of ideas that were held about science, the arts, and philosophy.

Philosophic Ideas: Rationalism and Empiricism

Over the centuries, philosophers of epistemology have developed a number of methodologies for examining knowledge. One is to view knowledge as something that occurs largely within the human mind. This approach is known as rationalism, the belief that knowledge is produced largely within the mind through thoughtful processes. René Descartes was a major supporter of the rationalist school of thought.

A second methodology suggests that knowledge is acquired primarily by using the senses, and interpreting what comes to us through our eyes, ears, and other senses. This second view is known as empiricism. John Locke, George Berkeley, and David Hume were important proponents of the empirical school of thought.

Rationalism

Rationalism emphasizes the importance of reason in finding truth. Reason is more important than sensory experience, emotions, or traditional authority in the search for truth. Extreme rationalism, which was first espoused by the natural philosophers of ancient times, suggests that all human knowledge is based on reasoning. Parmenides said that our reason is correct in concluding that change cannot occur, regardless of what conflicting evidence is presented to us by our senses. Zeno supported this view with his paradox of the race between Achilles and the tortoise. Even Plato, to some extent, was an extreme rationalist in that he claimed that the mind was the primary source of knowledge, certainly over our senses.

Language, Ideas, and Truth

What do words refer to: our inner ideas alone, the external world alone, or something different from either of these? For the empiricists of the seventeenth and eighteenth century, language was seen as a direct link to the world of ideas. One problem with this view, however, is that it is difficult to see how external things can be represented, either by ideas or by language. To what degree, if at all, does the idea of a dog, or the word "dog" itself, resemble a real dog in the "real" world? The word "dog" is a symbol only of the external four-legged creature. How do we construct, or model this creature, in our minds as ideas?

A second problem is that competence in language is not the same as comprehending, although the two are definitely related. That is, we can use language without necessarily understanding ideas in the same way someone else does. Our idea of a dog, a stream, or a person, may be different from the idea held by the person telling us about it, even though we use the same words to describe it.

Twentieth century philosopher G. Frege (*Philosophical Writings*, 1960) emphasized the objective and public, or shared, aspects of understanding. For example, if someone describes the Rocky Mountains to you, there is a shared idea of some kind, although what this is, Frege did not say. However, some philosophers rejected the idea that sentences could ever express single thoughts, or "propositions," to the point of scepticism. These philosophers stressed that language depends on socially agreed meanings that may or may not bear relationships to ideas, or to external reality. That is, language is a game all of its own without necessary reference to anything else. This idea is hard to accept, however, since language seems to work so well in giving and getting directions, and for other practical purposes.

A mind enclosed in language is in prison.
Simone Weil

Noam Chomsky

Noted linguist Noam Chomsky (1928–) brought a whole new view of language, revolutionizing both the philosophy and psychology of language. Chomsky wondered how it was that children, with varying backgrounds and experiences, without explicit training, and at much the same age, learn to speak a language so quickly and so readily. Chomsky argued that there is an innate biological capacity in humans that contains a universal grammar, a set of fundamental principles of language. When exposed to language, children learn it naturally and quickly. Research in recent years has shown that if a person is not exposed to language in these early years, they will have difficulty later in understanding the structure of language. Again, Chomsky forces us to ask the question: To what degree does language reflect innate ideas or at least innate ways of viewing the world.

Common sense is the collection of prejudices acquired by age eighteen.
Albert Einstein

More moderate rationalism recognizes that we must acquire some information from the senses, in order for the mind to have something to work on. Moderate rationalists claim, however, that the mind also brings important processes to bear in order to process information gained from our senses. Moderate rationalists, such as Immanuel Kant, also believe that we can understand some things, that is to say, have some knowledge, *a priori* (beforehand). We understand, for example, that everything with size has a shape. Kant said that we must explore the world using our understanding, or else we would not be able to acquire further knowledge from that world. Twentieth century philosopher and linguist Noam Chomsky argued that certain grammatical structures are innate in our minds, so all human languages share common features.

The term rationalism has also been used to mean opposition to authority, because rationalists argue that we must process our own information individually, and think critically about it individually, rather than just accept ideas from others.

Empiricism

Empiricism refers to any view that bases knowledge on what we experience through our five senses. Classical empiricism, partic-ularly, is associated with the philosophy of John Locke, the first of the British empiricists. Two other philosophers, George Berkeley and David Hume, continued to develop theories of empiricism, but in more extreme ways.

Classical empiricism is based on the idea that we know about the world only what the world reveals to us through our senses. Any attempt to reshape this information through rational thought will only lead to distortion. Locke's analogy portrays our minds as blank pages upon which experience writes its story. Once the sensory data have been entered in the mind, they can be combined or manipulated to form ideas and concepts.

Empiricism contained within it this inherent problem: If we are dependent solely on sensory data, then how can we know anything beyond our senses? Berkeley and Hume were particularly perplexed by this question. How, they asked, can we know anything at all about the outer world? Extreme empiricism led to scepticism about whether we could, in fact, know anything about the world.

In many ways, everyone is an empiricist; much of what we do and how we do it is based on sensory information. The question is: How accurate and real is this information.

Nineteenth century cartoon depicting the five senses.

Understand Concepts

1. (a) Which approach do you relate to most, rationalism or empiricism?
   (b) Do some life issues make you choose one approach over the other? Give reasons for your answer.

Think Critically

2. Use a chart to compare the characteristics, strengths, and weaknesses of rationalism and empiricism.

Communicate Ideas

3. In a paper of up to two pages, discuss how Plato and Aristotle would have responded to both empiricism and rationalism, as a way to search for truth.
4. Debate this issue: Truth can more readily be found through the senses than through rational thought.

Inquire and Research

5. (a) Research how we use language to express our ideas. Prepare a 400-word summary of your findings.
   (b) Discuss how language can affect our ideas about the world. Give some real-life examples that demonstrate that language can be a barrier to the truth as well as being a useful tool.

Francis Bacon:
False Beliefs Block the Truth

Francis Bacon (1561–1626) made significant contributions to the philosophy of science. Like many thinkers of his time, Bacon was involved in several fields, including philosophy, law, and politics, to name but a few. Bacon served the British royalty at the courts of Queen Elizabeth I and James I. He achieved great success and abysmal failure in his service to the monarchy. At one point, he was appointed Lord Chancellor, at another, he was imprisoned, probably unfairly, on charges of corruption. He also wrote non-philosophic works. Some people believe that Bacon wrote some of the plays attributed to William Shakespeare.

Today, Francis Bacon is remembered largely for his work in the philosophy of science. His major book, *The New Method (Novum Organum)* published in 1620, described how scientists should "interrogate nature," by using observation and experiment, to determine when a condition or a circumstance is present or absent. Such observations, Bacon wrote, would allow researchers to draw careful conclusions.

Bacon believed that science would ultimately bring great practical benefits to humanity by providing a world of ease and power. His faith in the value of science to humanity would eventually prove true, although it would take several hundred years before his vision was realized.

Bacon's enthusiasm for science may have contributed to his death. One of his last research questions was whether meat could be effectively preserved by freezing. Bacon ventured out in severe winter weather in order to stuff a chicken with snow. Whether or not this had an impact on his health, we cannot be certain. What we do know is that Bacon caught a bad cold and died a few days later at age 65. Today's scientific medical knowledge might have saved him.

Bacon argued that the truth could only be discovered if we go beyond superficial characteristics and question the accepted ideas of society. What are some barriers in contemporary life that block us from discovering the truth?

Bacon's Rebellion Against Intellectual Idols and False Beliefs

Like many pioneering philosophers, Francis Bacon rebelled against the commonly accepted views of his time. He disagreed with those traditional methods of seeking truth that had been taught in universities, especially by the scholastic school of philosophy, or "scholastics" as they were called, of the thirteenth and fourteenth centuries, who believed in deducing new ideas from apparently self-evident truths. Bacon was vehement in his belief that such practices led to nothing.

Bacon warned his contemporaries about complacency. We accept many ideas as truth, he said, that have little or no sound basis. He called these false beliefs "intellectual idols." Before we can discover truth, he argued, we must recognize and cast away these "intellectual idols," which he described as follows:

Idols of the tribe are illusions that stem from the manner in which human beings perceive the world. We tend to look only at the superficial appearance of objects, and therefore mistake our sensory impressions for the true underlying nature of things. An oar in water appears bent when observed from above the water's surface even though it is not; objects in the distance appear smaller than they really are. Plato was also concerned with this problem. Bacon, like most philosophers, thought that we need to get beyond the superficial appearance and nature, not only of things but of ideas as well. We must seek to understand what lies beneath to see the real nature of any thing or any idea.

Idols of the cave addresses the issue of how we allow private concerns and wishes to distort our perceptions. We see what we want to see rather than what really is. Focussing on our own needs and desires, we relate other events to ourselves, missing the truth in the process. Hundreds of years later, psychologists such as Sigmund Freud would elaborate on this idea, with the added perception that we may often not even be aware of these concerns and wishes. Buddhist philosophers, before and after, have also argued that in our false belief in our own permanence we connect all events to ourselves, and fail to understand the world around us correctly.

Idols of the marketplace are the beliefs of society. The customs of culture can often lead us to think and believe things which may not be true. All of us have points of view which are ingrained in us from childhood; we view our world through prejudices and stereotypes which we often fail to question or analyze. Assuming a stance in opposition to the ideas and beliefs of those around us often leads to friction and problems.

Idols of the theatre describes the false beliefs of traditional philosophy. Sometimes we pay too much respect and reverence to old schools of thought. Bacon made particular reference in this critique to the philosophies of the schools of his time, especially the "scholastic school." Bacon was a leading crusader in the movement to observe and draw individual and personal conclusions, ones that did not necessarily accept the ideas of traditional philosophers.

> You will never succeed in getting at the truth if you think you know, ahead of time, what the truth ought to be.
>
> *Marchette Chute*

> People only see what they are prepared to see.
>
> *Ralph Waldo Emerson*

Bacon's Scientific Methodology:
From Observation to Conclusion

Time Line

Rationalists and Empiricists in Science
- - - - - - - - - - -

FRANCIS BACON
(1561–1626)

contributes to development of scientific method

RENÉ DESCARTES
(1596–1650)
questions what is certain

JOHN LOCKE
(1632–1704)
says all our ideas come through our senses

GEORGE BERKELEY
(1685–1753)
argues that we have no real certainty of the world

DAVID HUME
(1711–1776)
proposes a different idea of empiricism

Bacon was a pioneer in the philosophy of science. He encouraged careful observation of the world, the collection of examples, and experimentation, before drawing general conclusions. Bacon's "new methodology" began with careful observation of the environment. One examines specific instances of objects and actions, particular leaves, tables, people, actions, or events. People using this method would discover three distinct types of observation. Bacon referred to these as "tables of observation."

The first table searches for instances where a given circumstance or phenomenon is present, for example, a green healthy lawn, a car that starts, or good philosophy grades. The second table looks for cases where a particular circumstance or phenomenon is absent, for example, the front lawn is burnt brown, a car will not start, or philosophy grades are embarrassing. The third table examines those situations where a given phenomenon exists in varying degrees, for example, the lawn is brown but shows promise, the car engine makes noises that indicate the starter mechanism may be functioning, or philosophy marks are improving.

Imagine, for example, that you are conducting an experiment that examines the effects of sunlight on a plant. You subject several plants to varying degrees of sunshine and observe the results. You sort these plants into categories, using Bacon's tables of observation: healthy, moderately healthy, or dead. Scientists making observations of particular instances, said Bacon, should aim to develop general laws or explanations. Your experiments on sunlight and plants might help you develop a general law that states that increased exposure to sunlight creates healthier plants. General laws applicable to the examples previously cited might include: watering the lawn improves its appearance, a car starts better when the engine is properly maintained, and studying usually improves philosophy marks.

Bacon's methodology involved using the process of studying specific cases, to develop more general truths or laws from them. From Chapter 2, we learned that this is inductive reasoning, a process of which Aristotle would have approved. Bacon was optimistic that induction would reveal broad and powerful new knowledge about the natural world. He was also hopeful that inductive reasoning would increase our knowledge about human affairs. By observing people and social activities carefully, Bacon believed that we would develop a deeper understanding of humanity and society. This belief eventually would become the bedrock on which the social sciences, such as sociology, anthropology, and psychology, developed.

Nagarjuna

The Sceptical Buddhist

Scepticism, the view that we cannot really know the external world, has been held by a number of philosophies, both East and West. Nagarjuna (c. 150 CE) was the greatest sceptic-mystic of the Voidist school of Mahayana Buddhism. Nagarjuna interpreted Buddha's "middle way" as emptiness of all things.

Nagarjuna argued in the following way about external reality. The most reliable means of knowledge that we generally accept depends on an appeal to the reality of the objects that make us know. But the reality of these objects is, in turn, established by the means of knowing, that is, the mind. So, said Nagarjuna, the establishing of any knowledge is hopelessly circular; we know because objects appear to be real, but they appear to be real because we know. Therefore, how can we know the real nature of anything?

In what ways is Nagarjuna's argument similar to, or different from, that of Berkeley? How convincing do you find it?

Novum Organum
(The New Method)

Francis Bacon

As all the sciences we now have do not help us in finding out new works, so neither does the logic we now have help us in finding out new sciences. The logic now in use serves rather to fix and give stability to the errors which have their foundations in commonly received notions…. So it does more harm than good….

The discoveries which have hitherto been made in the sciences are such as lie close to vulgar [everyday] notions, scarcely beneath the surface. In order to penetrate into the more and further recesses of nature, it is necessary [to determine] a more sure and guarded way; and that a method of intellectual operation be introduced altogether better and more certain….

It is idle to expect any great advancement in science from the … engraving of new things upon old. We must begin anew from the very foundations, unless we would revolve forever in a circle with … contemptible progress.

One method of discovery alone remains to us, which is simply this. We must lead men to the particulars themselves … while men on their side must force themselves for a while to lay their notions by and begin to familiarize themselves with facts.

The idols and false notions which are now in possession of the human understanding, and have taken deep root therein, … so beset men's minds that truth can hardly find entrance….

[Francis Bacon, *Novum Organum* (*The New Method,* 1620), Book 1. Trans. by Ellis and Spedding. London: Routledge, 1905, 259–66, 302, 303, 307–9.]

IDEAS AND ISSUES

Understand Concepts

1. What criticisms did Bacon make of how science operated up to his time?
2. (a) Summarize the meaning of Bacon's four "idols."
   (b) To what extent would Bacon suggest that we may still be entrapped by the four "idols" today?
   (c) For each of the four "idols" suggest an example from contemporary life.
3. What method did Bacon say should be followed to discover new knowledge?

Apply and Develop

4. Use Bacon's four "idols" to analyze a position piece, such as an argumentative essay, an editorial, or discussion of a social issue. You can ask these questions of the communication:
   (a) To what extent does the writer or speaker allow personal concerns and interests to shape his or her views?
   (b) To what extent is the writer or speaker failing to delve deeply into the truth?
   (c) To what extent does the communication reflect the accepted views of the culture?
   (d) In what ways does the communication reflect an uncritical acceptance of traditional ideas?
5. Identify how inductive reasoning may be used in each of these cases:
   (a) learning a language
   (b) learning to play a game such as chess or football
   (c) doing a science experiment
   (d) deciding how your friends will react to your idea for Friday night
   (e) solving a math problem

Think Critically

6. Discuss the benefits or strengths that Bacon's "new method" has over other existing methods for getting new information.

Communicate Ideas

7. How would Plato or Aristotle have reacted to Bacon's ideas? Write a paragraph responding as each of them might have to Bacon's "new method."

Inquire and Research

8. Ask your science teacher how important inductive reasoning is in science today. Make sure your teacher illustrates the importance with examples. Summarize your discussion and present it to a classmate.
9. Read about the life of Francis Bacon. Develop a hypothesis about the significance of his work. Present this in a paper that uses evidence to support your hypothesis, which will then become your thesis.

René Descartes: "I Think, Therefore I Am"

René Descartes (1596–1650) has been called the father of modern philosophy. He is described as the "chief architect of the seventeenth century intellectual revolution which devastated the traditional doctrines … and laid down the philosophical foundations for what we think of as the 'modern scientific age'."(Honderich, 1995, 188)

Descartes was born in Touraine, France, in a well-to-do family. His parents were able to send him to school, a privilege out of reach for most people at that time. Descartes studied mathematics, logic, and philosophy. Although he was impressed with the certainty and the precision of mathematics, he was disappointed with philosophy. "It contained no point which was not disputed and hence doubtful," he wrote. (Descartes, 1637, Part 1)

By the time he was a young man, Descartes despaired of finding truth in school. He was convinced that most of what he had been taught was faulty. Descartes decided to travel, hoping that he would learn how to reason well from that "great book of the world." He wandered through much of Europe, and even spent time as a soldier, but was disappointed in the knowledge that he found in everyday life as well. He realized that ordinary people had as many differences of opinion as did the philosophers he had studied in school.

Descartes lecturing to Queen Christina of Sweden in 1649. These lectures took place at 5:00 o'clock in the morning and lasted 5 hours. They are said to be the cause of Descartes' death.

Descartes concluded that true knowledge could only emerge from the power of human reason. On November 10, 1619, at the age of twenty-five, Descartes decided that he would no longer rely on the ideas of other philosophers, even the great Aristotle, just because these thinkers were accepted authorities. Instead, Descartes would use his own rational powers to determine truth.

Descartes settled in Holland, a country where diversity of opinion was tolerated. It was an environment that encouraged philosophic work. There, Descartes wrote his major works: *Discourse on Method* (1637), *Meditations on First Philosophy* (1641), *Principles of Philosophy* (1644), and *Passion of the Soul* (1649).

In 1649, Queen Christina of Sweden invited Descartes to instruct her in philosophy. She was willing to pay well, but on condition that he live in Sweden. Descartes accepted the offer, but, it turned out to be a serious mistake. The only time that Christina could discuss philosophy was at 5 o'clock in the morning. The bitter cold and the damp palace air wreaked havoc on Descartes' health. In 1650, at age fifty-four, Descartes caught a fever and died.

> We are drowning in information but starved for knowledge.
>
> *John Naisbitt*

Descartes' Philosophy: From Intuitive Certainty to Truth

From time immemorial, philosophers have sought truth and certainty. This was also Descartes' goal. He spent the early years of his life investigating commonly accepted sources: the opinions of other philosophers, the ideas held by people in their everyday lives, and information acquired through the senses. Descartes eventually rejected all of these, claiming they were uncertain and contradictory methods for determining truth. He concluded that all knowledge began with ideas in the mind, ideas which he considered carefully, using the following method.

"[I]t was necessary for me," wrote Descartes, "… to reject as absolutely false everything concerning which I could imagine the least ground of doubt." Descartes believed it was possible to doubt virtually everything. Even the fact that he was sitting by the fire could be doubted, he wrote one evening, for "How do I know that I am not dreaming?" Chuang Tzu, centuries before, had the same doubts.

Yet Descartes did not conclude his search with doubt. He continued to seek the one solid certainty upon which he could build knowledge. "If I am fortunate enough to find a single truth which is certain," he said, "I will reserve doubt and build a philosophy." That single certain truth, he found, was that he must exist. For even in the act of doubting everything, there is a being who doubts. In one of the most famous phrases in philosophy, Descartes wrote: "I think, therefore I am," or in Latin, *Cogito ergo sum*.

From this foundation of certainty, Descartes proceeded to determine what else he could know with certainty. He examined his thoughts, and found within them the idea of God as an infinitely independent, all-knowing, and all-powerful being. He wondered where such an idea came from. It must have come from God, he concluded, since an imperfect being such as himself could not have developed such an idea of perfection. Therefore, God must exist.

Descartes then looked around him and

asked himself whether he could be certain that external physical objects existed. We certainly receive impressions of physical objects, he noted, often against our will. Is it possible we are fooled? Perhaps God wishes to deceive us? No, Descartes concluded, because God is perfect and would not deceive us. Therefore, external objects must also exist.

Thus Descartes proved, to his satisfaction, three major truths of which he could be certain: that he existed, that God exists, and that external objects exist.

Descartes' method of philosophic inquiry employed orderly and systematic thinking. An aimless search for the truth, he said, is like a person wandering the streets hoping to find treasures that someone might have dropped. Orderly thinking, on the other hand, consists of two major elements: intuitive certainty and deductive logic.

Descartes believed that we *can* be certain of a truth when we recognize it intuitively, absolutely, and without question. We know intuitively that we are conscious of our own existence, for example, or that two plus two equals four, that a person cannot be in two different places at the same time, or that when an object is split in two each piece will be smaller than the original. Intuitive

Person touching fire.

certainty, then, is one essential characteristic of truth, according to Descartes.

Secondly, said Descartes, we use deductive reasoning to move with certainty from one truth to another. Mathematics is a prime example of effective deduction at work because it moves with certainty from one idea to another. Since two plus two equals four, then four minus two must equal two. If a pie is cut in two, then each piece must be smaller than the original pie. Deductive reasoning means that if you accept a statement or premise, then you must accept its deductive conclusion.

Descartes developed several other rules of reasoning to achieve what he believed to be certain knowledge and to move deductively to new knowledge:

- Do not begin with what others say but with what is clear and certain.
- Reduce each step to its simplest components.
- Move step by step from easy to more difficult ideas.
- Review carefully to ensure nothing is omitted.
- Stop when you arrive at a step that is unclear.

Willard van Orman Quine

The Quest for Truth

American philosopher Willard van Orman Quine (1908–) replaced the question mark on his typewriter with a logical symbol. Quine didn't miss the question mark because he said, "I deal in certainties." Quine's work in logic and epistemology challenged philosophy's search for the truth beyond human experience, which Quine claimed actually stood in the way of the pursuit of knowledge. Quine believed that philosophy had to recognize that it had no special claim to truth.

Quine developed a new type of philosophy, which he called naturalized epistemology. He claimed that the role of epistemology was to describe the way knowledge is actually obtained, that is, how science arrives at the beliefs accepted by the scientific community. The totality of our existing knowledge or beliefs, said Quine, is artificial and impinges very little on actual experience. Anything can be held "true" if we make drastic enough adjustments to our belief system. In 1951, Quine challenged accepted ideas of knowledge, meaning, and truth, by arguing that logic and mathematics need to be revised when they conflict with experience. Quine's ideas are central to the philosophy of language and the philosophy of science.

> I am attacked by two very opposite sects—the scientists and the know–nothings.
>
> *Luigi Galvani*

Meditations of First Philosophy

René Descartes

For several years now, I have been aware that I accepted many falsehoods as true in my youth, that what I built on the foundation of those falsehoods was dubious, and therefore that, once in my life, I would need to tear down everything and begin anew from the foundations if I wanted to establish any firm and lasting knowledge....

Of course, whatever I have so far accepted as supremely true I have learned either from the senses or through the senses. But I have occasionally caught the senses deceiving me, and it would be prudent for me never completely to trust those who have cheated me even once....

But, while my senses may deceive me about what is small or far away, there may still be other things taken in by the senses which I cannot possibly doubt—such as that I am here, sitting before the fire, wearing a dressing gown, touching this paper....

This would be perfectly obvious—if I weren't a man accustomed to sleeping at night whose experiences while asleep are at least as far-fetched as those that madmen have while awake. How often a dream has convinced me that I was here, sitting before the fire, wearing my dressing gown, when, in fact, I was undressed and between the covers of my bed!

Suppose then that I am dreaming. Suppose, in particular, that my eyes are not open, that my head is not moving, and that I have not put out my hand. Suppose that I do not have hands, or even a body....

Yesterday's meditation has hurled me into doubts so great that I can neither ignore them nor think my way out of them. I am in turmoil, as if I have accidentally fallen into a whirlpool and can neither touch bottom nor swim to the safety of the surface. But I will struggle and try to follow the path that I started on yesterday. That is, I will reject whatever is open to the slightest doubt just as though I have found it to be entirely false, and I will continue until I find something certain—even if it is just that nothing is certain....

I suppose, then, that everything I see is unreal. I believe that none of what my unreliable memory presents to me ever happened. I have no senses. Body, shape, extension, motion, and place are fantasies. What then is true? Perhaps only that nothing is certain....

I have convinced myself that there is nothing in the world—no sky, no earth, no minds, no bodies. Doesn't it follow that I don't exist? No; surely I must exist if it's me who is convinced of something. But there is a deceiver, supremely powerful and cunning, whose aim is to see that I am always deceived. Then surely I exist, since I am deceived. Let him deceive me all he can, he will never make it the case that I am nothing while I think that I am something. Thus having fully weighed every consideration, I must finally conclude that the statement "I am, I exist" must be true whenever I state or mentally consider it.

[René Descartes, *Meditations of First Philosophy*. Trans. by Ronald Rubin. CA: Arete Press, 1985.]

Understand Concepts

1. (a) Identify problems or questions to which both Bacon and Descartes turned their attention.
   (b) How did Bacon and Descartes view the existing state of philosophic knowledge?
2. Summarize Descartes' method of acquiring true and certain knowledge.
3. What knowledge did Descartes conclude was true and certain using this method?

Apply and Develop

4. For each statement below, provide reasons for believing it is certain and reasons why it could be doubted.
   (a) There are people inside the house next door.
   (b) There is a geographic location called Antarctica.
   (c) The grass will grow again next spring.
   (d) Your classmates are real people and not computerized robots.
   (e) The philosopher Socrates once existed.
   (f) You are a real person and not a robot that thinks it is a real person.
5. Make a list of the things that you believe you know, intuitively and without doubt, to be true. You may begin with $2 + 2 = 4$. Compare your list with the person sitting beside you. Determine if each of you can agree with each other's list. Try to raise doubts in the mind of the other person about his or her list.

Think Critically

6. Descartes criticized a number of other ways of obtaining true and certain knowledge, such as ideas handed down from other thinkers and philosophers, ideas of society, and knowledge acquired through the senses. To what extent do you agree or disagree with his criticisms?
7. Make two lists of your opinion on Descartes' method: one listing the strengths, and the other the possible problems or weaknesses.
8. Is it possible to doubt any conclusions that Descartes said were true and certain? Provide reasons.

Communicate Ideas

9. Debate this issue: Descartes' method is the right way to find true and certain knowledge.

John Locke: The Mind is a Blank Slate

John Locke (1632–1704) was born into a home that emphasized the virtues of hard work and a love of simplicity. He studied the classics, logic, moral philosophy, rhetoric, and Greek at Westminster School. He went on to study medicine and the newly developing experimental sciences at Oxford University. Upon graduating, Locke became personal physician to several important figures of his day.

England during the seventeen century was a country of great political, social, and intellectual upheaval. Monarchs were overthrown and parliamentary democracy developed. New social classes, lifestyles, and forms of religion emerged and the scientific revolution was proceeding at breakneck speed.

Locke was involved in many of these changes. He was active in politics, especially in the movement to prevent English Stuart monarchs from acquiring absolute power. In 1683, Locke's political activities caused him to be exiled to Holland. He did not return to England until 1689, when the Stuarts were overthrown. Locke's writings reflect his wide interests in education, economics, government, theology, science, medicine, and, of course, philosophy.

Unlike many of the philosophers we have examined so far, John Locke lived to the age of 72 and achieved significant public success during his lifetime. His work and writings have had wide and lasting influence. Locke's political writings helped shape the developing democratic systems of Britain, France, and the United States, and would continue to have significant impact on these governments for the next century or more. Locke's ideas about knowledge and understanding became the foundation of empiricism, the philosophy that studies how we understand the world through our senses.

Locke believed that innate knowledge is not possible and that knowledge can only be acquired through the senses and through experience. What concerns would you have about such a philosophy?

Locke's Theory of Knowledge: From Experience To Ideas

One evening, John Locke met with friends to discuss philosophy. Soon, however, they found themselves hopelessly entangled in an argument they could not settle. As a result of that evening Locke decided that before any topic can be discussed successfully it is necessary to "examine our own abilities and see what objects our understandings were … fitted to deal with." His *Essay Concerning Human Understanding* was written to "enquire into the original certainty, and extent of human knowledge; together with the grounds and degrees of belief, opinion and assent." (Locke, 1690)

In this essay, Locke asked, what is the "origin, certainty, and extent of human knowledge?" Although Descartes investigated this same question only a few years earlier, Locke rejected Descartes' solution, and denied the existence of innate, or inborn, ideas which needed only to be discovered or unearthed. Belief in innate ideas, Locke argued, was not only wrong, but potentially dangerous. Someone who believes that an idea is innate, Locke wrote, will tend to accept that idea without further question or examination. Many of the ideas we hold, Locke argued, need to be questioned. A skillful ruler, for example, might convince people that an idea or principle was innate in order to govern more easily and eliminate the development of opposing points of view. Locke cited the example of England's Stuart monarchy, which insisted that its rulers held authority by divine right, by the authority of God. The Stuarts believed their authority was inviolable, not to be questioned by anyone, including Parliament. The concept of innate ideas and innate behaviour continues to be used in our own society to discount opposing ideas.

Locke argued that all our ideas come to us through our senses. We are not born with undiscovered ideas already existing in our mind; we acquire them through experience. All ideas are learned.

Locke illustrated his view of learning with the image of a blank sheet of paper, or *tabula rasa* in Latin. Locke asked his readers to imagine that the human mind at birth was like a blank sheet of paper, with no markings or ideas yet written upon it. Life's experiences write their stories upon this blank sheet, providing us with knowledge and ideas.

Primary and Secondary Qualities

Locke asked another important question: To what degree can we truly understand the world around us? Are things around us really as we perceive them? Locke answered by suggesting that all material things possess two qualities: primary and secondary. Primary qualities reside within the object itself; secondary qualities are those powers within the object that actively produce ideas within our mind.

Primary qualities existing within the object include solidity, extension, figure, and mobility. Primary qualities can produce simple ideas in our minds. For example, we may experience a candle. We know that the candle contains these primary qualities: there is one of them, it is solid to the touch, it is about ten centimetres high, and it sits unmoving on the table. Locke wrote that we all have a fairly direct and certain idea of primary qualities.

Secondary qualities, however, are powers within an object that allow us to experience such things as colour, sound, taste, and

> The most important of my discoveries have been suggested to me by my failures.
> *Humphrey Davy*

heat. These characteristics are not within the object itself. The heat and light of the candle, for example, are not within the candle; it is the power of the candle that causes us to experience heat and light within our own bodies. Thus, according to Locke, we are less certain of secondary qualities.

Simple and Complex Ideas

Experience comes to us through our senses, from which we receive perceptions about external objects. From the senses we acquire simple ideas such as yellow, white, hot, cold, soft, hard, bitter, sweet, and other sensible qualities. We look at a flower and receive the ideas of white colour and sweet smell. We pick up a piece of ice and our senses transmit simple ideas of hard and cold.

The mind reflects upon these simple ideas and from them produces complex ideas. Complex ideas are assembled as a composite of simple ideas. The mind merges these simple ideas to produce general or abstract ideas. Whiteness, hardness, and sweetness coalesce through reflection to form the complex idea of sugar. Knowledge, then, is a product of reason working out the connections between simple ideas acquired through the senses.

Locke's views on how we can attain knowledge and the degree to which we can be certain of that knowledge were ground-breaking. Ideas are not innate, he said, rather we obtain them through observation and reflection on those observations. This means that we have an active, analytical role in organizing our ideas. We classify and collate sensory information into complex ideas. This classification is shaped by our own interests and our own convenience. General ideas, such as humanity, books, freedom, or philosophy do not exist in nature but are developed by human beings as we reflect on the world. We can create a true idea of some aspects of the external world through observation, Locke believed, although we need to accept the fact that some qualities may not be exactly what we think they are. Locke's views became the basis for scientific research and thought. He and his successors became the founders of philosophic empiricism, the doctrine that we learn through observation.

Simple ideas are acquired through the senses.

Essay Concerning Human Understanding

John Locke

All ideas come from sensation or reflection. Let us suppose the mind to be, as we say, white paper, void of all characters, without any ideas; how comes it to be furnished?... Whence has it all the materials of reason and knowledge? To this I answer, in one word, from experience. Our observation, employed either about external sensible objects, or about the internal operations of our minds ... is that which supplies our understandings with all the materials of thinking. These two are the fountains of knowledge, from which all the ideas we have, or can naturally have, do spring.

The object of sensation one source of ideas. First, our senses ... do convey into the mind several distinct perceptions of things, according to those various ways wherein those objects do affect them; and thus we come by those ideas we have of yellow, white, heat, cold, soft, hard, bitter, sweet, and all those which we call sensible qualities.... This great source of most of the ideas we have, depending wholly upon our senses, and derived by them to the understanding, I call sensation.

The operations of our minds the other source of them. Secondly, the other fountain, from which experience furnisheth the understanding with ideas, is the perception of the operations of our own mind within us, as it is employed about the ideas it has got; which operations ... do furnish the understanding with another set of ideas which could not be had from things without; and such are perception, thinking, doubting, believing, reasoning, knowing, willing, and all the different actings of our own minds; which we, being conscious of, and observing in ourselves, do from these receive into our understandings as distinct ideas.... I call this reflection ... understood to mean that notice which the mind takes of its own operations....

All our ideas are of the one or the other of these. The understanding seems to me not to have the least glimmering of any ideas which it doth not receive from one of these two. External objects furnish the mind with the ideas of sensible qualities, which are all those different perceptions they produce in us; and the mind furnishes the understanding with ideas of its own operations ...

Observable in children. He that attentively considers the state of a child at his first coming into the world, will have little reason to think him stored with plenty of ideas that are to be the matter of his future knowledge. It is by degrees he comes to be furnished with them....

Men are differently furnished with these according to the different objects they converse with.
Men then come to be furnished with fewer or more simple ideas from without, according
as the objects they converse with afford greater or less variety; and from the operations of
their minds within, according as they more or less reflect on them.

[John Locke, *Essay Concerning Human Understanding* (1690), Book 2. Washington. D.C.: Henry Regnery Co.,
1956, chap. 1, 17–9.]

Locke's ideas about acquiring new knowledge paved the way for scientific research and inquiry.

IDEAS AND ISSUES

Understand Concepts

1. Identify the questions and problems that Locke was considering.
2. (a) How does Locke distinguish between primary and secondary qualities, and simple and complex ideas?
   (b) Use these concepts to explain Locke's view of what we can learn of the world around us, and how we use these ideas in our mind.

Apply and Develop

3. Determine which qualities are primary or secondary according to Locke: heat, cold, five, round, tasty, nutritious, bright, sun, two metres wide, and big.
4. Some statements are empirical, in that they can be checked by observation of the world around us. Others are statements of preference, or value statements. Still others are conclusions reached through reasoning. Which statements are most clearly empirical?
   (a) Mohammed just got a haircut.
   (b) Olga prefers classical music.
   (c) The death penalty should be reinstated in Canada.
   (d) Politicians are generally honest.
   (e) The Earth is round.
   (f) Apples are cheaper than oranges.
   (g) It is illegal to cheat on your income tax form.
   (h) It is unethical to cheat on your income tax form.

Think Critically

5. (a) Compare the views of human understanding that Locke and Descartes had. Indicate areas of agreement and disagreement.
   (b) In your opinion, which of Locke or Descartes appears to have made the most convincing argument? Put your position into a thesis statement and provide arguments to support this thesis.
6. (a) To what degree do Locke's ideas of human understanding continue to be accepted today?
   (b) In what ways, if at all, do you think that Locke's ideas of understanding have been surpassed by more recent research? After reviewing Locke's ideas, consult with your science teacher to help with this question.

Inquire and Research

7. Find out more about the philosophic school of thought called empiricism. Describe how important it has been in the history of philosophy. State your opinion about this school of philosophy. Explain this to your class.
8. Philosopher and linguist Noam Chomsky theorized that humans have an innate readiness to learn languages at a certain point in their lives. Explain what this tells us about ideas of innate and learned behaviour.

Views of Two Empiricists:
Bishop George Berkeley and David Hume

John Locke argued that our understanding of the world comes to us through learning, not through innate ideas. His explanation of this was so clear and profound that it had a long lasting impact on philosophy. Others who followed him accepted this idea, which became known as empiricism. Bishop George Berkeley and David Hume, for example, were both empiricists. They took Locke's views to conclusions that were different from his and with which he probably would not have agreed. From the empirical idea that we understand much of the external world through our senses, Berkeley and Hume cast doubt on the degree to which we can, in fact, know about that world.

George Berkeley: Objects Exist Primarily as Ideas

George Berkeley (1685–1753) was born and educated in Ireland. When Berkeley began to study philosophy, he became familiar with the ideas of John Locke. He commended Locke's *Essay Concerning Human Understanding* as a good effort for one so advanced in years. Nevertheless, he criticized a number of Locke's principal theories.

Berkeley disagreed with Locke's distinction between primary and secondary qualities. Locke, as we have seen, believed that primary qualities existed within an object, while secondary qualities were the powers within objects to produce sensations within us. Thus, according to Locke, we might experience primary qualities more directly, while secondary qualities are not necessarily as they appear. For example, the size of a dog exists within the dog while the dog's barking sound is produced within us by a power the dog has.

For Berkeley, however, both primary and secondary qualities must come through the senses, and so there is no reason to believe that either of these is as it seems.

We must interpret all aspects of the external world through our senses and with our mind. Therefore, said Berkeley, we can have no real certainty about the external world. We have no reason to think that we have direct and true knowledge of external objects. Objects only exist for us because we perceive and think about them. All we are aware of are the ideas produced in our minds.

Berkeley did not deny that objects exist. He simply asserted that what we know about them is what we think of them in our minds. Do objects exist, then, when we are not perceiving them? Berkeley answered yes, objects are always perceived by God. This view of knowledge is called idealism because it emphasizes the concept that objects exist primarily as ideas.

Berkeley had pointed out an important consequence of Locke's empiricism. If we are dependent on our senses for understanding the external world, then we are not connected directly with that external world. What exists externally may be quite different from what we think it is.

The experience each person has of the external world is somewhat different from that of another person. For those with poor eyesight or with exceptional hearing, the mental representation of the world will be somewhat unique. The experience of a walk in the city or in the forest for someone who cannot see or hear at all would be quite a different experience.

> Facts are the raw material for thinking.
> *Robert E. Sparks*

Principles of Human Knowledge

George Berkeley

It is evident to anyone who takes a survey of the objects of human knowledge that they are either ideas actually imprinted on the senses; or … are perceived by attending to the … operations of the mind.…

That neither our thoughts, nor passions, nor ideas formed by the imagination, exist … [outside of] the mind, is what everybody will allow. And it seems no less evident that the various sensations or ideas imprinted on the sense … cannot exist otherwise than in a mind perceiving them.…

It is indeed an opinion strangely prevailing … that houses, mountains, rivers, and in a word all sensible objects, have an existence natural or real, distinct from their being perceived by the understanding.… For what are the forementioned objects but the things we perceive by sense? And what do we perceive besides our own ideas or sensations? And is it not plainly repugnant that any one of these or any combination of them should exist unperceived?

… Light and colours, heat and cold, extension and figures … the things we see and feel—what are they but so many sensations, notions, ideas or impressions on the sense? And is it possible to separate, even in thought, any of these from perception?…

But, say you, surely there is nothing easier than to imagine trees, for instance, in a park, or books existing in a closet, and nobody to perceive them. I answer, … there is no difficulty in it; but what is all this … more than framing in your mind certain ideas which you call books and trees, and at the same time omitting to frame the idea of anyone that may perceive them? But do not you yourself perceive or think of them all the while? This therefore is nothing to the purpose. It only shows you have the power of imagining or forming ideas in your mind; but it does not show that you can conceive it possible [that] the objects of your thought may exist without the mind.…

[George Berkeley, *Principles of Human Knowledge* (1710, 2nd ed. 1734). In *Western Philosophy*, trans. and ed. by John Cottingham. Oxford: Blackwell Publishers Ltd., 1997.]

David Hume: Impressions, Ideas, and Causality

David Hume (1711–1776) was also heir to the ideas of empiricist John Locke. Hume decided that existing philosophy contained "little more than endless disputes and set out to find a way to establish truth."

David Hume was an empiricist in that he accepted that ideas come to us through the senses. He divided the contents of the mind into impressions and ideas. Impressions are our sensations, passions, and emotions. Ideas are the "faint image of these in thought, reflection, and imagination." Simple ideas enter the mind only as copies of our impressions. Complex ideas are composed of simple ideas.

Hume applied his empiricism to causality, the way in which we come to believe that one thing causes another. Hume argued that we believe in causality only because we have

Like John Locke, David Hume believed that knowledge comes to us through the senses.

repeated experience of one thing connected to another; repeated exposure to fire brings the experience of heat and sometimes pain. So when we see a flame we expect to experience warmth. Repeated experience of an accumulation of clouds in the sky, followed by rain, brings the expectation that the same sequence of events will occur the next time we see such clouds in the sky. We come to associate events, and think of them in terms of cause and effect.

Where is Hume going with this idea? Hume's thesis is that there is no necessary connection between flame and heat in the external world, but only in our mind. There is no necessary connection between any cause and any effect, he argues, only an expectation in the mind. We will discuss Hume and causation in more detail in Chapter 10.

Of the Origin of Our Ideas

David Hume

All the perceptions of the human mind resolve themselves into two distinct kinds, which I shall call *impressions* and *ideas*. The difference betwixt these consists in the degrees of force and liveliness, with which they strike upon the mind, and make their way into our thought or consciousness. Those perceptions which enter with most force and violence, we may name *impressions*; and, under this name, I comprehend all our sensations, passions, and emotions, as they make their first appearance in the soul. By *ideas*, I mean the faint images of these in thinking and reasoning.... I believe it will not be very necessary to employ many words in explaining this distinction. Every one ... will readily perceive the difference betwixt feeling and thinking. The common degrees of these are easily distinguished; though ... in particular instances, they may very nearly approach to each other. Thus, in sleep, in a fever, in madness, or in any very violent emotions of soul, our ideas may approach to our impressions: as, on the other hand, it sometimes happens, that our impressions are so faint and low, that we cannot distinguish them from our ideas. But, notwithstanding this near resemblance in a few instances, they are in general so very different....

There is another division of our perceptions, which it will be convenient to observe, and which extends itself both to our impressions and ideas. This division is into *simple* and *complex*. Simple perceptions, or impressions and ideas, are such as admit of no distinction nor separation. The complex are the contrary to these, and may be distinguished into parts. Though a particular colour, taste, and smell are qualities all united together in this apple, it is easy to perceive they are not the same, but are at least distinguishable from each other.

Having, by these divisions, given an order and arrangement to our objects, we may now apply ourselves to consider, with the more accuracy, their qualities and relations. The first circumstance that strikes my eye, is the great resemblance betwixt our impressions and ideas in every other particular, except their degree of force and vivacity. The one seems to be, in a manner, the reflection of the other; so that all the perceptions of the mind are double, and appear both as impressions and ideas. When I shut my eyes, and think of my chamber, the ideas I form are exact representations of the impressions I felt; nor is there any circumstance of the one, which is not to be found in the other....

Upon a more accurate survey I find I have been carried away too far by the first appearance, and that I must make use of the distinction of perceptions into *simple* and *complex*, to limit this general decision, *that all our ideas and impressions are resembling*. I observe that many of our complex ideas never had impressions that corresponded to them, and that many of our complex impressions never are exactly copied in ideas. I can imagine to myself such a city as the New Jerusalem, whose pavement is gold, and walls are rubies, though I never saw any such. I have seen Paris; but shall I affirm I can form such an idea of that city, as will perfectly represent all its streets and houses in their real and just proportions?

I perceive, therefore, that though there is, in general, a great resemblance betwixt our *complex* impressions and ideas, yet the rule is not universally true, that they are exact copies of each other. We may next consider, how the case stands with our *simple* perceptions. After the most accurate examination of which I am capable, I venture to affirm, that the rule here holds without any exception, and that every simple idea has a simple impression, which resembles it, and every simple impression a correspondent idea....

The full examination of this question is the subject of the present treatise; and, therefore, we shall here content ourselves with establishing one general proposition, *That all our simple ideas in their first appearance, are derived from simple impressions, which are correspondent to them, and which they exactly represent.*

[David Hume, *A Treatise of Human Nature*, Book 1, Ed. by L.A. Selby-Bigge. Oxford: Clarendon Press, 1896. In *The Age of Enlightenment*, by Isaiah Berlin. The New American Library, 166–70.]

When you learn to skydive, your repeated jumps lead you to expect your parachute to open. However, according to Hume, the connection between skydiving and a functioning parachute exists only in our minds.

Understand Concepts

1. In what ways did Berkeley build upon Locke's ideas? In what ways did he depart from them?
2. Using your own words, summarize the theories of knowledge presented by Berkeley and Hume. Write a paragraph for each.

Think Critically

3. With whom do you tend to agree: Locke, Berkeley, or Hume? Explain.
4. Present an argument to Berkeley, indicating what you think is wrong with his theory. Present this in a position paper of one to two pages. Use specific examples, if you can, to support your argument.
5. (a) In what way is Berkeley's theory of knowledge similar to Hume's theory of causality?
   (b) In what way do Berkeley and Hume both use Locke's ideas of primary qualities as a starting point to disagree with him?

Inquire and Research

6. Find out more about Buddhist theories of knowledge. Use Nagarjuna's ideas as a starting point. Determine what modern Buddhist philosophers, such as the Dalai Lama, believe about our ability to understand the world around us.
7. Research the psychological field of human perception and Gestalt psychology. Focus on how we "construct" our reality from sensory information and the actions of the mind.
8. Determine what cognitive psychologists have to say about how we develop "models" of reality. How does this relate to the philosophic theories of Berkeley and Hume?

Twentieth Century Philosophers of Science

The sixteenth and seventeenth centuries witnessed the introduction of new philosophies of science, including new methods for deciding what knowledge was possible, and how certain we could be of that knowledge. To a large extent these new ways of thinking resulted from the work of such philosophers as Bacon, Descartes, Locke, Berkeley, and Hume.

By the eighteenth century, science was being used to create new technologies that could be applied to solve human problems in ways that Francis Bacon would have appreciated. Physics and engineering were combined to develop new machines that expanded the power of human efforts. Chemistry was used to develop new products and processes. Biology was used to develop medicines to prevent and combat diseases.

This scientific and technological transformation of the human condition came to be known as the Industrial Revolution. Where most work once consisted of heavy or repetitive physical labour, we could now use technology to perform these tasks. The standard of living of industrial nations increased, although many parts of the world have not benefitted from this scientific and technological revolution.

During the early years of the twenty-first century, we witnessed a new coming together of science and technology as the Information Revolution emerged. Increasingly, computer technology is being used to perform tasks and expand the bounds of our knowledge.

Science and technology have been highly beneficial to the human race. Yet many questions remain about what scientific knowledge is, and how it can be best utilized.

Philosophers of science continue to ask questions about the nature and the potential of science.

Science and technology have provided us with a lot of the consumer and commercial goods we know today. However, not all the world has benefitted from such progress. How would you account for the uneven benefits brought by science and technology?

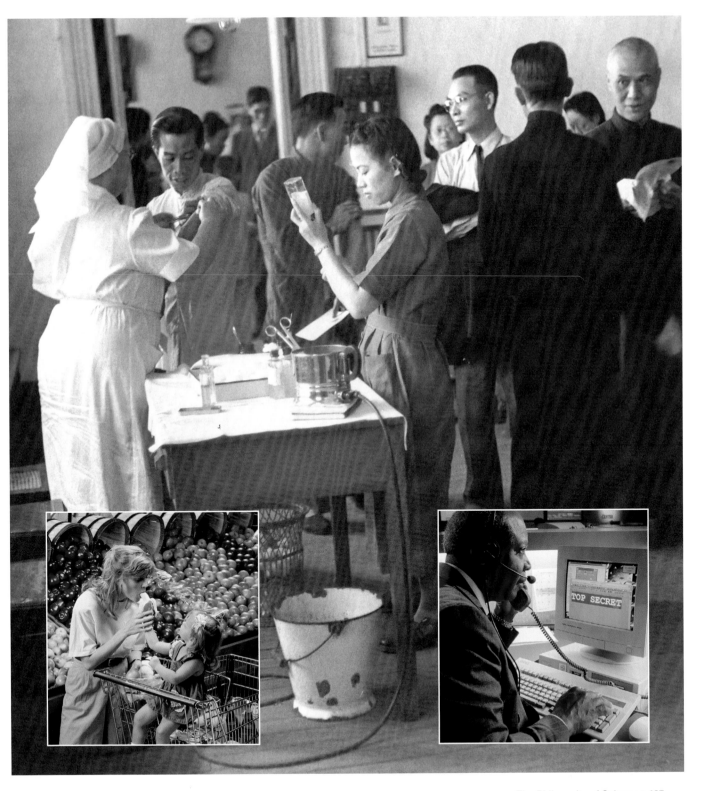

Karl Popper: Science and Society

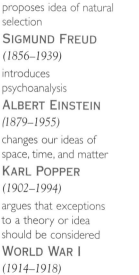

Time Line

Modern Era of Science
- - - - - - - - - -

CHARLES DARWIN
(1809–1882)
proposes idea of natural selection

SIGMUND FREUD
(1856–1939)
introduces psychoanalysis

ALBERT EINSTEIN
(1879–1955)
changes our ideas of space, time, and matter

KARL POPPER
(1902–1994)
argues that exceptions to a theory or idea should be considered

WORLD WAR I
(1914–1918)

THOMAS KUHN
(1922–)
says science is influenced by social and historical forces

RISE OF NAZISM
(1930s)

WORLD WAR II
(1939–1945)

Karl Popper's life (1902–1994) spanned most of the twentieth century, and his concerns reflected many of the major events of that century. Popper was raised in Austria, moving later to Britain. Although primarily a philosopher of science, Popper could not ignore the political and social events of his time. In the middle years of the twentieth century, fascist and communist military dictatorships expanded throughout much of the world. These totalitarian and repressive regimes had a powerful influence on Popper's views of the role and importance of knowledge and science. He argued that it is only through the free investigation and testing of ideas that knowledge can be moved forward.

Popper believed that it is not generally possible to prove the truth of any theory or idea with certainty. We can have only probable knowledge, he said, and tend to search for evidence with examples that support our views. For example, we may be taken in by horoscope predictions that tell us what we want to hear—that we will be rich or will meet someone tall, dark, and intriguing. We also tend to look for those cases that confirm our beliefs, for example, red-haired people have fiery tempers or Friday the thirteenth is an unlucky day. Thus, Popper noted, much of our knowledge may be supported by doubtful evidence and it should be questioned.

It is possible, however, to disprove any idea by noting exceptions to it. In fact, said Popper, we should actively look for such exceptions, situations, or conditions that might deny or weaken our ideas. We should take mental risks. If our ideas are refuted, or are shown to have exceptions, we should pay attention, question them, and be willing to modify them. If, after stringent testing, we are still confirmed in our beliefs, they will be that much more powerful.

Popper denied the premise that science proceeds from observation to theory. Science begins with an idea or a hypothesis, he said, one that is tested through observation. This concept is now accepted by most scientists and researchers.

Popper believed that his views on science were also applicable to social concerns. In *The Open Society and Its Enemies* (1945), he discussed the need to allow open discussion of social issues. Only by allowing, and encouraging, a variety of opinions to be heard, will the truth, or at least the best way to proceed, be determined. Totalitarian and authoritarian societies, he said, that impose on many people

Albert Einstein

Science without religion is lame; religion without science is blind.
Albert Einstein

Science Turned Upside Down

By the early twentieth century, new scientific theories were being developed that would revolutionize our views of ourselves and the universe. Charles Darwin challenged existing views of living species, including humans, by arguing that they were in a constant state of change and development. Sigmund Freud challenged our view that we understand ourselves and others on a conscious and rational level, putting forward the idea that we are unaware of much of our mental experiences, and are motivated more by emotions and drives than by rational thought. Albert Einstein (1879–1955) forced us to look at the world of physics in a way that rejected the Newtonian view of a universe where time and space, and mass and energy were unique and separate elements.

In Einstein's special theory of relativity (1905), he argued that time and space are relative to the point of view of the observer, and that only the speed of light is constant from all points of view in the universe. Imagine, he explained, that you were riding a beam of light through the universe, while images riding other beams at the same speed started out just after you did. As you looked back, it would appear that time was standing still for them.

Einstein's work was based on problems that appeared using the existing scientific theories. His ideas about space and time, and mass and energy irrevocably changed the world of the twentieth century. The physical universe was no longer as clear-cut as it had been in Newtonian physics.

the views of one person or of a small group of people, cannot find the truth because they do not allow discussion and debate. Thus these societies will eventually weaken themselves and become vulnerable.

Referring to the fascist and communist regimes of his time, Popper noted that such societies fail to consider views that disagree with our ideas or that expose potential weaknesses. This is similar to a faulty scien-tific investigation that fails to consider contrary evidence that may deny the truth of a theory or hypothesis. It is essential to allow those people who may be critical of a plan, a policy, or a social position to express their views and ideas, so that, when necessary, the opinions of society's rulers can be modified. This is the idea of an "open society," Popper argued.

Science and Falsifiability

Karl Popper

The problem which troubled me ... was [that] I wished to distinguish between science and pseudo-science [non-science or false science], knowing very well that science often errs, and that pseudo-science may happen to stumble on the truth.

I know, of course, the most widely accepted answer to my problem: that science is distinguished from pseudo-science ... by its empirical method, which is essentially induc-tive, proceeding from observation or experiment. But this did not satisfy me. I often formulated my problem as one of distinguishing between a genuinely empirical method and a non-empirical or even a pseudo-empirical method—that is to say, a method which, although it appeals to observation and experiment, nevertheless does not come up to sci-entific standards. The latter method may be exemplified by astrology, with its stupendous mass of empirical evidence based on observation—on horoscopes and on biographies.

I found that those of my friends who were admirers of Marx, Freud and Adler, were impressed by a number of points common to these theories, and especially by their appar-ent explanatory power. These theories appeared to be able to explain practically every-thing that happened within the fields to which they referred.... The world was full of verification of the theory. Whatever happened always confirmed it....

... A Marxist could not open a newspaper without finding on every page confirming evidence for his interpretation of history .... The Freudian analysts emphasized that their theories were constantly verified by their "clinical observations."...

With Einstein's theory the situation was strikingly different. Take one typical instance—Einstein's prediction ... that light must be attracted by heavy bodies. [This was

It is the theory that decides what can be observed.

Albert Einstein

confirmed by Eddington's expedition, which measured the shift in the light coming from a star.]

Now the impressive thing about this case is the risk involved in a prediction of this kind.

These considerations led me in the winter of 1919–20 to conclusions which I may now reformulate as follows.

1. It is easy to obtain confirmations, or verifications, for nearly every theory—if we look for confirmations.
2. Confirmations should count only if they are the result of risky predictions....
3. Every "good" scientific theory is a prohibition: it forbids certain things to happen. The more a theory forbids, the better it is.
4. A theory which is not refutable by any conceivable event is non-scientific....
5. Every genuine test of a theory is an attempt to falsify it ....
6. Confirming evidence should not count except when it is the result of a genuine test of the theory....

The belief that science proceeds from observation to theory is still so widely and so firmly held that my denial of it is often met with incredulity....

But in fact the belief that we can start with pure observations alone, without anything in the nature of a theory, is absurd; as may be illustrated by the story of the man who dedicated his life to natural science, wrote down everything he could observe, and bequeathed his priceless collection of observations to the Royal Society to be used as inductive evidence. This story should show us that though beetles may profitably be collected, observations may not.

... I tried to bring home the same point to a group of physics students in Vienna by beginning a lecture with the following instructions: "Take pencil and paper, carefully observe, and write down what you have observed!" They asked, of course, what I wanted them to observe. Clearly the instruction, "Observe!" is absurd.... Observation is always selective. It needs a chosen object, a definite task, an interest, a point of view, a problem.

[Karl Popper, "Science: Conjectures and Refutation." In *British Philosophy in Mid-Century*, ed. by C.A. Mace, 1957. London: Routledge, 1963 (3rd ed. 1969), chap. 1.]

Thomas Kuhn: Science and Progress

Does science proceed from one advancement to another, in an even and unbroken process of achievements? Thomas Kuhn (1922–) does not believe so. His book *The Structure of Scientific Revolutions* has been described as "the most influential book in modern philosophy of science." (Honderich, *The Oxford Companion to Philosophy*, 1995, 451)

Kuhn's view is that scientists work within an unquestioned theory or set of beliefs. This mental paradigm, or accepted view, shapes scientists' thinking as they work. Within this set of beliefs, scientists search for information and work out the details of an accepted theory or set of beliefs. For example, until the time of Copernicus, the accepted paradigm of the universe was that the sun revolved around the Earth, which was located at the centre of everything. Observers for thousands of years accepted and worked within that paradigm, gathering evidence to support it. Copernicus examined the night skies and the evidence, and reached a different conclusion. The movements of the stars and other heavenly bodies made much more sense, and could be more sim-

Thomas Kuhn

ply explained if one pictured the planets, like Earth, moving around the sun.

At some point, says Kuhn, an existing paradigm fails to explain events properly, because there are too many exceptions. Without a reasonable alternative, however, scientists continue to accept and support the status quo. When an alternative point of view, theory, or paradigm emerges, with a more satisfactory explanation of events, a scientific revolution occurs. Copernicus hypothesized that the sun was at the centre of the universe and the Earth circled around it. Soon others, such as Galileo, were supporting this new view or paradigm and providing evidence to support it.

Thomas Kuhn, like Popper, drew connections between science and society. Kuhn compares scientific revolutions with social and political upheavals. Political revolutions occur, he says, when existing ideas and institutions no longer work. At some point, alternative ideas and methodologies emerge to produce a new social or political paradigm.

Kuhn suggests that science, like other human institutions, is shaped by historical and social forces. Scientists are not immune from the generally accepted ideas of their time and place. There are many examples of this phenomenon. In Hitler's Germany, the racist doctrines of the Nazi regime produced erroneous paradigms and bad science. The controversy over global warming in industrial societies is often shaped by social and economic factors. Cutting back on pollution from industry and automobiles would have significant impact on the economy and on how we live. Scientists who work within that social framework will be influenced by this knowledge. Most scientists today accept that the scientist has a mental framework, an accepted paradigm within which science operates. The important thing is to be as aware as possible of the possible biases that may result.

Kuhn believed that there may be more than one way to view scientific evidence. He went so far as to say that there is likely more than one truth about nature, although some truths are simply more useful than others.

The Structure of Scientific Revolutions

Thomas Kuhn

In the development of any science, the first received paradigm is usually felt to account quite successfully for most of the observations and experiments easily accessible to that science's practitioners…. [This] leads, on the one hand, to an immense restriction of the scientist's vision and to a considerable resistance to paradigm change. The scientist has become increasingly rigid. On the other hand, within those areas to which the paradigm directs the attention of the group, normal science leads to a detail of information and to a precision of the observation–theory match that could be achieved in no other way….

So long as the tools a paradigm provides continue to prove capable of solving the problems it defines, science moves fastest and penetrates most deeply through confident employment of those tools. The reason is clear. As in manufacture so in science, retooling is an extravagance to be reserved for the occasion that demands it. The significance of crises is the indication they provide that an occasion for retooling has arrived….

Let us … ask next how scientists repond to [crises]…. Though they may begin to lose faith and then to consider alternatives, they do not renounce the paradigm that has led them into crisis…. Once it has achieved the status of a paradigm, a scientific theory is declared invalid only if an alternate candidate is available to take its place….

The decision to reject one paradigm is always simultaneously the decision to accept another....

When ... an anomaly [an out of the ordinary or unexpected observation] comes to seem more than just another puzzle of normal science, the transition to crisis and extraordinary science has begun. The anomaly itself now comes to be more generally recognized as such by the profession. More and more attention is devoted to it by more and more of the field's most eminent men.

[Thomas Kuhn, *The Structure of Scientific Revolutions*, 2nd ed., 1962. Chicago: University of Chicago Press, 1970, chap. 6–8.]

In the past, many scientists believed that lightning bolts travel from charged particles in clouds to the ground. However, scientists have found that lightning bolts actually travel from the ground to the charged particles in clouds.

Understand Concepts

1. (a) What questions or problems are Karl Popper and Thomas Kuhn addressing?
   (b) Summarize Popper's responses or answers to the questions referred to in part (a).
   (c) How does the idea of paradigms help Kuhn answer these questions?
2. Explain the examples Popper uses to illustrate his main ideas, in particular the example of astrology or of the experiment to have students "observe."

Apply and Develop

3. Explain how Popper's idea of the way in which we fail to look for contradictions to our ideas helps to explain each of these issues:
   (a) stereotypes of ethnic or racial groups
   (b) addiction to gambling
   (c) our views of the poor, or of the rich
   (d) falling in love
   (e) beliefs listed on the second page of this chapter
4. What mental paradigms do you have? In other words, what views and what assumptions do you make about the world around you? In what ways might your paradigms of the world change in the future?
5. Using a chart with the headings below, apply Popper's idea of paradigms to each of these areas of your life: Existing Paradigm, Limitations, and Possible Future Changes to the Paradigm.
   (a) your immediate family
   (b) your career choice
   (c) the process of education
   (d) the effects of electronic technology
   (e) how to travel with speed and safety
   (f) life on other planets
   (g) how poverty can be eliminated

Think Critically

6. (a) Why does Popper believe it is not sufficient to search only for evidence to support an idea or action?
   (b) What does this tell you about the importance of varied and opposing points of view in science and society?

Review and Reflect

In the ancient world, Plato, Aristotle, and Chuang Tzu asked questions about what we can know and with what certainty we can know it. For centuries, their ideas held sway because there was no way to disprove their theories, and there were few alternatives from which to choose. The social conditions of the time were also not conducive to questioning, at least in the Western world.

Then, at the beginning of the sixteenth century, Europe experienced renewed interest in such questions. Many thinkers began to believe that the formulators of accepted traditions and ideas had not explored all there was to know, and that better ways to think about and acquire knowledge needed to be developed.

New techniques were emerging in science; these involved logical thinking, observation, and experimentation. Yet scientists still needed solid ground upon which to develop their research and their findings. Philosophers began to investigate new methodologies for finding truth. Francis Bacon stressed the careful drawing of conclusions from detailed observations. René Descartes provided pathways for the rational processes of the mind to find truth (rationalism). John Locke, Bishop George Berkeley, and David Hume discussed how truth should be acquired through the use of the senses (empiricism).

During the nineteenth and twentieth centuries, the application of science and technology to human problems and concerns changed our lives significantly. The debate is still going on about whether these changes have produced an improvement in the human condition, although the weight of opinion would generally be on the positive side. Philosophers of science continue to examine what scientists do and how they can do it better. Karl Popper emphasized open questioning and tolerance of dissenting views, and a search for opposing cases in science and in society. Thomas Kuhn brought the concept of paradigms to us, when he indicated that scientists and non-scientists alike, all operate within a mental framework or paradigm, which shapes our views and indicates to us what to look for. When the paradigm fails to maintain its satisfactory explanation and new, more likely answers become available, a great leap in science may occur. Philosophers of science continue to study how scientists do their work, and how science can be developed more effectively.

ETHICS

From the beginning of recorded history, and probably long before that, people have asked themselves, "How should I live my life?" "How should I treat other people?" "What constitutes right behaviour and how does it differ from wrong behaviour?"

The study of ethics, or moral philosophy as it is sometimes called, began in historical times with early philosophers, such as the Sophists in Greece and Confucius in China, who began to ask questions about what ethics and morality are, and why they should exist. Those philosophers and the ones that followed searched for rules and philosophies that could guide human beings in their ideas of ethical behaviour, morality, and how we should live our own lives and interact with others.

All study, including the study of ethics, begins with the posing of questions. Perhaps you have thought of some ethical questions you would like to investigate. Perhaps these are questions about your own life or about important issues in the world today. How would you answer these questions:

- Why should we act ethically?
- Where do ethical ideas originate?
- Why do we act ethically?
- How can we judge if an action is ethical or not?
- Why do people have different views about what is ethical?
- Is it possible for all people to eventually reach consensus about ethical ideas?
- How can we apply ethical principles to real-life situations?
- Are we free to act ethically or otherwise, or is our fate guided by conditions beyond our control?

In this unit, we will explore all of these questions. We will look at classical views of ethics and their origins, and then we will investigate several modern ethical theories. Throughout this unit, we will apply ethical and logical principles to contemporary issues.

How does ethics apply to daily life? How can you judge if the actions of an individual are ethically correct?

Classical Views of Ethics

Ethics is the study of how to live life and how to treat other people. Of all philosophical studies, ethics is perhaps the most closely related to everyday life. From our early years, we are taught what is good or bad, right or wrong. Gradually we become aware of and acquire the ethical values and behaviours of those around us, and of our culture.

As we encounter other people, we begin to understand that not everyone shares the same ethical point of view. We come in contact with or hear about people whose views differ widely from our own. The ethical beliefs that people hold often vary widely on controversial issues, and these beliefs are supported with ethical arguments that may not agree with our own. Eventually, each one of us must determine for ourselves which ethical views and supporting arguments best suit us individually.

Philosophers recognize the importance of ethics in human life, and are intrigued by ethical diversity. Philosophers, like others, also apply ethical views to issues in life, striving to find better answers to important questions.

Children's Peace Monument in Peace Memorial Park, Hiroshima, Japan

For many people, the teachings found in religious traditions provide helpful ways to judge ethical behaviour. These scriptures contain ethical codes that can be applied to the challenges and issues that we face in contemporary life.

The Relevance of Ethics in Contemporary Life

What does it mean to think and act rightly or wrongly? Do you know? Do others agree with your definition? How sure are you of your methods for judging right and wrong? These are the types of questions that lead to moral philosophy, or the study of ethics.

When we are children, others tell us what is right and wrong. Parents and teachers praise us when we do right, and scold us when we do wrong. They tell us what they believe is the right thing to do and encourage us to believe likewise. So, why do we need a philosophy of ethics? Surely everyone knows what is right and wrong.

A philosophy of ethics often emerges when, at some point, an individual or a society realizes that not everyone holds the same ethical views. Encounters with people of different religions, with different points of view, and with different value systems lead us to think about our own ethical positions. We may wonder why others hold beliefs different from ours, and whether there are any points of agreement between their views and our own.

Diversity of opinion about human affairs is everywhere. A glance at the evening news indicates just how much people disagree over the correct, right, or best, way to act in any situation. Consider these questions:

- To what ethical standards should politicians be held?
- How should we help the poor?
- How should we deal with individuals who break the law?
- How should we help the mentally ill?
- What obligation do people have to help others?
- What right, if any, do people have to harm themselves, or other living things?
- What obligation do people have to take care of the environment?
- What standards should individuals support and maintain as they deal with others?

These questions and many more are ethical issues that we face daily in our everyday lives.

The Causes of Diverse Opinions on Ethics

As we discuss such issues, and the problems which relate to them, we often hear divergent opinions, each of which is supported by a strong argument. We may also feel the need to explain or justify our own opinions on the subject to other people. How is it possible, we wonder, that two "good" people can be so opposed to each other on such important issues as euthanasia, abortion, poverty, animal rights, and the criminal system? Why are there so many differences of opinion?

One reason is that we live in a dramatically changing world. Changes bring new challenges, new questions, and new ethical dilemmas. How do we know the right way to act in new situations? Do the old rules still apply? What precepts do we use to guide our behaviour and our lives?

Another reason for differences in opinion is heightened awareness of the ideas and values of others in this world. Today, we live in a global village, and all of us are increasingly aware that citizens of other countries have customs widely divergent from our own. There are many different ideas of what is right and what is wrong. In some countries, people wear clothing that covers the body completely while other countries allow revealing clothing. Punishment for crimes that are committed or that are perceived to have been committed can range from death or mutilation in some countries, to imprisonment and fines in others. Women in some societies become political leaders, while in other societies they are not allowed to vote.

Since the world is filled with widely divergent beliefs and credos, let's turn our attention to our own lives. How should we conduct ourselves and how should we act in everyday circumstances? What do we want from life, in the short term, and over the long haul? When we assess our place in the universe at the end of our lives, by what standards will we judge success or failure? Is fame or fortune our life's goal? Will we tally up whatever good we may have done for others and make our judgement accordingly? What is "the good life" in our own private world?

The study of ethics can help us determine and defend our own ethical positions, while understanding those of others. The study of ethics can also help us make well-reasoned decisions in tough situations when several possible courses of action are presented to us. For example, you may ask: How much should I give to a homeless street person? How should I vote in the next election? Studying ethics may help us decide, in a larger sense, how we want to live our lives. Simply thinking about what is right and wrong will not guarantee that good choices will be made. However, some philosophers believe that knowledge is a necessary first step to right action, and that people who reason carefully about such things will make better decisions than those who do not.

The philosophical study of ethics occurs on two levels. At one level, the philosophy of ethics investigates how we should act in specific situations, in our personal lives and in relation to others. This level of ethics deals with the question of what we should do.

Another level is the question of how we can explain and justify our own ethical positions, while understanding the ethical positions of others. Put another way, what are the foundations upon which ethical philosophies and points of view are built?

What feminism means is to change … our vision, which means we must also change our ethics.
Griselda Gambaro

The great decisions of human life have as a rule far more to do with the instincts and other mysterious unconscious factors than with conscious will and well-meaning reasonableness.
Carl Jung

Capital punishment is a very contentious issue in many states in the United States. Some people are in favour of it because they claim it is a deterrent for crime. Many oppose it because they see it as an inhumane way of dealing with criminals that does not lead to a reduction in the rate of crime. What are your views on this issue? How would you justify your choice?

Key Questions in the Philosophy of Ethics

One important question in the philosophy of ethics concerns the origin of ethical principles. Some suggest that ethical ideas originate outside of humanity, that they are of divine or universal origin. People who believe in this position may suggest that a particular ethical view is beyond discussion because its origin is outside human thought. Others believe that ethical views originate from human social interaction, emerging from the need to find ways to live harmoniously with others. People taking this position may believe that ethics is open for thought, discussion, and change.

Another important question in ethical philosophy is whether it is possible to come to an ethical agreement or whether we should accept that people in different times and places will always develop unique but equally valid ethical views. In other words, is it possible to find moral absolutes that are true for all times and places, or are ethics particular to a specific time and place?

A third question is to what extent general theories of ethics can help us in specific situations. Can we apply an ethical theory to a specific case, and be sure of the answer? Suppose another person applies a different ethical theory to the same situation, and comes up with a different answer. Perhaps we can make better decisions, and have a better life by understanding ethics more fully.

A fourth question deals with how to judge an action as ethically correct. Some philosophers have argued that the intention

Moving up the Career Ladder

Shirley is applying for a job with a computer company, one of the best in its field. It is offering her an excellent opportunity to do the type of work she loves. She knows that she will be an asset to the company.

The problem is that, on the application, the company requires references from Shirley's last two jobs. She left her most recent workplace on extremely good terms, and knows that she will get an excellent reference. However, her place of employment before that turned out to be a disaster, through no fault of her own. Shirley's manager took an immediate dislike to her and made her life miserable. Shirley knows that any reference from that company will be terrible, and may possibly ruin her chances at pursuing a new career path. What should Shirley do?

- Be honest with the new company about what happened, although they may not believe her.
- Omit this employer from the application form, and provide another reference, although this, if discovered, might arouse suspicions about her and affect her chances of getting the job?
- What other choices can she make? What choice would you make in such a situation? How would you justify your choice?

behind the action is most important, while others believe the consequence is the way to judge the action. Consider the person who lies to another in order to avoid an uncomfortable situation, but makes someone happier in the process. Or to take another example, consider the person who, in trying to save the life of another, inadvertently causes the death of several others. How does one judge the ethics of these situations?

Yet another central question in ethics is whether we have free will to act as we wish, and believe to be right, or whether our actions are guided by forces and conditions beyond our control. If we believe we have free will to choose, then ethics is an important subject for study. We can then sincerely ask: What is the best way for us to act in any specific situation? A number of religious traditions such as Christianity, and philosophic schools such as existentialism, support the belief in free will.

On the other hand, some religions, such as Taoism, and philosophies such as Stoicism, stress that we have less control over our lives than we think, that our fate is guided by unseen forces or wills. The study of ethics, in such cases, means determining what is the right, or pre-ordained, path to take under such circumstances.

Before we examine in detail the ethical questions mentioned at the beginning of this section, let us consider two situations. One involves a woman wanting to get a job with a company that she really wants to work for. The other involves a waiter asking questions about the way his colleagues treat each other regarding tips. In each situation, ask yourself: What choices would I make? Are my choices ethically correct? How can I justify my choices to myself and other people?

Sharing Tips

While reading a newspaper column called "Ethics in Everyday Life," you stumble across this letter that was recently addressed to the columnist:

Reader: I work as a waiter in a restaurant where the staff pool their tips and split the total amount at the end of the evening. The purpose is to give everyone the same amount of money, and to encourage teamwork as well. The problem is that some waiters take part of their tips, rather than put it in the common pot. Should I do the same? What other options do I have?

What do you think this person should do? Why? Before going further, write down what you would do, and provide your reasons.

You continue reading the article and find the columnist's reply:

Columnist: You should not cheat others. But you should not allow others to cheat you as well. You might tell the manager what is happening, without saying who the guilty parties are. If nothing is done, you may have to consider taking another job, rather than being part of a corrupt system, or being its victim. Another answer, though not very likely, is to eliminate the practice of tipping and raise wages to a decent level.

What do you think of the columnist's response? Are the suggestions ethically correct? How do you know?

Overview of Ethical Theories and Issues

Philosophers have taken a number of theoretical positions about ethics, largely in pondering the types of questions we have presented so far. We will now examine in detail the answers to some of these questions:

- Is it possible to have ethical views that are absolute?
- Are there any underlying theories that can help us make ethically correct choices in specific life situations?
- How do we judge if an action is ethically correct? Is it our intentions that count or do we only consider the consequences?
- Do we have free will in making ethical choices or are we governed by forces beyond our control?

As you read the brief descriptions that follow, ask yourself: Which of these theoretical positions seems to be true for me?

Absolute or Relative Ethics

Can we identify ethical values that are true for all people, at all times and in all places? Plato argued that ethical values, ideas of right and wrong, are independent of people and circumstances, and that these values are eternally and universally true. He also believed that they could be deduced through the use of rational thought. A number of philosophers since the time of Plato have agreed with his ideas. Philosophers such as the Stoics, Kant, and others, believed that universal ethical principles could be found that are applicable to all people. The great religions of the world—Christianity, Buddhism, Judaism, Islam, and Hinduism—are based on the idea that revealed religion contains universal ethical principles.

Other philosophic traditions take the position that ethics are relative and unique to different human situations. Of course, a look at the world around us soon reveals a number of different ethical points of view. The ethical relativist would go farther and say that there are, in fact, no overriding or superior ethical principles beyond this diversity. For example, Aristotle, and the Epicureans of ancient times, argued that there are no universal principles of ethics, external to human experience. These and other philosophers since have argued that right or wrong actions should be judged by the degree of happiness the actions created.

Theory or Practice

There are many circumstances in our lives where the distinction between right and wrong behaviour is difficult to make and not clear-cut. Can ethical theory be used to guide our behaviour, and provide us with any certainty? How are we to know if a specific action is good or bad, right or wrong?

One response to these questions is to argue that some ethical ideas are held by many people and cultures, and thus have some widespread validity. Many people would accept a rule such as "Thou shalt not steal" to be as a widespread, even universal, ethical principle. However, even here, there are incidences when no one rule is applicable to all cases. Suppose it was necessary to steal in order to bring about a greater good, such as providing medicine for a seriously ill person. Now we have two competing rules, "Thou shalt not steal" and "Do unto others as you would have others do unto you." How do we know which rule should prevail? This type of ethical or moral conflict has led philosophers to develop more complete theories of ethics.

Intentions or Consequences

Should we judge an action by the intention of the person performing the action, or by the results that the action achieves? Immanuel Kant believed that intent was of supreme importance; if someone intended that an action would benefit another, the result of that action would not be important. If, for example, you intended to rescue a person from the water, yet unintentionally caused that person to drown, according to Kant, you still acted ethically. The Stoics believed that we can only do our best, and must then accept the consequences without regret.

On the other hand, other philosophers believed that we should consider carefully the consequences of any action before doing it. They believed people should govern their actions according to the degree that these actions will result in the greatest happiness for the greatest number of people. The Utilitarians of the nineteenth century put forward such a view.

> We have two kinds of morality side by side; one which we preach but do not practice, and the other which we practice but seldom preach.
>
> *Bertrand Russell*

Sometimes ethical issues can be fairly complex. In recent years, for example, UN peacekeepers have come under fire for unethical behaviour. But, is it fair to expect people we train as fighters to play the role of peacekeepers?

Free Will or Fate

How free are we to behave rightly or wrongly? How much responsibility should the individual bear for his or her actions? Plato believed that any person who knows what is right will do the right thing. In modern times, existentialists have emphasized that we are free to choose our own destinies, and that we must also accept the responsibility for our choices.

The Stoics, however, believed that our fate was predetermined. Although we must necessarily act in this life, our actions are predestined. In modern times, certain aspects of human nature have been used to illustrate how our choices are limited in a number of ways. Sigmund Freud revealed to us how our psyche, our deepest feelings and self, influences the actions and thoughts that we choose. Freud and others have also stressed the influences of early childhood, and of cultural conditions, which can limit the decisions we make in our lives. A criminal may have childhood experiences that shape his or her character in negative ways, and that may predispose him or her to a life of crime. If this is so, should criminals, then, be held totally responsible for their transgressions against society or should we as a society try to understand and rehabilitate these people?

It is often easier to fight for principles than to live up to them.

Adlai Stevenson

Mosaic of Death and the three Fates with the thread of Human Life.

Understand Concepts

1. Identify important reasons why philosophers and other people study ethics.
2. Use an organizer to identify four ethical issues, and two contrasting positions taken by philosophers to each of these issues.
3. List important ethical questions that you may be dealing with in your life right now.
4. List four major issues in ethics and briefly explain their importance.

Apply and Develop

5. What do you believe to be the right and wrong action in each of these situations? Explain how you would justify your point of view.
   (a) You and your friend go to the store to look at some new song releases. You don't buy anything, but as you leave the store your friend pulls a CD from underneath her jacket. What should you do?
   (b) You have been studying very hard during your last year of high school. You also have a part-time job for twenty hours a week, because you intend to go to university next year. With several assignments coming up, you know you haven't the time to do your best. You find a site on the Internet that sells essays on several topics you must write about. What should you do?
   (c) You want to belong to a group of friends. You have spent time with them recently and have gone out with them on weekends. One day a member of the group makes a racist comment at which everyone laughs. A friend of yours is a member of that racial group. What should you do?

Think Critically

6. In cooperation with several others in your class, respond to one of these issues. Take a tentative position and back it up with argument. Report back to the class.
   (a) Will it be possible in the future for all humans to agree on one set of ethical principles upon which to live? How would they come to such an agreement? Would such a set of principles have value?
   (b) Is there any one moral or ethical principle that you can think of that would provide a basis for human action in all, or most, everyday situations? Show how this would work in a number of specific situations.
   (c) Which is most important to you in judging someone's behaviour as ethical or unethical: intentions or results? Provide examples.

Communicate Ideas

7. Identify one ethical or moral question that you think is important in the world today. With the rest of the class, compile a list of such questions that you can return to later in this unit.

Classical Ethical Philosophies: Why Behave Ethically?

> He whom love touches not walks in darkness.
>
> *Plato*

Many philosophers throughout the ages have asked the question: What motivates us to act ethically? Plato believed that many people behave ethically even if they could be unethical without others knowing. Other philosophers, such as the Stoics, developed different views. They believed that all things are predetermined and that we should accept our circumstances. The Stoics believed in accepting things as they are.

As you read the different views presented in this section, consider these questions:
- What motivates you, personally, to act ethically?
- Is behaving ethically a characteristic that is within all of us?
- Do you behave ethically because you want to be rewarded or because you fear punishment?
- Is it because others will respect you or is it so you will respect yourself?
- Do you choose to behave ethically out of your own free will or because of social or other pressures placed upon you?
- Do you behave ethically because you agree with the teachings you have been taught?
- Why should anyone be ethical and do the right thing?

Plato's Views on Ethics

Suppose, through some accidental means, a large sum of money is deposited into your bank account. You are reasonably sure there is no way that this money can be traced to you. On the other hand, it is very likely that someone else's account has been wrongly debited by the same amount; however, you do not know and cannot find out who that person might be. What would you do?

In *The Republic*, Plato created a fictional scenario to investigate why anyone would behave ethically: a Sophist named Glaucon claims that people are not willingly good, but behave ethically only for what reward they will receive as a result. Most people do right, says Glaucon, because they do not have the power to do otherwise and get away with it. To illustrate his point, Glaucon tells the fable of the shepherd Gyges.

If you knew you could do anything without people knowing, would you behave differently than you do now? Would you want to live in a society where everyone had that ability? In *The Republic,* Plato said that although such a situation would be difficult, many people would continue to be ethical and do the right thing. Plato believed that ethics, or virtue, was valuable for the person, despite consequences. Like food for the body, virtue is healthy for the soul (character or personality), because it makes us more complete human beings. In Plato's view, the healthy or virtuous personality has a clear moral vision, good judgement, and strength of will. This person knows where he or she is going.

Plato believed that each of us is made up of three elements: a physical body, spirit, and

The Fable of Gyges

Plato

... One day there was a great storm and an earthquake in the district where [a shepherd] was pasturing his flock and a chasm opened in the earth. He was amazed at the sight, and descended into the chasm and saw many astonishing things there, among them, so the story goes ... a corpse which seemed to be of more than human size. He took nothing from it save a gold ring it had on its finger, and then made his way out. He was wearing this ring when he attended the usual meeting of shepherds which reported monthly to the king on the state of his flocks; and as he was sitting there with the others he happened to twist the bezel of the ring toward the inside of his hand. Thereupon he became invisible to his companions and they began to refer to him as if he had left them. He was astonished, and began fingering the ring again, and turned the bezel outwards, whereupon he became visible again.... [He] found that every time he turned the bezel inwards he became invisible, and when he turned it outwards he became visible. Having made this discovery he managed to get himself included in the party that was to report to the king, and when he arrived seduced the queen, and with her help attacked and murdered the king and seized the throne.

Imagine now that two such rings existed and the just one put on one, the unjust the other. There is no one, it would commonly be supposed, who would have such iron strength of will as to stick to what is right and keep his hands from taking other people's property. For he would be able to steal from the market whatever he wanted without fear of detection, to go into any man's house and seduce anyone he liked, to murder or to release from prison anyone he felt inclined.... And in all this the just man would differ in no way from the unjust, but both would follow the same course. This, it would be claimed, is strong evidence that no man is just of his own free will, but only under compulsion, and that no man thinks justice pays him personally, since he will always do wrong when he gets the chance.

[Plato, *The Republic*, Book 2. Trans by Desmond Lee. New York: Penguin Classics, 1987, 105, 106]

Always do right.
This will gratify some people and astonish the rest.

Mark Twain

intellect. In the healthy soul, these three components are balanced. The physical body, the spirited or emotional part of us, and the intellect all have equal roles to play, and the well-balanced individual makes good ethical decisions. In the unhealthy soul, these three components are out of balance. If, for example, our desire for physical or emotional pleasures, is stronger than our intellect, our ideas and beliefs will be skewed. Lack of control over any one of these elements leads to bad decisions, and unethical behaviour. The result of wrongdoing, Plato stated, is to hurt others and oneself as well. Telling a lie can clearly harm another, but it also causes harm to the liar, by further damaging an unbalanced human being.

According to Plato some behaviours are absolutely right and others are absolutely wrong. These ethical absolutes have been true for all people at all times. Plato believed ideal "forms" existed for everything in the universe, including ethical ideals. We may not know what these ideals are, although we can learn and develop our knowledge of these universal

Crime has always been a prevalent human activity. How does Plato describe wrongdoing?

ethics through rational thought. Plato was sure that those people who learned the right way to act, would act accordingly. Knowledge creates ethical behaviour, while ignorance encourages unethical behaviour. Plato disagreed with Glaucon's claim that the just person would act as badly as the unjust person if there were no consequences attached.

Aristotle's Views on Ethics

Aristotle did not agree with Plato's view that an ethical way of life could be understood solely through rational means, simply by thinking. Aristotle believed that we must look around, and examine the everyday behaviour of the people in the world to discover what it means to live in an ethically correct manner. Aristotle believed that this ethical lifestyle may vary from one person to another, and from one culture to another. Aristotle, unlike Plato, proposed a view of ethics that is relative to the individual and the situation.

Aristotle said that we become ethical individuals as a result of two major influences: knowledge that we acquire, and the habits that we develop. We learn what is right and wrong from teachers, experience, and life, he said. However, we also become ethical persons through habit.

In this aspect, Aristotle recognized that while we may know what is right, there is still the element of action, of doing the right thing.

If ethical ideas vary from one social group to another, asked Aristotle, are there any of these ideas upon which all people can agree? For example, most people consider happiness to be a good thing. As a result, Aristotle reasoned that the good life is one of happiness. He reasoned that happiness is an activity rather than a goal, and is present when we behave ethically. That is, happiness is a by-product of living an ethical life. But what is meant by happiness? Here again, Aristotle had a suggestion. He reasoned that moderation, or the "golden mean," is the key to happiness. In other words, too much of anything is not healthy—too much food, too much work, too much socializing, or too much partying.

The good should be grateful to the bad—for providing the world with a basis for comparison.

Sven Halla

Ethics

Aristotle

Virtue is of two kinds: intellectual and ethical. Intellectual virtue owes its origins and growth more to teaching, and so needs experience and time; but ethical virtue comes about from habit…. It is clear from this that none of the ethical virtues arises in us by nature; for none of the things that exist by nature can be radically altered by habituation…. Hence the ethical virtues do not come about by nature—but neither do they come about contrary to nature: we are naturally constituted so as to acquire them, but it is by habit that they are fully developed….

The causes and means whereby every virtue is cultivated or destroyed are the same, just as in the case of all the arts. It is by playing the lute that people become good or bad lute players…. By building well, people get to be good builders, and they become bad builders from building badly. If this was not the case, there would be no need for teachers, and everyone would be born good or bad. It is just like this with the virtues. By behaving in a certain way in our dealings with human beings some of us become just and others unjust; by what we do in the face of danger, and by acquiring habits of timidity or boldness, we become brave or cowardly. And the same holds good with respect to desires and feelings of anger; some people become temperate and patient, while others become self-indulgent and bad-tempered, depending on the way they behave in the relevant situations. In a word, activities of a certain kind produce corresponding dispositions. This is why the activities we perform must be of a certain kind; for as these differ, so the dispositions that follow from them will differ. Thus the kinds of habits we form from early childhood are of no small importance; they matter a great deal—indeed, they make all the difference….

[Aristotle, *Nichomachean Ethics*. In *Western Philosophy*, trans. and ed. by John Cottingham. Oxford: Blackwell Publishers Ltd., 1997]

> The needs of a society determine its ethics, and in the Black American ghettos the hero is that man who is offered only the crumbs from his country's table but by ingenuity and courage is able to take for himself a Lucullan feast.
> *Maya Angelou*

Hellenistic Ethical Philosophies: Search for the Right Way to Live

During Aristotle's lifetime, Philip of Macedon from the north conquered the Greek city-states. This marked the end of the "golden age of Athens." Philip's son, Alexander the Great (356 BCE– 323 BCE) was in fact a student of Aristotle. During his short lifetime, Alexander conquered vast territories as far east as India. Then, from the third century BCE, Romans from Italy conquered all the lands surrounding the Mediterranean. The period between Alexander's death in 323 BCE and the height of the Roman empire in 31 BCE is known as the Hellenistic period.

Development of Classical Ethics

ZENO
(489 BCE–? BCE)
founds Stoicism

PLATO
(428 BCE–347 BCE)

DIOGENES
(412 BCE–323 BCE)
becomes notable Cynic

ARISTOTLE
(384 BCE–322 BCE)

EPICURUS
(342 BCE–270 BCE)
founds Epicureanism

ALEXANDER THE GREAT
(356 BCE–323 BCE)
expands Greek empire

HELLENISTIC PERIOD
(323 BCE–31 BCE)
represents height of Stoics, Cynics, and Epicureans

The conquering Romans brought to Greece a knowledge of law and administrative organization, but little in the way of philosophy. They recognized, however, the work that Greek philosophers and scholars had done, and brought many educated Greeks to Italy as slave tutors for rich young Roman men. The result was that Greek culture and philosophies spread, both west and east, throughout the Roman empire. Greek philosophy also came into contact with Eastern philosophies from the Middle East, India, and China.

Historians suggest that during times of change, when people are exposed to a variety of lifestyles, they search for ways to live their lives well. Our own time period has been seen in this light. The Hellenistic period was a time when cultures and ideas from all over came into contact with each other. It was an era of enormous change, and as the turmoil of ideas travelled from one country and civilization to another, people searched for certainty in an uncertain world, for guidelines to thought and action. This search resulted in the development of several major ethical philosophies of life including Cynicism, Scepticism, Epicureanism, and Stoicism.

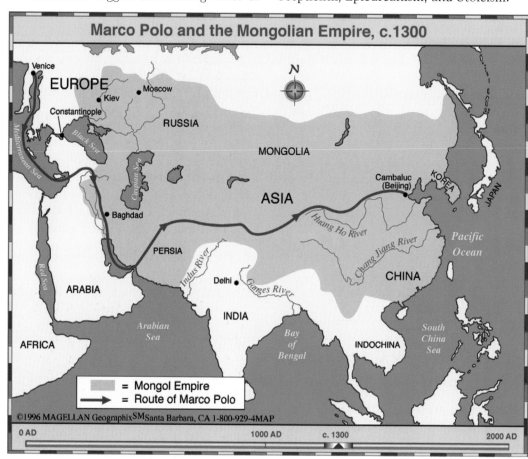

In ancient times, waterways were the best way to travel long distances. People and ideas spread this way, probably more than we know. The regions and civilizations surrounding the Mediterranean shared and further developed many philosophical ideas.

Stoicism:
Indifference to External Things

Stoicism was a highly influential doctrine of the ancient Western world, and was, for some time, the dominant philosophy for many people in the Roman empire. The origins of Stoicism can be traced back to its founder Zeno (489 BCE–? BCE), who often lectured to his students from a porch or "stoa."

Stoicism is based on the belief that all things, including human actions, are predetermined. Since a person has no control over external events, or how others act, there is little reason to struggle against these occurrences.

The only thing human beings can control, according to Stoics, is *how* we react to events. Zeno suggested that the best thing to do is to accept and be indifferent to external influences. In so doing, we become independent of the events that affect us.

Critics of Stoicism argue that if all things are determined beforehand, then our own reactions must be predestined as well. How, then, can we control our individual thoughts and actions? If all things are predetermined, how can there be any free decisions at all?

Marcus Aurelius with admirers. Stoicism was highly influential in the Western world particularly in the Roman empire. Marcus Aurelius, emperor of Rome from 161 CE–180 CE was a passionate follower of Stoicism.

It is customary these days to ignore what should be done in favour of what pleases us.
Plautus

Cynicism:
The Philosophy of a Simpler Life

Cynicism began as a rejection of the values, especially materialistic values, of ancient society. Socrates, wandering through the marketplace of Athens, was said to have commented, "There are so many things that I do not need or want." In fact, some believe that Antisthenes, one of Socrates' followers, began the philosophy of Cynicism. However, it was Diogenes (412 BCE–323 BCE)—whom Plato described as Socrates gone mad—who has remained as a major figure, some say caricature, of Cynicism.

We know of him largely through anecdotes, as a wandering sage, happy in his poverty. He lived in a barrel on the street at one time. For awhile he possessed a cloak and a cup, but when he saw a boy drink with cupped hands, he threw away the cup. When he was sold into slavery, Diogenes pointed out a purchaser and called out, "Sell me to him. He needs a master." He proceeded to raise his owner's children well, in good health and spirits. He was devoted to what he thought of as the "natural life." In an attempt to prove that cooking food was unnatural, he ate an octopus raw, so the story goes, and died of unknown causes.

After forty, a man is responsible for his own fate.
Abraham Lincoln

The Cynics rejected all luxury in favour of living a frugal life. They believed that civilization and its social institutions, such as government, property, marriage, and religion, could not provide the answers to life. Cynics rejected society totally, advocating a return to a simpler, unhindered lifestyle. The one true answer to life, they argued, would only be found from within oneself.

Later, the word "cynicism" acquired a somewhat different meaning as a result of the antisocial behaviour of the Cynical philosophers. Cynicism would come to mean misanthropy, a dislike of humanity in general, as Cynics looked with disdain on most human and social endeavours.

The Cynic Diogenes lived in a barrel. One day, Alexander the Great visited the philospher and asked if there was anything he could do for him. Diogenes replied : "Yes, stand out of the light and let me see the sun."

Epicureanism:
Enjoy Life While You Can

Even moderation ought not to be practised to excess.
Anon

Epicureans, named after their teacher Epicurus (342 BCE–270 BCE), argued that the goal of life was to live solely for pleasure. This idea was not entirely new; Aristotle, for example, believed that happiness was the goal of most people.

The Epicureans based their ethical views on the belief that there is no overall plan or rationality to the universe. There are no reasons outside one's own self to motivate or explain life. Therefore the response to life was to enjoy it while one can.

They did not advocate a life of excess of food, drink, and merriment. Like Aristotle,

they said that it was important to live moderately. Extreme searches for pleasure only result in long-term pain. Too much of anything, such as food, drink, or partying, causes unpleasant consequences—illness, dependence, and an unbalanced life.

Critics of Epicureanism point out that not all people act in ways that bring them pleasure. Some people act for the benefit of others, even at the expense of their own happiness or well-being. How, these critics ask, can an Epicurean explain the actions of someone who willingly gives up his or her own life to save another?

Understand Concepts

1. Using an organizer, summarize and comment on the ethical ideas of Plato and Aristotle. Show in what ways they agree, if at all, and in what ways they disagree.
2. (a) What reason is suggested for the rise in ethical theories and philosophies of life during the Hellenistic period.
   (b) Are there any similarities with our own society today? Why or why not?

Apply and Develop

3. With which of these statements would Plato or Aristotle tend to agree? Explain your reasoning.
   (a) There is only one right answer to any ethical problem or issue, if only we knew what it was.
   (b) To find out what is right, ethical behaviour, ask those who know in a given society.
   (c) Ultimately we must judge the rightness of an action by whether or not it makes people happy.
   (d) As I become wiser and more knowledgeable, I will become a better person.
   (e) Right action and moral behaviour are divinely ordained.
4. Determine how a Cynic, a Stoic, or an Epicurean would respond to these statements.
   (a) Since there is no universal order, we must find our own way to live life.
   (b) Since all things are pre-ordained and beyond our control, we can only control our responses to events.
   (c) The material goods of this world will not bring happiness.

Think Critically

5. Take the position of any one of Plato, Aristotle, a Stoic, an Epicurean, or a Cynic. In a brief response paper, state their general position on how to find the right way to live life, why they believe the way they do, and what this means for living an ethical life. Complete the paper by presenting your own point of view on their ideas.

Communicate Ideas

6. Debate this issue: Aristotle's view of ethics is more defensible than that of Plato.

Eastern Ethical Theories

No discussion of Eastern ethics would be complete without examining Confucianism, Hinduism, and Buddhism. These represent major traditions in Eastern ethical thought. The ethical theories of Confucius were primarily based on human interactions in daily life. Over time, his teachings have been modified to reflect a theological dimension. Hinduism and Buddhism represent two major religious traditions and have influenced all Asian philosophers to some degree. Hinduism, Buddhism, and Confucianism have formed the basis of social organization for many Asian countries, including India, Tibet, and China.

Hindu Ethics:
Transcending Birth and Death

Hindu culture and philosophy arose in the Indus Valley and flourished in northwest India between 2500 and 1500 BCE Later Indo-Aryan immigrants assimilated this culture, resulting in the body of orally preserved literature called *Vedas*—hymns, texts, and philosophic ideas about ultimate reality and the goal of life. Hinduism is the Western name given to a family of diverse religious beliefs and practices that are called *Vaidika*, after these sacred texts. Hinduism, unlike Christianity or Islam, for example, does not try to convince or convert others to one set of beliefs, because the Vedas say that "Reality is one, but different religious teachers speak of it differently."

Hindu philosophy is based on the law of karma, which itself is based on two principles: all things are determined; and individual souls are eternal through reincarntion, or rebirth. Karmic determinism says that our present state in life, whether of suffering or enjoyment, is a result of our own past actions, in this life or a previous life. We are the authors of our fate. As the *Bhagavadgita*, a holy text, says: "The Lord does not create human agency or actions." If we live well, we can be released from worldly existence after death. If we do not live well, we will be reincarnated in a new life, which will be determined by the karma we

*In Eastern philosophy, all our actions, whether they are good or bad, are called **karma**. During the course of our lives, the choices that we make on a daily basis affect the balance of good and bad karma. When we die, this sum total of good or bad karma affects the type of life form we will assume when we are reincarnated. If we acquire enough good karma, we may eventually escape the karmic wheel of reincarnation and achieve liberation from human suffering.*

practised in our previous life. According to Hinduism, it is possible to understand how to live life better through study, meditation, and yoga (a form of self-discipline for controlling the mind and body).

The Vedas set out rules, known as *dharma*, to guide how people should live. An individual's dharma describes his or her duty to gods, neighbours, family, and self. Dharma is a principle that connects people to one another and to the gods, but everyone can practise dharma in a different way.

By following your dharma, you can be released from the karmic cycle of rebirth. The dharma that is right for you changes as you grow older. When you are young, you ought to study hard, for example. As you become an adult, you should focus on your work and on raising a family. When you are even older, you should meditate and practise yoga. By this time, you will have mastered your worldly desires and possibly be released from worldly existence forever.

Buddhism:
The Principle of Detachment

Siddhartha Gautama (563 BCE– 483 BCE), who came to be known as the Buddha, was an Indian prince who grew up living a sheltered life of luxury. Against his family's wishes, he went out into the world and was shocked at the suffering he saw everywhere: poverty, hunger, sickness, toil, and death. He became motivated to do something about such suffering, and devoted himself to that quest.

Time Line

Development of Eastern Ethics
- - - - - - - - - - -

HINDUISM
(2500 BCE–PRESENT)
begins in Indus Valley

VEDAS
(C. 500 BCE)
oldest Hindu scriptures are written

SIDDHARTHA GAUTAMA
(563 BCE–483 BCE)

BUDDHISM
(C. 528 BCE)
begins being practised

CONFUCIUS
(551 BCE–479 BCE)

The study of ethics is concerned with finding right ways to live and act. What motivated Siddhartha Gautama to begin his search for right ways to live? What would Plato or Aristotle have said about Siddhartha Gautama's approach in developing new ethical principles?

Legend has it that the answer to life's suffering came to Buddha as he meditated under a lotus tree. The right way to live was neither to pursue pleasure, nor to deny oneself unnecessarily. We will not be happy by trying to satisfy our desires, for that will only lead to new desires, nor will denying ourselves the necessities of life lead to wisdom. With this enlightenment, Buddha developed the Four Noble Truths:

1. Life is suffering.
2. Suffering involves a chain of causes.
3. Suffering can cease.
4. There is a path to such cessation.

The right way to live is to gain the wisdom that allows us to see beyond the mistaken idea of the "self." In Buddhist philosophy, the self is an illusion that keeps people from achieving *Nirvana*, freedom from suffering. The way out of suffering, then, is to eliminate selfish desire by following the Eightfold Path which consists of: right seeing, right thinking, right speaking, right acting, right lifestyle, right effort, right mindset, and right meditating. The "right" way is not the same for everyone; rather it is a way to focus on enlightenment.

Buddhist ethics are also summarized by five moral precepts called the *Pancha Shila*.

1. Avoid killing, or harming any living thing.
2. Avoid stealing, taking what is not yours to take.
3. Avoid sexual irresponsibility, which for monks and nuns means celibacy.
4. Avoid lying or any hurtful speech.
5. Avoid alcohol and drugs, which diminish clarity of consciousness.

PHILOSOPHERS' FORUM

The Eightfold Path

"The Noble Eightfold Way, monks, I will expound and analyse to you. Listen to it, reflect on it well, I will speak." "Even so, Lord," the monks replied to the Lord.

The Lord said, "What, monks, is the Noble Eightfold Way? It is namely right view, right intention, right speech, right action, right livelihood, right effort, right mindfulness, right concentration."

"And what, monks, is the right view? The knowledge of pain, knowledge of the cause of pain, knowledge of the cessation of pain, and knowledge of the way that leads to the cessation of pain: that, monks, is called right view."

"And what is right intention? The intention … not to hurt, the intention not to injure: that, monks, is called right intention."

"And what is right speech? Refraining from falsehood, from malicious speech, from harsh speech, from frivolous speech: that, monks, is called right speech."

"And what is right action? Refraining from taking life, from taking what is not given, from sexual intercourse: that, monks, is called right action."

"And what is right livelihood? Here a noble disciple abandoning a false mode of livelihood gets his living by right livelihood: that, monks, is called right livelihood."

"And what is right effort? Here a monk … exerts his mind; with the dispelling of bad and evil thoughts that had arisen he exercises will…. [W]ith the producing of good thoughts … he exercises will, puts forth effort…. [W]ith the fixing, freeing from confusion, increasing, enlarging, developing and filling up of good thoughts that had arisen he exercises will, puts forth effort, … that, monks, is called right effort."

"And what is right mindfulness? Here (1) on the body: a monk abides contemplating the body, … dispelling his longing and dejection towards the world; (2) on feelings: he abides contemplating the feelings, … dispelling his longing and dejection towards the world; (3) on thoughts: he abides contemplating thoughts … dispelling his longing and dejection towards the world. That, monks, is called right mindfulness."

"And what is right concentration? Here (1) a monk free from passions and evil thoughts attains and abides in the first trance of joy and pleasure, which is accompanied by reasoning and investigation and arises from seclusion. (2) With the ceasing of reasoning and investigation, … with his mind fixed on one point, he attains and abides in the second trance of joy and pleasure arising from concentration, … (3) With equanimity and indifference towards joy he abides mindful and self-possessed, and with his body experiences pleasure that the noble ones call 'Dwelling with equanimity, mindful and happy,' and attains and abides in the third trance. (4) Dispelling pleasure and pain, and even before the disappearance of elation and depression, he attains and abides in the fourth trance, which is without pleasure and pain, and with the purity of mindfulness and equanimity: that, monks, is called right concentration."

[E.J. Thomas, trans., *Early Buddhist Scriptures*. New York: Krishna Press, 1935, 94–6.]

Confucius' Views on Ethics

A generation before Plato, the Chinese poet and teacher Confucius (551 BCE–479 BCE) was considering how people should treat each other. Self-educated, he tried to bring about social change by holding political office, but could not get such a position. So he acquired a small group of students and spent his life teaching them his philosophic beliefs. The *Analects* contain his ideas, written down by those who remembered his lectures. In them, he describes his ethical and social ideas.

According to Confucius, there are five basic relationships in life, ways that people should treat each other, and that contribute to good social order:

1. Father to son—There should be kindness in the father, obedience and respect (filial piety) in the son.
2. Elder brother to younger brother—There should be gentility in the elder brother and humility in the younger.
3. Husband to wife—There should be righteous behaviour in the husband and obedience in the wife.
4. Elder to junior—There should be consideration among the elders and deference among the juniors.
5. Ruler to subject—There should be benevolence among the rulers and loyalty among the subjects.

If you don't want anyone to know it, don't do it.
Chinese proverb

> Be careful with your words, for someone will agree with them. Be careful with your conduct, for someone will imitate it.
>
> *Lie Zi*

Confucian ethics arose in the sixth to fifth century BCE. They continue to be developed today, and are highly influential in Eastern thought. Confucianism today sets up an ethical and political ideal wherein its members are motivated by social and political concerns. Confucian scholars and others believe that cultivation of the self, of character and integrity, are necessary elements for those who are involved in public life. There are several important elements in Confucian ethics.

Tao is "the way" or the ideal way of life,

Portrait of Confucius

and *te* refers to virtue and moral power. Both *tao* and *te* refer to those qualities of generosity and humility that give one social authority. *Jen* refers to qualities of goodness, humanity, and benevolence; more generally with sensitivity to the well-being of others. *Li*, meaning rites, rituals, or propriety, now refers to the appropriate behaviour that is necessary for one's place in society. Observance of *li* in everyday life generally means having respect for others. *Yi* refers to the ability to weigh relevant considerations in specific situations before acting rightly.

Analects

Tzu Kung asked: "Is there any one word that can serve as a principle for the conduct of life?" Confucius said: "Perhaps the word 'reciprocity': Do not do to others what you would not want others to do to you." [XV: 23]

Tzu Chang asked Confucius about humanity. Confucius said: "To be able to practice five virtues everywhere in the world constitutes humanity…. courtesy, magnanimity [nobility of feeling and generosity of mind], good faith, diligence, and kindness. He who is courteous is not humiliated, he who is magnanimous wins the multitude, he who is of good faith is trusted by the people, he who is diligent attains his objective, and he who is kind can get service from the people." [XVII: 6]

[Confucius, *Analects*. Originally in *Sources of Chinese Tradition*, Vol. 1 20–33. In *Introduction to Religions of the East*, trans. by Charles S. Prebish. Dubuque: Kendall/Hunt Publishing Co., 1974.]

Understand Concepts

1. Describe how both Hinduism and Buddhism judge ethically correct behaviour. In each case, is the action or its consequences more important? Provide reasons for your answer.
2. How is ethical behaviour viewed in Hinduism?
3. (a) What ethical principles does Confucius mention in this section?
   (b) Explain why you think these principles are considered important to Confucius.
4. How is the method of inquiry of Confucius different, or similar to, that of Aristotle or Plato?

Think Critically

5. Comment critically on the ideas of Confucius presented in this section. Determine if there are any you particularly support or especially oppose. Provide reasons for your answer.
6. Summarize the nature of the ethical principles of the Eightfold Path.
7. What appears to be a primary goal of Buddhism?
8. Explain how Hinduism and Buddhism differ from, or seem similar to, other ethical systems you have studied so far.

Judeo-Christian and Islamic Ethical Theories

In the previous section, we examined the ethical theories that originated in Asia: Hinduism, Confucianism, and Buddhism. Confucius developed his ideas about ethical behaviour at about the same time that the *Vedas*, the oldest of the Hindu scriptures, were written (c. 500 BCE). Confucius' ideas consisted primarily of practical behaviours that could be applied in daily life, and his ethical theories did not extend into the realm of spirituality. In this way, Confucius' ethics differed widely from the ethical views presented in Hinduism. Later, in the sixth century B.C., the Buddha

Moses breaking the tablet Ten Commandments.

rejected certain ethical principles of Hinduism: the caste system, animal sacrifice, and unnecessary asceticism (self-denial in order to achieve spiritual purity). He developed his own ethical theories based on the Four Noble Truths. It is only by removing all desires, the Buddha said, by following the Eightfold Path that we are able to achieve *Nirvana* and be free of suffering.

In the Middle East, another set of ethical ideas developed independently from those found in Asia. These ethical ideas were centred on the belief in one all-powerful and jealous God, and these ideas formed the basis of Judaism. The Jewish people based their code of ethics on the Ten Commandments, the set of rules that God gave Moses on Mount Sinai in Egypt.

Later, in about 27 CE, Jesus Christ began to teach the people in Judea ethical principles that were based on Judaism but differed on several major points. Jesus' teachings portrayed God as forgiving and all-loving. God is not a supernatural Being far removed from us, but is found within each of us. Jesus also advocated that we love each other and "do unto others as we would want others to do unto us." And very importantly, Jesus said he was the expected Messiah, the Son of God, not a prophet. Then, around 610 CE, Mohammed, an Arab merchant, developed ethical ideas that built on both Judaism and Christianity.

In this section, we will examine the ethical principles found in the three religions of Judaism, Christianity, and Islam. As you read these ideas, consider these questions: How do Judeo-Christian and Islamic ethics differ from those in Hinduism and Buddhism? What would Plato, Aristotle, or Confucius have to say about these ethical principles? Which code of ethics do you believe applies to you? Does your personal code of ethics come from theories from various sources? What ethical behaviours are common to all the ethical theories you have encountered thus far?

Ethics of Judaism: The Ten Commandments

In the Middle East, over a long period of time, the concept of monotheism arose—the idea that there is only one God, and that such a God created the universe and is all-powerful and good. Such a concept formed the base of the religions and cultures of several people in that area. Judaism, Islam, and Christianity all shared in that idea, and continue to do so today.

In each of these religions, a rich legacy of texts developed, deemed to be revealed by God. For Jewish people, the Torah consists of the holy scriptures revealed to humanity by God, and contains Jewish history, codes of behaviour, poetry, and prophecy. As with Islam, Judaism developed a tradition of Biblical interpretation and commentary, and in this way a philosophic tradition of questioning and reasoning. Jewish scholars continually interpreted the scriptures and applied them to changing social circumstances.

In the Judaic tradition, the primary goal of ethical behaviour is not salvation, gaining entry to heaven or an afterlife. Rather, it is faithfulness to God by adhering to the "laws of life" that enables individuals and communities to be fulfilled. These ethical laws are obtained through reason, and are based on the scriptures and tradition.

Time Line

Judeo-Christian and Islamic Ethics

ABRAHAM
(C. 2000 BCE)
founds Judaism

MOSES
(14TH OR 13TH CENTURY BCE)
receives Ten Commandments

TORAH
(9TH CENTURY–4TH CENTURY BCE)
is written

TALMUD
(6TH CENTURY CE)
Jewish law is written

JESUS CHRIST
(C. 4 BCE–29 CE)
begins teaching in Judea c. 27 CE

MOHAMMED
(570 CE–632 CE)
develops religious beliefs c. 610 CE

*In Judaism, the **Talmud** represents scholarly interpretations of the **Torah**. It embodies Jewish law and describes how a practising Jew should live.*

The Ten Commandments

Thou shalt have no other gods before Me.

Thou shalt not make unto thee any graven image.

Thou shalt not take the name of the Lord thy God in vain.

Remember the sabbath day, to keep it holy.

Honour thy father and thy mother.

Thou shalt not kill.

Thou shalt not commit adultery.

Thou shalt not steal.

Thou shalt not bear false witness against thy neighbour.

Thou shalt not covet thy neighbour's house, … nor anything that is thy neighbour's.

[*The Bible* (King James version). Exodus 20:2–17.]

Christian Ethics:
Love Your Neighbour as Yourself

Be not deceived; God is not mocked: for whatsoever a man soweth, that shall he also reap.

Galatians 6:7

Christian philosophy, ethics, and religion are based on the teachings of Jesus Christ (c. 4 BCE–29 CE), who lived in Judea, a Roman province at the eastern end of the Mediterranean Sea. After His death and resurrection, Jesus' disciples continued spreading His teachings throughout the Mediterranean world. Eventually, these ideas gradually replaced Stoicism as the dominant belief system in Rome. Over the centuries, Christianity spread all over the world, and assumed a number of different forms. Yet the core elements of this philosophy, ethical principles, and religion remain the same.

Christian ethics are essentially the same as those found in Judaism. However, the differences arise from Jesus' teachings. The Sermon on the Mount presents a set of ethical behaviours that are based on forgiveness and love, between God and humans and among humans. Jesus also spoke about God being present within each one of us, not as a supernatural Being far removed from us both personally and physically. This idea then implies that because we are all parts of one and the same Being, we know internally what constitutes ethically correct behaviour.

The Sermon on the Mount is one of Christianity's fundamental teachings because it presents Jesus' view of God and right behaviour. It draws our attention to the divergent view that Jesus had regarding the ethics in Judaism.

According to Christians, the good life can be achieved through the love of God and adherence to His wishes. Problems arise when we resist God's will and disregard our own internal wisdom of what is right and wrong behaviour. Not all Christians agree about how to discover God's will. The Catholic Church, for example, believes that

During the Sermon on the Mount, Jesus explained the Beatitudes. The ethics of Christianity are described, in part, by this sermon.

The Sermon on the Mount

Blessed are the poor in spirit: for theirs is the kingdom of heaven.
Blessed are they that mourn: for they shall be comforted.
Blessed are the meek: for they shall inherit the earth.
Blessed are they which do hunger and thirst after righteousness:
    for they shall be filled.
Blessed are the merciful: for they shall obtain mercy.
Blessed are the pure in heart: for they shall see God.
Blessed are the peacemakers: for they shall be called the children of God.
Blessed are they which are persecuted for righteousness sake:
    for theirs is the kingdom of heaven.
Blessed are ye, when men shall revile you, and persecute you,
    and shall say all manner of evil against you falsely, for my sake.

[*The Bible* (King James version). Matthew 5:1–11.]

the Church is the "vicar" of God, and that God's will is expressed through the teachings and statements of the Church. Protestant churches place greater emphasis on the personal relationship that exists between God and the individual and through individual study of the Bible.

Critics of Christian ethics point to several elements of the philosophy that are unclear. One is the problem of how God can be good and all-powerful when there is so much evil in the world. Another is the problem of free choice. In Christian ethics, God has given people the freedom to choose how they will act, for good or for evil. But if God has knowledge of all things past, present, and future, do we really choose or do we simply think that we do? Thirdly, the Bible is the written source of Christianity, the revealed word of God. Yet it is not always clear and we do not necessarily know how the Bible should be interpreted, especially when we apply its teachings to modern circumstances.

Islamic Ethics: The Direct Word of God

If you adhere to the things that I am leaving behind, you shall never be misguided.
Mohammed

The Islamic religion, and the ethics that its followers hold came after the Hellenistic period during the seventh century A.D. Islam is the most recent of the major world religions. It is held by vast numbers of followers around the world, especially in the Middle East, the Persian Gulf, North Africa, and parts of Asia and Europe. It is a revealed religion, in that its beliefs were revealed word for word to its prophet, Mohammed, who memorized it over time. These words were eventually written down in the Qu'ran and are believed to be the direct word of God, or Allah, to Muslims.

BEHIND THE MIND

Mohammed

Scribe to Allah

Mohammed (570–632) was born near the city of Mecca in modern Saudi Arabia. Orphaned at a young age, Mohammed was raised by his uncle, a chief of the Quraysh tribe. With no chance for a formal education, he spent his early years travelling across the Middle East as a trader. During these travels, he came into contact with many cultures, and with a number of religions: Christianity, Judaism, and Zoroastrianism. All of these religions believed in one God, had a scripture that was held to be the word of God, and a belief system that taught that the world would one day end and that the righteous would be rewarded.

As a young man, Mohammed began to go into the hills around Mecca and think about the way his people were living, and he worried about the day of judgement. During one of these times of meditation, he reported that he had a visit from Gabriel, an angel, who spoke to him. Throughout his life, he continued to receive revelations from God. Mohammed memorized these divine messages and eventually they were written down. They became the scriptures of Islam, the Qu'ran.

Mohammed was convinced that there was but one God, called Allah. He said that he was the last prophet of Allah, and his revelations were to be the final ones. Over the years, more and more converts joined the

Painting of Mohammed

Muslim movement, largely from the younger and poorer groups in Mecca. However, the older, richer, and established leaders of Mecca opposed both Mohammed and his growing movement. Many of his followers had to leave the city for their own safety. Finally, Mohammed himself left Mecca, invited to become the judge of the city of Medina. The journey from Mecca to Medina is called the *Hijrah* (migration) and is the time from which Muslims have since dated their calendars. Over the next few years, the number of followers of Islam increased rapidly. By 629 CE, Mohammed, with 10 000 followers, returned to Mecca.

By 632, in poor health, Mohammed gave a farewell message to his followers and died. At his funeral, a central belief of his followers was stated this way: "O ye people, if anyone worships Mohammed, Mohammed is dead, but if anyone worships God, He is alive and dies not."

Although all things are within the power and knowledge of Allah, people are responsible for their own actions. They will be judged by the good or evil they commit in this lifetime, and they will be rewarded or punished after death. Central to these actions are the "five pillars of Islam" that indicate essential ways to live one's life.

1. Muslims must repeat the creed, "There is no God but Allah; Mohammed is the messenger of Allah."
2. Daily prayer, five times a day, is expected.
3. Almsgiving is required. Muslims are expected to share their possessions with the poor.
4. Each year during the month of Ramadan, Muslims must fast. During this month, they must abstain from food and drink during the daylight hours.
5. Muslims should make at least one pilgrimage to Mecca during their lifetime, if at all possible.

Excerpt from the *Qu'ran*

… he is pious who believeth in God, and the last day, and the angels, and the Scriptures, and the prophets; who for the love of God disburseth [pay out] his wealth to his kindred, and to the orphans, and the needy, and the wayfarer, and those who ask, and for ransoming; who observeth prayer, and payeth the legal alms, and who is of those who are faithful to their engagements when they have engaged in them, and patient under ills and hardships, and in time of trouble; these are they who are just, and these are they who fear the Lord.

[Excerpt from the *Qu'ran*, ch. 172. In S.E. Frost Jr., *The Sacred Writings of the World's Great Religions*. New York: The New Home Library, 1943.]

Understand Concepts

1. (a) Summarize the central ethical principles of each of these religions: Judaism, Christianity, and Islam.
   (b) For each of the principles in part (a), how would followers argue for their ethical position?
2. (a) In what ways do all of the religions discussed in this section share similar ethical ideas?
   (b) Describe the differences that you see between them.

Apply and Develop

3. Use an organizer to explain how the religions discussed in this chapter view:
   (a) the source of ethical ideas
   (b) the purposes of behaving ethically
   (c) whether ethical ideas are relative or absolute
   (d) whether acts should be judged by intentions or consequences
   (e) whether we possess free will or are guided by fate

Think Critically

4. Prepare a comparison chart to indicate similarities and differences between Judaism, Christianity, and Islam. From the information in this chart, draw conclusions about the essential nature of ethics in these religions.

Communicate Ideas

5. Take part in a panel discussion of the ethics of Hinduism, Buddhism, Judaism, Christianity, and Islam. Panel members should be made up of those who have studied one of these religions.
6. Invite a member of one of the world's major religions to speak to your class on the nature of that religion. Prepare questions ahead of time to ask about the ethics of that religion and about other aspects of the religion that interest you.

Inquire and Research

7. Interview someone who belongs to, or has a leadership position in Hinduism, Buddhism, Judaism, Christianity, or Islam. Find out more about the ethical views of that religion. How are teachings applied to everyday events? How should people live their lives? Why do people want to live ethically in that religion? Summarize your findings in a three to four page paper that outlines essential elements and draws major conclusions.
8. Research the life of one of the prophets of Judaism, Christianity, or Islam.

Review and Reflect

Ethics, the search for ways to live, and ways to act towards others, began early in human history. Many people share different views on what constitutes ethically correct behaviour and these views are apparent when you experience people from other cultures and of different religious backgrounds.

In fifth-century-BCE Athens, Socrates, Plato, Aristotle, and others began a serious discussion of ethics: how to live life well in society. Plato believed that universal rules of right and wrong existed if only we searched for them rationally. Aristotle, on the other hand, argued that we should study the way people live to determine right from wrong.

During the Hellenistic era that followed, a number of ethical theories emerged. The Stoics believed that since all events are predetermined, the best course of action for us is to accept what cannot be changed. The Epicureans, on the other hand, believed that we should live life while we can but that we should exercise moderation at all times. The Cynics espoused a simpler life and rejected society totally.

In the Eastern world, a number of philosophies and religions were developing that contained important ethical principles. Confucius concerned himself largely with social organization and how people related to each other. Followers of Hinduism and Buddhism developed ethical principles based on an understanding of the human condition and finding ways to deal with it.

In the Middle East, over a period of time, Judaism, Christianity, and Islam developed ethical principles based on revelations from God. These three religions would become powerful influences on ethical ideas around the world.

Modern Views of Ethics

What do you believe is most important in ethics, the intentions a person has, or the consequences of the action a person takes? Suppose someone who, while trying to help another person cross the street, involves both in an accident in which both are injured. Is the person who attempts to do good, but fails, an ethical person? Suppose a person accomplishes a positive result for someone else, by accident and with no good intention in mind. Has that person acted in an ethically correct manner?

Some philosophers such as Immanuel Kant believed that actions alone, not the consequences, should be used to judge the ethics of any situation. Even though we might not be found out, we will not hand in the "borrowed" term paper. We know we might lose our job, but we inform authorities that our employer is polluting the river. In each case, we believe we have a duty to act in a certain manner because the act itself is right or wrong. The consequences are not our primary consideration—perhaps we do not consider them at all!

Other philosophers, such as Jeremy Bentham and John Stuart Mill, believed that the consequences of an action should be considered when deciding to act in an ethically correct manner. They regarded actions as having no ethical value in themselves, those values residing in the consequences resulting from the actions. To these philosophers, an ethically correct action would produce the greatest pleasure or good for the majority of people concerned.

Philosophers in the recent past have considered the importance of action and consequence in human behaviour from many more perspectives than these. For some, culture plays an important role in evaluating the ethics of a group of people; for others, it is the dark, unconscious of our psyche. There are arguments to be made for and against each of these philosophies. As you examine the ethics of our recent past, consider whether you would accept those views. What arguments would you use to support those views? What arguments can be put forward against such ethics?

For many of us justice involves impartiality in judging right and wrong behaviour. Is it possible to be truly impartial when judging the ethical correctness of an action?

The Principles of
Action-Oriented Ethics

Many philosophers throughout the ages have considered how we can judge if a course of action is ethically correct. Some thinkers such as Immanuel Kant emphasized considering the ethics of the action only, without considering the effect or the consequences. This position is known as action-oriented ethics, or deontology. Deontology means that it is necessary to carry out the action based on principle or duty alone, without taking into account the consequences. This approach of judging the ethics of a situation considers the ethics of the action separately from its consequence. For example, an action-oriented ethicist may state that people must always tell the truth, despite the consequences, because telling the truth is the right thing to do.

Kant went further to say that the motivations behind our actions determine whether we are acting in an ethically correct manner, regardless of the outcome. What arguments can you make for and against action-oriented ethics?

Immanuel Kant:
The Idea of Right Action

Immanuel Kant (1724–1804) lived his whole life in the small town of Königsberg, East Prussia, now Germany. He attended the University of Königsberg from 1740 to 1746, and then worked as a private tutor. In 1755, he returned to the university, received a master's degree, and then began lecturing.

Kant had a reputation, probably exaggerated, for leading a highly regimented life. It is said that his daily schedule was so predictable that the townspeople set their clocks by him. Every day, at exactly the same time, he took his afternoon walk up the street. Without such organization, however, he would probably not have written the many books that

shaped modern philosophy: *Critique of Pure Reason* (1781), *Metaphysics of Ethics* (1785), *Critique of Practical Reason* (1788), and many others.

Kant was a highly successful lecturer, gathering a large following of students. He also had a reputation as an interesting conversationalist and a charming host, according to those who were invited to his home.

While his personal life appeared unremarkable, Kant's philosophic life was profound. He was interested in a wide range of philosophic problems, as illustrated by his comment, "two things fill the mind with ever new and increasing admiration and awe ... the starry heavens above and the moral law within."

Immanuel Kant

Kant was familiar with the philosophies of empiricists such as David Hume, and rationalists such as Descartes. Kant had respect for each of these schools, especially empiricism, but viewed them both as limited.

Kant's writings delved more deeply, seeking to know more about underlying realities of things studied, and questioning the assumptions held by philosophers who study in each field.

Criteria for Judging Right Action

Kant believed that an action is ethically correct because the act itself is the right thing to do, not because of the consequences. The question is: How do we know what is the ethically correct action to take in any situation? Here, Kant provided several guidelines on which to base our judgement.

Kant asserted that human beings, simply by being human, have certain unique characteristics and therefore must be treated in certain distinct ways. Humans are different from all other creatures because we set goals for ourselves, and we wish to control our own lives. As a result, we must respect that goal-setting quality of other human beings, and treat them with the dignity they deserve. We should act only in a manner that is respectful of the needs and nature of other free and rational beings. People should never, said Kant, be treated as objects for our own purposes. He wrote, "Act in such a way that you treat humanity, whether in your own person or in the person of any other, always … as an end and never simply as a means."

Another of Kant's rules for ethical behaviour is that motives, rather than consequences, are the most important element of any action. We should act with goodwill towards others, and have good intentions towards others. Do we try to treat others with respect? Do we acknowledge other people's worth as human beings when we initiate an action? If we do, Kant concluded, then our motives are good, and our actions will be ethically correct, regardless of the consequences.

A third way of judging whether an action is right is to determine if we would want all people to act in the same way under the same circumstances. Perhaps you may think that it would be acceptable to tell a lie in a specific situation in order to escape responsibility for an action. Would you want everyone to lie under similar circumstances? Kant believed this test helped to indicate whether an action is ethically correct or not.

Kant believed that these guidelines could determine correct action, and that once an action is determined to be ethically correct, it must be carried out in all cases, without exception. Kant used the phrase "categorical imperative" to describe this theory, that right action *must be done* (imperative) in all similar cases *without exception* (categorical).

One advantage of action-oriented ethics is that we know clearly which actions are ethically correct and which are not. Moreover, a wrong action today is a wrong action tomorrow, or any other time. Kant's approach lets us develop an ethical standard from the point of view of who we are as human beings. We are free, goal-setting individuals, and we want others to respect that freedom, rationality, and dignity.

Sometimes, however, we may come across circumstances where action-oriented ethics is difficult to apply. Any good ethical theory should help us understand the grey

Morality, like physical cleanliness, is not acquired once and for all: it can only be kept and renewed by a habit of constant watchfulness and discipline.
Victoria Ocampo

A truth that's told with bad intent beats all the lies you can invent.
William Blake

areas as well as those that are black and white. How would you develop a rule for action, following Kant's principles, if someone burst into your classroom, and demanded to know where you were sitting, so that he or she could hurt you? It might seem better to lie, in this instance, rather than to reveal where you are. How would Kant respond to such a situation?

Groundwork of the Metaphysics of Morals

Immanuel Kant

It is impossible to conceive anything at all in the world, or even out of it, which can be taken as good without qualification, except a good will…. A good will is not good because of what it effects or accomplishes—because of its fitness for attaining some proposed end: it is good through its willing alone—that is, good in itself…. Even if … this will is entirely lacking in power to carry out its intentions; if by its utmost effort it still accomplishes nothing … even then it would still shine like a jewel for its own sake as something which has its full value in itself. Its usefulness or uselessness can neither add to, nor subtract from, this value….

Our second proposition is this: An action done from duty has its moral worth, not in the purpose to be attained by it, but in the maxim [rule or law] in accordance with which it is decided upon.

But what kind of law can this be … which, even without regard to the results … has to determine the will … ? [It is that] I ought never to act except in such a way that I can also will that my maxim should become a universal law.

Take this question, for example. May I not, when I am hard pressed, make a promise with the intention of not keeping it? … Is it prudent, or is it right, to make a false promise? To tell the truth for the sake of duty is something entirely different from doing so out of concern for inconvenient results…. "Does a lying promise accord with duty?" I have then to ask myself "Should I really be content that my maxim (the maxim of getting out of a difficulty by a false promise) should hold as a universal law (one valid for myself and others)? And could I really say to myself that every one may make a false promise if he finds himself in a difficulty from which he can extricate himself in no other way?" I then become aware at once that I … can by no means will a universal law of lying; for by such a law there could properly be no promises at all, since … others … would not believe my profession or … if they did so … would pay me back in like coin…. [M]y maxim, as soon as it was made a universal law, would be bound to annul itself….

[Immanuel Kant, *Groundwork of the Metaphysics of Morals*, chap. 1 and 2. In *The Moral Law*, trans. by H.J. Paton. London: Hutchinson, 1948.]

Understand Concepts

1. What are the primary assumptions and rules that Kant used to develop his ethical views?
2. In a brief paragraph, explain Kant's ethics to someone who has never encountered it.

Apply and Develop

3. Using Kant's ethical views for each of these situations, develop what you would defend as a universal law that should be followed in all similar cases (a categorical imperative). Defend your law to others in the class.
   (a) Your friend has just bought a new outfit that cannot be returned. You don't think it suits him at all. Should you tell him a lie, that you think the suit is nice, so as not to hurt his feelings?
   (b) You are about to hand in your exam paper, one that will determine your final mark in science. As you accidentally glance over at your neighbour's desk, you see that you have misunderstood one of the diagrams on the exam. It will make a significant difference to your mark. Should you make the change before handing in your exam?
   (c) You have just met someone that you think you might like to date, but are not sure until you get to know that person a little better. This new person invites you out. The problem is that you have an understanding with your boyfriend that you will not date anyone else. You know that your boyfriend would be upset if you did, and upset if he found out you lied to him. What should you do in this situation?
   (d) Your friend has been charged with theft. You know this is true because he admitted it to you under promise of secrecy. You must go to court to testify. What should you do?
   (e) Your family is poor. You have siblings who do not have enough nutritious food to remain healthy. You work for a small family-run grocery store. You have tried all other means to get food. Is it all right to take some groceries from the store?
   (f) Your friend is seeing someone you know is a bad influence for her. You have tried to tell her the truth but she refuses to listen. Now she is thinking of living with this person. Should you lie to her or tell her something negative about this person to encourage her to end the relationship?

Think Critically

4. (a) In two lists, identify what you believe to be the strengths and weaknesses of Kant's ethics.
   (b) To what degree, if at all, can you accept his ideas?
5. What is the source of Kant's ethics: divinely revealed ideas, empirical observation, or rational thought? Explain your answer.

The Principles of Results-Oriented Ethics

In contrast to Kant's view of ethics, other philosophers reasoned that the consequences of an action, not the action itself, determine if it is ethically correct. Thinkers such as Jeremy Bentham and John Stuart Mill believed that the outcome of our actions should be the criteria for judging the ethical correctness of our behaviour. This position is known as results-oriented ethics, or teleology (from the Greek word *telos* meaning "end" or "goal"). Utilitarianism is one major school of thought that employs the teleological approach, and is based on the belief that the ethics of an action depend on the harm or good resulting from it. The way to judge the ethical correctness of an action based on its consequences, Bentham said, involved examining how much pleasure or good was created and determining how many people were affected. As the Utilitarian philosophers put it, ethical actions can be measured by their result in "the greatest good for the greatest number."

Jeremy Bentham: A Utilitarian Approach to Ethics

Jeremy Bentham (1748–1832) was born in London, England. Very early in life he showed advanced intellectual abilities: studying Latin grammar at four, entering Oxford University at twelve, and graduating with a B.A. at fifteen.

Bentham went on to study law at Oxford, listening to the lectures of the famous jurist William Blackstone. Bentham was immediately intrigued by, and disagreed with, Blackstone's idea of "natural rights," rights that people were born with and

Jeremy Bentham believed that social action is good to the degree that it promotes happiness for others.

had as a right of being human. "Nonsense in stilts," Bentham called it. He decided not to practise law. He determined to study the ideas behind the law, the philosophy of law. Bentham founded a group of philosophers he called "Utilitarians." Their ideas were strongly based on those of the empiricists John Locke and David Hume. Specifically, Bentham's philosophic goal was to establish a perfect system of laws and government. Since he rejected the idea of natural rights, Bentham needed a methodology for measuring social good, a way by which he could determine how best to live in society. Like Aristotle many centuries earlier, Bentham and his followers chose the "greatest happiness principle," that is, social action is good and useful to the degree that it promotes the happiness of people in society.

Jeremy Bentham became close friends and associates with James Mill and his son John Stuart Mill, two major philosophers of the nineteenth century. The Mills accepted many of Bentham's ideas, but developed them further.

One strange but intriguing part of Bentham's life was his desire to remain present after death, as a symbol or reminder of his ideas. He willed his body to be preserved and kept in a glass box in University College, London. To this day, meetings of Benthamites often take place in the presence of Jeremy Bentham's remains. No one knows, however, how carefully the philosopher follows the discussions of his followers.

Time Line

Modern Ethical
Ideas

IMMANUEL KANT
(1724–1804)
JEREMY BENTHAM
(1748–1832)
founds Utilitarianism
JOHN STUART MILL
(1806–1873)
develops his own
Utilitarian views

The Greatest Good
For the Greatest Number

Bentham was highly impressed by empiricism, the philosophy that said knowledge should be based on objective and observable physical evidence. Bentham argued that an empirical approach was the best way to improve society, and he believed actions and policies should be judged on the basis of how much observable good they produced. He called his approach Utilitarianism, to indicate that an action should be judged on the basis of how much benefit, or utility, it has for improving people's lives. Unlike Kant, Bentham argued that an action is not good or bad in itself. Rather, an action is morally good to the extent that it produces more pleasure than pain to the largest number of people involved.

Bentham devised a method to determine how much pleasure or pain an action can produce, using these categories:

- intensity of pleasure or pain
- duration of pleasure or pain
- the certainty that an action will produce pleasure or pain
- how soon pleasure or pain will be experienced
- future likelihood of more pleasure or pain
- the number of people affected

Do you think an action can be judged solely by the degree of pleasure or pain it produces? Suppose you exaggerated the truth to obtain a promotion, preventing someone else from getting the job. In so doing, you provide your family with a better standard of living, and maybe the other person gets a good job as well. No one appears to be hurt. Does that make it right? Consider the ethical views of both Kant and Bentham as you read the situation on the next page. Which point of view do you support? How would you defend your choice?

A Moral Dilemma

You are on a hiking trip through a remote part of the world, and suddenly you come upon a village. There, you see armed soldiers holding the men of the village hostage, at gunpoint, in the village square. The leader of the soldiers provides you with these options: if you shoot one of the hostages in retaliation for some imagined insult, he will consider releasing all the others. If you refuse, the leader threatens that all the men will be massacred. The hostages beg you to do this act.

- What would Immanuel Kant do? How would he reason?
- What would Jeremy Bentham do? How would he reason?
- What would you do? How would you reason?

John Stuart Mill:
Progressive Thinker of the Nineteenth Century

John Stuart Mill (1806–1873) was born into a family of thinkers and philosophers. His father, James Mill, was a close friend of Jeremy Bentham, founder of Utilitarianism. Other great thinkers of the time were regular guests in the Mill household, and John Stuart enjoyed great intellectual advantages by being around these philosophers at such an early age.

John Stuart Mill was the object of an educational experiment by his father. Between the ages of three and fourteen, he

John Stuart Mill

received rigorous and intense training in the classics, languages, and history. He was expected to memorize, analyze, and criticize the great works, a gruelling task for one so young.

This early education, said John Stuart, gave him a quarter century learning advantage, but it also took its toll. By the age of twenty, Mill experienced an emotional breakdown. He later said that there had been too great an emphasis on the intellectual and analytical side of his development, without equal care for his emotional development. He was stranded at the commencement of his voyage, "with a well equipped ship and a rudder, but no sail." As a result, the young scholar turned to the poetry of Coleridge, Carlyle, and Wordsworth to develop his emotional self.

When John Start Mill was twenty-five, he met Harriet Taylor, with whom he had a strong friendship for twenty years. They eventually married though, sadly, Harriet died only six years later.

Harriet Taylor had an important impact on Mill's life and ideas. He said that if she had been a man, she would have been recognized as a leading thinker. However, women were not expected to have public lives or serious intellectual pursuits during the nineteenth century. Because of Harriet Taylor, John Stuart Mill took a leading and progressive role in writing about women. In 1869, he published *The Subjection of Women*, which presented advanced views about the role of women and their rights in British society. The work was poorly received at the time, largely because it criticized contemporary social patterns, and put forward advanced ideas about gender roles. It later gained wide acceptance.

MILL'S LOGIC, OR FRANCHISE FOR FEMALES
"Pray clear the way, there, for these—ah—persons."

The Quantity and Quality of Pleasures

John Stuart Mill accepted Bentham's idea that the standard for judging action is pleasure or happiness. Mill rejected, however, the idea that all pleasures are equal. Some pleasures, he argued, are more desirable and valuable than others. It is necessary to judge not only the quantity of pleasure, but also the quality, because higher-quality pleasures outweigh lower-quality pleasures.

How can the quality of pleasures be judged? Who is to make this judgement? One person might enjoy playing tennis, while another enjoys basketball. One person loves to listen to classical music, while another believes jazz to be best. Mill believed that those persons who have experienced both types of pleasures are most qualified to make such judgements. If these people decide that one pleasure is of higher quality than another, the rest of us should trust their judgement.

PHILOSOPHERS' FORUM

Utilitarianism

John Stuart Mill

Utilitarianism or the Greatest Happiness principle, holds that actions are right in proportion as they tend to promote happiness, wrong as they tend to produce the reverse of happiness. By happiness is intended pleasure, and the absence of pain; by unhappiness, pain and the privation of pleasure....

Now such a theory of life excites in many minds ... dislike. To suppose that life has (as they express it) no higher end than pleasure ... they designate as utterly mean and grovelling; as a doctrine worthy only of swine, to whom the followers of Epicurus were, at a very early period, contemptuously likened....

When thus attacked, the Epicureans have always answered that it is not they, but their accusers, who represent human nature in a degrading light; since the accusation supposes human beings to be capable of no pleasures except those of which swine are capable.... Human beings have faculties more elevated than the animal appetites, and when once made conscious of them, do not regard anything as happiness which does not include their gratification.... [T]here is no known Epicurean theory of life which does not assign to the pleasures of the intellect, of the feelings and imagination, and of the moral sentiments, a much higher value as pleasures than to those of mere sensation.... [S]ome kinds of pleasure are more desirable and more valuable than others.... [Q]uality is considered as well as quantity.... If I am asked what I mean by difference of quality in pleasures, or what makes one pleasure more valuable ... except being greater in amount, there is but one possible answer. Of two pleasures, if there be one to which all or almost all who have experience of both give a decided preference ... that is the most desirable pleasure....

...[T]hose who are equally acquainted with ... appreciating and enjoying both, do give a most marked preference to the manner of existence which employs their higher faculties ... A being of higher faculties ... can never really wish to sink into what he feels to be a lower grade of existence.... It is better to be a human being dissatisfied than a pig satisfied; better to be Socrates dissatisfied than a fool satisfied. And if the fool, or the pig, are of a different opinion, it is because they only know their own side of the question. The other party to the comparison knows both sides....

According to the Greatest Happiness Principle, as above explained, the ultimate end ... is an existence exempt as far as possible from pain, and as rich as possible in enjoyments, both in point of quantity and quality....

Again, defenders of Utility often find themselves called upon to reply to such objections as this—that there is not time, previous to action, for calculating and weighing the effects of any line of conduct on the general happiness.... The answer to the objection is that there has been ample time, namely the whole past duration of the human species. During all that time, mankind have been learning by experience the tendencies of actions [to produce happiness or unhappiness]....

[John Stuart Mill, *Utilitarianism* (1861), chap. 2. Originally in *Collected Works of John Stuart Mill*, vol. 10. London: Routledge, 1969. In *Western Philosophy*, trans. and ed. by John Cottingham. Oxford: Blackwell Publishers Ltd., 1997, 388, 389.]

According to Utilitarianism, experimenting on animals, such as this Japanese Macaque, is ethically right when these experiments produce the greatest good for the greatest number of people. Recently, however, people have begun to question the ethics of animal testing.

Problems With Mill's Utilitarianism

Some thinkers have criticized Mill for appearing to say that "the ends justify the means." Does this mean it is acceptable to do something bad if good things are the result? What if members of your family opened your mail to prevent you from making what they consider to be a major mistake in your life? What if someone who is smart, but did not have time to study, cheated in order to get into medical school? Are these types of actions acceptable? Mill suggested that such actions would produce greater unhappiness in the long run. Nevertheless, he opened the door to questions and actions like those we just mentioned.

Another problem with Mill's Utilitarianism is that what appears to be right in one circumstance may be wrong in another; what is good today may be wrong tomorrow. This makes the process of developing a clear and consistent ethical way of living extremely difficult.

The Golden Rule

Some ethical ideas, such as the Golden Rule, seem to transcend time and place. As you read the statements below, determine how they are similar.

- "What you do not want done to yourself, do not do to others." (*Confucius, sixth century BCE*)

- "Hurt not others with that which pains yourself." (*Buddha, fifth century BCE*)

- "Do nothing to others which if done to you would cause you pain." (*Hinduism, third century BCE*)

- "What is hateful to yourself do not do to your fellow man." (*Hillel, first century BCE*)

- "Whatsoever you would that men should do to you do you even so to them." (*Jesus Christ, first century CE*)

- "Treat others as you would be treated yourself." (*Sikhism, sixteenth century BCE*)

How would Kant, or John Stuart Mill, respond to the Golden Rule?

Understand Concepts

1. (a) What is the central idea of results-oriented, or teleological, ethics?
   (b) Identify the main ethical principle of Utilitarianism.
2. Explain John Stuart Mill's argument for Utilitarianism.
3. Describe Mill's criteria for judging between pleasures. To what degree do you think he provides a clear statement?

Apply and Develop

4. How would a Utilitarian act in each case? How would you act? Explain your answer.
   (a) The head of a large corporation knows that his company has made a sizeable profit this year. If she reinvests it back into the company, it will more than double the profits. She knows, however, that if she reveals this success to the shareholders of the company, they will demand the profits be immediately distributed. She considers hiding the facts, knowing the shareholders will appreciate her actions next year.
   (b) An armed undercover detective is following a man believed to be a dangerous criminal. The man has robbed banks and shot people in the process. The detective follows the man into a bank, where he reaches into his pocket and pulls out a gun. If the detective warns him, someone may be shot.
   (c) Your rich distant relative has promised to leave you his fortune if you join an organization of which you disapprove. If you get this money it will help you go to university, and assist your family as well. If you refuse to go along with your relative's wishes, he will leave all the money to the organization.
   (d) Your best friend phones, upset because of something that happened to him that day. You know that he will calm down if you talk with him for awhile. You also know, from past experience, that this will take most of the evening. You have a major assignment due tomorrow, upon which your term mark depends.
   (e) You are planning a party and deciding whom to invite. You plan to invite several popular people who get along well. You have two other friends, who would not get along well with this group. You know they would not have a good time at the party. You consider not even telling them about your party, even though you feel that you are betraying their friendship.

Think Critically

5. What appears to be the strengths and weaknesses of Utilitarianism?
6. Compare and contrast Utilitarianism with action-oriented ethics, or deontology. Is it possible for an action to be ethically correct according to both types of ethics? Give an example.

Communicate Ideas

7. Debate this issue: Kant's ethical position is superior to that of John Stuart Mill and the Utilitarians.

Ethics From the Depths of the Human Psyche

What is morality in any given time or place? It is what the majority then and there happen to like, and immorality is what they dislike.

Alfred North Whitehead

Although action-oriented ethics and Utilitarianism seem to be at opposite ends of the ethical spectrum, they are not the only ideas concerning ethically correct behaviour. The great spiritual masters believed that ethically correct behaviour was determined by examining how we wish others to treat us in a particular situation. "Do unto others as others would do unto you," is an idea with which both Immanuel Kant and John Stuart Mill would have agreed. However, other philosophers, such as Friedrich Nietzsche (1844–1900), believed that these ideas represented weakness and only reflected ideas with which the majority of people felt comfortable. Nietzsche saw ethically correct behaviour in a different way, one that was based on the dark, unconscious aspects of ourselves. These parts of our psyche, he argued, had a power of their own that rose above the ordinariness of everyone else. These psychological drives, he said, should be heeded since they are an important life force. He believed that individuals who could act on these forces had an obligation to transcend, or contradict, the ethical standards of others, and of their society.

The Devil's boots don't creak.
Scottish proverb

Beginning in 1921, psychiatrist Hermann Rorschach used a series of inkblots to diagnose psychological or personality disorders. The inkblots are purposely ambiguous and structureless, and the subject "interprets" them according to his or her personality or psychological makeup.

Friedrich Nietzsche:
Beyond Good and Evil

Friedrich Nietzsche was one of the major philosophers of the nineteenth century. Nietzsche was extremely critical of most traditional ethics. He called Utilitarianism the "morality of the herd." Nietzsche viewed most ethical ideas, such as the principle of happiness or the Christian idea of loving one's neighbour as attempts by people to protect themselves against dynamic and powerful individuals. He rejected Kant's morality of intentions by stating that the value of any action lay in the unintentional, especially those motives that are below the surface of the conscious mind.

Nietzsche completely overturned the idea of conventional morality, based on what most people in a society agree upon as right behaviour. For Nietzsche, the Golden Rule and respect for others were the types of ethical principles that led to the weakening of a society. The drives and energy of the individual, he argued, especially the darkness and power of unconscious forces and emotions, must be respected and exalted. He believed that the strong and the determined few in a society were essential for social progress. Conventional morality, he said, hampered these essential, superior individuals. He believed that the dark, dangerous, and more passionate aspects of human existence must be emphasized.

One has to ask whether the type of society Nietzsche advocated is one in which most people would want to live. Many thinkers view his approach as both sinister and arrogant. Although Nietzsche would probably have been appalled by the evil of the Nazi regime in Germany, the leaders of that movement used many of his ideas to justify their inhumane actions.

Other thinkers respect Nietzsche's vision because it challenged accepted ideas in Western ethical philosophy.

Friedrich Nietzsche overturned conventional morality.

Beyond Good and Evil

Friedrich Nietzsche

During the longest part of human history—so-called prehistorical times—the value or disvalue of an action was derived from its consequences. The action itself was considered as little as its origin.... [I]t was the retroactive force of success or failure that led men to think well or ill of an action....

In the last ten thousand years, however, one has reached the point, step by step, in a few large regions on the earth, where it is no longer the consequences but the origin of an action that one allows to decide its value. On the whole this is a great event which involves a considerable refinement of vision and standards ... the sign of a period that one may call moral in the narrower sense....

But today—shouldn't we have reached the necessity of once more resolving on a reversal and fundamental shift in values, owing to another self-examination of man, another growth in profundity? Don't we stand at the threshold of a period which should be designated negatively, as extra-moral? After all, today at least we immoralists have the suspicion that the decisive value of an action lies precisely in what is unintentional in it, while everything about it that is intentional, everything about it that can be seen, known, "conscious," still belongs to its surface and skin—which, like every skin, betrays something but conceals even more. In short, we believe that the intention is merely a sign and symptom that still requires interpretation.... We believe that morality in the traditional sense [is] something that must be overcome....

There is no other way: the feelings of devotion, self-sacrifice for one's neighbour, the whole morality of self-denial must be questioned mercilessly and taken to court.... In the last analysis, "love of the neighbour" is always something secondary, partly conventional and arbitrary, illusory in relation to fear of the neighbour....

The highest and strongest drives, when they break out passionately and drive the individual far above the average and the flats of the herd conscience, wreck the self-confidence of the community, its faith in itself, and it is as if its spine snapped. Hence just these drives are branded and slandered most....

There is a point in the history of a society when it becomes so pathologically soft and tender that among other things it sides even with those who harm it, criminals, and does this quite seriously and honestly.

[Friedrich Nietzsche, *Beyond Good and Evil* (1886). Trans. by Walter Kaufmann. New York: Random House, 1966, 43, 44.]

IDEAS AND ISSUES

Understand Concepts

1. (a) Describe Nietzsche's view of the history of ethical philosophy.
   (b) What ethical philosophies considered thus far in this chapter fall under his historical description?
2. Describe what Nietzsche puts forward as his own philosophy of ethics.
3. Why does Nietzsche think that the unconscious part of ourselves is important in understanding ethics and actions?

Think Critically

4. Assess the pros and cons of Nietzsche's ideas of ethics.
5. In what ways is Nietzsche in opposition to much ethical philosophy?

Communicate Ideas

6. Debate this issue: Nietzsche's ideas lead to no ethics at all, but rather to a new concept of ethics.

Inquire and Research

7. Read Nietzsche's book *Beyond Good and Evil*. Analyze his major ideas in terms of the type of social world he would like to see. Conclude for yourself if he has something of importance to say, or whether his ideas are primarily destructive. Write an essay in which you state and argue your position on this issue.

Ethical Relativism:
Ethics That Depend on Culture

Many moral philosophies attempt to find ethical doctrines that are true for all times and places. Kant offered us the categorical imperative, and the need to treat humans in a distinct and unique way as "goal-developing beings." The Utilitarians, in a resurgence of Aristotle's happiness principle, suggested that "the greatest good for the greatest number" was universally true. Even Nietzsche, in some ways, was searching for ethical rules suitable for all people. Ethical relativism, by contrast, states that there are no common, universal, or objective values. Instead, moral values are developed by individual peoples, groups, or cultures to fit their unique conditions.

Ethical relativism's roots are deep. In ancient Athens, the Sophist Protagoras argued with Socrates, taking the position that no absolute values exist which can be true for all times and places. The Sophists claimed that the power of argument and rhetoric made an action right or wrong. Protagoras' motto was that "a man or a woman is the measure of all things." That good or evil begins with the judgement of the people involved, is a clear-cut statement of ethical relativism.

Ethical relativism is widely accepted in our modern world. Increased awareness of the world's many lifestyles, and many cultures, has likely encouraged such a position. Twentieth century psychologist B.F. Skinner (1904–1990) wrote: "Each culture has its own set of goods and what is good in one culture may not be good in another. What is good for the Trobriand Islanders is good for the Trobriand Islander, and that is that." Anthropologists such as Ruth Benedict (1887–1948) agree with this position, as can be seen in the following excerpt.

Patterns of Culture

Ruth Benedict

Every society, beginning with some slight inclination in one direction or another, carries its preference farther and farther, integrating itself more and more completely upon its chosen basis, and discarding those types of behavior that are uncongenial.... Normality, in short ... is culturally defined.... The very eyes with which we see the problem are conditioned by the long traditional habits of our own society....

We do not any longer make the mistake of deriving the morality of our own locality and decade directly from the inevitable constitution of human nature. We do not elevate it to the dignity of a first principle. We recognize that morality differs in every society and is a convenient term for socially approved habits. Mankind has always preferred to say, "It is really good," rather than "It is habitual."

[Ruth Benedict, "Anthropology and the Abnormal," *Journal of General Psychology* 10, 1934: 72.]

Anthropological View of Ethics: There Are No Moral Absolutes

By the late nineteenth and early twentieth centuries, anthropologists were investigating cultures all over the world, finding as many ways of doing things as there were cultures. In each case, the people involved considered their own practices to be right, and those of others to be wrong. Anthropologists such as Ruth Benedict needed to find ways to explain this wide range of customs, values, and ideas from around the world. Anthropology developed the point of view that all cultures and ethical systems should be respected as valid answers to the circumstances under which each society developed.

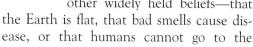

Ruth Benedict

Ethical relativism is the philosophical view that agrees with this position. Ethical relativists point out the existence of wide cultural differences in ideas, actions, and ethics around the world. Even within one society, there are often many conflicting positions concerning such controversial issues as capital punishment, abortion, and poverty.

Critics of ethical relativism argue that the existence of many different views of morality and ethics does not necessarily mean all views have equal value. They note that many other widely held beliefs—that the Earth is flat, that bad smells cause disease, or that humans cannot go to the moon—have been shown to be false. Therefore, they maintain it is also possible that one ethical view might be more correct than the others.

Critics of ethical relativism also point out that few people believe in, or practise, ethical relativism in their personal or social lives. You would probably have problems if your friend suddenly decided that theft is ethical and regularly took your possessions without permission. Most people have difficulty remaining neutral, or not passing judgement, when they hear how people treat each other in other cultures and societies. In Nazi Germany, a society based on racism and extreme nationalism, millions of people were put to death; and war was considered an acceptable way to deal with problems of the state. Most people, however, condemn such beliefs and actions, and, in fact, those who led Nazi Germany were put on trial and punished for their "acts against humanity."

In many Aboriginal cultures, chiefs, in consultation with the elders of their particular tribe, decide on the ethics of situations when there are disputes among tribal members.

Understand Concepts
1. (a) Identify the idea central to ethical relativism.
   (b) What factors appear to have encouraged this view in our modern world?

Apply Ideas
2. Are you an ethical relativist? Suppose each of these social activities have existed.
   For each, answer these questions.
   Would I disapprove and try to stop this behaviour in myself or in those I know personally?
   Would I disapprove and try to stop this behaviour in other parts of the country?
   Would I disapprove and support efforts to stop this behaviour in other countries
   where it existed?
   (a) Men and women go nude in public.
   (b) People eat the flesh of humans who have died.
   (c) People can legally have several spouses at the same time.
   (d) Capital punishment is the penalty for murder.
   (e) Parents are encouraged to discipline their children by using physical punishment.
   (f) Discrimination is allowed against a racial or ethnic minority.
   (g) People must believe in one religion.
   (h) People must support one political party.
   (i) Certain topics, such as religion or politics, must not be discussed in public.
   (j) Individuals can have others as slaves.
   (k) Males experience political and economic discrimination.
   (l) People practise infanticide to allow the strong to survive.

Think Critically
3. To what degree do you think ethical relativism is an acceptable philosophy? That is, do
   you accept that all ethical views are of equal value, and dependent on the society or
   social group only, to validate them, or do you think that there are moral and ethical
   ideas that do, and must, transcend social agreement? Take a position, and present your
   supporting arguments in a position paper.
4. Are there any ethical principles to which all people on earth should adhere? Identify
   these, and support your choices with argument and examples.

Communicate Ideas
5. Debate this issue: Kant's categorical imperative is a superior philosophic principle
   compared to ethical relativism.
6. Watch a film or video of a society that has values quite different from your own. What
   social values and ethics exist in this society? How would an anthropologist approach the
   society and its values? Is the cultural relativism of the anthropologist an acceptable
   approach for an ethical philosopher? What is your position? Discuss these issues with
   other members of the class.

Existentialist Ethics: Behaviour Based on Our Existence

Existentialism has roots in the nineteenth century, but became widely accepted from the mid-twentieth century on. This view of ethics is based on the idea that each of us must create our own being and character. We must do this as individuals, each in our own situation and environment, through the decisions we make in life. Sören Kierkegaard (1813–1855) was the first person to develop this idea of ethics, and many other philosophers, such as Albert Camus (1913–1960) and Jean-Paul Sartre (1905–1980), soon accepted these views. Each of these thinkers developed Existentialism in specific ways.

A central principle of Existentialism, as the name indicates, is the fact that we exist and are conscious of that existence. Sartre's phrase "existence precedes essence" means that first we exist, then we develop our ideas and decisions to act. Put another way, first we exist, then we identify who and what we are. For an Existentialist like Sartre, choice is fundamental in all human life. We choose who we are, what we think, and how we act. Ethics is central to this belief, especially for Sartre.

In 1967, Jean-Paul Satre chaired a mock tribunal which questioned the United States and its role in the Vietnam War. The tribunal was called the Bertrand Russell Tribunal in tribute of the noted pacifist philosopher.

Jean-Paul Sartre

"Condemned to Be Free"

Jean-Paul Sartre (1905–1980) is one of the primary philosophers of the twentieth century. Many of the ideas we hold today are, often unknowingly, borrowed from his writings. Sartre lived his life not only as a philosopher but also as an activist who became deeply involved in the events of the twentieth century.

Jean-Paul Sartre was born into a French family. His father was a navy officer, his mother a cousin of Albert Schweitzer, theologian and doctor in central Africa. Sartre wrote in his autobiography that he had a happy childhood, often reading in his grandfather's library. He went on to study philosophy at the Ecole Normale in Paris. By 1931, he was teaching philosophy in Le Havre. In 1937, he moved to Paris, where he published his brilliant philosophical novel *Nausea* in 1938.

World events, however, intruded upon his philosophic life. The Nazis were beginning their reign of terror and military expansion, and invaded France in 1940. Sartre said later that World War II was the turning point in his life. It changed him from an academic philosopher and well-known avant-garde writer into a man deeply committed to the fate of the poor and powerless, the "wretched of the Earth."

Sartre became a resistance fighter against the Nazi invaders. He was captured and imprisoned. There, under extreme circumstances of interrogation and torture, he realized how alone he was. He also realized that only he, and no one else, could make this terrible situation meaningful for himself.

Sartre supported communism for a while, impressed with the communists' fight against Nazism and their support of the poor of the world. He left the party, in protest, after the Russians invaded Hungary in 1956, but continued to support liberation movements in developing countries such as Algeria and Vietnam. In 1964, Sartre was awarded the Nobel Prize in Literature but refused to accept it on the grounds that he did not want to be "transformed into an institution."

As a young man at the Ecole Normale, Sartre met Simone de Beauvoir. She was a brilliant student who was forging her own career as initiator of the twentieth-century feminist movement. The two remained lifelong companions. Sartre never published anything before de Beauvoir read and approved it.

Sartre's work and reputation gained him the respect and imagination of a generation of younger thinkers in the post war years. He was offered several academic positions but

Development of Existentialism

SÖREN KIERKEGAARD (*1813–1855*) founds Existentialism

JEAN-PAUL SARTRE (*1905–1980*) influences attitudes during the 1960s

SIMONE DE BEAUVOIR (*1908–1986*)

ALBERT CAMUS (*1913–1960*)

GABRIEL MARCEL (*1889–1973*) disagrees with Sartre's ideas about God

decided to make his living as a writer, concerned with the social and political issues of the day. By the 1950s, his ideas were influencing a whole generation of young philosophers. Much of the youth movement in Europe and North America during the 1960s was based, in major ways, on Sartre's philosophic ideas of freedom, respect for the individual, and the assumption of responsibility for one's own decisions.

Sartre's eyesight deteriorated as he grew older, although he continued to work as well as he could. Asked once why he did not dictate his ideas to someone else, Sartre replied that he needed to be able to see what he wrote in order to think. Towards the end of his life, Sartre lived simply, with few possessions, in a small apartment on the left bank of the Seine in Paris.

Sartre's Existentialism:
We Are Responsible for Our Choices

Sartre has been called the "last significant Existentialist philosopher." Unlike Kierkegaard, Sartre was an atheist; he did not believe in God. As a result, according to Sartre, there are no objective and transcendent values. The individual trying to define himself or herself, determining how to choose and act, finds no external answers. In Sartre's words, we are "condemned to be free," unshaped by any external moral law or values.

How do we determine, then, what is the right thing to do? According to Existentialist ideas, we must choose for ourselves how we will act, and it is through such choices that we become who we are. Having chosen, we also must accept the full burden and responsibility of our freedom, and of our choices. If we choose to take one path in life, that of a student, an employer, or a parent, we can blame no one else but ourselves for how things turn out.

There is a further responsibility we face when we choose, said Sartre. By choosing one way over another, we become examples to others. We are making a personal statement in our choice which is: This is how I think I should act. The manner in which we act, as student, employer, friend, teacher, or parent is interpreted by others as a decision we have made consciously, a decision which may be emulated by those around us.

Sartre also provided another guideline for action. Because each of us is free to choose, and indeed must choose, how we will live and exist, we should act in such a way that we respect the freedom of others. Only by having respect for others and for their freedom can everyone have the freedom to be themselves.

Having to find the right way to live ethically is difficult when this must be found within oneself. But choosing wisely, taking responsibility for these choices, and having respect for one's own and others' freedom offers some guidance. Sartre, for example, fought as a member of the French resistance against Nazi military dictatorship during World War II. He must have determined that, in the interests of human individual freedom, the ethical choice was to oppose Nazism.

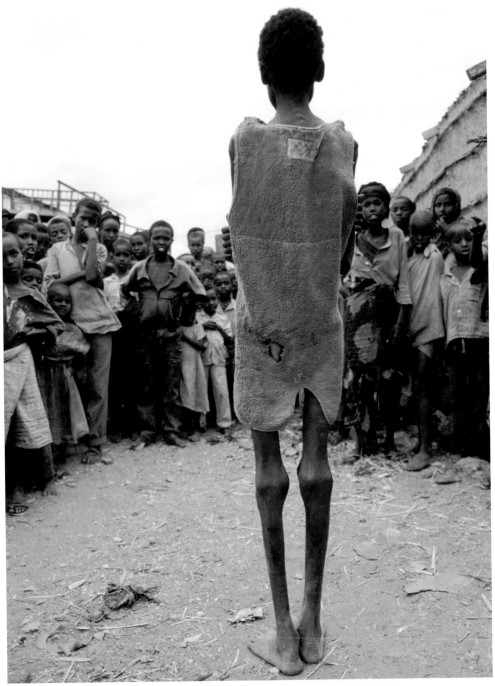

This fifteen-year-old boy is a product of the heinous conditions in war-torn Somalia. Power struggles between various warlords since the ousting of President Siad Barre have left the country ravaged by famine. Mohammed died of starvation a few hours after this picture was taken.

Existentialism has had a powerful impact on thinkers of the late twentieth century. The ideas of Sartre and other Existentialists have been accepted by many who despaired of the atrocities that human beings have committed upon each other. If right or wrong truly exists, Existentialists believe, it must be found from within oneself.

However, some Existentialist philosophers disagreed with Sartre's ideas of God. Gabriel Marcel (1889–1973) was a Christian Existentialist. Marcel agreed with Sartre that one begins with existence, with oneself as a person. However, he disagreed with Sartre that we create and choose our own values. How is this possible, he asked, unless we have something to choose from? Values are discovered, said Marcel, and some values are better than others. From where do we acquire values and meaning? From God, answered Marcel.

Marcel pointed to Sartre's own example of resistance to the Nazis. Sartre himself fought against them, and also wrote a book praising heroes of the Resistance. Marcel raised the question: If there is no external or objective value system, how can one judge Resistance fighters as different from, and ethically superior to, those who fought for the Nazis? The answer, he said, is that some behaviours are better than others, and that ethical values are real and outside the creation of individuals.

Existentialism

Jean-Paul Sartre

What is meant here by saying that existence precedes essence? It means that, first of all, man exists, turns up, appears on the scene, and, only afterwards, defines himself.... [A]t first, he is nothing. Only afterward will he be something, and he himself will have made what he will be. Thus, there is no human nature, since there is no God to conceive it. Not only is man what he conceives himself to be, but he is also only what he wills himself to be after this thrust toward existence.

Man is nothing else but what he makes of himself.... For we mean that man first exists, that is, that man first of all is, the being who hurls himself toward a future and who is conscious of imagining himself as being in the future. Man is at the start a plan which is aware of itself, rather than a patch of moss, a piece of garbage, or a cauliflower.... But if existence really does precede essence, man is responsible for what he is. Thus, existentialism's first move is to make every man aware of what he is and make the full responsibility of his existence rest on him. And when we say that a man is responsible for himself, we do not only mean that he is responsible for his own individuality, but that he is responsible for all men.

[Jean-Paul Sartre, "Existentialism." In *Existentialism and Human Emotions*, trans. by Bernard Frechman. New York: Citadel Press, 1957, 12–8.]

Understand Concepts

1. Explain the phrase "existence precedes essence."
2. (a) How would you describe Sartre's idea of individual responsibility for one's actions?
   (b) How would he respond to the argument that our ideas, and our character, are largely shaped by our environment?

Apply and Develop

3. How well does Sartre's Existentialism explain this situation: the person, who grows up in a deprived environment, without any advantages or opportunities, turns to a life of crime. Can we really say that this person is the author of his or her own fate and must accept responsibility for it?

Think Critically

4. In the 1960s, many young people interpreted Existentialism, as they understood it, to mean extreme individualism, freedom to be yourself, to do as you wished. To what degree do you think Sartre would have agreed with this?
5. To what extent do you accept the idea that we make ourselves the people we are, and the characters we become, through the decisions we make, and therefore must accept full responsibility for our lives and our ethical decisions?

Communicate Ideas

6. Describe the responsibility that an individual has to take for his or her own actions in a society that helps to shape the individual. Take the position of Kant, Nietzsche, or Sartre on this question and present your views in a panel discussion to the class.
7. Both Nietzsche and Sartre, in their own way, focus on the power of the individual in making ethical decisions. Explain how their ethical philosophies differ in the conclusions they reach for the role of the individual.

Inquire and Research

8. Read Sartre's essay "Existentialism," and a general work on Sartre's views of existential existence. In a response paper, critically analyze his main ideas and respond to them from your own point of view.
9. Existentialist philosophy grew in power and influence during the mid-twentieth century as a response to world events such as the horror of totalitarian governments with their lack of respect for, and destruction of, individuals and their rights. Read Albert Camus' book *The Plague*, a commentary on the Nazi invasion of France. Discuss *The Plague* and its meaning in an essay.

Contemporary Ethical Points of View

Interest in ethics, and the desire to find some certainty in the philosophy of ethics, has produced a wide range of ideas and theories over time, as we have seen. Yet, as with many areas of philosophy, new conditions and social situations produce new ideas and philosophies. In this section, we will see several views of ethics that have arisen from contemporary conditions. Moreover, each of these ethical philosophies emerges from unique background conditions: science, psychology, and feminism.

Modern determinism has roots in our increased knowledge of science and social science. Determinists believe that, to a large extent, we are not in control of our own lives and actions. This may remind us of the similar Stoic belief of ancient times, but this determinism is based on our knowledge of natural and social forces that shape our lives.

Other theories of ethics stem from the field of psychology, and an understanding of how we develop and become adult human beings. Psychologist Lawrence Kohlberg (1927–1987), for example, argued that all humans go through a series of psychological stages, and that our ethical decisions are based on our psychological development. For Kohlberg, human beings have the potential to develop into fully ethical human beings given the right circumstances. He also put forward his own view of what a fully ethical human being would be like.

A third area that we will look at stems from the study of gender. Feminist philosophers believe that we cannot understand ethics unless we understand what it means to be a man or a woman in society.

Psychologist testing a six-year-old boy. Twentieth-century psychologists such as Lawrence Kohlberg believe that our ethical decisions are based on our psychological development.

Determinism:
Everything Is Beyond Our Control

Determinism is the view that since all things are caused by something else, nothing can be different from the way it is at any given moment in time. We are who we are because of our upbringing. We are born into a specific culture, and society has shaped us in particular ways. To some degree, we are also the result of our genetic make-up, in that we are men or women, large or small, with certain inherited characteristics. Determinists argue that our actions and behaviours all result from our own individual background and other surrounding conditions of our time.

Being a determinist has a powerful impact on one's view of ethics. If it is true that all things, including our own actions, are caused by other things, then we really have no free will to choose. And if there is no free will with which to choose, then it would seem that there can be little discussion of morality or ethics. What is there to praise or blame in a person if his or her choices are shaped by circumstances beyond human control?

Society recognizes that our choices are, to some degree, limited and shaped by external circumstances. When a person is sentenced in a court of law, extenuating circumstances such as a deprived childhood or peer pressure may often be taken into account. When a person behaves poorly in a social situation, we may excuse that individual by pointing to a lack of opportunity or to a lack of appropriate role models.

The human being who looks upon his own future as already determined by fate ... only acknowledges a lack of will power to struggle and win through.

Max Planck

Determinists believe that we have absolutely no control over the events in our lives—that our actions are determined by external forces. How would a determinist explain the ethical issues surrounding some of the more horrific events in history, such as the mass execution of all the people found in this grave?

There are two major categories of determinists: hard determinists and soft determinists. Hard determinists believe that social forces outside of our control shape everything. These forces include birth, upbringing, environment, and genetics. As a result, hard determinists find it difficult to praise or blame someone for their actions. They believe that successful people have had innate or environmental advantages; that people with problems should be treated; and that rehabilitation, not punishment, is the right response to deal with criminals.

Soft determinists also believe that, because of a number of reasons, our choices in life cannot be other than they are. However, the soft determinist focusses on the causes that lie within us, in our own character. This can, therefore, be changed, and the individual can still struggle to make decisions, despite these internal forces that push us in one direction or another. The soft determinist believes that morality can still exist, despite the forces that shape us, internal or otherwise.

Ethics From a Psychological Point of View

Lawrence Kohlberg put forward a theory of moral development which has had a powerful impact on educators and others concerned with the study of ethics. Kohlberg was a psychologist and based his views on research done in different cultures, with people of different ages.

Kohlberg suggested that people develop through several ethical stages during their lifespan. Each stage brings about different types of moral reasoning. Kohlberg reported that individuals pass through the same stages in all parts of the world, although the rate of development varies according to the culture and life experiences of each individual. He described six stages which are grouped into three levels: preconventional moral level, conventional moral level, and post-conventional moral level.

Preconventional Moral Level

A child is aware of cultural rules of good and bad, and interprets these rules in terms of reward and punishment, or in terms of the

How would our ideas about ethics change as we go through life's stages?

power of those who state the rules.

Stage 1: punishment and obedience orientation. The child determines if something is right or wrong by seeing if the consequences are good or bad for that child. The value here is to avoid punishment. Obedience generally ensures that punishment is avoided.

Stage 2: instrumental relativist orientation. At this stage of moral development, the individual judges whether an action is right if it satisfies his or her own needs, and occasionally the needs of others. Helping others is a matter of "you scratch my back and I'll scratch yours." Human relations are similar to that of the marketplace where one helps another in order to receive goods oneself, rather than through ideas of loyalty, gratitude, or justice.

Conventional Moral Level

At this level the individual values the family, group, or nation most highly and as the source of correct ethical decisions. The individual believes that the most important thing is to conform to, and be loyal to, the group. The person will support and justify the actions of the group, and identify strongly with the people in it.

Stage 3: interpersonal agreement or "good-boy–nice girl" orientation. At this stage, good behaviour is seen as that which pleases and helps others. The individual earns approval by acting as the group expects.

Stage 4: "law and order" orientation. Authority is highly valued at this stage, whether it be that of officials, governments, or the laws of nations. Rules are seen as things to be rigidly followed. Ethically correct behaviour consists of doing one's duty and respecting authority.

Post-Conventional Moral Level

At this level, there is effort to define moral values that are valid apart from the authority of the group.

Stage 5: social-contract legalistic orientation. Right action is defined in terms of individual rights and standards agreed upon by the whole society. The individual is aware that views may differ and may look for ways to reach agreement. At this stage, the individual is willing to change the rules if other ways of doing things are more useful. This is the level upon which many constitutional societies such as Canada's are based.

Stage 6: universal ethical-principle orientation. At this stage, the individual believes that right action is defined by one's conscience in accordance with ethical principles that are consistent and comprehensive. Such principles as the Golden Rule, Kant's categorical imperative, and universal principles of justice, such as respect for the dignity of others, are at this level. Right action, at this stage, would have universal applications, Kohlberg said. That is, what is right for one group of people, would be right for all.

Kohlberg argued that moral development can be hastened through education and experience. Individuals who confront moral issues, and who are aware of how others at a higher level of moral development deal with such issues, will move more quickly towards the next stage, because they see people at higher levels of development dealing more effectively with the challenges of life.

According to Kohlberg, the reasons given for doing something, not the act itself, reveal the level of moral decision-making of an individual. In other words, two people might do the very same thing, such as help a friend, for very different reasons. One might do this to get something in return, the other because he or she believes it is right to help others in general. Moreover, two people at one stage might act differently from each

… Sometimes the very faults of parents produce a tendency to opposite virtues in their children.…
Maria Edgeworth

The child learns more of the virtues needed in modern life—of fairness, of justice, of comradeship, of collective interest and action—in a common school that can be taught in the most perfect family circle.
Charlotte Perkins Gilman

other in similar circumstances. They may have different universal principles about a particular moral issue, for example.

Psychologist and philosopher Carol Gilligan (1936–) disagrees with Kohlberg's view of moral development. Gilligan argues that human relations are an important element in ethics. She argues that women more often consider this as an important element in making ethical decisions, and that Kohlberg ignored this element in his research. Gilligan raises the important question of whether ethical systems are related in an important way to one's gender. Furthermore, even if this is true, is it because men and women have inherently different natures, or is it because they are raised differently in society?

> Thus changes in women's rights change women's moral judgements, seasoning mercy with justice by enabling women to consider it moral to care not only for others but for themselves.
>
> *Carol Gilligan*

Moral Imperative of Men and Women

Carol Gilligan

The moral imperative that emerges repeatedly in interviews with women is an injunction to care, a responsibility to discern and alleviate the "real and recognizable trouble" of this world. For men, the moral imperative appears rather as an injunction to respect the rights of others and thus to protect from interference the rights to life and self-fulfillment. Women's insistence on care is at first self-critical rather than self-protective, while men initially conceive obligation to others negatively in terms of noninterference.

[Carol Gilligan, *In a Different Voice*. Cambridge: Harvard University Press, 1982.]

Carol Gilligan argues that men think in terms of rules and justice, while women are more inclined to think in terms of caring and relationships.

Understand Concepts

1. Identify and describe the two forms of determinism.
2. What are the factors that Kohlberg suggests influence our sense of ethically correct behaviour?

Apply and Develop

3. Categorize each situation as a belief in determinism or freedom of choice. Explain your choices.
   (a) A father sends a child to his room for bad behaviour.
   (b) A person consults a horoscope before venturing out during the day.
   (c) A person is given a light sentence for a crime in consideration of their deprived upbringing.
   (d) A person plans her day carefully in her daytimer.
4. The statements below are ones that people might make in defence of an action. Do you think these statements reflect a preconventional, conventional, or post-conventional level of ethical thinking? Explain your reasoning.
   (a) I am not going to speed because I know there is a radar trap down the road.
   (b) Good citizens should help keep order in a society, whether or not this agrees with the law.
   (c) The law should be followed, whether or not I agree with it.
   (d) It's important to look out for number one, no matter what.
   (e) In any conflict, the right to life and liberty must be upheld.
   (f) Each of us should support laws that promote individual rights.
   (g) If a law is not good, it can be changed through the democratic process.

Think Critically

5. Outline the differences and similarities between ethical relativism and the idea of moral development.
6. Prepare a comparison chart of the major ethical philosophies in this chapter. Use such headings as: place and date, central ideas, major supporting arguments, criticisms, and overall assessment. Identify your own view so far of ethically correct behaviour.

Inquire and Research

7. Read further about one of the ethical writers or schools discussed in this chapter. You might begin by looking into encyclopedias of philosophy and textbooks for survey courses in philosophy. You might then read one of the books written by these philosophers. Develop a point of view about the writer or school, for example, what you believe are the central ideas of that writer or school or a critical assessment of their worth. Present your point of view as a thesis statement supported by argument in a paper of 1500 to 2000 words.

Ethics in a Contemporary Setting

Each area of our lives requires our having a sense of what is right and wrong, and making ethical decisions. This occurs in our family life, in our relations with friends and acquaintances, and in our dealings with groups, organizations, and institutions. What may be ethically correct in one area of life may not be in another. For example, it may be ethically correct to tell your spouse or family that

Sometimes ethically correct behaviour in one situation is morally wrong in another.

you quit working at your previous workplace because of sexual harassment, but it is likely not a good idea to mention it to your prospective employer.

As we make ethical decisions each day, many factors affect our choices. Our gender is a powerful influence on our perception of most situations; women have a different perspective based on their experience as women. Our culture and the way that our culture is perceived by certain groups in society also affect our ethical decisions. Furthermore, our age, plans, and goals may also influence our ethical behaviour.

As we examine different areas of daily life, consider these questions: How do the ethical views presented in the previous sections apply to our everyday lives? It is necessary to consider new ethical views in deciding what is right and wrong today? Can we agree on ethically correct behaviours that can be applied in most work or personal situations?

Feminist Ethics:
Women Voicing Their Own Views

Is there such a thing as feminist ethics? Is there an ethical theory or philosophy that stems from the experience of women alone? Reflecting on the ideas presented thus far, it is clear that men have been at the forefront of main philosophic views. In recent years, however, the views of women have come to be recognized, challenging the idea that men should dominate philosophic discussion. Some women philosophers argue that since philosophers have largely been men, ideas about ethics have to a large extent reflected a male point of view. Others say that the experience of women is essentially different from men and must therefore be expressed by women.

In reading the excerpt below, determine whether the author makes the point that there is a good reason to consider feminist philosophy in its own right or as a separate category.

Feminist Ethics:
Some Issues for the Nineties

Alison Jaggar

… Feminist ethics … seeks to identify and challenge all those ways … in which western ethics has excluded women or rationalized their subordination.…

While those who practice feminist ethics are united by a shared project, they diverge widely in their views as to how this project might be accomplished.…

Even though my initial characterisation of feminist ethics is quite loose, it does suggest certain minimum conditions of adequacy for any approach to ethics that purports to be feminist.

1. … [A] feminist approach to ethics must offer a guide to actions that will tend to subvert rather than reinforce this subordination;
2. Since so much of women's struggle has been in the kitchen and the bedroom, as well as in the parliamentary chamber and on the factory floor, a second requirement for feminist ethics is that it should be equipped to handle moral issues, in both the so-called public and private domain[s].…
3. Finally, feminist ethics must take the moral experience of all women seriously, though not, of course, uncritically.

[Alison Jaggar, "Feminist Ethics: Some Issues for the Nineties," *Journal of Social Philosophy* 20, no. 1–2, Spring/Fall 1989, 91–107.]

Work Ethics:
Values in the Workplace

The study of work ethics has increased significantly in recent years. This is partly the result of people in a particular field behaving unethically and causing others problems as a result. Overall, however, it is the result of rapid social changes that have raised new questions about how to deal with long-standing situations. There is a growing realization in many occupations and professions that a study of ethics is important in order to do the work well, and is important to those working within or being served by those professions. For example, we trust that mechanics, electricians, medical practitioners, and teachers have an ethical system that we can trust and that will work for our own benefit and that of society as a whole.

The ethical principles that operate in a particular work situation come from several sources. The overall ethical principles of society, such as honesty and reliability, will shape the ethical system and values of a profession or a corporation. There will be specific values and ethical systems that have developed within each profession or occupation: service to the client or patient or a search to increase profit. These values will generally, but not always, be consistent with overall social values. Furthermore, individuals who enter a profession will bring with them their own values and ethical systems.

For example, in the teaching profession, society as a whole has a significant impact on what is considered appropriate ethical behaviour, particularly in situations involving students of different cultural backgrounds and perceived and explicit sexual behaviours. The teaching profession itself has developed its own value systems over time. Those individuals who choose to go into teaching will bring with them their own sense of what constitutes ethically appropriate behaviour. However, regardless of the type of work we do, our ideas about ethics must conform to established acceptable behaviours in our society.

Business Ethics:
Values Shared in the Business World

Business has been around for a very long time and, at one level, so has business ethics. Those who stole, cheated, or provided shoddy goods have always been looked down upon, and usually punished. Like other ethical studies, however, business ethics increased during the latter part of the twentieth century.

Business ethics is concerned with the economic systems that exist in our world, such as capitalism and socialism. Business ethics considers the morality of the economic system, how it works within a society, and how it affects workers, consumers, and the environment. Within a given economic system, such as our own mixed economy, with its public and private components, business ethics studies the structures and the practices that exist. For example, an ethicist who is studying our own economic system would consider how it provides for people. Does it encourage effort? Does it allow for fair distribution of important goods to a large number of people? Does it lead to long-term growth and prosperity, while preserving the environment? These are the types of questions that might be considered when analyzing economic systems as a whole.

Another aspect of business ethics involves how individual corporations and other businesses operate. It asks what the ethical responsibilities of an individual business are: how should it treat its workers, consumers, and the environment. Often the media will report on a business that has been found guilty of polluting the environment or of knowingly producing faulty goods.

Business ethics also investigates the behaviours of individuals within a business. What is expected of them? Is there a code of ethics they should follow? What happens if they break this code? Are there conflicts within the business that lead to unethical behaviour? Consider these questions as you read the following case study which is used in the ethical education of Certified General Accountants.

When men harass, it should not be women's characters that are on trial.
Deborah L. Rhode

The bar's ethical code miscasts professional self-interests as moral necessities.
Deborah L. Rhode

The McMullin Plumbing Case

The case was created by J.T. Stevenson for "Ethics and Values in the Workplace," a seminar for the Certified General Accountants Association of Ontario Annual Provincial Conference, November 9, 1989, in Toronto.

Deepak Ramachan, CGA, works for Bill McMullin, the sole proprietor of McMullin Plumbing, Heating and Air-Conditioning. Deepak is a thoughtful, refined man with a passion for accuracy. Since taking over as chief accountant for McMullin, he has tried hard to put its finances in order and to maintain the highest standards of modern accounting practice. He likes his job, which pays well and has generous fringe benefits, including an annual bonus.

Bill McMullin is a large, burly man who came up the hard way from journeyman plumber to owner of a successful business. Technically, he is very good and, when he needs to be, can be a charming salesman. If thwarted, however, he can be very headstrong and rough-tongued. He gets along well with the people in general construction and is good at picking up sub-contracts. Although shrewd with a dollar and good at driving a hard bargain, he is not good at the details of accounting and finance—which is why he hired Deepak….

Although it is not strictly necessary to maintain his financial credibility, Bill always has another CGA do an annual external audit of the firm. Thanks in large part to Deepak's careful competence, the auditor has always been able to give a very favourable report. However, this month McMullin has suddenly run into a cash flow crisis.

Bill subcontracted and completed the plumbing, heating, and air-conditioning of a row of townhouses with Executive Renovations. Now it appears these homes are seriously overpriced and are not selling. Although the account receivable from Executive Renovations is overdue, Bill feels it very unwise in the long run to press them too hard, lest he drives them into bankruptcy. Consequently, his own account payable to Glacier Air is overdue, and that firm's credit manager has been making serious threats about collecting.

The obvious solution is a bank loan as bridge financing. Bill has spoken about this with his bank manager, Nancy Chun. She has his last audited statements, now six months old. She is sympathetic, but she is cautious because her head office has been warning branch managers about risky loans in tight money situations. She wants Bill to give her a carefully documented case with complete current financial statements. Bill has instructed Deepak to present the financial statements for his perusal, and Deepak has done so. The following conversation ensues.

Bill: Look, Deepak, this is no good. You're painting too gloomy a picture. We're in better shape than this.
Deepak: I'm sorry you say that, Bill, for that statement is very accurate.
Bill: Accuracy is relative. You're good with the pennies, but you don't see the big picture, and you don't see that I have a selling job to do. You don't sell something by playing it down. You have to dress your product up to make it look good.
Deepak: But, Bill, we wouldn't want to practise deceptive advertising with our bank manager.
Bill: Hold on there. Who's putting bread in your mouth—me, or those damned, tight-fisted bankers? Don't you want me to survive so that I can keep you and my crews at work?
Deepak: Of course, but …
Bill: Never mind the buts, here's what I want you

to do. First, I don't like this bad debt business. Executive Renovations will eventually pay up, they always have…. I don't want you to make any of our customers look bad. Get rid of this item.

Next, you've undervalued our inventory again. We're going to have another hot summer and those air-conditioners are going to sell like ice cream on a hot day. We'll get premium prices for them. While you're at it, you can put up the value of our copper pipe and fittings, because there is a rumour going around that the price of copper is going up.

Third, you don't seem to understand the conditions of the real estate market. Things are booming. Increase the value of our land and buildings.

Finally, I want you to send out right away the invoices for those Loon Lake condos. We're almost finished, so we'll only be jumping the gun by a few weeks. That will make our accounts receivable look a hell of a lot better….

Deepak: I don't know, Bill, it doesn't seem …

Bill: Come on, Deepak. We're not really lying. I wouldn't ask you to do that. Those accounts will be receivable; Executive Renovations will pay up. We're just putting things positively. Be optimistic!

Things will work out. This is merely a temporary measure to tide us over.

Just draw up nice, neat, professional-looking statements that I can use to get the loan. Don't worry about getting into trouble. Do you think I got where I am today by being a worry wart about taking a risk? Take it easy; I'll take full responsibility. Just do your job.

What should Deepak do? What would you do if you were in Deepak's situation?

[Michael McDonald, ed., *Ethics Readings Handbook,* CGA Canada. Vancouver: Certified General Accountants Association of Canada, 1995.]

Medical Ethics:
Behaviours Between Doctor and Patient

Ethics has long been an important part of the medical profession, going back as far as Hippocrates (460 BCE–377 BCE). In fact, medical graduates still take the Hippocratic oath which begins: "First, do no harm…." The study of ethics is part of every medical doctor's training. Major medical institutions, such as hospitals, have ethics counsellors or committees to help make decisions about tough cases.

Medical ethics stems from general ethical philosophy, and is applied specifically to medical situations. For example, someone who draws their medical ethics from a Utilitarian philosophy might argue that the goal of medicine is to maximize human health, extend life, and therefore increase human happiness. A Kantian ethicist might argue that any action should be considered in light of whether it could be applied in all similar cases. Still other medical ethicists apply moral rules derived from religious or philosophic sources.

Medical ethics has increased in importance for a number of reasons. For one, the range of decisions made by doctors, and their power to intervene in life processes, has increased. For example, advances in medical science and technology such as *in vitro* fertilization, or genetic engineering have raised new questions, and require new ethical decision-making. For another, the types of major decisions to be made, such as those involving euthanasia, abortion, and others have come about with changing, often conflicting, social attitudes. Thirdly, everyday decisions about how to practise medicine require ethical thought.

There are also ethical decisions to be made about how limited resources should be used in medicine when there are so many needs for it. Should medical care be paid for by government, or by private citizens? Should efforts be put into preventive, broad-based health care, or into high-technology and expensive procedures such as transplants and artificial organs?

Medical ethics, like other workplace ethics, usually originates from the study of problem situations in which decisions have to be made. This is certainly true when ethical training is involved. Sometimes these are life and death situations, while at other times they involve decisions about treatment in less dramatic conditions. Consider the following reported situation.

What behaviours do you think Hippocrates would have approved of? Do you think the medical profession has changed its views on ethics?

… I have to ask if our society's current rage at the ghastly errors doctors occasionally commit might not actually be, in part, rage at our own helplessness, facing down death as we must at every moment—and ultimately failing.

Lisa Alther

Teaching Ethics on Rounds

Jacqueline J. Glover et al.

… We had visited several other patients when we came to the room of Mr. S, who had suffered for many years from Parkinson's disease and had been admitted on this occasion because his medications were proving less and less effective in preserving his stability. He was a fairly well educated man in his late sixties who was still working as a structural engineer on a consulting basis.

Outside of Mr. S's room, the resident explained the case to the team and told us that over that last week a variety of dosages of medications had been tried in order to reduce Mr. S's dizziness and unsteadiness when he walked. Unfortunately the dosage needed to control his neurological symptoms had the side-effect of confusing Mr. S and weakening his memory. "What we have to determine," said the attending [physician], "is whether we should trade stability for clear-headedness or the other way around." ...

"Well it's obvious," said the resident, "that [Mr. S] would choose in favour of stability on his feet, so he can walk around and interact effectively with his environment."

"Oh, no," said the attending [physician]. "Obviously he would prefer to be clear-headed."

Both doctors looked at me. This conversation was the first time they had realized that they differed on this matter, in spite of several months of work side-by-side.

[Jacqueline J. Glover et al., "Teaching Ethics on Rounds: The Ethicist as Teacher, Consultant, and Decision-Maker." In *Ethics and Social Concern*, ed. by Anthony Serafini. New York: Paragon House, 1989, 108.]

What decision would you make? Upon what grounds would you base that decision? These are the types of situations that call for ethical ideas throughout the day of a medical doctor. In this particular case, the ethicist who was accompanying the doctors on their rounds asked them, "Why don't you ask the patient?"

Mr. S was sitting up in his chair next to the bed. The attending doctor sat on the bed facing him and began to chat. It was clear that Mr. S was having a good day and was very lucid. Before long, the attending [physician] was discussing Mr. S's situation with him, explaining the problems which they had uncovered in trying to find a dosage level which would preserve his stability without confusing him. Mr. S understood the matter and responded thoughtfully, first with a few questions to complete his understanding, and then with a clear choice.

[Ibid., 109.]

IDEAS AND ISSUES

Understand Concepts
1. For each of the cases in this section, drawn from business and medical situations, identify the problem faced, the alternatives suggested, the reasons given for these alternatives, and the course of action taken, if any.

Apply and Develop
2. Recently, a number of cases have been reported of senior executives of companies selling their shares in their own company days before the company makes an announcement that negatively affects their stock prices. What ethical principles should be applied here? Make an argument for a particular course of action.
3. Describe the obligations that a seller has to inform a buyer of possible defects or faults in a product. For example, if you are selling your second-hand car to someone and know that the engine has a serious problem that will likely burn it out in a few thousand kilometres, should you inform the buyer? Suggest what you think is the correct course of action and back it up with an argument.
4. Suppose you work for a large corporation. You know that your office manager discriminates against certain social groups in his hiring practices. If you say anything about this, you know that you may suffer consequences as serious as losing your job. What should you do, and why should you do it?
5. A physician knows of a new medicine, untested and unproven as yet, that might help a patient with a debilitating disease for whom nothing else has worked. This new medicine is not yet approved for use. Should the physician use this new and untried medicine, with its unknown risks, or should the physician follow established procedures? Take a position and present arguments in support.

Think Critically
6. (a) List several other circumstances that would call for an ethical decision to be made in business or in medicine.
   (b) For any one of these circumstances, briefly describe a possible scenario, the options available, and reasons for a particular course of action.

Inquire and Research
7. Choose an occupation of interest to you. Research the ethical ideas that are central to that occupation. Use the questions below as a starting point.
   • What are the primary goals of the occupation or profession?
   • How should one act to achieve these goals?
   • Is there a code of behaviour widely known and accepted within that field?
   • How do the most respected people in that profession think and act when doing their work?
   • How do people in the field make decisions when faced with problem situations?
   • What behaviours are rewarded or punished in that occupation or profession?

Review and Reflect

Over the centuries different ethical views have been put forward as ways to determine what is ethically correct behaviour. Traditionally, variations of the Golden Rule were used by some individuals as their code of ethical behaviour. Some philosophers, such as Kant, emphasized the importance of the action and our underlying motives for it. Others, such as the Utilitarians, believed the consequences of our actions should be used to determine what is ethically correct.

More divergent views on ethics were proposed by Nietzsche, Existentialists, and ethical relativists. Nietzsche viewed the dark side of our psyche as being an important element in evaluating ethical behaviour. Existentialists believed that humans must create their own existence from their environment and their own situations. Ethical relativists proposed the idea that ethical behaviours are relative to each culture and that these differences must be considered when evaluating behaviour. To the ethical relativist, there are no universally right and wrong actions.

Ethics continues to be an important issue in our modern society. Attitudes from society, business, and the workplace influence our ideas about what constitutes ethically correct behaviour. People in various professions have developed codes of ethics by which they abide, and we as a society expect that systems be in place to safeguard us from individuals who participate in inappropriate behaviour. What may have been acceptable in the past is no longer so because our awareness of certain issues has increased. One example of this is feminist ethics, where women express their view of ethical behaviour in contrast to the dominant male views of the past.

There is no doubt that without ethics a society could not function. Our ideas about ourselves shape our views on ethics, and our views on ethics create the society that we live in. Social changes make the re-examination of ethics an ongoing process.

Human Nature

Over the centuries, philosophers have pondered what it means to be human. They asked questions about whether there are central qualities that make up a human being, or if the definition of humanity changes from time to time, and from place to place. If we can identify those central qualities that constitute all human beings, where do these qualities reside? Are they apparent in the physical appearance of humans, or in some other less visible element? With the development of new scientific theories, and the presence of new social structures, new ideas about human nature caused us to change our perception about ourselves.

Gender also plays a role in defining who we are as individuals, particularly if we consider the sex-roles that are portrayed in the society we live in. These perceptions affect our behaviour in conscious and unconscious ways, and this in turn creates the type of society that we live in. Over time, the perceptions of ourselves from a gender point of view have changed allowing us to consider social issues in a different light.

Defining who we really are is not as easy as it may sound. In the past, some people argued that the physical body a person possesses represents the real person. However, according to ancient religious beliefs, the idea of the real self is far greater than the physical body. A major issue in the philosophic search to define human beings is whether there is a non-physical component to ourselves that all humans share.

In this unit, we will explore all of these ideas as we attempt to define who we are. We will look at classical views of human nature, and how social and scientific changes initiated new ideas about what it means to be human. Throughout this unit, we will critically analyze contemporary issues that deal with our human nature.

What does it mean to be human? Is it only the physical elements of the body that make us human? Are there non-material elements that define the essential elements of humanity? Many cultures, religions, and philosophies have struggled with such questions.

Images of Human Nature

Each of us has our own idea of what it means to be human, and usually, our image is composed of many different concepts of what we are physically, intellectually, socially, and spiritually. This human image we have of ourselves shapes how we live our lives and how we treat others.

The more completely we define our image of what it means to be human, the more fully we can live our lives. If, for example, we believe that humans are driven by unalterable forces such as instinct or fate, we may become passive, giving up control over how we act and what we believe. On the other hand, if we believe human beings are free decision-makers, then we may tend to act and think in a decisive way and feel in control of our lives.

Philosophers from both Eastern and Western cultures have developed different ideas about human nature. In some cases they agreed; in others their ideas diverged. Over the years, developments in science, and changes in social structures and world events caused thinkers to develop new ideas about what it means to be human. Some thinkers, such as Freud, considered human behaviour from the point of view of the unconscious; others, such as Darwin, believed that genetics were important in shaping who we are.

Even today, as we look at our species from a global perspective, questions about human nature continue to be important as we struggle to find peace and harmony. What essential characteristics do all humans share? How are we different from other species?

Native North Americans traditionally have a highly developed concept of what it meant to be human. This involves a close relationship with nature. Native North Americans also believe that human beings are part of a larger, non-material spiritual world that influences their lives and the afterlife.

Conflicting Views on What It Means to Be Human

What is a human being? How can you determine what is human from what is non-human? Philosophers have considered this question for a very long time. More recently, social scientists have also contributed to this debate. What are your own ideas about the essential elements that all humans share?

You might begin by considering the physical qualities that make up a human being. Anthropologists have determined that a number of physical characteristics are important human qualities that separate us from other species: upright locomotion, a large brain, and an opposable thumb, for example. However, are these traits enough to identify what is human and what is not? Clearly, someone who has lost the ability to walk, who has no thumbs, or who is mentally challenged is still human. Conversely, today's technology allows us to create robots that can walk, and computers that can "think."

During the last several decades, biologists have researched the behaviours of various animal species and noted some interesting abilities. Jane Goodall, one of these researchers, observed that chimpanzees have the ability to walk on two legs, to think and plan, and to use their hands to make tools. Other animals have equally interesting abilities: sea otters use stones as tools to open abalone; parrots can speak; elephants use sticks to clean their toes; ants and bees have highly structured social hierarchies; whales communicate with each other using echolocation across hundreds of kilometres of ocean; loons mate for life; and beavers are master architects. Where does that leave humans? Philosophers and others have suggested that in order to characterize humans we must move beyond purely physical attributes.

Essentialist Definition of a Human

The "essentialist" position is based on the idea that all humans possess a core of basic elements. The essentialists believe that human nature is a unique entity, just as there are essential characteristics for all other material objects in the universe, whether they are animal, plant, or mineral. Some of the essential characteristics of bluebirds, for example, are that they fly, nest, and migrate during winter. Only when essential human elements, such as mind, con- science, and soul, are identified, can we describe what a human being is. Difficul- ties arise when these essential elements are defined differently depending on the philosopher. Try to define what you believe are the essential elements required to characterize a human being. Once you have compiled your list, delete one ele- ment after another and ask yourself, as each element is removed, whether the remaining elements still characterize a human being.

> Man is nothing else but what he makes of himself. Such is the first principle of exis- tentialism.
>
> *Jean-Paul Sartre*

Constructivist Definition of a Human

The "constructivist" position is that there are no essential qualities pos- sessed by all humans upon which all people could eventually agree. Construc- tivists believe there is no essential human nature, and point to the fact that many def- initions and descriptions of humanness have been developed by different cultures around the world, and throughout time. For this reason, they say, it is impossible to define human beings by using a set of universal characteristics. The constructivist point of view became popular in modern times, as people travelled around the world and encountered a wide variety of cultures and behaviours. Existentialists, such as Jean-Paul Sartre, support this point of view, suggesting that there is no such thing as an essential human nature; they claim that each human being is defined by the choices that he or she makes, or by how each person lives his or her individual life.

> I realized that if what we call human nature can be changed, then absolutely *anything* is possible.
>
> *Shirley MacLaine*

permission of John Hart and Field Enterprises, Inc.

According to Existentialism, these babies have no common essential nature. Their personalities will depend on the experiences they have and the choices they make.

Understand Concepts

1. Why is an understanding of human nature important?
2. Identify and briefly summarize two positions on human nature.

Apply and Develop

3. (a) What are five elements that you believe are essential human characteristics?
   (b) Defend each of these characteristics to the class.
4. Do you think that it is possible to build a complex computerized robot that would have characteristics that would make it human? Explain your position.
5. Do you think some animals have human-like characteristics that qualify them as a "person"? Defend your position.

Think Critically

6. In small groups, discuss the pros and cons of the essentialist and the constructivist positions on human nature. Develop arguments and examples on each side. Report back to the whole class.
7. Explain why you think it might be more difficult to define the term "human" than any other thing that exists.

Communicate Ideas

8. Debate this issue: There are no non-material elements of humanity. We are made up of physical elements only, as are stones, trees, and giraffes.
9. In a reflection paper of three to four pages, discuss your own ideas of what it means to be human, and how that is different from all non-human things and beings.

Classical Views of Human Nature

The philosophers in ancient Greece were very interested in determining the characteristics that all humans share. Both Plato and Aristotle agreed that the ability to reason sets humans apart from other creatures. However, their ideas differed in how they viewed the soul and desires. As you examine Plato's and Aristotle's ideas about human nature, consider these questions: How would you define "soul" or "desire"? In what ways would soul and desire affect human nature?

Plato's View:
Humans have a Body and a Soul

Plato described human beings as consisting of body and soul. The body is the material self we perceive through our senses. The soul is the non-material self contained within the body. The soul is composed of three parts: thought, which aspires to wisdom; spirit, which makes us angry, excited, or courageous; and appetites, which make us feel hunger, thirst, and want. Plato believed that each part of the soul is important, playing a vital role in making us human. He also believed that rational thought was the most important element of human existence. Here is how he described the parts of the soul and their interrelationships in *The Republic*.

Plato used the image of a charioteer to illustrate his idea of soul. The charioteer represents reason, controlling both the noble horse, spirited and energetic, and the ignoble horse, with its irrational and uncontrollable appetites. The truest self, said Plato, occurs when the reasoning charioteer rules over both the spirited and desire-based horses. We are free when our rational selves

Plato argued that reason sets us apart from other creatures. How would he respond to a situation such as this, where an animal and a human share a unique and personal bond?

Parts of a Human

Plato

... "[E]ach one of us will be just and doing his own work if the parts within him are doing severally their own work." ... [said Socrates] "Then is it not fitting that the rational part should rule, inasmuch as it is wise and has foresight for the whole soul, and that the spirited part should be its subject and ally?"

"Undoubtedly," ... said [Glaucon].

"And these two so nurtured, finely taught and trained in their own offices, will be set over the desiring elements, which of a truth makes the greatest part of each man's soul, and is by nature insatiably covetous. Over it they will keep guard, lest it fill itself with the false pleasures of the body, and becoming great and strong no longer attend to its own work, but try to get the rule and mastery over those matters, that do not belong to it, and so quite overturn the life of the whole."

[Plato, *The Republic*. Book 1, Part 4. Toronto: Fitzhenry & Whiteside, 1980, 443.]

---

are in control over our will and our appetites. In this way, Plato described his vision of the major elements of humanness, and the interrelationship of these elements.

Plato argued that reasoning sets us apart from other creatures and makes us truly human. Non-human species are willful and controlled by their appetites. Only humans have the ability to reason and reflect on abstract and eternal ideas. Therefore, according to Plato, the ability to reason is the most human element, and closest to the eternal world.

Some people might ask: Does that mean we are less human when our appetites and our will are in control? What happens to our humanity when we are enjoying a good meal, or are cheering for our favourite hockey team? Plato's view is clearly open for discussion.

Plato's *Phaedo* portrays Socrates in his cell waiting to be executed. Despite Socrates' death sentence, he continues to discuss philosophy with his friends. The discussion eventually turns to the immortality of the soul, and how this immortality distinguishes the soul from the body, and the changeable material world of the senses.

Socrates explains to his students how parts of the soul relate to each other, and how the whole relates to the body, by noting that human beings are made up of an invisible soul. Socrates and Plato both believed the soul, which includes the rational mind, is the immaterial part of humanness, only temporarily united with a body. When we use the rational part of the soul to learn and think, we are able to discover eternal truths. Use of our senses, however, results in dramatically different experiences.

Do you accept that there is a non-material part of human beings? Or can all human existence be thought of as material things working together in the body?

The Body and the Soul

Plato

"Now were we not saying … [Socrates begins] that when the soul makes use of the body to investigate something through vision or hearing or some other sense … it is dragged by the body towards objects that are never constant, and itself wanders in a sort of dizzy drunken confusion, inasmuch as it is apprehending confused objects?"

"Just so."

"But when it investigates by itself alone, it passes to that other world of pure, everlasting, immortal, constant being … apprehending unchanging objects. And is not the experience which it then has called intelligence?" …

"… [W]hich of the two kinds of things do you find that soul resembles and is more akin to?"

"On the strength of our present line of inquiry, Socrates, I … agree that the soul has a far and away greater resemblance to everlasting, unchanging being than to its opposite."

"And what does the body resemble?"

"The other kind."

"Now consider a further point. When soul and body are conjoined, nature prescribes that the latter should be slave and subject, the former master and ruler. Which of the two, in your judgement, does that suggest as being like the divine, and which like the mortal? Don't you think it naturally belongs to the divine to rule and lead, and to the mortal to be ruled and subjected?"

"Yes, I do."

"Then which is soul like?"

"Of course it is obvious, Socrates, that soul is like the divine, and body like the mortal."

"Would you say then … that … on the one hand we have that which is divine, immortal, indestructible, of a single form, accessible to thought, ever constant and abiding true to itself; and the soul is very like it: on the other hand we have that which is human, mortal, destructible, of many forms, inaccessible to thought, never constant nor abiding true to itself; and the body is very like that? Is there anything to be said against that?"

"Nothing."

[Plato, *Phaedo.* Trans. by R. Hackforth (Cambridge: Cambridge University Press, 1952). Found in *Introduction to World Philosophies,* by Eliot Deutsch (Upper Saddle River: Prentice Hall, 7).]

Aristotle's View:
Humans Are Unique Because They Can Think

Aristotle, the great Athenian philosopher and student of Plato, had his own ideas about human nature. Aristotle described humans as having three basic characteristics. First, we share with all living things, the ability to absorb nourishment, to grow, and to have offspring. Second, we share with animals the ability to perceive the world and to move about in it. Third, and unlike all other creatures, we can think in abstract and complex ways. Therefore, human beings do share some characteristics with other living things, but remain unique in our ability to think.

Aristotle also had a different view of the human soul. He believed that the soul gives life to any human being, a type of animating factor within the body. A person's soul is revealed through the behaviour of his or her body. Aristotle also believed that plants and animals had souls of their own, and that no soul could exist outside a living body.

Do we build character traits in the same way we learn other skills? What did Aristotle believe? What do you think?

In *Ethics*, Aristotle discusses how life should be lived in order to achieve one's fullest potential as a human being. The purpose of life, he wrote, is to achieve happiness, which comes in three forms: a life of pleasure and enjoyment; a life as a free citizen; and a life as a thinker and philosopher. Aristotle believed humans should enjoy all three forms of happiness—the physical, the social, and the intellectual pleasures—in a harmonious balance.

Aristotle also wrote about the origins of human qualities. Today, we call this the "nature–nurture debate." Are we born to be the way we are, or do we acquire our characteristics through experience? Are you the person you are largely as a result of your genes, or did you become who you are by living, learning, and experiencing the world? Aristotle addressed these questions in the following excerpt.

Of all the wonders of the universe, the greatest is man.
Aristotle

All men by nature desire knowledge.
Aristotle

Concerning the Soul

Aristotle

Knowledge we regard as a fine and worthwhile thing, and one kind as more so than another, either in virtue of its accuracy or in virtue of its being concerned with superior and more remarkable things. On both these grounds we should … place the study of the soul in the first rank. It would seem also that an acquaintance with [the soul] makes a great contribution to truth as a whole, and especially to the study of nature; for the soul is as it were the *first principle of animal life*. We seek to inquire into and ascertain both its nature and its essence….

… First surely we must determine how to classify the soul, and what it is; I mean whether it is a particular thing and substance or quality or quantity or some other….

For as things are, people who speak and inquire about the soul seem to study the human soul only. But we must take care not to overlook the question whether there is one definition of the soul, as of animal, or whether there is a different one for each animal, as of horse, dog, man and god....

There is also the problem whether the properties of the soul are all common to that which has it, or whether they are peculiar to the soul itself.... It appears that in most cases the soul is not affected nor does it act apart from the body—for example in being angry, being confident, wanting and perceiving in general. Thinking, however, looks most special to the soul; but if this too is a form of imagination, or does not exist apart from imagination, it would not be possible for it to exist apart from the body....

It seems that all the affections of the soul involve the body— passion, gentleness, fear, pity, confidence, and also joy and both loving and hating. For at the same time as these occur, the body is affected in a certain way....

If this is so, it is clear that the affections of the soul are principles involving matter. Hence their definitions are such as "Being angry is a particular movement of a body of such and such a kind ... as a result of so and so, and for the sake of such and such." Hence an inquiry concerning the soul ... is the province of the natural scientist.

But the natural scientist and the conceptual inquirer would define each of these differently.... For the latter would define it as a desire for retaliation, or something of that sort, while the former would define it as the boiling of the blood and hot material round the heart....

... We say that the soul is grieved, rejoices, is confident and afraid, and again is angry, perceives and thinks. And all these seem to be movements. One might conclude from this that the soul itself is moved; but this is not necessary.

... It is surely better not to say that the soul pities, learns or thinks, but that the human being does this by means of soul.

So it is clear that the soul, or certain parts of it, if it is divisible, cannot be separated from the body; for in some cases it is the actuality of the parts themselves.... Let this suffice as a rough definition and sketch about the soul....

What has soul is distinguished from what has not by life. But life is spoken of in many ways, for we say that a thing lives if one of the following is present: intellect, perception, movement and rest ... and also the movement involved in nutrition and both decay and growth.

For the present, let it suffice to say the soul is the source of the things mentioned above, and is defined by them—by the faculties of nutrition, perception, thought, and by movement.... [C]oncerning the intellect and the potentiality for contemplation, the situation is not so far clear, but it seems to be a different kind of soul, and this alone can exist separately, as the everlasting can from the perishable. But the remaining parts of the soul are not separable...

[Aristotle, *De Anima*, Book 1, chap. 4; Book 2, chap. 1–3 (c. 325 B.C.). In *Aristotle's De Anima*, ed. and trans. by D.W. Hamlyn, Oxford, UK: Clarendon, 1968, 1–16. Found in *Western Philosophy*, ed. by John Cottingham. Oxford, UK: Blackwell Publishers, Ltd.,1997, 134.]

IDEAS AND ISSUES

Understand Concepts

1. Identify the elements of human beings, according to Plato.
2. Draw a concept map, or other visual aid, to illustrate the relationship Plato says exists between: the body, the soul, the material world, and divine unchangeable truths.
3. (a) In one paragraph, summarize your understanding of Plato's view of human nature.
   (b) Assess Plato's view of human nature and give your reasons.

Apply and Develop

4. How would you describe the human species to someone who knows nothing about us, to an extraterrestrial being for example? What essential and common elements of human beings would you identify? Which of these elements separate us from all other species? Write a description of the major elements of any human being.
5. Our idea of "human nature" guides our thoughts and actions, and how we react to others. Briefly describe your reactions to each of these situations. What do your reactions tell you about your view of what people are like?
   (a) Your friend blurts out a secret you told her, then is immediately sorry.
   (b) You hear about someone who has overcome great odds to be successful. Coming from a poor family this person had to struggle for an education.
   (c) Several of your friends make jokes about a cultural group that dresses differently than most people in your community.
   (d) A technology exists that will do away with the need for anyone to work.
   (e) You read about a man who has committed crimes all of his life. His lawyer argues that the sentence should take into account his abusive childhood. The prosecution insists that he should take responsibility for his actions.

Think Critically

6. How would Plato react to Aristotle's views of human nature? Prepare a comparison chart that indicates important human characteristics according to both Plato and Aristotle. Identify similarities and differences in their points of view.
7. In two to three paragraphs write a critical response to Aristotle's views of human nature. Identify and assess major ideas.
8. Do you think the ability to reason is the most important aspect of human nature? Would our definition of humanity change if another creature were discovered that could reason better than humans?

Inquire and Research

9. Research recent psychological ideas on the impact of heredity and our environment on human personality. You may include the ideas of sociobiology, a school of thought that argues that behaviour is primarily the result of genetics. Other psychologists and philosophers argue that learning is primary in forming the human personality. Where do you think Aristotle or Plato would stand on this issue?

Eastern and Western Ideas About Human Character

The question of whether we, as humans, are basically good or bad has been investigated by many philosophers, and non-philosophers alike. It is an important question to ponder when we consider the entire human race and its widely diverse range of human beings, with their many, different thoughts and actions. How can one person be so good, wise, and selfless while another so evil, ignorant, and exploitative?

Philosophers have questioned the idea about our human character. Are we born with distinctly human characteristics or are these acquired through experience and learning? Are these basic human characteristics generally good or bad?

Thinkers from both Asia and the Western world developed differing ideas. However, there were some characteristics upon which they agreed. One of these was the idea that humans are not bad by nature. Another was that behaviour and personal choices during one's life have an impact on whether someone has a good or bad nature.

Confucian Views:
Noble Character Through a Life Well-Lived

Traditional Chinese philosophy was shaped by the ideas of Confucius (551–479 BCE). Confucius' approach was humanistic in that it focussed on humanity, and the role of human beings in the world. Confucius did not address himself to the issues of spirituality or life after death. Instead he focussed on good government, harmonious human relations, filial piety, and the good person.

A key element of Confucian thought is the identification of the *chun-tzu*, or Superior Person. Historically, this term had been associated with people of noble blood. Confucius shifted the word's meaning, using it to denote an individual with noble character. The *chun-tzu* treats others with dignity, respect, and benevolence. The *chun-tzu* becomes wiser, and acquires noble characteristics, through a life well-lived. "The Superior Person so acts that his actions blaze a common trail for all generations. He so conducts himself that his conduct becomes law for all generations. He so speaks that his words are a valid precept for all generations."

Confucius believed that one important way to live life well was to find the proper balance, the harmonious way. He believed firmly in the Golden Rule: "Do unto others as you would have others do unto you." "Repay evil with justice," he said, "and good with good."

In the following excerpt, a Confucian follower named Mencius (c. 372–289 BCE) set out the Confucian view of human nature using an interesting analogy. All people are basically good, he said, because their original nature contains several good characteristics. The good person is the one who has developed his or her human potential, mind, and feelings to the fullest. The evil person is the one who has not developed this original potential for good.

The Book of Mencius

Mencius

Mencius said ... , "[M]ust you ... violate human nature in order to make it into humanity and righteousness?" ...

Kung-fu Tzu [Confucius] said, "Man's nature is like whirling water. If a breach in the pool is made to the east it will flow to the east. If a breach is made to the west it will flow to the west. Man's nature is indifferent to good and evil, just as water is indifferent to east and west." ...

Mencius said, "If you let people follow their feelings (original nature), they will be able to do good. This is what is meant by saying that human nature is good. If man does evil, it is not the fault of his natural endowment.... Humanity, righteousness, propriety, and wisdom are not drilled into us from outside. We originally have them with us." ...

Kung-fu Tzu asked, "We are all human beings. Why is it that some men become great and others become small?"

Mencius said, "Those who follow the greater qualities in their nature become great men and those who follow the smaller qualities in their nature become small men." ...

... Now, when men suddenly see a child about to fall into a well, they all have a feeling of alarm and distress, not to gain friendship with the child's parents, nor to seek the praise of their neighbors and friends.... From such a case, we see that a man without the feeling of commiseration [sympathy] is not a man; a man without the feeling of shame and dislike is not a man; a man without the feeling of deference and compliance is not a man; and a man without the feeling of right and wrong is not a man. The feeling of commiseration is the beginning of humanity; the feeling of shame and dislike is the beginning of righteousness; the feeling of deference and compliance is the beginning of propriety; and the feeling of right and wrong is the beginning of wisdom.

[Mencius, *The Book of Mencius*. In *A Source Book in Chinese Philosophy*, comp. and trans. by Wing-tsit Chan. Princeton: Princeton University Press, 1963.]

St. Augustine's Views:
Humans Are Evil by Vice, Not by Nature

St. Augustine (354–430 CE) lived in Algeria, a province of the Roman empire. As a young man, he converted to Christianity. Augustine wrote his major work, *The City of God*, while Germanic tribes were attacking Rome, and the once formidable empire was crumbling. Critics of Christianity claimed that the Christian faith

St. Augustine, an important Christian philosopher, had a view about human nature, its origins, and good and evil. How would you describe that view?

undermined the Roman empire by replacing the harsh codes of the Roman gods with Christian ethics, which made citizens of the empire soft and weak. Augustine's goal was to develop a political and social philosophy based on Christian ethics.

According to Augustine, human nature has worsened because of original sin, Adam and Eve disobeying God in the Garden of Eden. The ills of the world, he believed, were the direct result of the punishment that befell Adam and Eve to posterity. Humans are not evil by nature, he said, but evil by vice. Augustine felt that although God has condemned us, God would redeem those individuals who accepted Christianity.

Time Line

Ideas About Human Nature

CONFUCIUS
(551–479 BCE)
develops his idea of *chun-tzu*

MENCIUS
(c. 372–289 BCE)
writes Confucius' view of human nature

ST. AUGUSTINE
(354–430 CE)

FALL OF WESTERN ROMAN EMPIRE
(476 CE)

RISE OF CHRISTIANITY
(c. 2 CE)

BEHIND THE MIND

Mother Teresa

Selfless Example of Human Nature

Mother Teresa (1910–1997), originally named Agnes Gonxha Bojaxhiu, was born in Albania in a devoutly Catholic family. At the age of eighteen, Agnes had a strong desire to be a missionary in India. After joining the Sisters of Loreto in 1928, she spent nineteen years teaching at the convent school in Calcutta. Here, Sister Teresa witnessed poverty and suffering that she had never imagined possible.

In 1946, Sister Teresa experienced a "call within a call," a divine inspiration to devote her life to the care of the poor and sick of India. After waiting for the Catholic Church to accept her new vocation, she moved to the slums of Calcutta and began her tireless work to help the poor, sick, dying, and abandoned. There was never anyone who came to her who was turned away. In fact, she brought many people from the slums, too sick to come themselves, to various missions. Living in poverty herself, Sister Teresa's work began to spread among the people in India. She soon had a number of young women who wanted to follow her example of selfless giving.

In 1950, Sister Teresa and her followers became officially recognized as a separate order, the Missionaries of Charity. Today, more than 3000 sisters and novices and 70 000 Co-Workers help the poor, sick, abandoned, dying, and outcasts all over the world. In 1979, Mother Teresa received the Nobel Peace Prize for her humanitarian work.

The City of God

St. Augustine

God ... created men with such a nature that the members of the race should not have died, had not the first two [Adam and Eve] ... merited this with their disobedience; for by them so great a sin was committed, that by it the human nature was altered for the worse, and was transmitted also to their posterity.

That the whole human race has been condemned in its first origin, this life itself ... bears witness by the host of cruel ills with which it is filled. Is not this proved by the profound and dreadful ignorance which produces all the errors that enfold the children of Adam, and from which no man can be delivered without toil, pain, and fear? Is it not proved by his love of so many vain and hurtful things ... ?

But because God does not wholly desert those whom He condemns ... , the human race is restrained by law and education, which keep guard against the ignorance that besets us and oppose the assaults of vice.... Why all these punishments, save to overcome ignorance and bridle evil desires—these evils with which we come into the world?...

But ... the man who lives according to God, and not according to man, ought to be a lover of good, and therefore a hater of evil. And since no one is evil by nature, but whosoever is evil is evil by vice, he who lives according to God ought to cherish toward evil men a perfect hatred, so that he shall neither hate the man because of his vice, nor love the vice because of the man....

[St. Augustine, *The Political Writings of St. Augustine*. Lake Bluff: Regnery Gateway, Inc., 1985.]

Understand Concepts

1. Explain the views of human nature held by Mencius and St. Augustine. Compare their views using the headings: human characteristics, source(s) of these characteristics, effect of inborn nature, effect of life and experience, major assumptions made.
2. (a) How would Mencius and St. Augustine define good and evil?
   (b) What is the origin of good and evil, according to these philosophers?

Apply and Develop

3. Identify events or conditions in the world today or in your own personal experience that tend to support the points of view of Mencius or St. Augustine. Briefly describe the events or conditions and show how they seem to support one or the other point of view.
4. (a) How would you define good and evil? Provide examples in your answer. To what degree, if at all, do you think that people naturally tend towards good or evil? Provide reasons for your position.
   (b) Using your own definition of good and evil, do you think humans naturally tend towards one or the other?

Think Critically

5. Write a position paper stating and arguing the position of Mencius, St. Augustine, or your own on the existence of good and evil in human nature.

Communicate Ideas

6. Interview someone knowledgeable about Confucian or Christian beliefs. Prepare questions about human nature ahead of time. Report to the class on your findings.
7. Debate this issue: Human nature is basically good, while experience makes people bad.

Inquire and Research

8. Read further in either Confucian or Christian works. Describe a view of human nature based on one or the other.

Human Nature in Relation to Society

One issue that classical philosophers raised was whether human nature is innate or acquired. As new social orders, especially nation-states, emerged in the modern world, philosophers began to ask about the nature of humans within social groups. The question of whether basic human nature is good or bad or somewhere in between becomes an important factor when philosophers think about social structures. If, for example, human nature is at heart bad, then society probably should be organized in order to control the evil potential of humankind. If, on the other hand, people are basically good, then social structures might possibly be organized to provide opportunities to allow human beings to progress and improve, as their natural inclinations take them. A third alternative suggests that people are neither basically good nor bad, but respond and develop according to the social circumstances in which they find themselves.

Some philosophers take the view that humanity is only fully realized when the individual is involved in society. This position tends to emphasize the rational mind as the means whereby people become most human. Such a belief was common during the Enlightenment of the eighteenth century. In today's world, this view is consistent with a belief in science and technology, coupled with a strong faith in future human progress.

Other philosophers argue that human nature is most obvious and most natural before it is affected by society. Thinkers who take this position often believe that society distorts or corrupts the natural qualities of human beings. Jean-Jacques Rousseau (1712–1778), an eighteenth century philosopher and forerunner of the Romantic movement, and the "flower children" or hippies of the 1960s took this view. They believed natural reactions, often those stemming from emotions, were the most real, the most human, and should be the most trusted. These thinkers sought to find human nature in an unspoiled, rural, and isolated condition. They also searched for an idealized past where such conditions were more common.

Whichever view we take affects how we live our lives. The parent who believes that the natural feelings and reactions of a child are the best examples of real and honest human nature will tend to raise that child with respect for his or her wishes, impulses, and "natural" development. The parent who believes that people become most human through interaction with the social world will focus on teaching the child to become part of that world.

Do you believe there is a natural state for human beings, one that is most real and evident before being influenced by others? Or do you think humans need to interact with society in order to become fully human? What do you think your own life would be like if you lived apart from society: away from family, school, laws, or other social organizations?

The Enlightenment

The Enlightenment was an intellectual movement that began in mid-eighteenth century France, before spreading to most of Europe and North America. Philosophers during that period put forward the idea that human beings, and the social worlds they created, could be understood and shaped using the power of reason. These thinkers believed social change was possible and necessary, and progress could be achieved using reason and science. Although this view is widely accepted today, it was revolutionary for its time. Before the Enlightenment, during the Middle Ages for example, social conditions were generally thought of as static, and unchangeable, no matter how unpleasant the circumstances.

Enlightenment thinkers believed that, through the use of reason, ways could be found to bring about social progress. Where societies of the past tolerated unequal social class privileges, Enlightenment thinkers argued for greater social and legal equality. Where historically, political power had resided in the hands of a few aristocrats who inherited their position, Enlightenment thinkers argued for wider participation in government. Where historically the rights of individuals had been suppressed, Enlightenment thinkers envisioned a future where the rights of individuals were protected.

Enlightenment thinkers believed it was necessary to have an informed population to accomplish these social goals and to bring about a better society. These philosophers based many of their ideas on the work of John Locke. They believed human nature was capable of learning and developing to its maximum potential when provided with the right opportunities. In time, this belief in the potential of young children to grow and learn, and the recognition that social progress required that all people have opportunities to learn, encouraged societies to provide public education for all children. It was during the nineteenth century that most Western nations, including Canada, began to set up school systems for all people, not just for the wealthy.

Over a longer period, the Enlightenment also affected our views of human nature and how we look at social change. Movements to ensure the rights of women, cultures, social classes and others gained momentum as a result of Enlightenment ideas. Philosophers and non-philosophers of our modern era are the intellectual products of the Enlightenment. Modern ideas about human nature, the purpose of life, and the nature of society have been shaped by the eighteenth century Enlightenment.

The idea that human progress continues as a result of the development of a reasoning population remains with us, although perhaps not as optimistically as during the Enlightenment. Two World Wars, the Holocaust and other ethnic genocides, coupled with a general awareness that human thought and rationality can be put to evil, as well as good purposes, have dampened the Enlightenment's optimism and belief in progress. To what degree do you and your generation believe in social progress? How might future social progress be achieved?

Jean-Jacques Rousseau's View: How Education and Society Affect Children

One notable philosopher who emerged during the Enlightenment was Jean-Jacques Rousseau. (1712–1778). Although he held the ideas of Enlightenment thinkers, he ushered in ideas of the nineteenth century. Rousseau believed that nature was all-important, that natural ways of raising children were essential, and that the emotional part of human nature must be respected and encouraged. These ideas would become a core element of the Romantic movement.

Rousseau's early years were not happy, and this situation may have influenced his philosophy. Rousseau's mother died a few days after he was born, not an unusual event in those days. He was sent to a boarding school, where he was not impressed with the education. Rousseau noted he had to learn insignificant facts that obscured any real education. At the age of sixteen, he ran away to hike around Europe, reading extensively and developing his own ideas.

Rousseau focussed on the emotional element of human nature. He believed in allowing children to develop naturally, and freely as the flowers do. His book *Emile* (1762) presents Rousseau's views on raising and educating a young person. Ironically, Rousseau left his own five children to be raised in foundling homes, something he deeply regretted later in life.

Before Rousseau's work, children were regarded as willful beings who needed to be brought under control. Education, which was usually only provided for the rich, was often based on the idea that young people must be trained to rid them of their basic nature.

Rousseau's views of human nature and education were much different. He believed that human nature is basically good, although it can often be corrupted by society. For this reason, Rousseau said, society should have a minimal influence on educating the young, except to provide love and nurture. Children should be allowed to develop naturally.

Rousseau's ideas had a powerful impact on how people thought about children and how children should be raised. Many people thought Rousseau's ideas made good sense, and over time some parents began to raise their children according to his ideas. Rousseau's influence continues today, as educators still study *Emile*, some reacting against Rousseau's concept of education, while others remain highly influenced by the book.

Rousseau's personal life contrasted in many ways with his philosophic views and ideals. Do you think that, generally, one's personal life should have any bearing on how one's philosophy is judged?

What image did Rousseau have of human nature, children, and child-raising? Would he have agreed with ideas of child-rearing today?

On Education

Jean-Jacques Rousseau

God makes all things good; man meddles with them and they become evil. He forces one soil to yield the products of another, one tree to bear another's fruit.... He mutilates his dog, his horse, and his slave. He destroys and defaces all things; he loves all that is deformed and monstrous; he will have nothing as nature made it, not even man himself, who must learn his paces like a saddle-horse, and be shaped to his master's taste like the trees in his garden.

Yet things would be worse without this education.... [A] man left to himself from birth would be more of a monster than the rest. Prejudice, authority, necessity, example, all the social conditions into which we are plunged, would stifle nature in him and put nothing in her place. She would be like a sapling chance sown in the midst of the high-way, bent hither and thither and soon crushed by the passers-by.

We are born weak, we need strength; helpless, we need aid; foolish, we need reason. All that we lack at birth, all that we need when we come to man's estate, is the gift of education. This education comes to us from nature, from men, or from things. The inner growth of our organs and faculties is the education of nature, the use we learn to make of this growth is the education of men, what we gain by our experience of our surroundings is the education of things....

… All his life long man is imprisoned by our institutions…. The child has hardly left the mother's womb, it has hardly begun to move and stretch its limbs, when it is deprived of its freedom. It is wrapped in swaddling bands, laid down with its head fixed, its legs stretched out, and its arms by its sides; it is wound round with linen and bandages of all sorts so that it cannot move…. Thus the internal impulses which should lead to growth find an insurmountable obstacle in the way of the necessary movements….

Is not such a cruel bondage certain to affect both health and temper? Their first feeling is one of pain and suffering; they find every necessary movement hampered; more miserable than a galley slave, in vain they struggle, they become angry, they cry….

Fix your eyes on nature, follow the path traced by her. She keeps children at work, she hardens them by all kinds of difficulties, she soon teaches them the meaning of pain and grief. They cut their teeth and are feverish, sharp colics bring on convulsions, they are choked by fits of coughing and tormented by worms, evil secretions corrupt the blood, germs of various kinds ferment in it, causing dangerous eruptions. Sickness and danger play the chief part in infancy. One half of the children who are born die before their eighth year. The child who has overcome hardships has gained strength, and as soon as he can use his life he holds it more securely. This is nature's law; why contradict it? Do you not see that in your efforts to improve upon her handiwork you are destroying it?…

I shall not take pains to prevent Emile hurting himself; far from it, I should be vexed if he never hurt himself, if he grew up unacquainted with pain. To bear pain is his first and most useful lesson. It seems as if children were small and weak on purpose to teach them these valuable lessons without danger. If the child has such a short distance to fall he will not break his leg; if he knocks himself with a stick he will not break his arm….

With our foolish and pedantic methods we are always preventing children from learning what they could learn much better by themselves …. Can anything be sillier than the pains taken to teach them to walk, as if there were anyone who was unable to walk when he grows up through his nurse's neglect?…

Emile shall have no padded caps, no strollers, no restrainers…. Instead of keeping him confined to a stuffy room, take him out into nature every day; let him run about, let him frolic and fall…. [H]e will learn all the sooner to pick himself up. The delights of liberty will make up for many bruises. My pupil will hurt himself oftener than yours, but he will always be merry; your pupils may receive fewer injuries, but they are always restricted, constrained, and sad….

Nature provides for the child's growth in her own fashion, and this should never be thwarted. Do not make him sit still when he wants to run about, nor run when he wants to be quiet…. Let them run, jump, and shout to their heart's content. All their own activities are instincts of the body for its growth in strength….

[Jean-Jacques Rousseau, *Emile*. In *On Education*. trans. by Barbara Foxly. (London: J.M. Dent & Sons, Ltd., 1911).]

Antoine Nicolas de Condorcet's View: Equality and Education for All

Another philosopher during the Enlightenment was Antoine Nicolas de Condorcet (1743–1794). Unlike Rousseau, Condorcet was born into an aristocratic French family, and he reaped the rewards and benefits of his station in life. However, Condorcet believed in and supported the reforming ideas of the Enlightenment. He fought against the privileges of the nobility and the established Church, and devoted his efforts to social and political reform. When the French revolution broke out in 1789, Condorcet was an enthusiastic supporter, involved in political and social movements for change. Several of his ideas to broaden the scope of education became law.

Ultimately, however, the French Revolution moved to a more extreme stage of terror and violence. Within a short period of time, under this more radical political regime, Condorcet found himself accused of being an enemy of the revolution. He was forced to flee Paris, and live as a fugitive. While in hiding, he wrote *Sketch for a Historical Picture of the Progress of the Human Mind*, a testament to his continuing faith that the use of reason would achieve social progress.

Soon after completing his book, Condorcet was arrested and taken to prison. The very next day he was found poisoned in his cell, supposedly a suicide.

When a more moderate government assumed power in France in 1795, Condorcet's views again became popular. His book remains an impassioned example of the Enlightenment belief in progress.

Although Condorcet's prophecies remain unfulfilled even today, his predictions were amazingly accurate. Many of his ideas about medicine, genetics, geriatrics, social insurance, women's rights, education, and computer technology have become reality.

Time Line

Paradigm Shift in Social Ideas
- - - - - - - - - - -

THOMAS HOBBES
(1588–1679)

ENLIGHTENMENT
(C. 1700–1750)

JEAN-JACQUES ROUSSEAU
(1712–1778)

ANTOINE NICOLAS DE CONDORCET
(1743–1794)

FRENCH REVOLUTION
(1789) begins

ROMANTIC MOVEMENT
(C. 1800–1850)

CHILD LABOUR
(C. 1830–1900) is abolished in Canada and other Western nations

PUBLIC EDUCATION
(C. 1850–1900) is legislated in Canada

SOCIAL RIGHTS AND EQUALITY MOVEMENTS
(1960s) begin

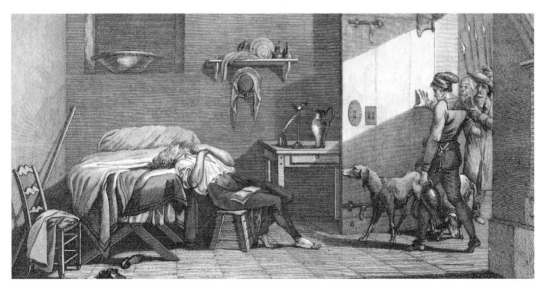

Although Condorcet had an unfortunate demise, his ideas about social progress were centuries ahead of his time. What aspects of human nature do you think Condorcet believed contribute to social progress?

The Progress of the Human Mind

Antoine Nicolas de Condorcet

... I have undertaken ... to show by appeal to reason and fact that nature has set no term to the perfection of human faculties....

The first stage of civilization observed among human beings is that of a small society whose members live by hunting and fishing, and know only how to make rather crude weapons and household utensils.... The uncertainty of life, the difficulty man experiences in providing for his needs ... do not allow him the leisure in which he can indulge in thought and enrich his understanding.... Thus the progress of the human species was necessarily very slow....

[At later stages of human civilization] life that was less hazardous and more leisured gave opportunities for meditation.... In consequence there arose a class of men whose time was not wholly taken up in manual labor.... Industry was born; the arts ... were spread and perfected ... , the dawn of science had begun to break....

This ... brings us up to the stage when the influence of progress ... ceases to be a slow imperceptible affair, and produces a revolution ... that must one day include in its scope the whole of the human race.

After long periods of error ... publicists have at last discovered the true rights of man and how they can all be deduced from the single truth, that man is a sentient being, capable of reasoning and of acquiring moral ideas.... At last man could ... submit all opinions to his own reason.... Every man learned ... that nature had not forever condemned him to base his beliefs on the opinions of others; the superstitions of antiquity and the abasement of reason....

The time will therefore come when the sun will shine only on free men who know no other master but their reason... when tyrants and slaves ... will exist only in works of history and on the stage.... The ... result [will be] the absolute perfection of the human race ... by producing ampler sources of supply, more extensive education, more complete liberty, so equality will be more real and will embrace everything ... for the happiness of human beings....

[The practical] arts ... can be perfected ... ; new instruments, machines, and looms can add to man's strength and can improve at once the quality and the accuracy of his productions, and can diminish the time and labor that has to be expended.... [A]ccidents will be foreseen and prevented, the insanitary conditions that are due either to the work itself or to the climate will be eliminated....

[W]ill not the general welfare that results from the progress of the useful arts once they are grounded on solid theory, or from the progress of legislation once it is rooted in the truths of political science, incline mankind to humanity, benevolence, and justice?... [T]he moral goodness of man ... is capable of indefinite perfection....

... [O]f the utmost importance to the general happiness, we must number the complete annihilation of the ... inequality of rights between the sexes.... It is vain for us to look for a justification of this principle in any differences of physical organization, intellect, or moral sensibility between men and women. This inequality has its origin solely in an abuse of strength....

Once people are enlightened ... they will gradually learn to regard war as the most dreadful of scourges, the most terrible of crimes.... Nations will learn that they cannot conquer other nations without losing their own liberty; that permanent confederations are their only means of preserving their independence....

... [A]s preventive medicine improves and food and housing become healthier, as a way of life is established that develops our physical powers by exercise, ... as ... misery and excessive wealth, are eliminated, the average length of human life will be increased and a better health and a stronger physical constitution will be ensured. The improvement of medical practice ... will mean the end of ... illnesses brought on by climate, food, or working conditions.... [D]eath will be due only to extraordinary accidents or to the decay of the vital forces.... Certainly man will not become immortal, but will not the interval between the first breath that he draws and the time ... he expires, increase indefinitely?

[Antoine Nicolas de Condorcet, *Sketch for a Historical Picture of the Progress of the Human Mind*. Trans. by June Barraclough. London: Weidenfeld & Nicholson Ltd., 1979.]

Thomas Hobbes' View: Humanity Requires Social Organization

Thomas Hobbes (1588–1679) lived at a time when societies in the Western world and their governments were undergoing tremendous change. In England, Hobbes' native country, new social classes were growing in power, religions were transforming themselves, and parliamentary government was being developed. The British aristocracy and members of the wealthier classes controlled the nation's political power, but the opinions of a wider society were increasingly being voiced and heard.

The development of new forms of government and changing social structures gave rise to many questions about the essential nature of human beings and the essential nature of human society. It has become difficult to discuss what a human being is without including the idea of humans in a social setting. Most of us live within social settings and it is within that environment that we become the people we are. Rarely, if ever, do we encounter individuals who have been socially isolated as children or adults. When we do, we often look to see whether these people have been negatively or positively affected, and whether their development has been delayed as a result of social isolation.

In the following excerpt, Hobbes speculated about what life might have been like before people organized societies and governments. Hobbes believed that unorganized civilization would result in chaos, creating conditions so horribly unpleasant that people would be forced to organize into social and political groups. Without such social organization, Hobbes believed, people could not develop their full humanity.

The Leviathan

Thomas Hobbes

I put for a general inclination of all mankind, a perpetual and restless desire … after power…. [I]f any two men desire the same thing … they become enemies; and … endeavour to destroy, or subdue one another…. [I]f one plants, sows, builds, or possesses a convenient seat, others may probably be expected to come prepared with forces united, to dispossess and deprive him, not only of the fruit of his labor, but also of his life or liberty….

So that in the nature of man, we find three principal causes of quarrel. First, competition; second, diffidence [insecurity]; thirdly, glory.

The first maketh men invade for gain; the second, for safety; and the third, for reputation. The first use violence to make themselves masters of other men's persons, wives, children, and cattle; the second, to defend them; the third, for trifles, as a word, a smile, a different opinion….

… [D]uring the time men live without a common power to keep them all in awe, they are in that condition which is called war; and such a way as is of every man against every man…. In such condition there is no place for industry, because the fruit thereof is uncertain: and consequently no culture of the earth; no navigation; … no knowledge of the face of the earth; no account of time; no arts; no letters; no society; and which is worst of all, continual fear, and danger of violent death; and the life of man, [is] solitary, poor, nasty, brutish, and short ….

[Thomas Hobbes, *Leviathan* (1651). Ed. by Herbert Schneider. Indianapolis: Bobbs-Merrill Co., 1958, chap. 13.]

IDEAS AND ISSUES

Understand Concepts

1. (a) Prepare two lists: one listing the type of education with which Rousseau disagreed; the other the type of education he recommended.
   (b) How would he defend his vision of education?
2. Identify the topic, questions, and thesis of Condorcet's work.
3. Why did Condorcet think that progress is possible, even inevitable?
4. Describe Hobbes' perception of life before the development of government and laws.
5. What did Hobbes say about basic human nature? Describe what human nature reveals when there is neither government nor law.

Apply and Develop

6. (a) Do you think contemporary education reflects Rousseau's views?
   (b) Is there a significant difference in the way young individuals are treated at different levels of education: pre-school, elementary, secondary, and post-secondary? Provide reasons.

Think Critically

7. Describe the concept of human nature stated or implied by Rousseau.
8. In a paragraph, describe Hobbes' view of human nature. Take into account his view of "natural" humans and social humans.

Communicate Ideas

9. What goals would Rousseau have had in education, and what methods would he have employed? Interview teachers at different levels of education to determine if they agree or disagree with Rousseau and provide reasons.
10. Using the ideas of Rousseau, Condorcet, and Hobbes as a starting point, develop your own view of human nature that includes the concepts of: what we are born with, what we must develop through experience, and the best way to organize society to help us become most human.
11. Compare Rousseau's and Condorcet's views on human nature. Which of these two do you think is most represented or most outdated in the modern world? Provide reasons.
12. To what extent, if at all, have Condorcet's predictions occurred?
13. In a brief paragraph, outline how Condorcet would probably answer the question: What are the most important elements of human nature?

Inquire and Research

14. Describe the views of raising children that are present in child-rearing manuals or child psychology texts today. Is the emphasis on allowing or encouraging the natural development of the child, or on shaping the child in socially acceptable ways?
15. Read William Golding's *Lord of the Flies*. What vision of human nature is put forward here? To what degree do you agree with the vision?

How Science Affected Our Ideas About Human Nature

The nineteenth century was a time of rapid change in science and technology, and in social and political thinking. Science increased our existing knowledge of the human mind and body. Technology was applied to the industrial production of material goods. New social and political ideas evolved with the rise of new social classes and different lifestyles. The result raises even more new questions about what it means to be human.

Charles Darwin (1809–1882) and Sigmund Freud (1856–1939), two nineteenth century thinkers, put forward new ideas about our origins as a species and how our mind affects our behaviour. Darwin was a naturalist who examined the origin of different species. Freud was a psychiatrist who investigated the relationship between human conscious and unconscious aspects, and their manifestations in human behaviour. Both Darwin and Freud presented ideas that were controversial and revolutionary, and they forced us to consider different aspects of ourselves as humans, whether or not we agree with their original ideas.

Nineteenth-century people had to rethink their place in the universe and their nature as human beings. Charles Darwin and Sigmund Freud led the assault against long-accepted ideas of humanity.

Charles Darwin and His Idea of Natural Selection

As a young man, Charles Darwin prepared for the life of a church minister, but he became increasingly interested in science, especially biology. When asked to study plants and animals on a voyage around the world aboard the ship "Beagle," Darwin jumped at the opportunity. The ideas that emerged from his observations during this voyage changed our views of life on this planet, the place of human beings, and the nature of humans ever since.

His voyage took place between 1831 and 1836, sailing across the Atlantic to South America, and then to the Galapagos islands. There, he was amazed at the tremendous variety of plants and animals he found. Darwin noted that birds and other species exhibited minor variations in appearance and behaviour, from one island to another. He speculated on the causes of these changes, and began to develop his theories of biological selection and evolution.

When Darwin returned to England, he took up life as a country gentleman, reflecting on his findings. He had observed that all plant and animal species descended and developed from other species, changing in the process from one generation to the next. He concluded that these changes resulted because more offspring were always born than eventually survived. Those that did survive had some characteristics that enabled them to adapt more adequately to their environment. They were better able to escape prey, to gather food, to mate, and to pass on their unique characteristics.

The idea of evolutionary change amongst species was not new, although how the change took place was not known. Darwin proposed a theory that explained how evolution occurred, and provided detailed observations and examples as evidence of this.

Darwin waited for over twenty years before he published his conclusions, fearing the social impact his ideas might have. Then, he discovered that Alfred Russell Wallace, another biologist who had independently deduced the same results, was about to publish his findings. In 1859, Darwin finally published *On the Origin of Species by Means of Natural Selection*.

Charles Darwin

Man is descended from some less highly organized form.
Charles Darwin

… [O]ur ancestral proto-hominids "were not striving to become human; they were … trying to stay alive."
Philip Van Doren Stern

The concept of biological evolution had been in existence for some time. Darwin's research provided many examples to illustrate the theory, and to provide an explanation for how it might happen. His theories aroused great controversy, and changed our views of humanity and our place in nature.

His ideas were, and still are, controversial. *The Origin of Species* and Darwin's later work, *The Descent of Man* (1871), caused great public and philosophic discussion. Many people were outraged. They felt that Darwin's ideas were a denial of God creating humans directly. Other critics felt that evolution minimized the distinction between human beings and other species. Darwin's supporters, however, proclaimed his theory of evolution to be one of the most powerful explanations of life, and of the nature of the human species.

Some scientists and philosophers applied Darwin's evolutionary theories far beyond biology, to society, and to human ethics and behaviour. Social Darwinists used the idea of survival of the fittest to argue that unbridled competition should reign in society, as it did in the natural world. Karl Marx (1818–1883) used Darwin's theories as a rationale for class struggle and progress towards socialism. Darwin himself never applied broad social applications to his theories; he never ventured beyond the biological limits of his hypotheses. Yet he influenced every aspect of study about human nature and the social world. Since 1859, philosophers of human nature have had to take Darwin's ideas into account in determining their own views, whether or not they agree with his position.

The Origin of Species

Charles Darwin

Nothing at first can appear more difficult to believe than [the fact] that the more complex organs and instincts have been perfected … by the accumulation of innumerable slight variations, each good for the individual possessor. Nevertheless, … there is a struggle for existence leading to the preservation of profitable deviations…. [A]ccording to the theory of natural selection, an interminable number of intermediate forms must have existed, linking all the species in each group by gradations as fine as are our existing varieties….

ing to the theory of natural selection, an interminable number of intermediate forms must have existed, linking all the species in each group by gradations as fine as are our existing varieties….

More individuals are born than can possibly survive. A grain in the balance may determine which individuals shall live and which shall die, which variety or species shall increase in number, and which shall decrease, or finally become extinct…. The slightest advantage in certain individuals … over those with which they come into competition, or better adaptation in however slight a degree to the surrounding physical conditions, will, in the long run, turn the balance….

If, then, animals and plants do vary, let it be ever so slightly or slowly, why should not variations or individual differences, which are in any way beneficial, be preserved and accumulated through natural selection, or the survival of the fittest?… What limit can be put to this power, acting during long ages … favoring the good and rejecting the bad? I can see no limit to this power, in slowly and beautifully adapting each form to the most complex relations of life. The theory of natural selection … seems to be in the highest degree probable….

[Charles Darwin, *The Origin of Species by Means of Natural Selection*, 6th ed. New York: D. Appleton & Co., 1892.]

The Descent of Man

Charles Darwin

Man, like every other animal, has no doubt advanced to his present high condition through a struggle for existence resulting from his rapid multiplication; and if he is to advance still higher, it is to be feared that he must remain subject to a severe struggle….

The main conclusion arrived at in this work, namely that man is descended from some lowly organized form, will, I regret to think, be highly distasteful to many. But there can hardly be a doubt that we are descended from barbarians….

Man may be excused for feeling some pride at having risen, though not through his own exertions, to the very summit of the organic scale; and the fact of his having thus risen, instead of having been simply placed there, may give him hope for a still higher destiny in the distant future.

[Charles Darwin, *The Descent of Man,* 2nd ed. (rev). New York: D. Appleton & Co., 1898, 633, 634.]

Sigmund Freud and the Power of the Unconscious

Sigmund Freud is considered by many people to be the father of modern psychology. His ideas have shaped our view of human nature in a broad philosophic way.

Freud was born into an upper middle class Austrian family in the mid-nineteenth century. After completing medical school, Freud specialized in disorders of the nervous system. He learned to use scientific methods, such as observation of symptoms, to analyze the human body. At that time, physicians assumed that all physical symptoms have a physical cause.

As he proceeded in his career, however, Freud soon began to note that such an assumption was not always correct. Some physical symptoms, for example, seemed to have no detectable physical origin. Freud began to think that emotions might be at the root of some symptoms. He asked his patients about their early years, their feelings, and their problems. Gradually, Freud developed the theory that people are often governed by elements of the unconscious mind about which they are largely unaware. This part of the mind, Freud believed, can have a powerful, if little understood, impact on our thoughts, feelings, and actions.

Freud also believed that people inherit certain instincts, which act as drives. Our genetic make-up provides us with instinctive drives towards pleasure and aggression. Freud proposed that as we mature and become socialized, we realize that we cannot give free reign to these drives. We must control them in order to survive and to live with other human beings. While drives can be directed towards constructive ends and redirected in other ways, they do not disappear. Understanding our own unconscious mind, and the instinctive drives that often motivate us, Freud believed, will help us live fuller and happier lives. Freud called this process of understanding the self "psychoanalysis," literally "analysis of the mind."

World events in the early twentieth century reinforced Freud's view that humans are often at the mercy of their primitive instincts and emotions. Civilized behaviour, he wrote, was only a thin skin over instincts and emotions that erupt violently from time to time. World War I, an irrational and horrific war, was one such event. The rise of Nazi brutality and aggression during the 1930s, with its appeal to the worst and most base human emotions, further supported Freud's beliefs. In the late 1930s, Sigmund Freud was forced to flee Nazi occupied Austria and seek refuge in England.

Freud's view of human nature continues to exert a powerful influence on the world. He challenged the old view of the self as primarily a conscious, rational being. He provided an explanation of the unconscious mind,

Sigmund Freud

Freud's ideas of the unconscious mind had a powerful impact on how we view ourselves. While many disagree with his theories, Freud directed our attention to the emotional and unconscious parts of human nature.

The brutality and destruction due to the wars in the twentieth century, such as Khmer Rouge, made many people question the essence of human nature. What aspects about our human nature make us choose war in certain situations?

It seems we discover the meaning of our unconscious behavior only when we are confronted with the unconscious behavior of others.
Minako Ohba

and worked to increase our awareness and insight into the less conscious parts of human existence. Today, Sigmund Freud's influence is evident in modern psychiatry, literature, art, and social thought.

Not everyone, however, accepts Freud's views. Many of his ideas are hotly debated, and some are widely rejected. Many psychologists, philosophers, and others dispute the idea that we are largely shaped by inborn drives. Instead, they argue such instincts, if they exist at all, are largely shaped by learning and experience.

In a letter written to the great physicist Albert Einstein (1879–1955) in 1932, Freud discussed whether it is possible to avoid warfare in the future. He used his ideas about human nature to think about this issue. Avoiding future wars, Freud argued, depends on whether or not the human intellect will be able to control the instinctive forces that directed human behaviour.

The intention that man should be "happy" is not contained in the plan of Creation.
Sigmund Freud

PHILOSOPHERS' FORUM

Why War?

Sigmund Freud

… [C]onflicts of interest between men are settled by the use of violence. This is true of the whole animal kingdom, from which men have no business to exclude themselves….

You express astonishment at the fact that it is so easy to make men enthusiastic about a war and add your suspicion that there is something at work in them—an instinct for hatred and destruction—which goes halfway to meet the efforts of the warmongers. Once again, I can only express my entire agreement. We believe in the existence of an instinct of that kind….

According to our hypothesis human instincts are of only two kinds: those which seek to preserve and unite—which we call erotic ... or sexual with a deliberate extension of the popular conception of "sexuality"—and those which seek to destroy and kill and which we class together as the aggressive or destructive instinct. As you see, this is in fact no more than a theoretical clarification of the universally familiar opposition between Love and Hate.... Neither of these instincts is any less essential than the other; the phenomena of life arise from the operation of both together, whether acting in concert or in opposition....

It is very rarely that an action is the work of a single instinctual impulse.... In order to make an action possible there must be as a rule a combination of such compounded motives.... A lust for aggression and destruction is certainly among them: the countless cruelties in history and in our everyday lives vouch for its existence and its strength. The gratification of these destructive impulses is of course facilitated by their admixture with others of an erotic and idealistic kind. When we read of the atrocities of the past, it sometimes seems as though the idealistic motives served only as an excuse for the destructive appetites; and sometimes—in the case, for instance, of the cruelties of the twentieth century, it seems as though the idealistic motives had pushed themselves forward in consciousness, while the destructive ones lent them an unconscious reinforcement....

... [T]his [destructive] instinct is at work in every living being and is striving to bring it to ruin and to reduce life to its original condition of inanimate matter. Thus it quite seriously deserves to be called a death instinct, while the erotic instincts represent the effort to live. The death instinct turns into the destructive instinct if ... it is directed outward.... This would serve as a biological justification for all the ugly and dangerous impulses against which we are struggling....

... [T]here is no use in trying to get rid of men's aggressive inclinations.... [I]t is enough to try to divert them to such an extent that they need not find expression in war.... If willingness to engage in war is an effect of the destructive instinct, the most obvious plan will be to bring Eros, its antagonist, into play against it. Anything that encourages the growth of emotional ties between men must operate against war.... The second kind of emotional tie is by means of identification. Whatever leads men to share important interests produces this community of feeling, these identifications. And the structure of human society is to a large extent based on them....

Yours sincerely,
Sigm Freud

[Sigmund Freud, "Why War?", *Collected Papers*, Vol. 5. Trans. and ed. by James Strachey. New York Basic Books, Inc., 1959, 273–87.]

IDEAS AND ISSUES

Understand Concepts

1. Summarize the views of human nature put forward by Darwin and Freud.
2. How did each of these scientists reach his conclusions?
3. Define these terms: natural selection, adaptation, unconscious, and psychoanalysis.

Apply and Develop

4. Explain how Freud's view of aggression agrees with current ideas of learned behaviour. For example, aggression and violence vary from culture to culture, and group to group. How would he explain this?
5. Some have said that, instead of adapting ourselves to the environment, human beings increasingly adapt the environment to suit their needs. To what degree, if at all, do you believe that human evolution will continue in the future?

Think Critically

6. Outline the types of arguments and evidence put forward by Darwin and Freud. How convincing do you find each argument?
7. Critically assess the ideas of either Darwin or Freud.
8. Using Freud's letter to Einstein as a starting point, describe your view of whether humans will ever achieve peace on a global scale. Support your argument with evidence.

Communicate Ideas

9. In what ways, if at all, did Darwin and Freud make similar assumptions in their theories?

Inquire and Research

10. Read more about Freud's understanding of the mind. You may begin with an introductory psychology text, then look at one of his books, such as *The Interpretation of Dreams* or *Two Short Accounts of Psycho-Analysis*. Write a critical assessment of his main ideas.
11. Read about Darwin's life and research. Summarize the essence of his theory of evolution. Write an argumentative essay taking a position on the theory.

Is There a Fixed Human Nature?

Some issues about human nature have been around for a long time. For example, the nature–nurture debate is argued as hotly today as it was in previous times. That is, while some philosophers believe our humanness is something that we are born with, others believe we acquire it through experience and learning. If you review the philosophers discussed so far, it is not hard to categorize their views into one or the other of the two camps. Some thinkers straddle the issue by saying that we acquire our humanness in both ways. What do you think Aristotle, St. Augustine, Rousseau, or Freud would have added to the nature–nurture debate?

In modern times, behavioural psychologists, such as B.F. Skinner, have argued that the environment is the primary factor in shaping the human psyche. Skinner was so certain of the importance of a controlled environment that he raised his daughter in a "Skinner box," an enclosed and controlled playpen. Skinner argued that human behaviour can be shaped into any desired shape, by controlling positive and negative reactions.

Other philosophers and psychologists focussed on the innate, genetic qualities of humans. Recently, sociobiologists have renewed the argument that many of our qualities are inherited and genetic. Current work on the "genome project," which maps out our genetic blueprint in an attempt to provide information about our individual innate qualities, may shed more scientific light on this issue.

Existentialism is another important twentieth century philosophic movement which came to prominence in the 1950s. Existentialist philosophers, such as Jean-Paul Sartre and Albert Camus, searched

Is there such a thing as a fixed human nature? If so, how can we explain the extremes in human behaviour?

to find answers about human nature. One question they asked was: How can human beings exhibit such a wide range of behaviour, from the most unselfish to the most brutal? Existentialists tried to grasp the horrors of both World Wars and the mass murder of the Holocaust.

Most Existentialists believe that there is no such thing as a fixed human nature. We are thrown into the world to make of ourselves what we can through our own actions. Who we are and what we become depends on the decisions we make and the actions we take. Literally, we create ourselves as we live our lives. Therefore, the responsibility for who we are, good or evil, rests solely with ourselves.

Sartre's View of Human Nature

Jean-Paul Sartre's view of human nature outlines some essential ideas of existentialism. We are born, then we make of ourselves what we can, or in his words, "Existence precedes essence." We are not born with a predetermined nature; we create our own nature through our actions.

Sartre believed that we are free to choose how we will act, and so we must make decisions. We are "condemned to be free," since we have no other choice. We cannot avoid responsibility for our actions, by blaming human nature, fate, or God. In choosing to act in one way or another, we shape who we become.

Sartre believed that we can only live authentically, as an individual person, by accepting our freedom and the responsibility that goes with it. Others will try to define us in their own view of what we are like. However, we must try to be true to ourselves, and what we think is right. Moreover, in choosing to act, we are also setting an example for others. If we decide to act unselfishly, or bravely, or wrongly, others will see and be influenced.

> We are left alone, without excuse. That is what I mean when I say that man is condemned to be free.
>
> *Jean-Paul Sartre*

PHILOSOPHERS' FORUM

An Existentialist View of the Self

Jean-Paul Sartre

What do we mean by saying that existence precedes essence? We mean that man first of all exists, encounters himself, surges up in the world—and defines himself afterwards…. Man is nothing else but that which he makes of himself. That is the first principle of existentialism …. If, however, it is true that existence is prior to essence, man is responsible for what he is, thus the first effect of existentialism is that it puts every man in possession of himself as he is, and places the entire responsibility for his existence squarely upon his shoulders. And, when we say that man is responsible for himself, we do not mean that he is responsible only for his own individuality, but that he is responsible for all men…. [I]n choosing for himself he chooses for all … an image of man such as he believes he ought to be…. If … I decide to marry and to have children … I am thereby committing not only myself, but humanity as a whole, to the practice of monogamy. I am thus responsible for myself and for all men, and I am creating a certain image of man as I would have him to be….

… [O]ne will never be able to explain one's action by reference to a given and specific human nature; in other words, there is no determinism—man is free…. We are left alone, without excuse. That is what I mean when I say that man is condemned to be free. Condemned, because he did not create himself, yet is nevertheless at liberty, and from the moment that he is thrown into this world he is responsible for everything he does….

If people condemn our works of fiction, in which we describe characters that are base, weak, cowardly and sometimes even frankly evil, it is not only because those characters are base, weak, cowardly or evil. For suppose that ... we showed that the behavior of these characters was caused by their heredity, or by the action of their environment upon them, or by determining factors, psychic or organic. People would be reassured, they would say, "You see, that is what we are like, no one can do anything about it." But the existentialist, when he portrays a coward, shows him as responsible for his cowardice. He ... has not come like that through his physiological organism; he is like that because he has made himself into a coward by his actions.... What people would prefer would be to be born either a coward or a hero.

[Jean-Paul Sartre, *Existentialism*. Trans. by Philip Mairet. London Methuen & Co., 1946.]

Which philosophic view do you feel best characterizes Terry Fox's human nature?

An Alternative View of Human Nature

Freud, and sociobiologists, believe that our actions are determined by inborn qualities. Freud said that human nature has instincts that shape our behaviour. Sociobiologists point to genetic, innate qualities of human nature that determine our behaviour. On the other hand, Existentialist Jean-Paul Sartre denied any such determining human nature. Sartre said that humans are capable of almost anything. They become what they are by acting freely, and as such, they must take responsibility for their actions.

Is it possible that there still is some innate entity called human nature, which yet allows for freedom of action? How is it possible that all human beings share the same human nature, yet are so different from one another? Consider the argument American philosopher Mortimer Adler makes and the conclusions he draws as you read the following excerpt. How are Adler's views similar to, or different from, those presented so far?

In China, literature is ... viewed as ... an effective means of education, of inspiring readers with high ideals and the belief that these can be attained.

Gladys Yang

Human Nature

Mortimer Adler

... [A]ll human beings alive today, and all that have been alive since *Homo sapiens* first appeared on earth, are members of one and the same species. Nevertheless, in the twentieth century, the essential sameness of all human beings, by virtue of their participating in the same specific nature, has been widely challenged.... What can possibly be meant by the denial of human nature? We are all human beings, are we not?... Let me now try to explain what it is that leads to a denial of human nature.

... If you were to investigate [any animal species] ... you would find that the members ... manifest a remarkable degree of similarity. You might find differences in size, weight, shape, or coloration.... But, by and large, you would be impressed by the similitudes [resemblances]....

Now consider the human species. It inhabits the globe ... under the most widely divergent environmental conditions. Let us suppose you were to take the time to visit human populations wherever they existed.... Let the visit not be a casual one, but one in which you lived for a time with each of these populations and studied them closely. You would come away with the very opposite impression from the one you took away from your investigation of ... animal species. You were there impressed by the overwhelming similitude.... Here, however, you would find that the differences were dominant....

There are many different ways of being human.

Carl Sagan

Of course human beings … have certain biological traits in common…. But when you come to their human traits, how different one human population … [can] be from another. They will differ in the languages they speak, … in their adornments, … in their customs and manners, … in the institutions of their societies, in their beliefs, in their standards of conduct…. It is this that might lead you to the conclusion that there is no human nature in the sense in which a certain constant nature can be attributed to other species of animals….

Looked at one way, the denial of human nature is correct. The members of the human species do not have a specific or common nature *in the same sense* that the members of other animal species do…. But [this] … is not to admit that they have *no specific nature whatsoever*….

In what sense then is there a human nature, a specific nature that is common to all members of the species? The answer can be given in a single word: *potentialities*. Human nature is constituted by all the potentialities … common to all members of the human species.

It is the essence of a potentiality to be capable of a wide variety of different actualizations. Thus, for example, the human potentiality for syntactical speech is actualized in thousands of different human languages. Having that potentiality, a human infant placed

at the moment of birth in one or another human subgroup, each with its own language, would learn to speak that language…. What has just been said about one human potentiality applies to all the others that are the common, specific traits of the human being….

Man is to a great extent a self-made creature. Given a range of potentialities at birth, he makes himself what he becomes by how he freely chooses to develop those potentialities by the habits he forms. No other animal is a self-made creature in the sense indicated above. On the contrary, other animals have … natures genetically determined in such a way that they do not admit of a wide variety of different developments as they mature.

Human nature is also genetically determined; but, because the genetic determination consists, behaviorally, in an innate endowment of potentialities that are determinable in different ways, human beings differ remarkably from one another as they mature. However they originated in the first place, most of those differences are due to differences in acculturation, to nurtural differences. To confuse nature with nurture is a philosophical mistake of the first order. That philosophical mistake underlies the denial of human nature….

The correction of the philosophical mistake just mentioned is of the greatest impor-

What does Adler think that all human beings have in common? How does he say we are different?

tance because of the consequences that follow from doing so. Most important of all is overcoming the persistent prejudice—the racist, sexist, elitist, even ethnic prejudice—that one portion or subgroup of mankind is distinctly inferior by nature to another. The inferiority may exist, but it is not an inferiority due to nature, but to nurture. When, for most of the centuries of recorded history, the female half of the population was nurtured—reared and treated—as inferior to the male half, that nurturing made them apparently inferior when they matured.... What I have said about the sexist prejudice ... applies to all the racist and ethnic prejudices about human inequality that still exist among mankind. All these apparent inequalities are nurtural. None is a natural inequality between one human subgroup and another....

If a world cultural community is ever to come into existence, it will retain cultural pluralism or diversity with ... such things as cuisine, dress, manners, customs, and the like. These are the things that vary ... according as these subgroups differ in the way they nurture their members.

In contrast, the common elements that will unite all human beings in a single, cultural community will be related to such essentials as truth in science and philosophy, moral values and human rights, man's understanding of himself, and the wisdom that is the highest good of the human mind. When that happens, we will have at last overcome the nurtural illusion that there is a Western mind and an Eastern mind, a European mind and an African mind, or a civilized mind and a primitive mind. There is only a human mind and it is one and the same in all human beings.

[Mortimer Adler, *Ten Philosophical Mistakes*. New York: Macmillan Publishing Co. 1985, 156–66.]

IDEAS AND ISSUES

Understand Concepts

Summarize the main ideas of human nature discussed by Sartre and Adler.

Explain the meaning of each statement:
(a) "Existence precedes essence."
(b) "To confuse nature with nurture is a philosophical mistake of the first order."

Think Critically

Using one statement for each thinker, identify the main thesis of the excerpts from Sartre and Adler.

Prepare an argument in support of or against Sartre's view of human nature.

Communicate Ideas

Review the ideas of human nature presented in this chapter. Organize these in chart form. Look for points of similarity and points of uniqueness. Draw your own conclusions about the essential nature of human beings.

Inquire and Research

Read B.F. Skinner's *Walden Two*. Determine the image of human nature he puts forward.

Research Abraham Maslow's theory of human needs in a psychology text or encyclopedia. In essence, what did he say about human nature? To what extent do you agree with him?

Review and Reflect

P hilosophers since ancient times have attempted to define and understand what it means to be human. Plato believed the body and soul were the two major elements of human nature. For him, the goal of human life was to escape the bounds of the material body into the rational and eternal world of the soul. Aristotle focussed on learning and habit as determiners of human nature.

Mencius and St. Augustine asked if humanity was good or evil. Both Mencius and St. Augustine concluded that humans are basically good; however, St. Augustine believed that vice makes human beings evil.

In the early modern period, Hobbes, Condorcet, and Rousseau looked at human nature within society. Hobbes and Condorcet were sure that it was only through society, and civilization, that humans could become truly fulfilled, although the view each took of human nature was quite different. Rousseau foreshadowed a later view in looking to the more natural element of humanity. He believed that nature was a good indicator of how we should live our lives and treat others.

Nineteenth century scientific, technological, and social developments caused the question of human nature to be framed in new terms. Darwin and Freud asked to what degree we are the products of our biological development and our hereditary instincts.

In the twentieth century, the discussion about human nature continued. Existentialist Jean-Paul Sartre argued that we are free to shape our own nature through the decisions we make. Adler defined human nature as the potential to shape ourselves in a wide variety of ways. Reflecting on what it means to be human is still important today as we struggle to deal with the issues of our modern world.

CHAPTER 8

How Men and Women See Themselves

Throughout history, many philosophers and non-philosophers alike have questioned what makes a man a "man" and a woman a "woman." Are men and women intrinsically different from a strictly biological point of view, or does society play a major role in shaping male and female identities? Although the terms "gender" and "sex" are used interchangeably in everyday speech, philosophers use the term gender to mean how a society and culture shapes our identities as men and women in addition to the biological differences.

Many of the dominant ideas about this issue have been put forward by men. Some have argued that males and females have natures that are very different. This argument has resulted in the long-standing, and often rigid, sex roles particularly visible in patriarchal societies. For example, men have often been expected to be the major providers for their families. Similarly, women have certain expectations put upon them from birth, such as the emphasis on their physical appearance. Such gender expectations have often restricted both men and women in their choices of identity and social roles.

Other thinkers have argued that despite the visible biological differences between men and women, they share the same basic human nature and have the same aspirations and desires, emotionally, intellectually, and spiritually. Philosophers who hold this position believe that gender differences are largely created by culture and socialization. Without such influences both men and women would enjoy greater choices and, perhaps, live fuller lives.

Still other philosophers believe that, although there are significant differences in nature between men and women, these differences do not justify either sex being placed in an inferior social position to the other. Such thinkers argue that sexual differences are important, and that each sex contributes its own uniquely valuable social benefits to society as a whole.

Mexican fertility goddess

Regardless of which point of view you support, there is no doubt that gender affects the way we view ourselves and others in society. Many modern writers and thinkers have challenged our previously held ideas about men and women. There is no doubt that social changes require new definitions of gender roles and that these new definitions will, in turn, contribute to more social changes.

Since ancient times, men and women have sought to define their identities. How do we define ourselves as men and women today?

Perceptions of Gender in Ancient Greece

Ancient Greek society did not, for the most part, consider men and women to be of equal status. Each sex was expected to play a distinct social role. Only men participated in public affairs, speaking and voting on political issues. Women usually confined their activities to the home, taking a secondary place in most other areas as well.

Plato and Aristotle lived within this social setting and were influenced to some degree by the commonly held ideas of the time. Nevertheless, these two thinkers were accustomed to philosophic debate, often arguing on behalf of non-traditional points of view. This is precisely what each of them did as they explored the nature and social position of men and women.

In most societies, including ancient Greece, women were excluded from most public activities, including government. What did Plato and Aristotle say about this? What reasons did each give?

> Now perhaps you may think it not fitting for a woman to philosophize, just as it is not fitting for her to ride horses or speak in public. But I think that some things are peculiar to a man, some to a woman, some are common to both…. I say that courage and justice and wisdom are common to both.
>
> *Phintys of Sparta*

> Why are males usually larger than females? Is it because they are hotter, and heat is productive of growth? Or is it because the male is complete in all its parts, whereas the female is defective? Or is it because the male takes a long time to achieve perfection, the female a short time?
>
> *Aristotle*

Plato's View of Women

In *The Republic*, Plato describes a Utopian society. In the following excerpt, Plato lets Socrates become his voice. Socrates did not deny that men and women may have different natures, although he did argue that such differences are irrelevant to performing the necessary tasks of society. Socrates said that men and women can both be equally skilled at most occupations and so the best qualified person should be awarded the job. Socrates concluded that men and women must receive similar education, an early argument for belief that gender differences are more the result of culture than biology.

As you read Plato's excerpt, consider these questions: Do men and women share common human natures or are the sexes fundamentally different in important ways? Should men and women perform similar and equal roles in society, or should these roles be separate and distinct?

The Nature and Role of Women

Plato

"Can you," [asked Socrates,] "use any living creature for the same work as another unless you rear and train it in the same way?"

"No."

"Then if we employ women at the same tasks as men, we must give them the same instruction?"

"Yes."

"The men were given music and gymnastic."

"Yes."

"Then we must assign to the women also these two arts, and the art of war in addition, and treat them in the same way."

"That follows from what you say," he said....

"But must we not first come to an agreement as to whether these proposals are practical or not, and allow any one, whether he is a jester or a serious person, to raise the question whether female human nature is capable of sharing with the male in all his occupations, or in none of them, or whether it is capable of some and not of other?..."

"How could we do otherwise?"

"But is not a woman by nature very different from a man?"

"Certainly she is different."

"And ought not different tasks to be assigned to different individuals in accordance with the nature of each?"

"Yes."

"Then are you not mistaken and inconsistent now in maintaining, as you do, that men and women would do the same things, seeing that they have widely different natures? Will you be able to offer any defence to that, my wonderful friend?"

"It is certainly not easy just at the moment," he said....

"When we insist that what are not the same natures ought not to have the same pursuits, we ... have never inquired at all of what kind were the sameness and the difference and with reference to what we were then distinguishing them, when we proposed to give different pursuits to different natures, and the same pursuits to the same natures."

"No," he said, "we did not inquire."

"In the same way," [Socrates] said, "we might evidently ask ourselves whether bald and hairy men had the same or opposite nature; and, agreeing that they have opposite nature, might forbid hairy men to be shoemakers if bald men are, or forbid bald men if hairy men are."

"Well, that would be ridiculous," he said.

"But would it not be ridiculous," [Socrates] said, "simply because, in that proposition, we did not mean same and different in general? Our rule was only directed against that particular form of likeness and difference which concerns those particular pursuits. We meant, for example, that the soul possessed of medical capacity and a doctor have the same nature. Do you agree with me?"

"I do."

"But a doctor and a carpenter have different natures."

"Of course."

"Then," [Socrates] said, "if we find either the male or the female sex excelling the other in any art or other pursuit, then we shall say that this particular pursuit must be assigned to one and not to the other; but if we find that the difference simply consists in this, that the female conceives and male begets, we shall not allow that that goes any way to prove that a woman differs from a man with reference to the subject of which we are speaking, and we shall still consider that our guardians and their wives ought to follow the same pursuits."

"And quite rightly," he said....

"When you say that one man has a natural talent for anything, and another is naturally unfitted for it, do you mean that the first learns it easily, while the second learns it with difficulty?... Are these not the only signs by which you meant to determine in any case natural talent or the want of it?"

"No one," he said, "will name any others." ...

"Then, my friend, there is not one of those pursuits by which the city is ordered which belongs to women as women, or to men as men; but natural aptitudes are equally distributed in both kinds of creatures. Women naturally participate in all occupations, and so do men; but in all women are weaker than men."

"Certainly."

"Shall we, then, assign all occupations to men and none to women?"

"Of course not."

"But shall we say, I fancy, that one woman is by nature fit for medicine, and another not; one musical, and another unmusical?"

"Surely."

"And is not one woman a lover of gymnastic and of war, and another unwarlike and no lover of gymnastic?"

"I should think so."

"And one a lover and another a hater of wisdom; one spirited, another spiritless?"

"Yes."

"Then one woman will be capable of being a guardian and another not. For did we not select just this nature for our men guardians?"

"We did."

"Then for the purpose of guarding the city the nature of men and women is the same, except that women are naturally weaker, men naturally stronger?"

"Apparently."

"Then we must select women of the necessary character to share the life of men of like character and guard the city along with them, inasmuch as they are capable and of a kindred nature?"

"Certainly."

"Then must we not assign the same occupations to the same natures?"

"Yes."

"So we are come round to what we said before, and allow that there is nothing unnatural in assigning music and gymnastic to the wives of the guardians?"

"Most certainly." …

"Then surely if women are to become fit to be guardians, we shall not have one education to make guardians of the men and another for the women, especially when education will have the same nature to work upon?"

"No."

[Plato, *The Republic*, Book 5., trans. by A.D. Lindsay. Toronto: Fitzhenry & Whiteside, 1980, 139–45.]

Aristotle's View of Women

Plato's view was but one in the ancient world, and not a very widely held one at that. His student, Aristotle, disagreed. Aristotle believed the essential nature of men and women to be determined by biology. Nature not nurture, biology and not experience, is the determining factor which makes us the men and women we are, he thought. Artistotle's view has been commonly accepted, both in the ancient and in the modern world.

Aristotle believed all our important human potentials and possibilities are shaped by biological nature, and so he suggested that society should be organized around biology. That is, since women should be primarily defined by their biological and reproductive roles, their role should be restricted to the family. Men, he said, should embody power in the family and in society as a whole.

Aristotle's beliefs led to problems, because they are often used as justification for keeping women and men in separate, usually unequal, situations. Examine the following two excerpts to understand and assess Aristotle's views on men and women. What do you think of these views?

Men and Women

Aristotle

The male is by nature superior, and the female inferior; and the one rules, and the other is ruled; this principle, of necessity, extends to all mankind. Where there is such a difference as that between soul and body, or between men and animals … the lower sort are by nature slaves, and it is better for them as for all inferiors that they should be under the rule of a master.

[Aristotle, *Politics.* In *The Basic Works of Aristotle*, trans. by Benjamin Jowett, ed. by Richard McKeon. New York: Random House, 1941, 1254b.]

Marital Authority

Aristotle

…[W]hile the head of the household rules over both wife and children, and rules over both as free members of the household, he exercises a different sort of rule in either case…. His rule over his wife is like that of a statesman over fellow citizens; his rule over his children is like that of a monarch over subjects. The male is naturally fitter to command than the female….

…[W]hen one body of citizens is ruling, and the other is being ruled, the former desires to establish a difference—in outward forms, in modes of address, and in titles of respect…. The relation of the male to the female is permanently that in which the statesman [temporarily] stands to his fellow citizens.

[Aristotle, *Politics.* In *The Politics of Aristotle*, ed. by Ernest Barker. London: Oxford University Press, 1958, Book 1, chap. 12.]

IDEAS AND ISSUES

Understand Concepts

1. (a) Identify the major questions being addressed by Aristotle and Plato in the excerpts, even though they may not have stated them outright.
   (b) How did Aristotle and Plato respond to each of these questions?
   (c) How would you respond?
2. Use a comparison chart to organize similarities and differences in the ideas of Aristotle and Plato.

Apply and Develop

3. To what degree, if at all, does our own society implement the ideas of Plato?
4. How would Plato or Aristotle react to a policy that encourages women or men to apply for positions in previously segregated occupations?

Think Critically

5. What are the strengths of the arguments presented by Aristotle and Plato? How would you be critical of each philosopher's arguments?
6. Does it seem that the state envisioned in *The Republic* would consider men and women as equals and allow them equal opportunities?

Gender Roles Throughout Human History

Despite Socrates' arguments to the contrary, Aristotle's view of women has often carried the day. Many philosophers and non-philosophers believe men and women have separate natures and should, therefore, fulfill distinct and separate social positions.

Gender roles, however, have varied from one culture to another throughout human history. There are a number of different possible reasons for this. Some argue that traditional gender roles are rooted in the distant past, when hunting was performed largely by men, and gathering by women.

Anthropologists have often put forward such theories, arguing that the economic systems of a culture are primary in shaping the roles of men and women. When many societies developed agriculture about 10 000 years ago, gender roles changed to adapt to this major economic shift. Often, but not always, women became the primary agriculturalists, and as a result gained a great deal of political power. For example, the Haudenonsaunes (Iroquois) living near the Great Lakes were an established matriarchal society. The women had significant social influence because they provided most of the food, cultivating the land through agriculture.

However, many societies, such as the ancient Greeks, developed as a result of war. Men were expected to be good warriors to defend their country and provide honour for their people. In such societies, men assumed greater social and political power and women were expected to support their cause. These patriarchal societies left little room for flexibility in the gender roles.

Boadicea, Queen of ancient Britain, leads a revolt against the Romans who had taken control of Anglia. How would Plato and Aristotle have reacted to a woman being such a fierce and courageous warrior?

The same situation arose in societies based on patriarchal religions, such as Judeo-Christianity. In such cultures, religion was cited as a reason for maintaining rigid gender roles. During the Middle Ages in Europe, although men and women toiled in the fields together, and both sexes were active in trade, women continued to have less social and political power.

Paradigm Shift in Human Rights in Western Societies

As the Western world developed during the seventeenth and eighteenth centuries, human rights, more democratic government, and social equality became increasingly important issues for many people. Philosophers were not immune from this social upheaval, and thinkers of this period wrote extensively on these rights and the revolutions that followed in England, France, and America.

"We hold these truths to be self-evident: That all men are created equal; that they are endowed by their Creator with certain unalienable rights; that among these are life, liberty, and the pursuit of happiness (*United States Declaration of Independence 1776*)."

In France, the *Declaration of the Right of Man and Citizen,* published in 1789 during the early years of the French Revolution, put forward broad claims to liberty and equality:

"Article 1: Men are born and remain free and equal in rights.

"Article 2: The aim of all political associations is the preservation of the natural and inalienable rights of man. These rights are liberty, prosperity, security, and resistance to oppression....

"Article 4: Liberty consists of the freedom to do everything which injures no one else...."

Views of liberty and equality, however, were usually restricted to white, middle-class males; for the most part non-whites, the poor, and women were excluded from this new order. Yet once the idea of liberty and equality was recognized within one group, it became increasingly difficult to ignore the logic of extending such rights to others.

Two philosophers of this period, John Locke and Jean-Jacques Rousseau, wrote extensively on the topics of human rights, equality, and liberty. Locke was the philosopher of the English and American Revolutions, while Rousseau is associated with the French Revolution. Both men wrote about political power in the state, advocating

Aphra Behn, England's first female professional writer, was once a spy in Charles II's court. She turned to writing after being imprisoned for debt.

wider participation in government by the people.

Locke and Rousseau discussed the role and authority of men and women within the family, recognizing that social roles and human relations are important to family structure. Today we continue to examine the roles of each person within the family. Who should be the nurturer or caregiver? Who should work? Who should make decisions? All of these issues are important and timeless. Think about your own family and how people within it relate to one another. Is yours the type of family you wish to be part of in the future? Why or why not?

Political Power and the Family

John Locke

To understand political power … we must consider what state all men are naturally in … a state of perfect freedom to order their actions…. A state also of equality, wherein all the power and jurisdiction is reciprocal, no one having more than another….

It may perhaps be censured as an impertinent criticism … to find fault with words and names…. [Y]et possibly it may not be amiss to offer new ones, when the old are apt to lead men into mistakes, as this of paternal power probably has done…. [I]t seems so to place the power of parents over their children wholly in the father, as if the mother had no share in it: whereas, if we consult reason or revelation, we shall find she hath an equal title. This may give one reason to ask, whether this might not be more properly called parental power? For whatever obligation nature and the right of generation lays on children, it must certainly bind them equally to both [parents]….

But what reason can hence advance this care of the parents due to their offspring into an absolute arbitrary dominion of the father…. [I]n this power the mother too has her share with the father…. And what will become of this paternal power … when the husband and wife part … the children are all left to the mother, follow her, and are wholly under her care and provision?… [D]o they not owe the same obedience to their mother, during the minority, as to their father … ?

[John Locke, *Second Treatise of Civil Government*. Originally in *The Works of John Locke* (London: C. & G. Rivington, etc., 1824). In *History of Ideas on Women*, by Rosemary Agonito. New York: G.P. Putnam's Sons, 1977, 106, 109.]

Are there any good reasons for educating children separately according to gender? What are the results of doing this?

Paternity and the Origin of Political Power

Jean-Jacques Rousseau

In the family … the father ought to command. In the first place, the authority ought not to be equally divided between father and mother; the government must be single, and in every division of opinion there must be one preponderant voice to decide…. Besides, the husband ought to be able to superintend his wife's conduct, because it is of importance for him to be assured that the children, whom he is obligated to acknowledge and maintain, belong to no one but himself. Thirdly, children should be obedient to their father, at first of necessity, and afterwards from gratitude: after having had their wants satisfied by him during one half of their lives, they ought to consecrate the other half to providing for his. Fourthly, servants owe him their services in exchange for the provision he makes for them, though they may break off the bargain as soon as it ceases to suit them.

[Jean-Jacques Rousseau, *A Discourse on Political Economy.* Originally in *The Social Contract and Discourses*, trans. by G.D.H. Cole (London: J.M. Dent & Sons, Ltd., 1913) In *History of Ideas on Woman*, by Rosemary Agonito. New York: G.P. Putnam's Sons, 1997, 119.]

How should authority be divided in the family? What roles should men and women play?

IDEAS AND ISSUES

Understand Concepts

1. (a) What position would Locke and Rousseau have taken on the question: "Where should authority in the family reside?"
   (b) What reasons would each give for his position?

Apply and Develop

2. How would most people today feel about where the authority in a family should reside? How would they act within the family? Give reasons for your answer.
3. What conditions exist today that affect the arguments made by Locke or Rousseau?

Think Critically

4. What factors do you believe are important in shaping the roles played by men and women in the family today?
5. How should authority be shared within a family? Support your position with argument.

Inquire and Research

6. Research further into the ideas of Plato, Aristotle, Locke, and Rousseau on the nature of men and women. Read a major work by each, and identify what each says about the nature of each sex, and the roles each should play in society.

Work, Education, and Equality

If the two sexes were to make equal social contributions, Plato wrote, they must receive equal education. Yet this view has been set aside for much of human history. During the Middle Ages, a small minority of people were educated. These were upper class men, and men who chose the clergy for their vocation. Most philosophers and others viewed human nature as predetermined at birth and sharply distinct between the sexes.

During the eighteenth century, the European Enlightenment introduced a new view of human nature to public consciousness. Many philosophers believed that human beings were shaped more significantly by learning, experience, and culture, and that individual character was not set at birth but developed according to lived experiences. This view of the power of experience and education was ultimately understood as being equally applicable to men and women. Philosopher John Locke and his ideas about learning were highly influential in shaping this line of thinking. Movements to provide education widely to the poor and to women grew stronger.

At the same time, forces such as industrialization were at work. Men, women, and children often worked together in factories during the early stages of the Industrial Revolution. This was not by choice, since such work was unpleasant and dangerous, but through economic necessity. As the nineteenth century progressed, increased wealth began to make its way into the hands of the middle class, and to a lesser degree into the hands of the working class. Gradually, society idealized woman's role in the family; she would stay home and look after the house and children, while her husband went out to work. Soon, the ideas of separate and distinct sexual natures and separate and distinct economic roles according to gender became popular, particularly in the world's industrial nations through most of the twentieth century.

For a long time, women have toiled in the workplace and the family. What are current attitudes towards women's roles at work and in the family in our society?

Mary Wollstonecraft:
Pioneer of Gender Equality

One woman writer of note in late eighteenth century England was Mary Wollstonecraft (1759–1797). She was a champion of the rights of women, and some historians consider her to be the first modern feminist writer. Born in London, and largely self-taught, Wollstonecraft worked as a governess and schoolteacher, founding a small village school with her sister Eliza. Wollstonecraft wrote extensively, and she spent several years in France observing the events of the French Revolution.

Wollstonecraft's book *A Vindication of the Rights of Women* (1792) earned her worldwide recognition and a lasting place in the history of ideas. In *Vindication*, Wollstonecraft discussed the types of education available to women of the eighteenth century. She explained how the lack of learning opportunities ensured that women would be unable to fulfill their potential and would, in fact, remain enslaved to their male counterparts. Wollstonecraft argued for a society with equal education for both sexes, where women would be free from restrictions caused by ignorance and prejudice, and where both men and women could be honest and open with each other. Unfortunately, Wollstonecraft died of septic poisoning a few days after the birth of her second daughter, Mary (who would create the Western world's first literary monster in *Frankenstein*).

Not everyone in the nineteenth century agreed with Wollstonecraft. Another point of view was put forward by Mrs. John Sandford, a popular writer of the time. She was very much in favour of maintaining the socially accepted roles for women at that time. As you read both these women's points of view on the following pages, consider what response you think Mary Wollstonecraft would have given to Mrs. Sandford's point of view.

Time Line

Change in Awareness of Women's Rights

ENLIGHTENMENT
(c. *1700–1750*)
MARY WOLLSTONECRAFT
(*1759–1797*)
argues that equal educational opportunities for women will allow them to be equal in society
JOHN STUART MILL
(*1806–1873*)
confronts societal issues that keep women subordinate to men

Mary Wollstonecraft was a woman who had ideas about gender equality centuries before her time. How do you think Wollstonecraft would respond to the situation of most women in Canada today?

A Vindication of the Rights of Women

Mary Wollstonecraft

Contending for the rights of woman, my main argument is built on this simple principle, that if she be not prepared by education to become the companion of man, she will stop the progress of knowledge and virtue; for truth must be common to all, or it will [not] influence ... general practice.... If children are to be educated ... their mother must [as well]; but the education and situation of woman, at present, shuts her out from such investigations....

... Why should ... [women] be kept in ignorance under the ... name of innocence? Men complain, and with reason, of the follies and caprices of our sex, when they do not keenly satirize our headstrong passions and grovelling vices. Behold, I should answer, the natural effect of ignorance! The mind will ever be unstable that has only prejudices to rest on.... Women are told from their infancy, and taught by the example of their mothers, that ... softness of temper, outward obedience, and ... propriety, will obtain for them the protection of man; and should they be beautiful, everything else is needless, for at least twenty years of their lives....

How grossly do they insult us who thus advise us only to render ourselves gentle, domestic brutes!... Men indeed appear to me to act in a very unphilosophical manner when they try to secure the good conduct of women by attempting to keep them always in a state of childhood.... Children, I grant, should be innocent; but when the epithet is applied to men, or women, it is but a civil term for weakness....

In treating, therefore, of the manners of women, let us ... trace what we should endeavour to make them.... By individual education, I mean ... such an attention to the child as will slowly sharpen the senses, form the temper, regulate the passions as they begin to ferment, and set the understanding to work ... [and] begin the important task of learning to think and reason....

To gain the affections of a virtuous man, is affectation necessary? Nature has given woman a weaker frame than man; but ... must a wife ... feign a sickly delicacy in order to secure her husband's affection? Weakness may excite tenderness, and gratify the arrogant pride of man; but the lordly caresses of a protector will not gratify a noble mind that ... deserves to be respected. Fondness is a poor substitute for friendship....

I lament that women are systematically degraded by receiving the trivial attentions which men think it manly to pay to the sex, when in fact they are insultingly supporting their own superiority.... I scarcely am able to govern my muscles when I see a man start with eager and serious solicitude to lift a handkerchief, or shut a door, when the lady could have done it herself, had she only moved a pace or two....

That women at present are by ignorance rendered foolish or vicious is, I think, not to be disputed; and that the most salutary effects tending to improve mankind might be expected from a REVOLUTION in female manners....

Asserting the rights which women in common with men ought to contend for, I have ... attempted to ... prove them to be the natural consequence of their education and station in society.... [T]hey will change their character, and correct their vices and follies, when they are allowed to be free in a physical, moral and civil sense.

[Mary Wollstonecraft, *A Vindication of the Rights of Women* (1792), Introduction, chap. 2, 4, and 13. In *Western Philosophy*, trans. and ed. by John Cottingham. Oxford: Blackwell Publishers Ltd., 1997, 433–40.]

What image of women did Wollstonecraft describe as prevalent in her time? How would women in our society react to that image? How would men in our society react?

Woman in Her Social and Domestic Character

Mrs. John Sandford

> ... [T]here are still those who would claim that women's reason is less reliable than men's, or that it occurs in a different—perhaps even in an intuitive—manner.
>
> *Carolyn W. Korsmeyer*

A woman may make a man's home delightful, and may thus increase his motives for virtuous exertion. She may refine and tranquilize his mind—may turn away his anger, or allay his grief. Where want of congeniality impairs domestic comfort, the fault is generally chargeable on the female side; for it is for woman, not for man, to make the sacrifice, especially in indifferent [less important] matters. She must, in a certain degree, be plastic [mouldable] herself, if she would mould others, and this is one reason why very good women are sometimes very uninfluential. They do a great deal, but they yield nothing.

In everything that women attempt, they should show their consciousness of dependence. There is something so unpleasant in female self-sufficiency, that it not infrequently prejudices instead of persuading.

Their sex should ever teach them to be subordinate; and they should remember that, by them, influence is to be obtained ... by a delicate appeal to affection or principle. Women, in this respect, are something like children: the more they show their need of support, the more engaging they are.

[Mrs. John Sandford, *Woman in her Social and Domestic Character* (1837). In *The Western Tradition*, 3rd ed., ed. by Eugen Weber. Toronto: D.C. Heath & Co., 1972.]

> One of the things about equality is not just that you be treated equally to a man, but that you treat yourself equally to the way you treat a man.
>
> *Marlo Thomas*

Women and Social Expectations

Almost one hundred years after Mary Wollstonecraft published *Vindication*, Utilitarian philosopher John Stuart Mill also wrote about the role of women in society. His book *The Subjection of Women* (1869), written with stepdaughter Helen Taylor, argued that male dominance was an abuse of power. The authors believed female inequality violated the principle of individual rights and hindered human progress. Two years earlier, Mill, as a member of Parliament, had proposed that women should have the right to vote. His proposal was defeated, and it would be another fifty years before women in most Western nations acquired the right of suffrage.

The Subjection of Women

John Stuart Mill

The object of this Essay is to explain ... that the principle which regulates the existing social relations between the two sexes—the legal subordination of one sex to the other—is wrong in itself, and is now one of the chief hindrances to human improvement; and that it ought to be replaced by a principle of perfect equality, admitting no power or privilege on the one side, nor disability on the other.

In the first place, the opinion in favour of the present system, which entirely subordinates the weaker sex to the stronger, rests upon theory only; for there never has been trial made of any other: so that experience ... cannot be pretended to have pronounced any verdict. And in the second place, ... this system of inequality never was the result of deliberation ... , or any notion whatever of ... the benefit of humanity or the good order of society. It arose simply from the fact that from the very earliest twilight of human society, every woman (owing to the value attached to her by men, combined with her inferiority in muscular strength) was found in a state of bondage to some man.

But, it will be said, the rule of men over women ... is accepted voluntarily; women make no complaint, and are consenting parties to it. In the first place, a great number of women do not accept it.... [A]n increasing number of them have recorded protests against their present social condition: and ... have petitioned Parliament for their ... parliamentary suffrage [vote]. The claim of women to be educated as solidly ... as men, is urged with growing intensity; ... while the demand for their admission into professions and occupations ... closed against them becomes every year more urgent....

All causes ... make it unlikely that women should be collectively rebellious to the power of men. They are so far in a position different from all other subject classes, that their masters require something more from them than actual service ... , not a forced slave but a willing one.... The masters of women wanted more than simple obedience, and they turned the whole force of education to effect their purpose. All women are brought up from the very earliest years in the belief that their ideal of character is the very opposite to that of men; not self-will, and government by self-control, but submission, and yielding to the control of others. All the moralities tell them that it is the duty of women, and ... that it is their nature, to live for others; ... and to have no life but in their affections.... When we put together three things—first, the natural attraction between opposite sexes; secondly, the wife's entire dependence on the husband ... and lastly, that ... all objects of social ambition, can in general be sought or obtained by her only through him—it would be a miracle if the object of being attractive to men had not become the polar star of feminine education and formation of character.

[John Stuart Mill, *The Subjection of Women*. Suffolk: Richard Clay, Ltd., 1869, chap. 1 and 3. In *History of Ideas on Women*, by Rosemary Agonito. New York: G.P. Putnam's Sons, 1977, 225.]

Sylvia Pankhurst after her release from prison in 1921. Pankhurst along with her mother and sister formed a militant suffragette movement in England. The fight to gain the right to vote sometimes resulted in women going to prison.

IDEAS AND ISSUES

Understand Concepts

1. Make a comparison chart of the most important ideas of Wollstonecraft, Sandford, and Mill. Select the most important ideas relating to the social position of women, the causes of that position, and what should be done about it.

Apply and Develop

2. Suppose Wollstonecraft, Sandford, or Mill were transported to Canada in the twenty-first century. Determine what they would say about the position of women today.

3. Set up a panel discussion where individuals role-play Locke, Rousseau, Wollstonecraft, and Mill. Each person should explain and support their ideas of human nature, education, gender roles in society, and human potential.

Think Critically

4. Critically analyze the arguments used by Wollstonecraft, Sandford, and Mill. In your analysis indicate question asked or implied, hypothesis stated or implied, major subtopics, major arguments, evidence used to support arguments, and your reaction to the argument of each.

Inquire and Research

5. In 1879, *A Doll's House*, a play by Norweigan playwright Henrik Ibsen was presented to the public for the first time. At the time, it was regarded as highly controversial because of its championship of women's rights, and its careful analysis of gender and society. Today, *A Doll's House* is a classic. If possible, read the play. What views of human nature and social roles does it present? Write a review of this work. What relevance does *A Doll's House* have to our world today? Explain your reasoning.

6. Find out about the efforts of the Suffragists of the early years of this century. Identify their goals, and the methods they used to attain them.

Twentieth Century Feminism

By the early twentieth century, the world was undergoing significant changes that would eventually revolutionize the way men and women would live their lives. In many parts of Africa, India, and China, contact with the West, often through colonialism, was shaking traditional ways of doing things. New ideas, new products, and new influences and powers often brought questions about how life should be lived. For much of the history of these countries, traditional ways had governed the roles of men and women. These roles varied from place to place, and so it is difficult to generalize. In many cases, men and women had worked side by side in fields and in other hard physical labour. In other cases, roles were separated according to gender. There were cases where women ruled, often in hereditary monarchies. During the early years of the twentieth century, for example, Empress Dowager ruled in China, although this was only until the young emperor was to take over.

In some parts of the world, women such as Empress Dowager of China had positions of power.

Factors that Led to Different Female Gender Roles

In Western nations, several historical forces were leading to dramatic changes in the lives of men and women. The eighteenth-century Enlightenment led to the view that liberty and equality were essential human rights, at least for men. It was logical, as Mary Wollstonecraft and John Stuart Mill pointed out, that such rights should be extended to women. The Industrial Revolution had a powerful impact on gender roles. For one thing, it made it possible for both men and women to work in factories and businesses, although less from choice than necessity. It also provided access to material products and wealth for increasing parts of the population. In Canada and in other Western nations, public education enabled most people to become literate. By the early twentieth century, conditions were ready for changes in the roles of men and women.

There had been a strong movement in the late nineteenth and early twentieth centuries to gain equal political rights for women, a movement called the suffrage movement to gain voting rights for women.

During World War I (1914–1918), mass warfare involving whole populations, including women, brought about great changes. Women worked at all types of jobs, such as in munitions factories and as military nurses, demonstrating that they could handle a wide range of occupations. In most Western nations, they acquired political rights to vote and hold office during the postwar years.

During the 1920s, a social revolution occurred in Canada and the rest of the Western world. Some say this revolution in morals and manners was a reaction to the horrors of war. Others point to such technological and communications innovations as radio and movies as important factors in spreading "modern" ideas faster. The result was that young people embraced new ways of thinking, acting, and speaking, rejecting traditional attitudes in many cases. Many young women began to go out without chaperones, dressing in new fashions, smoking cigarettes, and asserting their independence.

Change took different forms in other parts of the world. In the former Soviet Union, starting from the 1920s under the Communist regime of Stalin, women took part in many non-traditional occupations, such as medicine, law, and other professions, as well as in factory work. In this case, the rapid development of industrialism and political leadership that favoured everyone working outside the home contributed to this.

In Canada and much of the rest of the Western world, during the 1920s and 1930s, women increasingly took part in the world of work, and in a variety of professions (such as teaching and nursing) and as office and clerical workers, among other occupations. Yet men and women still maintained separate social roles. Women were expected, generally, to work for a while before they married, then stay home to raise children after marriage. Most women still received less education, were trained for lower paying jobs, and were paid less than men for the same work.

> Let me listen to me and not to them.
> *Gertrude Stein*

> Learning to cherish and emphasize feminine values is the primary condition of our holding our own against the masculine principle….
> *Emma Jung*

The All-American Girls Baseball League was established in 1943 in response to the lack of available male players. Once the war was over, though, fans returned to men's baseball. The AAGBL was formerly abolished in 1954, when professional baseball banned women from the sport.

World War II (1939–1945) came along to change conditions throughout the world. This was truly a world war involving every part of the globe. Men and women everywhere felt its impact, and took part in military efforts and in industrial production. New ideas were spread via radio, and after the war, through television. A new generation grew up after the war aware of efforts to bring about social change wherever this was happening. Social changes in gender roles and in other areas of life increased their pace during the mid- and later twentieth century, rapidly in Canada and other industrialized nations, but significantly everywhere else.

Two mid-twentieth century intellectuals, Simone de Beauvoir and Betty Friedan were important feminist writers, pushing for understanding of the issues. They presented their analyses of social conditions of their time, and suggested solutions to the problems they saw. De Beauvoir argued that, despite the fact that the world was changing, women were still prevented from becoming independent individuals or from assuming their rightful place as the equals of men. Because of women's failure to escape the psychological trap of secondary status, she maintained they lack confidence and creativity in their work. Although de Beauvoir was addressing conditions in Western nations during the middle of the twentieth century, it is interesting to ask whether her observations and analyses are still valid for our current time.

Today, many women still work in traditionally feminine — pink collar — occupations, despite the inroads made by feminists. What kinds of jobs do you consider suitable for women only?

Simone de Beauvoir

An Existentialist View of Feminism

Time Line

Feminist Movements

SIMONE DE BEAUVOIR
(1908–1986)
writes about feminism

BETTY FRIEDAN
(1921–)
presents issues around women in relationships with men

SOCIAL RIGHTS AND EQUALITY MOVEMENTS
(1960s)
confront old attitudes regarding gender and race

SECOND WAVE FEMINISM
(1970s)
begins

Simone de Beauvoir (1908–1986) was one of the first major feminist writers of the mid-twentieth century. Existentialist philosopher, novelist, and essayist, de Beauvoir was also the lifelong companion of Existentialist philosopher Jean-Paul Sartre. Each partner strongly influenced the ideas of the other.

De Beauvoir's most famous book was *The Second Sex* (1949), which described the role of women in traditional society in which most women married, depended on men for their livelihood, and were tied to home and children. Only a minority of women led independent lives.

In *The Second Sex*, de Beauvoir took the

Simone de Beauvoir was an influential feminist during the twentieth century.

Existentialist view that we are all free and must accept responsibility for this freedom. As time went on, however, de Beauvoir changed her view, recognizing society as a powerful force that helps shape who we are. De Beauvoir sought to reach a compromise in her writings arguing that people often find it difficult to move beyond, or transcend, their environment.

Throughout her life, de Beauvoir took strong critical stands not only on feminism, but on war, aggression, and other issues. Later in life, she wrote *Old Age,* in which she blamed poverty and exploitation for worsening the conditions of the elderly.

The Second Sex

Simone de Beauvoir

… Woman has always been man's dependant, if not his slave; the two sexes have never shared the world in equality. And even today woman is heavily handicapped, though her situation is beginning to change. Almost nowhere is her legal status the same as man's, and frequently it is much to her disadvantage. Even when her rights are legally recognized in the abstract, long-standing custom prevents their full expression…. In the economic sphere men and women can almost be said to make up two castes; … the former hold the better jobs, get higher wages, and have more opportunity for success than their new competitors. In industry and politics men have a great many more positions and they monopolize the most important posts. In addition to all this, they enjoy a traditional prestige that the education of children tends in every way to support…. [I]t is still a world that belongs to men….

Marriage is the destiny traditionally offered to women by society. It is still true that most women are married, or have been, or plan to be, or suffer from not being…. Marriage has always been a very different thing for man and for woman. The two sexes are necessary to each other, but this necessity has never brought about a condition of reciprocity … making exchanges and contracts with the male caste upon a footing of equality. A man is socially an independent and complete individual; he is regarded first of all as a producer whose existence is justified by the work he does for the group…. [T]he reproductive and domestic role to which woman is confined has not guaranteed her an equal dignity…. The young girl's freedom of choice has always been much restricted; … marriage is her only means of support and the sole justification of her existence. It is enjoined upon her for two reasons.

The first reason is that she must provide the society with children…. [T]he second reason why marriage is enjoined is that woman's function is also to satisfy a male's sexual needs and to take care of his household. These duties … are regarded as a service rendered to her spouse: in return he is supposed to give her presents, or a marriage settlement, and to support her….

Thus for both parties marriage is at the same time a burden and a benefit; but there is no symmetry in the situations of the two sexes; for girls marriage is the only means of integration in the community….

It must be said that the independent woman is justifiably disturbed by the idea that people do not have confidence in her…. Most women, in particular, steeped in adoration for man, eagerly seek him out in the person of the doctor, the lawyer, the office manager, and so on. Neither men nor women like to be under a woman's orders….

Woman must constantly win the confidence that is not at first accorded her: at the start she is suspect, she has to prove herself....

[Simone de Beauvoir, *The Second Sex*. Trans. and ed. by H.M. Parshley. New York: Alfred A. Knopf, Inc. & Jonathon Cape Ltd., 1952.]

According to de Beauvoir, the professional and domestic choices available to women during the 1950s were greatly restricted. Apart from a few jobs such as nursing and teaching, most employment opportunities were closed to women.

Betty Friedan:

The "Problem With No Name"

Betty Friedan (1921–) was a leading thinker in the feminist movement during the 1960s. After graduating from college with a psychology degree, she married in 1947 and became a housewife and mother of three children.

During the period immediately following World War II, the roles of men and women in Western societies became more traditional and stereotypical, as great emphasis was placed on marriage and family. Women were encouraged to leave the work they had done during the war and assume the role of homemaker. Men were expected to be the breadwinners.

Friedan examined her own experiences, in addition to interviewing other women of her generation. She sensed that many women felt restricted in their life choices, especially because of social

Although Betty Friedan focussed her attention on issues that affected women like her, her ideas were important in challenging the social roles and expectations of women in general.

pressures that forced them to give up careers in favour of becoming wives and homemakers. Friedan called these feelings of female dissatisfaction the "problem with no name." Critics attacked Friedan because they felt her concerns focussed on what was really a relatively privileged social group—well-educated, middle class women. Friedan's work, however, did reflect a reality of the times, pinpointing some of its problems.

In 1963, Betty Friedan published *The Feminine Mystique*, a best-seller that coincided with the emerging feminist movement. Ideas of social change were widespread in society and feminist ideas were reaching a larger audience than ever before. Increasingly, young women were searching for changes in the roles portrayed by both sexes.

In 1966, Friedan founded and became president of the National Organization for Women (NOW), the largest of the feminist organizations. She continued to be a leader in the movement as its goals and methods changed in the later twentieth century.

The Feminine Mystique

Betty Friedan

I discovered a strange thing, interviewing women of my own generation over the past ten years. When we were growing up, many of us could not see ourselves beyond the age of twenty-one. We had no image of our own future, of ourselves as women.

I remember the stillness of a spring afternoon ... in 1942 when I came to a frightening dead end in my own vision of the future.... I had received a notice that I had won a graduate fellowship. During the congratulations, underneath my excitement, I felt a strange uneasiness .... "Is this really what I want to be?" ... I lived in a terror of indecision for days, unable to think of anything else.

The question was not important, I told myself. No question was important to me that year but love. We walked in the Berkeley hills and a boy said: "Nothing can come of this, between us. I'll never win a fellowship like yours." Did I think I would be choosing, irrevocably, the cold loneliness of that afternoon if I went on? I gave up the fellowship, in relief. But for years afterward, I could not read a word of the science that once I had thought of as my future life's work; the reminder of its loss was too painful.

I never could explain, hardly knew myself, why I gave up this career. I lived in the present, working on newspapers with no particular plan. I married, had children, lived according to the feminine mystique as a suburban housewife. But still the question haunted me. I could sense no purpose in my life, I could find no peace, until I finally faced it and worked out my own answer....

The feminine mystique permits, even encourages, women to ignore the question of their identity. The mystique says they can answer the question "Who am I?" by saying "Tom's wife ... Mary's mother." But I don't think the mystique would have such power over American women if they did not fear to face this terrifying blank which makes them unable to see themselves after twenty-one. The truth is ... an American woman no longer has a private image to tell her who she is, or can be, or wants to be.

The public image, in the magazines and television commercials, is designed to sell washing machines, cake mixes, deodorants, detergents, rejuvenating face creams, hair tints. But the power of that image ... comes from this: American women no longer know who they are. They are sorely in need of a new image to help them find their identity....

A ... college junior from South Carolina told me: "I don't want to be interested in a career I'll have to give up. My mother wanted to be a newspaper reporter from the time she was twelve, and I've seen her frustration for twenty years.... Maybe education is a liability. Even the brightest boys at home want just a sweet, pretty girl. Only sometimes I wonder how it would feel to ... learn all you want, and not have to hold yourself back...."

The strange, terrifying jumping-off point that American women reach—at eighteen, twenty-one, twenty-five, forty-one ... has been blamed on the education which made American girls grow up feeling free and equal to boys—playing baseball, ... going away to college, going out in the world to get a job, ... testing and discovering their own powers in the world. All this gave girls the feeling they could be and do whatever they wanted to.... It did not prepare them for their role as women. The crisis comes when they are forced to adjust to this role....

It is my thesis that the core of the problem for women today is ... a problem of identity—a stunting or evasion of growth that is perpetuated by the feminine mystique.... [O]ur culture does not permit women to accept or gratify their basic need to grow and fulfil their potentialities as human beings.... The expectations of feminine fulfillment that are fed to women by magazines, television, movies, and books, ... and by parents, teachers and counselors ... [are] keeping most women ... from achieving the maturity of which they are capable....

More and more women are asking themselves ... "Where am I ... what am I doing here?" For the first time in their history, women are becoming aware of an identity crisis ... which ... will not end until they ... make of ... their lives the new image that so many women ... need.... I think this is the crisis of women growing ... from an immaturity that has been called femininity to full human identity. I think women had to suffer this crisis of identity ... simply to become fully human.

[Betty Friedan, "The Crisis in Woman's Identity." In *The Feminine Mystique,* by Betty Friedan. New York: W.W. Norton & Co., Inc., 1963.]

Betty Friedan felt that education made women aware of the restrictions society put on them. In some parts of the world, however, women have been denied this education. How can social change occur if women are denied this basic right?

IDEAS AND ISSUES

Understand Concepts

1. (a) What social disadvantages did de Beauvoir say women face?
   (b) What is the impact of these social disadvantages on women?
2. Summarize the problem identified by Friedan in the excerpt.
3. (a) What is meant by "the feminine mystique?"
   (b) What needs to be done about it, according to Friedan?

Apply and Develop

4. From the statements below, choose those that accurately describe social conditions in Canada today.
   (a) The working world is one of equal opportunity for both men and women.
   (b) Women are prevented from achieving the highest positions in the corporate world.
   (c) Women, rather than men, most often take time from work to look after young children.
   (d) Men and women generally take on different responsibilities in the family.
   (e) Women who go out to work continue to look after most household responsibilities.
5. Using an interview or questionnaire, identify the future plans held by the young men and women in your school. Are there significant differences between the sexes? Does this indicate the continued existence of Friedan's "feminine mystique"?

Think Critically

6. (a) To what degree, if at all, do you agree with de Beauvoir?
   (b) Do you think conditions have changed significantly since she wrote her book?
7. Do you think the problem Friedan identified in the 1960s still exists? Provide reasons for your answer.

Inquire and Research

8. Find out about the social revolution that occurred in the position of women during the 1920s. What changes took place in attitude and behaviour, and what were the causes of these changes?
9. Research the roles of Canadian women during both World Wars. What types of work did they do, and how did their expected roles change after each war?
10. Find out about the roles of Canadian men and women during the 1950s. Use old advertisements as one source, and several Canadian social histories as another source. What were the expected roles for men and women? What do you think brought these about?
11. Read and report on Betty Friedan's *The Feminine Mystique*. Outline the concerns she pointed out, and the solutions she suggested.

Second Wave Feminism

The emerging feminist movement which began during the early 1970s is called the "Second Wave" to distinguish it from the efforts of feminists during the earlier years of the twentieth century. Second wave feminism tackles the issues and concerns of importance to men and women at the end of the old millennium and on into today's world.

The "second wave" of feminism has practical problems with which to deal. While women have gained political rights they are not well represented in government. Most women work outside the home but are paid less than men and are restricted to job ghettos. The "glass ceiling" prevents competent women from being promoted. Women work outside the home, but are primarily responsible for the home and children. Home responsibilities often reveal inequities.

Second wave feminists use a number of philosophic ideas to analyze feminist issues. They use political theories to understand power relationships and to consider ways to bring about change. They also use psychological theories to discuss relations within the family, how children are socialized into gender roles, and why people accept or resist change.

Different Types of Second Wave Feminism

The second wave of feminists emerges from a variety of political positions, liberal, socialist, and radical. Each of these positions has an impact on the way different women view the problems of inequality and what can be done to rectify it.

Liberal feminists in the tradition of Mary Wollstonecraft and Betty Friedan seek equal rights and opportunities for women. They base their efforts on the view that the position of women can be improved through education, equal opportunity laws, and improved social facilities such as day-care.

Socialist feminists believe that sexism reflects fundamental values and institutions of the society, and is a way to exploit women economically. They point out that conditions of working-class women have been ignored

Have women gained equal rights and opportunities in the workplace today?

in most analyses. Socialist feminists argue that fundamental social and economic changes are required to improve the position of women.

Radical feminism sees the source of women's oppression in the nature of gender relations. They say that physical strength and male social power, or patriarchy, are at the source of sexism. They believe it is necessary for women to organize politically to gain their share of social power.

Work and Family

During the last three decades, women have increasingly entered the work force outside the home. In 1951 only twenty-four percent of Canadian women were part of the paid labour force. By 1990 the percentage had increased to fifty-nine percent. The percentage of working women today is almost equal to that of working men. A social revolution has occurred.

At the same time, families continue to be raised, children cared for, and homes looked after. Sometimes these tasks are shared with a partner; sometimes they are done by a single parent. While some people may look back fondly on past times when mothers stayed at home and fathers went out to work, this division of roles does not appear to be practical in today's economic climate, as many women must earn money to survive.

One commentator, Danielle Crittenden, author of *What Our Mothers Didn't Tell Us*, argues that women should stay home while the children are young. She believes working full time has negative consequences for the family, especially for children. She wonders why society cannot return to earlier times when women stayed home to look after the house and children.

Crittenden's critics and most women who work say that this point of view is unrealistic. Women have always worked outside the home, unless they had the economic luxury of not having to do so. Most women work today, these critics say, because they must in these new economic times. Making working mother's feel guilty about their work helps no one.

Statistics indicate that Canadians have mixed feelings about the issue. In a 1997 survey, Statistics Canada reported that most Canadians, seventy-three percent of women and sixty-eight percent of men, believe women should contribute to family income. On the other hand, slightly over half, fifty-one percent of women and fifty-nine percent of men, are concerned that two-career families may cause harm to preschool children.

The fact is that our economy today is based on most people, both men and women, working outside the home for most of their lives. Business and industry are constantly exploring new methods of increasing productivity, often providing flexible work hours, extended maternity leaves, and child-care provisions to accommodate the increasing number of parents in the work force. In addition, parents are finding ways to handle the pressures of work and home, through part-time employment, shift work, and other means.

These practical problems and their solutions are based on practical concerns, but discussion and debate about these concerns is often based on philosophic beliefs about the nature of men and women and the social roles each should play. Do women have a greater obligation than men to stay home with children? Is it essential for children to have a mother or a father at home with

To me feminism is not simply a struggle to end male chauvinism or a movement to ensure that women will have equal rights with men; it is a commitment to eradicating the ideology of domination that permeates Western culture on various levels—sex, race, and class, to name a few....

bell hooks

... [M]en are very important to women; they want them at the center of their lives; they want to be sure they're at the center of their lives. But women are not at the center of men's lives.... [M]en want their relationships with women to be controllable; they want them in a compartment that they can visit at will. And women don't have that same feeling. They want ... to share somebody else's life....

Germaine Greer

them for an extended period of time? What types of life should women or men enjoy in the social world? How should society, and its social institutions help parents care for children through better day-care and improved working conditions?

Social and Racial Concerns in the Feminist Movement

Second wave feminism focusses its attention on the concerns of a wider range of women than had often been considered in the past. Early and mid-twentieth century writers, such as Virginia Woolf and Betty Friedan, were writing largely about the desire of middle class women for equal rights and career opportunities. Second wave feminism deals with the fact that women occupy a range of social situations; some women are economically well-off while others are hard-working but poor. One criticism made of earlier feminists was that they ignored working class women and the poor while focussing on problems faced by middle-class women.

Starting from the 1970s, second wave feminists increasingly have been dealing with the problems faced by poor working women and minority women. Feminist philosophers, such as Germaine Greer, Rosemary Radford Ruether, Sister Prudence Allen, Maryann Ayim, Barbara Houston, Gloria Steinem, and Kathryn Pauly Morgan, have written extensively on how the problems faced by many women are not only the result of their gender, but are related to their social class and ethnic identity as well. In other words, problems of work and of economic survival are made worse because of sexism, classism, and racism.

PHILOSOPHERS' FORUM

New Woman, New Earth

Rosemary Radford Ruether

… [W]omen must become more critical about their own class and racial contexts. Women are not a class or a race. Models of liberation drawn from Marxism or racial liberation are misleading when applied to women. Women must find an analysis of their social condition which is appropriate. Women are sociologically a sexual caste within every class and race. All women share certain common oppressions as women: dependency, secondary existence, domestic labour, sexual exploitation, and the structuring of their role in procreation into a total definition of their existence. There is, in this sense, a common condition of women in general. But women are also divided against each other by their integration into oppressor and oppressed classes and races.

[Rosemary Radford Ruether, *New Woman, New Earth*. Boston: Beacon Press, 1995.]

American writer bell hooks says that the problem faced by most working and poor women is not primarily how to gain and be successful in a career, or whether to work part time or not at all. These are not options for most women. The problem faced by most women is lack of choices and lack of social power. As a result, problems of job discrimination and lack of opportunities are immensely important.

Re-Shaping Feminist Theory

bell hooks

Feminism in the United States has never emerged from the women who are most victimized by sexist oppression; women who are daily beaten down, mentally, physically, and spiritually—women who are powerless to change their condition in life. They are a silent majority. A mark of their victimization is that they accept their lot in life without visible question, without organized protest, without collective anger or rage. Betty Friedan's *The Feminine Mystique* is still heralded as having paved the way for the contemporary feminist movement—it was written as if these women did not exist. Friedan's famous phrase, "the problem that has no name," often quoted to describe the condition of women in this society, actually referred to the plight of a select group of college-educated, middle and upper class, married white women—housewives bored with leisure, with the home, with children, with buying products, who wanted more out of life…. That "more" she defined as careers. She did not discuss who would be called in to take care of the children and maintain the home if more women like herself were freed from their house labor and given equal access with white men to the professions. She did not speak of the needs of women without men, without children, without homes. She ignored the existence of all non-white women and poor white women….

… Friedan never wondered whether or not the plight of college-educated, white housewives was an adequate reference point by which to gauge the impact of … sexist oppression on the lives of women…. I say this not to discredit her work. It remains a useful discussion of the impact of sexist discrimination on a select group of women….

Friedan was a principal shaper of contemporary feminist thought. Significantly, the one-dimensional perspective on women's reality presented in her book became a marked feature of the contemporary feminist movement. Like Friedan before them, white women who dominate feminist discourse today rarely question whether or not their perspective on women's reality is true to the lived experiences of women as a collective group. Nor are they aware of the extent to which their perspectives reflect race and class biases, although there has been a greater awareness of biases in recent years….

Privileged feminists have largely been unable to speak to, with, and for diverse groups of women because they either do not understand fully the interrelatedness of sex, race, and class oppression or refuse to take this … seriously.

Black women … often have a lived experience that directly challenges the prevailing classist, sexist, racist social structures…. It is essential for continued feminist struggle that [B]lack women recognize the special vantage point our marginality gives us and make use of this perspective to criticize the dominant racist, classist, sexist hegemony [dominant influence over another]…. I am suggesting that we have a central role to play in the making of feminist theory and a contribution to offer that is unique and valuable…. Though I criticize aspects of the feminist movement as we have known it so far, a critique which is sometimes harsh and unrelenting, I do so not in an attempt to diminish a feminist struggle but to enrich, to share in the work of making a liberatory ideology and a liberatory movement.

[bell hooks, "Black Women: Shaping Feminist Theory." In *Yearning*, by bell hooks. Boston: South End Press, 1990.]

Angela Davis was dismissed from her post as a philosophy professor at the University of California in 1969 because she was heavily active in the civil rights and feminist movements.

Feminism and Immigrant Women

Bell hooks writes about the American social reality. Her work and that of others in the second wave of feminism have broadened the scope of feminism. Do her analyses and theories have relevance for Canadians? Do Canadian feminists think in similar terms?

Roxana Ng writes about race and gender

relations, and feminist thought and teaching. Ng teaches feminist studies and sociology at the Ontario Institute for Studies in Education in Toronto. She has discussed the position of Canadian immigrant women. In some ways her concerns apply the ideas described by bell hooks in the previous excerpt. Ng also shows that philosophy has its roots in the real-life concerns of real people. Philosophy analyzes the underlying nature of social concerns, such as feminism, and can point the way to dealing with these concerns in practical ways.

Racism, Sexism and Immigrant Women

Roxana Ng

Immigrant women have always been part of the Canadian historical landscape. The contributions of pioneer gentlewomen such as Catharine Parr Traill and Susanna Moodie are well known. Less visible is the fact that ... working-class women from Britain were recruited into Canada in the early days of settlement as wives and domestic workers.... Later, as a result of the postwar boom and the relaxation of immigration policy, many non-white immigrants came to Canada. While immigrant men integrate relatively quickly into Canadian society through their paid work, many immigrant women, especially if they do not speak English, become marginal members of society. Together with Native women they became the most disadvantaged and invisible group in our society....

Specifically, I argue that sexism and racism ... underpin many immigrant women's and domestic workers' experiences in Canada.... [W]hen I use the terms I am referring to the system of oppression and inequality based on the ideology of the superiority of one gender and/or race over the other.... In the lives of immigrant women we see how this system of oppression produces the specific experiences they have in Canada....

The official view of the immigrant family, according to immigration procedures, is that of one "independent" member upon whom others depend for their sponsorship, livelihood, and welfare. Thus the immigration process systematically structures sexual inequality within the family by rendering one spouse (usually the wife) legally dependent on the other....

Once she is classified as a dependent immigrant, a whole series of consequences follow, placing a woman in a progressively disadvantaged position.... In general, family-class immigrants are ineligible for most forms of state assistance during the five- to ten-year sponsorship period. They cannot obtain family benefits, welfare, and other benefits unless there is a break in the sponsorship....

The story of Maria, a fifty-nine-year-old semi-retired worker, epitomizes the experience of many non-English-speaking immigrant women in the "captive labour force." Maria came to Canada in 1955 with her husband and five children.... They were sponsored as immigrants to Canada by Maria's brother, and Maria held a variety of jobs after arriving. Two days after the family arrived in Toronto, she got a job in a restaurant washing dishes. For ten years, Maria's daily routine went something like this:

She started her day cleaning people's houses at 8 a.m. and worked until 4 p.m. At 4 she went to work at the restaurant until 1 a.m…. On the weekend she did house-work with the help of her eldest daughter, who was responsible for looking after the younger children. She also did the shopping and banking on weekends.

Maria did stay home for a couple of years after the birth of her sixth child. Then she went back to work because the family needed the money. At one time she got a job cleaning in a bank, and she would go to work between 4 and 8 in the morning, before the bank employees arrived. She got home just in time for her oldest daughter to leave for school. She stayed home during the day looking after the baby and went around cleaning houses and offices again at night. Maria is proud that she now has a nice house and that her children all had a good education. At the time of the interview she was still working as a cleaner in a textile factory. "Now," said Maria contentedly, "I go to work because I enjoy it. When I am tired, I go home."

Maria's experience reveals that … non-English-speaking immigrant women … are dependent upon good personal relationships with employers or supervisors. As individual workers, they have few rights. The wages they earn are inadequate to maintain them-selves and their families. As workers they are completely unprotected and vulnerable to exploitation.

Occasionally in the garment industry, if a woman shows initiative, works hard, and learns a bit of English quickly, she may become an assistant to the supervisor. But most often women are confined to operating sewing machines. The more prestigious positions, such as garment-cutting and supervisory positions, are usually occupied by men, and women are rarely promoted to them…. [I]mmigrant women are confined to the bottom layers of the labour force, with the worst working conditions and wages….

Within the feminist movement, immigrant women, together with women of colour, have begun to … draw attention to the fact that the demands of the feminist movement are defined according to white middle-class women's perspectives…. [T]he emphasis on women working outside the home, one of the major efforts of the feminist movement in the 1960s and 1970s, stemmed largely from the concerns of middle-class women who had the privilege to be full-time homemakers. Immigrant and [B]lack women have always worked outside the home…. [T]heories about women's oppression, based mainly on the experiences and perspectives of white women, are being challenged by immigrant women, women of colour, and Third World women….

[Roxana Ng, "Racism, Sexism and Immigrant Women." In *Changing Patterns: Women in Canada*, 2nd ed., ed. by Sandra Burt, Lorraine Code, and Lindsay Dorney. Toronto: McClelland & Stewart, 1993.]

Understand Concepts

1. (a) What is meant by second wave feminism?
   (b) Why is it called a "second wave," what goals does it have, and what are the branches of ideas within this second wave?
2. (a) What criticism does bell hooks make of liberal feminism?
   (b) Describe what she suggests in its place.
3. Summarize the experience of Maria in the excerpt by Roxana Ng.

Apply and Develop

4. Interview several parents, both male and female. Ask them for their opinions on the issues discussed in the excerpts in this section.

Think Critically

5. What branch of second wave feminism does bell hooks appear to be part of? Give reasons for your answer.
6. In what ways, if at all, are the experiences of Maria and other immigrant women caused by sexism and racism? Defend your position.

Communicate Ideas

7. Interview working women that you know. Ask them about their work and domestic lives. Prepare questions ahead of time. What are their major concerns at work and at home? Do they fit within the ideas presented in the excerpts of this section?

Inquire and Research

8. Research the early years of the "second wave" of feminism—also called the Women's Liberation Movement. Authors such as Gloria Steinem and Shulameth Firestone in the United States, and Doris Anderson in Canada are good ones to start with. What were the issues of concern at that time and have they changed since then?

Contemporary Gender Issues

What important gender issues do you believe men and women face today? What problems must either sex deal with in their relations with each other and as members of society? What solutions would you propose to these issues and problems?

Feminist theory and philosophy of the early twentieth century dealt with such important concerns as the legal and political rights of women, access to equal education, and greater occupational opportunities. In most Western nations, a new generation had come of age by the late 1960s. These men and women, born after World War II, explored and developed new ideas about themselves and society. This new generation demanded and struggled for new lifestyles, new attitudes, and new solutions to old problems.

The Men's Movement: Men Seeking New Identities

How do men view their gender roles and who they are? It is fair to say that, like women, there is no one view of what it means to be a man. Ideas of what it means to be male in the twenty-first century range widely, from highly traditional to emerging views. On the one hand, there are those who hold that men and women are quite different by nature, and therefore should have distinct social roles. On the other hand, there are those who believe, and live in a way that accepts that men and women have a variety of natures that overlap extensively and significantly. From such points of view, it is acceptable and worthwhile to have men and women perform a full range of activities according to their nature and interests.

Social and economic conditions play an important role in shaping our views of women and men. During the late twentieth century, in Canada as in other post-industrial nations, jobs and careers were increasingly created that could be done by both men and women. The nature of the skills required in the working world were becoming less dependent on heavy physical activity. Careers in the service industries, in offices, and in the emerging information and communications industries became available. Moreover, for a number of reasons, it became increasingly essential for both men and women to remain in the work force in order to acquire the standard of living that

was considered adequate. Today, the percentage of both men and women in the work force is about the same, close to seventy percent. Such changes in the working world have had an impact on the roles of men and women in their families and personal lives as well. Men are increasingly participating in domestic duties and active parenting, realms that have been associated with women's roles for a long time.

A great deal of recent literature and philosophy about the role of men and about male self-perception has focussed on the need for men to acquire a new definition of themselves. The traditional roles and self-perceptions seem out of place in the new social order. In most cultures, men have traditionally been raised to be highly competitive, and often aggressive—the "Rambo" image. While this might have been more appropriate when humans were hunter-gatherers, such characteristics have led to numerous social problems throughout human history. In our modern world, high rates of crime and violence, feelings of isolation, and parenting concerns among divorced fathers are some of the issues that men of all age groups have been facing.

Current literature in the area of gender definition discusses the psychological limitations that traditional male roles have placed on men. Men, like women, have been forced to ignore or reject parts of their personalities that do not conform to the stereotypical male role; the nurturing or compassionate parts of their personalities have traditionally been associated with female gender roles. Many men are finding it easier in the modern world to allow these parts of their personalities to emerge. Less often is the stereotype of the absent or rigid father a part of contemporary culture.

What the "new man" of the twenty-first century will be is still an open question. There is no doubt that it will be different from the past. Men and women are both searching for their identities as their old gender roles are being cast aside.

> Men, even more than women, are fettered to gender roles. Women at least have had the guts to break out of bondage. Only gay men have had the courage to expose themselves to the woman inside them and to challenge the current masculinity.
>
> *Gloria Anzaldúa*

The Effect of the Media on Sex Roles

Second wave feminism analyzes the attitudes and belief systems of men and women. It asks what these attitudes and beliefs are and tries to determine from where we get them. For example, how do you define what is male and what is female? To what degree does the mass media shape who we think we are?

It is pretty clear that our views of men and women are shaped by socialization and the culture within which we live. A survey of men and women in different cultures and at different historical periods reveals a wide range of images of gender. A look at advertisements and movies over the course of the last hundred years shows varying images of what it means to be a man or woman.

In the following excerpt, writer Naomi Wolf analyzes our image of beauty, specifically female beauty. Where do we get such images? What impact do they have upon us? Why is this important? Her point of view and her theory of beauty adds a great deal to our understanding of ourselves and others. It also provides us with insight into the things that we may take for granted, or do not think consciously about. Fuller understanding of unconscious or subconscious assumptions can be important, as Freud said, and allow us to live fuller lives.

> … [T]he media is still dominated by men, many of whom think of women in a very sexist way. They cover them in a sexist way, and they do *not* cover them because of sexism.
>
> *Gloria Allred*

The Beauty Myth

Naomi Wolf

I hate the beauty business. It is a monster industry selling unattainable dreams. It lies. It cheats. It exploits women. Its major product lines are packaging and garbage. It is no wonder that Elizabeth Arden once said that the cosmetics business was the "nastiest in the world."

*Anita Roddick,
founder of
The Body Shop*

... In the two decades of radical action that followed the rebirth of feminism in the early 1970s, Western women gained legal and reproductive rights, pursued higher education, entered the trades and the professions, and overturned ancient and revered beliefs about their social role. A generation on, do women feel free?

The affluent, educated, liberated women of the First World, who can enjoy freedoms unavailable to any women ever before, do not feel as free as they want to. And they can no longer restrict to the subconscious their sense that this ... has something to do with ... apparently frivolous issues.... Many are ashamed to admit that ... physical appearance, bodies, faces, hair, clothes—matter so much. But ... more women are wondering if ... something important is indeed at stake that has to do with the relationship between female liberation and female beauty....

During the past decade, women breached the power structure; meanwhile, eating disorders rose exponentially and cosmetic surgery became the fastest-growing medical specialty. During the past five years, consumer spending doubled, pornography became the main media category, ... and American women told researchers that they would rather lose ten to fifteen pounds than achieve any other goal. More women have more money and power and scope and legal recognition than we have ever had before; but in terms of how we feel about ourselves physically, we may actually be worse off than our unliberated grandmothers....

It is no accident that so many potentially powerful women feel this way. We are in the midst of a violent backlash against feminism that uses images of female beauty as a political weapon against women's advancement: the beauty myth....

The beauty myth tells a story: The quality called "beauty" objectively and universally exists. Women must want to embody it and men must want to possess women who embody it. This embodiment is an imperative for women and not for men ... because it is biological, sexual, and evolutionary: Strong men battle for beautiful women, and beautiful women are more reproductively successful....

None of this is true. "Beauty" is a currency system.... Like any economy, it is determined by politics, and in the modern age in the West it is the last, best belief system that keeps male dominance intact. In assigning value to women ... according to a culturally imposed physical standard, it is an expression of power relations in which women must unnaturally compete for resources that men have appropriated for themselves.

"Beauty" is not universal or changeless, though the West pretends that all ideals of female beauty stem from one Platonic Ideal Woman.... Nor is "beauty" a function of evolution: Its ideals change at a pace far more rapid than that of the evolution of species....

Anthropology has overturned the notion that females must be "beautiful" to be selected to mate....

Nor has the beauty myth always been this way.... [I]n the matriarchal Goddess religions that dominated the Mediterranean ... to about 700 BCE, the ... pattern is of an older woman with a beautiful but expendable youth.... Among the Nigerian Wodaabes, the women hold economic power and the tribe is obsessed with male beauty; Wodaabe men spend hours together in elaborate makeup sessions, and compete ... in beauty contests judged by women. There is no legitimate historical or biological justification for the beauty myth; what it is doing to women today is a result of ... the need of today's power structure, economy, and culture to mount a counteroffensive against women....

How have our ideas about male and female beauty changed during the last 100 years? Does our society value beauty more in women than in men? Why or why not? How does beauty and image influence "success"?

... Before the Industrial Revolution, the average woman could not have had the same feelings about "beauty" that modern women do.... Before the development of technologies of mass production—daguerreotypes, photographs, etc.—an ordinary woman was exposed to few such images.... Since the family was a productive unit and women's work complemented men's, the value of women ... lay in their work skills, economic shrewdness, physical strength, and fertility. Physical attraction, obviously, played its part; but "beauty" as we understand it was not ... a serious issue in the marriage marketplace.... Most of our assumptions about ... "beauty" date from no earlier than the 1830s....

For the first time new technologies could reproduce ... [on film] images of how women should look.... [A]dvertisements using images of "beautiful" women first appeared in mid-century. Copies of classical artworks, postcards of society beauties ... , Currier and Ives prints, and porcelain figurines flooded the separate sphere to which middle-class women were confined....

... The modern arsenal of the myth is a dissemination of millions of images of the current ideal.... And the unconscious hallucination grows ever more influential.... [P]owerful industries—the $33-billion-a-year diet industry, the $20-billion cosmetics industry, the $300-million cosmetic surgery industry, and the $7-billion pornography industry ... , through their influence on mass culture, ... reinforce the hallucination....

Why does the social order feel the need to defend itself by evading the fact of real women, our faces and voices and bodies, and reducing the meaning of women to these formulaic and endlessly reproduced "beautiful" images?... Western economies are absolutely dependent now on the continued underpayment of women. An ideology that makes women feel "worth less" was urgently needed to counteract the way feminism had begun to make us feel worth more.... It did so to substitute both a new consumer imperative and a new justification for economic unfairness in the workplace....

... The contemporary ravages of the beauty backlash are destroying women physically and depleting us psychologically. If we are to free ourselves from the dead weight that has once again been made out of femaleness, it is not ballots or lobbyists or placards that women will need first; it is a new way to see.

[Naomi Wolf, *The Beauty Myth*. New York: William Morrow & Co., 1991, 9–19.]

Understand Concepts
1. (a) What is meant by the "beauty myth"?
   (b) Why is it a myth?
2. What causes this myth in our society and how is it promoted?
3. What is the social and psychological impact of this myth for both men and women?

Think Critically
4. (a) Where do you get your ideas of physical ideals of women and of men?
   (b) To what degree are these reinforced by the media—movies and advertisements for example?
5. Debate Wolf's thesis. Is it just an interesting hypothesis or is there evidence to support it?
6. (a) Why are men now seeking new gender roles?
   (b) What are some barriers that still face men seeking new male identities?
   (c) How can these barriers be overcome?

Inquire and Research
7. Research the area of abnormal body image—men using steroids to "bulk up" and women suffering from eating disorders. Identify the social and psychological influences that encourage these behaviours. Does the evidence support Wolf's ideas?
8. To what degree do people, especially young people, use media images to shape their personal dress and style? Who are the media personalities at the moment? Use questionnaires to gather information.

Do men and women share a common nature or are there significant differences in their natures? How should we view ourselves and live our lives as men and women in society? Throughout history, philosophers and non-philosophers have differed in their answers to such questions. The debate continues even today.

From ancient to modern times, the discussion focussed on whether biological and cultural differences imply different human natures for men and women. Some arguments suggested that men and women should have distinct and separate social roles; these suggestions were primarily put forward by men. However, some men argued that men and women should share these roles. Over the ages, women began to voice their concerns about rigid gender roles, and their arguments added further to this debate.

During the past century, significant changes took place in our awareness of human rights. Women and men began to rebel against the old gender roles; however, the struggle is far from over. Modern women have achieved a great deal in legal and civic rights, in the working world, and in their personal lives. Philosophers such as Mary Wollstonecraft, John Stuart Mill, Simone de Beauvoir, Betty Friedan, bell hooks, and many others have been leaders in stating the problems and suggesting solutions.

The second wave of feminism that began in the 1970s analyzed contemporary problems and argued for changes in new ways. The people involved in this movement broadened the scope of the discussion to include more women, and analyzed the situation in more critical terms. When the men's movement began, men began to challenge old beliefs about male gender roles. Although there have been many gains in human rights for women, both men and women are still searching for their identities as they cope with the stresses of modern society.

METAPHYSICS AND UNIVERSAL QUESTIONS

Who are we? Where did we come from? What is the reality that appears to exist around us? Is there such a thing as time or space? Does God exist? Do we really possess free will or are events pre-determined? These questions go to the heart of who we are and the nature of the universe, and have been asked throughout history by every culture. We still ask ourselves these questions today—but often during periods of crisis. They are the types of questions dealt with in metaphysics.

Metaphysics is the branch of philosophy that asks questions about the ultimate reality of human existence and the natural world. Throughout the world, Aboriginal cultures developed myths to address these issues. In the ancient world, the pre-Socratic, or natural, philosophers also asked metaphysical questions when they speculated on the ultimate components of the natural world, or whether or not change was possible. These were questions that could not be answered easily. Generally, metaphysics refers to those questions that are, or appear to be, beyond the natural or physical world of observation and that we suspect might be the ultimate basis of reality.

We will begin this unit by examining the question of personal identity: Who are we really as persons? Are we primarily our thoughts, our physical being, or something altogether different? Are we really in control of our actions and our lives? We will then consider the area that deals with several large questions that are universally puzzled over. As philosophers observed aspects of the world around them, they asked such questions as: What is time? What is cause and effect? Finally, we will ask questions about the nature and existence of God, and the problem of evil in this universe.

Many scientists, including noted physicist Stephen Hawking, have put forward various theories about the origin of the universe and ourselves, and the nature of reality. In what ways can science help us answer metaphysical questions?

Personal Identity

Many of us have asked at some time in our lives the questions: Who am I? Am I the body in which I live? Do I exist primarily in my mind and thoughts, or is there some part of my identity beyond these, a spirit or soul?

Statue of Shiva

Philosophers and other thinkers since ancient times have often wondered who the real self is, where it resides, and what happens to us when we die. Plato believed in a soul that was different from the body, and that could connect with the ideas of the universe. Gurus from various religious traditions, such as Hinduism and Buddhism, have suggested that the ego, our sense of self, distorts our view of our own reality making us believe that our identity is primarily our physical body. These philosophies and religions use techniques such as meditation to transcend the ego and discover the true self.

In Western religious philosophies, such as Judaism, Christianity and Islam, there is a strong sense of the body and the soul, the latter of which resides within the body for a time, but which is immortal as well. The idea that there is more to a person than their body was also known by Aboriginal people around the world.

In modern philosophy, the connection between the mind and the body has been widely discussed. Does the self exist primarily in the mind or in the body? And if it exists in one or the other, how does it relate to the other part of our earthly existence? Such questions were raised by Descartes, and his ideas have influenced philosophy ever since.

Despite all our scientific achievements, there is still a lot we do not know and understand about the mind, the body, and the soul. The question about defining our personal identity is very pertinent to our troubled times. Many people in our society suffer from mental illnesses, such as schizophrenia and Alzheimer's disease, and the question of personal identity is much more complicated. Wars continue to be waged based on perceived differences of personal identities. Regardless of where we come from or what we look like, the quest to discover our true self unites us all.

Questions about mind, body, and personal identity have been asked by Eastern and Western thinkers alike.

The Connection Between Mind and Body

Does the real you exist in the thoughts you are thinking at this moment, the memories you have of the past, and the plans for the future? Does the real you exist in your physical body? Or is the real you found in *both* your mind and body? One way to think about this is to ask whether you could continue to be yourself if, for a moment, you did not possess either your mind or your body?

Although each of us has a brain enclosed within a body, our mind is far greater than just a physical brain. The mind contains a never-ending stream of thoughts, past, present, and future. But where exactly is the mind located, and what is the relationship between the mind and body?

There are some philosophers who deny that there is any such thing as a personal identity; they claim that it is an illusion. Often such philosophers accept that we have a momentary sense of ourselves; they deny however, the existence of a personal identity over time. Since humans are changing all the time, they argue, how can we possibly think that who we were as a baby is the same person we are today, and that this idea of ourselves will be the same in twenty years?

The Relationship Between the Mind and Personal Identity

René Descartes viewed the mind and body as being two distinct entities. The mind was a non-material substance, Descartes reasoned, and that was where an individual's real identity resided. Others since have rejected Descartes' view, and insist that the mind is simply the result of material events, as are all other things in this world. How we define mind, body, and the relationship between them will be important in our determination of personal identity.

Developments in the modern world have added to the complexity of determining where personal identity resides. With the advent of complex information technology and artificial intelligence, the possibility of "conscious" thinking machines is more than mere speculation, and may become a reality in the near future. Will such technology possess a personal identity?

In the mid-twentieth century, British mathematician Alan Turing (1912–1954), an early developer of computer science, suggested how this issue might be explored. Turing imagined a complex computer hidden behind a curtain. Then he imagined a person approaching the curtain, without knowing whether a computer or a human being was behind it. The person can only ask questions of the unknown object or person. If, said Turing, the nature of the answers received convinces the questioner that he or she is speaking with a human being, then thinking has occurred.

Not long ago, a world-class chess master, Garry Kasparov, played against Deep Blue, a computer programmed to play chess. Deep Blue won the series. Afterwards, Kasparov declared that there were moments during the competition when he detected an intelligence behind his opponent's moves, which

---

A human being is a part of the whole ... a part limited in time and space. He experiences himself, his thoughts and feelings as something separated from the rest— a kind of optical delusion of consciousness.

Albert Einstein

Mind and spirit together make up that which separates us from the rest of the animal world, that which enables a man to know the truth and that which enables him to die for the truth.

Edith Hamilton

could not be totally explained by a rigid mechanistic programmed response. At times, the computer took chances that were almost human in their intuitive nature. Will computers eventually develop personal identities? Will they possess self-conscious thought processes as humans do? Consider the following hypothetical scenario.

Can a machine be created that possesses self-conscious thought processes? Will it then have a personal identity?

Human Identity, Thoughts, and Bodies

Many people believe it will be possible in the future to transfer all the thoughts, memories, and emotions of a human being to a highly sophisticated computer. What if a man or woman allowed some scientist to transfer his or her mind, with all its contents, to a robot? The robot would assume all of that person's mind and would become fully conscious, once its "on" switch had been activated. Then the scientist, through carelessness, may cause the body of the human donor to die. The scientist would be arrested, charged with manslaughter, and brought to trial. Suppose the defence lawyer claims that there has been no death, because the mind of the human donor now exists within the robot, and the robot agrees. How could the prosecutor rebut the defence? Should the scientist be found guilty of manslaughter, or of bad ethical judgement? What do you think a judge or jury would decide? Explain your reasons.

Descartes' View of the Mind and Body

I want, by understanding myself, to understand others.
Katherine Mansfield

Plato was one of the first philosophers to say that the soul was, in important ways, separate from the body. We must remember that, for Plato, the soul referred to, among other things, the thinking part of a human being. Plato argued that rational thought at its best was not dependent on the senses, perception, or the physical body.

Aristotle rejected Plato's view that ideas and thoughts were separate from matter. Aristotle believed that all things, both form and substance, were firmly situated within the objects themselves, not in some other non-physical place. Experience of the world, largely through the senses, was crucial for Aristotle, who saw a much greater connection between the mind, the body, and the external world than did his teacher.

The issue of the nature of mind and body was subjected to sharp scrutiny again during the seventeenth century. This time, it was René Descartes who provided food for thought with his views of the mind, the body, and their interrelationship. Descartes believed that the mind and the body were composed of two different elements. He suggested that the essence of the mind consists of the fact that it can think, and that it is indivisible and does not extend in space. The essence of the body, he wrote, is that it is extended in space and divisible. Descartes concluded that these two types of substances are essentially different and distinct from one another.

Where did Descartes believe the real person resided? Only thought, he wrote, cannot be separated from the self. As for the body, Descartes believed, it enjoys a unique union with the mind. It is clear that the body and its sensations, thirst and hunger for example, have an impact on the mind. Nevertheless, according to Descartes, the body is a different substance entirely, and does not constitute our true personal identity. Had Plato been privy to Descartes' line of thinking, he probably would have agreed.

There was a difficulty with this separation, one that Descartes himself recognized. It arose as a result of Descartes' conception of two distinct substances, mind and body. If the mental and physical worlds are separate and distinct, how do they interact with each other? How can mind, which is without physical substance and composed of thought alone, have any connection with body, which consists entirely of physical substance? We know through observation that a connection between the two substances does exist. If we wish to raise our arm, lo and behold, our arm goes up. If our body feels hunger, this feeling is transmitted to our mind, which in turn begins to think of food. How does this interaction happen?

Descartes tried to develop a satisfactory explanation of the mind–body interaction, but his hypothesis did not hold up well to scrutiny. Without any real proof, Descartes suggested that the pineal gland, which lies at the base of the brain, somehow was able to connect mind with body and transfer messages from one to the other. This explanation still failed to show how two different forms of substance, mind and body, could interact with each other within this gland.

Descartes' view of the distinct nature of mind and body had a long and powerful impact on philosophers and on the general public. The belief that mind and body were distinct entities with only a partial interaction influenced how many people viewed humankind. Our mental being and our physical being were thought to be co-existing somewhat uneasily in the same structure. Treatment of mental or physical illness was applied to one element or the other, and not holistically to the mind–body as a single unit.

In more recent times, however, Descartes' distinction between mind and body has been increasingly attacked and rejected by philosophers and others. Today, there is significant support for the idea that there is a close connection between mind and body, while some would say that these two form a single identity.

There are other criticisms of Descartes' distinction between mind and body to consider. For example, Descartes went from the realization that because thinking occurred, (*cogito* or "I think,") the resultant conclusion was that he existed, (*ergo sum* or "therefore I am.") Many philosophers have pointed to this conclusion as a fallacy, suggesting that, while Descartes could assert that thinking is going on, he could not support the position that there is, therefore, an "I," or an identity doing the thinking.

Another criticism of Descartes is that he could not explain how a thinking mind experiences interaction with others in the world. Suppose you have an idea—of a beautiful morning, for example—how would you communicate this idea to someone else's mind without using physical means such as speech, gestures, or writing? If we accept Descartes' idea of mind and body as distinct entities, it becomes difficult to understand how a thought can be transferred to a physical substance and then translated back into thought again.

Descartes' idea that our real selves reside in our thoughts, our memories, our images, and our desires seems to make sense if we reflect on it. Yet, as we have seen, there remain some serious problems with the idea of separating the physical body and the physical world in general, so clearly and distinctly from the mind.

Happy the man who freed himself from his "self" and united himself with the Infinite.

Rumi

Meditations of First Philosophy

René Descartes

I do not yet have a sufficient understanding of what this "I" is, that now necessarily exists.... I will therefore go back and meditate on what I originally believed myself to be, before I embarked on this present train of thought. I will then subtract anything capable of being weakened, even minimally, by the arguments now introduced, so that what is left at the end may be exactly and only what is certain and unshakeable.

What then did I formerly think I was? A man. But what is a man? Shall I say "a rational animal"? No; for then I should have to inquire what an animal is, what rationality is, and in this way one question would lead me down the slope to other harder ones.... Instead I propose to concentrate on what came into my thoughts spontaneously and quite naturally whenever I used to consider what I was. Well, the first thought to come to mind was that I had a face, hands, arms and the whole mechanical structure of limbs which can be seen in a corpse, and which I called the body. The next thought was that I was nourished, that I moved about, and that I engaged in sense-perception and thinking; and these actions I attributed to the soul. But as to the nature of this soul, either I did not think about this or else I imagined it to be something tenuous, like a wind or fire or ether, which permeated my more solid parts. As to the body, however, I had no doubts about it, but thought I knew its nature distinctly. If I had tried to describe the mental conception I had of it, I would have expressed it as follows: by a body I understand whatever has a determinable shape and a definable location and can occupy a space in such a way as to exclude any other body; it can be perceived by touch, sight, hearing, taste or smell, and can be moved in various ways, not by itself but by whatever else comes into contact with it....

But what shall I now say that I am, when I am supposing that there is some supremely powerful and, if it is permissible to say so, malicious deceiver, who is deliberately trying to trick me in every way he can? Can I now assert that I possess even the most insignificant of all the attributes which I have just said belong to the nature of a body? I scrutinize them, think about them, go over them again, but nothing suggests itself; it is tiresome and pointless to go through the list once more. But what about the attributes I assigned to the soul? Nutrition or movement? Since now I do not have a body, these are mere fabrications. Sense-perception? This surely does not occur without a body, and besides, when asleep I have appeared to perceive through the senses many things which I afterwards realized I did not perceive through the senses at all. Thinking? At last I have discovered it—thought; this alone is inseparable from me. I am, I exist—that is certain. But for how long? For as long as I am thinking. For it could be that were I totally to cease from thinking, I should totally cease to exist. At present I am not admitting anything except what is necessarily true. I am, then, in the strict sense only a thing that thinks; that is, I am a mind, or intelligence, or intellect, or reason.... But for all that I am a thing which is real and which truly exists. But what kind of a thing? As I have just said—a thinking thing.

What else am I? I will use my imagination. I am not that structure of limbs which is called a human body. I am not even some thin vapour which permeates the limbs—a wind, fire, air, breath, or whatever I depict in my imagination; for these are things which I have supposed to be nothing. Let this supposition stand; for all that I am still something....

But what then am I? A thing that thinks.... A thing that doubts, understands, affirms, denies, is willing, is unwilling, and also imagines and has sensory perceptions....

Thus, simply by knowing that I exist and seeing at the same time that absolutely nothing else belongs to my nature or essence except that I am a thinking thing, I can infer correctly that my essence consists solely in the fact that I am a thinking thing. It is true that I may have ... a body that is very closely joined to me. But nevertheless, on the one hand I have a clear and distinct idea of myself, in so far as I am simply a thinking, non-extended thing; and on the other hand I have a distinct idea of body, in so far as this is simply an extended, non-thinking thing. And accordingly, it is certain that I am really distinct from my body, and can exist without it....

Nature also teaches me, by these sensations of pain, hunger, thirst and so on, that I am not merely present in my body as a sailor is present in a ship, but that I am very closely joined and, as it were, intermingled with it, so that I and the body form a unit....

There is a great difference between the mind and the body, inasmuch as the body is by its very nature always divisible, while the mind is utterly indivisible. For when I consider the mind, or myself in so far as I am merely a thinking thing, I am unable to distinguish any parts within myself; I understand myself to be something quite single and complete. Although the whole mind seems to be united to the whole body, I recognize that if a foot or arm or any other part of the body is cut off, nothing has thereby been taken away from the mind.... By contrast, there is no corporeal or extended thing that I can think of which in my thought I cannot easily divide into parts; and this very fact makes me understand that it is divisible. This one argument would be enough to show me that the mind is completely different from the body, even if I did not already know as much from other considerations.

[René Descartes, *Meditationes de Prima Philosophia* (*Meditations Of First Philosophy*, 1641). In *The Philosophical Writings of Descartes*, trans. by John Cottingham. Cambridge: Cambridge University Press, 1986 (rev. ed. 1996), 17–19, 51–59.]

Three Positions on Mind and Body

Besides Descartes, there have been, over the years, different ideas put forward about the mind and body. Some of these ideas resulted from psychological studies of human behaviour, particularly in relation to family dynamics. Others came from a strictly medical point of view that was based on physical observations in the body. Recently, many medical doctors have put forward even more interesting ideas about the nature of the mind and body, as well as the relationship between the two. Despite our knowledge, there is still a lot about the mind and body that we do not know or understand.

The Materialist View

Materialists argue that there is no real difference between mind and body. Seventeenth century thinkers such as Thomas Hobbes (1588–1679) and behavioural psychologists in the twentieth century, believed that mental events, like physical actions, are combinations of matter. As we use sophisticated technology to gain knowledge about the way the brain functions this point of view seems to have merit. If the mind is primarily or completely physical in nature, then it seems possible that scientists will someday be able to create a machine that thinks.

On the other hand, when we consciously examine our thoughts, or when we feel we have a new idea, materialism does not seem to provide a very satisfactory explanation. Can ideas present in our consciousness really be explained by chemical and electrical processes occurring in our brains? Can the emotions we feel, the enjoyment of a sunset or the experience of seeing an old friend for example, really be

explained as a combination of chemical and electrical elements?

The Modified Materialist View

Some philosophers believe that, while thoughts are caused by physical processes, thoughts are themselves something other than simply physical processes. These doubters, called epiphenomalists, say that thoughts are the by-product of physical processes, as smoke is a by-product of fire. Epiphenomalists try to keep a foot in both materialist and non-materialist camps.

Still, questions remain. If thoughts are by-products of physical processes, then what are the thoughts themselves composed of? How does a thought emerge from a physical process?

The Idealist View

Idealists reject the materialist view completely. Idealists believe that thoughts, and in fact all things, are basically mental not physical. According to idealists, we think of things and create them in the mind. These thoughts do not exist in any way beyond or external to the mind; nor can they exist without the mind. They are products of the mind alone.

To some degree, modern psychology agrees with this concept, in that each of us constructs our individual view of the world rather than having it arrive ready-made in our minds. Our attitudes and emotional development will influence the types of images that we create. If we examine the images of the world created by siblings within a family, we can see that they will not all share the same views.

There are some problems with the

idealist view. It is clear that external physical conditions, such as the pain experienced when stubbing a toe, *can* shape our thoughts. In addition, factors such as weariness, drugs, disease, and damage to the brain can also affect our thoughts in different ways. This means that the actual external world may not correspond to the images that we have of it in our minds, and that those images may change at different times, depending on our physical or emotional state.

Where Is the Mind Located?

Many physicists, psychologists, and medical researchers have begun to question the idea that the mind is localized in the brain, that it is separate from the body, and that it is separate from one individual to another. Furthermore, the idea that the act of observing something changes the very nature of a physical system, an idea that came out of quantum mechanics in physics, has added a sense of scepticism about previously held views about mind and matter. What is interesting is that many scientists are starting to seriously consider ideas that were known by Eastern philosophies such as Buddhism and Hinduism. What are your views on the mind–matter debate?

PHILOSOPHERS' FORUM

Mind–Matter Interaction

Dean Radin

… [D]oes mental intention directly affect the physical world, without an intermediary? This question concerning the ultimate role of the human mind in the physical world has intrigued philosophers for millennia. Indeed, the concept that mind is primary over matter is deeply rooted in Eastern philosophies and ancient beliefs about magic. For the past few hundred years, such beliefs have been firmly rejected by Western science as mere superstition. And yet, the fundamental issues remain as mysterious today as they did five thousand years ago. What is mind, and what is its relationship to matter? Is the mind caused, or is it causal?…

While the general idea of mind–body connections is now widely accepted, forty years ago it was considered dangerously heretical nonsense. The change in opinion came about largely because of hundreds of studies of the placebo effect, psychosomatic illness,

We have to see all becomings as developments of the movement in our true self and this self as one inhabiting all bodies and not our body only.

Sri Aurobindo

psychoneuroimmunology, and the spontaneous remission of serious disease…. The implication is that the body's hard, physical reality can be significantly modified by the more evanescent [transient] reality of the mind….

While the idea that the mind can affect the physical body is becoming more acceptable, it is also true that the mechanisms underlying this link are still a complete mystery. Besides not understanding the biochemical and neural correlates of "mental intention," we have almost no idea about the limits of mental influence. In particular, if the mind interacts not only with its own body but also with distant physical systems, … then there should be evidence for what we will call "distant mental interactions" with living organisms. And there is….

[Dean Radin, *The Conscious Universe*. San Francisco: HarperCollins Publishers Inc., 1997, 127, 148, 149.]

… [C]onsciousness does not just passively reflect the objective material world; it plays an active role in creating reality itself.
Stanislav Grof

I D E A S A N D I S S U E S

Understand Concepts

1. (a) What questions can be raised about the nature of mind and body, and the relationship between them?
    (b) Briefly outline your own immediate responses to these questions.
2. What positions do materialists, epiphenomenalists, and idealists take on these issues?
3. Why are questions about mind and body important in our modern world?
4. Summarize Descartes' argument in a brief paragraph.
5. How did Descartes describe the mind, body, and external objects?

Apply and Develop

6. Are you an idealist or a materialist? Respond to these questions to find out.
    (a) Will it ever be possible to communicate telepathically with another person?
    (b) Is it possible for the human mind to continue to exist after the death of the body?
    (c) Do you believe that the experience of stress is primarily a mental, rather than a physical, event?
    (d) Will it always be impossible to physically capture a thought in the same way one can capture a butterfly?
    If you answered "yes" to most or all of these questions, you tend toward idealism, believing that mental processes are quite different from physical processes. If you answered "no" to most or all, you tend to be a materialist, believing that all things, including thought, can be converted into physical elements.
7. (a) We now know that psychosomatic illnesses, illnesses that result from mental or emotional states, do exist. What would Descartes say about this?
    (b) Our frame of mind, our emotions, and even our rational abilities are affected by our physical states. What would Descartes say about this?

Think Critically

8. Describe the problems that you can see with Descartes' separation of mind and body as different substances.
9. If we are unconscious or in a coma, are we still ourselves, according to Descartes? What do you think?

Communicate Ideas

10. Write a position paper that responds to the question: What are the advantages of a life involved in physical activities as opposed to pursuits of the mind?

Inquire and Research

11. Find out what recent medical science indicates about the mind–body connection. In what ways does the mind react to physical conditions? Find out how the body is affected by mental states and emotions. For those who, through accidents, have lost the use of their physical bodies, what impact has this had on their mental states?

Gilbert Ryle: The "Ghost in the Machine"

The distinction that Descartes made between mind and body has had a long and powerful impact on philosophic thinking, although many philosophers have objected to his dualism. Twentieth century British philosopher Gilbert Ryle (1900–1976) was one of Descartes' strongest critics.

There Is No Separation Between Mind and Body

Ryle attacked the notion of a split between the observable world of matter and the private inner mind. He also argued that the concept of the mind as a separate realm existing alongside a bodily realm is a mistake. Ryle suggested that mental events are not separate and above bodily events and properties, any more than a school is a separate item existing alongside the libraries, laboratories, administration, students, and so on that make it up. According to Ryle, when we say that someone is in a mental state, we are describing how that person is disposed to behave and react under certain circumstances; we are not making a statement about private, inaccessible occurrences taking place in the subjective theatre of the mind.

Ryle's approach is similar to that of twentieth-century behavioural psychologists. Behaviourists believe that it is useless to discuss mental events at all since one can never know exactly what transpires inside the mind. Behaviourists observe the behaviour of humans and other living organisms, and restrict conclusions to what has been observed, and to an organism's tendency or disposition to behave in certain ways. Thus, instead of concluding, "That person is in an angry or thoughtful state of mind," the behaviourist would note, "That person behaves in an angry or thoughtful way."

Materialist philosophers have suggested that scientists should discuss brain states rather than mental states. These thinkers believe we should analyze how a particular brain state is linked to both a sensory input and a behavioural output. Modern behavioural studies offer a hope of a new framework for understanding the mind, a framework which leaves behind the problems of Descartes' dualism.

No line of thought is free from criticism, however, and critics of Ryle and materialism argue that such behavioural approaches do not explain subjective experience and consciousness. What is it like to think a thought, to smell a rose, or touch a soft surface? How does one describe what happens when, for example, someone sits in an armchair ruminating about a problem? The philosophic quest to understand our mental life and how it relates to our minds and bodies is far from concluded.

This painting by Otto Rogers, a prairie artist, is called "City of Lights."

The Concept of Mind

Gilbert Ryle

The official doctrine

There is a doctrine about the nature and place of minds which is so prevalent among theorists and even among laymen that it deserves to be described as the official theory.... It will be argued here that the central principles of the doctrine are unsound and conflict with the whole body of what we know about minds....

The official doctrine, which hails chiefly from Descartes, is something like this.... [E]very human being has both a body and a mind. Some would prefer to say that every human being is both a body and a mind. His body and his mind are ordinarily harnessed together, but after the death of the body his mind may continue to exist and function....

Human bodies are in space and are subject to the mechanical laws which govern all other bodies in space. Bodily processes and states can be inspected by external observers. So a man's bodily life is as much a public affair as are the lives of animals and reptiles and even as the careers of trees, crystals and planets.

But minds are not in space, nor are their operations subject to mechanical laws. The workings of one mind are not witnessable by other observers; its career is private. Only I can take direct cognizance of the states and processes of my own mind. A person therefore lives through two collateral histories, one consisting of what happens in and to his body, the other consisting of what happens in and to his mind. The first is public, the second private....

... [T]he problem [of] how a person's mind and body influence one another is notoriously charged with theoretical difficulties. What the mind wills, the legs, arms and the tongue execute; what affects the ear and the eye has something to do with what the mind perceives; grimaces and smiles betray the mind's moods and bodily castigations [punishments] lead, it is hoped, to moral improvement. But the actual transactions between the episodes of the private history and those of the public history remain mysterious, since by definition they can belong to neither....

... It is assumed that there are two different kinds of existence or status. What exists or happens may have the status of physical existence or it may have the status of mental existence....

The absurdity of the official doctrine

Such in outline is the official theory. I shall often speak of it, with deliberate abusiveness, as "the dogma of the Ghost in the Machine." I hope to prove that it is entirely false, and false not in detail but in principle. It is not merely an assemblage of particular mistakes. It is one big mistake and a mistake of a special kind. It is, namely, a category-mistake....

I must first indicate what is meant by the phrase "category-mistake." This I do in a series of illustrations.

A foreigner visiting Oxford or Cambridge for the first time is shown a number of colleges, libraries, playing fields, museums, scientific departments and administrative offices. He then asks "But where is the University? I have seen where the members of the Colleges live, where the Registrar works, where the scientists experiment and the rest. But I have not yet seen the University in which reside and work the members of your University." It has then to be explained to him that the University is not another collateral institution, some ulterior counterpart to the colleges, laboratories and offices which he has seen. The University is just the way in which all that he has already seen is organized. When they are seen and when their coordination is understood, the University has been seen....

... The representation of a person as a ghost mysteriously ensconced in a machine derives from this argument. Because, as is true, a person's thinking, feeling and purposive doing cannot be described solely in the idioms of physics, chemistry and physiology, therefore they must be described in counterpart idioms. As the human body is a complex organized unit, so the human mind must be another complex organized unit, though one made of a different sort of stuff and with a different sort of structure....

Origin of the category-mistake

... When Galileo showed that his methods of scientific discovery were competent to prove a mechanical theory which should cover every occupant of space, Descartes found in himself two conflicting motives. As a man of scientific genius he could not but endorse the claims of mechanics, yet as a religious and moral man he could not accept ... that human nature differs only in degree of complexity from clockwork. The mental could not be just a variety of the mechanical. He and the subsequent philosophers naturally but erroneously availed themselves of the following escape route.... Minds are things, but different sorts of things from bodies; mental processes are causes and effects, but different sorts of causes and effects from bodily movements....

Now the dogma of the Ghost in the Machine ... maintains that there exist both bodies and minds; that there occur physical processes and mental processes; that there are mechanical causes of corporeal movements [movements relating to a physical body] and mental causes of corporeal movements. I shall argue that these and other analogous conjunctions are absurd; but it must be noticed, the argument will not show that either of the illegitimately conjoined propositions is absurd in itself. I am not, for example, denying that there occur mental processes. Doing long division is a mental process and so is making a joke. But I am saying that the phrase "there occur mental processes" does not mean the same sort of thing as "there occur physical processes," and, therefore, that it makes no sense to conjoin or disjoin the two....

Time Line

Ideas About the Mind–Body Connection

- - - - - - - - - -

RENÉ DESCARTES
(1596–1650)

believes mind and body are two distinct entities

JOHN LOCKE
(1632–1704)

suggests that our memory provides our sense of personal identity

DAVID HUME
(1711–1776)

claims that the self is an illusion

GILBERT RYLE
(1900–1976)

proposes that mind and body are not separate but integrated together to form our idea of self

It is perfectly proper to say, in one logical tone of voice, that there exist minds and to say, in another logical tone of voice, that there exist bodies. But these expressions do not indicate two different species of existence.... They indicate two different senses of "exist," somewhat as "rising" has different senses in "the tide is rising," "hopes are rising," and "the average age of death is rising." ... "Mental" does not denote a status, such that a person can sensibly ask of a given thing or event whether it is mental or physical, "in the mind" or "in the outside world." ...

[Gilbert Ryle, *The Concept of Mind*. London: Hutchinson, 1949, chap. 1 and 7.]

Why does Ryle refer to Descartes' theory of personal identity as "the Ghost in the Machine"? Do you agree with Descartes' or Ryle's position?

IDEAS AND ISSUES

Understand Concepts

1. Briefly describe the position against which Ryle is arguing.
2. What reasons does he suggest help to explain why Descartes took the view that he did?
3. (a) Summarize Ryle's view of the distinction between mind and body.
   (b) What reasons does he give for his position?

Apply and Develop

4. (a) Where do Descartes and Ryle fit within the three categories of materialist, epiphe-nomenalist, or idealist?
   (b) Provide evidence for your categorization.

Think Critically

5. Compare the ideas of Descartes and Ryle regarding the mind–body issue.
6. Do you believe there is a difference in quality between mind and body? Give reasons for your point of view.
7. If mind is of a different quality than body, what is it?

Communicate Ideas

8. Write a response paper that discusses Descartes' and Ryle's views of the mind. Develop your own point of view on the subject: Of what does the mind consist?
9. Debate this issue: Personal identity no longer exists when there is a loss of consciousness.

Inquire and Research

10. Do research into current knowledge of the brain. Determine if this knowledge tends to support the idea that thought can be understood in physical terms or if it is something non-physical.
11. Research current medical views of the connection between mind and body. Look, for example, at recent ideas of the ability of the mind to affect physical illnesses.

John Locke: The Enduring Self Through Memory

Are you the same person you were ten years ago? You may not look the same; and probably you do not think in the same way. Over the last ten years, you have experienced a number of life events which have affected you in immeasurable ways. Medical science tells us that over a ten-year period of time it is probable that all the cells in your body have been replaced by new cells. So, are you the same person with the same identity that you were ten years ago?

Although we pass through many changes in life, it seems important for us to have a sense of enduring selfhood, of personal identity. Such a sense of self seems necessary for us to understand our lives. Many of us keep old photographs, which we occasionally go over nostalgically, remembering times past. We treasure memories of who we were once upon a time, and the older we become, the more treasured such memories often are.

One of the most influential philosophic writers on personal identity was John Locke (1632–1704). Locke identified the self as a conscious "thinking thing" with memories of past events. It is this memory and consciousness that links who we are today with the person we were in the past.

The Identity of Humans Is Not the Same as Other Things

Locke discussed the identity of a variety of objects, such as a diamond, a tree, a cat, or a person. In the case of the diamond, Locke believed identity existed in the continuance of the same atoms, or "minute particles," over a period of time. In the case of a tree or a cat, Locke suggested a different definition of identity. The tree does not continue to contain the same atoms as it grows, sheds leaves, or loses branches in storms. The tree has a continuous life that follows a normal cycle. The kitten grows, matures, and ages; its cells change but the cat remains the same cat throughout its life cycle.

Locke described the identity of human beings as being different both from non-living and other living things. He believed a human being is not only an animal, but also a person. Human identity therefore is based on mental life, thought, consciousness, and especially memory. According to Locke, if we remember that we were born and raised in a small town, that we went to university in Calgary, and that we have lived our life since then in Vancouver, our personal identity will consist of these events.

Like Descartes, Locke did not believe a specific physical or bodily existence to be necessary for personal identity. He imagined a "body-swap," where a prince assumes the body of a shoemaker. As long as the prince retains all his conscious memories after waking up in the shoemaker's body, he is, in Locke's view, the same person, although not the same physical human being.

Some aspects of Locke's philosophy agree with parts of Descartes' philosophy. Both thinkers believed that consciousness and self-awareness were *the* essential characteristics of personal identity, rather than just physical existence. However, Locke argued that the idea of continuity develops through memory.

Can you accept a theory that identifies a person's unique self through his or her memories? What if someone suffers from anmesia, has a false memory, or suffers from a mental illness? Who is the self of someone who believes himself to be Napoleon?

Some critics suggest that persons are simply human animals, that a person is the physical human being recognized by others as such. What do you think? Is your self the body in which you live or are you the composite of memories that you possess?

If every part of one's body is replaced several times over a lifetime, and if one's thoughts change radically over that same lifetime, where does continuity of identity exist?

The Self

John Locke

To find wherein *personal identity* consists, we must consider what *person* stands for; which, I think, is a thinking intelligent being that has reason and reflection and can consider itself as itself, the same thinking thing in different times and places; which it does only by that consciousness which is inseparable from thinking.... When we see, hear, smell, taste, feel, meditate, or will anything, we know that we do so.... For since consciousness always accompanies thinking, and it is that which makes everyone to be

We know that we do so.

think intelligent being – can reflect

person thinking back still same person.

> One of the oddest things in life, I think, is the things one remembers.
> *Agatha Christie*

what makes a person not skin and bones. Sleeping/changing = Same person what happens when we forget.

> God gave us memories that we may have roses in December.
> *James M. Barrie*

Doesn't matter what your made of - same "person".

Body is a part of us. ↑ substance/personal self.

Personal Identity doesn't change Still same person.

Memory is not part of the body. Memories are the Same. In your Brain/Soul.

Consciousness - can't Judge by it. Dr Jeckel and Hyde.

what he calls *self* and thereby distinguishes himself from all other thinking things, in this alone consists *personal identity*, i.e. the sameness of a rational being. And as far as this consciousness can be extended backwards to any past action or thought, so far reaches the identity of that *person*. It is the same *self* now it was then, and it is by the same *self* as this present one that now reflects on it, that that action was done.

But it is further inquired whether it [personal identity] be the same identical substance.... [T]hat which seems to make the difficulty is this: that this consciousness is interrupted always by forgetfulness, there being no moment of our lives wherein we have the whole train of all our past actions before our eyes in one view, ... and in sound sleep have no thoughts at all.... I say, in all these cases, our consciousness being interrupted, and we losing the sight of our past *selves*, doubts are raised whether we are the same thinking thing, i.e. the same substance, or no. Which ... concerns not *personal identity* at all: the question being what makes the same *person*, and not whether it be the same identical substance, which always thinks in the same person.... For, it being the same consciousness that makes a man be himself to himself, *personal identity* depends on that only, whether it be annexed solely to one individual substance, or can be continued in a succession of several substances. For as far as any intelligent being can repeat the idea of any past action with the same consciousness it had of it at first, and with the same consciousness it has of any present action, so far it is the same *personal self*.... [It] would be by distance of time or change of substance no more two *persons* than a man be two men by wearing other clothes today than he did yesterday, with a long or a short sleep between. The same consciousness unites those distant actions into the same *person*, whatever substances contributed to their production.

That this is so, we have some kind of evidence in our very bodies, all whose particles, whilst vitally united to this same thinking conscious self (so that we feel when they are touched and are affected by and conscious of good or harm that happens to them) are a part of our *selves*, i.e. of our thinking conscious *self*. Thus, the limbs of his body are to everyone a part of *himself* he sympathizes and is concerned for them. Cut off a hand, and thereby separate it from that consciousness he had of its heat, cold, and other affections, and it is then no longer a part of that which is *himself* any more than the remotest part of matter. Thus we see the *substance* whereof *personal self* consisted at one time may be varied at another, without the change of personal *identity*....

Self is that conscious thinking thing ... which is sensible or conscious of pleasure and pain, capable of happiness or misery, and so is concerned for itself.... Upon separation of this little finger, should this consciousness go along with the little finger and leave the rest of the body, it is evident the little finger would be the *person*, the *same person*, and self then would have nothing to do with the rest of the body....

This may show us wherein *personal identity* consists not in the identity of substance but, as I have said, in the identity of *consciousness*, wherein, if Socrates and the present mayor of Queenborough agree, they are the same person. If the same Socrates waking and sleeping do not partake of the same *consciousness*, Socrates waking and sleeping is not the same person. And to punish Socrates waking for what sleeping Socrates thought,

Personal Identity is not the same substance but same consciousness and waking Socrates was never conscious of, would be no more right than to punish one twin for what his brother-twin did, whereof he knew nothing, because their outsides were so like that they could not be distinguished....

But yet possibly it will still be objected, suppose I wholly lose the memory of some parts of my life beyond a possibility of retrieving them: ... yet am I not the same person that did those actions, had those thoughts that I once was conscious of, though I have now forgot them? To which I answer that we must here take notice what the word I is applied to, which, in this case, is the man only. And the same man being presumed to be the same person, I is easily here supposed to stand also for the same person. But if it be possible for the same man to have distinct incommunicable consciousness at different times, it is past doubt the same man would at different times make different persons; which, we see, is the sense of mankind in the solemnest declaration of their opinions, human laws not punishing the mad man for the sober man's actions, nor the sober man for what the mad man did, thereby making them two persons....

Are you the same person if you lose your memory? Would you be a different person after losing/gaining new experiences?

Does personal identity continue to exist when one is asleep, according to Locke? What do you think?

But is not a man drunk and sober the same person—why else is he punished for the fact he commits when drunk, though he be never afterwards conscious of it? Just as much the same person as a man that walks and does other things in his sleep is the same person and is answerable for any mischief he shall do in it. Human laws punish both … because … they cannot distinguish certainly what is real, what counterfeit; and so the ignorance in drunkenness or sleep is not admitted as a plea.… But in the Great Day, wherein the secrets of all hearts shall be laid open, it may be reasonable to think no one shall be made to answer for what he knows nothing of, but shall receive his final judgement, his conscience accusing or excusing him.

[John Locke, *Essay Concerning Human Understanding* (1690), Book 2, chap. 27, sec. 9–19, 22–3. Ed. by P.H. Nidditch. Oxford: Clarendon Press, 1975.]

IDEAS AND ISSUES

Understand Concepts

1. What issue is Locke addressing in the excerpt?
2. Overall, how does John Locke define personal identity? What is, and what is not, a part of personal identity for Locke?
3. How does Locke use and explain each of these terms: personal identity, substance, person, and consciousness?
4. Although Locke did not know that such technologies and medical triumphs as computers and brain transplants would someday be possible, he would have been intrigued by the implications. For each of the scenarios below, how would Locke have replied? How would you reply?

    (a) Angelo has a disease that is ravaging his body; yet his mind is functioning well. Rubin has a healthy body, but is brain-dead as the result of an accident. After long consideration, doctors and family decide to transplant Angelo's brain into Rubin's body. The operation is a success, and the patient awakes. Who will he be—the person who donated the body; the person who donated the brain; or someone else altogether?

    (b) Mimi has lost her memory altogether, and is wandering in a strange city. Attempts to find out who she is fail, and she gets on with a new life—new job, new family, and new goals. Then Mimi, after a blow to the head, remembers her former life but has no memory of the intervening second life. What is the identity of this person now; the first identity, the second, or someone else entirely?

    (c) Kwan is seventy years old. Scientists tell us that over time every cell in our body changes as some die and others are created. Over the years, we become an entirely different person physically. From a physical point of view, of course, the evidence is apparent; a small baby becomes an adult and then an older person, each person quite different from the one that came before. Mentally, we become quite different people as we experience life. The thoughts of the seventy-year-old bear little or no resemblance to that of the infant. To what degree, if at all, can we say that the identity of seventy-year-old Kwan is the same as when he was seven years old?

    (d) Twyla, in the mid-twenty-first century, has all the contents of her mind scanned and transferred to a computer. For a while, Twyla continues to live, while the computer begins to function. In a few years, Twyla passes away. The computer continues on, however, with all of her thoughts, memories, ideas, and desires. The computer believes that it is the continuation of Twyla, since it possesses her mind. Is the computer now Twyla?

5. How convincing do you think Locke's ideas are? Provide arguments that you believe are most powerful, and those that are not as strong.
6. How would you argue against Locke's position?

David Hume:
The Self Is an Illusion

Although many philosophers believed that personal identity comes from the mind, as in the case of Descartes, or from our memories, as in the case of Locke, not everyone was convinced. Some thinkers were particularly opposed to the idea of a personal identity. To them, the idea of a self is an illusion.

There Is No Evidence of a Personal Identity

Scottish philosopher David Hume (1711–1776) was harshly critical of the whole concept of personal identity; he called it an illusion. In his *Treatise of Human Nature* (1739–40), Hume pointed out that the idea of the *self* is not based on any one experience or impression. When one thinks about the self, he wrote, all one encounters are particular perceptions of heat, cold, love, or anger. There is no awareness of any specific object that can be identified as the self, he argued. Human beings are nothing other than bundles of perceptions rapidly succeeding each other.

In Chapter 4, we saw how Hume took the idea of empiricism to its logical conclusion, by denying the existence of solid proof for the concept of a continuing external world. Hume believed that no tangible evidence existed for the reality of the table in front of you, for example. All we can know

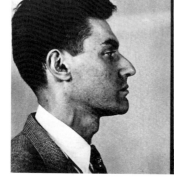

How can you argue against Hume's position?

about external objects, he argued, is a series of impressions, of sensory images of colour, shape, and texture. We draw the conclusion, falsely he believed, and these impressions make up some single enduring object that is a table in this case.

Hume took the same approach to his discussions of the self when he suggested that all we can really experience and be aware of are sensory impressions of things of the moment. Human beings simply connect these individual sensory impressions and conclude that they are conscious of a continuing self.

We may intuitively reject Hume's explanation, but it is a difficult theory to argue against. Hume's idea that the sense of an enduring self is an illusion has been a cornerstone philosophy for many writers, including those of the Buddhist tradition.

A Treatise of Human Nature

David Hume

There are some philosophers who imagine we are every moment intimately conscious of what we call our SELF; that we feel its existence and its continuance in existence; and are certain, beyond the evidence of a demonstration, both of its perfect identity and simplicity....

Unluckily all these positive assertions are contrary to that very experience which is pleaded for them, nor have we any idea of self after the manner it is here explained. For from what impression could this idea be derived?... It must be some one impression that gives rise to every real idea. But self or person is not any one impression.... If any impression gives rise to the idea of self, that impression must continue invariably the same through the whole course of our lives.... But there is no impression constant and invariable. Pain and pleasure, grief and joy, passions and sensations succeed each other, and never all exist at the same time. It cannot, therefore, be from any of these impressions, or from any other, that the idea of self is derived; and consequently there is no such idea.

... For my part, when I enter most intimately into what I call myself I always stumble on some particular perception or other, of heat or cold, light or shade, love or hatred, pain or pleasure. I never can catch myself at any time without a perception, and never can observe anything but the perception. When my perceptions are removed for any time, as by sound sleep, so long am I insensible of myself and may truly be said not to exist. And were all my perceptions removed by death, and could I neither think, nor feel, nor see, nor love, nor hate after the dissolution of my body, I should be entirely annihilated....

Don't exist when you sleep.

I may venture to affirm, of the rest of mankind, that they are nothing but a bundle or collection of different perceptions, which succeed each other with an inconceivable rapidity, and are in a perpetual flux and movement. Our eyes cannot turn in their sockets without varying our perceptions ... and all our other senses and faculties contribute to this change.... The mind is a kind of theatre, where several perceptions successively make their appearance, pass, re-pass, glide away, and mingle in an infinite variety of postures and situations....

We have a distinct idea of an object that remains invariable and uninterrupted through time; and this idea we call that of identity or sameness. We have also a distinct idea of several different objects existing in succession, and connected together by a close relation; and this ... affords a notion of diversity.... But though these two ideas of identity, and a succession of related objects, be in themselves perfectly distinct, and even contrary; ... they are generally confounded with each other.... This resemblance is the cause of the confusion and mistake, and makes us substitute the notion of identity, instead of that of related objects....

Sameness > diversity.

... [S]uppose any mass of matter, of which the parts are contiguous and connected, to be placed before us; it is plain we must attribute a perfect identity to this mass, provided all the parts continue uninterruptedly and invariably the same, whatever motion or change of place we may observe either in the whole or in any of the parts. But suppose some very small or inconsiderable part to be added to the mass, or subtracted from it: though this absolutely destroys the identity of the whole, strictly speaking, yet as we seldom think so accurately, we scruple not to pronounce a mass of matter the same....

We now proceed to explain the nature of personal identity.... And here it is evident the same method of reasoning must be continued which has so successfully explained the identity of plants, and animals, and ships, and houses, and of all the compounded and changeable productions either of art or nature. The identity which we ascribe to the mind of man is only a fictitious one, and of a like kind with that which we ascribe to vegetables and animal bodies....

The whole of this doctrine leads us to a conclusion ... that all the nice and subtle questions concerning personal identity can never possibly be decided, and are to be regarded rather as grammatical than as philosophical difficulties. Identity depends on the relations of ideas; and these relations produce identity ... [and] gives rise to some fiction or imaginary principle of union.

[David Hume, *A Treatise of Human Nature* (1739–40), Book 1, part 5, sec. 6. Ed. by L.A. Selby-Bigge, revised by P.H. Nidditch. Oxford: Clarendon Press, 1978, 251–63.]

What reasons does Hume give to deny the existence of a self? How might Locke respond?

Understand Concepts

1. Describe Hume's position on personal identity.
2. Summarize the arguments Hume used to support his position.

Apply and Develop

3. (a) Analyze and write down your own experience at this moment. To what degree does your experience support or negate Hume's view of personal identity?
   (b) How useful do you think such self-analysis is in dealing with the question of personal identity?

Think Critically

4. What arguments can be used to support or deny Hume's view of personal identity? Write these down in two lists: for and against. Come to your own conclusion on the issue.
5. How would Descartes and Locke reply to Hume if they had the opportunity? Do you think they could provide arguments against his position? If so, what would they be?

Communicate Ideas

6. In teams of three, take part in a conversation or a panel discussion between Locke, Descartes, and Hume. Begin by outlining the position taken by each of these philosophers about personal identity. Continue by arguing for the position of one or the other.

Inquire and Research

7. Using the ideas of Descartes, Locke, and Hume as a starting point, investigate the concept of personal identity. Develop your own view as to which one of these, if any, has the most defensible position.

The Eastern View of Personal Identity

Hinduism and Buddhism have always associated the term "personal identity" with life in some type of existence. Beings are born; they die; and the cycle of rebirth begins again. Buddhists believe that there are six types of existence for beings, each of which is characterized by a negative trait that prevents the being from achieving freedom from the cycle of rebirth: Pride leads to rebirth as a god, jealousy as a demi-god, attachment as a human being, stupidity as an animal, greed as a hungry ghost, and hatred as a hell creature. These modes of existence represent psychological states formed by the mind, and are therefore figurative, not literal, beings. Only existence as a human is conducive to future spiritual growth. Predominance of any one particular type of negativity results in rebirth in the most appropriate mode.

Eastern religions see our goal as humans to be one of freedom from the cycle of reincarnation. This freedom can only be achieved by developing ourselves spiritually. The doorways to any level of spiritual realization, which represent boundless states of mind, are boundless love, compassion, sympathetic joy, and equanimity (steady calmness). The root psychological traits that prevent us from being freed from reincarnation are ignorance, greedy attachment, and hatred. These traits determine the moral quality of our actions and the spiritual residue of these actions determines the manner of our rebirth. According to Buddhists, there are four possible ways for a being to be reborn: from eggs, wombs, moisture, or miraculously.

The body is viewed as being composed of the elements: earth, water, fire, air, and space. If any of these elements are out of balance, sickness results. When we are in the process of dying, we go through a transition where one element turns into another. Earth gives way to water, which gives way to fire, which gives way to air, and finally to space. In the process of death, our personal identity dissolves, and our minds are freed of their self-imposed limitations and experience limitless expansion.

Everything in life, and indeed in the world around us, is changing, and Tibetan Buddhists refer to these transitional phases, the actual moments of change, as "bardo." There are six transitional phases: life, dying, death, rebirth, dreaming, and meditation. The bardo is the only real state because everything is impermanent. According to Eastern religions, when a person is able to see the bardo as a moment of great opportunity, that person has the power to orchestrate changes rather than be controlled by change. Such a person is called a "yogin" and can see the truth in the bardo.

Buddhist Ideas About the Mind

According to Tibetan Buddhism, the mind creates and projects images of the world using its collection of memories and habits. These projections are usually negative in nature and, as a result, we do not experience reality as it truly is. Buddha's Fourth Noble Truth says that the path to avoid suffering is to follow a structured program of morality, insight, and meditation. By living a life according to Buddha's teachings (the dharma), it is possible to train the mind and develop spirituality, and these projections can be modified.

The mind is conditioned through habit to be ignorant of fundamental reality, a reality that occurs during meditation and after death. The space between our thoughts presents us with a sense of freedom to be in harmony with this reality and be in control of our destiny. The mind has two aspects: primordial enlightenment and a corrupted version of enlightenment. The primordially enlightened mind, pure in nature, is believed to be the only thing that represents reality. All our thoughts and desires, which originate from our ego, and our conditioned ignorance of the true meaning of life are illusions. Primordial enlightenment, or awareness, has a vast open nature and consists of five different types of awareness.

1. The *intrinsic primary awareness* represents ultimate reality.
2. The *subtle awareness that sees colour and form* is free of judgement yet sees the web of cause and effect. It remains quietly detached, uninvolved, and unconcerned.
3. The *compassionate awareness* recognizes that all sentient beings desire happiness and wish to avoid pain. It holds all these beings equally in immeasurable love.
4. The *spontaneously discriminating awareness* recognizes the potential for bliss in all beings, and the useful qualities of every aspect of the material world.
5. The *accomplishing awareness* shows the way in which a being can successfully accomplish all the things that beings need for fulfillment of their purposes.

Buddhist Ideas About the Ego

Buddhists say that the ego is a parasitical illusion that serves as a defence mechanism to deal with the experience of impermanence. The ego has no basis in reality and is continually reinvented as reality chips away at it. It is created by desire and demands constant attention in order to maintain its illusory status. From the moment we cease to be an infant, the ego presents us with the duality of "me" versus "you," and gives us a false sense of self-importance. Anything that does not fit this scope is viewed with suspicion, mistrust, jealousy, and hatred. As an infant we are unaware of a separation of ourselves from each other, or of the rules society has placed or will place on us. The world and our physical bodies support the ego.

The ego consists of forms, feelings, perceptions, and motivations, all of which act as barriers to the mind's primordial enlightenment. The ego uses the negative emotions of attachment and dislike to ensure its survival. Both of these emotions are the main causes of our suffering. Buddha's First Noble Truth says that all life is suffering. Our goal as sentient beings is to achieve freedom from the ego, so that we can experience primordial enlightenment.

When we die, our ego is unable to dominate our mind in the same way as during our life because we have cast away our physical bodies. However, according to Tibetan Buddhists, when we die, we will experience projections of our mind, first as pure awareness, then as visions of peaceful deities, followed by visions of stern deities, and then by visions of wrathful deities. Each

It is almost an absurd prejudice to suppose that existence can only be physical. As a matter of fact, the only form of existence of which we have immediate knowledge is psychic [in the mind]. We might as well say … that physical existence is a mere inference, since we know of matter only in so far as we perceive psychic images mediated by the senses.
Carl Jung,
The Structure and
Dynamics of
the Psyche

The influence which is most truly valuable is that of mind over mind.

Lydia Howard
Sigourney

of these projections and visions are experienced in sequence if we do not accept the primordial enlightenment within our mind. Tibetan masters are known to read the sacred text called the *Great Liberation through Hearing in the Bardo* during the first 49 days after someone dies. The purpose of reading the text is to help the spirit of the deceased achieve liberation from reincarnation.

Siddhartha Gautama

The Enlightened One

Siddhartha Gautama (563 BCE–483 BCE) was born into a royal family along the southern edge of Nepal. The young Siddhartha lived a sheltered and luxurious life. He was isolated from the reality of unhappiness, sickness, and death that existed outside his palace walls. Yet, on occasion he would escape from the palace grounds and encounter the real world outside. Siddhartha was overwhelmed by the terrible misery, sickness, ignorance, and death that he observed.

Eventually, Siddhartha left his protected environment for good. He wanted to understand life, and to find a way in which he could help others transcend suffering. Siddhartha travelled extensively, seeking various teachers, or gurus, for advice and instruction. Once, he even joined a group of monks who practised extreme measures such as fasting to find the truth. But none of these practices worked for Siddhartha. He was dissatisfied with the teachings of all the gurus.

Siddhartha resolved to gain enlightment through personal meditation. He meditated for hours, sometimes days, for as long as necessary to gain true understanding. Finally, Siddhartha found the enlightenment he sought. He also gained a new name, Buddha, which means "the enlightened one." Buddha travelled to Benares in northern India where he

These footprints are a shrine to Siddhartha.

delivered his most famous sermon outlining the Four Noble Truths of Buddhism.

The first truth says that all life is suffering (duhkha). Everything in life is subject to death and discord. The wishes of human beings are endless, and will always be frustrated. Impermanence is stamped on all things. The second truth says that all suffering is caused by selfish desires, based on human ignorance and on the human belief in a permanent self. The third truth says that such suffering can be overcome. The fourth truth sets out an ethical and mental discipline by which the flame of desire can be extinguished.

Today, the ideas of Buddhism are practised in many countries, such as Thailand, Laos, Cambodia, Sri Lanka, China (Tibet), Bhutan, and Japan. Many Westerners are also Buddhists.

No Continuous Personal Identity

Translated from the Milindapanha

"Bhante Nagasena," said the king, "is a person when just born that person himself, or is he someone else?"

"He is neither that person," said the elder, "nor is he someone else." …

"What do you say to this, your majesty? When you were a young, tender, weakly infant lying on your back, was that your present grown-up self?"

"Nay, verily, bhante. The young, tender, weakly infant lying on its back was one person, and my present grown-up self is another person."

"If that is the case, your majesty, there can be no such thing as a mother, or a father, or a teacher, or an educated man, or a righteous man, or a wise man…. Is it one person who is a student, and another person who has finished his education? Is it one person who commits a crime, and another person whose hands and feet are cut off?"

"Nay, verily, bhante. But what, bhante, would you reply to these questions?"

Said the elder, "It was I, your majesty, who was a young, tender, weakly infant lying on my back, and it is I who am now grown up. It is through their connection with the embryonic body that all these different periods are unified."

"Give an illustration."

"It is as if, your majesty, a man were to light a light—would it shine all night?"

"Assuredly, bhante, it would shine all night."

"Pray, your majesty, is the flame of the first watch the same as the flame of the middle watch?"

"Nay, verily, bhante."

"Is the flame of the middle watch the same as the flame of the last watch?"

"Nay, verily, bhante."

"Pray, then, your majesty, was there one light in the first watch, another light in the middle watch, and a third light in the last watch?"

"Nay, verily, bhante. Through connection with that first light there was light all night."

"In exactly the same way, your majesty, do the elements … join one another in serial succession: one element perishes, another arises, succeeding each other as it were instantaneously. Therefore neither as the same nor as a different person do you arrive at your latest aggregation of consciousnesses."

"Give another illustration."

"It is as if, your majesty, new milk were to change in … time into sour cream, and from sour cream into fresh butter, and from fresh butter into clarified butter. And if any one, your majesty, were to say that the sour cream, the fresh butter, and the clarified butter were each of them the very milk itself—now would he say well, if he were to say so?"

"Nay, verily, bhante. They came into being through connection with that milk."

"In exactly the same way, your majesty, do the elements … join one another in serial succession: one element perishes, another arises, succeeding each other as it were instantaneously. Therefore neither as the same nor as a different person do you arrive at your latest aggregation of consciousnesses."

[Henry Clark Warren, trans., *Buddhism in Transition*. Cambridge: Harvard University Press, 1896 (President and Fellows of Harvard College, 1953).]

Buddhists believe that meditation helps us experience reality directly.

IDEAS AND ISSUES

Understand Concepts

1. Summarize the Eastern idea of the mind, the body, and the ego.
2. What is the point of the illustrations of the light and of the milk in the excerpt?

Apply and Develop

3. How would Locke, Hume, or a Buddhist respond to each scenario below? How would you respond?

   (a) A young man takes part in an extremist political movement in which he believes strongly. Part of the activities involve terrorism and even murder. He leaves the movement after a time, increasingly regretful for having taken part in it. He spends the rest of his life as a good citizen and doing good deeds. As an old man, however, his past is uncovered by the authorities. Is he the same person he once was? Should he be held responsible for the actions of the person he was many years ago?

   (b) A man marries, has children, and is raising a family. One day, however, while travelling in a strange country, he falls down and hits his head. When he recovers consciousness he finds that he has no memory of who he is. Unable to recover his past life, he proceeds to carve out a new one, again marrying and raising a family. Ten years later he trips, falls, and hits his head again. Now he remembers his first life, but has no memory of his second. Who is he?

   (c) It may be possible in the foreseeable future to download a person's full conscious mind into a computer. Imagine this has been done to Chitra. In the course of time she ages and dies. But her mind survives in the computer. For whatever reason, the consciousness of Chitra is now transplanted in a new body that now thinks it is Chitra. Is it?

Think Critically

4. Explain to what degree Buddhism agrees or disagrees with Hume's idea of personal identity.

Inquire and Research

5. Find out more about Eastern views about the mind, body, and the ego. How do these ideas compare with current medical and psychological knowledge?

The Self, the Unconscious, and Archetypes

Being entirely honest with oneself is a good exercise.

Sigmund Freud

Sigmund Freud (1856–1939) put forward the idea that there is a significant part of us about which we are not conscious, yet still forms part of our identity. Freud, founder of psychoanalysis (analysis of the mind), was one of the most controversial figures of the twentieth century. His book *The Interpretation of Dreams* (1900) was a pioneering work that explored the hidden recesses of the unconscious mind, and was based on documented case studies of his patients. In *Psychopathology of Everyday Life* (1901), Freud argued that many of our actions, especially unintended ones, have deeper, unconscious causes. Freud worked to develop therapies to treat the various emotional disorders he identified.

Psychological View of Personal Identity

If you wish to shine like the daylight, burn up the night of self-importance

Rumi

Freud believed his ideas brought about a major revolution in the human conception of self. What is interesting to note is that Freud's work and especially that of Carl Jung, one of Freud's students, validated ideas that had already been known in Eastern religions for many centuries. Freud believed in the existence of an unconscious self (which he called the "id"), a part of our mind that is essentially irrational and pleasure seeking. Freud believed that the id exerted a major influence on our everyday waking experience, and its existence was at the heart of his concept of human nature and personal identity. Freud also identified the ego as our conscious, rational self. The ego, he wrote, deals not only with the unconscious id, but also with the demands of society and with reality. In addition, the ego must work with what Freud called the superego, or the rules of conduct and moral attitudes that every child learns from his or her parents.

Because childhood experiences

Sigmund Freud

are so important, said Freud, our personality becomes determined to a high degree at an early age. Moreover, there are important forces operating within our unconscious mind, forces about which we may be only vaguely aware, or about which we know nothing at all. Nevertheless, these unconscious forces can have a dramatic effect on our well-being and our relationships with others. Using analysis to help us understand our own thoughts, both conscious and unconscious, can help free us from these forces and enable us to face ourselves, others, and the world.

Carl Jung (1875– 1961) was a psychologist, and he developed a different understanding of personal identity from that of Freud. Jung suggested that the fundamental structure of the mind consists of aspects called archetypes. Each of us possesses archetypes of a hero, a god, or a goddess, among others. These archtypes represent inherited unconscious patterns of ourselves

Carl Jung

that can be observed only by examining their effects, such as recurring images in dreams, and behaviour patterns. When we examine the archetypes that are dominant within us during different stages of our lives, we gain a truer insight into our true personal identity. Jung went further, to say that these archetypes form a major part of a larger consciousness, called the collective unconscious, which we all share.

Introductory Lectures on Psychoanalysis

Sigmund Freud

[The id, the unconscious part of the mind that includes the drives and ideas of which we are unaware] is the dark, inaccessible part of our personality; what little we know of it we have learnt from our study of the dream-work and of the construction of neurotic symptoms.... It is filled with energy reaching it from the instincts, but it has no organization, produces no collective will, but only a striving to bring about the satisfaction of the instinctual needs subject to the observance of the pleasure principle. The logical laws of thought do not apply in the id....

... Every time we meet with a symptom [of anxious or neurotic behaviour] we may conclude that definite unconscious activities which contain the meaning of the symptom are present in the patient's mind.... You will perceive at once that here is an opening for therapy, a way by which symptoms can be made to disappear....

By thus emphasizing the unconscious in mental life we have called forth all the malevolence in humanity in opposition to psychoanalysis.... Humanity has in the course of time had to endure from the hands of science two great outrages upon its naive self-love. The first was when it realized that our earth was not the centre of the universe, but only a tiny speck in a world-system of a magnitude hardly conceivable; this is associated in our minds with the name of Copernicus.... The second was when [Darwin's] biological research robbed man of his privilege of having been specially created, and relegated him to a descent from the animal world.... But man's craving for grandiosity is now suffering the third and most bitter blow from present-day psychological research which is endeavouring to prove to the "ego" [the conscious part of the mind] of each one of us that he is not even master in his own house, but that he must remain content with the veriest scraps of information about what is going on unconsciously in his own mind.

[Sigmund Freud, *New Introductory Lectures on Psychoanalysis*. Trans. by James Strachey, W.W. Norton and Co. Inc., 1964, 1965. Sigmund Freud, *Introductory Lectures on Psychoanalysis*. Trans. by J. Riviere, London, UK: Allen and Unwin, 1922, chap. 17 and 18.]

Time Line

Ideas About the Unconscious
- - - - - - - - - - -
SIGMUND FREUD (1856–1939) suggests that our unconscious forms part of our identity

CARL JUNG (1875–1961) introduces the idea of archetypes and the collective unconscious

The Structure and Dynamics of the Psyche

Carl Jung

... [T]he instinctive processes ... make the supplementary concept of the unconscious necessary. I define the unconscious as the totality of all psychic phenomena that lack the quality of consciousness. These psychic contents might fittingly be called "subliminal," on the assumption that every psychic content must possess a certain energy value in order to become conscious at all. The lower the value of a conscious content falls, the more easily it disappears below the threshold. From this it follows that the unconscious is the receptacle of all lost memories and of all contents that are still too weak to become conscious. These contents are products of an unconscious associative activity which also gives rise to dreams. Besides these we must include all more or less intentional repressions of painful thoughts and feelings. I call the sum of all these contents the "personal unconscious." But, over and above that, we also find in the unconscious qualities that are not individually acquired but are inherited, e.g., instincts as impulses to carry out actions from necessity, without conscious motivation. In this "deeper" stratum we also find the *a priori*, inborn forms of "intuition," namely the *archetypes* of perception and apprehension, which are the necessary *a priori* determinants of all psychic processes. Just as his instincts compel man to a specifically human mode of existence, so the archetypes force his ways of perception and apprehension into specifically human patterns. The instincts and the archetypes together form the "collective unconscious." I call it "collective" because, unlike the personal unconscious, it is not made up of individual and more or less unique contents but of those which are universal and of regular occurrence. Instinct is an essentially collective, i.e., universal and regularly occurring phenomenon which has nothing to do with individuality. Archetypes have this quality in common with the instincts and are likewise collective phenomena....

The collective unconscious consists of the sum of the instincts and their correlates, the archetypes. Just as everybody possesses instincts, so he also possesses a stock of archetypal images. The most striking proof of this is the psychopathology of mental disturbances that are characterized by an irruption [eruption] of the collective unconscious. Such is the case in schizophrenia; here we can often observe the emergence of archaic impulses in conjunction with unmistakable mythological images.

[Carl Jung, *Collected Works: The Structure and Dynamics of the Psyche*, Vol. 8. In *The Portable Jung*, ed. by Joseph Campbell, trans. by R.F.C. Hull. New York: Penguin Books, 1971, 51–3, 57, 58.]

Understand Concepts

1. What is Freud's essential position on personal identity?
2. Define and describe id, ego, superego, and archetype.

Think Critically

3. Use Freud's concept of the unconscious to critically analyze Locke's view of personal identity.
4. How does Jung's idea of personal identity compare with Freud's? In what ways is it the same? In what ways is it different?

Inquire and Research

5. What methods do you think Freud and Jung would suggest for learning more about our individual personal identities? Find out more about the use of psychoanalysis for this purpose.
6. Research either Freud's or Jung's concept of the mind and the unconscious. Report your ideas in an essay that develops a thesis about their views of personal identity.

Review and Reflect

Philosophers from ancient times to the present have asked questions about personal identity. Where does the real "you" exist? Is it in your mind, your body, or even in both your mind and body? Is it possible that the real you does not exist at all, or is constantly changing?

Plato believed that every human possesses a soul, which represented the rational part of that person, and a body. Aristotle argued that there was a greater connection between the body, soul, and the external world. In modern philosophy, Descartes initiated the discussion of personal identity by asserting that one's thoughts were the only certain starting point for any examination of this topic. Descartes influenced generations of idealist philosophers who saw the mind and body as essentially distinct from each other. Locke, on the other hand, believed that memory provided the continuity of personal identity for a person as he or she changes throughout his or her life. In recent times, Gilbert Ryle and others have adopted a materialist position that suggests thought is the product of physical processes, just as are all other things in this universe.

Eastern religions have viewed only one reality, primordial enlightenment, which is one aspect of the mind. Everything else is an illusion. Buddhism says that the ego is a parasitical illusion that confuses and tricks the mind into believing that things are unchanging. Many centuries later, modern psychoanalysis and psychology have studied the nature of the ego, and have suggested that there are significant parts of our identity that we are not aware of at all.

Reality, Time, Cause, and Free Will

What is real? What is time? What causes things to happen? Is there a fate that guides our destiny? Many people associate these questions with philosophy. The questions are fascinating to consider, yet are difficult for us to

answer with certainty. In everyday life, we may reflect upon them for awhile, and then carry on, simply accepting the fact that we do not know the answers to these phenomena.

Philosophers encounter similar difficulties when they tackle questions pertaining to reality, time, causality, and fate. It is often difficult to come up with, or even to agree upon, solid answers to their existence, so philosophers will also often assume the fact and move on to other issues.

Questions about reality, time, and causality are part of metaphysics. The term "metaphysical" originated when editors placed these topics in Aristotle's writings after the material on the physical world. Since that time, metaphysical has come to refer to those questions that extend beyond, or above, the physical realm.

Despite the difficulties in establishing final answers to metaphysical questions, they are interesting, if puzzling, to consider. There are times in our lives when the assumptions we make about reality, time, and causality have practical importance: when we wonder about our perceptions of reality; when time seems to be different for one person than for another; or when we would like to know what causes other people or ourselves to act in certain ways. We may wonder if we really have freedom of action in certain circumstances.

Philosophers understand that reality, time, and causality, assumed as these concepts may be, tend to shape other ideas we have about the world. They and other thinkers continue to grapple with such puzzles.

From the beginning of time, people everywhere have asked questions about the nature of reality, the passage of time, and why things happen.

Different Views of Reality

I s there a reality that exists beyond our bodies? If so, what is it like, and how do we experience it? We usually assume that our experience of reality is similar to that of others, but sometimes we are led to question this assumption. This may happen, for example, when we disagree with others, and wonder why they view things so differently from the way we do. We may, in a moment of reflection, ask if there is a reality beyond our own existence about which we and others can agree.

People from every time and place have asked questions about reality: What is this world in which we live? How did it come about? Philosopher Martin Heidegger (1889–1976) said that the most fundamental philosophic question of all is: Why is there something rather than nothing?

Curiously, what may appear obvious when you don't think about it becomes more complex when you do. Like fish swimming in water, we usually assume the reality around us without being aware of it. When we try to understand and explain what reality is, the task becomes much more difficult.

Major Approaches to Understanding Reality

S everal major approaches to understanding the nature of reality have been suggested: idealism, materialism, and mysticism.

Idealism: Reality Through Reasoning

Idealism, generally, is the view that there are differences between mind and matter and that the mind is central to understanding reality. Plato was one of the first philosophers to suggest that there was an important distinction between appearance and reality. He believed that what we experience through our senses is not the ultimate reality and that only through reasoning can we understand what is real. Various forms of idealism have been built upon this basis. Platonists and idealists ask: What is the relationship between our ideas of things and the things themselves?

Materialism: Reality Through Discovery

Materialism assumes a material reality that exists beyond our knowledge, a reality waiting to be discovered. Philosophers such as Aristotle believed that experience was, in fact, the best way to understand the truth of this reality. In the modern world, scientists often assume a materialistic view of reality. A central question for Aristotelians and materialists is: What are the principles that shape all things in the world?

Mysticism: Reality Through Spirituality

Mysticism is another approach to understanding reality. In the mystic tradition, reality cannot be understood either through the senses or through reasoning, but only through intense spiritual experience. Mysticism challenges the assumption that there is a separate world of reality beyond the conscious self. The mystic asks: Why do we believe in an independent world of sense experience?

We can never arrive at the real nature of things from the outside. However much we investigate, we can never reach anything but images and names. We are like a man who goes round a castle seeking in vain for an entrance and sometimes sketching the facades.

Arthur Schopenhauer

I don't know what you could say about a day in which you have seen four beautiful sunsets.

John Glenn
(astronaut in orbit around the Earth, February 20, 1962)

Understand Concepts

1. (a) What are some major metaphysical questions?
   (b) What are three more specific questions that can be asked about each of these questions?
2. Define several views of reality outlined in this section.

Apply and Develop

3. Provide three examples in your own life of circumstances in which you may have pondered the nature of reality, the concept of time, or the way things are caused.
4. (a) Does the fact that people see and understand the world in different ways cast doubt on the existence of an external reality?
   (b) What possible explanations are there for this?

Think Critically

5. (a) Why do you think that metaphysical questions and answers are usually assumed rather than investigated by philosophers and non-philosophers alike?
   (b) Discuss why this might be a problem.
6. (a) State a question of interest to you, for any one of the topics time, space, or cause.
   (b) Develop a brief, preliminary response to the question you wrote in part (a), one that might form the basis for a later investigation.

Communicate Ideas

7. Before reading further, discuss these questions in small groups.
   (a) Does an external reality exist outside me?
   (b) If so, how do I know that such a reality does exist?
   (c) How accurate is my view of what is external to myself?
   (d) Is it possible to be more clear about what reality is?

Ancient Explanations for Reality

Philosophers since ancient times have attempted to explain what reality is and to determine what its constituent components are. The natural philosophers offered explanations for the objects that they experienced; some believed these objects could be understood by experiencing them through the senses, while others believed reason was the primary method of investigation. These early thinkers held widely different opinions about what the components of this reality were. Plato later proposed ideas of his own. He did not believe that the senses provided a true description of what reality is. Aristotle, on the other hand, believed that our experience of reality comes through our senses.

The Natural Philosophers' Idea of Reality

The natural philosophers of the ancient world wanted to understand the world of reality. They developed a number of theories to explain what reality is and how it comes about.

Some natural philosophers were materialists. They identified reality with what could be experienced through the senses. Several of them tried to identify the one single element that made up reality. Thales believed water to be the essential element because water is abundant, found in virtually everything, and is necessary for life. Anaximenes believed air to be the primary substance. Air, he thought, produces everything around us when it becomes thicker or thinner. Heraclitus believed that fire is the underlying element of all things. Although fire is continually transformed into other elements, Heraclitus reasoned that it is the central substance of all reality.

Other materialist natural philosophers sought to identify reality with more than one element. Empedocles believed that the universe is composed of four elements: earth, air, fire, and water. He suggested that Love and Strife were the forces drawing these elements together and pulling them apart

in endless cycles. Aristotle took up Empodocles' ideas and passed them on. Anaxagoras maintained that all things are made up of an infinite number of divisible particles of different qualities, and that particles dominating a particular substance give it its quality. Mind, he believed, controlled the whole. Leucippus and Democritus explained that everything arises out of an infinite number of atoms that cannot be divided further.

Each of these early philosophers was seeking an essential quality or qualities to account for reality. You may find some of these theories to be not very convincing, even far-fetched. What we discover in each of them, however, is a search for an underlying principle to explain everything in existence. Scientists today continue this search in order to increase the strength of their hypotheses, although it is an accepted theory that energy and mass are the building blocks of reality.

The natural philosophers in Italy searched for the essential structure of reality in ideas rather than in something sensed. These philosophers were moving away from the world of experience. Pythagoras believed all existence to be essentially numbers. Although Pythagoras ultimately became quite mystical about this view, modern scientists also investigate the universe using mathematics. Parmenides believed that only *being* exists, and that being is one and indivisible.

These natural philosophers asked important questions. They also suggested ideas that prompted other thinkers after them to contemplate the nature of reality. The natural philosophers were among the first to provide rational arguments to support their ideas of reality. Plato, Aristotle, and others built upon their theories.

Plato's Idea of Eternal Forms

You may have heard someone say there is no single principle or standard by which the world can be understood. That is, my view of the world and its activities is as good as your view. Each individual must be the judge of what is true or false, of what exists or does not exist. In Plato's day, such views were also

Plato believed that for each physical thing that existed there was a perfect idea, or form, which that thing resembled to some degree. How could we explain why we call a wide variety of things, such as different people, vegetables, or furniture, by one name?

held by Sophist philosophers such as Protagoras, when they said, "A man is the measure of all things." There is no external reality to be known in the same way by all people.

Another explanation of reality prevalent both today and in fifth century BCE Athens is that there is no permanent reality. All things are constantly changing. Natural philosopher Heraclitus, for example, pointed to the act of putting one's foot into a river once, and then again. Each time, both the experience and the river are different.

Plato disagreed with both of these views. He could not accept that reality depended on the point of view of the observer. Nor could he accept that all things were in constant change. When one accepted such views, he said, there was little point in talking about anything. Such views make reality, truth, and morality whatever anyone wants them to be. There must be an external reality, Plato believed, one independent of our sense experience, because our senses are incapable of providing us with clear answers. Plato believed it was possible to understand a reality that was constant and certain for all people at all times.

Accordingly, Plato developed his Theory of Forms, wherein he proposed two levels of reality. The senses provide us with what only *appears* to be real, while reasoning leads us to what is *actually* real. The appearance of reality, said Plato, is revealed to us through our senses. This is the world of individual things: chairs, buildings, people, and trees. These are particular, imperfect, and impermanent objects. Through reasoning, on the other hand, we understand what is real and permanent. Through reasoning we can understand the ideas, or forms, that go beyond time and space—the eternal models for all individual things and ideas in existence. This world of ideas contains models of chairs, tables, horses, mountains, triangles, and ideas of justice and truth.

Plato put forward the idea that there are two levels of reality in order to answer two philosophic problems. The first problem was how to explain that several different looking objects—a variety of tables, for example—can be understood as the same thing and called by the same name, even though they may be made of different materials, have various heights, colours, or numbers of legs. Regardless of the variety, we call them all tables. Clearly, we have an idea, he said, of what constitutes a table even if each individual table we see is different.

The second philosophic problem of reality that Plato needed to solve was that of change. How can we think of or understand a permanent object such as a human being when it is constantly changing? Plato felt there must be some permanent existence of each thing somewhere, even if we cannot see this permanence in the everyday sensory world.

Plato's Theory of Forms suggested a two-tier concept of reality. There are ideas, or forms, of all things existing somewhere, such as in the mind, but not in the world of sensory information. These ideas, or forms, are permanent, unchanging, and perfect models for all of the impermanent and imperfect things in the everyday world. The degree to which a particular object shares characteristics with an idea, or form, is the degree to which it can be called truth, justice, beauty, or a table.

Aristotle's Idea of Forms

Aristotle disagreed with Plato's theory of ideas, or forms, for two reasons. First, he saw no way these forms could shape things in this world without being within them. Secondly, Aristotle could not see how the forms could cause things to change in this world if the forms existed separately from the world. However, Aristotle still faced the same philosophic dilemmas of reality that Plato did: What determines the nature of things in this world? What determines how they change?

Aristotle supported Plato's theory insofar as he continued to believe in the existence of forms. Forms were necessary, agreed Aristotle, in order to understand how things can vary in size, shape, and other ways, and yet still be part of one category of thought. If we are going to discuss trees, truth, or justice, Aristotle believed, we must have a

The very essence of all life is growth, which means change....

Jean Baker Miller

How would Plato have explained the development of a tree such as this Bonsai. How different would Aristotle's explanations have been?

shared idea of what we are thinking about. The idea of forms helped to explain how it is that something, such as an acorn, can become something else, such as an oak tree, in that it is striving to fulfill its potential in that particular form.

Aristotle made a crucial change in the idea of forms, however, because he believed that forms were not ideas that existed somewhere else. A form was an essential essence which existed within each thing in the natural world. Specific tables, chairs, cats, donkeys, and dogs each contain within them the unique form of table, chair, cat, donkey, or dog. The form of an object shapes the object, ensuring that it develops into the goal for which it exists. The form that exists in the acorn allows it to grow into an oak tree. If we rephrased this theory in modern terms, we might say that an acorn or a child contains within it the potential to become an oak tree or an adult.

Aristotle's theory of forms introduced an important shift in his view of reality. Instead of understanding reality through the mind alone, Aristotle believed that we should all be encouraged to look at, examine, and understand objects around us in our sensory world. Each object contained within itself, he believed, the information to help us understand what the object is and what it will become.

IDEAS AND ISSUES

Understand Concepts

1. (a) Identify the major views of reality put forward by the natural philosophers, Plato, and Aristotle.
   (b) In each case, what reasons did they give for their particular view of reality?

Apply and Develop

2. (a) What problems were Plato and Aristotle trying to solve by using the idea of forms?
   (b) Compare the concept of forms developed by Plato and Aristotle.
   (c) To what degree, if at all, do you think their ideas of forms solved the problems they faced?

3. Explain how Plato and Aristotle would have used the idea of forms to explain each of the following situations:
   (a) how people of all ethnic backgrounds, shapes, and sizes are still called people
   (b) how a tiny baby becomes a full-grown adult
   (c) how we can find the truth about the reality of the world around us

4. The term "concept" is now used to describe physical and non-physical things in the world around us. We may say that we have the concept of a table, a game of chess, a human being, or justice.
   (a) How do we acquire, and hold, such concepts?
   (b) What would Plato or Aristotle have to say about our views of concepts?

Think Critically

5. Take the point of view of one of the philosophers of reality discussed in this section. Convince others, in a position paper and presentation, of the value of that point of view.

6. Assuming you found the views of reality presented in this section inadequate in some way, present your own view. Describe this in a paragraph. Convince others of your position.

Inquire and Research

7. Find out more about any one of the philosophers of reality described so far. Describe their views in more detail. To what degree were their ideas significant in influencing future thinkers?

René Descartes: Reasoning of What Is Real Without Doubt

Like Plato, René Descartes also rejected the use of our senses as a means of understanding reality. Like Plato, Descartes turned to the mind and to rational thought to discover truth. Descartes believed that it is only through the process of deduction and insight that we can find what is possible to understand about the world around us.

Descartes began his deliberations by doubting the existence of everything that could be doubted and by accepting only those truths that he knew with complete and intuitive certainty. When Descartes was absolutely, rock-solid certain about something, and could not deny it in any way, he accepted that idea as a truth or building block from which he could deduce other certainties.

Using this process, Descartes decided that almost everything in existence could be doubted. Soon, however, Descartes realized that the process of doubting required a mind that was, in fact, doubting. He concluded that he, Descartes, or at least his mind, must exist in order to doubt. His famous phrase "I think, therefore I am," became, for Descartes, a solid foundation upon which he could determine other truths.

Descartes also considered the existence of God, a being he defined as perfect in all ways. Descartes asked himself: How could he, Descartes, as an imperfect being, have developed any idea at all of perfection? Descartes concluded that the idea of perfection could only have been communicated to him from a perfect being, a being he called God. Descartes' reasoning led him to two conclusions of which he was sure, without a doubt: the existence of his own mind and the existence of God.

According to Descartes, there are three things that exist for certain, God, mind, and matter. He reached these conclusions through rational thought. He accepted ideas if they seemed clear and distinct, and if other clear and distinct ideas could be deduced from them.

Descartes' Idea About Material Objects

Is there any doubt of the world of reality, of material objects? Is it possible, asked Descartes, to doubt the existence of apparent reality? Using deduction and insight, Descartes noted that we experience and believe in the existence of a material, real world. Descartes had already deduced the existence of a perfect being, God. A perfect God, he concluded, would not deceive or allow human beings to believe falsely in the existence of a material reality. Therefore, Descartes concluded, the world of material objects must exist.

Next, Descartes turned his attention to the investigation of the nature of a material reality. The investigative process used was deductive reasoning. Descartes reasoned that the material world is different from the mind, which is a thinking substance, and different from God, a perfect being. Although material objects may not be exactly as we experience them—in colour or texture, for example—he reasoned that they do contain some characteristics of which we can be certain. Material objects occupy space; they possess shape, size, position, and movement. These aspects of the physical world affect our sensory organs, causing us to experience light, colour, smell, taste, sound, heat, and cold.

Descartes used this line of reasoning, coupled with certain intuitive insights and deduction, to determine, to his satisfaction, the existence of three major substances: mind, God, and material reality.

One problem Descartes left others to deal with was the distinction between mind and matter as different substances. Descartes himself was firmly convinced that the mind was of a different quality than material objects. This point of view has troubled many philosophers to this day. The issue has become known as the mind–body problem, and it raises a number of questions.

If mind and body are different substances, how do they communicate? How can the material world have an impact on the mind? How can the mind influence the material world? We all understand that there exists some connection between mind and matter, but what is it? When we decide to pick up an object from the floor, we succeed in communicating to our body that it must do so. Events that happen in the external world often affect the way we think on many levels. Descartes attempted to deal with this conundrum by suggesting that the human pineal gland at the base of the brain is the switching station that facilitates communication between the mind and matter. Scientific research, however, has proved his theory incorrect.

> Spirit is the real and eternal; matter is the unreal and temporal.
> *Mary Baker Eddy*

Descartes' idea of mind and body having distinct and separate characteristics had a profound impact on future thinkers and artists like Salvador Dali, pictured here.

IDEAS AND ISSUES

Understand Concepts
1. State the problems of reality that Descartes was trying to solve.
2. (a) What conclusions did he reach about reality in its different forms?
   (b) Upon what basis did he establish each of these conclusions?

Apply and Develop
3. Descartes developed his own method of searching for truth, which involved: looking for intuitively true, clear, and distinct ideas; and using deduction to build upon these ideas and find other clear and distinct ideas. Show how he did this in his search for reality.

Think Critically
4. Assess Descartes' views on reality by answering the questions below:
   (a) Do you think that his acceptance of intuitively clear and distinct ideas is justifiable?
   (b) What do you think of the conclusions he reached using this method?
5. Could alternative conclusions about mind, external reality, and God be reached using Descartes' method?
6. How would a materialist or a mystic respond to Descartes' views?

Communicate Ideas
7. Debate this issue: Descartes' views of reality are fundamentally flawed.

Inquire and Research
8. Descartes put forward his reasoning about the nature of mind, God, and material things in his *Meditations*. "Meditation 2" deals with the nature of the human mind; "Meditation 3" is called "Of God; that He exists"; "Meditation 5" and "Meditation 6" deal with the essence of material things. Choose one of these "Meditations" to read. Prepare a summary of the argument used in the "Meditation." Explain the argument in a brief response paper.

John Locke: Reality Is Learned Through the Senses

John Locke took up the problem of reality where Descartes left off. In the process, Locke began the modern redevelopment of idealism. Idealists hold that mind is central to reality; that all things are based to some degree on mind and ideas. Objective idealists believe that although the mind creates images of objects and ideas, these things do exist in some form in the external world. Plato was an objective idealist. Subjective idealists, on the other hand, believe that objects have no existence outside the mind.

Locke's Idea About Mind and Matter

Like Descartes, Locke believed in the existence of distinct substances of matter and mind. Matter, he wrote, is composed of size, shape, colour, position, sound, and movement. Mind is something that thinks, wills, denies, and doubts. Locke believed that both the mind, which exists within the knower, and matter, that which is known, are involved in the act of knowing.

Locke theorized that what is known is not the same as that which exists in the external world. What is known in the mind

is a mental representation of that which exists externally, although what is known in the mind may have some relationship to the external world. A flower in the garden, he reasoned, will correspond to our mental representation of what that flower is like. A bee, however, will have a different mental representation of the flower, seeing the flower in ultraviolet light with different patterns, as it approaches looking for pollen. Both bees and human beings have a concept of flower, but each concept is dependent on an individual's sense and the ability of an individual's mind to convey the image and develop the appropriate mental representation at the same time.

Locke asked if there was anything at all we can be sure of in the external world. The answer to such a question, suggested Locke, meant that we must first understand that matter—

According to Locke, what are primary and secondary qualities? Which of these reside within the object, and which are mere powers within the object to affect our ideas?

substances in the external world—is composed of two qualities: primary and secondary. The primary quality exists within the external object itself and would exist without observers or external participants, such as a bee. Size, position, shape, and movement are primary qualities. Locke believed there is a close resemblance between primary qualities and the ideas in our mind. Secondary qualities depend on observers for their existence. Examples of secondary qualities are warmth, fragrance, colour, sweetness, and loudness. Secondary qualities, Locke suggested, are powers that an object possesses to produce sensations from observers or external participants. Secondary qualities do not reside within the object itself. There is, he said, no necessary resemblance between secondary qualities and the ideas in our mind.

So, according to John Locke, a veil exists between our sensory awareness of the world and the world as it truly exists. Furthermore, Locke believed that secondary qualities filtered our understanding of the world through our senses, and consequently these qualities were only a reflection of that reality. Unlike Descartes, however, Locke firmly believed that the senses are the only true means we have to gain understanding of reality. Locke denied the existence of any innate ideas or certainties on which we can rely. His emphasis on the importance of the senses in gaining knowledge developed into the empiricist school of philosophy.

Essay Concerning Human Understanding

John Locke

… [Our ideas are not] exactly the images and resemblances of something inherent in the subject…. Whatsoever the mind perceives in itself, or is the immediate object of perception, thought, or understanding, that I call idea; and the power to produce any idea in our mind, I call quality of the subject…. Thus a snowball having the power to produce in us the ideas of white, cold, and round … I call qualities; and as they are sensations, or perceptions, in our understandings, I call them ideas….

… [Primary] qualities … are … inseparable from the body … e.g., take a grain of wheat, divide it into two parts, each part has still *solidity, extension, figure,* and *mobility*…. [P]*rimary qualities* … produce simple *ideas* in us … solidity, extension, figure, motion, or rest, and number.

… [*Secondary*] *qualities* … are … powers [in the object] to produce various sensations in us…. For the power in fire to produce a new colour, or consistency in wax … is as much a quality in fire, as the power it has to produce in me a new *idea* or sensation of warmth or burning ….

… [So] the *ideas of primary qualities* of bodies, *are resemblances* of them, and their patterns do really exist in the bodies themselves; but the *ideas produced* in us by these *secondary qualities, have no resemblance* of them at all. There is nothing like our *ideas* existing in the bodies themselves. They are … only a power to produce those sensations in us….

Flame is denominated *hot* and *light* … from the *ideas* they produce in us. Which qualities are commonly thought to be the same in those bodies that those *ideas* are in us, the one the perfect resemblance of the other…. And yet he that will consider that the same fire, that at one distance produces in us the sensation of *warmth*, does, at a nearer approach, produce in us the far different sensation of *pain*, ought to bethink himself what reason he has to say that his *idea* of *warmth*, which was produced in him by the fire, is actually *in* the fire; and his *idea* of *pain*, which the same fire produced in him the same way, is *not* in the fire….

The particular *bulk, number, figure,* and *motion of the parts* of fire, or snow, are *really in them*, whether anyone's senses perceive them or no…. But *light, heat, whiteness,* or *coldness*, are [not]….

[John Locke, *Essay Concerning Human Understanding* (1690), Book 2, chap. 8, 7–22. Ed. by P.H. Nidditch. Oxford: Clarendon Press, 1975.]

Locke argued that there was a difference between qualities within objects, and ideas, which are mental representations of objects. Primary qualities in objects, such as size, shape, and number, are represented very closely in our ideas. Secondary qualities such as texture, smell, and colour are powers in the object to produce ideas in us. Such ideas may bear some correspondence to the object.

IDEAS AND ISSUES

Understand Concepts

1. What is the difference between an idea and a quality, according to Locke?
2. What are the differences between primary and secondary qualities?
3. Describe how objects produce ideas in us, according to Locke.
4. To what degree did Locke say that the ideas produced by primary and secondary qualities resemble the objects themselves?

Apply and Develop

5. Analyze objects according to Locke's views of primary and secondary qualities. For example, analyze a flower, a food, a teacher, a book, the sun, a blade of grass, or any other object of interest to you. Summarize your analysis in two to three paragraphs.

Think Critically

6. (a) Do you think that objects and their qualities produce the same ideas in dogs, cats, or fleas as they do in humans? Explain your answer.
   (b) What does this tell us about Locke's theory?
7. Do you think Locke's ideas are valuable? Why?

Communicate Ideas

8. Use a panel discussion to explain the ideas below to the class.
   (a) Descartes' view of reality and his method of inquiry
   (b) Locke's idea of reality and his method of inquiry
   (c) how the two views are different from each other
   (d) how these views are significant contributions to philosophy

Inquire and Research

9. Read Chapter 20 of John Locke's *Essay Concerning Human Understanding*. Summarize and comment on the ideas in the chapter in a response paper.

Bishop George Berkeley: Perception Implies Existence

Locke believed that external objects have two qualities, primary and secondary, that create ideas in the mind. While primary qualities actually exist in objects, he wrote, secondary qualities are powers within the objects to create ideas in us.

George Berkeley agreed with Locke that ideas exist only in the mind, but he wanted to know how we distinguish between primary and secondary qualities. How, he asked, do we know that primary qualities exist in objects in the same way as we perceive them? Our only guidance in the question of nature of primary qualities is our mental concept of these objects. Berkeley's phrase, *Esse est percipi*, or "To be is to be perceived," is famous in the history of philosophy.

Does Berkeley mean that there is no external reality outside our minds? Do things only exist when someone is observing them? When you walk out of this room, does the room cease to exist? No, Berkeley wrote, all things continue to exist because they are perceived by God.

PHILOSOPHERS' FORUM

Principles of Human Knowledge

George Berkeley

It is indeed an opinion strangely prevailing ... that houses, mountains, rivers, and ... all sensible objects, have an existence ... distinct from their being perceived by the understanding.... For what are the forementioned objects but the things we perceive by sense? And what do we perceive besides our own ideas or sensations? And is it not plainly repugnant that any one of these ... should exist unperceived?...

Some truths there are so near and obvious to the mind that a man need only open his eyes to see them. Such I take this important one to be.... [A]ll those bodies which compose the mighty frame of the world, have not any subsistence without a mind; ... so long as they are not actually perceived by me ... they must either have no existence at all, or else subsist in the mind of some Eternal Spirit....

But, say you, though the ideas themselves do not exist without the mind, yet there may be things like them ... copies or resemblances, which things exist without the mind, in an unthinking substance. I answer, an idea can be like nothing but an idea; a colour or figure can be like nothing but another colour or figure. If we look but ever so little into our thoughts, we shall find it impossible for us to conceive a likeness except only between our ideas....

Some there are who make a distinction betwixt *primary* and *secondary* qualities. By the former, they mean extension, figure, motion, rest, solidity or impenetrability and number; by the latter they denote all other sensible qualities, as colours, sounds, tastes, and so forth. The ideas we have of these they acknowledge not to be the resemblances of anything existing without the mind or unperceived; but they will have our ideas of the primary qualities to be patterns or images of things which exist without the mind, in an unthinking substance which they call *matter*…. But … extension, figure, and motion are only ideas existing in the mind … and … neither they nor their archetypes can exist in an unperceiving substance….

[George Berkeley, *Principles of Human Knowledge*, Part 1 (1710, 2nd ed. 1734). In *The Empiricists*, by Margaret Atherton. Garden City: Anchor, 1974.]

What Does Science Have to Say About Reality?

Western science has long believed that the best way to understand a physical phenomenon is to dissect it and study its parts. But if, as quantum physics has shown, we are not separate from the world we thought was "out there," then how can there be "parts" to study? Just as the religions of the East believe the material world is an illusion, the belief that we are physical beings moving through a physical world is also an illusion.

Some physicists have tried to explain the world using a holographic paradigm. Holographic theory is based on the belief

> He who confronts the paradoxical exposes himself to reality.
> *Friedrich Dürrenmatt*

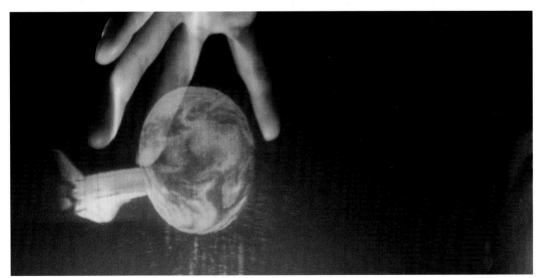

What would Berkeley or Locke have said about the holographic theory? What do you think?

that objective reality does not exist, that despite its apparent solidity the universe is basically a giant hologram. A hologram is a three-dimensional photograph created using a laser. The object to be photographed is flooded with the light of a laser beam. Then a second laser beam is bounced off the reflected light of the first and the area where the two laser beams interfere is captured on film. The developed film is then illuminated by a third laser beam, resulting in a three-dimensional image of the original object. Unlike a normal photograph, every part of a hologram contains all the information possessed by the whole. If we try to take apart a hologram, we will not get the pieces of which it is made; we will only get smaller wholes. This "whole in every part" nature of a hologram has led to an entirely new way of understanding the world and how we perceive it.

Although many scientists have greeted the holographic paradigm with scepticism, a small but growing group of researchers believe it may be the most accurate model of reality science thus far. Some, such as Michael Talbot, believe it is the key to understanding the mysterious phenomena that science has not been able to explain, including the mystical and the paranormal (supernatural).

PHILOSOPHERS' FORUM

The Holographic Universe

Michael Talbot

... [T]here is evidence to suggest that our world and everything in it—from snowflakes to maple trees to falling stars and spinning electrons—are also only ghostly images, projections from a level of reality so beyond our own it is literally beyond both space and time.

The main architects of this astonishing idea are two of the world's most eminent thinkers: University of London physicist David Bohm, a protégé of Einstein's and one of the world's most respected quantum physicists; and Karl Pribram, a neurophysiologist at Stanford University.... Bohm and Pribram arrived at their conclusions independently and while working from two very different directions....

However, after arriving at their views, Bohm and Pribram quickly realized the holographic model explained a number of ... mysteries ... , including the apparent inability of any theory, no matter how comprehensive, ever to account for all the phenomena encountered in nature....

But the most staggering thing about the holographic model was that it suddenly made sense of a wide range of phenomena so elusive they generally have been categorized outside the province of scientific understanding. These include telepathy, precognition, mystical feelings of oneness with the universe, and even psychokinesis, or the ability of the mind to move physical objects without anyone touching them.

... [I]t quickly became apparent to the ever growing number of scientists who came to embrace the holographic model that it helped explain virtually all paranormal and mystical experiences, and in the last half-dozen years or so it has continued to galvanize researchers and shed light on an increasing number of previously inexplicable phenomena. For example:

- In 1980 University of Connecticut psychologist Dr. Kenneth Ring ... , who is president of the International Association for Near-Death Studies, believes [that near-death] experiences, as well as death itself, are ... nothing more than the shifting of a person's consciousness from one level of the hologram of reality to another.
- In 1985 Dr. Stanislav Grof, chief of psychiatric research at the Maryland Psychiatric Research Center and an assistant professor of psychiatry at the Johns Hopkins University School of Medicine, ... concluded that existing neurophysiological models of the brain are inadequate and only a holographic model can explain ... archetypal experiences, encounters with the collective unconscious, and other unusual phenomena experienced during altered states of consciousness.
- At the 1987 annual meeting of the Association for the Study of Dreams ... , physicist Fred Alan Wolf ... asserted that ... [lucid dreams (unusually vivid dreams in which the dreamer realizes he or she is awake)] are ... visits to parallel realities....
- In his 1987 book ... Dr. F. David Peat, a physicist at Queen's University in Canada, asserted that synchronicities (coincidences that are so unusual and so psychologically meaningful they don't seem to be the result of chance alone) ... are actually "flaws in the fabric of reality." They reveal that our thought processes are much more intimately connected to the physical world than has been ... suspected.

... Many of these ideas are extremely controversial. Indeed, the holographic model itself is highly controversial and is by no means accepted by a majority of scientists. Nonetheless ... many important and impressive thinkers do support it and believe it may be the most accurate picture of reality we have to date.

The holographic model has also received some dramatic experimental support. In the field of neurophysiology numerous studies have corroborated Pribram's various predictions about the holographic nature of memory and perception. Similarly, in 1982 a landmark experiment performed by a research team led by physicist Alain Aspect at the Institute of Theoretical and Applied Optics, in Paris, demonstrated that the web of subatomic particles that compose our physical universe ... possesses what appears to be an undeniable "holographic" property....

One final piece of evidence in favor of the holographic model is the paranormal itself.... [I]n the last several decades a remarkable body of evidence has accrued suggesting that our current understanding of reality, the solid ... sticks and stones picture of the world ... , is wrong. Because these findings cannot be explained by any of our standard scientific models, science has in the main ignored them. However, the volume of evidence has reached the point where this is no longer a tenable situation.

... [I]n 1987, physicist Robert G. Jahn and clinical psychologist Brenda J. Dunne ... after a decade of rigorous experimentation by their Princeton Engineering Anomalies Research Laboratory, ... had accumulated unequivocal evidence that the mind can psychically interact with physical reality.... Jahn and Dunne found that through mental concentration alone, human beings are able to affect the way certain kinds of machines operate. This is an astounding finding and one that cannot be accounted for in terms of our standard picture of reality.

It can be explained by the holographic view, however. Conversely, because paranormal events cannot be accounted for by our current scientific understandings, they cry out for a new way of looking at the universe, a new scientific paradigm.

[Michael Talbot, *The Holographic Universe*. New York: HarperPerennial/HarperCollins, 1991, Introduction.]

IDEAS AND ISSUES

Understand Concepts

1. Can objects exist without being perceived, according to Berkeley? Why does he say this?
2. Are there existing things that resemble our ideas, according to Berkeley?
3. What does Berkeley think about Locke's primary and secondary qualities?

Think Critically

4. Show how Berkeley critiqued Locke's view of reality. On the left side of a page, list Locke's major ideas. On the right side of the same page, list arguments Berkeley used to refute Locke's ideas.

Communicate Ideas

5. Set up a panel discussion where three individuals role-play these philosophers and their views of reality: Descartes, Locke, and Berkeley. Allow each philosopher five minutes to explain his point of view, and fifteen minutes for each to criticize the ideas of the others. Allow fifteen minutes or more for the audience to ask questions, make critical comments, and suggest their own points of view.

Inquire and Research

6. Compare the perceptions of reality according to any two of Descartes, Locke, or Berkeley, in a written paper of three to four pages. Analyze and critique their views of reality. Determine who had the most powerful influence on modern ideas of reality.

Materialist Concepts of Reality: Matter, Not the Mind, Forms Reality

Descartes developed the concept of metaphysical dualism—the idea that there are two different substances, mind and matter. We can see origins of this concept in Plato's view that ideas were a more accurate view of reality than sensory information. Locke, followed by Berkeley, led philosophy and metaphysics increasingly down an idealist road. Locke wrote of a partial veil between substance and matter. Berkeley believed that ultimate reality existed in the mind and its ideas, although he did not deny the existence of other elements outside the mind.

Materialists disagree with Descartes' concept of dualism. They believe that matter, not mind, constitutes ultimate reality. Democritus, for example, believed that all things are made of indivisible particles or atoms, while Epicurus argued that all things, even the soul, were material. Thomas Hobbes (1588–1679) declared that everything existing in the universe is matter.

The Western world experienced a scientific revolution during the seventeenth and eighteenth centuries, and these dramatic changes encouraged materialist views of reality. Isaac Newton's (1642–1727) laws of motion suggested that everything could be explained as a mechanical process. The universe was likened to a complex watch in motion, and operated according to precise and predictable universal laws. It was up to humankind to discover precisely what those laws were. Materialism retains its popularity today. Some people have no problem equating human beings and human thought with computers. Scientist and philosopher Carl Sagan (1934–1996) expressed the views of many when he said, "Each human being is a superbly constructed, astonishingly compact, self-ambulatory [self-propelled] computer."

This painting by William Blake is called "Newton." What does this painting reveal about Blake's view of Newton and the materialist view of reality?

Modern Materialist Views:
Distinction Between Mind and Matter Is Not Clear

Not all thinkers supported this position. Recently mechanistic views of the universe and the concept of human beings as machines have generated strong and eloquent opposition. Modern physics no longer accepts Newton's mechanistic view of the universe. Werner Heisenberg's (1901–1976) uncertainty principle in quantum mechanics denies that causal determinism operates at the level of atomic and subatomic particles. Most scientists today believe an observer cannot observe the material world without influencing what it is that he or she is observing. Such scepticism suggests that there may not be any clear distinction between mind and matter, or between experience and that which is experienced.

In the following excerpt, James Feibleman argues that materialism, the concept that reality is composed of matter, has more support from science than ever before. Feibleman suggests that such elements as consciousness, memory, and intentions are readily explained in materialist rather than idealist terms.

Can a thought, the beauty of a sunrise, the purpose of life, belief in God, consciousness, memories, and the awareness of time passing be explained from a materialist point of view? If so, will we be able to program such experiences into a machine, such as a computer?

Werner Heisenberg

PHILOSOPHERS' FORUM

Matter, Including the Mind, Is Ultimately Real

James Feibleman

With the ... development of science has come an increased knowledge of matter.... Matter is ... a highly dynamic agent capable of sustaining the most complex activities.... "Mind," "consciousness," "spirit," "purpose," "goodness," and "beauty" will serve as typical items....

In the traditional materialism, there was no explanation for mental events.... In the newer materialism, mental events take place in the brain, and consist in [material] signals and ... systems.... "Consciousness" would seem to depend upon a particular area of the brain....

Next we have to examine the property of "purpose." For individual man it means ... his reason for existence. Purpose lies in the present, and consciousness of purpose belongs to sentient organisms. Ends lie in the future.... In material terms, this could be the

Time Line

Different Ideas About Reality
- - - - - - - - - - -

PLATO
(428 BCE–347 BCE)
believes reality exists in the mind

ARISTOTLE
(384 BCE–322 BCE)
claims senses provide the mind with information about reality

RENÉ DESCARTES
(1596–1650)
"proves" that God, mind, and matter exist

JOHN LOCKE
(1632–1704)
argues that reality is acquired through the senses

GEORGE BERKELEY
(1685–1753)
says that perception implies existence

THOMAS HOBBES
(1588–1679)
believes all that exists is matter

ISAAC NEWTON
(1642–1727)
says that ordered laws govern the universe

WERNER HEISENBERG
(1901–1976)
proposes that the universe has uncertainty

service of society.... For society itself it is necessary to appeal to the principle of biological evolution. *Homo sapiens* is working itself out to an end which lies invisible in the greater expanses of the material universe. But we do know this much. A state of maximum entropy would seem to be the ... [end point] of the universe....

That "goodness" could be considered a property of matter is not a currently conventional proposition, yet ... could conceivably be entertained. Let us define the good as the quality which emerges from the attraction between material objects.... Thus the quality of goodness at the level of the physical is the pull of gravitation. At the psychological level, it is friendship or love. The good, in the conventional ethical sense, would be ... an attraction between human individuals. In the domain of logic the good is represented by completeness.

"Beauty" as a property of matter is perhaps more unfamiliar.... We can define beauty as the ... relation of perfection between the parts of a material object. Beauty is thus an internal property. Art in the conventional aesthetic sense is the quality of beauty produced in a material object through human agency. In the domain of logic beauty is represented by consistency. It does not belong in the eye of the beholder ... but is a quality of the object: a sunset, a tree....

We conclude, then, that the spiritual values are ... incorporated in matter....

[James Feibleman, *The New Materialism*. The Hague: Martinus Nijhoff, 1970, 39–51. Reprinted by permission of Kiuwer Academic Publishers.]

Can materialism explain the beautiful, the spiritual, or the good? Is some wider explanation necessary?

IDEAS AND ISSUES

Understand Concepts

1. What is the major thesis presented by Feibleman in the excerpt? Outline his views of materialism and idealism.
2. (a) Why does Feibleman consider these terms in his argument: mind, consciousness, spirit, purpose, goodness, and beauty?
   (b) For each of the terms in part (a), state the materialist argument he presents.

Apply and Develop

3. If all human experience is composed of material elements, then does it follow that a very complex computer could undergo human experiences such as consciousness, a sense of self, sadness, and joy?

Think Critically

4. Overall, to what extent do you think that Feibleman has argued his case well, considering specific elements of human experience?
5. Respond to Feibleman's position from the point of view of an idealist or a mystic.
6. Present your own point of view in response to the arguments presented by materialists.

Communicate Ideas

7. Write a position paper in which you identify some aspect of reality or some belief that you think cannot be explained in materialist terms. Provide arguments to support your position. Anticipate and respond to possible arguments opposing your position.

The Nature of Time

What time is it? Do you have time? Where does the time go? Is time a line along which all events flow? Does the past or the future exist in the present? Do you think that someday we will be able to travel in time? Most of us take time for granted. Time is something that moves behind us in the background from one day to the next or from one year to another. Once in a while, but not often, we become highly aware of time passing, perhaps when we have a deadline looming or are late for an appointment. Only then do we become conscious of time's importance in our lives.

Perception of Time: Our Experience of Time

Perceptual time is time as we experience it. Our perception or experience of time often seems to vary from one situation to another. We experience time with friends differently from time spent in a dentist's chair. Even time spent in philosophy class may be experienced differently by two people, and differently by the same person at various moments.

Does the actual movement of time vary with experience? Sundials, followed by clocks, were developed as a way to standardize time, and to coordinate human plans and efforts, because humankind's perceptual time seemed so inconsistent. Clock time, however, is an arbitrary measure, geared to the movements of the Earth and sun, with little relevance to any other part of the universe.

How do you define time? Is it absolute and unchanging, relative to events, or does it even exist?

Indeed, clock time may have little relevance to your own experience of time. Two accurate watches in the same philosophy class register the same duration, despite their owners' perceptions. Nevertheless, the invention of clocks and watches strengthened the view that a constant unvarying time actually existed.

So what, then, is this concept of time, if we experience and measure it in so many ways? Is time a constant factor, an unchanging measuring stick which tracks all events, including our own lives, at an even unvarying rate? Or does time vary from place to place and person to person?

Conception of Time: Our Understanding of Time

Conceptual time is time as we think about it, even as we try to understand what it means. As soon as we try to define time, however, we stumble into difficulties and contradictions. St. Augustine, when asked about time, said, "If no one asks me, I know; if I wish to explain it to one that asks, I know not."

We know time is an interesting, if difficult, concept. Some philosophers consider time as absolute, independent of events, moving with unchanging regularity. Others view it as dependent on events, and varying with those events. Still others suggest that time does not exist. With which of these three positions do you intuitively tend to agree?

Absolute Time: Time That Is Independent of Events

Absolute time is the idea that time is independent of events. Absolute time stops for nothing and no one, moving forward at its own constant and relentless pace. Isaac Newton believed in absolute time because he saw time as a detached, impartial container through which events transpired. Newton believed that time was measured identically by all observers in the universe. Time, he thought, was unaffected by events, and could also be empty: "Absolute, true and mathematical time, of itself, and from its own nature, flows equably without regard to anything external."

Newton's concept of time as absolute, unaffected by events, has been challenged by modern science, particularly by Einstein's special theory of relativity. Newton's theory also does not seem to agree with our present-day experience of time. Consider this scenario: Suppose everything ceased to move. If all living and non-living things, even the atoms and their electrons, suddenly became static, frozen, and unable to move, would time stop, or would time continue to exist?

Zen Buddhist View of Time: Time *Is* Events

Zen Buddhist Dogen (1200–1253) had a different concept of time. He argued that time is not separate or isolated from events; it is not a container within which things happen. Dogen believed that time *is* the events, the things that happen. He believed that events defined time. Spring, he said, is the blooming of flowers, and not the time or season when flowers bloom. Our lives and the experiences within our lives, he wrote, define the time that we live; time does not measure our lives with clockwork precision.

If a multitude of events occur in many places, as we know they do, how would Dogen define time? How does Dogen's definition differ from absolute time?

Time Line

Different Ideas About Time
- - - - - - - - - -

DOGEN
(1200–1253)
believes time *is* events

ISAAC NEWTON
(1642–1727)
suggests that time is absolute and unchanging

IMMANUEL KANT
(1724–1804)
believes time is a mental construct to help us organize events

ALBERT EINSTEIN
(1879–1955)
theorizes that time is not constant throughout the universe but depends on the speed and location of the observer

STEPHEN HAWKING
(1942–)
suggests that time is based on three elements or arrows of time: thermodynamic, psychological, and cosmological

Being Time

Dogen

… You should perceive that each … thing of this whole world is an individual time…. You should learn that each single blade of grass, each single form, is on the whole earth…. Because it is only right at such a time, therefore being time is all the whole time….

In spite of this, when people … have not studied the Buddha's teaching, the views they have are such that when they hear the expression a time of being … they think, "Even though those mountains and rivers may exist still, I have passed them and am now in the vermilion tower of the jewel palace—the mountains and rivers and I are as far apart as sky and earth."

However, … [i]n the time one climbed the mountains and crossed the rivers, there was oneself. There must be time in oneself. Since oneself exists, time cannot leave. If time is not the appearances of going and coming, the time of climbing a mountain is the immediate present of being time. If time preserves the appearances of going and coming, there is in oneself the immediate present of being time….

… The principle of yesterday and today is just the time of directly entering the mountains and gazing out over the thousand peaks, … it is not a matter of having passed…. Though it seems to be elsewhere, it is right now…. To tell the gist of it, all existences in the whole world, while being lined up, are individual times….

[Thomas Clearly, trans., *Shobogenzo: Zen Essays by Dogen.* Hawaii: University of Hawaii Press, 1986.]

Relative Time: Time Associated with Events

The relative concept of time connects time to events as they occur. Subjective relativity links time to the observer, the person having the experience. Time spent in a dentist's chair, for example, is experienced differently than time spent with friends. Objective relativity relates the concept of time to the events or changes that occur within a specific time frame. Thus time happens because events happen; if events ceased to happen, time would be nonexistent.

In what ways does time seem to vary according to the circumstances? Does this mean that time really does proceed at varying speeds?

Subjective Relativity of Time: Time Viewed from the Mind

Immanuel Kant (1724–1804) believed that the idea of time originated in the structure of the human mind, as a mental construct devised to organize our experiences. Kant believed humankind could only understand the world by defining it through time. In Kant's view, time is an essential and preliminary, or *a priori*, part of the human mind. Human beings use time to change the chaos of sensory experience into an ordered understanding of the world. Time is not something that exists separately from our own human psyche, and it does not exist separately from our inner experience, but is relative to individual experiences.

The Moving Finger writes; and having writ, Moves on....
Omar Khayyam,
The Rubaiyat

Objective Relativity of Time: Time Viewed Relative to an Observer

Is it possible for time to vary as the events that occur within it vary? Can time vary not only in the perception of the person experiencing time, but in a reality beyond our experience? Can two different times occur in two different segments of the universe?

In the early twentieth century, physicist Albert Einstein (1879–1955) introduced his special theory of relativity. Einstein believed that time is not constant, but rather is dependent on the speed and position of an observer. Time slows down, Einstein suggested, at very high speeds, and when speeds approach the speed of light, time is at a standstill.

According to this theory of relativity, interesting things would happen to time travellers should they be able to move fast enough. Imagine twin sisters twenty years old. One, an astronaut, travels in a spaceship at 2.4×10^8 m/s to a star four light years away. At that speed, the clocks on her ship would slow to three-fifths of their normal rate, as measured by the twin sister on Earth. The astronaut would make her journey into space and back in less than five years. Meanwhile, her sister on Earth would have aged eight years.

Einstein's special theory of relativity has been supported by observable evidence. When atomic particles are accelerated to high speeds, and collide with other particles, they disintegrate more slowly than they would otherwise. The "time experience" of the particle slows to a fraction of what it was at rest. Scientists accept Einstein's special theory of relativity, even though it seems to go against what we think of as "common sense."

Does relativity mean it is possible to travel through time given enough speed? As yet, scientists are unable to answer this question. However, Einstein raised interesting questions about our perception of space and time.

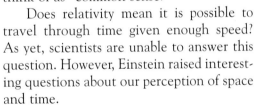
Albert Einstein

The idea that time can vary from place to place is a difficult one, but it is the idea Einstein used, and it is correct—believe it or not.
Richard Feynman

The Direction of Time:
Is There a Past, Present, and Future?

Does time move on? If so, in what direction? What is the difference between the past, the present, and the future? Do all these concepts exist and, if so, in what sense?

Some physicists describe time as a straight line with a beginning and an end. They believe time began with the creation of the universe and will end with the death and destruction of the universe. Before and after the existence of the universe, there are states where time does not exist at all. This linear, almost "common sense" view of time allows one to place the concept of time on the backburner while investigating other questions.

The linear view of time, however, raises several persistent questions. What is the difference between past time, present time, and future time? Often, we humans experience these time frames as very much the same. Suppose you are listen-

ing to a piece of music. At the same time, you also remember hearing an earlier rendition of the same piece of music, a memory that is as clear to you as if that past experience were part of your present. You are so entranced by the piece that you can imagine another future performance in your head. Usually, you are very conscious of the difference between your past, present, and future experiences but sometimes a dream or a very vivid memory will cloud your perception. How can your future anticipatory experience of music be different from the experience you are enjoying in the present and have enjoyed in the past?

If the future is constantly slipping into the past, is there really any such concept as the present? Does time have duration? The moment you have experienced something, does time dictate that that experience becomes part of your past and thus part of your memory?

DENNIS THE MENACE

"ISN'T IT ALWAYS NOW?"

Stephen Hawking's View of Time

Renowned physicist Stephen Hawking analyzed the concept of time in his book, *A Brief History of Time*: Why do we believe there is a difference between the past and the future? Why do we remember the past but not the future?

Hawking hypothesizes that all human beings have a sense of the right order of time in their everyday lives. This sense governs how we experience and understand the events around us. Suppose, for example, a cup falls from the table, smashing into pieces on the floor. We recognize that this is an event to which we are accustomed; it is the way things happen. Should the cup return to the top of the table and reassemble itself, we would be confused and bewildered. Why does that not occur?

Hawking reasons that time and our experience of it does indeed exist, and that time is based on three elements, or arrows of time: the thermodynamic, the psychological, and the cosmological.

Thermodynamic Arrow of Time

Hawking's first explanation of time is grounded in twentieth-century physics.

According to Hawking, the universe began with the Big Bang. At the moment of that explosion, the state of the universe was as uniform and orderly as it would ever be. As the universe expanded, it became increasingly disordered, with a growing complexity of densities, as galaxies, stars, planets, and human beings came into being. The result was an increasing lack of uniformity, something Hawking refers to as the thermodynamic arrow of time.

Psychological Arrow of Time

As observers in the universe, we human beings recognize and expect the thermo-

My goal is simple. It is complete understanding of the universe, why it is as it is and why it exists at all.
Stephen Hawking

Short then is the time which every man lives, and small the nook of the earth where he lives....
Marcus Aurelius

Why can't time sometimes go backward instead of always going forward? Is time travel possible?

dynamic arrow of time of the universe to move towards increasing disorder. We also measure time psychologically, in the direction of the thermodynamic arrow. Hawking cites as an example the arrangement of jigsaw puzzle pieces in a box. There are many more ways in which the pieces can be assembled in a disorderly state rather than in an orderly one. As puzzle players, we may assemble the pieces in an orderly manner, but as we do so, we expend energy, which in turn increases the amount of disorder in the universe overall.

Cosmological Arrow of Time

Cosmological time refers to the fact that the universe is presently expanding. What will happen when the universe stops expanding and begins to contract? Although we know this phenomenon will not happen for at least ten thousand million years (and thus is not of immediate personal concern), the question poses an interesting problem. Will teacups jump back up off the floor? Will we be able to predict the stock market? Will people die, live, then be born? What does happen when the universe reverses itself?

> Every saint has a past and every sinner a future.
> *Oscar Wilde*

The Arrow of Time

Stephen Hawking

> Time present and time past
> Are both perhaps present in time future
> And time future contained in time past.
> *T.S. Eliot*

… Conditions in the contracting phase [of the universe] would not be suitable for the existence of intelligent beings…. By then all the stars will have burned out and the protons and neutrons in them will probably have decayed into light particles and radiation. The universe would be in a state of almost complete disorder. There would be no strong thermodynamic arrow of time…. However, a strong thermodynamic arrow is necessary for intelligent life to operate. In order to survive, human beings have to consume food, which is an ordered form of energy, and convert it into heat, which is a disordered form of energy. Thus intelligent life could not exist in the contracting phase of the universe….

To summarize, the laws of science do not distinguish between the forward and backward directions of time. However, there are at least three arrows of time that do distinguish the past from the future. They are the thermodynamic arrow, the direction of time in which disorder increases; the psychological arrow, the direction of time in which we remember the past and not the future; and the cosmological arrow, the direction of time in which the universe expands rather than contracts. I have shown that the psychological arrow is essentially the same as the thermodynamic arrow, so that the two would always point in the same direction…. And the reason we observe this thermodynamic arrow to agree with the cosmological arrow is that intelligent beings can exist only in the expanding phase. The contracting phase will be unsuitable because it has no strong thermodynamic arrow of time.

The progress of the human race in understanding the universe has established a small corner of order in an increasingly disordered universe. If you remember every word in this book, your memory will have recorded about two million pieces of information: the order in your brain will have increased by about two million units. However, while you have been reading the book, you will have converted at least a thousand calories of ordered energy, in the form of food, into disordered energy…. This will increase the disorder of the universe by about twenty million million million million units.…

[Stephen Hawking, *A Brief History of Time*. New York: Bantam Books, 1990, 151–3.]

Achilles and the Tortoise

In the fifth century BCE, the philosopher Zeno travelled to Athens to put forward a series of paradoxes for Socrates and others to consider. Zeno wanted to illustrate the fact that some of our basic assumptions about time and space should be questioned. One of Zeno's most famous paradoxes was the story of a race between Achilles and a tortoise. The tortoise began the race some distance ahead of Achilles. By the time Achilles reached the point where the tortoise began, the tortoise had moved ahead by a small distance. When Achilles reached that new point, the tortoise had moved still further. Thus, Zeno concluded, there will never be a point in time when Achilles will catch up to the tortoise. Are you convinced? Can you logically argue against this conclusion?

An Argument that There Is No Time

The question of time continues to perplex people in many different fields. In the following excerpt, a theoretical physicist argues that there is no such thing as time.

Moreover, he claims that all existence, even the existence of this moment, will continue to exist forever. What do you think of his argument? Is it convincing?

From Here To Eternity

Tim Folger

Millions long for
immortality who
do not know what
to do with themselves
on a rainy Sunday
afternoon.

Susan Ertz

Eternity is not some-
thing that begins
after you are dead. It
is going on all the
time. We are in it
now.

*Charlotte Perkins
Gilman*

Time seems to stand still in South Newington, a secluded village … about 20 miles north of Oxford, England. The … church, the thatched roof houses, and the tidy gardens along narrow lanes all appear unchanged by the passage of centuries. Standing on the roof of the church's bell tower on a warm, late summer day, Julian Barbour, a theoretical physicist with some extraordinary notions about the nature of time, points to his home, known as College Farm, which borders the ancient church.

"It looks almost exactly as it did when it was built 340 years ago," says Barbour…. "Virtually all the houses you see around are from about 1640 to 1720…." The entire scene is so placid one can't help but imagine that … the village and the surrounding landscape, will remain unchanged for the next 340 years.

… Barbour … is convinced the static harmony of South Newington extends past the horizon to the universe at large. In his view, this moment and all it holds … will never change. There is no past and no future. Indeed, time and motion are nothing more than illusions.

In Barbour's universe, every moment of every individual's life—birth, death, and everything in between—exists forever. "Each instant we live," Barbour says, "is, in essence, eternal." That means each and every one of us is immortal…. "[W]e are forever … young." We are also forever aged and decrepit, on our deathbeds, in the dentist's chair, at Thanksgivings with our in-laws, and reading these words.

Barbour fully realizes how outrageous the notion of a world without time sounds…. But then, common sense has never been a reliable guide to understanding the universe—physicists have been confounding our perceptions since Copernicus first suggested that the sun does not revolve around Earth. After all, we don't feel the slightest movement as the spinning Earth hurdles through the void at some 67 000 miles per hour. Our sense of the passage of time, Barbour argues, is just as wrongheaded as the credo of the Flat Earth Society….

Barbour's central argument is that a mistaken belief in the reality of time prevents physicists from achieving their ultimate goal: the unification of the submicroscopic atomic world of quantum mechanics with the vast cosmic one of general relativity. The problem arises because each theory provides a radically different conception of time, and physicists simply don't know how to reconcile the two views….

What makes the two versions of time so different? Time in the quantum realm has no remarkable properties at all; … it simply regularly ticks away in the background, just as it does in our own lives. Like a clock at a sporting event, it provides an invisible framework in which events unfold. That's not the case in Einstein's general theory of relativity.

To describe the universe on the largest scale, Einstein had to weave time and space together into the very fabric of the universe. As a result, in general relativity, there is no invisible framework, no clock ticking outside the universe against which to measure events.... Space and time curve around stars and other massive bodies and make light bend away from straight-line paths. Near black holes, time seems to slow down or even come to a full stop.

Barbour is not alone in recognizing that the pictures of time in general relativity and quantum mechanics are fundamentally incompatible.... But Barbour has taken perhaps the most unorthodox approach by proposing that the way to solve the conundrum is to leave time out of the equations that describe the universe entirely....

... [Barbour says that time] is nothing but a measure of the changing positions of objects. A pendulum swings, the hands on a clock advance. Objects—and their positions—he argues, are therefore more fundamental than time. The universe at any given instant simply consists of many different objects in many different positions.

... But the next part of his argument ... is much harder to swallow: Every possible configuration of the universe, past, present and future, exists separately and eternally. We don't live in a single universe that passes through time. Instead, we—or many slightly different versions of ourselves—simultaneously inhabit a multitude of static, everlasting tableaux that include everything in the universe at any given moment. Barbour calls each of these possible still-life configurations a "Now." Every Now is a complete, self-contained, timeless, unchanging universe. We mistakenly perceive the Nows as fleeting, when in fact each one persists forever.... Barbour coined a new word for it: Platonia. The name honors the ancient Greek philosopher [Plato] who argued that reality is composed of eternal and changeless forms, even though the physical world we perceive through our senses appears to be in constant flux....

... Barbour ... likens his view of reality to a strip of movie film. Each frame captures one possible Now, which may include blades of grass, clouds in a blue sky ... and distant galaxies. But nothing moves or changes in any one frame.... Don't we then somehow shift from one "frame" to another?

No. There is no movement from one static arrangement of the universe to the next. Some configurations of the universe simply contain little patches of consciousness—people—with memories of what they call a past that are built into the Now. The illusion of motion occurs because many slightly different versions of us—none of which move at all—simultaneously inhabit universes with slightly different arrangements of matter. Each version of us sees a different frame—a unique, motionless, eternal Now....

The parish church next to Barbour's home contains some of the rarest murals in England. One painting, completed in about 1340, shows the murder of Thomas à Becket, the twelfth-century archbishop whose beliefs clashed with those of King Henry II.

The mural captures the instant when a knight's sword cleaves Becket's skull. Blood spurts from the gash.

If Barbour's theory is correct, then the moment of Becket's martyrdom still exists as an eternal Now … , as do our own deaths. But in Barbour's cosmos, the hour of our death is not an end; it is but one of the numberless components of an inconceivably vast, frozen structure. All the experiences we've ever had and ever will have lie forever fixed, set like crystalline facets in some infinite, immortal jewel. Our friends, our parents, our children, are always there. In many ways it's a beautiful and comforting vision…. Could it possibly be true?

Only time will tell.

[Tim Folger, "From Here To Eternity," *Discover* Magazine, December 2000, 54–6.]

Julian Barbour argues that all possible configurations of the universe, past, present, and future, exist as separate and eternal entities. Do you agree with his view? Is it possible to prove that he is right?

IDEAS AND ISSUES

Understand Concepts

1. What is the difference between perceptual and conceptual time?
2. How would Dogen respond to the idea that we move through time, as a train moves through a tunnel?
3. What is the difference between the thermodynamic and the psychological arrows of time?
4. What will happen when the universe stops expanding? How important is this?
5. Summarize Julian Barbour's concept of time.

Apply and Develop

6. How is it that there is no constant sense of time in everyday life?
7. Does the movement of a clock make time any more regular, and in what ways? Explain your answer.
8. Time in a dentist's chair and time watching a movie may be experienced differently. Describe the implications for the nature of time itself.

Think Critically

9. Who has the most to say about perceptual or "experienced" time — Dogen or Hawking? Describe what each of them says.
10. (a) Do you think that Barbour's idea of time is worth considering?
    (b) What evidence does he provide to support his view?
    (c) How would you argue for or against Barbour's view?

Communicate Ideas

11. In a panel discussion, present the ideas of time put forward by each of the theorists in this section. Be prepared to defend their point of view in each case.
12. Debate this issue: It is possible that at some time in the future time travel will occur.

Causality:
The Dynamic of Cause and Effect

What causes things to happen? Why did you choose to study philosophy rather than another subject? Why does the sun rise in the east, instead of in the west? Why did it snow today, and rain two days ago? Why did your friend decide not to play ball today? You probably can come up with an answer for each of these questions. Notice that in some cases the question concerns human actions and their causes, while in other cases the question is about natural events.

Under most circumstances, we usually accept that events and actions are caused by other events and actions. Often we disagree, however, over what cause is in operation, and how it has its effect. Suggest a cause for each of the situations below. When you are finished, compare your causes with others in your class.
- Night follows day.
- Shaken from the tree, an apple falls to the ground.
- Many car accidents occur at the corner of Main and Elm.
- Periods of prosperity are often followed by economic recession.
- World War II followed the rise of Hitler in Germany and the Great Depression of the 1930s.
- Two children were raised in abject poverty. One became a criminal, while the other became a highly respected social worker.
- For four years, you study hard to achieve high grades. Your goal is to earn a scholarship at university.
- The race-car driver, determined to win, rounds the last turn at high speed. He loses control of his car, and is lucky to escape with his life.
- I was hungry, so I went to lunch early.
- Even though I was hungry, I continued to study philosophy.

In this previous exercise, you no doubt noticed that events have different causes. For example, a natural event, such as an apple falling to the ground, often has a different sort of cause than does a human action, such as the student who goes to lunch early. How would you characterize this difference? Another causal difference appears to be between social events that occur on a large scale, such as wars, and the actions of individuals.

Consider this scenario. A homeowner allows his house to fall into serious disrepair. The shingles are loose, the paint is peeling, and the furnace has a strange smell of gas around it. One day the homeowner goes down to the basement. All the lights are burned out, and he cannot see. He lights a match, and a massive gas explosion erupts, starting a fire. The homeowner is injured, and he cannot call the fire department for help because his telephone has been disconnected due to lack of payment. The house burns down to the ground. What are the causes of these events?

What Is a Cause?

Have you ever seen a cause? David Hume asked the same question, and concluded that there was no such thing as a cause, only the expectation that one event will follow another. While Hume's answer seems to run counter to our experiences of life, he does raise an important point. Consider, for example, a simple action such as a home run in baseball. What we see is a person swinging a bat, from which a ball rebounds high over the field and into the stands. Where in this sequence of visible events is there a cause? According to Hume we see sequences, but nowhere do we see "causes."

Hume's consideration of the notion of cause raised many related questions. How does one event that we call "cause" bring about another event that we call "effect"? Is there some necessary connection between the two events? Maybe the universe just evolves from one state to another, and human beings try to explain this evolution by arbitrarily creating the concept of cause. Scientists studying the natural world agree that they have difficulty predicting the effect of any action with certainty; the best they can do is to predict the probability of an action's occurrence.

When we begin to consider human actions, questions of cause and effect take very interesting turns. Suppose two children are raised in poverty. One becomes a happy and successful person, while the other becomes unhappy and bitter about life, and turns to crime. How could there be such widely divergent results from a common beginning? How do we explain the causes of human actions? Do we look to genetics, the environment, intentions, fate, or chance? What has made you the person you are today, and what will shape or cause you to do other things in the future?

> In shallow ponds, even little fish can stir up a commotion. In the oceans, the largest whales make hardly a ripple.
> *Hindu proverb*

> Nature is but a name for an effect Whose cause is God.
> *William Cowper*

Aristotle's View of Causality

Many philosophers have tackled the problem of causality, especially Aristotle. His views on this issue have had a long-lasting impact.

Aristotle identified four types of causes he said we must consider: efficient, material, formal, and final. He used the example of a sculptor fashioning a marble statue to illustrate each of these distinctions. What causes a statue, or any human product, to come into existence? Here is how Aristotle answered this question.

Efficient Cause

Aristotle believed every product of the universe has an efficient cause, which is the effort of someone or something to bring about an effect. Aristotle provided the example of the sculptor as an efficient cause, as the sculptor chisels away to create a statue. All of us certainly recognize efficient causes in our own lives. If you tidy up your room, it looks neat. If you study hard, you will more likely do well in school.

Material Cause

The material cause, according to Aristotle, is the material out of which something is made. In the case of the sculpture, the material cause is marble. The lumber, bricks, and mortar are the material causes of a house. Books, pens, classrooms, and libraries are some material causes of student success.

Today, we generally do not consider material elements as causes. We do not consider the books we use for our study as a cause of good marks. We do not usually consider bricks and mortar as a cause of a house. Nevertheless, without the materials, such as books and mortar, events would not come about.

Formal Cause

Aristotle identified the form or shape of an event or product as its formal cause. Artistotle, as we discussed earlier, believed that the potential form of an object resided within that object. The adult oak tree, for example, resided within the acorn as potential. The final shape of the marble statue resided within the unformed block of marble. One might think of a formal cause as the blueprint, plan, or organizing principle towards which an event or object proceeds.

Today we do not normally consider the outcome or final shape as a cause, certainly in the case of natural objects. Nevertheless, there are many ways in which we do use the idea of a formal cause. Formal causes might be construed as the goals towards which people aim, goals such as building a house, passing an exam, or sculpting a work of art. Moreover, when one considers that all living things, such as birds, salamanders, trees, antelope, and human beings, have specific genetic qualities embedded within them which define individual growth potential, the idea of formal causes is not that far-fetched.

Final Cause

Aristotle believed that all things were created for a final purpose. A stone, he wrote, fell towards the earth because the earth is its natural resting place. A sculpture is made for the final purpose of decorating a building; a house is made to provide a home. Today, we very rarely use the idea of final causes when we are speaking of inanimate objects. We do not believe that stones, bridges, or statues have a final goal towards which they move.

We do, however, speak of the goals or purposes of some things. People involved in the study of life sciences, such as biology or genetics for example, speak of the goals or purposes of organs. The purpose of the heart is to pump blood, while the purpose of pain is to warn of danger.

Aristotle believed all things in the natural world had a final cause or purpose, and that final cause is God. For Aristotle, the final cause was the most important cause. This idea and its importance remains a central element in many religions. In science, however, the idea of final causes has minimal effect. In fact, much of modern science has eliminated the very idea of final causes.

Well begun is half done.

Aristotle

It is absurd to suppose that purpose is not present because we do not observe the agent.

Aristotle

The Revolt Against Final Causes

Aristotle's ideas of causality exerted a powerful influence on philosophers for hundreds of years. The scientific revolution of the seventeenth century, however, introduced a new way of looking at things. In many ways, the scientific revolution was a revolt against final causes and an affirmation of efficient causes. Scientists, such as Galileo and his contemporaries, were more interested in finding out *how* things happened than in trying to determine *why* they happened. Scientific philosophers of the day emphasized observation and experimentation. This helped them determine the processes by which events happened and how these events affected other events. Galileo, for example, was much more interested in the manner, speed, and direction with which objects fell to the earth than in why they moved in a downward direction.

The search for efficient causes is a core element of modern science. It has facilitated the discovery of new knowledge in every area of medicine, biology, chemistry, and physics. The search for the causes of illnesses has led to an understanding of illness and its treatments. The detection and definition of humankind's genetic blueprint, the genome project, is one of the most recent research projects studying the causes of human illnesses and behaviour.

David Hume:
Expectations Help Explain Sequences of Events

Have you ever seen a "cause"? What did it look like? Perhaps you saw one thing occur, and expected something else to happen as a result. How often did your expectation come to pass? Empiricists such as David Hume held two major principles: the information we have about the world comes to us through our senses; and the ideas that we have about the world exist within our minds. Hume used these two principles of empiricism to investigate the idea of causation.

Hume had great difficulty with unseen events. Why do we believe there is such a thing as a "cause," anyway? When we play a game of billiards, for example, we use a cue to strike the cue ball, which, in turn, moves and strikes a coloured ball, which also moves. In each case, we see movement, but where do we see a cause? If there is such a thing as a cause that was occurring, it must certainly have been invisible. We see a hammer strike a nail; we also see the nail enter the wood. When a ball goes through a glass window, we hear glass break. But where and what is a cause, asked Hume?

Hume suggested that our ideas of causal connections are composed of four elements. First is the fact that the cause and the effect must be in close proximity to each other; the hammer, for example, must approach and touch the nail. Second, the cause must precede the effect, that is, the hammer swing must come before the nail moves. Third, there must be a transmission of force from cause to effect; the hammer must somehow transmit force to the nail so that the nail moves. Fourth, there must also be a necessary connection between cause and effect; when the hammer hits the nail, the nail is driven into the wood.

Hume wanted to know which of these four elements of cause and effect could be observed, and which could not. He concluded that we can observe closeness (the hammer touches the nail), and we can observe order of time (the swing occurs before the nail moves). We cannot, however, observe the other two elements, transmission of force and necessary connection. No one, Hume believed, is able to see a "transmission of force" or a "necessary connection." Where does the transmission of force or the necessary connection appear when you hit the nail with the hammer?

Hume suggests that these two causal elements occur only in our minds as we seek to explain a sequence of events. When a sequence of events occurs often, we expect that it will continue to occur, although there is only a probability, not an absolute certainty, that the sequence will happen again in the future. According to Hume, there is no necessary connection or transmission of force that exists beyond our own expectations.

Here is an illustrative example. A turkey noticed that when the farmer came to the barnyard, there would be corn scattered on the ground. The turkey was hungry, but it did nothing for several days. Finally it connected the appearance of the farmer and the scattering of corn on the ground. Every day the farmer appeared and every day the corn appeared. Finally the turkey ventured into the barnyard when the farmer appeared. Unfortunately, it was Thanksgiving and the farmer was in the barnyard not to feed the turkey, but to deliver it to the dinner table. There was no necessary connection between the farmer and the corn. The turkey came to a false expectation, one that proved contrary to its continued best interest.

Hume's analysis of causation has had a strong impact on how scientists view their work. Today, many scientists look for correlation between events, rather than searching for something called a cause. Correlation means that two events tend to happen together, although the reasons for such simultaneous occurrences may not be immediately obvious. For example, a doctor may note a correlation between diet and heart disease, or between pollution and lung disease. An engineer discovers a correlation between a certain type of bridge construction and long-term safety. Eventually, reasons for such connections may be found, but correlations provide good beginnings.

Immanuel Kant: Cause Involves the Mind

Immanuel Kant studied the work being done by scientists of his time. It seemed to him that this work was too successful to be simply a record of things that seemed to occur together. Kant decided that causality is not a relation between things in themselves. Cause, he said, is a principle of order that our minds impose on events to make sense of experience.

Kant was trying to understand a number of aspects of human thought in the field of metaphysics. Cause, like our concepts of space and time, he said, are built into our mind—"hardwired" as we might say today. He called such elements of thought *a priori*, meaning that they come first, before we experience things in this world. As such, they are largely beyond our ability to critically analyze them, or to investigate them empirically, and so are "synthetic." Statements such as "God exists" or "Every event has a cause" are such *synthetic a priori* statements. Searching for understanding of such metaphysical topics and questions, he said, is the fundamental goal of philosophy.

We use this built-in concept of cause, as we use concepts of time and space, to understand the world existing around us. The knowledge that we gain in this way, said Kant, is analytic. That is, we use existing knowledge, definitions, and logic to find out more about the world. Analytic knowledge such as "God is all-powerful" or "a balanced diet increases healthy living" is in this category.

Understand Concepts

1. (a) What are Aristotle's four types of causes?
    (b) Which of these is still considered important, and which is no longer thought of as a cause? Explain your answer.
2. How would Aristotle and Galileo answer the question, Why did the apple fall to the ground?
3. How did Hume analyze our concept of causality?
4. What conclusions did Hume reach about each of the elements of causality?

Apply and Develop

5. Consider any project that you are currently involved in. Analyze it in terms of Aristotle's four types of causes. Draw conclusions about his theory based on this application.
6. Determine the causal explanation you would provide for each series of events listed below. How is each explanation different from, or similar to, Aristotle's concept of causes? In each case, provide a plausible causal explanation. Categorize the types of causal explanations in some way that organizes them logically. In what cases do goals or intentions have a part in your explanations?
    (a) A person risks her life to save another.
    (b) A person continues to work hard at a job after winning a million dollar lottery.
    (c) A parent does everything in life to ensure the happiness and success of her children.
    (d) A person who has had every advantage as a child becomes an adult who is hurtful and unethical towards others.
    (e) An airplane, examined carefully before flight, develops engine problems soon after take-off.
    (f) Lightning strikes a historical building, setting it on fire and destroying it, while all the surrounding buildings are left intact.
    (g) Despite predictions of rain made by forecasters, the day of a camping trip turns out to be beautiful.
    (h) The Earth continues to orbit around the sun at just the right distance to provide us with seasons, warmth, and life.
    (i) The plants and animals on Earth all have a part to play in creating an interdependent ecosystem.
    (j) Sometimes I feel like working hard, and sometimes I feel like relaxing.

Think Critically

7. Why is it important that different forms of causality be identified in science and in everyday life?
8. Is there a difference between causality in natural events and in human events? In what ways does the causality differ?

Comparison of Human and Natural Causes

What differences are there between events caused by human behaviour and events caused by non-human natural actions? One major difference that comes immediately to mind is the fact that human events are often the result of human intentions. Human beings plan, or strive towards, goals in life. Natural events, on the other hand, are usually not regarded as goal-oriented, or as occurring with intention. Lightning strikes in one place or another through the interactions of physical elements and their associated forces, not through conscious intention. A volcano erupts as a result of certain physical conditions, not as a result of intention.

Some philosophers, such as Aristotle, believed that natural events possess conscious direction, or intention. If one has a mystical or religious view of the universe and of nature, one might also see Divine intention therein. Twentieth-century philosopher Douglas Gasking (1911–1994) suggests that our ideas of causality in the natural world stem from observations of human behaviour. We act in the world and things happen as a result. We mix substances in a test tube, and an interesting reaction might occur. We place fresh vegetables in a hot wok and a delicious meal may develop. Gasking believes that we mistakenly take human intentions, behaviours, or results, and extrapolate them to the rest of the natural world. Humans envision cause and effect in terms of things that can be done to change nature. According to Gasking, we, like Aristotle, probably see intentionality in most of the natural events around us.

Causality Applied to Human Behaviour

What are the major elements causing human beings to behave as they do? Some philosophers and scientists say that our behaviour is largely the result of biology or genetics. Others believe behaviour is largely the result of learning and life experiences. These two positions provide an important platform for debate, as we seek to understand to what extent we are in control of our own destinies, and to what extent our own intentions can shape our behaviour. If behaviour is shaped primarily by inborn, genetic characteristics, we have less control over our lives. However, if human behaviour is largely the consequence of learning and experience, we are able to exercise more control over our destinies. The arguments on behalf of both positions are strong and wide-ranging.

Consider your own behaviour, for example. Which of your characteristics appear to be the result of biological inheritance from your parents? Which seem more to result from your life experiences? Making these distinctions is not an easy task.

If we find it so difficult to perform an analysis on our own behaviour, how can we possibly analyze other people? Suppose the local newspaper has a story about a man with a lifetime history of violence and other criminal behaviour. He has served a jail term of twenty years, and is seeking a parole review. The prisoner claims he has changed; he has become a different person and is a good candidate for parole. The prisoner's intentions are to live a very different type of life than he did previously. What factors will affect his behaviour? What type of person will he be if he is released?

Empathetic Explanation

One methodology for explaining the causes of human behaviour is to attempt an understanding of the individual person—his or her characteristics, motives, intentions, and any outside influences which may affect that person. We often use our own life experiences when we attempt to understand another person, that is, we empathize with the other individual.

Robin Collingwood (1889–1943), a philosopher of history, argued that the only way to understand the actions of others is by projecting ourselves into their own situation as much as possible. If we want to understand the actions of another person, living or dead, we must view the world through that person's eyes. Canadian philosopher John Eisenberg expanded Collingwood's view by suggesting that we should understand the goals and intentions of the individual, the means or methods available to achieve those goals, the external factors that shape the individual's life and choices, and the decisions the individual makes.

When studying the lives of others, we want to learn as much as we can about specific causes and effects in their lives. This helps us to understand their intentions and actions. Knowing a person's character may give us some chance to predict how he or she will act in the future. This traditional historical approach to understanding human behaviour is also the approach used by psychoanalysts as they seek to understand the problems of individuals.

The Idea of Universal Law

How can we explain human events that take place on a large scale? How can we use the concepts of cause and effect to explain changing crime rates, economic recessions, or wars? These events require complex explanations. Moreover, unlike many events in nature, they can only be recorded after they occur; they cannot be predicted with certainty.

One way to explain widespread human events is to attempt to find general, or universal, laws within which these events can be understood. For example, one might explain a stock market crash by developing a "law" such as: Stock markets crash when stocks are highly overvalued. Migration of people from one place to another might be explained by a "law" such as: People will move to seek better circumstances for themselves wherever possible. The concept of such universal or "covering laws" to explain human behaviour was

In his famous turn-of-the-century experiments, Ivan Pavlov rang a bell everytime he fed his dogs. Eventually, the dogs began to salivate whenever they heard a bell, regardless of whether food followed. Pavlov named this behaviour a "conditioned reflex."

It is indeed high time for the clergyman and the psychotherapist to join forces.

Carl Jung

suggested by Karl Hempel (1905–), a philosopher of science. In some ways, it is like applying the scientific methods that work so well in the natural sciences to human behaviour. Social scientists use the universal law concept in sociology and anthropology as they seek a general rule, or principle, with which they can understand large groups of people: the forces that operate, why certain behaviours occurred, or why certain actions may result.

Sociologists and criminologists note that the rate for several crimes has continued to decline in the last decade, whereas it grew steadily during the 1970s and 1980s. A covering law explanation of this occurrence might be that crime is more often committed by younger adults. The number of young adults during the 1970s and 1980s was increasing, while more recently this number has decreased.

Insurance companies use universal laws to make predictions about the likelihood of accidents, based on the age, sex, and habits of people. If you are young and male, some insurers may believe that you will more likely drive fast and cause accidents. Is this judgement fair or unfair? A universal explanation of cause will give us statistical, probable information about large numbers of people in any given situation, but it provides little predictable information about individuals within the group.

Probabilistic Explanations

Probabilistic explanations put forward in recent times deny that a "covering law" such as Hempel's provides a satisfactory explanation for human actions, especially for the actions of individuals. Probabilistic explanations say that it is not possible to predict human behaviour from existing conditions, except that a particular behaviour or behaviours might occur. For example, two young people, twins perhaps, grow up in what appear to be identical circumstances. One turns to a life of crime, while the other does good deeds all her life. How can this happen?

Philosophers such as J.L. Mackie (1917–1981) argue that we can only look back to find conditions that were present and necessary for the behaviour to happen. These conditions do not necessarily guarantee that a specific result will ensue, but they increase the likelihood of a particular outcome.

Is this because we simply do not know all the factors that are involved in human decisions? Or is there really significant freedom to make decisions and to act, despite existing conditions?

Recent theories in physics suggest that even in the natural world events can only be predicted with some degree of probability, not with absolute certainty. We cannot know beforehand in what direction an individual animal or atom will move. We can only predict what the probability of movement is by looking at many animals or atoms. Such explanations involving probability appear to operate in the human social realm as well. We can only know with some degree of probability how an individual human being will turn out, or the decision an individual will make in a particular case. Predicting human behaviour with certainty is difficult to impossible in most cases.

IDEAS AND ISSUES

Understand Concepts
1. What views did Kant and Gasking have about causality?

Apply and Develop
2. How might cause and effect operate in the cases of human activity below? In each case, identify the effect to be explained. Then provide explanations that use each of these concepts of causality applied to human actions: empathetic explanation, universal law, and probabilistic explanation. In each case, indicate how investigation into the causes of the event or situation might be conducted.
   (a) A young music student decides to make music her career. She goes on to study music at university and eventually joins a major symphony orchestra. When asked later why she was successful, she says that it is because of the encouragement she received from her family and teachers, as well as her dedicated regular practising.
   (b) Research indicates that behaviour is shaped most effectively by random reinforcement, rewards, or punishments that occur with no predictable pattern. Students study more when they are given surprise tests and tests at irregular intervals.
   (c) Automobile insurance companies set their premiums using a variety of factors: driver's age, years of driving experience, record of accidents and serious highway offences, and other factors. Some people argue that it is unfair to judge an individual simply by their age, since young drivers, for example, vary widely in their driving habits and attitudes. How can you predict who will be a good or bad driver? Are there better ways to determine car insurance rates?

Think Critically
3. Organize and compare the views of Hume, Kant, and Gasking regarding causality. Are there any general conclusions you can reach about causality based on these philosophers' ideas?
4. In what ways must we separate human behaviour and natural events when we speak of causality?

Inquire and Research
5. Find out what theory of human causation police officers, school principals, guidance counsellors, parents, teens, younger children, and older people hold about teenage behaviour. You may have to develop examples and scenarios to help get answers. Draw conclusions about these theories.
6. Research Abraham Maslow's theory of needs and actions. Report on the essence of the theory. Critically analyze it.

Free Will, Fate, and Responsibility

Most of us generally live under the assumption that we enjoy the freedom to make decisions and control our lives. However, we are also part of a universe that operates in ways that are beyond our control and that has an impact on us in many ways. As human beings, are we largely free to make life choices, or are our actions governed primarily by external forces and circumstances beyond our control? Philosophers and people in everyday life face this issue when they examine the ideas of free will and fate. Here are several possible positions in the free-will-and-fate debate.

Determinism:
Our Choices Are an Illusion

Determinism is the view that our actions are determined by forces beyond our control. One form of determinism considers that, since all things are caused by events that precede them, any action can only be the result of previous conditions. For example, if you are playing billiards, and you set the ball up directly in front of the corner pocket, the fact that the next player will sink the ball is determined by your placement of the ball. If you study for tomorrow's philosophy test and you know what the major questions will be and you get a good night's sleep, you will probably do well on the test. This form of determinism looks to natural and physical forces

in the universe that shape our destinies in much the same way as they shape other natural objects.

Another type of determinism suggests that unknown forces, such as God or fate, control our destinies. This type of determinism goes beyond the natural universe to find an explanation for all events. There are several forms of this type of determinism. In Hinduism and Buddhism, for example, there is a belief in karma, that our fates are determined by our past actions, even in previous existences. Other forms of this supranatural determinism hold that a supreme intelligence, such as God, knows all things, past and present; therefore this intelligence also knows the future. So even though we think we have free will, our actions are known beforehand by a supreme intelligence. Debate has proceeded for a very long time over whether knowledge of future events negates free will and choice. That is: Is free will an illusion? In Christian theology, for example, it is generally held that while God is all-knowing and therefore knows the future, God has still provided humans with free will and choice.

Natural Determinism and Pierre Laplace

Nineteenth-century scientist and mathematician Pierre Simon de Laplace (1749–1827) wrote that if there was an intelligence great enough to know all forces acting in nature at any given moment, and the positions of all things at that very same moment, this intelligence would be able to predict the future. Laplace argued that every event is connected with all previous events by universal causality. He described the universe as a complete and integrated system, and suggested that the human belief in chance arises solely from our ignorance of causes. He cited the appearance of comets, believed in ancient times to be supernatural omens, but later proven to travel in regular, predictable orbits, as part of a determinist universe.

Pierre Laplace

Laplace believed human actions are also part of the deterministic system. Freedom is an illusion, he wrote; there are motives behind every human action. When people believe that they have freedom to select specific options, they are simply ignorant of those hidden causes leading them to choose one option over the other. Nothing avoids the universally necessary chains of causality.

Laplace believed a complete intelligence would have the ability to provide a formula that explained the universe in total—past, present, and future. Human beings, he thought, are only just beginning to devise general laws to explain events, and humans have a long way to go.

Belief in determinism persists into this century, although not in the sciences of

Philosophical Essay on Probability

Pierre Laplace

All events, even those which because of their small scale do not appear to keep to the great laws of nature, are just as necessary a result of those laws as are the revolutions of the sun. In ignorance of the ties which bind these events to the entire system of the universe, people have made them depend on final causes, or upon chance.... But these imaginary causes have been gradually pushed out of the way as the boundaries of our knowledge have increased....

Present events have a connection with previous ones that is based on the self-evident principle that a thing cannot come into existence without a cause that produces it.... The freest will is unable to give birth to them without a determinate motive.... Believing in ... uncaused events is an illusion of the mind....

We must therefore regard the present state of the universe as the effect of its preceding state and as the cause of the one which is to follow. An intelligence which in a single instant could know all the forces which animate the natural world, and the respective situations of all the beings that made it up, could, provided it was vast enough to make an analysis of all the data so supplied, be able to produce a single formula which specified all the movements in the universe from those of the largest bodies in the universe to those of the lightest atom....

Let us recall that in former times, still not so very far away, a heavy rainfall or prolonged drought, a comet trailing a very long tail, eclipses, the aurora borealis, and in general all of the ordinary phenomena, were regarded as so many signs of celestial anger.... Thus the comet of 1456, with its long tail, spread terror throughout Europe.... The knowledge of the laws of the world-system acquired during the interval had dissipated the fears produced by ignorance of the true relationship of man to the universe; and Halley, having recognized that the appearances of 1531, 1607 and 1682 all related to the same comet, predicted its next return for the end of 1758 or the start of 1759.... There is no doubt that this regularity which has been demonstrated by astronomy in the movement of the comets also obtains in all other phenomena.

[Pierre Laplace, *Essai Philosophique sur les Probabilités* (1819). Trans. by John Cottingham from *Œuvres de Laplace* (Paris, 1847), Vol. 7, vi–viii. In *Western Philosophy*, trans and ed. by John Cottingham. Oxford: Blackwell Publishers, Ltd., 1997.]

mathematics and physics. Some determinists believe our actions in later life are determined by a genetic blueprint set down at conception. Psychoanalytic psychologists are convinced that our actions and our characters are determined by childhood events. Some thinkers combine these two views.

Behaviourial psychologist B.F. Skinner argued that every human action is the result either of a specific genetic blueprint, or of reinforcing experiences. Like many determinists, Skinner insisted that belief in free will is not based on reason but on superstition.

> The gods help them that help themselves.
> *Aesop*

Libertarianism:
We Have Free Will

Libertarianism is the belief that we have free will and we can make free choices in life. We can choose to buy an ice cream cone or not, to get married or not, or to become a teacher or not. Existentialist philosophers such as Sartre have told us that we must accept this freedom, and the responsibilities that go with it, whether we like it or not. Many religions, including Christianity, assume that all human beings have the choice to do good or evil in their lives.

Sartre distinguished between natural objects, "things in themselves," and the human agent, "being for itself." According to Sartre, a human being has conscious plans, purposes, and intentions, plotting a course from a given situation to a future possibility.

Sartre believed that the stage is never set unalterably for human beings. When you say you are "constrained" by external circumstances, this statement often conceals your *decision* to interpret these influences in a certain way. Sartre believed no one was confined by personal motives, as was suggested by some determinists. Instead, he wrote, while individuals may conceptualize cause and motive as actual entities, they are hiding from themselves the fact that we, ourselves, interpret such causes and motives, giving them the meaning we wish.

Determinism, wrote Sartre, is a process by which we deny our freedom to determine how to live our lives. The truth is, we are, all of us, responsible for our lives, whether we like it or not. Human beings are, in Sartre's famous phrase, "condemned to be free."

> Freedom is not for the timid.
> *Vijaya Lakshmi Pandit*

Being and Nothingness
Jean-Paul Sartre

It is strange that philosophers have been able to argue endlessly about determinism and free-will, ... without ever attempting first to make explicit the structures contained in the very idea of *action*. We should observe first that an action is on principle *intentional*. The careless smoker who has through negligence caused the explosion of a powder magazine has not *acted*. On the other hand the worker who is charged with dynamiting a quarry, and who obeys the given orders, has acted when he has produced the expected explosion; he knew what he was doing or, if you prefer, he intentionally realized a conscious project....

... In order to be a *cause*, the *cause* must be *experienced* as such.... If I accept a ... [low] salary it is doubtless because of fear; and fear is a motive. But it is *fear of dying from starvation*.... And this fear is understood in turn only in relation to the *value* which I implicitly give to this life.... [I] must assume the situation with the proud consciousness of being the author of it.... It is therefore senseless to think of complaining, since nothing foreign has decided what we feel, what we live, or what we are....

Thus there are no *accidents* in a life; a community event which suddenly bursts forth and involves me in it does not come from the outside. If I am mobilized in a war, this war is my war; it is in my image and I deserve it. I deserve it first because I could always get out of it by suicide or by desertion; these ultimate possibilities are those which must always be present for us when there is a question of envisaging a situation. For lack of getting out of it, I have *chosen* it. This can be due to inertia, to cowardice in the face of public opinion, or because I prefer certain other values to the value of the refusal to join in the war (the good opinion of any relatives, the honour of my family, etc.). Any way you look at it, it is a matter of a choice.... There was no compulsion here.... Therefore it remains for me only to lay claim to this war....

... Someone will say, "I did not ask to be born." ... I am responsible for everything, in fact, except for my very responsibility, for I am not the foundation of my being. Therefore everything takes place as if I were compelled to be responsible. I am *abandoned* in the world ... in the sense that I find myself suddenly alone and without help, engaged in a world for which I bear the whole responsibility without being able, whatever I do, to tear myself away from this responsibility for an instant.... Thus in a certain sense I *choose* being born.... I never encounter anything except my responsibility. That is why I cannot ask, "Why was I born?" or curse the day of my birth or declare that I did not ask to be born, for these various attitudes toward my birth—i.e., toward the *fact* that I realize a presence in the world—are absolutely nothing else but ways of assuming this birth in full responsibility and of making it *mine*. Here again I encounter only myself and my projects so, that finally my abandonment ... consists simply in the fact that I am condemned to be wholly responsible for myself.

[Jean-Paul Sartre, *L'Etre et le Néant* (1943), part 4, chap. 1, sec. i and iii. Trans. by H.E. Barnes. London: Methuen & Co., 1957, 433–7, 440,441, 553–6.]

Compatibilism: Outside Forces Act on Us But We Still Have Freedom

A third position, compatibilism, or soft determinism, attempts to reconcile freedom with determinism. This position suggests that, while outside forces do indeed act on human beings, an individual's action is still free when it is caused by a decision made as a result of that person's beliefs and wishes.

Why does it really matter whether our thoughts and actions are free or determined? Philosophically, this question remains a matter of practical concern to us all in our everyday world. If we are not free to make our own decisions, how can we be held responsible for our actions? If, on the other hand, we are free to act, it seems only right that we should be held totally responsible for everything we do.

Our real-life situations offer a variety of answers to the question of freedom versus determinism, as we are held responsible for some of our actions in our everyday social encounters, and not for others. If we break the law intentionally, we are held

The Buddha can only tell you the way: it is for you yourself to make the effort.
The Dhammapada

I was born to be a remarkable woman; it matters little in what way or how....
Marie Konsantinovna Bashkirtseff

responsible; if we break the law unintentionally, we are not. If we accidentally cause harm to someone's property or person, we may not be held legally responsible, although we may feel morally responsible. We sometimes feel compelled to replace the damage or to right an unintentional wrong. In a court of law, the background or upbringing of the accused may often be used as a reason for mitigating the sentence.

To what degree do you hold yourself or others responsible for actions committed in your own life? To what degree do you think that people must act in certain ways because of forces acting on them, either from within or from without?

If you don't have a goal, any road will do.

Charles Tart

Human Freedom and Divine Providence

Many of the ancient philosophers believed that their lives were subject to fate. Stoic philosophers such as Chrysippus (third century BCE) defined fate as "a certain natural everlasting ordering of the whole: one set of things follows on and succeeds another, and the interconnection is inviolable." In modern times, scientific writers often regard the universe as a deterministic system, in which every event must follow as a result of fixed causal laws.

Such an idea gives rise to what philosophers call the problem of free will and determinism. That is, How can humans be truly free in a world where life is predetermined or preordained?

Many religions, such as Christianity and Islam, have held that God knows all things, past, present, and future, including every human action which has or will take place. Some infer from belief that human actions are fixed, and cannot be altered or avoided by any means available to the human race. Since God knows which actions are good and which are bad, God also knows in advance which people are destined for heaven and which for hell.

Some sects of Christianity argue that God granted humanity free will. This position is supported by the argument that God's punishments and rewards, heaven and hell, would make no sense unless mortals were free to choose between good and evil.

Early Christian writer St. Augustine (354–430) asked, Since there is an all-powerful and all-knowing God who "knows ... all things which shall be," how can we have freedom of will? St. Augustine's answer was, "It does not follow that because there is for God a certain order of all causes, there must therefore be nothing depending on the free exercise of our wills; for our wills themselves are included in that order of causes which is certain to God and embraced by his foreknowledge."

If God knows the past, present, and future, do we really have free will?

Not even the gods fight against necessity.

Diogenes Laertius

St. Augustine's position was a compatibilist view of freedom and determinism, because he believed that a universal causality does not rule out human freedom. Our wills still exist as wills, St. Augustine wrote. If everything is unalterably determined according to divine laws, would this not mean we have to act in a particular way? St. Augustine's answer was reassuring. He believed that the necessity of acting always according to divine law only becomes a dilemma when it seems we have to do something whether or not we want to. Usually, St. Augustine noted, we do something because we will it, and we should have no fear of necessity taking away our free will.

De Civitate Dei (The City of God)

St. Augustine

...Cicero addresses himself to the task of refuting the Stoics ... by denying that there is any knowledge of future things, and maintains with all his might ... that there is no prediction of events. Thus he both denies the foreknowledge of God, and attempts ... to overthrow all prophecy.... Nevertheless ... to confess that God exists, and at the same time to deny that He has foreknowledge of future things, is the most manifest folly.... [Cicero] ... thinks that, the knowledge of future things being once conceded, fate follows as so necessary a consequence that it cannot be denied.

... What is it, then, that Cicero feared in the prescience [foreknowledge] of future things? Doubtless it was this—that if all future things have been foreknown, they will happen in the order in which they have been foreknown ... then is there nothing in our own power, and there is no such thing as freedom of will; and if we grant that, says he, the whole organization of human life is subverted [overthrown]. In vain are laws enacted. In vain are reproaches, praises, chidings [scoldings], exhortations [warnings] had recourse to; and there is no justice whatever in the appointment of rewards for the good, and punishments for the wicked....

... [W]e assert both that God knows all things before they come to pass, and that we do by our free will whatsoever we know and feel to be done by us only because we will it.... But it does not follow that, though there is for God a certain order of all causes, there must therefore be nothing depending on the free exercise of our own wills, for our wills themselves are included in that order of causes which is certain to God ... for human wills are also causes of human actions....

Are our wills ruled by necessity?

It follows that there is also nothing to fear in that necessity—it is manifest that our wills by which we live uprightly or wickedly are not under such a necessity; for we do many things which, if we were not willing, we should certainly not do....

Consequently, it is not in vain that laws are enacted, and that reproaches, exhortations, praises, and vituperations [abusive condemnations] are had recourse to; for these also He foreknew, and they are of great avail, even as great as He foreknew that they would be of. Prayers, also, are of avail to procure those things which He foreknew that He would grant to those who offered them; and with justice have rewards been appointed for good deeds, and punishments for sins. For a man does not therefore sin because God foreknew that he would sin....

Therefore God is supreme and true, with His Word and Holy Spirit (which three are one), one God omnipotent, creator and maker of every soul and of every body; ... who made man a rational animal consisting of soul and body, who, when he sinned, neither permitted him to go unpunished, nor left him without mercy....

[St. Augustine, *De Civitate Dei* (*The City of God*, 413–26), Book 5, chap. 9–11. In *The Works of Aurelius Augustine*, trans. and ed. by M. Dods, Edinburgh: T. & T. Clark, 1872, 190–8. Included in *The Hellenistic Philosophers*, ed. by A.A. Long and D.N. Sedley, Cambridge: Cambridge University Press, 1987, 336.]

According to St. Augustine, God knows all things; however, we have free will, which causes our actions. Do you agree with this view? Why or why not?

IDEAS AND ISSUES

Understand Concepts
1. (a) Why did Laplace believe that all events are determined?
   (b) What illustration did he provide?
2. Outline Sartre's argument for free will.

Apply and Develop
3. For each scenario, decide whether you would hold the person responsible for their actions, and what you would do.
   (a) Carlyle has a temporary bout of amnesia, caused by a blow to the head. He cannot remember anything that happened during a two-day period of time. During that time, he behaved in a way that caused others to wonder whether or not he was in full possession of his faculties; he held up a store and struck the owner.
   (b) Devita has had too much to drink, and has a blackout for most of the evening. When she awakens, she finds that she hit her best friend over the head with a bottle, causing serious pain and potential long-term damage.
4. In each of the following cases, people perform certain actions. To what extent is the person free in performing that action? An action can be considered free if it is the person's deliberate action and the person could have acted in a different way. It cannot be considered free if it is the result of forces beyond the person's control. To what degree should the person be held responsible, and praised or blamed for the action?
   (a) Aya goes to a party and has several alcoholic drinks. As she leaves, she refuses an offer of a ride home, and insists that her date come with her. As she approaches an intersection, she decides to go through an amber light. Another car jumps the gun and there is a crash. Aya's friend is seriously injured in the accident.
   (b) Sarah was raised in a very poor home. Her mother had to struggle to raise the family, and they were often without proper food and clothing. When Sarah became a teenager she determined that this would not happen to her. She worked very hard at school, got a scholarship, and became a well-paid engineer. She was also able to help her mother have a better life.

Think Critically
5. Present an argument against determinism, as it is put forward by Laplace.
6. If God knows all things past, present, and future, is it still possible to have free will? What would St. Augustine say? State your own opinion.

Communicate Ideas
7. Present an argument for freedom of will. Convince your audience that they really can make free decisions.

Inquire and Research
8. Read B.F. Skinner's book *Beyond Freedom and Dignity*. Summarize his position in two to three paragraphs. Explain how he argues his point.

Review and Reflect

Many people throughout the ages—philosophers, gurus, and scientists—have attempted to answer metaphysical questions concerning reality, time, causality, and freedom. What is reality? Is there such a thing? And if so, what is it? Some thinkers have suggested that the most real things are those that we create in our minds; others have argued that our experiences of our external world are most real.

For a long time, time was perceived in a very linear way. The past and future were seen as abstract, while the present was a tangible, if momentary, slice of existence. Most early scientists believed that time was the same for all observers, an impartial silent witness to events. With Einstein's special theory of relativity, the whole notion of "standard time" and linear events was turned upside down. Einstein suggested that time was no longer uniform for every observer, and events that happened in the past for one person may in fact be observed in the future by another.

Aristotle was one of the first philosophers to consider causality. David Hume and Immanuel Kant believed that our minds see cause in terms of explaining the observed sequences of events. Other thinkers considered the question of whether there is a difference between human and natural causes, while still others sought to determine the causes of human behaviour.

The question of causality led many thinkers to question whether we possess free will or if we live in a pre-determined universe. Pierre Laplace believed that the universe, including human action, was totally determined by the laws of nature. Sartre, on the other hand, believed that we are born free and must take responsibility for our actions. Other thinkers have taken a middle road, suggesting that although there are outside forces that act on us, we are still free to choose our actions.

No definitive answer exists yet for questions about reality, time, causality, and freedom. However, definitive answers may not be as important as the reasoning process we use to discover meaning in our lives.

God and Evil

What is God? Can God's existence be demonstrated through reason, or through faith alone? Why is there evil in the universe? Many of us try to answer such questions in our daily lives, in moments of quiet contemplation, or in times of trial. Philosophers also struggle with such questions. The philosophical approach to this topic, as with all others, is to begin by understanding the ideas and arguments presented by others, and then to draw one's own conclusions.

Since ancient times, humans have attempted to answer questions about God and evil. Most cultures have developed ways to understand these important concepts, and to explain the existence of humans and the universe in which we live. Most of these ways describe some supernatural force at work that created all things. Philosophers also put forward ideas about the existence and nature of God, and the presence of evil. Some argued that God's existence could not be determined with certainty; others believed that there is no God in the universe.

Many of us have preconceived ideas about God and evil, usually as a result of some religious upbringing. As we go through many life experiences, questions about God and evil will come to the forefront. Does God really exist? What is our relationship to God? Is it possible for God to be present in the face of evil? Why does evil exist? Although there are few absolute answers to these questions, it is important to keep an open mind to new ideas as we develop our own points of view.

According to Eastern philosophies, our existence in this life is connected to the supernatural and the idea of reincarnation. We cannot escape from life or suffering unless we become enlightened beings.

Human Inquiry in Religious Knowledge

Human concern with religious questions predates written records by hundreds of years. Modern day discoveries of prehistoric civilizations indicate that very early people had developed some concept of an afterlife, often burying tools and other implements with the dead, so that these would be available to them in the next world. Bodies of the ancient Egyptian pharaohs were preserved through mummification, and were buried in huge tombs called pyramids, along with favourite possessions and keepsakes of their life on Earth. Unfortunately, servants of the Pharaohs were often killed so that they too could accompany their masters.

Most, if not all, human cultures created myths and legends to explain important spiritual ideas; often these stories included an all-powerful deity. Native North Americans believed in an afterlife that was a better form of earthly life. They believed in a powerful, infinite being, called the Great Spirit or the Transformer, who was maker of the Earth and all of its creatures.

PHILOSOPHERS' FORUM

Bella Coola Image of the Universe

Joseph Campbell

The Bella Coola First Nation of British Columbia, a Salishan people from the south, now settled inland of Queen Charlotte Sound ... [have a mythic image] of a universe of five levels; two above, and two beneath the earth, those above being of the gods, those below of the dead, the earth-plane being everywhere alive with the in-dwelling spirits of rocks and trees, watercourses, mountain peaks, and the ocean—also the Elders of the animal species.... The first of the two realms below the earth is of the remembered dead, who will be reborn. The second is of those forgotten, who have thus died a "second death" and passed into oblivion. The first of the heavens above is a mansion known as the House of Myths, where dwell the gods to whom prayers are addressed and of whom the Sun is the master. But the second heaven is a windswept, treeless plain occupied by a single female presence named Qamaits ... known as "Our Woman and Afraid of Nothing," for it was she who conquered inhospitable mountains and made them habitable.

[Joseph Campbell, *Historical Atlas of World Mythology*, vol. 1, part 2. New York: Harper & Row, 1988, 199.]

How Philosophers Approach Religious Questions

The concepts of God, heaven, and the beginning and end of all things constitute the core of religious beliefs. In important ways, however, religious knowledge is different from other types of knowledge. Most areas of investigation, such as history, science, or philosophy, are usually studied through empirical observation and rational thought processes. Generally, most people in these fields agree about what constitutes acceptable evidence. In religious matters, however, additional sources of ideas are present. All religious scriptures, such as the Vedas, the Bible, and the Qu'ran, contain material provided by a divine being or a prophet. To religious followers, such holy scriptures provide knowledge that may be interpreted in a number of ways. Moreover, religious beliefs, such as the existence and nature of God,

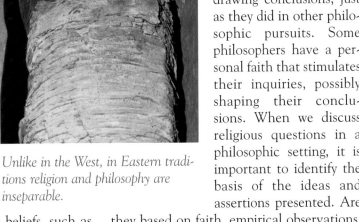

Unlike in the West, in Eastern traditions religion and philosophy are inseparable.

are often accepted on faith as true knowledge. It becomes the task of each individual to determine whether this information is to be trusted or not.

Philosophy concerns itself with religion and religious questions in a number of ways. We know that for centuries philosophers have sought to find truth about the nature of God, and of good and evil. Often they used rational methods of inquiry, considering the evidence and drawing conclusions, just as they did in other philosophic pursuits. Some philosophers have a personal faith that stimulates their inquiries, possibly shaping their conclusions. When we discuss religious questions in a philosophic setting, it is important to identify the basis of the ideas and assertions presented. Are they based on faith, empirical observations, or reasoning?

> I maintain that all attempts to employ reason in theology in any merely speculative manner are altogether fruitless.
> *Immanuel Kant*

> A philosopher is a blind man in a dark room looking for a black cat that isn't there. A theologian is the man who finds it.
> *H.L. Mencken*

Different Perceptions of God

How do people think about God? If you ask ten people to describe their concept of God, you are likely to get ten different views. In ancient times, people often projected human characteristics on divine beings. In many traditional Western religions, God is portrayed in human, generally male, form reflecting

social circumstances and values of the societies in which these religions developed. In other cases, God is seen as absolutely unique, and quite different from any earthly being. What type of being do you think God is? Before reading further, define your own idea of God. Compare your definition with those of others in your class.

Pantheism: God Exists in Nature

Pantheism is the belief that God exists within the forces and substance of nature. God is a part of all existence, not a separate entity. Philosopher Baruch Spinoza (1632–1677) wrote that God and nature are one and the same substance. Pantheists understand the Divine Spirit as part of all things, and that God is revealed to us through the workings of the natural world.

Pantheism is the spiritual view held by many people and cultures throughout time. The traditional beliefs of many Aboriginal cultures, including those of North America, are pantheistic in nature. Pantheists see a deep connection between humanity, other living creatures, and nature as a whole. To pantheists, spirit resides in all things. North American Aboriginal cultures also believed in a Great Spirit that created all things.

The gender of god, god's presumed masculinity, has functioned as the ultimate religious legitimization of the unjust social structures which victimize women.

Sandra Marie Schneiders

O millet, thou hast grown well for us; we thank thee, we eat thee.

Ainu prayer

Aboriginal spiritual beliefs and Zen Buddhism are examples of pantheism. Here a group of North American Aboriginal priests pray around a sacred tree.

The Idea of a God

Joseph Campbell

The idea of a god, whether of gods or of a High God ... is not theological, but mythical—transtheological. The god, that is to say, is not a final term (like Yahweh), but the personification or agent of a power that is transcendent of deification and definition.

American names for this *mysterium* include: Manitou (of the Algonquians), Wakan (of the Sioux), Orenda (of the Iroquois), and Tirawa (of the Pawnee). Personified, the power can be thought of as a being "out there" to whom prayers are addressed. Absolutely, however, it is the informing life and energy of all things; so that the prayer is actually a meditation, the calling up of a power from within. Ramakrishna, the great Hindu saint and teacher of the [nineteenth] century, used to ask those coming to him for consolation: "How do you like to speak of God, with form or without?"... [T]he African Bushman experiences this energy as *ntum*, a supernatural potency "put by the great god into a number of things: medicine songs, ostrich eggs, certain plants and fruits, the sun, falling stars, rain, bees, honey, giraffes, aardvarks, blood, redwing partridges, and fires made in certain situations; also into certain persons, who might function then as medicine men and healers.... "

[Joseph Campbell, *Historical Atlas of World Mythology*, vol. 1, part 1 and 2. New York: Harper & Row, 1988.]

> Religion is ... the organization of all duties as divine commands.
>
> *Immanuel Kant*

Deism: The Universe Follows God's Laws of Order

Deism is the belief that God created the universe and its physical laws, and then set the universe in motion before moving away from any future involvement with this creation. Deists believe God has no involvement in the workings of the universe, and does not interfere in the affairs of humanity. Deists do not believe that God creates miracles.

Deism is a product of the eighteenth century Enlightenment and its faith in science. When Isaac Newton discovered the universal laws of gravity and motion, the rational and orderly nature of the universe became clearer. Newton's scientific discoveries and those of his contemporaries had a powerful impact on philosophers' ideas about God as the creator of a complex and orderly universe. Eighteenth century thinkers likened God's creation of the universe to a clockmaker's creation of a timepiece. As the clockmaker creates and winds up the clock, God created the universe and set it in motion. This rationalist theory left little room for a personal connection between individuals and God. Deism, like most Western theologies, generally represents God as a male figure.

Theism: God and Humans Have a Personal Relationship

Theism is in direct contrast with deism and suggests that God has a direct and personal relationship with human beings.

> All ages before ours believed in gods in some form or other.
>
> *Carl Jung*

Theists believe that God is aware of, and concerned with, the actions of humanity and the actions of individual human beings. Many religious traditions, such as Judeo-Christianity and Islam, are founded on the principles of theism. Theists believe that God and human beings are in direct communication through such methods as prayer, ritual, or meditation. Theism can be polytheistic, based on the belief in a number of gods, or monotheistic, supporting a belief in a single God. Hinduism and Buddhism are examples of religious traditions that are polytheistic, with their gods possessing androgynous characteristics, while Judeo-Christian and Islamic religions are monotheistic, with God being represented as a male figure.

Atheism: God Does Not Exist

Atheism is the belief that no God exists at all. Atheists deny the existence of a divine being. Atheists argue that there is no certain proof of God's existence available to us that we can acquire from our observations or through the use of reasoning. Therefore there is no reason to believe that God does exist.

Atheism is probably a more commonly held belief in our modern scientific world than it was in the past. As science increasingly has been able to explain natural events through observation and rational processes, many people have discovered less of a need to believe in the existence of God in the universe.

It is true that many natural events can be explained by scientific reasoning, but other events remain elusive. We still do not know, for example, the origins of the universe or the nature of thought and reality. Atheists argue that such mysteries will all be explained at some future date through scientific endeavour.

Critics of atheism counter that some knowledge will forever be beyond human powers of rational thought, that such knowledge is only possible because of the existence of God. Critics of atheism also reply that lack of proof does not necessarily mean that God does not exist. The fact that we have no proof that other life exists in the universe does not negate the possibility that such life exists somewhere. Similarly, lack of proof of God's existence may mean simply that we have not yet found such proof.

Agnosticism: God's Existence Is Not Certain

Agnostics believe that nothing is known, or can be known, about the existence of God. The word agnostic comes from Greek and means "one who does not know." Agnostics believe there is not enough evidence to prove that God does or does not exist. Agnostics do not deny that God exists, but they do suggest that even if God exists, the human mind will never understand the nature of such a supreme being. The agnostic prefers to withhold judgement until more evidence is available.

> The mysteries of faith are degraded if they are made into an object of affirmation and negation, when in reality they should be an object of contemplation.
>
> *Simone Weil*

> If only God would give me some clear sign! Like making a large deposit in my name at a Swiss bank.
>
> *Woody Allen*

Personal Views of God

In the following selections, several individuals present their personal views of God. How do these views reflect the concepts of God we discussed earlier? How do they differ from your own personal views?

The Face of God

Archbishop Desmond Tutu

When I was young, I thought of God as a grandfatherly figure, which made God very accessible. Now, inside me is an almost imageless conception, a dark light, or a light darkness. I find God through the clues given in Jesus Christ—that God is caring and compassionate, that God has deep feelings about us. And God is always available....

There is a beautiful story about a Jew in a concentration camp, who was made to clean out toilets. His Nazi guard taunted him, "Where is your God now?" The Jew quietly replied, "He is right here with me, in the muck."

Joanna Ashong

I think that God is both black and white, because the Bible says He created man in His image. Why would there be black people if God was not part black?...

In heaven, everybody will be happy and everybody will be equal. There will be no rich and no poor. We will be married and have children, because this is how God started it. We will live in houses and drive cars, but everybody will be one color. I think everybody will be black.

David "B"

I didn't set out to kill him, but I did.... I thought that I would shrug it off the way I had successfully ignored all my other crimes.

But I soon discovered that a man who commits murder sets himself apart from all other human beings for the rest of his life. One day I woke and felt that I had been permanently stained by my act.... The feeling of horror, of disgust, of shame grew. I consulted a priest in prison. He gave me a Bible and, as I began to read, I was somewhat comforted, not initially by a sense of God's forgiveness but by the conviction that he was present. The sense of separation I felt suggested the existence of a Being who was offended, who cared enough for me to be ashamed for me....

What most impresses me now is the mercy of God, His refusal to be shocked by anything I could do. The God I know is a knowing but forgiving God.... I still feel guilty, but ... I can face it because I know that I am not alone in the universe.

Stephen Pieters

I come from a family of Presbyterian ministers, but in my youth I rejected God because my understanding was that God didn't love gay people.... [I listened to a speaker on television] who ... spoke about the gay issue, and I made some comment like "Gosh, she's stupid." ... My father asked me if I thought I might be gay. I said yes. I was terrified. But my father and mother both grabbed my hands. My mother cried, and my father said how much he loved me. He said it didn't change a thing....

... To have a minister say, "God loves you just the way you are" can bring about a radical change. They suddenly get it: ... God created me, therefore I must be good.

Cody Faircloth

If somebody wants God, all they've got to do is look. He's all around. That don't mean He's busy shoveling out the goods when you ask for them, but God watches over us, all right. He allows us the privilege of raising 40 head of cattle a year. God lets us grow our vegetables. You can see God in a butter bean patch.

Baldeva Ram

I worship Lord Sankara. I picture Him in my mind as His idol in the temple.... I was an ordinary laborer. Then four years ago I was stricken with leprosy and my life changed. Brahma has written out my fate. I am being punished for sins I must have committed in my last life.... There is no escape from the consequences of sin. I pray that heaven will be better than this.

Chana Meier

I believe that God has many attributes, which He shows at different times. In Hebrew there are about 60 names for God. Each one denotes a characteristic. When God is using judgment more, we say one name. When God is being merciful more, we say another. He can be angry, and He can be kind....

I don't see him as moody, but He is emotional, and He wants an emotional relationship with man. He's creative ... ! Look at the world He has made.... He's witty. Not sarcastic, but witty. And sharp, very, very sharp. If He were to say something, it would be a one-liner. Just perfect.

Dr. Arthur Peacocke

There is no necessary conflict between what science and Christian faith affirm about ultimate realities. You'll never prove religion from science. That's not what people are trying to do. They're seeing how these two enterprises of the human spirit can come into a common focus....

In my youth I became an agnostic. But I was terribly impressed, as I did research, that the universe was intelligible. Why does nature always turn out to be more intellectually coherent than anything we can conceive before we do the studies?... I believe the universe is rational because there is a suprarational Being behind it.

["The Face of God," *Life* Magazine, 13, no. 15, Dec. 1990, 47.]

IDEAS AND ISSUES

Understand Concepts

1. Identify the major questions that can be asked about God and evil.
2. What different approaches can be used to investigate such questions?
3. What views in this section are discussed by philosophers and by others about the nature of God?

Apply and Develop

4. Identify your own belief system about God and evil. Determine from where you derived this belief system. Explain how you would characterize it based on faith, reasoning, or both.

Think Critically

5. What conclusions would you reach about the nature of God based on the information in this section and on your existing belief system?

Inquire and Research

6. If you belong to an organized religion, research the basis of the belief system. Interview a religious leader or someone else knowledgeable in that religion. What are the sources of knowledge in that religion, the major elements of belief, and the questions of interest in that religion? Summarize your research in two to three pages.

Ways We Reach Out to God

There are many ways that we as humans have attempted to understand and reach out to God. In some cultures, particularly Aboriginal ones, males or females endowed with extraordinary powers and a keener sense of vision serve as intermediaries between the world of the supernatural and human existence. These people are called shamans, and they are called upon when a direct link to the world of the supernatural is required. In other cultures, rational thought is used as the means to reach God and acquire answers to universal questions. For Hindu and Buddhist gurus, meditation is used as a means to understand the great mysteries of life and death by directly coming into contact with universal knowledge.

Shamanism: Human Intermediaries Between Person and Spirit

Shamanism is the belief that it is possible to have direct contact with the spirit world. Often this is done by one individual, a shaman, who leads other individuals into a state of mind where they are accessible to spiritual influence. Shamanism has played a major role in the religions of many cultures, particularly Aboriginal cultures that are close to nature. In recent times, people from many walks of life have embraced shamanism as a way to handle difficult personal or health issues, or as a way to understand themselves more clearly.

PHILOSOPHERS' FORUM

A Return to the Earth

Susan McClelland

It is the first day of the basic shamanic workshop, a weekend retreat where participants learn how [N]ative cultures contact the spirit world. A small group is beginning to gather in a second-floor room at Northern Edge Algonquin Retreat and Awareness Centre…. Everyone is barefoot, quietly taking seats on floor mats. Shari Geller sets a small drum and two rattles beside her, and in a soft voice introduces herself. "I've wanted to be here for a while now," says the 32-year-old psychotherapist. "It's a natural progression in my spiritual growth." …

The journey to the spirit world is one of the most sacred exercises among almost all indigenous cultures. It involves entering an altered state of consciousness and communicating in the dimension experienced normally in dreams—one that benefits emotional and spiritual well-being. Anthropologists today refer to the journey as shamanism, and over the past few decades people from various religious backgrounds have embraced it.

Prayer is not an old woman's idle amusement. Properly understood and applied, it is the most potent instrument of action.
Mohandas K. Gandhi

Through making God in his own image, man has almost forgotten that woman once made the Goddess in hers. This is the deep secret of all mythologies….
Barbara G. Walker

Shamanic-based retreats and sweat lodges—places for communal prayer among [N]ative North Americans—have burgeoned from coast to coast....

Native cultures that practise shamanism are often referred to as earth-based and are grounded in a belief that all things—the environment, humans and the spirit world—are interconnected. At one time, people "knew there were spirits in the land and in animals," explains Sharon Van Raalte, a Quebec-based therapist who conducts shamanism workshops. "It was part of the tapestry of survival for humans to contact and respect them." ...

... [T]he healing powers of shamanism have impressed some members of the medical profession. Calgary psychologist Margaret McLeod sends some clients to shamanic healers in addition to the therapy she provides. There are similarities, McLeod says, between the messages people receive during the shamanic journey and the images her patients see through hypnosis and visualization—standard techniques to help them reach the subconscious.... Carl Jung and Sigmund Freud believed dreams were important sources of information; Jung thought they provided clues to what is needed to restore harmony in a person's life.

Oliver Pruden embraced shamanism in the final few months of his life. Raised a Christian, Pruden was aware that he was Métis but unaware of the culture's belief system. That changed in 1999, shortly after he was diagnosed with an inoperable brain tumour. The former school trustee and principal in Fort McMurray, Alberta, travelled to Anzac, about 40 km to the southwest, to attend a sweat lodge—a small igloo-shaped building covered in cloth. Inside an elder keeps the heat high by pouring water over hot rocks. The heat combined with prayer, says Pruden's wife, Vickie, transported Pruden to the altered state of consciousness. During his journey, he felt none of the pain that accompanied his illness. He also reported having conversations with spirits who were waiting for him when he crossed over. When he died last year, at age 59, "he was trusting of his fate," says Vickie. "It was as if a peace had come over his entire body."

[Susan McClelland, "A Return to the Earth," *Maclean's* Magazine, April 16, 2001, 46.]

Different Theologies for Understanding God

A major issue in theology and philosophy is how to reach out, find out about, or understand God. Several avenues are available to people seeking to understand God. Three major routes are through natural theology, revealed theology, and mystic theology. Each of these methods is based on a different idea about the nature of God's knowledge.

Natural Theology: Understanding God Through Reason

Natural theology is the study of God through the use of reason. Natural theology uses an intellectual or logical approach to explore the meaning of God. Deism is one form of natural theology. Many arguments for the existence of God that you will encounter in this chapter are based on natural theology.

Revealed Theology: Using Faith to Discover God

Fideism is the view that rational processes are not enough to prove God's existence. Natural evidence, fideists believe, can never provide knowledge of God. Faith alone is the way to understand and believe in God. Revealed knowledge through human prophets or divinely inspired scriptures is the only true source for the existence of God. Religious knowledge, therefore, is different from natural knowledge. For example, in the Muslim tradition, the Qu'ran represents Allah's words directly spoken to his prophet Mohammed.

Mystic Theology: Altering Awareness to Reach God

Mystical theologians believe God can only be reached by altering the state of the human body or mind. Such a transformation leads to a holy communion with God, and a greater understanding of God's being.

PHILOSOPHERS' FORUM

Excerpt from the *Qu'ran*

[T]here is [no] god but He, the
    Living, the Everlasting.
Slumber seizes Him not, neither sleep;
    to Him belongs
all that is in the heavens and the earth.
Who is there that shall intercede with Him
    save by His leave?
He knows what lies before them
    and what is after them,
and they comprehend not anything of His knowledge
    save such as He wills.
His Throne comprises the heavens and earth;
    the preserving of them oppresses Him not;
He is the All-high, the All-glorious.

[Excerpt from the *Qu'ran*, 2:255.]

Identifying the Form of Theology

Before embarking on a discussion of religious matters, such as the existence and nature of God, it is important to be clear which theological approach is to be employed: natural, revealed, or mystic theology. Although each approach can be considered a valid method for the investigation of religion, we must bear in mind that each approach contains different assumptions, and uses different methods to solve the problems being studied.

Most people approach religious questions from an existing belief system. They already have a view of the supernatural world, God, good and evil, and how to understand these entities. While an established system of beliefs provides a good starting point for thinking about religion, it must be remembered that the philosophic approach is primarily a rational approach; philosophers usually investigate concepts of God, and good and evil through rational processes or natural theology. St. Thomas Aquinas (1225–1274) presented several arguments in support of the use of reason to understand God. As you read the excerpt on the following page, consider these questions: What are Aquinas' arguments? Are they convincing?

Religious Ideas About God and Evil

HINDUISM
(2500 BCE–PRESENT)
begins in Indus Valley

ABRAHAM
(C. 2000 BCE)
founds Judaism

TORAH
(9TH CENTURY BCE–
4TH CENTURY BCE)
is written

SIDDHARTHA GAUTAMA
(563 BCE–483 BCE)

BUDDHISM
(C. 528 BCE)
begins being practised

VEDAS
(C. 500 BCE)
oldest Hindu scriptures are written

JESUS CHRIST
(C. 4 BCE–29 CE)

CHRISTIANITY
(30 CE)
starts

MOHAMMED
(570 CE–632 CE)

ISLAM
(6TH CENTURY CE)
starts

BEHIND THE MIND

Thomas Aquinas

Celebrated Christian Theologian

Thomas Aquinas (1225–1274) was born to a noble family in Roccasecca, midway between Rome and Naples. He began his studies at age five and eventually was exposed to the ideas of various philosophers, including Aristotle, Augustine, and Plato. His contact with the Dominican monks at the University of Naples led him to choose to become a Dominican himself. Aquinas was strongly influenced by the ideas of the philosophers he had encountered during his education. However, he formulated his own ideas about eternity, the soul, the intellect, and faith, to name a few.

Although he was a celebrated Christian theologian, some of his beliefs were condemned after his death by the Bishop of Paris. This decision was soon revoked, and Aquinas was cannonized as a saint.

Summa Contra Gentiles
(On the Truth of the Catholic Faith)

St. Thomas Aquinas

... There is a twofold mode of truth in what we profess about God. Some truths about God exceed all the ability of the human reason. Such is the truth that God is triune [three in one]. But there are some truths which the natural reason also is able to reach. Such are that God exists, that He is one, and the like. In fact, such truths about God have been proved demonstratively by the philosophers, guided by the light of the natural reason....

Since, therefore, there exists a twofold truth concerning the divine being, one to which the inquiry of the reason can reach, the other which surpasses the whole ability of the human reason, it is fitting that both of these truths be proposed to man divinely for belief....

Now, although the truth of the Christian faith ... surpasses the capacity of the reason, nevertheless that truth that the human reason is naturally endowed to know cannot be opposed to the truth of the Christian faith. For that with which the human reason is naturally endowed is clearly most true.... If ... contrary knowledges were implanted in us by God, our intellect would be hindered from knowing truth by this very fact. Now, such an effect cannot come from God....

There is also a further consideration. Sensible things [things perceived by the senses], from which the human reason takes the origin of its knowledge, retain within themselves some sort of trace of a likeness to God. This is so imperfect, however, that it is absolutely inadequate to manifest the substance of God. For effects bear within themselves, in their own way, the likeness of their causes, since an agent produces its like; yet an effect does not always reach to the full likeness of its cause.

[St. Thomas Aquinas, *Summa Contra Gentiles (On the Truth of the Catholic Faith)*. Trans. by Anton C. Pegis. Garden City, New York: Doubleday, Dell Publishing Group, Inc., 1955, 63–86.]

IDEAS AND ISSUES

Understand Concepts

1. (a) Identify the different concepts of God described in this section.
   (b) Explain how pantheism, theism, deism, atheism, and agnosticism differ.
2. (a) What are the possible ways that gurus, theologians, and philosophers have developed to reach out to, or understand, God?
   (b) What reasons can be given in support of each of these ways?
3. Describe the issues raised about God in this section. Are there other issues that you can suggest?
4. In a brief paragraph, explain your image of God.

Think Critically

5. What factors do you think would lead people to support one or another of pantheism, theism, deism, atheism, and agnosticism?

Communicate Ideas

6. Debate this issue: It is possible to prove the existence of God through the use of reason.
7. Discuss this issue: There are certain characteristics possessed by God on which all theologies would agree.

Ideas on the Existence of God

Does God exist? How do we know? Most of us have asked these questions at some time in our lives. Perhaps our religious upbringing provided answers to these questions before we even considered them. Perhaps we pursued these questions because we felt that something was missing from our lives.

Philosophers and other thinkers have pondered these questions since ancient times. For some of them, their religious beliefs influenced their ideas about the existence of God. Others denied the existence of God, and still other thinkers felt that reason alone could not provide a definite answer.

Philosophic Reasoning About the Existence of God

Philosophers often take the position that there is much value in discussing the existence of God from a rational position. Natural theologians also believe that knowledge of God can be obtained through reason.

Philosophers and natural theologians have developed several major arguments to support the idea that God exists. Three of these positions are of special importance: the teleological argument, or argument from design; the cosmological, or causal argument; and the ontological argument, or argument from definition.

Teleological Argument: God Is a Master Designer

How did the universe and all it contains come to exist? When we look around our world, we see that everything, including human beings, seems to be too complex and wonderfully designed to have appeared without some designer or creator. The more that modern science reveals about the nature of the universe, the more the design, complexity, and regularity of the universe continue to amaze us. Even chaos has some type of predictability and regularity about it.

The teleological argument is based on this evidence of design and purpose; its premise is the conviction that a universe of such complex and regular design could not possibly have appeared spontaneously, that only the hand of a master creator could have devised such a world.

One analogy often used to explain the argument by design is that of a clock or other piece of machinery, found in a remote forest by someone who has never seen such an object. The finder concludes that the clock must have been designed and made by some other rational being, because it is much too complex to have occurred by chance or accident.

The teleological argument proceeds on a similar basis: the universe is so obviously complex, with everything in it so intricately related and working so wonderfully together, its creator must be a divine designer or God.

Not all philosophers agree. David Hume, for one, absolutely rejected the teleological argument. It was human vanity, he wrote, to suggest that planning of the universe was even remotely similar to the laws we all associate with human planning. "Can you pretend to show any ... similarity between the fabric of a house and the generation of a universe?" Our human need to make sense of the universe means that we impose an order upon it that may not exist. Hume believed the universe may be the result of blind chance.

Today, explorations and discoveries in contemporary science indicate several possible scenarios that may describe how the complexity of the universe may have evolved over time. Physicists describe the development of the universe from its origin. Biologists discuss the evolution of living things as they developed from simple to complex forms. We now know that at least some of the complexity of the universe can be explained scientifically, without resorting to divine explanations. Nevertheless, the teleological explanation for all the world's creations remains a major argument for the existence of God.

Eastern and Western philosophers discuss the question of God's existence in different ways.

Cosmological Argument: A Primary Cause Must Exist

The cosmological, or causal, argument suggests that everything in existence must have a cause. We know from our own experience that all things that move or change around us do so because of some preceding event that effects change. The cosmological argument incorporates this knowledge and provides the conclusion that there must, therefore, exist a first or primary cause. According to proponents of the causal argument, lack of a first cause creates two impossible results: first, there exists no concept of beginning, so time recedes infinitely into the past; and second, if no first cause exists, there can be no other subsequent events.

David Hume was among the many philosophers who took exception to this argument. He refuted it by declaring that no proof of a first cause exists. Why, he asked, must there be a beginning or a first event? Why can we not trace the succession of events back indefinitely? What is wrong with the idea of an infinite progression? Immanuel Kant also criticized the cosmological argument. He reasoned that while every event in our own human sensory experience may have a cause, that is no reason to accept the doctrine that all things in the universe must have a cause.

Ontological Argument: God Is Perfect by Definition

The ontological, or definitional, argument is not based on the human experience of the world. Rather, this argument relies on

The more we learn of science, the more we see that its wonderful mysteries are all explained by a few simple laws so connected together and so dependent upon each other, that we all see the same mind animating them all.
Olympia Brown

The best remedy for those who are afraid, lonely or unhappy is to go outside, somewhere where they can be quiet, alone with the heavens, nature and God. Because only then does one feel that all is as it should be and that God wishes to see people happy, amidst the simple beauty of nature.
Anne Frank
(Feb. 23, 1944)
The Diary of a Young Girl

our definition of God, and on rational human reasoning about what that definition means.

The main premise of the ontological argument is the idea that God is defined as perfect. St. Anselm (c.1033–1109), Archbishop of Canterbury, stated this idea very succinctly when he argued that God must be greater than any other being we can imagine. If God were not supremely perfect, another even greater supremely perfect being must exist, and if not that being, yet another, and so on. St. Anselm concluded that such an infinite progression of increasingly superior beings was an impossibility.

The second century BCE yoga system of Patanjali was based on a similar argument: "God's pre-eminence is … without anything equal to or excelling it. God cannot be excelled by any other pre-eminence, because the very idea of God is that which is the uttermost limit of a real and existing perfection."

Another form of the ontological argument says that because God is perfect, God must therefore exist. Using this definition of a perfect being, St. Anselm reasoned two possible consequences: first, that God exists only in the mind of the believer; second, that God exists in reality. He concluded that God must exist, because existence in reality is more perfect than existence only in our mind. Descartes used this ontological argument as well, when he wrote that since God is by definition complete and perfect, God must exist. If God did not exist, God would not be perfect.

The ontological or definitional argument has been criticized by many philosophers. St. Thomas Aquinas argued that the establishment of God's existence should precede any discussion of perfection as one of his characteristics. Immanuel Kant said that existence is not the type of thing that can be part of a definition of a concept. We may have an idea of one hundred dollars but our idea is not the same thing as a real stack of bills; we may have an idea of God but that does not prove the existence of God.

St. Anselm's Ontological Argument for God

St. Anselm was a strong defender of Christian faith through the use of reason, and supported the ontological, or definitional, argument for the existence of God. He did not draw his definitional argument from experience or from observations of the world, as did other philosophers before him. Instead he began his argument from the concept or definition of God as an utterly supreme being, the greatest being the mind can conceive. St. Anselm's argument assumes that we all have an idea of God as a perfect being, beyond which no greater being can be imagined. He also assumed that God's very existence requires that God be complete in greatness and perfection.

St. Anselm asked if it is possible that God exists only in the mind of the believer and not in reality. He rejected this possibility by reasoning that it is greater to exist in reality than to exist only in someone's mind. If God exists only in the mind, the greatest conceivable being cannot be the greatest conceivable being. St. Anselm concluded that God must exist not only in human understanding but also in actual reality.

His argument was not universally accepted, even in his own time. The monk Gaunilo was a particularly strong dissenter, who argued that if we accept the idea that it is greater to exist in reality than to exist only in the mind, all mythical ideas would become fact. St. Anselm responded by declaring that the logic of his argument applied not to such mythological creations, but only to the greatest conceivable object, "that than which a greater cannot be thought." What follows are the arguments made by St. Anselm and Gaunilo about the ontological, or definitional, proof for the existence of God.

The Proslogion (Discourse)

St. Anselm

The mind stirred up to the contemplation of God

Come now, wretched man, escape for a moment from your preoccupations.... Lay aside for now your burdensome worries and put off your wearisome tasks. Empty yourself to God for a little while, and rest a short time in him. Enter the private chamber of your mind, shut out everything except God and whatever may help you to search for him....

... I will not attempt, Lord, to reach your height, for my understanding falls so far short of it. But I desire to understand your truth just a little.... I do not seek to understand in order that I may believe, but I believe in order that I may understand....

God truly exists

So, Lord, you who give understanding to those who have faith, grant me to understand, so far as you judge it fit, that you indeed exist as we believe, and that you are what we believe you to be. Now we believe that you are something than which nothing greater can be thought. Is there then no such being?... For it is one thing for an object to exist in the understanding, and another to understand that the object exists. When an artist thinks in advance of what he is about to paint, he has it in his understanding, but does not yet understand it to exist, since he has not yet painted it. But when he has painted it, then he both has it in his understanding and also understands that it exists.... Yet surely that than which a greater cannot be thought cannot exist in the understanding alone. For once granted that it exists, if only in the understanding, it can be thought of as existing in reality, and this is greater.... Hence something than which a greater cannot be thought undoubtedly exists both in the understanding and in reality....

God cannot be thought not to exist

And this being is you, O Lord our God. So truly do you exist, O Lord my God, that you cannot even be thought not to exist.... For if some mind could think of something better than you, then a created being would rise above its creator and judge its creator, which is utterly absurd….

I give you thanks, good Lord, that what I formerly believed through your gift of faith, I now understand through the light which you bestow; so much so that the truth of your existence … is now something I cannot fail to understand.

[St. Anselm, *Proslogion* (1077–8), chap. 1–5. In *The Many-Faced Argument*, ed. by Arthur C. McGill and John Hick, trans. by Arthur C. McGill. New York; Macmillan Publishing Co., 1967.]

On Behalf of the Fool

Gaunilo

Consider this example. Certain people say that somewhere in the ocean there is an island which they call the "Lost Island." … They say that it is more abundantly filled with inestimable riches and delights than the Isles of the Blessed….

When someone tells me that there is such an island, I easily understand what is being said…. Suppose, however, … he then goes on to say: you cannot doubt that this island, more excellent than all lands, actually exists somewhere in reality…. Since it is more excellent, not simply to [be understood] … but to be in reality as well, therefore this island must necessarily be in reality. Otherwise any other land that exists in reality would be more excellent than this island, and this island … would then not be the most excellent.

If, I repeat, someone should wish by this argument to demonstrate to me that this island truly exists and is no longer to be doubted, I would think he were joking; or, if I accepted the argument, I do not know whom I would regard as the greater fool, me for accepting it or him for supposing that he had proved the existence of this island with any kind of certainty. He should first show that this excellent island exists as a genuine and undeniably real thing, and not leave it standing in relation to my understanding as a false or uncertain something.

[Gaunilo, *On Behalf of the Fool*. In *The Many-Faced Argument*, ed. by Arthur C. McGill and John Hick, trans. by Arthur C. McGill. New York: Macmillan Publishing Co., 1967.]

The Response

St. Anselm

My reasoning, you claim, is as if someone should say that there is an island in the ocean, which surpasses the whole earth in its fertility, but which is called a "Lost Island" because of the difficulty, or even impossibility, of finding something that does not exist, and as if he should then argue that no one can doubt that it actually does exist because the words describing it are easily understood.

I can confidently say that if anyone discovers for me something existing either in fact or in thought alone, other than "that than which a greater cannot be thought," and is able to apply the logic of my argument to it, I shall find that lost island for him and shall give it to him as something which he will never lose again.

[St. Anselm, *Reply*. In *The Many-Faced Argument*, ed. by Arthur C. McGill and John Hick, trans. by Arthur C. McGill. New York: Macmillan Publishing Co., 1967.]

What arguments support the teleological view? What are the arguments against it?

Understand Concepts

1. Define teleological, cosmological, and ontological.
2. Identify and explain the proof St. Anselm claims for the existence of God.
3. Summarize St. Anselm's argument that God must exist.
4. Summarize Gaunilo's criticism of St. Anselm's argument.
5. How does St. Anselm reply to Gaunilo?

Apply and Develop

6. Are the statements below based on teleological, cosmological, or ontological arguments? Indicate why you think so.
   (a) The universe is such a wonderfully intricate and integrated place that it must have been created and designed by a supreme being.
   (b) All things have a cause; so the universe and everything in it must as well.
   (c) One cannot imagine a God that is imperfect, therefore such a being must exist.

Think Critically

7. Develop an organizer that describes all of the items listed below:
   (a) the essential meanings of the teleological, cosmological, and ontological arguments
   (b) the strengths of these arguments
   (c) the weaknesses of these arguments

Communicate Ideas

8. Stage a debate between St. Anselm and Gaunilo.
9. Using any one of the traditional philosophic arguments for the proof of God as a basis, write a position paper in which you analyze that argument, its pros and cons, and come to your own conclusion.

Arguments For and Against the Existence of God

Many arguments throughout human history have been presented for and against the existence of God. St. Thomas Aquinas, for example, stated several major arguments in support of God's existence. Others, such as Jean-Paul Sartre, believed that we cannot pass any responsibility for ourselves to a supreme being. Some thinkers, such as Karl Marx, felt that belief in God and religion in general was a means used to control the masses. Sigmund Freud thought that there was no real evidence for God's existence beyond human need for such a Being. The debate about the existence of God continues.

St. Thomas Aquinas: The Five Proofs of God

Many people today believe that St. Thomas Aquinas (1224–1274) was the greatest philosopher–theologian of the Middle Ages. He presented five proofs of the existence of God based on what we know about the world around us, and on Aristotle's principles about causal factors of world events. He did not use the ontological, or definitional, argument, because he could not completely accept its validity.

In the first and second proofs, Aquinas addressed the cosmological, or causal, argument to prove the existence of God. All things, Aquinas argued, are caused to move by some outside force. This meant that either the causal chain extends infinitely into the past or there exists an original source of motion. St. Thomas Aquinas did not believe that the

What arguments does Aquinas make for the existence of God? How convincing do you find them?

first possibility is conceivable; he did, however, consider the second possibility to be proof that God, the original source of motion, exists.

Aquinas' third proof focussed on the impermanence of all life as we know it, compared to the permanence of God. All life comes into being and passes away, but if everything is truly impermanent, Aquinas argued, there must have been some time in the past where nothing existed at all. If nothing at all existed, then nothing could have come into existence. Therefore, there must have been a permanence that has always existed, some force or supreme being that necessarily created existence. St. Thomas Aquinas' conclusion to his third proof was that there must always be an eternal being that causes all things to exist.

Aquinas' fourth and fifth proofs are teleological, arguments from design. His fourth proof focussed on the degrees of perfection found in the world. He argued that because objects or concepts exist in the world which are more or less good, a supreme being, or God, the source of all being and goodness, must have had a hand in their creation. This argument reminds us of Plato's view that ordinary objects are good and beautiful to the degree that they reflect pure forms of ideas. In his fifth proof, Aquinas argued that non-conscious objects exist for the sake of some goal or purpose. Goal-oriented actions, such as the acorn developing into an oak tree, or the structure of animal teeth for biting and chewing, would not occur unless they were designed or directed by some supreme intelligent being, or God.

> Cause me to pass from the unreal to the real, from darkness to light, from death to immortality.
>
> *Brihadaranyaka*
> *I.3/28*

The Five Proofs of God

St. Thomas Aquinas

The first and quite obvious way [to prove God's existence] is taken from a consideration of motion. It is certain and agreed on the basis of what our senses tell us that some things in this world are in motion. But whatever is in motion is moved by something else…. For example, something which is actually hot, like fire, makes wood, which is hot in potentiality, hot in actuality, thereby moving and altering it…. Hence whatever is in motion is moved by something else…. But the sequence cannot continue *ad infinitum*, since … there would not be any first mover, and hence nothing would move anything else…. Hence it is necessary to arrive at a first mover which is moved by nothing else; and this everyone understands to be God.

The second way is taken from the notion of an efficient cause…. But it is not possible for the series of efficient causes to go on *ad infinitum*. For in each ordered series of efficient causes, the first item is the cause of the next item, and this in turn is the cause of the final item … and if any one cause is taken away, the effect will also be absent…. But if the series of efficient causes stretches back *ad infinitum*, there will be no first efficient cause, which will mean that there will be no final effect, and no intermediate efficient causes, which is patently not the case. Hence it is necessary to posit some first efficient cause; and this everyone calls "God."

The third way … goes as follows. We come across some things … coming into being and passing away…. So if all things have the possibility of not being, at some time there was nothing at all. But if this were the case, then there would still be nothing now, since what lacks being does not begin to be except through something which is. So if nothing was in being, it was impossible for anything to begin to be, and so there would still be nothing, which is patently not the case…. So it is necessary to posit something which … does not have the cause of its necessity from elsewhere but is itself the cause of necessity in other things; and this everyone calls "God."

> Supposing science ever became complete so that it knew every single thing in the whole universe. Is it not plain that the questions, "Why is there a universe?" "Why does it go on as it does?" would remain just as they are?
>
> *C.S. Lewis*

The fourth way is taken from the gradations to be found in things. We come across some things which are more or less good, or true or noble than others, and so on. But "more" and "less" are terms used of different things by reference to how close they are to what is greatest of its kind (for example, something is "hotter" if it is closer to what is hottest). Hence there is something which is truest and best and noblest, and consequently greatest in being…. Now what we call the greatest in any kind is the cause of everything of that kind, just as fire, which has the greatest heat, is the cause of everything hot…. Hence there is something which is the cause of being and goodness and every other perfection in things; and this we call "God."

The fifth way is taken from the manner in which things are directed or guided. We see some things, … namely natural bodies, working for the sake of a goal or end. This is clear from the fact that they always or often act in the same way to pursue what is best; and this shows that they reach their goal not by chance but from directedness. But things which do not have knowledge do not tend towards a goal unless they are guided by something with knowledge and intelligence, as an arrow is by the archer. Hence there is some intelligent being by whom all natural things are directed to their goal or end; and this we call "God."

[St. Thomas Aquinas, *Summa Theologiae* (*On Theology*, 1266–73), part 1, question 2, article 3. In *Western Philosophy*, trans. and ed. by John Cottingham. Oxford: Blackwell Publishers Ltd., 1996.]

Arguments Against the Existence of God

Not everyone is convinced of God's existence. Karl Marx believed that religion was a result of the basic belief systems of culture and economy. Religion, he argued, with its basic concept of an afterlife, was a belief encouraged by the ruling classes to keep lower classes from revolt. Existentialist Jean-Paul Sartre, also a non-believer in God, was convinced that no human being can pass responsibility for his or her actions onto any other being except themselves. We exist, he wrote, and must shape our own character and destiny without sharing the responsibility with others, or with an outside supreme being.

Most of the philosophers who deny God's existence believe that the arguments presented for such an existence are not convincing. Sigmund Freud stated that people accept arguments in favour of God's existence, because people intrinsically need to believe in that fact. Despite such human needs, he says, the existence of God is not a certainty. Carl Jung, a student of Freud, proposed a much different argument concerning religious experience. Jung's argument is not really an argument for the existence of God, but rather for the value of religion. As you read the following excerpt, ask yourself these questions: To what degree, if at all, are Freud and Jung arguing about the same idea or belief? What different conclusions do they reach?

Freud argued that belief in God is an illusion resulting from psychological need. Does this in any way disprove God's existence?

The Psychical Origin of Religious Ideas

Sigmund Freud

... [Religious ideas] ... are not ... of experience or end-results of thinking: they are illusions, fulfillments of the oldest, strongest and most urgent wishes of mankind.... As we already know, the terrifying impression of helplessness in childhood aroused the need for protection—for protection through love—which was provided by the father; and the recognition that this helplessness lasts throughout life made it necessary to cling to the existence of a father, but this time a more powerful one. Thus the benevolent rule of a divine Providence allays our fear of the dangers of life....

When I say that these things are all illusions, I must define the meaning of the word. An illusion is not the same thing as an error; nor is it necessarily an error. Aristotle's belief that vermin are developed out of dung ... was an error.... On the other hand, it was an illusion of Columbus's that he had discovered a new sea-route to the Indies....

What is characteristic of illusions is that they are derived from human wishes.... Illusions need not necessarily be false.... For instance, a middle-class girl may have the illusion that a prince will come and marry her. This is possible; and a few such cases have occurred.... Thus we call a belief an illusion when a wish-fulfillment is a prominent factor in its motivation, and in doing so we disregard its relations to reality....

... [L]et us return once more to the question of religious doctrines. We can now repeat that all of them are illusions and insusceptible of proof.... [J]ust as they cannot be proved, so they cannot be refuted.... [T]here are many questions to which science today can give no answer. But scientific work is the only road which can lead us to a knowledge of reality outside ourselves. It is once again merely an illusion to expect anything from intuition and introspection; they can give us nothing but particulars about our own mental life....

At this point one must expect to meet with an objection. "Well then, if even obdurate [unyielding] sceptics admit that the assertions of religion cannot be refuted by reason, why should I not believe in them, since they have so much on their side—tradition, the agreement of mankind, and all the consolations they offer?" Why not, indeed? Just as no one can be forced to believe, so no one can be forced to disbelieve. But do not let us be satisfied with deceiving ourselves that arguments like these take us along the road of correct thinking....

[Sigmund Freud, *The Future of an Illusion*. Trans. by James Strachey (1961), renewed by Alix Strachey (1989). New York: W.W. Norton & Company, Inc., 1989.]

PHILOSOPHERS' FORUM

Religious Experience

Carl Jung

Religious experience is absolute. It is indisputable. You can only say that you have never had such an experience and your opponent will say: "Sorry, I have." And there your discussion will come to an end. No matter what the world thinks about religious experience, the one who has it possesses the great treasure of a thing that has provided him with a source of life, meaning and beauty and that has given a new splendor to the world and to mankind.... Where is the criterium by which you could say that such a life is not legitimate, that such experience is not valid and that such ... [faith] is mere illusion? Is there ... any better truth about ultimate things than the one that helps you to live?

[Carl G. Jung, *Psychology and Religion*. New Haven: Yale University Press, 1938, 113ff.]

Understand Concepts

1. Identify and summarize St. Thomas Aquinas' five proofs of the existence of God.
2. State Freud's major thesis.
3. What is the origin of religion, according to Freud?
4. Are illusions necessarily false, according to Freud?
5. Does Freud deny that people should believe in religion? State his position.
6. What is Jung's main point?

Think Critically

7. Present criticisms that can be made against each of St. Thomas Aquinas' arguments.
8. Compare St. Thomas Aquinas' arguments with St. Anselm's.
9. (a) Does Freud present a strong argument against the existence of God?
   (b) Is this really an argument against the existence of God?

Communicate Ideas

10. Stage a debate between two people who begin from the positions held by Freud and Jung. Debate this issue: Religious experience is absolute and indisputable.

The Concept of Evil in the Universe

What is evil? Why does it exist? How can evil exist in the same universe as a divine being? Such questions have been asked since time immemorial by those who observe evil in the world, and those who have been

the victims of evil or affected by evil. We ask such questions when an innocent person is killed in an accident, when someone is murdered, when a generation goes to war, when a baby acquires an incurable illness, or when an earthquake destroys the lives of thousands. Sometimes natural disasters cause the misfortunes and horrors that we call evil, while other evil events are perpetrated by human actions. Such situations force us to ask what evil is and why it exists.

Why Does Evil Exist?

One explanation of evil is that it exists for some greater good beyond human understanding. This argument suggests that while evil things happen apparently senselessly, without further or better goals, such events may not, in fact, be evil to God. Our idea of God is shaped by human concepts of kindness and love. Perhaps God's understanding of good and evil may be greater and different than our own.

Another explanation of evil suggests that because human beings are able to exercise their free will, we will sometimes choose evil rather than good. This argument can only address the issue of human evil. It does not explain such natural events as earthquakes or plagues. It also does not explain why it is often the weak and innocent people who suffer most from evil actions or events.

In our modern scientific world, some people have suggested that there is no such thing as evil, only events that can be explained through science and life's natural processes. Someone is stoned to death; millions of people are systematically murdered in concentration camps; a kitten is tortured; hundreds of people die while fleeing an erupting volcano; thousands die in a terrorist attack. We cannot help but react when these terrible acts of violence happen; we want to say there is some evil influence at work. But evil need not always manifest itself in acts of physical violence. How would you characterize those businesses which con people out of their life's savings, or those persons who prey upon the weak or elderly, convincing them that some nonessential, expensive object is vital to life's happiness or security?

In philosophy, we often ask the question: How can evil exist in a universe where God exists? Some philosophers argue that it is possible to accept the existence of evil in a universe where God exists. This argument is called theodicy, the concept of God and evil existing together in the same universe. Others believe that the existence of evil causes us to question the nature of God, or at least the existence of an all-powerful and all-benevolent God. David Hume put it this way: If God allows evil to exist in the world, then He is not all-loving. If evil exists outside the control of God, then He is not all-powerful. Therefore, God cannot be both all-powerful and all-benevolent, although God may be either one or the other.

Some thinkers suggest that the presence of evil serves a purpose to humanity. If all our experiences were pleasant and there was no pain and suffering, we would never grow, or mature as individuals. If God were to remove evil from the world, our free will as humans would be taken away. When someone chooses to do good deeds even though evil is present, that person is making a conscious choice to build character.

> He who passively accepts evil is as much involved in it as he who helps to perpetrate it.
> *Martin Luther King, Jr.*

> Evil being the root of mystery, pain is the root of knowledge.
> *Simone Weil*

How is it that evil can exist in the same universe as God? Is there an important difference between human and natural evils? How does religion explain evil?

The Irenaean Theodicy

John Hick

For many people … the appalling depth and extent of human suffering, together with selfishness and greed which produce so much of this, … makes the idea of a loving creator implausible.

John Hick

Evil is obvious only in retrospect.

Gloria Steinem

The Negative Task of Theodicy

… The Scriptures reflect the characteristic mixture of good and evil in human experience. They record every kind of sorrow and suffering from the terrors of childhood to the "stony griefs of age": cruelty, torture, violence, and agony; poverty, hunger, calamitous accident; disease, insanity, folly; every mode of man's inhumanity to man and of his painfully insecure existence in the world. In these writings there is no attempt to evade the clear verdict of human experience that evil is dark, menacingly ugly, heart-rending, crushing. And the climax of this biblical history of evil was the execution of Jesus of Nazareth. Here were pain and violent destruction, gross injustice, the apparent defeat of the righteous, and the premature death of a still-young man. But further, for Christian faith, this death was the slaying of God's Messiah, the one in whom mankind was to see the mind and heart of God made flesh…. And yet throughout the biblical history of evil, including even this darkest point, God's purpose of good was moving visibly or invisibly towards its far-distant fulfillment…. And even the greatest evil of all, the murder of the son of God, has been found by subsequent Christian faith to be … the greatest good of all….

The aim of a Christian theodicy must thus be … one of showing that the mystery of evil, largely incomprehensible though it remains, does not render irrational a faith that has arisen … from … religious experience….

The Value of Soul-Making Theodicy

As well as the "majority report" of the Augustinian tradition, which has dominated Western Christendom, both Catholic and Protestant, since the time of Augustine himself, there is the "minority report" of the Irenaean tradition….

Instead of regarding man as having been created by God in a finished state, as a finitely perfect being … , then falling disastrously away from this, the minority report sees man as still in process of creation…. [M]an as a personal and moral being already exists in the image, but has not yet been formed into the finite likeness of God. By this "likeness" Irenaeus means something more than personal existence as such; he means a certain valuable quality of personal life which reflects finitely the divine life. This represents the perfecting of man, the fulfilment of God's purpose for humanity….

And so man, created as a personal being in the image of God, is only the raw material for a further and more difficult stage of God's creative work. This is the leading of men as relatively free and autonomous persons, through their own dealings with life in the world … , towards that quality of personal existence that is the finite likeness of God….

… But the second stage of the creative process … cannot be performed by omnipotent power as such. For personal life is essentially free and self-directing. It cannot be perfected by divine fiat [order], but only through the uncompelled responses and willing co-operation of human individuals in their actions and reactions in the world…. Men may eventually become the perfected persons whom the New Testament calls "children of God," but they cannot be created ready-made as this.

The value-judgement … here is that one who has attained to goodness by meeting and eventually mastering temptations, and … making responsible choices in concrete situations, is good in a richer and more valuable sense than would be one created … in a state either of innocence or of virtue….

… Antitheistic writers … assume that the purpose of a loving God must be to create a hedonistic paradise [a paradise full of pleasure]; and therefore to the extent that the world is other than this, it proves to them that God is either not loving enough or not powerful enough to create such a world. They think of God's relation to the earth on the model of a human being building a cage for a pet animal to dwell in. If he is humane he will naturally make his pet's quarters as pleasant and healthful as he can….

… But if we are right in supposing that God's purpose for man is to lead him from human Bios, or the biological life of man, to that quality of Zoe, or the personal life of eternal worth, which we see in Christ, then the question we have to ask is not, Is this the kind of world that an all-powerful and infinitely loving being would create as an environment for his human pets? or, Is the architecture of the world the most pleasant and convenient possible? The question that we have to ask is rather, Is this the kind of world that God might make as an environment in which moral beings may be fashioned, through their own free insights and responses into "children of God"?… For if our general conception of God's purpose is correct the world is not intended to be a paradise…. Men are not to be thought of on the analogy of animal pets, whose life is to be made as agreeable as possible but rather on the analogy of human children, who are to grow to adulthood in an environment whose primary and overriding purpose is not immediate pleasure but the realizing of the most valuable potentialities of human personality.

… This characterization of God as the heavenly Father … lies at the heart of the Christian faith. Jesus treated the likeness between the attitude of God to man, and the attitude of human parents at their best towards their children, as providing the most adequate way for us to think about God…. [A] parent who loves his children, and wants them to become the best human beings that they are capable of becoming, does not treat pleasure as the sole and supreme value. Certainly we seek pleasure for our children … but … not … at the expense of their growth in such even greater values as moral integrity, unselfishness, compassion, courage, humour, reverence for the truth, and perhaps above all the capacity for love…. A child brought up on the principle that the … supreme value is pleasure would not be likely to become an ethically mature adult or an attractive or happy personality…. If, then, there is any true analogy between God's purpose for his human creatures, and the purpose of loving and wise parents for their children, we have to recognize that the presence of pleasure and the absence of pain cannot be the supreme and overriding end for which the world exists. Rather, this world must be a place of soul-making….

[John Hick, ed., *Classical and Contemporary Readings in the Philosophy of Religion*, 2nd ed. Englewood Cliffs: Prentice Hall, Inc., 1970.]

> If there were not a Devil, we would have to invent him.
> *Oscar Wilde*

> The spiritual poverty of the western world is much greater than the physical poverty of our people.
> *Mother Teresa*

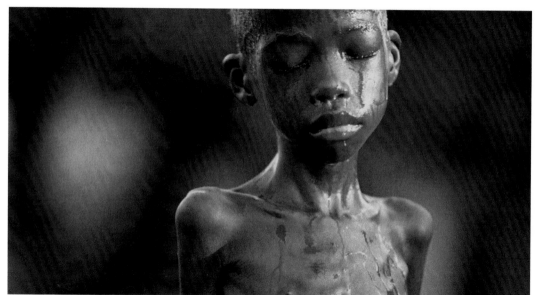

What purposes does evil serve, if any? Is the existence of evil consistent with the existence of God? Must we give up the idea of God as all-powerful or all-good, in the face of the existence of evil?

Arguments Against God Being All-Good and All-Powerful

Not all people share the view as expressed in the previous excerpt. The problem of God being all-good and all-powerful while co-existing in a universe with evil is difficult to resolve. Some philosophers have put forward arguments that oppose the idea of God being all-good and all-powerful. We may never find an absolute answer to this problem. One thing is certain: Humans will continue to question the existence of both God and evil existing together in the universe.

Evil and Omnipotence

J.L. Mackie

The problem of evil … is a problem only for someone who believes that there is a God who is both omnipotent and wholly good…. In its simplest form the problem is this: God is omnipotent; God is wholly good; and yet evil exists. There seems to be some contradiction between these three propositions, so that if any two of them were true the third would be false….

However, to show [the contradiction] we need some additional premises…. These additional principles are that good is opposed to evil … and that there are no limits to what an omnipotent thing can do. From these it follows that a good omnipotent thing eliminates evil completely, and then the propositions that a good omnipotent thing exists, and that evil exists, are incompatible.

Now once the problem is fully stated it is clear that it can be solved … if one gives up at least one of the propositions that constitute it. If you are prepared to say that God is not wholly good, or not quite omnipotent, or that evil does not exist, or that good is not opposed to the kind of evil that exists, or that there are limits to what an omnipotent thing can do, then the problem of evil will not arise for you….

There are, in fact, many so-called solutions which purport to remove the contradiction without abandoning any of its constituent propositions. These must be fallacious…. I suggest that in all cases the fallacy has the general form suggested above: in order to solve the problem one … of its constituent propositions is given up, but in such a way that it appears to have been retained….

1. *"Good Cannot Exist Without Evil…."*

It is sometimes suggested that evil is necessary as a counterpart to good, that if there were no evil there could be no good either…. It is true that it points to an answer to the question "Why should there be evil?" But it does so only by qualifying some of the propositions that constitute the problem.

First, it sets a limit to what God can do, saying that God cannot create good without simultaneously creating evil, and this means either that God is not omnipotent or that there are some limits to what an omnipotent thing can do….

But, secondly, this solution denies that evil is opposed to good in our original sense. If good and evil are counterparts, a good thing will not "eliminate evil as far as it can." …

2. "Evil Is Necessary as a Means to Good"

It is sometimes suggested that evil is necessary for good not as a counterpart but as a means.…[T]his … implies a severe restriction of God's power.… [I]f God has to introduce evil as a means to good, he must be subject to at least some causal laws.…

3. "The Universe Is Better With Some Evil In It Than It Could Be If There Were No Evil"

Much more important is a solution … that the universe as a whole is better … with some evil in it.… This solution may be … supported by an aesthetic analogy, … that contrasts heighten beauty, that in a musical work, for example, there may occur discords which somehow add to the beauty of the work as a whole. Alternatively, it may be worked out in connection with the notion of progress, that … the gradual overcoming of evil by good [in the universe] is really a finer thing than would be the eternal unchallenged supremacy of good.…

4. "Evil Is Due To Human Free Will"

Perhaps the most important proposed solution … is that evil [comes from] … the independent actions of human beings … endowed by God with freedom of the will.… To explain why a wholly good God gave men free will although it would lead to some important evils, it must be argued that it is better on the whole that men should act freely, and sometimes err, than … [act] rightly in a wholly determined way.…

… [I]f God has made men such that in their free choices they sometimes prefer what is good and sometimes what is evil, why could he not have made men such that they always freely choose the good?… Clearly, his failure to avail himself of this possibility is inconsistent with his being both omnipotent and wholly good.…

… [I]f men's wills are really free this must mean that even God cannot control them, that is, that God is no longer omnipotent. It may be objected that God's gift of freedom to men does not mean that he cannot control their wills, but that he always refrains from controlling their wills. But why, we may ask, should God refrain from controlling evil wills? Why should he not leave men free to will rightly, but intervene when he sees them beginning to will wrongly?… The present solution of the problem of evil, then, can be maintained only in the form that God has made men so free that he cannot control their wills.

Conclusion

Of the proposed solutions of the problem of evil which we have examined, none has stood up to criticism.… [T]his study strongly suggests that there is no valid solution of the problem which does not modify at least one of the constituent propositions.… God's omnipotence must in any case be restricted in one way or another.…

[J.L. Mackie, "Evil and Omnipotence," Mind, vol. 64, 254. Oxford: Oxford University Press, 1955.]

Understand Concepts

1. Why is the death of Christ a problem in the discussion of evil?
2. What is the "minority report" of the Irenaean tradition?
3. Explain Hick's discussion of "God's pet."
4. What is the value of considering God as a parent?

Apply and Develop

5. How does Hick's idea solve the problem of evil?
6. What is the central element of the problem of evil, according to Mackie? Consider the ideas of omnipotence, goodness, and evil in your answer.
7. (a) Briefly explain the solutions to the problem of evil documented by Mackie.
   (b) What are the problems with these solutions, according to Mackie?

Think Critically

8. State Hick's major thesis, and summarize his argument in support of this thesis.
9. Assess the pros and cons of Hick's argument.
10. Present additional arguments you would suggest to support or oppose Hick's thesis.
11. Which solutions to the problem of evil does Hick suggest?

Communicate Ideas

12. Debate this issue: It is possible to accept the co-existence of God and evil in the universe.

Inquire and Research

13. Choose one of the margin quotations in this chapter with which you disagree. In a position paper of less than two pages, provide an argument against it.

Review and Reflect

Questions about the existence and nature of both God and evil have been of concern to humanity since the beginning of human history. Does God exist? What is God like? Why does evil exist? Many thinkers have proposed different answers to these questions.

There are those who believe in God because of faith alone; others, such as St. Thomas Aquinas, have used reason to "prove" the existence of God. Sartre, among other philosophers, did not believe that God existed. Still others are uncertain.

Questions about the nature of God usually involve questions about evil. Some thinkers believe that God cannot be all-powerful or all-loving if evil exists. Others have suggested that the presence of evil is necessary for us to develop character.

Discussions about God and evil continue today as most of us grapple with making sense of events around us. Regardless of our personal opinions, it is important to keep an open mind as we continue to find answers.

POLITICAL AND SOCIAL PHILOSOPHY

Human beings have been referred to as "social animals" because most of us live our lives as members of a number of social groups. We begin our lives as members of a family, eventually moving on and joining other social groups. Throughout our lives we encounter many different social situations and challenges. We must learn how to live with others and reach agreements about how we should behave as a group.

Philosophers since ancient times have investigated the social nature of human beings, and the types of societies that groups of individuals can form. Political and social philosophers ask such questions as:

- Why do we have governments and laws?
- What forms of government are best?
- How can societies provide for human needs?
- What constitutes a just and fair society?
- What are the best ways to deal with social issues and problems?
- What are the shortcomings in our own society, and how can we deal with them?

In this unit, we will explore all of these questions. We will look at classical views of political and social philosophy and will then investigate several modern theories. Throughout this unit, we will apply reasoning and an investigative approach in analyzing contemporary domestic and world issues.

Political and social philosophy affects every aspect of our lives. What influences our ideas of government and various social groups? How can we make informed decisions about these?

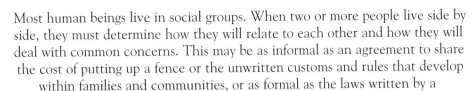

CHAPTER 1 2

Political Philosophy

Most human beings live in social groups. When two or more people live side by side, they must determine how they will relate to each other and how they will deal with common concerns. This may be as informal as an agreement to share the cost of putting up a fence or the unwritten customs and rules that develop within families and communities, or as formal as the laws written by a nation's government.

Political philosophy is the result of people thinking about and discussing issues pertaining to authority and freedom. Some questions considered in political philosophy are:

- Why do we have governments?
- What are the best forms of government?
- How can society balance freedom and authority?
- What should be done when authority is unjust?

In the twenty-first century, as in most times past, various forms of political authority and types of government exist. These forms of authority and types of government are tested during times of change, as nations seek to solve problems that they face. What type of government or political authority do you think is best, most just, and capable of solving the problems that face our nation and our world today? Consider this overriding question as you examine the ideas presented in this chapter.

Political philosophy is concerned with questions about the nature of government, and the balance between state authority and the freedom of citizens.

Personal Political Philosophies

Some people believe politics has little impact on their lives. The fact is that the political systems we live within shape our lives in countless ways. Political decisions influence how we make a living, what legal rights we enjoy as individuals, what opportunities are available to us, and how we must treat others, including children. Politics decides what we can read, what television programs we can watch, and the quality of education we receive. It also affects how people experience justice, and how much liberty and equality exists in a society. In some countries, politics even affects who we can marry.

It is in our own best interest to be aware of the political systems and decisions at work in our society. We need to be knowledgeable about major political issues, so that we can make informed opinions about them and, when appropriate, act on those opinions.

Most people already have a personal political philosophy. Each of us has concerns and opinions about current issues and what should be done about them. We see homeless people and want to help them. We hear about a law intended to reduce pollution and we approve. We admire the views of certain political leaders and disagree with others. Our personal political philosophy consists of all the beliefs and values we have about the social world around us.

We form our personal political philosophy from many sources. Parents, media, friends, teachers, and books all contribute to our political ideas and beliefs. Studying the political philosophies of others can add to our own understanding of current issues and the political leadership of our country.

PHILOSOPHERS' FORUM

Good Government

Confucius

The ancients, wishing to set an example of supreme virtue in the land, first put their country in order. In putting their country in order, they first worked on themselves. In working on themselves, they purified their hearts. In purifying their hearts, they endeavoured to be sincere in their thoughts. In being sincere in their thoughts, they extended their knowledge. In extending their knowledge, they explored matters. When these matters had been explored, their knowledge became comprehensive. When their knowledge was comprehensive, their thoughts became sincere. When their thoughts were sincere, they themselves became decorous. When they themselves were decorous, their families became orderly. When their families were orderly, their country became well-governed. And when their country became well-governed, the whole world lived in peace and contentment.

[Arthur Waley, trans., *Analects of Confucious*. New York: Macmillan, 1938 (Foundation for Classical Reprinta, 1991).]

IDEAS AND ISSUES

Understand Concepts

1. Define politics, political philosophy, and personal political philosophy.
2. From where do we get our personal political philosophy?
3. What questions would you ask about the nature of politics in Canada, or in other countries, today?

Apply and Develop

4. Choose a particular social or political issue of importance to you and to others you know. Write this as a question to be asked to a variety of people you know. Ask them to provide reasons for their answers. Organize the results of your interviews and report these results to the class. What do these responses tell you about the personal political philosophies of those you interviewed?
5. What type of government do you think is best? Take five or ten minutes to describe this form of government on paper. What would it look like? What would it do? How would it deal with problems? Compare your answers with those of others in the class.

Communicate Ideas

6. Read the first section of a daily newspaper or watch the television news in the evening. What news items are related to government and politics? What problems does each item describe? What solutions, if any, are suggested? Use an organizer to analyze these items. Discuss the items with the rest of the class. Choose issues that need more investigation.

Do We Need a Government?

Why do we need governments? Would it be possible to have a society without a government, where people looked after themselves and treated others well? Governments are created to make decisions and enact laws about how people live together. They possess the authority to carry out those decisions and to enforce those laws. One way to think about the need for government is to imagine, as many philosophers have, what it would be like to live in a society where there was no constituted authority to create and carry out laws.

Before examining the need for government and political philosophies that address this, we need to identify the scope of the topic. Political systems, political processes, and forms of government exist at many different levels. The most formal and powerful levels of government exist at the national level; for example, the federal government of Canada. Other formal political systems exist at the provincial or regional and municipal levels.

We need to recognize, however, that governments and politics also exist in informal social groups and relationships. In smaller groups such as families, schools, workplaces, friendship groups, and others, when rules are determined and decisions are made, formally or informally, we can say that politics and government are present. Think of the groups within which you live and/or participate. What rules exist or are assumed? What types of personal relationships exist? How are decisions made?

What forms of government do you think are best? Would it be possible to live in a society with no government?

How Modern Philosophic Ideas About Government Emerged

Seventeenth and eighteenth century Europe saw the formation of many nation-states and national governments. Often this occurred when a number of smaller political units, such as principalities, united to form a larger nation. New forms of government were necessary to allow large and often diverse groups of people to be ruled in an orderly manner. Determining what new forms of government should be developed, and why, was suddenly a matter of great practical importance, as was the need to shape a philosophy upon which governments might be structured. Who should make the important decisions? What role, if any, should a nation's population play in government? What role should its rulers play? What sorts of laws would prove most useful? The newly emerging social and political worlds of the seventeenth and eighteenth centuries required new concepts in political philosophy.

One avenue of investigation open to political philosophers of the time was to imagine a social existence devoid of governments and political authority. It is very probable that such conditions never existed in reality, but philosophers found it useful to imagine what life might be like when people interact in an untouched "state of nature." These thinkers could then use logic to determine why, and how, a political system might emerge from such a "state of nature" existence.

What do you think life would be like if the social groups to which you belong had no legitimate ruling authority? What if there were no forms of government in your school, workplace, or social club? How would people act? Would people's personal relationships change dramatically? Would any organized activities take place?

Time Line

Examples of
Political Change

BILL OF RIGHTS
(1689)
establishes supremacy of parliament in England

DECLARATION OF INDEPENDENCE
(1776)
takes place in the U.S.

FRENCH REVOLUTION
(1789)
begins

BOLSHEVIK REVOLUTION
(1917)
takes place in Russia

Thomas Hobbes' View: Individuals Relinquish Freedom for Personal Security

In his book *Leviathan,* Thomas Hobbes speculated about what social life might have been like before the existence of established authority or government. Hobbes' thoughts revealed much of his views concerning human nature and the way it would operate without political or social controls, or government.

His imagined "state of nature" predates any form of government or authority. Living beings would constantly be quarrelling and competing for scarce resources. People would have only their physical and mental strength for protection. Hobbes imagined a life of continual fear, danger, and violence, one in which people would voluntarily join together because of the desperate circumstances.

These people, Hobbes concluded, would agree to a "social contract" wherein each individual relinquished his or her natural freedoms in exchange for security. A government would be established.

Thomas Hobbes

Given Hobbes' description of life in a "state of nature," and his view of how people would act under such circumstances, it is not surprising to discover that his description of the necessary form of government outlined an institution with very broad powers. Hobbes' hypothetical government was charged with a number of tasks: maintaining peace within society; ensuring that all citizens have the right to live free from fear, and protecting the population against foreign invasion. Such a government, Hobbes believed, must be endowed with enough power and strength to rule decisively by using fear to deter people from disobeying its laws.

Is there such a thing as a state of nature? What would people act like in such a state?

The Leviathan

Thomas Hobbes

… [D]uring the time men live without a common power to keep them all in awe, they are in that condition which is called war; and such a war as is of every man against every man…. In such condition, there is no place for industry, because the fruit thereof is uncertain; and consequently no culture of the earth … no arts; no letters; no society; and which is worst of all, continual fear, and danger of violent death; and the life of man, solitary, poor, nasty, brutish, and short.

It may … be thought there was never such a time…. Howsoever, it may be perceived what manner of life there would be, where there were no common power to fear….

And because [this] … is a condition of war of every one against every one … it follows that … every man has a right to everything, even to one another's body. And therefore … there can be no security … of living out the time which nature ordinarily allows men to live. And … every man, ought to endeavour peace, as far as he has hope of obtaining it; and when he cannot obtain it … he may seek … war. The … fundamental law of nature … is, to seek peace, and follow it. The second … is … to defend ourselves.

From this fundamental law of nature, by which men are commanded to endeavour peace, is derived this second law: That a man be willing, when others are so too … to lay down this right to all things; and be contented with so much liberty against other men as he would allow other men against himself….

The only way to erect such a common power, as may be able to defend them from the invasion of foreigners, and the injuries of one another … is to confer all their power and strength upon one man, or upon one assembly … to submit their wills … and their judgements to his judgement…. [It is] as if every man should say to every man: I authorize and give up my right of governing myself to this man, or to this assembly of men, on this condition, that you give up your right to him, and authorize all his actions in like manner….

For by this authority … so much power and strength [is] conferred on him, that by terror thereof, he is enabled to form the will of them all, to peace at home, and mutual aid against their enemies abroad…. And he that carries this person is called sovereign and said to have sovereign power; and every one besides, his subject.

[Thomas Hobbes *Leviathan* (1651). In *Western Philosophy*, trans. and ed. by John Cottingham. Oxford: Blackwell Publishers Ltd., 1997, chap. 13, 14, and 17.]

John Locke's View: Individuals and Rulers Draft a Social Contract

Locke also speculated on what life might be like in "a state of nature," although Locke's concept was different from Hobbes'. Locke imagined a state in which people lived together "according to rational self-interest." He believed that reasonable people would rightly look after their own interests. In addition, Locke said, that in this state of nature, each person possessed certain natural rights: property, personal safety, and the results of their labour.

Enjoyment of these rights, however, is not guaranteed when life exists solely in a "state of nature" because others will threaten, or even take away these rights. Locke agreed with Hobbes in the belief that, under such conditions, people would willingly give up their individual freedoms and rights to a ruler who could ensure individual enjoyment of life and property in peace and security.

Locke also described the type of social contract that would, or should, emerge from this need for government. Again, this was different from Hobbes' concept. Locke's social contract specified certain conditions to be accepted by any ruler. Should the leader, or person in power, fail to ensure the rights and security of the people, he or she would be breaching the contract. The social contract between the ruler and his or her subjects would therefore be nullified. The ruler would lose his or her authority and the people would no longer have reason to obey.

Civil Government

John Locke

Men being ... by nature all free, equal and independent, no one can be put out of this estate and subjected to the political power of another without his own consent.... [This] is done by agreeing with other men, to join and unite into a community for their comfortable, safe and peaceable living, ... in a secure enjoyment of their properties, and a greater security against [others]....

If man in the state of nature be so free; ... absolute lord of his own person and possessions; equal to the greatest and subject to nobody, why will he part with his freedom? Why will he ... subject himself to the dominion and control of any other power? To which it is obvious to answer, that though in the state of nature he has such a right, yet the enjoyment of it is very uncertain and constantly exposed to the invasion of others ... and the enjoyment of the property he has in this state is very unsafe, very insecure. This makes him willing to quit this condition which, however free, is full of fears and continual dangers....

... [I]n a constituted commonwealth, ... acting for the preservation of the community, there can be but one supreme power, ... the legislative, to which all the rest are and must be subordinate.... [Yet] there remains still in the people a supreme power to remove or alter the legislative when they find the legislative act contrary to the trust reposed in them.... [T]he trust must necessarily be forfeited, and the power devolve [be given] into the hands of those that gave it, who may place it anew where they shall think best for their safety and security.

And thus the community perpetually retains a supreme power of saving themselves from the attempts and designs of anybody, even of their legislators, whenever they shall be so foolish or so wicked as to lay and carry on designs against the liberties and properties of the subject.... And thus the community may be said in this respect to be always the supreme power....

[John Locke, *Second Treatise of Civil Government* (1690). In *Western Philosophy*, trans. and ed. by John Cottingham. Oxford: Blackwell Publishers Ltd., 1997.]

David Hume's View: Individuals Do Not Voluntarily Accept a Ruler

Hobbes and Locke both used the hypothetical idea of a social contract as a means for thinking about the powers of government. David Hume, on the other hand, attacked the very idea of the social contract because he believed it fostered false conclusions. Hume wrote that no people ever agree voluntarily to give up their rights to become subjects of a sovereign. Rulers, he noted, usually seize control by force, leaving individuals with no choice but to accept or reject the sovereign authority. Hume believed that the majority of human beings never have any part in shaping a social contract with the government. According to Hume, the average person struggles daily without rights, obeying laws that he or she did not make.

Hume's critics responded with the argument of "tacit consent" or consent by action. They suggested that by continuing to live in a country, a person is therefore agreeing to abide by that country's government and its laws. Hume denounced this position. Even if people wanted to leave a country, he noted, most do not have the means to do so, or to survive in a foreign land. According to Hume, the only person, who makes an active decision to become part of any society and its laws is the immigrant who deliberately moves to a new land or society.

In the end, however, Hume agreed that governments are necessary for practical reasons. We are all born into a society and, unless we leave it, we must obey its laws and authority. Without authority, Hume said, the strong would prey on the weak.

Of the Original Contract

David Hume

... [It is] said that, by living under the dominion of a prince which one might leave, every individual has given a tacit consent to his authority, and promised him obedience.... [It] may be answered, that ... implied consent can only have place where a man imagines that the matter depends on his choice. But where ... , by his birth, he owes allegiance to a ... certain form of government, it would be absurd to infer a consent or choice....

Can we seriously say that a poor peasant or artisan has a free choice to leave his country, when he knows no foreign language or manners, and lives, from day to day, by the small wages which he acquires? We may as well assert that a man, by remaining in a vessel, freely consents to the dominion of the master; though he was carried on board while asleep, and must leap into the ocean and perish, the moment he leaves....

The truest tacit consent ... is when a foreigner settles in any country, and is beforehand acquainted with the ... government, and laws, to which he must submit....

We are bound to obey our sovereign, it is said.… But why are we bound to observe our promise? It must here be asserted that … mankind … can have no security where men pay no regard to their engagements. In like manner may it be said that men could not live at all in society … without laws, and magistrates, and judges, to prevent the encroachments of the strong upon the weak, of the violent upon the just and equitable.

[David Hume, *Four Dissertations*, 1757. In *Essays Moral, Political and Literary by David Hume*, ed. by T.H. Green and T.H. Grose. London: Longmans Green, 1875, vol. 1, 443–60.]

Although many immigrants to Canada chose to leave their country of origin, some did not choose to accept or abide by some Canadian laws.

IDEAS AND ISSUES

Understand Concepts

1. Describe the natural condition of mankind imagined by Hobbes and Locke.
2. How does Locke's view of the social contract differ from that of Hobbes?
3. How does Hume disagree with both Locke and Hobbes?

Think Critically

4. What philosophic purposes does the idea of a social contract fulfill for Hobbes and Locke?
5. Assume for the moment that all governments and all laws were cancelled in Canada tomorrow. Also assume that you, and a representative group of other Canadians, are on a committee to draw up a social contract that would describe the rights and duties of government and citizens. This contract would also indicate the conditions under which this contract could be broken by either side. As a class, prepare a draft of this contract.
6. In what ways do you feel that you are a part of a "social contract" in Canadian society, psychologically or legally? How does such an implied "social contract" affect your thoughts, behaviour, and sense of loyalty and obedience? Do you feel that you have given up significant rights and freedoms to be part of this society?
7. Hobbes, and to some extent Locke, believed that without government human existence would be insecure. Is it necessary to accept this view of human nature?
8. Locke believed that individuals gave up their rights voluntarily, and could take them back if government failed to fulfill its part of the social contract. Do you believe such natural rights exist, or are rights possessed by any individual or group that can claim them?
9. Hume raised the question why we should obey constituted authority. Do the same arguments hold for obeying authority in other situations, such as in school or in a family? Are there advantages to doing so? What are the costs of disobeying?

Communicate Ideas

10. Debate this issue: Everyone in Canada today has the right and the opportunity to cease to be part of the implied "social contract" in this country if they are determined to do so.

Inquire and Research

11. Analyze the American Declaration of Independence, and the French Declaration of the Rights of Man and Citizen. In what ways do these documents reflect the idea of a "social contract"?
12. Read Henry David Thoreau's essay "Civil Disobedience." What position does he take on a social contract, if any? To what degree does he feel that obedience to established authority should be followed? Outline and comment on his ideas in a response paper.

A Negative View of Government

The philosophers we have examined thus far have all been convinced of the need for political and social authority, for government and law. Not one of these thinkers doubted the rationale for government, although each provided different reasons, and looked to different ideal forms.

Some philosophers, however, argue that governmental authority causes more harm than good. Before reading further on this topic, ask yourself whether you personally are convinced of the need for government and authority. Is it possible to live without such external controls and authority? Can people live a complete life only when they are within an organized society ruled by laws and governments?

Hobbes and Locke formulated their ideas during a time when nations were being created; many of their contemporaries were interested in determining what form state authority should take. By the nineteenth century, many of those new nations had taken shape. Centralized government authority was widespread throughout the Western world. Some philosophers began to wonder what life would be like without governments, laws, and state authority.

Anarchism: Central State Power Is Harmful

Anarchists believe central state authority is harmful. Anarchists are especially concerned with the coercive nature of state authority, and the power it has to make people act in certain ways. Anarchists speculate about what society would be like without coercive authority in government, business, religion, education, the family, and other social institutions.

Some people believe that anarchists have a positive view of human nature because they are convinced that human beings are usually capable of governing themselves in a cooperative, peaceful, and rational manner. Anarchists regard freedom as the most basic and important value in life. As a result, most anarchists view the ideal society as one where a small group of people comes together voluntarily in order to determine how they will live.

Anarchists have worked to develop such idealistic communities for a long time, beginning as far back as the nineteenth century. Some have tried to achieve this goal through violent overthrow of established authority; others have turned to education to change people's minds; still others formed communities with like-minded people to develop small cooperatives. A number of such communes were also established during the 1960s. These societies stressed cooperative efforts, hoping to minimize the need for rules. Most of these communal groups failed to survive over an extended period.

Peter Kropotkin (1842–1921) was a Russian aristocrat who became a revolutionary anarchist. He presented an anarchist point of view of society arguing that laws are unnecessary and even harmful. Are you convinced?

In politics, the more things change, the more they remain the same.

Marianne Means

Anarchism is ... the teacher of the unity of life; not merely in nature, but in man.

Emma Goldman

Views of an Anarchist

Peter Kropotkin

In existing States a fresh law is looked upon as a remedy for evil. Instead of themselves altering what is bad, people begin by demanding a law to alter it. If the road between two villages is impassable, the peasant says: … "There should be a law about parish roads." … In short a law everywhere and for everything! A law about fashions, a law about mad dogs, a law about virtue, a law to put a stop to all the vices and all the evils which result from human indolence and cowardice.

We are so perverted by an education which from infancy seeks to kill in us the spirit of revolt, and to develop that of submission to authority; we are so perverted by this existence under … law, which regulates every event in life … that … we shall lose all initiative, all habit of thinking for ourselves. Our society seems no longer able to understand that it is possible to exist otherwise than under the reign of law….

But times and tempers are changing. Rebels are everywhere to be found who no longer wish to obey the law without knowing whence it comes, what are its uses, and whither arises the obligation to submit to it…. [They] are criticizing the very foundations of society which have hitherto been held sacred, and first and foremost amongst them that fetish, law.

The critics analyze the sources of law; and find … bloodshed, conquest by fire and sword. They study the characteristics of law, and instead of perpetual growth corresponding to that of the human race, they find … a tendency to crystallize what should be modified and developed day by day…. [T]hey see … the axe, the cord, the rifle, the prison; … the brutalized prisoner, reduced to the condition of a caged beast….

They see a race of law-makers legislating without knowing what their laws are about; today voting a law on the sanitation of town, without the faintest notion of hygiene, tomorrow making regulations for the armament of troops, without so much as understanding a gun; making laws about teaching and education without ever having given a lesson of any sort…. Finally, they see the jailer on the way to lose all human feeling, the detective trained as a blood-hound, the police spy despising himself….

… [I]nstead of inanely repeating the old formula, "Respect the law," we say, "Despise law and all its attributes!" In place of the cowardly phrase, "Obey the law," our cry is "Revolt against all laws!" Only compare the misdeeds accomplished in the name of each law with the good it has been able to effect … and you will see if we are right.

[Peter Kropotkin, *Kropotkin's Pamphlets* (London, 1886). Ed. by Roger N. Baldwin. New York: Vanguard Press, 1927.]

Emma Goldman (1869–1940) is one of the best known anarchists of the twentieth century.

IDEAS AND ISSUES

Understand Concepts

1. What is Kropotkin's point of view and how does he support it?
2. How would Hobbes or Locke have responded to Kropotkin's anarchism?

Apply and Develop

3. (a) (i) Imagine there were no rules for behaviour in your philosophy class that were agreed on, nor any agreed method for making decisions about behaviour. Imagine that your class was out of touch with any external authority such as the principal or school board that could be called upon to make decisions and to establish rules. What do you think would result in the short and long term? Would chaos reign, or would some form of order and organization emerge? Develop and defend a scenario you think might occur.

   (ii) Imagine your town or city was cut off from all other people on Earth. Just before this happened, all established authority, the mayor, councillors, judges, police officers, and others went on vacation. Describe what you think would happen in your town or city. Would the results be different from part (i)?

   (b) On the basis of part (a), develop your own views about why governments exist and what life would be like without them.

Think Critically

4. Although anarchists vary in their views, many regard individual freedom to be the highest value. Any association of people, they argue, should be a free association where there is no external authority and power is shared equally by all concerned. Do you think that anarchy is a possible or desirable route for human organization?

Communicate Ideas

5. Debate this issue: It is possible for people to live together peacefully without delegating authority to anyone.

Inquire and Research

6. (a) Read William Golding's book *Lord of the Flies*. What happened to the group of young schoolboys on the island? What is Golding's view of human nature as described in the book?

   (b) Does *Lord of the Flies* tell us about human nature generally or only about English schoolboys under certain circumstances?

Who Should Govern?

Almost all people on Earth live under the authority of some form of government. At this moment, you live within the jurisdiction of municipal, provincial, and federal governments. Many questions can be asked about these governments, and about government in general. What types of government are best? What changes would you like to see in existing forms of government? Who should have the authority to govern?

These questions are as important today as they were in the past. Political philosophers, like ordinary people, recognize daily the power that governments have to influence our lives. We all recognize the ways in which governments operate: at

What characteristics would you look for in a leader? Why?

times, they may seem worthwhile, effective, and just, while at other times, they may seem less useful, ineffective, and unjust.

We live in a democracy, where all citizens have the right to take part in decisions. Yet, even with universal participation, we see problems in democracies. What happens when some representatives who are poorly prepared

or ill-suited to govern, support policies that seem wrong, resulting in laws with which we disagree? We know the dangers that can result from entrusting political power to one individual or a few. Twentieth century dictatorships have caused terrible harm and human suffering. What are the types of governments, and who are the types of political leaders you admire? What characteristics do they share?

Political philosophers use several methods to investigate questions about government and authority. Sometimes they analyze actual governments and political systems, using examples from these institutions to draw conclusions and general rules about good and bad government. Other political philosophers begin by identifying basic principles upon which governments are, or may be, formed. These essential core elements may include democracy, freedom, or equality. Still other philosophers may speculate on ideal forms of government, or utopias.

The question of who should govern is as important today as in ancient times.

Different Types of Governments

At one time or another throughout history, each of the types of government below have been recommended as ideal. Which form do you think is best? Why?

- Plutocracy: government by the rich
- Meritocracy: government by those who have ability
- Theocracy: government by religious people
- Aristocracy: government by "the best" people, however that is determined
- Oligarchy: government by the few
- Monarchy: government by one person who inherits that position
- Democracy: government by the people

Plato's View: Government Should Consist of Philosophers

The Republic was Plato's major work, and in it he described what he believed to be the perfect society. An important part of the book is Plato's discussion of possible forms of government, and his justification for the form he preferred. Plato also analyzed the qualities of those people he believed were best suited to occupy positions of authority.

Plato rejected several of the forms of government that existed in the city-states of ancient Greece at the time. He disapproved of "timocracy," government by those who are ambitious and seek honour. Such ambition, Plato noted, resulted in politicians who are motivated by the spirited and emotional aspects of their character, rather than the rational element. Plato also rejected "plutocracy," rule by the rich. Such leaders, he believed, were so involved in worldly matters, that they made poor deci-

sions. Moreover, Plato suggested, wealthy rulers would tend to make laws that discriminated against the poor, resulting in class warfare. Nor was Plato impressed by "democracy," rule by the people. He believed that government by the majority led to mob rule.

Plato's preferred form of government was "aristocracy." Today we think of aristocracy as an inherited form of rule, but this was not Plato's meaning. He defined aristocracy as "the rule of the best," the most enlightened people who could recognize reality, truth, and goodness. Plato recommended rule by the educated, rational thinkers. He wanted rulers who were not only knowledgeable about the world, but were also able to understand ideal and eternal truths. Plato believed that the most perfect form of aristocracy would be a government led by philosophers.

In a democracy, such as Canada's, we choose representatives by vote based on our assessment of how well they might rule. Normally there are no other legal requirements of our candidates, such as level of education, ethical behaviour, or demonstration of rational thought. We usually elect people who are clearly ambitious for the position. Some of those we elect are wealthy, others are not. Some are experienced, others are not. Should we require our political leaders to acquire their positions through training and education, and to demonstrate ethical behaviour, and the ability to think clearly and rationally? Or should we continue to elect our leaders based on whatever criteria we believe are important?

Plato explained his plan for a political system based on philosopher–rulers.

The Republic

Plato

Unless either philosophers become kings in their countries or … kings [are] inspired with a genuine desire for wisdom … there can be no rest from troubles…. [P]hilosophers … apprehend the eternal and unchanging…. Those who cannot do so, but are lost in the mazes of multiplicity and change, are not philosophers.

… [M]en who are entirely cut off from knowledge … have in their soul no clear pattern of perfect truth … before they proceed to embody notions of justice, honour, and goodness in earthly institutions…. It would be absurd not to choose the philosophers, whose knowledge is perhaps their greatest point of superiority….

… [The philosopher has] … passion for any knowledge that will reveal … that reality which endures forever and is not always passing into and out of existence…. [The philosopher possesses] a love of truth and a hatred of falsehood….

Again, in seeking to distinguish the philosophic nature, you must not overlook the least touch of meanness. Nothing could be more contrary than pettiness to a mind constantly bent on grasping the whole of things, both divine and human. And do you suppose that one … whose thought can contemplate all time and all existence will count this life of man a matter of much concern?… A mean and cowardly nature, then, can have no part in the genuine pursuit of wisdom.

[Plato, *The Republic*, 473C–E, 484B–487A. trans. by Francis MacDonald Cornford. New York: Oxford University Press, 1945.]

IDEAS AND ISSUES

Understand Concepts

1. (a) What personal characteristics does Plato believe are important to a political leader?
   (b) What reasons does he provide for such characteristics?

Think Critically

2. What personal characteristics would you find important in a political leader? Support your position with reasons.
3. Should political leaders be trained experts? If so, what training should they have? If not, provide reasons why not. For example, should we make it a requirement that those who take part in government be trained in philosophy or in other areas such as political science, history, and psychology?

Communicate Ideas

4. Debate this issue: Only those who are well educated should be able to run for elected political positions.

Inquire and Research

5. Read selections from Plato's *The Republic* where he discusses his ideal forms of leadership and government. Several chapters in "Part 2: Justice in the State and in the Individual," and "Part 3: The Philosopher King" have important ideas to discuss. Analyze these ideas using the questions below as a basis:
   • What type of leadership and government does Plato think is best?
   • What reasons does he give for his position?
   • What do you think of his political philosophy?

Democratic Government: Pros and Cons

One alternative to a government run by trained professionals is to involve all people within a society in the decision-making process. Democracy is rule by the people (or the *demos* as they were called in ancient Greece). Democratic government was first developed in Athens, the home city-state of Socrates, Plato, and Aristotle. Democracy is also the form of government that many people prefer today.

The democracy of ancient Athens, however, was very different from the democracy Canadians are familiar with today. Although Athenian democracy governed a city-state of only a few thousand people, it did not fully represent the population. Athenian government was run by the adult male citizens of Athens who gathered to discuss, debate, and vote on issues of importance. Women and slaves, who made up the majority of the Athenian population, were not allowed to participate.

Aristotle: All Citizens Should Participate in Democratic Government

Aristotle believed in democracy and provided arguments in its favour. He discussed the role that ordinary people, without wealth or special training, should have in government. Once again, Aristotle disagreed with his mentor Plato.

Under what form of leadership do you think government is best: by one person, by a few, or by all?

Politics

Aristotle

The principle that the multitude ought to be supreme rather than the few best … , though not free from difficulty, yet seems to contain an element of truth. For the many … when they meet together may very likely be better than the few good … as a feast to which many contribute is better than a dinner provided out of a single purse. For each individual among the many has a share of virtue and prudence, and when they meet together, they become in a manner one man, who has many feet, and hands, and sense…. Hence the many are better judges than a single man of music and poetry [and government]; for some understand one part, and some another, and among them they understand the whole….

… [W]hat power should be assigned to the mass of freemen and citizens, who are not rich and have no personal merit[?]… There is still a danger in allowing them to share the great offices of state, for their folly will lead them into error, and their dishonesty into crime. But there is a danger also in not letting them share, for a state in which many poor men are excluded from office will necessarily be full of enemies. The only way of escape is to assign to them some deliberative and judicial functions. For this reason Solon and certain other legislators give them the power of electing to offices, and of calling the magistrates to account, but they do not allow them to hold office singly. When they meet together their perceptions are quite good enough, and combined with the better class they are useful to the state … but each individual, left to himself, forms an imperfect judgement.

[Aristotle, *Politics*, 1281a-b. In *Basic Works of Aristotle*, trans. by Benjamin Jowett, ed. by Richard McKeon. New York: Random House, 1941.]

Problems with Democracy

Discussion of the strengths and weaknesses of democracy did not end in ancient times and continues today. Although most people in Canadian society believe it is one of—if not the—best forms of government, everyone recognizes the problems that go along with it.

Democracy relies on informed citizens making the best decisions, under the circumstances. Of course, this is not always the case, since all citizens may not be well informed about issues, and decisions may favour one group or discriminate against another. Voters and elected representatives may make decisions that are short term rather than long term, that fail to take all factors into account, or that do not represent important values of the society.

Nevertheless, although it may be flawed, as Winston Churchill noted, democracy appears to be the best form of government available.

The following excerpts, identify and discuss concerns about democracy, at least problems that democracy has to deal with if it is to continue. What are these concerns? What do you think about them?

Groups such as the Ku Klux Klan have ideas about how societies should be organized and who should have the power to make decisions. These ideas sometimes oppose the rights of certain individuals in a society. Do these groups threaten democratic societies?

Race Matters

Cornel West

In these downbeat times, we need as much hope and courage as we do vision and analysis; we must accent the best of each other even as we point out the vicious effects of our racial divide and the pernicious consequences of our maldistribution of wealth and power. We simply cannot enter the twenty-first century at each other's throats, even as we acknowledge the weighty forces of racism, patriarchy, economic inequality, homophobia and ecological abuse on our necks. We are at a crucial crossroad … and we either hang together by combating these forces that divide and degrade us or we hang separately. Do we have the intelligence, humour, imagination, courage, tolerance, love, respect, and will to meet the challenge? Time will tell. None of us can save the nation or the world. But each of us can make a positive difference if we commit ourselves to do so.

[Cornel West, *Race Matters*. Princeton: Beacon Press, Vintage, 1993, 1994.]

Democracy Has Its Problems

Susan Neiburg Terkel

Democracy is often thought of as an ideal form of government, but it is not without problems. Direct rule by the people is impractical: too many people are ignorant about important issues, and a general election cannot be held every time something needs to be decided. On the other hand, representatives sometimes act against the interests and wishes of the people who elect them. These problems may be mere technical, as in finding the best way to put into practice the will of the majority. Sometimes, however, serious moral problems arise. What happens if the majority desires a social policy that discriminates or harms the minority? Is it fair for an apathetic majority to use its votes to thwart a dedicated minority? What if some groups of people always end up on the wrong side of elections, and thus feel they are unrepresented?

[Susan Neiburg Terkel, ed. (consulting) and R. Shannon Duval, ed., *Encyclopedia of Ethics*. New York: Book Builders Inc., 1999.]

Noam Chomsky:
Mass Media Stifles Freedom of Speech

One feature that we as citizens of a democracy frequently fail to recognize is the effect that the mass media has in shaping our ideas and attitudes about the political system in our nation and the policies our government enacts. Noted linguist and political activist Noam Chomsky (1928–), among other scholars, has investigated this issue and the effect that it has had, and continues to have, in the United States. One central idea in democracies is freedom of speech and expression. According to this premise, the media should be "independent and committed to discovering and reporting the truth." (Noam Chomsky and Edward Herman, 1988) However, if an important aspect of the overall service of mass media is to serve the needs of powerful groups within that nation, then propaganda is present. In other words, our perception of what our government is like and what it is doing may be at odds with reality, if public opinion is being shaped by propaganda campaigns.

> Propaganda is to democracy what violence is to totalitarianism.
> *Noam Chomsky and Edward Herman*

Noam Chomsky

The Connection Between Language and Power

One of the best known dissidents and political activists in modern American society is Noam Chomsky (1928–). He was the elder son of working-class immigrants to the United States; his father had fled Russia in 1913, avoiding the draft into the czar's army. Both his parents were Hebrew teachers, and instilled in Chomsky a keen interest in language. Chomsky's family and early life experiences during the Great Depression set the stage for his desire to understand the world events around him and uncover the truth.

During the 1950s, Chomsky revolutionized the study of linguistics, changing it from a behaviourist subject based primarily on observation into one that united language, biology, and psychology. He proposed a theory stating that language is an innate ability based on a universal grammar. Language, says Chomsky, is the creative tool of

> Propaganda is not directed towards creating an inspiration; it closes, seals up all the openings through which an inspiration might pass; it fills the whole spirit with fanaticism.
> *Simone Weil*

intelligence and serves as the means for understanding human nature. In terms of the impact on his field, Chomsky's contributions have been likened to those of Einstein and Freud.

Chomsky's study of language led him to examine the relationship between language and freedom and language and politics. He has studied extensively the effect of mass media in shaping public opinion in democratic societies, particularly the United States. If human nature is not based on some instinct for freedom, Chomsky argues, then there really is no such thing as moral values. If humans are essentially ignorant and can be modified by experience and training, then those in power can control them for their own good.

Since the 1960s, Chomsky has actively written, demonstrated, and spoken out against injustices inflicted within and on many countries throughout the world, as well as exposing how mass media controls political and social thought in democratic societies. He participated in anti-Vietnam war activities, and exposed the atrocities in East Timor and Nicaragua, among many others. His criticisms of American foreign policy over the last several decades have been scathing and, as a result, his views have been met by criticism and marginalization on the part of the media.

A Propaganda Model

Noam Chomsky and *Edward Herman*

The mass media serve as a system for communicating messages and symbols to the general populace. It is their function to amuse, entertain, and inform, and to inculcate individuals with the values, beliefs, and codes of behavior that will integrate them into the institutional structures of the larger society. In a world of concentrated wealth and major conflicts of class interest, to fulfil this role requires systematic propaganda.

In countries where the levers of power are in the hands of a state bureaucracy, the monopolistic control over the media, often supplemented by official censorship, makes it clear that the media serve the ends of a dominant elite. It is much more difficult to see a propaganda system at work where the media are private and formal censorship is absent.

This is especially true where the media actively compete, periodically attack and expose corporate and governmental malfeasance [dishonest and illegal behaviour], and aggressively portray themselves as spokesmen for free speech and the general community interest....

A propaganda model focuses on this inequality of wealth and power and its multi-level effects on mass-media interests and choices. It traces the routes by which money and power are able to filter out the news fit to print, marginalize dissent, and allow the government and dominant private interests to get their messages across to the public....

... In assessing ... newsworthiness ... , the media do not stop to ponder the bias that is inherent in the priority assigned to government-supplied raw material, or the possibility that the government might be manipulating the news, imposing its own agenda, and deliberately diverting attention from other material.

[Noam Chomsky and Edward Herman, *Manufacturing Consent*. New York: Pantheon Books, 1988, 1, 2.]

The events that occurred on September 11, 2001, shocked most people in the Western world. Many began to question what precipitated those events. What image did the media portray of the events of September 11, 2001, and the circumstances before and after those events? What information did the media not disclose to the public? Why? How can the public find out the truth?

IDEAS AND ISSUES

Understand Concepts

1. What form of government does Aristotle recommend? Why?
2. What reservations does he have about this form of government?
3. Describe some of the problems that could arise in a democracy.

Think Critically

4. Do you agree with Aristotle's concern about allowing all people to be fully involved in decision-making?
5. What additional arguments can you provide in support of or against democracy?
6. (a) To what degree and in what ways is the present form of government in Canada a democracy?
   (b) How is Canada's government different from the form of government that existed in ancient Athens? Why is it different?
7. What form of government does Cornel West appear to be arguing for? How do you know?
8. (a) Do any of the problems with democracy discussed in this section exist in Canada today? How do you know? Provide three examples.
   (b) What courses of action would have to take place to prevent these problems from happening?
   (c) Do you think that individuals or government would pursue such courses of action? Why or why not?

Communicate Ideas

9. Debate this issue: The interests of mass media threaten democracy.

Inquire and Research

10. Read the book *Manufacturing Consent* by Noam Chomsky and Edward Herman. Write a paper that critically analyzes mass media in Canada and the effect that mass media has in shaping public opinion.

Government Rule by Individuals with Absolute Control

For most of human history, political power was exercised by individuals, and this took several forms. Often these individuals were monarchs, hereditary rulers who governed by virtue of belonging to a particular family. The British monarchy, which still exists today, began in this way. At other times, it took the form of tyranny, where an individual took and held power arbitrarily with no real justification, and may have ruled cruelly, causing oppression and suffering for the citizens of that nation. In modern times, dictators such as Napoleon, Hitler, and Stalin seized total control of their respective nations through military might, terror, and propaganda.

What arguments can be put forward that support rule by a powerful individual? Plato argued that a philosopher–king, who possessed wisdom and good character, would be the best ruler. This idea was renewed in eighteenth century Europe by those who wished their monarchs to be "enlightened" through education. Historically, monarchs justified their right to rule by claiming that this right was given to them by God. In seventeenth century France and England, for example, it was called the Divine Right of Kings.

In modern times, dictators have often justified their rule by claiming to represent the ideal of the nation or the will of the people. Yet concentrating political power in the hands of an individual can produce difficulties and often tragic results. The ruler may be ineffective, or he or she may rule in a manner harmful to the majority of their subjects. It may be difficult or impossible to remove an unfit ruler from power. Another argument against rule by a single person is that most people prefer to retain some control over their lives. Government by an individual tends to remove that element of self-control.

Louis XIV of seventeenth century France and his descendants claimed to possess a divine right to rule, given by God. If one accepts this claim, then it becomes very difficult to oppose such a ruler. Is such a justification ever put forward in today's world?

St. Thomas Aquinas:
Natural Law Is Best for Humans

In the thirteenth century, Christian philosopher St. Thomas Aquinas sought to determine a form of government that was most natural to human beings and to the natural world. He argued that we should look to nature as our guide to the best form of government. According to Aquinas, natural law is eternal law as it has been revealed to human reason and resides in human nature. Natural law provides direction for humanity's purpose in this world. Human governments and laws are good, Aquinas argued, only insofar as they reflect natural law.

Aquinas believed natural law was the best form of government. Do you agree?

How do we determine the form of government that best reflects natural law and divine law? Aquinas suggested that since our human reason has been given to us by God, reason can lead us in the search for the best form of government. Moreover, we can explore the world around us to discover examples of natural forms of government existing in nature. In his work *On Princely Government*, Aquinas described the type of government he thought human reason would determine, and provided his reasons why such a government would be beneficial.

Time Line

Examples of Absolute Control
- - - - - - - - - - -

ABSOLUTE MONARCHY IN FRANCE
(17TH CENTURY–1789)

POWERFUL FAMILIES IN ITALY
(12TH CENTURY – 14TH CENTURY)

SHOGUNS IN JAPAN
(12TH CENTURY–MID-19TH CENTURY)

MOGHULS IN INDIA
(1526–1857)

DYNASTIES IN CHINA
(C. 12TH CENTURY BCE–1911 CE)

RUSSIAN CZARS
(1533–1917)

COMMUNIST REGIME IN THE FORMER SOVIET UNION
(1917–1989)

NAZI GERMANY
(1933–1945)

PHILOSOPHERS' FORUM

On Princely Government
St. Thomas Aquinas

… Whenever a certain end [or goal] has been decided upon, … someone must provide direction if that end is to be expeditiously attained. A ship, for instance, will sail … according to the winds … and would never reach its destination but for the skill of the helmsman…. In the same way man … has an end toward which all his life and activities are directed; for it is clearly the nature of intelligent beings to act with some end in view. Yet the diversity of human interests and pursuits makes it equally clear that there are many courses open to men when seeking the end they desire. Man, then, needs guidance for attaining his ends.

When we consider all that is necessary to human life, however, it becomes clear that man is naturally a social and political animal, destined more than all other animals to live in community. Other animals have their food provided for them by nature.... They are also given the means of defence, be it teeth, horns, claws or ... speed in flight. Man, on the other hand, is not so provided, but having instead the power to reason must fashion such things for himself.... [N]ature has destined him to live in society, so that dividing the labour with his fellows, each may devote himself to some branch of the sciences....

... [S]ociety being thus natural and necessary to man, ... there must be some principle of government.... For, if ... people were to live, each intent only upon his own interests, such a community would surely disintegrate unless there were one of its number to have a care for the common good.... We differ in our particular interests and it is the common good that unites the community.... So in all multiplicity there must be some controlling principle....

... [I]t is now our further task to enquire whether it is better for a realm or a city to be ruled by one person or by many.... The aim of any ruler should be to secure the well-being of the realm.... But the welfare and prosperity of a community lies in the preservation of its unity; or, more simply, in peace.... So the most important task for the ruler of any community is the establishment of peaceful unity.... [M]any persons will never succeed in producing unity in the community if they differ among themselves.... So it is better for one to rule rather than many who must first reach agreement.

... [T]hat is best which most nearly approaches a natural process, since nature always works in the best way. But in nature, government is always by one. Among members of the body there is one which moves all the rest, namely the heart; in the soul ... one faculty ... is pre-eminent, namely reason. The bees have one king, and in the whole universe there is one God.... So, since ... [human institutions are] an imitation ... of nature, and ... better for being a faithful representation of its natural pattern, the best form of government in human society is that exercised by one person.

[St. Thomas Aquinas, *De Regimine Principum* (1265–67), book 1, chap. 1 and 2. In *Aquinas: Selected Political Writings*, by A.P. D'Entreves, trans. by J.G. Dawson. Oxford: Blackwell Publishers Ltd., 1948, 3–13.]

Niccolò Machiavelli: The End Justifies the Means

Another philosopher with particular opinions about the most suitable form of government was Niccolò Machiavelli (1469–1527). Descended from a long-time Florentine family, Machiavelli was born in Florence, a city-state governed by the powerful Medici family. When the Medici were driven out of Florence in 1494, Machiavelli became active as a diplomat for the new Florentine Republic, travelling on state visits to France and Austria, and accompanying Pope Julius II on one of his military journeys of conquest. In 1500, Machiavelli was elected military chancellor of the Republic. His troops participated in the capture of Pisa in 1509. When the Florentine Republic was defeated by the Spanish in 1512, the Medici returned to Florence. Machiavelli was imprisoned, tortured, and exiled from public life. He retreated to his country farm with his family to write and study. In 1520, he was commissioned to write a history of Florence, which he completed in 1525. Machiavelli died in 1527 at the age of 58. His principle works included *The Prince* (published in 1532), *The Art of War*, and *Discourses on the First Decade of Livy*.

The Prince is one of the most outstanding documents of political philosophy. Written during the enlightened period of the Italian Renaissance, *The Prince* establishes rules of conduct for a successful monarch.

Niccolò Machiavelli

Machiavelli argued that evil means were sometimes necessary to achieve desired ends. Cruelty, deceit, terrorism, ruthless use of force, and treachery were all permissible and desirable on occasion. Machiavelli was the first writer to use *raison d'état*, or "the good of the state," as an explanation and defence of political action. Nowhere did Machiavelli deny the idea of goodness or disguise the nature of evil. The consideration of goodness and evil was simply irrelevant to political success.

Whoever desires to found a state and give it laws, must start with assuming that all men are bad and ever ready to display their vicious nature, whenever they may find occasion for it.
Niccolò Machiavelli

The Prince

Niccolò Machiavelli

I was there to follow orders, not to think.
John Dean
(Watergate testimony)

When states newly acquired ... have been accustomed to living freely under their own laws, there are three ways to hold them securely: first by devastating them; next, by going and living there in person; thirdly, by letting them keep their own laws, exacting tribute, and setting up an oligarchy which will keep the state friendly to you. In the last case, the government will know that it cannot endure without the friendship and power of the prince who created it, and so it has to exert itself to maintain his authority. A city used to freedom can be more easily ruled through its own citizens provided you do not destroy it, than in any other way.

A prince … must have no other object or thought, nor acquire skill in anything, except war, its organization, and its discipline…. The first way to lose a state is to neglect the art of war; the first way to win a state is to be skilled in the art of war…. [T]he prince must read history, studying the actions of eminent men to see how they conducted themselves during war and to discover the reasons for their victories or their defeats, so he can avoid the latter and imitate the former…. [A] prince cannot practise the virtue of generosity in such a way that he is noted for it, except to his cost, he should if he is prudent not mind being called a miser. In time he will be recognized as being essentially a generous man, seeing that because of his parsimony his existing revenues are enough for him, he can defend himself against an aggressor, and he can embark on enterprises without burdening the people….

[Niccolò Machiavelli, *The Prince* (1532). In *The Great Political Theories*, vol. 1. Ed. by Michale Curtis. New York: Avon Books, 1981.]

Should Governments Behave Ethically?

Do you believe that governments should behave ethically in the same way that individuals behave ethically?

Should one state treat another fairly, or should it look out only for its own self-interest?

Should a government treat its citizens in a kind and humane way, or should it seek only to maintain power and create order?

How do you think governments today act in ethical ways or otherwise?

IDEAS AND ISSUES

Understand Concepts

1. What form of government does Aquinas recommend?
2. What arguments does Aquinas use to support his idea of good government?
3. How does Aquinas use the idea of natural law to support his position?
4. What characteristics of a monarch does Machiavelli say are necessary? What reasons does he give?

Think Critically

5. To what degree, if at all, do you agree with Aquinas' arguments for a particular form of government?
6. Compare Aquinas' and Machiavelli's views about absolute control. What are the similarities? What are the differences?

Communicate Ideas

7. Debate this issue: It is better to be ruled by one person than by many.
8. Debate this issue: St. Thomas Aquinas puts forward a better argument for government than does Aristotle.

Inquire and Research

9. Read Machiavelli's *The Prince*. Analyze his view of good government, and his ideas of how a ruler should govern. To what degree do you agree or disagree with his ideas? Are his ideas of any value in the world today? Write an argumentative essay in which you take a position on Machiavelli's ideas and present arguments in support of your position.

The Balance Between Individual Freedom and State Authority

In what ways should each of us be free to think and act as we wish? In what ways should governments have powers to direct our thoughts and actions? Most of us want to control our lives as much as possible. Yet we also realize that because we live within a society, we must give up some of our freedom and obey some authority. Political philosophers concern themselves with the tension that exists between individual rights and freedoms on the one hand, and state authority on the other.

Arguments For and Against State Authority

Several arguments exist in support of state authority. St. Thomas Aquinas provided one when he wrote that, because each individual has his or her own interests and pursuits, coordination is necessary in order to accomplish group goals. Thomas Hobbes believed it was in the nature of humans to be aggressive and to take what is not their own. Therefore, he argued, governments with strong powers were needed to ensure that individuals cooperate with others, even if such cooperation was achieved as a result of fear of punishment. Arguments for state authority are often based on the need for social order and peace.

In modern times, most people accept that some individual rights and freedoms must be given up for the greater benefit of all in a society. Restricting freedoms may include disallowing certain behaviours that cause harm to others. The illustration is often given that it would be wrong to allow freedom of speech to include yelling "Fire" in a crowded theatre if there is no fire. We restrict people from driving any way they want to on highways for

In 1990, Aboriginal Canadians and the federal government came to blows when Aboriginal Canadians protested the desecration of a sacred burial ground. The federal government sent in troops and much fighting ensued. How much authority should governments have, and how much force should they be able to use to deal with organized protest?

the safety of all concerned. Another way that freedoms are restricted is by requiring people to actively do things for the benefit of others or the society as a whole. For example, societies require people to pay taxes, to serve on juries, sometimes to offer humanitarian aid, and a host of other requirements.

There are others, philosophers among them, who focus on the rights and freedoms of individuals, disagreeing with limitations on these, unless absolutely necessary. They believe that rights and freedoms, not limitations and obligations, should be the primary social value.

In our modern world, individuals and groups have often demanded and attained the rights to have freedom of thought and action. In China and other nations there are those who are actively fighting to gain freedoms that have been restricted by their governments. In Canada, the boundaries of art and literature are often being tested by those who demand the elimination of censorship. There are times when freedom of expression and action cause harm or pain to others, such as in the case of hate literature and hate crimes.

Anarchists argue that coercive state authority should not exist, and some have been prepared to support that argument with violent, and sometimes deadly, protest. One historic example occurred on June 28, 1914. Anarchist Gavrilo Princip assassinated Archduke Franz Ferdinand of Austria and his wife Sophie, as they were travelling through the streets of Sarajevo in a motorcade. This event was one of the sparks that set off World War I, a war that lasted four years and cost millions of lives.

Modern-day libertarians also argue against what they perceive as excessive state authority, exercised through laws promoting such restrictions as gun control and taxation. Libertarians believe that individual freedoms are inalienable natural rights, and that such freedoms can only be restricted when there are very strong grounds for doing so.

Usually, however, the question of individual freedom is one of degree. Very few people believe in total individual freedom, or in complete state control. The question is, How much freedom should individuals have? And how much authority should the state possess, and in what areas of life should such authority be exercised? Some people believe that all firearms should be registered; others believe such registration is an infringement on their rights. Some people believe that all parents should be allowed to educate their children in any way they see fit; others argue that children should attend a publicly-funded school. These issues exist in almost every aspect of our lives.

What is your response to each of these questions involving freedom and authority?

- Should you have the right to print or publish anything you want, even if it has the potential to cause harm? Should you be allowed to make racist or sexist statements if you believe in those points of view?
- Should you have the right to harm yourself if you choose, by taking dangerous drugs, for example, or by acting in a reckless manner? Do you have the right to commit suicide?
- Should the state have the right to enforce certain behaviours on you, such as setting highway speed limits, forcing you to attend school, making you pay taxes, or filling out census forms?
- Should the government limit your freedom to prevent potentially dangerous situations from happening (for example, not allowing you to drive without a licence, or requiring that you register a firearm)?

I'm for anybody who's for freedom. I'm for anybody who's for justice. I'm for anybody who's for equality. I'm not for anybody who tells me to sit around and wait for mine.

Malcolm X

There are no new truths, but only truths that have not been recognized by those who have perceived them without noticing.

Mary McCarthy

- Should the state enforce beliefs and values through education or other organizations, in order to develop good attitudes and behaviour? Do teachers and religious leaders have the right to encourage you to act and believe in certain ways? Should the government sponsor television commercials discouraging smoking, violent behaviour, or excessive drinking, or commercials which encourage positive environmental and ecological actions?

Make a list of those areas in your life where you believe individual freedom should rule, and a second list of those areas in your life where you think state authority should be allowed to limit your freedom.

John Stuart Mill: A Statement of Individual Liberty

John Stuart Mill's book *On Liberty* (1859) is a classic statement of the freedoms that individuals should enjoy within any society. He argued that society should only interfere with an individual's ideas or actions if these have potential to harm others. According to Mill, no interference is justified when ideas or actions will only affect the life of the individual who originates them. His treatise presents a very strong statement of individual liberties, one which transcends what most modern societies accept today.

Mill also suggested that individuals owe duties to society in return for benefits received. One example of this duty, he believed, is conscription, since individuals should assist in protecting society and its members from harm.

Mill outlined his general principles of freedom, providing examples to reinforce his theories. He left it to his audience to determine the applications of these principles to specific situations. Consider, for example, if involuntary military service is a necessary duty of living in a successful society. Should an individual within any society be allowed the freedom to inflict physical or psychological harm on his or her person?

John Stuart Mill argued that as long as individual thought and action affected only the individual thinking or acting, he or she should think and do as he or she wishes. If the thought and action interfered with others, then society was justified in limiting the action. Mill also said that individuals owe certain duties in return to the society in which they live. What duties would you include in this?

On Liberty

John Stuart Mill

The ... sole end for which mankind are warranted ... in interfering with the liberty of action of any of their number, is self-protection.... [T]he only purpose for which power can be rightfully exercised over any member of a civilized community, against his will, is to prevent harm to others. His own good, either physical or moral, is not a sufficient warrant. He cannot rightfully be compelled to do or forbear because it will be better for him to do so, because it will make him happier, because, in the opinions of others, to do so would be wise, or even right. There are good reasons for ... remonstrating [protesting] with him, or reasoning with him, or persuading him, or entreating him, but not for compelling him.... To justify that, the conduct from which it is desired to deter him must be calculated to produce evil to some one else. The only part of the conduct of any one, for which he is amenable to society, is that which concerns others.... Over himself, over his own body and mind, the individual is sovereign....

If any one does an act hurtful to others, there is a *prima facie* case [an apparently clear case] for punishing him, by law, or ... [disapproval]. There are also many positive acts for the benefit of others, which he may rightfully be compelled to perform; such as, to give evidence in a court of justice; to bear his fair share in the common defence, or in any other joint work necessary to the interest of the society of which he enjoys the protection; and to perform certain [beneficial] acts ... such as saving a ... life, or ... protect[ing] the defenceless against ill-usage, things which whenever it is obviously a man's duty to do, he may rightfully be made responsible to society for not doing. A person may cause evil to others not only by his actions but by his inaction, and in either case he is justly accountable to them for the injury....

But there is a sphere of action ... which ... is the appropriate region of human liberty. It comprises, first, the inward domain of consciousness, demanding liberty of conscience, ... liberty of thought and feeling; absolute freedom of opinion; liberty of expressing and publishing opinions.... Secondly, the principle requires liberty of tastes and pursuits; of framing ... our life to suit our own character; of doing as we like ... so long as what we do does not harm [others], even though they should think our conduct foolish, perverse, or wrong. Thirdly, from this liberty of each individual, follows the liberty ... of combination among individuals; freedom to unite, for any purpose not involving harm to others....

We ... [recognize] the necessity ... of freedom of opinion, and freedom of the expression ... on [several] grounds. First, if any opinion is compelled to silence, that opinion may ... be true.... Secondly, though the silenced opinion be an error, it may ... contain a portion of truth.... Thirdly, even if the received opinion be ... the whole truth; unless it is ... contested, it will ... be held in the manner of a prejudice, with little comprehension or feeling of its rational grounds…. Fourthly, the meaning of the doctrine itself will be in danger of being lost, or enfeebled … preventing the growth of any real and heartfelt conviction from reason or personal experience….

… [L]et us next examine whether the same reasons do not require that men should be free to act upon their opinions … without hindrance … from their fellow-men, so long as it is at their own risk and peril…. No one pretends that actions should be as free as opinions….

The liberty of the individual must be thus far limited; he must not make himself a nuisance to other people. But if he … acts according to his own inclination and judgement in things which concern himself, the same reasons which show that opinion should be free, prove also that he should be allowed … to carry his opinions into practice….

What, then, is the rightful limit to the sovereignty of the individual over himself? Where does the authority of society begin?… To individuality should belong the part of life in which it is chiefly the individual that is interested; to society, the part which chiefly interests society.

… [E]very one who receives the protection of society owes a return for the benefit, and … should be bound to observe a certain line of conduct towards the rest. This conduct consists, first, in not injuring the interests of one another … and secondly, in each person's bearing his share … for defending the society or its members from injury and molestation. These conditions society is justified in enforcing….

… [I]f the consequences of misconduct could be confined to the vicious or thoughtless individual, ought society to abandon to their own guidance those who are manifestly unfit for it? If protection against themselves is … due to children … , is not society equally bound to afford it to persons of mature years who are equally incapable of self-government? If gambling, or drunkenness, … or idleness, or uncleanliness, are as injurious to happiness, and … improvement, as many or most of the acts prohibited by law, why … should not law … repress these also?…

… [T]he mischief which a person does to himself, may seriously affect … those nearly connected with him, and … society at large. When … a person is led to violate a distinct … obligation to any other person or persons, the case … becomes amenable to moral [disapproval]…. If, for example, a man, through intemperance or extravagance, becomes unable to pay his debts, or … incapable of supporting or educating [his family], he is deservedly … punished…. [B]ut it is for the breach of duty to his family or creditors, not for the extravagance…. George Barnwell murdered his uncle to get money for his mistress, but if he had done it to set himself up in business, he would equally have been hanged…. [A] man who causes grief to his family by addiction to bad habits … deserves reproach … but so he may for cultivating habits not in themselves vicious, if they are painful to those with whom he passes his life…. [W]hen a person disables himself, by conduct purely self-regarding, from the performance of some definite duty incumbent on him to the public, he is guilty of a social offence. No person ought to be punished simply for being drunk; but a soldier or a policeman should be punished for being drunk on duty. Whenever, in short, there is a definite damage, or a definite risk of damage, either to an individual or to the public, the case is taken out of the province of liberty, and placed in that of morality or law.

[John Stuart Mill, *On Liberty* (1859). In *Collected Works of John Stuart Mill*, ed. by J.M.Robson. London: Routledge, 1977.]

Benito Mussolini:
Argument for State Authority

One form of absolute state authority that arose in the mid-twentieth century was fascism. Among other things, fascism represented authoritarian control over citizens of the state, and the formal cessation of individual freedoms. Benito Mussolini (1883–1945) was the fascist leader of Italy during the early years of

Fascism glorified the state and submerged the rights of the individual into the will of the nation. What consequences can you see of such a political philosophy? To what degree should individuals obey state decrees without thinking critically about them?

the twentieth century. Although he was a political leader and not a political philosopher, he outlined his philosophy of government, providing a rationale for authoritarian government—a telling view of the fascist ideology. Mussolini argued that the only true social reality exists within the state. He expanded this view by suggesting that any individual exists as a person insofar as he or she is a member of a state. Mussolini believed that it was impossible to have a human or spiritual existence outside the state. As a result individual rights have no reality beyond a political entity.

The Doctrine of Fascism

Benito Mussolini

Against individualism, the Fascist conception is for the State; and it is for the individual in so far as he coincides with the State, which is the conscience and universal will of man in his historical existence. It is opposed to classical Liberalism…. Liberalism denied the State in the interests of the particular individual; Fascism reaffirms the State as the true reality of the individual…. Therefore, for the Fascist, everything is in the State, and nothing human or spiritual exists, much less has value, outside the State. In this sense Fascism is totalitarian, and the Fascist State, the synthesis of unity of all values, interprets, develops and gives strength to the whole life of the people.

… Fascism is opposed to Socialism, which confines the movement of history within the class struggle and ignores the unity of classes established in one economic and moral reality in the State.

… Fascism is opposed to Democracy, which equates the nation to a majority, lowering it to the level of that majority….

The Fascist State, the highest and most powerful form of personality, is a force, but a spiritual force, which takes over all the forms of the moral and intellectual life of man. It cannot therefore confine itself simply to the functions of order and supervision as Liberalism desired. It is not simply a mechanism which limits the sphere of the supposed liberties of the individual. It is the form, the inner standard and the discipline of the whole person; it saturates the will as well as the intelligence…. Its principle … pierces into the depths and makes its home in the heart of the man of action as well as of the thinker, of the artist as well as of the scientist: it is the soul of the soul.

[Benito Mussolini, *The Doctrine of Fascism* (1932). In *About Philosophy*, by Robert P. Wolff. Upper Saddle River: Prentice Hall, 1995, 165–7.]

Rights and Freedoms
in Canada Today

When do individual rights and freedoms give way to the authority of the state? Should they give way to the state at all? Thinkers throughout history have pondered these questions, and these questions have serious implications for everyday life and society. In Canada, we may take for granted the rights and freedoms that we have, at least until they are threatened. It is important to remember, however, that these rights and freedoms do not exist in some modern societies. Many countries have developed constitutions and charters to protect and enshrine the rights and freedoms of individuals and groups. In Canada, the Charter of Rights and Freedoms was written in 1982. As you read the following excerpt from the Charter, consider these questions: How would John Stuart Mill justify each of the rights and freedoms in the Charter? Would he disagree with any? What do you think about the Charter?

What rights does the Canadian Charter of Rights and Freedoms ensure? What limitations, if any, do you think there should be on such rights and freedoms?

Canadian Charter
of Rights and Freedoms

Rights and Freedoms guaranteed within the Canadian Charter of Rights and Freedoms are subject only to such reasonable limits prescribed by law as can be demonstrably justified in a free and democratic society.

Fundamental Freedoms
- freedom of conscience and religion;
- freedom of thought, belief, opinion and expression, including freedom of the press and other media of communication;
- freedom of peaceful assembly; and
- freedom of association.

Democratic Rights
- Every citizen of Canada has the right to vote in an election ....

Mobility Rights
- Every citizen of Canada has the right to enter, remain in, and leave Canada.
- Every citizen of Canada has the right to move to and take up residence in any province; and to pursue the gaining of a livelihood in any province.

Legal Rights
- Everyone has the right to life, liberty and security of the person, and the right not to be deprived thereof except in accordance with the principles of fundamental justice.
- Everyone has the right to be secure against unreasonable search or seizure.
- Everyone has the right not to be arbitrarily detained or imprisoned.

Equality Rights
- Every individual is equal before and under the law and has the right to the equal protection and equal benefit of the law without discrimination ... based on race, national or ethnic origin, colour, religion, sex, age or mental or physical disability.

Official Languages of Canada
- English and French are the official languages of Canada and have equality of status and equal rights and privileges as to their use in all institutions of the Parliament and government of Canada....

Minority Language Educational Rights
- Citizens of Canada whose first language learned and still understood is that of the English or French linguistic minority population of the province in which they reside ... have the right to have their children receive primary and secondary school instruction in that language in that province.

Enforcement
- Anyone whose rights or freedoms, as guaranteed by this Charter, have been infringed or denied may apply to a court of competent jurisdiction to obtain such remedy as the court considers appropriate and just in the circumstances.

[Canadian Charter of Rights and Freedoms, 1982.]

Understand Concepts

1. Summarize Mill's main thesis or position in a brief paragraph.
2. Under what circumstances, according to Mill, should individuals be prevented from acting as they wish?

Apply and Develop

3. In each of the areas of society described below, with which alternative do you most agree? Discuss your choices with others in the class.

   Marriage and Family
   (a) People are not bound by any marriage laws or restrictions.
   (b) Social pressure discourages people from marrying outside their ethnic or religious group.
   (c) The family chooses the spouse for a son or daughter.

   Beliefs
   (a) All beliefs can be practised.
   (b) Beliefs that threaten the health or security of people in society cannot be practised.
   (c) All people must accept one set of beliefs.

   Speech
   (a) Individuals may express any ideas they wish.
   (b) Freedom of speech is allowed only when it does not infringe on others.
   (c) Some speech is restricted in the interests of public morals and tastes.

   The State and the Individual
   (a) The state is viewed as the servant of the people.
   (b) Individuals must contribute to the good of the nation.
   (c) The government directs people to live and work in certain places.

4. For the following scenario, indicate how John Stuart Mill would probably respond and how you respond. Provide reasons.
   (a) A debating club has been established in your school. Topics include life, death, morality, and God. Your best friend joins this club and begins to develop opinions that you find strange and sometimes objectionable. Many others in the school are also offended by the views they hear. You and others believe that such opinions are destructive to the cohesion and unity of the school and its spirit. Someone suggests this club should not be allowed to exist in the school.

Think Critically

5. How would the fascist Mussolini reply to Mill's views on liberty?

Inquire and Research

6. Compare the Canadian Charter of Rights and Freedoms with the American Bill of Rights. How are they similar? How are they different? How would John Stuart Mill react to the various rights and freedoms in each? Do you think he would add any?

Obedience and Resistance to State Authority

Governments are established to make laws, and to see that they are enforced. Courts of law and police forces are created to ensure that these laws are obeyed. All of us, from our earliest years, are taught to obey the law, and, for the most part, we do. We know that governments and laws are necessary to the well-being of society and to the people within that society. We also know there are consequences for us if we do not obey the law.

Given the recognized need for law and authority, we must still ask ourselves if disobeying the law is ever justifiable. Are there circumstances where it is more ethical to resist established authority than to accept it? There are times when government and laws appear to go against our own beliefs and values. Under such circumstances, do we go along with these laws reluctantly, do we protest against them, or do we disobey? Consider these questions as you read "The Case of Rosa Parks."

The Case of Rosa Parks

On December 1, 1955, a woman named Rosa Parks (1913–) boarded a Montgomery, Alabama, city bus to ride home from her job at the Maxwell Field Army Air Force Base. Rosa Parks was forty-two years old and she was black.

In those days, Blacks paid their bus fare at the front of the bus, then got off the bus to re-enter it at the middle, because they were only allowed to sit at the back of the bus. Blacks were not even allowed to sit across the aisle from whites, and they were also required to give up their seat to a white person if no more white seats were available.

Rosa Parks paid the fare, and took a seat in the middle of the bus. "I didn't want to pay my fare and then go around to the back door, because many times, even if you did that, you might not get on the bus at all. They'd probably shut the door, drive off and leave you standing there."

When Rosa Parks refused to give her seat up to a white person, she was arrested, and charged with trespassing. "I did not get on the bus to get arrested. I got on the bus to go home."

Although she was released on bail, Rosa Parks decided she would not pay the fine. Instead, she elected to challenge the constitutionality of Montgomery's bus segregation law. Thousands of Black people, including newly appointed Montgomery church pastor, Martin Luther King, Jr., supported Rosa Parks by staging a boycott of the city buses. It would last over a year. On December 20, 1956, the United States Supreme Court declared Montgomery's bus segregation law unconstitutional, and on December 21, 1956, Rosa Parks boarded a Montgomery city bus and paid her fare. She sat at the front. The modern-day American Civil Rights movement had begun.

> We give credibility to unjust laws by obeying them.
> *Alan Boesak*
> *(protesting apartheid laws in South Africa, 1989)*

Reasons for Civil Disobedience and Its Consequences

Most cases of civil disobedience are not clear-cut, yet decisions to obey or disobey legal statutes must be taken. What happens if you live in a society such as ours where laws can be changed through democratic processes, and the majority of people vote to implement a law you consider unjust. Conscription, for example, has been mandated by law at various times throughout Canada's history. Young Canadian men and women were drafted into the army to fight during both World Wars. Yet a number of Canadians at the time, such as many in Quebec, resisted conscription, some for religious reasons, while others on political grounds. If you disagree with war on ethical grounds, are you justified in resisting?

Henry David Thoreau (1817–1862), an American naturalist and writer, was also concerned with the question of civil disobedience. He became increasingly disturbed by the trend in America and other industrialized nations towards increasing government authority over many aspects of life. His essay "On the Duty of Civil Disobedience" (1849) has become the basis for nonviolent protest throughout history and around the world. According to Thoreau, all citizens must resist, expose, and overturn all unjust or immoral action in order to maintain personal integrity. Thoreau believed nonviolent, or passive, disobedience was necessary whenever governmental edict conflicted with higher moral law—the ideal natural law, from which human law was derived.

> Under a government which imprisons any unjustly, the true place for a just man is also a prison.
> *Henry David Thoreau*

On the Duty of Civil Disobedience

Henry David Thoreau

I heartily accept the motto, "that government is best which governs least"; and I should like to see it acted up to more rapidly and systematically. Carried out, it finally amounts to this, which also I believe, "That government is best which governs not at all"; and when men are prepared for it, that will be the kind of government which they will have….

Can there not be a government in which majorities do not virtually decide right and wrong, but conscience?—in which majorities decide only those questions to which the rule of expediency is applicable? Must the citizen ever for a moment, or in the least degree, resign his conscience to the legislator? Why has every man a conscience, then? I think that we should be men first and subjects afterward. It is not desirable to cultivate a respect for the law, so much as for the right. The only obligation which I have a right to assume is to do at any time what I think right…. It is truly enough said, that a corporation has no conscience; but a corporation of conscientious men is a corporation *with* a conscience….

Action from principle—the perception and the performance of right—changes things and relations; it is essentially revolutionary…. It not only divides state and churches, it divides families; yes, it divides the *individual*, separating the diabolical in him from the divine….

Unjust laws exist: shall we be content to obey them, or shall we endeavor to amend them, and then obey them until we have succeeded, or shall we transgress them at once?…

Under a government which imprisons any unjustly, the true place for a just man is also a prison….

Thus the State never intentionally confronts a man's sense, intellectual or moral, but only his body, his senses. It is not armed with superior wit or honesty, but with superior physical strength. I was not born to be forced. I will breathe after my own fashion. Let us see who is strongest. What force has a multitude? They can only force me who obey a higher law than I….

They force me to become like themselves. I do not hear of *men* being *forced* to live this way or that by masses of men. What sort of life were that to live? When I meet a government which says to me, "your money or your life," why should I be in haste to give it my money? It may be in a great strait and not know what to do: I cannot help that. It must help itself; do as I do. It is not worth the while to snivel about it. I am not responsible for the successful working of the machinery of society. I am not the son of the engineer. I perceive that when an acorn and a chestnut fall side by side, the one does not remain inert to make way for the other, but both obey their own laws, and spring and grow and flourish as best they can, till one, perchance, overshadows and destroys the other. If a plant cannot live according to its nature, it dies; and so a man....

[Henry David Thoreau, "On the Duty of Civil Disobedience." In *Walden and Other Writings*, ed. by Joseph Wood Krutch. New York: Bantam Books, 1962.]

What conditions were Civil Rights activists protesting? What methods were they using?

Civil Disobedience and Nonviolence

Civil disobedience was a principle means of protest during the struggle against apartheid in South Africa, and against the Vietnam War during the 1970s. It can take many forms, such as boycotts, strikes, sit-ins, marches, demonstrations, tent cities, and so on.

Mohandas K. Gandhi (1868–1948), commonly referred to as Mahatma ("the great soul") Gandhi, advocated and practised civil disobedience during his thirty-year campaign to secure India's independ-ence from Great Britain. Martin Luther King, Jr. learned a great deal from Mahatma Gandhi about resisting unjust authority. King used similar methods in his struggle against the policy of racial segregation that existed in the American south. Segregation separated African-Americans from whites in education, jobs, business, housing, and most other areas of social life. Segregation meant that Black people had fewer opportunities and rights than whites.

Mohandas K. Gandhi

Nonviolent Leader of India's Freedom

Mohandas Gandhi (1869–1948) was a leading figure of nonviolence during the twentieth century. Gandhi was born in Porbandar, the capital of a small principality in western India. His father was a chief minister who knew how to avoid conflicts with the princes, their suffering subjects, and the British officers in power. His mother was a deeply religious woman who instilled in the young Gandhi values of nonviolence, *ahimsa* (non-injury to all living things), and tolerance for those who had different religious beliefs.

After Gandhi's early schooling in India, he went to London, England, to study law. During his stay, Gandhi found that he did not fit in with Western foods, dress, or etiquette. Eventually, his vegetarianism provided a way for him to break out of his shell and meet socialists and humanitarians, such as George Bernard Shaw, Annie Besant, and Edward Carpenter, who happened to be

God is Truth
MKGandhi

Mohandas Gandhi

vegetarian. These individuals, whose ideas rejected late Victorian values, exposed the flaws with capitalism, and stressed the significance of moral over material values, had a profound effect on Gandhi, and helped shape his personality and political views.

Gandhi returned to India in 1891 only to realize that his employment prospects were grim. He reluctantly accepted a legal position in an Indian firm in South Africa. There, Gandhi gained first-hand knowledge of the prejudice and oppression against Indians, which incited him to assert his rights, as an Indian and as a man, in opposition to the European rulers. He used his knowledge of British law to unite the Indians in South Africa in non-violent protest of unjust laws, and publicized the injustices in newspapers abroad.

In 1914, Gandhi returned to India. After a few years, he began to become proactive against the injustices of British colonialism in India, and aroused feelings of nationalism among his fellow Indians. He created an Indian solidarity that used nonviolent non-cooperation with the British and with those aided by the British. These actions, which included Gandhi's salt march, resulted in the arrest of thousands of Indians, including Gandhi himself, and led the British to inflict more oppressive measures in India. When tensions grew, as in the conflict between Hindus and Muslims, or in the British attempt to segregate the "untouchables," Gandhi used fasts as a means to achieve corrective action.

The British used whatever means they could to destroy Gandhi's influence over his people and to promote discord between Hindus and Muslims. However, the shackles of colonial oppression were soon to come off. In August, 1947, the independent countries of India and Pakistan were formed. The achievement of Indian freedom at the expense of Indian unity was to remain Gandhi's greatest disappointment. The Hindu–Muslim tensions continued, and in 1948 a Hindu fanatic assassinated Gandhi.

The role that Gandhi played in history was significant. The independence of India began a series of events that led to many British colonies around the world seeking and acquiring their own independence. Many have argued that Gandhi was the initiator of three major twentieth century revolutions: against racism, violence, and colonialism. For Gandhi, his deepest motivations were spiritual, not political, ambition.

Arguments For and Against Civil Disobedience

John Rawls (1921–), an American philosopher, writes that any democratic society will always have some laws we dislike. Yet, when we agree to live within a society, we accept majority rule: "Assuming that the constitution is just and that we accepted its benefits, we then have both an obligation and a natural duty… to comply with what the majority enacts even though it may be unjust…. In this way we become bound to follow unjust laws, not always, of course, but provided the injustice does not exceed certain limits." (John Rawls 1969)

Some argue that resistance to established authority must not be done lightly, and then only in exceptional circumstances. For example, if you do not accept a particular rule or law you have several options other than resistance. You can leave the place where that law is enforced. During the Vietnam War, many young men from the United States moved to Canada rather than fight what they considered to be an unjust war.

The Clayoquot Sound dispute, which began in the 1970s, led to the largest act of civil disobedience in Canadian history. The dispute arose because the B.C. government announced a logging zone that jeopardized B.C.'s old growth forest. Nonviolent protests ensued for five months and resulted in the First Nations and the B.C. government signing an interim agreement in 1993 that provided for local Native review of logging plans in Clayoquot Sound until the Nuu-Chah-Nulth land claim was settled.

Another option is to change the law through protest or other type of public pressure. Some people believe these kinds of actions are preferable to disobedience. They argue that disobedience to established authority only leads to social disorder and chaos.

There is also the related issue of what happens if you resist and refuse to obey the law. You are caught by the authorities, but what should you do? Should you accept the consequences, regardless of the punishment? Some philosophers, such as Marshall Cohen, argue that accepting appropriate punishment is necessary in order to prove that your resistance was done not for personal or selfish reasons, but to improve social conditions. After openly breaking the law, the traditional disobedient willingly pays the penalty. This is one of the characteristics that serve to distinguish him from the typical criminal … and it helps to establish the seriousness of his views and the depth of his commitment as well."

Understand Concepts

1. (a) Define the term "civil disobedience."
   (b) Provide three examples of civil disobedience that illustrate this definition.
2. In what ways, if at all, is civil disobedience different from the actions below?
   (a) simply breaking the law
   (b) active peaceful protest
   (c) violent protest

Think Critically

3. Review the excerpt from Henry David Thoreau. Using that as a basis, develop an organizer that indicates those circumstances in which you believe civil disobedience is and is not justified.
4. Do you think that civil disobedience is ever justified in a democracy, where laws are open to being changed through lawful means?
5. It has been said that if you break the law for ethical reasons, then you must accept the consequences to show that your reasons were other than to make a social statement. Do you agree with this position?

Communicate Ideas

6. Debate this issue: Individuals should participate in civil disobedience, no matter what the cost, if they disagree with certain government laws.
7. Many young Americans during the late 1960s and early 1970s disagreed with the Vietnam War. Some allowed themselves to be drafted into the army despite their feelings about the war; some went to jail rather than serve, while still others left the country. With which of these options do you most agree, and most disagree? Provide your reasons.

Inquire and Research

8. Find out more about Gandhi's nonviolent movement and how it led to the independence of India. Could India's independence have been gained in other ways? Present your response in a three to four page paper.
9. Research the American Civil Rights movement of the 1950s and 1960s. What methods to bring about change were used by such leaders as Martin Luther King, Jr. and Malcolm X? How effective do you think each of these methods were? With which methods do you most agree?

Review and Reflect

Do we need government? What type of government is best? How much freedom should individuals have and how much authority should government possess? Is it ever right to disobey state authority? Philosophers have debated these questions since ancient times. Over the ages, many groups of individuals have adopted different types of governments, including democracies, monarchies, and dictatorships. Each of these types of state authority had problems in varying degrees.

During the eighteenth and nineteenth centuries, many countries overthrew their respective monarchies and established democratic governments. These fledgling nations developed constitutions based on human rights and freedoms, although it would be many years in the future before those rights would be fully realized for certain individuals within those nations.

Civil disobedience was the catalyst that allowed nations to undergo social change. This occurred when India gained her independence, during the United States' Civil Rights movement, as well as during other events. In some cases, individuals who participated in civil disobedience lost their lives.

Each of us deals with political philosophy in our own personal lives when we must determine whether or not we agree with people and institutions who have authority. We must also decide what to do if we do not agree. Understanding political philosophy helps us make more informed and better-reasoned personal decisions.

Ideologies

How is our society and its political and social systems organized? What do you believe are the strengths and weaknesses of this social, political, and economic system? The answers you suggest for such questions indicate your personal ideology. An ideology is a set of beliefs and values about the social world as it has existed in the past, the way it is at present, and the direction it should go in the future. Your ideology is your concept of the way the social world is and should be.

There are many ways to think about the social world. There are many choices that can be made in shaping the society in which we and others live. One approach to understanding the range of choices available to us is to explore how people view the world, that is, to understand those ideologies already in existence. In this chapter, we will investigate several major ideologies. As you read, study, and discuss these views, consider these questions:

- How do people who believe in this ideology view the social world?
- What does this ideology assume about human nature?
- What types of political, economic, and social conditions does this ideology advocate or support?
- What methods do people who support this ideology consider acceptable to bring about social change?

An ideology provides a view of the past, an explanation of the present, and a goal for the future.

Why Different Ideologies Developed

Ideologies are not restricted to the world of philosophy; they can be shared by anyone who has opinions about the social world in which we live. Ideologies, however, are largely a product of the modern world. In earlier times, most people assumed that existing social conditions were inevitable. Scholars and rulers were usually the only persons who envisioned a social world governed by an organized belief system. Ideologies developed as an increasing number of people became aware of their social and political worlds, and began to believe that changes could be made in these worlds.

Two conditions in modern societies fostered the development of ideologies. First, as more and more of the general populace became aware of the social conditions that affected most of society, they began to seek ways in which their lives, and the lives of the people around them, could be improved. It is probably no accident that the great revolutions of the modern world occurred in countries where more people could read and write than ever before: for example, England in the seventeenth century, and France and the United States in the eighteenth century. Increasingly, the general population became aware of, and actively involved in, political issues and causes.

A second and related reason for the increase in ideologies was that more of the general public as well as those in power developed different ideas as to what the ideal society should be like. Many new ideas were introduced about how government should be organized and how it should operate, and the type of economy and society that would best suit the population it served. There were many different opinions as to who should govern, and how economic benefits should be distributed among the population. This wide divergence of ideological thought continues today. Almost everybody has opinions about political leaders and issues, how government operates, and how social institutions should be organized.

Factors That Shape Our Ideologies

Individual social views or ideologies are derived from several sources. Personal ideologies are shaped by the circumstances in which we are born and raised: the country in which we live; our social group; economic circumstances; the type of information we are exposed to; and the education we experience. The people in our immediate environment have an important impact on our values and belief system. As we live and experience the world around us, our ideology may grow and change, as we select some ideas and values from our social environment, while rejecting others. It is important to understand the nature of the views we select and what they mean. One method of doing this is to examine major ideologies in existence and determine to what degree, if at all, we agree with them. Important ideologies of the modern world include conservatism, liberalism, capitalism, communism, democratic socialism, fascist totalitarianism, and libertarianism.

Those who adhere to or support a

particular ideology tend to have similar beliefs and attitudes about a number of social conditions and circumstances. With which of these beliefs or values do you agree?

- It is better to invent new and untested procedures rather than follow procedures that have been tried and tested.
- The collected wisdom of many people tends to be superior to the ideas of any one individual.
- Individuals should be responsible for their own lives and welfare as much as possible.
- Governments should shape the lives of individuals rather than be restricted to maintaining order.
- People tend to be guided more by emotion than by rational thought.

Your responses to the previous statements indicate preference for one or another ideology. As you examine the different ideologies discussed in this chapter, consider these statements and your responses as you critically analyze those ideologies. It is important to note that the ideologies discussed in this chapter are not necessarily related to political parties of similar or the same names, although that is sometimes the case. That is, a political party may call themselves Conservative, Liberal, or Socialist and not accept the ideologies of conservatism, liberalism, or socialism. Nazism, or National Socialists, in Germany during the twentieth century, were not socialists at all, in fact were the enemies of any form of socialism.

An ideology is a set of values and beliefs about the social world, explaining what it is like and defining a path for the future. Ideologies are especially concerned with political and social institutions, government and economics. How would you describe the society you live in? In what direction would you like to see society progress?

What Is an Ideology?

An ideology is a collection of beliefs and values about government, the economy, and society. It is a set of lenses through which individuals and groups view and understand their social world. Ideologies are made up of several elements.

- An ideology allows us to explain why things are the way they are in a society. One ideology, for example, might explain the existence of economic inequality by discussing human nature; another might point to historical causes.
- An ideology represents a set of values about what society should be like. One person might hold individual liberty as the highest value; another person may believe equality is of greater importance. People supporting a particular ideology will have a specific view of how they would like society to change in the future.
- An ideology is also a call for action. It suggests how people can work to bring about the type of society and government they believe to be the best.

The Importance of Ideologies

Most people in the modern world have some sort of ideological point of view. We know, for example, that people often interpret events and conditions from a conservative, liberal, or socialist perspective. Many individuals may agree with the general thrust of a particular ideology, while others may cling tightly only to the vision of society a specific ideology espouses. As we analyze ideologies using a philosophic approach, we must first begin by understanding them, and then critically analyze them.

Ideologies have a profound impact on the lives of people, so it is important that we develop informed opinions about them. Political leaders and the mass media often believe in an ideology, a specific view of politics and society and the direction in which these elements should move. Ideologies can exercise a powerful influence on the type of society we live in and on the forms of government we will have. Concerned citizens need to be aware of existing ideologies in order to make informed choices about society and the direction it should go.

After years of being an outspoken consumer advocate, Ralph Nader, leader of the Green Party, ran for president during the 2000 U.S. election. What ideology does Ralph Nader support?

Understand Concepts

1. Define "ideology" and describe its elements.
2. Why is it important to understand ideologies?
3. What ideologies do you see operating in the world today?
4. Why are ideologies largely a product of the modern world?

Apply and Develop

5. Respond to the questions below using point-form answers. How have others in your class responded to these?
   (a) What do you think are the most serious social problems facing Canada today? What should be done about these problems?
   (b) What do you think are the strengths and weaknesses of our form of government? What should be done to improve it?
   (c) If you were to create a utopian society, what would it be like?
   (d) Where should ultimate authority lie: with the individual or with the state?
   (e) What should be the highest priority in a society: freedom or equality?

Think Critically

6. Ideologies are usually based on values that an individual holds as important such as respect for authority, liberty, or individual rights. Review the answers you provided for exercise 5. For each answer you provided, determine what are the basic values, stated or unstated, these answers are based on. One way to know that you are stating a value is to begin the sentence this way: "It is important that ... "

Conservatism:
Established Ways Are Best

During the late eighteenth, and early nineteenth centuries, the accepted attitudes and governments in the Western world changed dramatically. Although some people sparked events that would change the course of history, others sought to oppose these changes. Those who opposed change came to be known as conservatives, and they valued ideas and institutions with roots in the past.

Note that the term conservative, with a lowercase "c" does not imply allegiance to a particular political party. Conservatism refers to a specific set of attitudes, values, and beliefs that people hold that may vary from time to time, place to place, and person to person. Some attitudes and beliefs, however, are common to many conservatives. The characteristics described here are of conservatism as it evolved over the last two centuries.

One belief many conservatives share is that society should be rooted in long-standing traditions, and that the institutions of society should reflect how these traditions have evolved over generations. Conservatives believe that individuals identify themselves as being part of long-standing and evolving social patterns and institutions. Traditional conservatism does not support dramatic or revolutionary change.

Conservatives also believe that those customs and social structures that have successfully withstood the test of time are good guides for the future. They believe long-standing social customs are generally superior to those plans and policies that are deliberately and rationally developed. That which has lasted has an inner strength and wisdom that transcends rational thought and planning.

Conservatives have great faith in an individual's ability to plan and carry out his or her own life goals. According to conservatives, an individual is the best judge of his or her own choices and destiny. As a result, conservatives often support smaller scale government intervention, because they are suspicious of letting politicians and institutions make decisions that might more properly be made by an individual. Conservatives believe that large-scale attempts by government to change or plan society are inefficient and lessen individual initiative. Conservatives tend to argue that a healthy economy, for example, is more often the result of individual effort rather than government planning. One basic tenet of the conservative ideology is that individuals should be responsible for their own welfare.

Conservatives often believe that human beings are motivated by emotional elements such as self-interest and a search for power. According to conservatives, the goal of governments and institutions is to prevent the individual's natural self-interest from being destructive, while channelling his or her energies into socially useful behaviours.

Stripped of ethical rationalizations and philosophical pretensions, a crime is anything that a group in power chooses to prohibit.

Freda Adler

Those who ignore history are doomed to repeat it.

George Santayana

Edmund Burke:
A Conservative Criticizes Change

Beginning in 1789, the French people rose up in revolt against their long-established monarchy. They sought to overthrow the old order and establish a new society through revolutionary and increasingly violent means. English conservative politician Edmund Burke responded eloquently to these events. His words were directed not only against the French Revolution, but also against the rationalist and reformist views of the Enlightenment upon which the Revolution was based. In an open letter to the French revolutionaries, Burke outlined his criticisms of radical change, indicating how they were based on what he considered mistaken values and incorrect views. In the process, he presented a classic conservative view.

Reflections on the Revolution in France

Edmund Burke

… [I]t has been the uniform policy of our constitution to claim … our liberties as an … inheritance … from our forefathers…. By this means our constitution preserves a unity in so great a diversity of its parts. We have an inheritable crown, an inheritable peerage, and a House of Commons and a people inheriting privileges, franchises, and liberties from a long line of ancestors.

This policy [follows] … nature, which is wisdom without reflection, and above it. A spirit of innovation is generally the result of a selfish temper and confined views. People will not look forward to posterity, who never look backward to their ancestors…. [W]e receive, we hold, we transmit our government and our privileges in the same manner in which we enjoy and transmit our property and our lives…. Thus, by preserving the method of nature in the conduct of the state, in what we improve we are never wholly new….

We know that we have made no discoveries, and we think no discoveries are to be made, in morality, nor many in the great principles of government, nor in the ideas of liberty, which were understood long before we were born….

… [I]nstead of casting away all our old … [traditions] we cherish them … and … the longer they have lasted … the more we cherish them. We are afraid to put men to live and trade each on his own private stock of reason, because we suspect that the stock [of reason] in each man is small, and that the individuals would do better to avail themselves of the … [wisdom] of ages….

Time Line

Changes Throughout the World

- - - - - - - - - -

BILL OF RIGHTS (1689)
establishes supremacy of parliament in England

DECLARATION OF INDEPENDENCE (1776)
takes place in the U.S.

FRENCH REVOLUTION (1789)
begins

BOLSHEVIK REVOLUTION (1917)
takes place in Russia

Your literary men and your politicians … have no respect for the wisdom of others…. With them it is a sufficient motive to destroy an old scheme of things because it is an old one. As to the new, they are in no sort of fear with regard to the duration of a building run up in haste…. [D]uration is no object to those who think little or nothing has been done before their time, and who place all their hopes in discovery….

At once to preserve and to reform is quite another thing…. [T]he useful parts of an old establishment are kept, and what is superadded is to be fitted to what is retained…. But you may object—"A process of this kind is slow … [and] might take up many years." Without question it might; and it ought…. Time is required to produce that union of minds which alone can produce all the good we aim at….

But am I so unreasonable as to see nothing at all that deserves commendation in the … labors of this [French revolutionary] assembly? I do not deny that among an infinite number of acts of violence and folly, some good may have been done. They who destroy everything certainly will remove some grievance. They who make everything new, have a chance that they may establish something beneficial….

[Edmund Burke, *Reflections On The Revolution in France* (1790). In *The Works of Edmund Burke*. Boston, MA: Little Brown, 1881, part 3, 274–561.]

How does a conservative respond to demands for drastic or revolutionary action?

Understand Concepts

1. Identify the main elements of traditional conservative ideology, as outlined by Burke.

Think Critically

2. What arguments does Burke provide in support of a conservative ideology?
3. To what degree does Burke believe that governments should interfere in the lives of individuals?
4. Brainstorm the potential positive and negative impact on society of a conservative ideology.

Research and Communicate

5. Research conservative views in Canada today. A starting point is to interview members of conservative political parties, or someone who supports one. Members or supporters of the Progressive Conservative or Alliance parties would be useful to interview.

Liberalism: Individuals' Inalienable Rights Must Be Preserved

Great men can't be ruled.

Ayn Rand

Philosophers have only interpreted the world in various ways; the point, however, is to change it.

Karl Marx

Liberalism is an ideology that arose from a number of sources. One can be traced back to ancient Athens, where citizens were involved in the democratic guidance of their government. Later, during the early modern period, when

education and wealth were more widely accessible to increasing numbers of citizens, people in many countries began to demand a greater share of decision-making power. Gradually, the concepts of shared decision-making and representative government began to emerge. John Locke was an early proponent of such thinking in England, while Jean-Jacques Rousseau adopted a similar position in France. These political philosophers discussed the idea of a social contract, where individuals had the power to assert themselves if government failed to preserve their individual rights. The liberal ideas of these thinkers and others provided the incentive for the French and American revolutions of the eighteenth century, revolutions founded on a belief in the inalienable rights of people. Philosopher John Stuart Mill, writing in the nineteenth century, discussed respect and how it should be granted to the individual.

Classical liberalism has three major components:
- freedom from unnecessary government interference;
- the idea that the state must guarantee the liberties and rights of the individual; and,
- the belief that citizens should be represented in government decision-making, that is, a democracy.

What rights and freedoms for citizens has the Canadian government legislated?

How Liberals View Government and Citizens

Liberals believe that the best government is that controlled by, and representative of, a wide group of people. In ancient Athens, the city-state was so small that all male citizens were able to take an active and direct part in decision-making. Today, many modern nation-states, such as Canada, have such large populations that it is impossible for all people to be directly involved in all decisions. As a result, the concept of representation emerged: we elect representatives to speak for a group or groups of people in the Legislature (at the provincial level) or Parliament (at the federal level). In earlier times, only the rich and the nobility could vote for, or serve as, political representatives. Gradually, however, liberals pushed for wider and more inclusive representation, one which would allow all adults to have the vote and to participate in government. Today in Canada, we are fortunate to have the right to elect a representative of our choice to the Legislature or Parliament. If our candidate fails to perform as we wish, we are able to vote for someone else in the next election.

According to liberals, all citizens possess and should be guaranteed certain inalienable rights: such as the right to openly express a personal opinion or point of view; the right to vote (franchise); the right to practise a particular religion or faith; and, the right to be treated equally in the eyes of the law. Many liberals believe that such rights must be guaranteed, because the state would otherwise tend to trample over them.

Classic or early liberals also believe that individuals should be free from unnecessary government interference, and that the right of the individual to shape his or her own life, opinions, and actions is paramount.

Liberal economic ideas changed and developed somewhat during the late nineteenth and twentieth centuries. Earlier liberals had fought for the right of all individuals to compete and to succeed as much as their talents and abilities allowed. As time went on, however, they increasingly realized that the rights of the individual are not equal where economic disparity is widespread. In other words, a child living in poverty has fewer opportunities to develop individual talents than does a child living in wealth. Liberalism sought to address this disparity by suggesting that governments level the playing field by providing such benefits as education and health services to all people. Modern liberal thought accepts a growing obligation of government to provide those services necessary to allow the individual to make the most of his or her talents.

James Mill, father of John Stuart Mill, provided arguments for representative government, while his son, John Stuart, expressed concern about the use of power by representatives, and how people can work to prevent power abuse. James Mill expressed a view of human nature that many thinkers before him have observed: that human beings will take to themselves as much power as possible if they are not restrained by others. Do you agree with this view? If so, what methods would you suggest to ensure that democratically-elected representatives do not acquire more power than they should?

An Essay on Government

James Mill

Whenever the powers of government are placed in any hands other than those of the community—whether those of one man, of a few, or of several— ... those persons will make use of them to defeat the very end for which government exists. A man is never satisfied with a smaller degree [of power] if he can attain a greater.... If the powers of government are entrusted to one man or a few men, and a monarchy or governing aristocracy is formed, the results are fatal....

... [But] it is not yet proved that good government is unattainable. For though the people, who cannot exercise the powers of government themselves, must entrust them to some one individual or set of individuals, and such individuals will infallibly have the strongest motives to make a bad use of them, it is possible that checks may be found sufficient to prevent them....

In the grand discovery of modern times, the system of representation, [provides] the solution.... There can be no doubt that if power is granted to a body of men, called representatives, they, like any other men, will use their power, not for the advantage of the community, but for their own advantage, if they can. The only question is, therefore, how they can be prevented....

Each representative may be considered ... in his capacity of representative, in which he has the exercise of power over others, and in his capacity of member of the community, in which others have the exercise of power over him. If things were so arranged that, in his capacity of representative, it would be impossible for him to do himself so much good by misgovernment as he would do himself harm in his capacity of member of the community, the object would be accomplished....

[To accomplish this] the power assigned to the representative ... can be diminished ... in duration.... The smaller the period of time during which any man retains his capacity of representative, as compared with the time in which he is simply a member of the community, the more difficult it will be to compensate the sacrifice of the interests of the longer period by the profits of misgovernment during the shorter.

[James Mill, "An Essay on Government." In *Encyclopedia Britanica*, Chicago: Encyclopedia Britanica Inc., 1820.]

The Rights of the Minority

In his essay *Considerations on Representative Government*, John Stuart Mill discussed the idea of representative democracy. He addressed the question of minority rights in any democracy. How can the rights of the few be preserved when the majority have power in a democratic society? John Stuart Mill argued that any minority should continue to have representation and not be totally without power.

Native Canadians have consistently been underrepresented in government both at the federal and provincial levels. What problems exist with our democratic system that continue to perpetuate this problem?

Representative Government

John Stuart Mill

In a really equal democracy every or any section would be represented proportionately. A majority of the electors would always have a majority of the representatives, but a minority of the electors would always have a minority of the representatives. Man for man they would be as fully represented as the majority. Unless they are, there is not equal government, but a government of inequality and privilege: one part of the people rule over the rest ... contrary to the principle of democracy, which professes equality as its very root and foundation.

Such a representative democracy ... , representative of all, and not solely of the majority ... would be free from the greatest evils of the falsely-called democracies which now prevail.... But even in this democracy, absolute power, if they chose to exercise it, would rest with the numerical majority; and these would be composed exclusively of a single class.... Democracy is not the ideally best form of government unless this weak side of it can be strengthened, unless it can be so organized that no class, not even the most numerous, shall be able to reduce all but itself to political insignificance and direct the course of legislation and administration by its exclusive class interest. The problem is to find the means of preventing this abuse, without sacrificing the characteristic advantages of popular government.

[John Stuart Mill, *Considerations on Representative Government.* Ed. by Currin V. Shields. New York: The Liberal Arts Press, 1958, 103, 104, 127, 128.]

Understand Concepts

1. What major views of government are put forward in the excerpts from James Mill and John Stuart Mill?
2. How do views of human nature affect these concepts of ideal government?

Apply and Develop

3. To what degree does the Canadian political system follow traditional liberal principles?
4. Would a traditional conservative or liberal tend to agree with the statements below? Explain your reasoning.
   (a) Traditional ways of doing things are to be preferred. They have stood the test of time and have worked well.
   (b) It is important to provide equal opportunity, a "level playing field" for everyone. Only then can they develop their potential to the fullest.
   (c) Generally speaking, it is better for government to leave most things to the initiative of the individual, certainly of the private sector. Private individuals and groups are more efficient and competitive.
   (d) A good public education system is essential to allow all children, rich and poor, to make the most of their lives.
   (e) The values of the family and of the church have evolved over generations. In the process, the thoughts of many people have helped to make them what they are and these should be respected.
   (f) When the rights of any one individual are trampled upon, the rights of all are threatened.
   (g) Society is like a plant, an organism that has developed over time in a natural way.
   (h) Some social services are essential to help those who cannot look after themselves, through no fault of their own. Unemployment insurance, health care, old-age pensions, and other forms of public insurance provide more equal opportunities. These should not, however, infringe upon individual liberty.

Think Critically

5. Do you agree that, given the opportunity, most people in government will take as much power as they can?
6. Compare the ideas of traditional conservatism and liberalism. Develop your own categories for comparison. Which ideology do you tend to agree with most?

Research and Communicate

7. What does it mean to be "liberal" in Canada today? Research the views of today's liberals. To what degree do they follow traditional liberal ideas?

Opposing Ideologies: Capitalism and Socialism

Two ideologies that have often been in opposition to each other are capitalism, a society driven by profit, and socialism, a society based on distribution of wealth for all. Throughout the past century, these two ideologies have clashed as political leaders from the United States and the former Soviet Union rallied public support to perpetuate their respective ideologies. Propaganda was widespread and differing points of view often resulted in negative consequences, especially during the McCarthy years (1950–1954). The Cold War was one result of this difference of opinion, and generations of people became brainwashed into believing that their form of government was superior.

Joseph McCarthy, an American Republican senator, led a campaign against supposed communist infiltration in the American government.

Capitalism:

Self-Interest and Profit Are Important

Major social and economic changes taking place in England, Germany, and other Western nations during the late eighteenth century gave rise to a growing social class of entrepreneurs, traders, and others involved in commerce, who were becoming increasingly powerful. This "middle class" felt restricted by the political controls and social prestige of the nobility, as well as by the legal and economic systems the nobles controlled. The laws restricting the freedom to manufacture and to trade were particularly troublesome to new entrepreneurs who were aware that as manufacturing machinery improved, the basis of wealth would shift from agriculture to industrial production.

This new middle class pushed hard to reduce the old economic restrictions and regulations, and in the process, a new ideology was created, one that we call capitalism.

A major tenet of this new ideology was that wealth or capital should be in the hands of, and controlled by, individuals who would use it in the most productive and dynamic manner. Capitalists believe that freedom to produce and to trade without government restrictions is beneficial not only to business, but to society as a whole.

Adam Smith (1723–1790) is considered to be the philosophic founder of modern capitalism, or free enterprise as it is also called. Smith's book *Wealth of Nations* laid out rules for free economic development. Smith believed capitalism was based on a realistic view of human nature, and that it also complemented the structure of the universe. Whenever an individual buys, sells, or trades, Smith wrote, he or she makes such decisions with self-interest and personal gain in mind, not with the overt intention of benefitting society. Nevertheless, Smith argued, within the course of such commerce, the capitalist often provides unintentional benefit to others and to society as a whole. Suppose you wish to sell your product to the widest possible range of customers, and make the highest possible profit. You will probably sell your goods at a price that is more attractive to consumers than that of your higher priced competitor. Self-interest, according to Smith, is a natural human trait that benefits society.

Today, many nations have some form of capitalist, or free enterprise, economy. These have evolved over many years, yet no one nation's economy can be defined as purely capitalist. Most are more accurately described as mixed economies. A mixed economy is one in which some economic decisions are made by individuals or private businesses, and some by governments. Societies and economies have seen dramatic changes since Adam Smith wrote *Wealth of Nations*. Nevertheless, his portrait of capitalism remains a classic description of the principles involved.

What is the most effective way to have the economy operate according to the capitalist ideology?

The Wealth of Nations

Adam Smith

Every individual is continually exerting himself to find out the most advantageous employment for whatever capital he can command. It is his own advantage, indeed, and not that of the society, which he has in view. But the study of his own advantage, naturally, or rather necessarily, leads him to prefer that employment which is most advantageous to the society....

As every individual, therefore, endeavours as much as he can both to employ his capital in the support of domestic industry, and so to direct that industry that its produce may be of the greatest value, every individual necessarily labors to render the annual revenue of the society as great as he can. He generally, indeed, neither intends to promote the public interest, nor knows how much he is promoting it…. [H]e intends only his own gain, and he is in this, as in many other cases, led by an invisible hand to promote an end which was no part of his intention….

[Adam Smith, *The Wealth of Nations* (1776), Books 1 and 4. Ed. by James Rogers. Oxford: Clarendon Press, 1880.]

Factors That Led to Socialism

The Industrial Revolution moved forward at breakneck speed in Great Britain and Germany during the nineteenth century, and had moved to the United States and Canada by the end of the nineteenth century. The impact of industrialization was overwhelming. Primarily rural societies based on farming, and family "cottage" industries, were replaced by urbanization dominated by factories and mechanized production. The lives of individuals, and of whole populations, were transformed.

Industrialism did not benefit all equally. Although the industrial age was a time of great opportunity for factory owners and investors, life for working people in the new factories was often squalid and inhumane. Long work hours, dangerous and filthy work-

How did social conditions in early industrial nations help shape socialist and Marxist ideologies?

Capitalism
and Socialism
- - - - - - - - - -

ADAM SMITH
(1723–1790)
describes rules for the development of capitalism

INDUSTRIAL
REVOLUTION
(19TH CENTURY)
occurs in Great Britain, Germany, Canada, and the U.S.

KARL MARX
(1818–1883)
develops communism as an ideology

COLD WAR
(1945–1989)
creates world tension as the U.S. and the former Soviet Union build nuclear arsenals

McCARTHY YEARS
(1950–1954)
foster fear of communism in the U.S.

ing conditions, and low pay were common. Living conditions in the rapidly growing cities were horrendous, as these centres were unprepared for the massive influx of people, and were dedicated to a belief in minimal government and private initiative. Cities lacked sewers, clean water, building codes, health centres, food services, or transportation.

Conservatism and early liberalism, the dominant political ideologies at the time, both believed that government had a minimal role to play in economic affairs. The predominant view was that economic decisions should be guided by individual effort and private initiative.

Under such circumstances, various forms of socialism emerged. Most socialists shared the view that communal effort was necessary to make life bearable in any industrial society. Efforts and rewards should be shared in one way or another, as opposed to the concept of individual production and individual consumption of the finished products.

Socialism Comes in Several Forms

Most socialists share the view that members of a society should work for the good of others, sharing the results of their efforts with others in their society. How this sharing occurs varies from one socialist ideology to another. Democratic socialists, for example, believe that those in government should work to be elected through democratic processes, and that only some of the products and processes should be shared. Other socialists, such as followers of Karl Marx, often believe that only socialist political parties have the right to govern, and that all major elements of the economy should be controlled by, and run for, the benefit of all members of society.

Communism:
Sharing Wealth and Efforts Benefits All

Several small-scale socialist experiments were attempted in the early years of the nineteenth century, but most disappeared within a few years. German economist and social philosopher Karl Marx (1818–1883) condescendingly called these efforts "utopian socialism," because they relied on the initiative and efforts of individuals or small groups, coupled with the goodwill and hope of these people.

Marx claimed that his own form of socialism, which he called communism, and which eventually became known as Marxism, was scientific, unlike the other "utopian" socialist experiments. Marx believed that communism would come about naturally, dictated by the laws of history, and was not the result of the hopes and efforts expended by individuals or groups. Marx's views had a remarkable impact on philosophers, sociologists, political scientists, workers, and politicians—all people who were interested in the organization of society and forms of government.

Karl Marx based his philosophy to some degree on German philosopher Georg Hegel's (1770–1831) view of dialectic, the interaction of opposing ideas to produce a new idea. Hegel argued that change within the universe only occurred when a confrontation of ideas produced a new concept different from those that preceded it. Marx extended Hegel's argument by adding the element of materialism—the belief that it is the physical, material world, not the world of ideas, which is at the root of all existence.

Marx applied dialectical materialism to human affairs. He argued that the dominant and moving force in any society is its economic system, a system he labelled the social substructure. Once one identified how goods and services are produced and distributed within any given society, and who controlled these processes, one would discover all relevant facts about the rest of the society: its superstructure of ideas, institutions, values, family life, religion, and political make-up.

Marx developed his theory of history based on the following philosophic reasoning. Every society in the world, he wrote, consists of competing interests and opposing social classes struggling for dominance. This conflict increasingly reveals the weaknesses of the existing social, economic, and political systems. Those members of a social class struggling for power ultimately overturn the existing social order, with its power structure and dominant social class. A new social order is created, placing the rising social class in power. Marx viewed this process as a universal truth of history, one that has occurred regularly over time. Beginning with the Roman empire when slaves and slave owners struggled with each other, to the French revolution when aristocrats and the emerging middle class fought for control, class struggle has been the dominant and dynamic force of historical change.

Next, Marx turned his critical eye to the industrial society of the mid-nineteenth century of which he was part. He examined its existing social and economic structure, and the forces at work from within and without. His analysis made it clear that the middle classes, or bourgeoisie, owned and controlled the forces of production. Consequently, they also shaped and controlled the rest of the society: its political structure, its family life, its value system, and religion. The working class, or proletariat, defined by Marx as those people who worked for a wage, had no control or influence. Moreover, the proletariat was exploited in that its members received only a small part of the rewards of their labour.

Marx predicted that the struggle between the bourgeoisie and the proletariat would intensify. He suggested that as the number of workers eking out a subsistence-level living increased, the size of the ruling class would decrease, albeit growing richer all the time. Eventually, Marx predicted, the working class would rise up in revolution and take over the means of production and society as a whole.

Marx was vague about the manner in which the future would unfold, but he was firm in his belief that there would be a period of time, which he called the "dictatorship of the proletariat," when the old bourgeois social class would be eliminated from power and a classless society would result. A classless society required no government, according to Marx, who viewed government as only useful in subjugating the powerless classes. The communist society of the future, Marx wrote, would be based entirely on work done cooperatively with the products of the economy shared equally among all members of society, "from each according to his ability; to each according to his needs."

Marx's vision of the future did not unfold as he predicted. Several factors within the Western industrial nations, including Germany, Great Britain, the United States, and Canada, led to improvements in the life and economic welfare of working classes, so revolutionary socialism did not attract overwhelming support in those countries. Perhaps this was because the industrial system produced an ever-increasing quantity of goods, and developed increasingly sophisticated methods of distribution. Labour unions also fought for, and won, better pay and working conditions. Governments in the twentieth century strove to become more democratic in representing the interests of all citizens, not just the rich. Reforms were enacted which made working and living conditions more acceptable in cities and in factories. The overall result was a greater distribution of wealth to a larger portion of the population in industrial nations, and a lack of support for political movements that advocated overthrowing the existing economic system that was based on private enterprise and ownership.

Nevertheless, the view of history and society put forward by Karl Marx exerted a powerful impact on the world in many ways. Marx pointed out the importance of understanding a society's economic system, particularly the economic relations between groups of people. One of his most important legacies is the fact that economic interpretations of history and society are now regarded as a critical element of all social and historical analyses.

Marx's views of social change and revolution had an impact where he least expected they would, in the economically less developed parts of the world, in nations such as Russia, China, Cuba, and others. For much of the twentieth century, international relations have been dominated by the tensions and conflicts between communist and non-communist nations.

The Communist Manifesto

Karl Marx and *Friedrich Engels*

The history of all hitherto existing society is the history of class struggles.

Freeman and slave, patrician and plebeian, lord and serf, guild master and journeyman, in a word, oppressor and oppressed, stood in constant opposition to one another, carried on … a fight that each time ended either in a revolutionary reconstitution of society at large or in the common ruin of the contending classes.

In the earlier epochs of history we find almost everywhere a complicated arrangement of society into various orders, a manifold gradation of social rank. In ancient Rome we have patricians, knights, plebeians, slaves; in the Middle Ages, feudal lords, vassals, guild masters, journeymen, apprentices, serfs….

The modern bourgeois society … has but established new classes, new conditions of oppression, new forms of struggle…. Society as a whole is … splitting up into two great hostile camps, into two great classes directly facing each other: Bourgeoisie and Proletariat [industrial workers]....

The bourgeoisie, during its rule of scarce one hundred years, has created more massive and more colossal productive forces than have all preceding generations together. Subjection of nature's forces to man, machinery, application of chemistry to industry and agriculture, steam navigation, railways, electric telegraphs, clearing of whole continents for cultivation....

... [T]he means of production and of exchange, on whose foundation the bourgeoisie built itself up, were generated in feudal society. At a certain stage in the development of these means of production and of exchange, the conditions under which feudal society produced and exchanged ... became so many fetters. They ... were burst asunder. Into their place stepped free competition, accompanied by a social and political constitution adapted to it, and by the economic and political sway of the bourgeois class.

A similar movement is going on before our own eyes.... The productive forces at the disposal of society no longer tend to further the development of ... bourgeois property.... The weapons with which the bourgeoisie felled feudalism are now turned against the bourgeoisie itself.

But not only has the bourgeoisie forged the weapons that bring death to itself; it has also called into existence the men who are to wield those weapons—the modern working class—the proletarians.... [A]s the bourgeoisie ... developed, ... the modern working class, developed; a class of laborers, who live only so long as they find work, and who find work only so long as their labor increases capital. These laborers, who must sell themselves piecemeal, are a commodity, like every other article of commerce, and are consequently exposed to all the vicissitudes [changing circumstances] of competition, to all the fluctuations of the market.

Owing to the extensive use of machinery and to division of labor, the work of the proletarians has lost all individual character and, consequently, all charm for the workman. He becomes an appendage of the machine, and it is only the simplest, most monotonous, and most easily acquired knack that is required of him....

Modern industry has converted the little workshop of the patriarchal master into the great factory of the industrial capitalist. Masses of laborers, crowded into the factory, are organized like soldiers. As privates of the industrial army they are placed under the command of a perfect hierarchy of officers and sergeants. Not only are they slaves of the bourgeois class, and of the bourgeois State, they are daily and hourly enslaved by the machine, by the over-seer, and, above all, by the individual bourgeois manufacturer....

But with the development of industry the proletariat not only increases in number; it becomes concentrated in greater masses, its strength grows, and it feels that strength more.... [M]achinery obliterates all distinctions of labor and ... reduces wages to the same low level. The growing competition among the bourgeois, and the resulting commercial crises, makes the wages of the workers ever more fluctuating. The unceasing improvement of machinery … makes their livelihood … precarious.… Thereupon the workers began to form combinations (Trades' Unions) … in order to keep up the rate of wages.… Here and there the contest breaks out into riots.…

… The modern laborer … sinks deeper and deeper.… He becomes a pauper.… And here it becomes evident that the bourgeoisie is unfit any longer to be the ruling class … because it is incompetent to assure an existence to its slave.…

The immediate aim of the Communists is the … formation of the proletariat into a class, overthrow of the bourgeois supremacy, conquest of political power by the proletariat.…

… [T]he first step in the revolution by the working class is to raise the proletariat to the position of ruling class; to win the battle of democracy. The proletariat will use its political supremacy to wrest … all capital from the bourgeoisie; to centralize all instruments of production in the hands of the State … and to increase the total productive forces as rapidly as possible.

When … class distinctions have disappeared and all production has been concentrated in the hands of a vast association of the whole nation, the public power will lose its political character. Political power … is merely the organized power of one class for oppressing another.…

In place of the old bourgeois society with its classes and class antagonisms we shall have an association in which the free development of each is the condition for the free development of all.…

… Let the ruling classes tremble at a Communistic revolution. The proletarians have nothing to lose but their chains. They have a world to win.

Working men of all countries, unite!

[Karl Marx and Friedrich Engels, *Manifesto of the Communist Party* (1848). Trans. by Samuel Moore. New York: Socialist Labor Party, 1888, 7–21.]

Karl Marx predicted that worker revolutions to establish a communist state would occur in industrialized nations such as Germany, England, and the United States. However, they occurred in pre-industrial nations such as Russia and in rural agrarian countries such as China and Cuba. Why?

The following excerpt is from the book *True Believer* by American social philosopher Eric Hoffer (1902–1983). Entirely self-educated, Hoffer, who many referred to as "the longshoreman philosopher" because of his affinity for manual work, published nine books and was awarded the American Presidential Medal of Freedom. *True Believer: Thoughts on the Nature of Mass Movements* was published in 1951.

Excerpt from *True Believer*

Eric Hoffer

A rising mass movement attracts and holds a following not by its doctrine and promises but by the refuge it offers from the anxieties, barrenness and meaninglessness of an individual existence. It cures the poignantly frustrated not by conferring on them an absolute truth or by remedying the difficulties and abuses which made their lives miserable, but by freeing them from their ineffectual selves—and it does this by enfolding and absorbing them into a closely knit and exultant corporate whole....

To be in possession of an absolute truth is to have a net of familiarity spread over the whole of eternity. There are no surprises and no unknowns. All questions have already been answered, all decisions made, all eventualities foreseen. The true believer is without wonder and hesitation.... The true doctrine is a master key to the world's problems. With it the world can be taken apart and put together.... The true believer is emboldened to attempt the unprecedented and the impossible not only because his doctrine gives him a sense of omnipotence but also because it gives him unqualified confidence in the future.

An active mass movement rejects the present and centers its interest on the future. It is from this attitude that it derives its strength, for it can proceed recklessly with the present—with the health, wealth and lives of its followers. But it must act as if it had already read the book of the future to the last word. Its doctrine is proclaimed as a key to that book.

[Eric Hoffer, *True Believer: Thoughts on the Nature of Mass Movements*. New York: Harper & Row, 1951, 39, 80, 81.]

IDEAS AND ISSUES

Understand Concepts

1. Identify the social conditions within which Marx lived. How did this affect the ideology he developed?
2. What are the major elements of Marxist communist ideology? Discuss its philosophic basis, analysis of history, analysis of society, and predictions for the future.

Think Critically

3. Assess the pros and cons of Marxist ideology. Consider the validity of its explanation and criticism of the social world, and its value as a signpost for action.
4. (a) What is Eric Hoffer's view of "the true believer"?
   (b) Comment critically on Hoffer's position.

Communicate Ideas

5. Stage a round table debate between Edmund Burke, John Stuart Mill, and Karl Marx. The issue is: Which ideology is most accurate and most useful for Canadians in the twenty-first century?

Inquire and Research

6. Research the ideas of one of the major communists of the twentieth century. You may choose Vladimir Lenin, Leon Trotsky, Mao Tse-tung, or someone else. What are their major positions on communism, and how do they adapt the ideas of Marx to suit the needs of their own country? Write a paper that outlines and critically analyzes these views.
7. Read Eric Hoffer's *True Believer*. Does it accurately describe any mass movements with which you are familiar? In what ways does it do this?

Democratic Socialism: Socialism Without Revolution

Marxist philosophers argued that society would develop into two social classes increasingly divided in wealth, interests, and point of view. The end result, they predicted, would be the working class, or proletariat, taking control of the state and its institutions through revolution, installing first a socialist, and then a communist, state.

Not all of these predictions came to pass, as industrial societies of the late nineteenth century underwent many social and political changes, which Marxist philosophers had failed to take into account. Working people increasingly shared in the wealth produced by industrialism. Stronger labour unions won higher wages and better working conditions. Liberal governments enacted laws to reform the worst evils of early industrial factories and cities.

How Democratic Socialism Emerged

One response to conditions in industrialized Western countries was the development of democratic socialism. Democratic socialists agreed that some form of cooperative effort was necessary to any state, as was some redistribution of wealth to all its citizens. Eduard Bernstein (1850–1932), an early philosopher of democratic socialism, among others, disagreed with Marxist methods and, to significant degrees, with the outcome to be achieved as a result of those methods. Democratic socialists believed revolution was unnecessary, and that such turmoil was not even a foregone conclusion of class struggle. Democratic socialists believed that socialist goals could be achieved as a result of peaceful, democratic means, through the formation of socialist political parties which would use the electoral process to create a socialist government. This government would involve itself in the economy and in the institutions of private property, to effect reforms and reorganization which would result in evolutionary, rather than revolutionary, socialist changes.

Democratic socialism was practised widely in England and in Scandinavia during the twentieth century. During the Great Depression in the 1930s, liberal democracies were threatened and the whole idea of a capitalist economic system was almost destroyed altogether. Industrial systems suffered a severe slowdown, grinding almost to a halt. Millions of people all over the world were out of work. Poverty was rampant, spreading across social classes, even to groups that had previously been immune. The Great Depression dragged on for almost a decade, and suddenly, the

Tommy Douglas

It is not the consciousness of men that determines their existence, but on the contrary, their social existence determines their consciousness.

Karl Marx

Violent revolutions do not so much redistribute wealth as destroy it.... The only real revolution is in the enlightenment of the mind and the improvement of character. The only real emancipation is individual....

Will Durant

threat of a communist revolution was very real.

Industrial nations, such as Canada, enacted reforms providing a safety net for unemployment, health care, old-age pensions, and other socio-economic elements that historically favoured the rich. The concept of increased government involvement in the economy changed significantly. Today in Canada, we accept the fact that education, health care, public utilities, and a host of additional social supports are the responsibility of government. We also accept the fact that redistribution of the wealth produced by our industrial system is achieved through income taxes and public benefits. Many of the goals of democratic socialism became an integral part of most Western democratic systems. Today, we argue not whether public benefits should exist, but rather, to what extent and what forms they should take.

PHILOSOPHERS' FORUM

The Need to Revise Socialism

Eduard Bernstein

I set myself against the notion that we have to expect shortly a collapse of the bourgeois economy.... The adherents of this theory of a catastrophe, base it especially on the conclusions of the *Communist Manifesto*. This a mistake in every respect.

The theory which the *Communist Manifesto* sets forth of the evolution of modern society was correct as far as ... the general tendencies of that evolution. But it was mistaken ... in the estimate of the time the evolution would take.... [I]f social evolution takes a much greater period of time than was assumed, it must also take ... forms that ... could not be foreseen then.

Social conditions have not developed to such an acute opposition of things and classes as is depicted in the Manifesto.... The number of members of the possessing classes is today not smaller but larger. The enormous increase of social wealth is not accompanied by decreasing number of large capitalists but by an increasing number of capitalists of all degrees. The middle classes change their character but they do not disappear from the social scale....

In all advanced countries we see the privileges of the capitalist bourgeoisie yielding step by step to democratic organisations. Under the influence of this, and driven by the movement of the working classes which is daily becoming stronger, a social reaction has set in against the exploiting tendencies of capital.... Factory legislation, the democratising of local government, and the extension of its area of work, the freeing of trade unions and systems of cooperative trading from legal restrictions, the consideration of standard conditions of labour, in the work undertaken by public authorities—all these characterise this phase of the evolution.

But the more the political organisations of modern nations are democratised the more the needs and opportunities of great political catastrophes are diminished…. Friedrich Engels stated in … *War of the Classes* that the time of … "revolutions of small conscious minorities at the head of unconscious masses was today at an end … that social democracy would flourish far better by lawful than by unlawful means and by violent revolution…."

… [T]he task of social democracy is … to organise the working classes and develop them as a democracy and to fight for reforms … and transform the State in the direction of democracy….

No one has questioned the necessity for the working classes to gain the control of government. The point at issue is … whether … a sudden catastrophe would be desirable in the interest of the social democracy…. [I]n my judgment a greater security for lasting success lies in a steady advance than in … a catastrophic crash….

The conquest of political power by the working classes, the expropriation of capitalists, are not ends in themselves but only means for the accomplishment of certain aims and endeavours…. [T]he most important problem of tactics which German social democracy has at the present time to solve, appears to me to be to devise the best ways for the extension of the political and economic rights of the German working classes.

[Eduard Bernstein, *Evolutionary Socialism* (1899). In *Capitalism, Socialism, and Democracy*, ed. by Joseph A. Schumpeter. New York: Harper & Brothers, 1942, 1947.]

Understand Concepts

1. What factors led to the development of democratic socialism?
2. How do democratic socialists see change coming about?

Apply and Develop

3. With which of these statements do you agree?
   (a) Human beings can learn to live cooperatively.
   (b) All wealth should be taxed away at death so that everyone starts life on a level playing field.
   (c) There should be little variation in individual wealth. Economic equality is the ideal.
   (d) Most public utilities should be publicly, not privately, owned.
   (e) Most manufacturing and industry should be publicly, not privately, owned.
   If you agreed with any or all of these statements you share, to some degree, the ideas and values of democratic socialists.
4. In what ways do Canadian socialist parties, such as the New Democratic Party, stand for democratic socialist principles?

Think Critically

5. Compare the social processes leading to socialism described by Marx and Bernstein.
6. How would Marxists and democratic socialists be critical of each other?

Communicate Ideas

7. Debate the merits of democratic socialism over Marxism as an ideology that explains and predicts.
8. Write a position paper that responds to this issue: Democratic socialism is an ideology that would benefit Canadians in the long run.

Totalitarianism:
Total Control of the People by the State

All reactionaries are
paper tigers
Mao Tse-tung

In the early twentieth century, governments based on totalitarian ideologies seized power in several countries. Totalitarian ideologies are based on the conviction that the state is entitled to exercise absolute power over all institutions and individuals. A common characteristic of most totalitarian regimes is the centralization of power in the hands of a small group, and the removal of democratic and individual rights.

Totalitarian ideologies are often divided into those of the left, that are based on socialist or Marxist concepts, and those of the right, that idealize and elevate the nation to a supreme position. During the mid-twentieth century, countries ruled by totalitarian regimes were aggressive internationally. In some cases, particularly during the Great Depression of the 1930s, these countries appeared to be effective in solving social problems, such as poverty. Liberal governments at that time were on the defensive because they were unable to offer effective relief.

Insanity in individuals
is something rare—
but in groups, parties,
nations, and epochs,
it is the rule.
Friedrich Nietzsche

These men are clearing the road to a nearby railway station in Valcartier, Quebec. Canada's federal government was reluctant to offer relief during the Great Depression of the 1930s. Totalitarian governments, by contrast, appeared better able to solve such social problems as poverty and crime.

Totalitarianism of the Left:
Lenin and the Beginning of Communist Russia

In 1917, the Russian state collapsed, an event precipitated by the terrible conditions of World War I. The Communist party assumed control, under the leadership of Vladimir Lenin (1870–1924), and proceeded to structure an entirely new government. Lenin's Russian communism differed markedly from that proposed by Karl Marx. Marx had predicted that the oppressed people would rise up spontaneously and overthrow the government. In Russia, however, it was Lenin, supported only by a small group of followers, who took control of the revolutionary movement. Lenin's successor, Joseph Stalin (1879–1953), ruled Russia absolutely, exercising total power until his death in 1953.

Communism in twentieth-century Russia took new forms for several reasons. Although Marx had predicted that increasingly impoverished people in industrial nations would rise up and establish a communist society, people in industrial states shared increasingly more material goods, and revolutions tended to happen in pre-industrial states such as Russia, or in agricultural states such as China. Political leaders such as Vladimir Lenin in Russia and Mao Tse-tung (1893–1976) in China led smaller groups of communist party members to spearhead revolutions. When the revolutions in Russia and later in China were complete, these political leaders and their supporters took control of the state and proceeded to create new institutions and values.

Another factor that Marx did not predict, was the increasing ability of governments in the twentieth century to influence the ideas and control the activities of the people. New means of mass media, such as radio and movies in the early twentieth century, led to the ability to use propaganda to shape political and social beliefs. New means of transportation and technological developments allowed governments to assert their power in all parts of the nation in ways that were never before possible. The result was that totalitarian power was added to Marxist ideas.

In these ways totalitarian states of the left appeared in some ways similar to those of the right, in terms of the lack of freedom for people and restrictions on ideas and expression.

Totalitarianism of the Right:
Fascism in Italy and Germany

During the period of the 1920s and 1930s, ideologies of the right became dominant in Italy and Germany. Fascism under Benito Mussolini (1883–1945) became the governing ideology of Italy, while the people of Germany were ruled by Adolf Hitler (1889–1945) and his Nazi party (known as the *National Socialist German Workers' Party*). Both Germany and Italy were relatively new nation states, without established traditions of democracy. Both suffered from chaotic social and economic conditions during the 1920s, circumstances which paved the way for determined despots and their political parties to seize control. Benito Mussolini's fascists took control of the Italian government in the 1920s, while the Nazis assumed power in Germany in the 1930s.

The fascist and Nazi ideologies are based on several common elements, although each ideology was shaped to suit the conditions of its individual country. Neo-Nazism, in existence today, draws common elements from both creeds.

One important component of totalitarianism of the right is the principle of leadership and the destruction of democracy. Benito Mussolini was Italy's leader or "il Duce"; in Germany, Adolf Hitler was leader or "der Führer." Both fascism and Nazism are based on the belief that political leaders and single political parties should exercise total control, and all competing political parties are to be suppressed and eliminated. Although the Nazi party was originally based on a left-wing socialist doctrine, under Hitler it became more right-wing, incorporating fascist ideologies including racism, militarism, and totalitarian leadership. During the tumultuous times of the early twentieth century, dictatorships and the centralization of power were admired for their apparent effectiveness in controlling unrest and dealing with social problems such as economic depression. In fact, totalitarianism seemed to be the ideology of the future.

Extreme nationalism is another important element of right-wing totalitarianism. Loyalty to the nation becomes all-consuming, achieving an almost cult-like status; all other values are subservient to support the state. Right-wing totalitarians believe that the true purpose of life is service to the state, and not the provision of individual needs and wishes. Ultimately, extreme nationalism within a nation turns outward, leading to military aggression against other countries. After Hitler had consolidated his power within Germany by the mid-1930s, he began to execute the military expansion of Nazism throughout the rest of Europe.

Racism was an essential element of some right-wing totalitarian ideologies. Although racism, specifically anti-Semitism, was common in many nations, the Nazis made racism a central element of their ideology. Nazism was based to a large extent on a belief in which the racial superiority of the Aryan people gave them the right to control and even destroy other races. Aryans were classified, according to Nazis, as a Nordic race of pure Caucasian stock and were referred to as the "master race." Almost as soon as the Nazis came to power in Germany in 1933, they began their campaign against racial, political, and other minorities within the state. It was not long before the Nazis enacted laws to prevent many people from participating in most economic activities and from attending school. Eventually the Nazis forced minorities living in Germany into segregated quarters, or ghettos. The Nazis' ultimate solution was achieved through imprisonment and mass murder. As the Nazis expanded their territory in Eastern and Western Europe, they brought their racist policies with them, and by the end of World War II, they had succeeded in killing millions of Jewish people and other minorities.

Racist dogma reinforced other elements of Nazism. The emphasis upon extreme nationalism led to widespread suspicion of those individuals not readily identified as members of the Aryan German nation. Elimination of individual rights in the Nazi state provided an effective rationale for the persecution and eventual elimination of any group perceived to be in opposition or as a threat to the Nazi party and Hitler.

Right-wing Nazi totalitarianism expressed contempt for the individual and for individual rights. Hitler believed few people had the ability or the inherent right to lead, and that the majority of the population could be manipulated and led, without regard for their political and human rights. Hitler and his supporters were convinced that the masses were ruled by their emotions rather than by reason, and thus were easily swayed by rhetoric, propaganda, and lavishly produced political rallies.

In his book *Mein Kampf* (1926), Hitler presents his view of government and people. The book was not well received, and it is unfortunate that more people did not read it, because *Mein Kampf* was a blueprint for Hitler's attempt to control the world. Perhaps if more people had been aware of exactly what Hitler was planning to accomplish, stronger safeguards might have been devised to stop him before millions of people died.

Mein Kampf (My Struggle)

Adolf Hitler

Race and the Folkish Philosophy

For me and all true National Socialists there is but one doctrine: people and fatherland.

What we must fight for is to safeguard the existence and reproduction of our race and our people, the sustenance of our children and the purity of our blood, the freedom and independence of the fatherland, so that our people may mature for the fulfilment of the mission allotted it by the creator of the universe....

Everything we admire on this earth today—science and art, technology and inventions—is only the creative product of a few peoples and originally perhaps of *one* race.... We see this most distinctly in connection with the race which ... is the bearer of human cultural development—the Aryans.... The cultures which they found ... are ... determined by the existing soil, the given climate, and—the subjected people.... Without this possibility of using lower human beings, the Aryan would never have been able to take his first steps toward his future culture; just as without the help of various suitable beasts which he knew how to tame, he would not have arrived at a technology which is now gradually permitting him to do without these beasts.

The folkish [originating from and benefitting the people] philosophy finds the importance of mankind in its basic racial elements.... Thus, it by no means believes in an equality of the races.... [I]t recognizes their higher or lesser value and feels itself obligated ... to promote the victory of the better and stronger, and demand the subordination of the inferior and weaker....

The State

Thus, the highest purpose of a folkish state is concern for the preservation of those original racial elements which bestow culture and create the beauty and dignity of a higher mankind....

A folkish state must therefore begin by raising marriage from the level of a continuous defilement of the race, and give it the consecration of an institution which is called upon to produce images of the Lord....

Few things are as immutable as the addiction of political groups to the ideas by which they have once won office.
John Kenneth Galbraith

In violence we forget who we are.
Mary McCarthy

What is objectionable, what is dangerous about extremists is not that they are extreme but that they are intolerant.
Robert Kennedy

Ideologies • **529**

Propaganda

The broad masses of the people can be moved only by the power of speech. And all great movements are ... volcanic eruptions of human passions and emotional sentiments.... Only a storm of hot passion can turn the destinies of peoples, and he alone can arouse passion who bears it within himself....

In general the art of all truly great national leaders ... consists ... in not dividing the attention of a people, but in concentrating it upon a single foe. The more unified the application of a people's will to fight, the greater will be the magnetic attraction of a movement....

The function of propaganda does not lie in the scientific training of the individual, but in calling the masses' attention to certain facts ... whose significance is thus for the first time placed within their field of vision. The whole art consists in doing this so skillfully that everyone will be convinced that the fact is real.... But since propaganda ... consists in attracting the attention of the crowd, and not in educating ... , [it] must be aimed at the emotions and only to a very limited degree at the so-called intellect.

All propaganda must be ... adjusted to the most limited intelligence among those it is addressed to. Consequently, the greater the mass it is intended to reach, the lower its purely intellectual level will have to be. But if, as in propaganda for sticking out a war, the aim is to influence a whole people, we must avoid excessive intellectual demands on our public....

The receptivity of the great masses is very limited, their intelligence is small, but their power of forgetting is enormous.... [Therefore], propaganda must be limited to a very few points and must harp on these in slogans.... As soon as you sacrifice this slogan and try to be many-sided, the effect will piddle away, for the crowd can neither digest nor retain the material....

The magnitude of a lie always contains a certain factor of credibility.... [I]n view of the primitive simplicity of their minds, they [the masses] more easily fall a victim to a big lie than to a little one, since they themselves lie in little things, but would be ashamed of lies that were too big....

Foreign Policy and War

... [Humanitarian] concepts become secondary when a nation is fighting for its existence; ... they become totally irrelevant ... where they might paralyze a struggling nation's power of self-preservation....

Only an adequately large space on this earth assures a nation of freedom of existence. Moreover, the necessary size of the territory to be settled cannot be judged exclusively on the basis of present requirements ... the safeguarding of the existing soil itself must also be borne in mind.... Hence, the German nation can defend its future only as a world power....

[Adolf Hitler, *Mein Kampf* (1925–27). trans. by Ralph Manheim. Boston: Houghton Mifflin, 1943, 197.]

The essential thing is the formation of the political will of the nation: that is the starting point for political action.
Adolf Hitler

All animals are equal But some animals are more equal than others.
George Orwell, Animal Farm

What are the major elements of Nazi totalitarianism? How were they justified by Nazi propaganda? What were the costs?

Irony of Nazi Racism:
The Allies Were Not Immune

Germany during World War II was not the only country where racism was prevalent. Many other nations had long histories of anti-Semitic attitudes. During World War II, many Jewish people from Europe left German-occupied countries only to be denied entry into many Allied countries and the former Palestine. Political activist and Hungarian–Palestinian soldier Hannah Senesh (1921–1944) described an account of Jewish immigrants being left on their own near the British coast. Senesh was eventually executed by the Nazis.

PHILOSOPHERS' FORUM

Let Them Land!

Hannah Senesh

November 27, 1940

A ship filled with immigrants reached the coast. The British would not allow them to disembark, for "strategic reasons," and for fear there might be spies among them. The ship sank. Part of the passengers drowned, part were saved and taken to Atlit. I brood over this and ask, What is right? From a humane point of view there is no question, no doubt. One must cry out, Let them land! Haven't they endured enough, suffered enough? Do you want to send them far away until the end of the war? They came home; they want to rest; who has the right to prevent them from doing so? But from the point of view of the country ... really, who knows? They come from German-occupied countries. Perhaps there are elements among them likely to endanger the peace of the Land, particularly at a time when the Front is drawing closer.

[Hannah Senesh, *Hannah Senesh Her Life & Diary* (Hakibbutz Hameuchad Publishing House, Ltd., 1966). trans. by Marie Syrkin, ed. by Nigel Marsh, 1971. New York: Shocken Books, 1972.]

IDEAS AND ISSUES

Understand Concepts

1. What are the major elements of totalitarianism in general?
2. (a) What is meant by totalitarianism of the left and totalitarianism of the right?
   (b) How are they similar, and how are they different?
3. (a) Why did twentieth-century communism become, in many cases, a form of totalitarianism?
   (b) How did this differ from Karl Marx's view of communism?
4. (a) Summarize the major elements of fascist totalitarianism, as indicated by Hitler in *Mein Kampf*.
   (b) For each of the elements in part (a), speculate on the potential impact on human and social existence.

Think Critically

5. Respond to each element of Nazi ideology. Are there any positive or beneficial elements? What are the negative aspects?

Communicate Ideas

6. Develop a comparison chart that allows a consideration of the major elements of the ideologies you have studied in this chapter. Your chart may contain origins of the ideology, beliefs about human nature, explanations of history and society, plan of action, future possibilities, and others.

Inquire and Research

7. Research the history of Nazi Germany from 1933 to 1945. What were the results of this ideology on individuals, the German nation, and the world?
8. Write a research paper that compares totalitarian ideologies of the right and left in the early twentieth century. You may wish to use Stalin in the Soviet Union and Hitler in Germany during the 1930s.

The Future of Ideologies

I would hope to see this world a gentler place before I leave it. If not, I would prefer to leave it before it gets much worse.

Jim Guendert

Some philosophers believe that the age of ideologies ended when the former Soviet Union disintegrated beginning in 1989, abandoning its role as a major communist force. These thinkers claim that civilization no longer needs belief systems that attempt to explain the world and set it into structured social order. Today's world, they argue, is a global universe requiring global visions.

However, many people still recognize competing ideologies, or world views, each of which has its own idea of how political, economic, and social systems should be structured, within Canada and elsewhere around the world. Liberal democracies often have political parties to represent and express various world views or ideologies. Citizens of these countries vote for the party whose world view most closely approximates their own. Individual lives and the shape of society as a whole often depend on which ideology proves most convincing to the largest segment of the population.

It is not the cause for which men took up arms that makes a victory more just or less, it is the order that is established when arms have been laid down.

Simone Weil

The collapse of the Berlin wall in 1989 marked the beginning of the end of the communist ideology that had dominated Eastern Europe and former East Germany. What led to the disintegration of the former Soviet Union? Could such a change happen in nations with different political ideologies? Why or why not?

What to Consider When Forming Our Own Ideologies

As individuals we need to consider these questions: How much should government regulate the lives of individuals? To what extent and in what ways, should government affect society as a whole? To a large degree, modern day political and social ideologies are based on these questions.

Some ideologies argue that government should only minimally regulate the lives of individuals, and should have little or no influence on shaping society. Libertarianism, which places individualism and freedom above all other socio-political values, is an extreme representation of this view. Libertarians believe that economic decision-making should be done by individuals pursuing their own goals, and that governments should exercise very little influence on the economy.

Other ideologies expect government to assume a more active role in the lives of its citizens. These ideologies often stress the belief that in the natural order of things as people live and work together in society, conditions and problems necessitate government intervention and adjustment. Economic disparities in the lives of people, caused by the social structure, for example, require government assistance in equalizing the potential of success for all citizens by redistributing the benefits produced within the society. Liberal ideologies work to forge a combination of liberty and equality. Socialist ideologies, on the other hand, believe that the primary goal of society is to equalize the position of its people.

Conservative, libertarian, liberal, and socialist ideologies are all rooted in the past. The libertarian view stems from the conservative idea that emphasizes competition and individual initiative. Modern liberalism grew out of respect for the individual coupled with a belief in the responsibility of the state to preserve these rights and ensure equality of opportunity; John Stuart Mill was an early proponent of respect for the individual. Modern socialism, or democrat-

What ideology do you think will play a significant role in the next 100 or so years? Will there be any ideologies that will benefit the most people on this planet?

ic socialism, was born out of the socialist struggles during the last century and earlier. Socialism usually considers the existence of social inequalities as being largely outside the control of individuals. Socialists also believe the role of the state is to equalize opportunities and benefits.

As we begin the new millennium, individuals throughout the world face many of the same social and political challenges as before. Most nations still have some degree of disparity between their rich and their poor citizens. The respect for all individuals is continually being challenged in many nations, even within Canada. Women, children, and minority groups have historically been overlooked by most types of governments. In our modern world, the rapid developments in technology are adding a further dimension to our social and political challenges.

Many political and environmental activists are advocating that we as individuals need to develop ideologies that are more inclusive, considering not just our own country but the world as a whole. As human beings on this planet, we cannot afford to focus just on ourselves. The new questions we need to ask are: How will wealth be distributed among citizens in Canada and among countries throughout the world? What role will technology play in improving environmental and human conditions in Canada and throughout the world? How can individuals in Canada and in other nations create a new world order?

Understand Concepts

1. Is the age of ideologies over, or are there reasons why ideologies will continue to be part of many people's world views?
2. How have the major world ideologies evolved over time?

Think Critically

3. (a) Identify several major problems that exist in Canadian society and in other parts of the world today.
   (b) To what degree, if at all, do traditional ideologies (conservatism, liberalism, socialism, and capitalism) direct their attention to these problems, or have the will or the means to do anything about them?
4. The world has become increasingly interconnected over a very short period of time. Increased travel, television, the Internet, and other technologies have brought us closer to other people and countries in ways never before experienced. How do you think this will affect the world views, or ideologies, of your generation and succeeding generations of Canadians?

Communicate Ideas

5. Interview people, such as local politicians, who hold political and social views about Canada and the world, and where it is going. Ask them to identify what they believe to be important problems to be dealt with, and how they would describe an improved or ideal Canada and the world. Interview young people on the same questions. Compare points of view. Is there a need for a new world view, a new ideology, in your opinion? Present your research to the class and in written form.

Inquire and Research

6. Identify a political or social problem of importance in Canada or the world today. Interview a variety of people to determine their views about this problem. Read about how it is being dealt with by those involved. Determine possible solutions to the problem from different ideological positions, such as conservative, liberal, or socialist. Draw your own conclusions about the problem, and suggest potential solutions.

Review and Reflect

An ideology is a collection of beliefs and values about the social world. These ideas provide a view of the past social world, an explanation of what society is, and a vision of where it should go. Throughout human history, several ideologies have emerged: conservatism, liberalism, capitalism, communism, democratic socialism, and fascism. Ideologies in today's world often revolve around the questions: How much should governments regulate the lives of citizens, especially in economic matters? What do we want the future to be like?

During the twentieth century, a number of ideologies have come and gone. Beginning in the 1920s to the end of World War II, fascism and Nazism, totalitarian ideologies of the right, were powerful ideologies that threatened world peace because of their military expansion. Similarly, totalitarian ideologies of the left, which began in the former Soviet Union in 1917, were also powerful and threatening, and continue to exert a strong international presence today. Conservatism, liberalism, and democratic socialism have each played an important role in shaping societies during the twentieth century.

Individuals within nations continually struggle to define what is the best form of government. The balance between the power and control that government should have and the autonomy that individuals should possess is continually being tested. In this new millennium, individuals must consider the effect that their social and political ideologies will have on other nations throughout the world.

CHAPTER 14

Social Justice

What is a just or unjust social action? What reparations should a government or society make if it commits an unjust action? Should the reparations differ if an individual committed the injustice? Is there such a thing as justice that transcends time and place? The concept of justice, is in many ways, closely related to ethics, the study of right and wrong behaviour.

From our earliest life experiences, we continually develop a concept of justice throughout our lives. When we are children, we believe our siblings receive more than their fair share of toys, food, or attention. As we grow, we think our parents are wrong when they punish us for minor wrongdoings. We say that our teacher graded our last essay unfairly.

As we mature and acquire more knowledge about the world around us, our idea of what is just or unjust becomes more inclusive, involving more people within its scope. We may feel a sense of justice or injustice in events that happen on the other side of the world. We also discover that other people have different views of what is, or is not, just or fair.

Since the beginning of human history, philosophers and other thinkers have considered the question of justice. Some people have tried to find ways to determine justice within an individual society. Others have tried to develop rules of justice that are right for all times and places. Issues involving justice inevitably lead to questions about making amends for unjust actions. What is your view of a just or unjust action? How should amends be made if someone commits an unjust action? Is it possible for amends to be made regardless of the injustice committed?

Philosophers have long been concerned with social justice. Many have tried to define the essential elements of a just society.

The Search for a Principle of Justice

How can we determine whether justice is, or is not, being served? Consider, for example, how our legal system treats those who break the law. How would you decide if the treatment is just or not? Suppose someone has been unfairly treated by society, perhaps by being falsely imprisoned. How would you decide on what would be a just social response?

A philosophy of justice searches for some principle upon which to base right social actions. Without such a principle, or reason for action, ideas of justice become merely opinions. Perhaps you have an idea at this moment as to how you would determine whether or not justice is being served. How would you know if an action was just, or whether society was acting on just principles?

Justice in the Ancient World

The search for a principle of justice has a long history. In ancient times, laws were often based on the principle of "an eye for an eye," using retribution for the concept of justice. The Code of Hammurabi, established during the reign of King Hammurabi of Babylon (1792 BCE – 1750 BCE) stated: "If a man has knocked out the eye of a patrician [upper class person], his eye shall be knocked out." In the Judeo-Christian tradition, the Old Testament of the Bible contains a similar philosophy: "And thine eye shall not pity; but life shall go for life, eye for eye, tooth for tooth, hand for hand, foot for foot (*The Bible* (King James version), Deuteronomy 19:21)." This concept of justice, where retributions must be made for transgressions, continues to be a widely accepted principle for dealing with wrongdoers in society.

In ancient Greece, "might is right" was another principle of justice that was often accepted. In *The Republic*, Plato described a dialogue between Socrates and Thrasymachus that presents this principle of justice, and how it can be achieved. As you read the following excerpt, ask yourself: What do you think makes something just in a society?

Does justice depend on the society, as Thrasymachus thought, or are there universal principles of justice, as Socrates tried to argue?

Thrasymachus Argues that Might Is Right

Plato

Now, while we had been talking, Thrasymachus had several times tried to interrupt the argument, but had been restrained by those next him who wished to hear it to the end. When we stopped for a moment … he could keep still no longer; but … sprang at us like a wild beast.…

"What nonsense has possessed you two all this time, Socrates? What do you mean by all your polite bowing and scraping to one another? If you have a genuine desire to know what justice is, don't confine yourself to asking questions, and making a show by refuting any answer that is given. You know that it is much easier to ask questions than to answer them. But answer yourself, and say how you define justice; and don't dare to tell me that it is the obligatory, or the expedient, or the profitable, or the lucrative, or the advantageous, but make your answer precise and accurate, for I will not have any rubbish of that kind from you."

"Thrasymachus," [Socrates] said trembling, "don't be hard on us, for if Polemarchus and I have gone astray in our scrutiny of the argument, our sin has assuredly not been deliberate.… We are in earnest, my friend, believe me; but the task, I fancy, is beyond our powers; and, therefore, you clever people should rather pity than scold us." …

"Listen, then," he said. "I declare that justice is nothing else than that which is advantageous to the stronger. Well, where is your praise? You refuse it?"

"I must first learn what you mean," [Socrates] said. "As yet I do not know. You say that what is advantageous to the stronger is just. Now, what do you mean by that, Thrasymachus?…"

"Do you mean to say you don't know," he said, "that in some cities a tyrant is master, in others a democracy, in others an oligarchy?"

"Surely."

"Then it is the government which is master in each city, is it not?"

"Certainly."

"Well, every government lays down laws for its own advantage—a democracy democratic, a tyranny tyrannical laws, and so on. In laying down these laws they have made it plain that what is to their advantage is just. They punish him who departs from this as a law-breaker and an unjust man. And this, my good sir, is what I mean.…"

"Now tell me. Do you not also say that it is just to obey the rulers?" [said Socrates.]

"I do."

"Then are the rulers in every city infallible, or are they liable sometimes to make mistakes?"

"They are certainly liable to make mistakes," [Thrasymachus] said.

"Then in their legislation will they not lay down some right and some mistaken laws?"

"I fancy so."

"Are right laws those which are to their advantage, and mistaken laws those which are to their disadvantage?"

"Surely."

"And their subjects must do what they order and this is justice?"

"Yes."

"Then, according to your argument, not only is it just to do what is advantageous to the stronger, but also to do the opposite, what is not advantageous.... The rulers unwittingly prescribe what is to their own hurt, and you say that it is just for others to do what they have prescribed. Then, my most wise Thrasymachus, must it not necessarily follow that it is thus just to do the opposite of what you say? For obviously the weaker are commanded to do what is to the disadvantage of the stronger....Tell me, Thrasymachus, was this how you wished to define justice … ?"

"Most certainly not," he said. "Do you think that I call him who makes a mistake the stronger at the time of his mistake?"

"I certainly thought," [Socrates] said, "that that was what you meant when you admitted that the rulers are not infallible, but sometimes make mistakes."

"Well, you are a quibbler, Socrates. When a doctor makes a mistake about his patients, do you at that moment in so far as he is mistaken call him a doctor? Or do you call a man who makes a mistake in calculating an accountant at the moment of, and in respect to, his mistake? No.... To speak precisely, since you are for being precise, every craftsman is infallible. He who makes a mistake does so where his knowledge fails him; that is, where he is no craftsman. As with craftsmen and wise men, so with a ruler; he is always infallible so long as he is a ruler.... A ruler, so far as he is a ruler, is infallible, and being infallible he prescribes what is best for himself, and this the subject must do. So that, as I said originally, to do what is advantageous to the stronger is just."

"Well" [said Socrates]… "Answer me this. Is the doctor in the precise sense in which you have defined him a money-maker or a healer of the sick?…"

"A healer of the sick," he said.

"What of the ship captain? Is the genuine captain a ruler of sailors or a sailor?"

"A ruler of sailors." …

"Both for sick people and for sailors there is something which is advantageous, is there not?"

"Certainly."

"And is it not the natural end of the art to seek after and provide this?"

"It is," he said.…

"Then," [Socrates] said, "medicine seeks what is advantageous not to medicine, but to the body."

"Yes," he said....

"And no art seeks its own advantage (for it needs nothing), but the advantage of its subject." ...

To this he agreed, though very reluctantly.

"Then no science either prescribes or seeks the advantage of the stronger, but the advantage of the weaker over which it rules?"

This also he admitted in the end, though he tried to make a fight of it....

"Then, Thrasymachus, no one in any kind of government will, so far as he is a ruler, prescribe or seek his own advantage but that of the subject of his craft over which he rules; all that he says and does is said and done with the subject in view, and for his advantage and good."

When we had reached this stage in the argument, and it was plain to all that the definition of justice had been turned upside down, Thrasymachus, instead of answering, said:

"Tell me, Socrates, have you a nurse?"

"Why this?" [Socrates] said. "Should you not answer rather than ask questions of that kind?"

"Because," he said, "she lets you go on sniveling, and doesn't wipe your nose when you need it, for you have not learnt from her to distinguish sheep and shepherd."

[Plato, *The Republic*. Toronto: Fitzhenry & Whiteside, 1980, Book 1, Part 1.]

Problems with Early Ideas of Justice

Even during ancient times, the "eye for an eye" principle had problems. Wars did not necessarily resolve differences between groups of people, and tended to perpetuate feelings of violence and racism. Similarly, wrongdoers who were punished for offences to the state did not necessarily stop their wayward actions or contribute to society in meaningful ways.

A change in mentality occurred when Jesus Christ began preaching a different form of justice. The New Testament contains many instances where Jesus exacted justice. In the story of the moneychangers selling their wares in the temple, Jesus used physical punishment, whipping the moneychangers and overturning their tables. In the case of the female adulterer, who was condemned to be stoned to death, the acceptable punishment at the time, Jesus addressed the woman's accusers by saying that the person who had never sinned should cast the first stone. One by one the accusers dropped their stones eventually leaving Jesus and the woman by themselves. He then told the woman that he was not going to condemn her but that she should sin no more.

The idea of forgiveness, on the part of the person exacting justice, and changing the behaviour of the wrongdoer, eventually led to states developing rehabilitation programs such as counselling, therapy, and community work for many individuals who broke the law. Canada is an example of a state where such programs have allowed some wrongdoers to lead more meaningful lives and contribute positively to society.

Early religious leaders such as Jesus Christ urged new concepts of justice that departed from the idea of revenge, retribution, and an "eye for an eye."

Aboriginal Forms of Justice

Although many of us may think of the "eye for an eye" principle as a primitive form of justice, this was not the form used by Aboriginal people around the world. Most Aboriginal people had very democratic forms of government within their tribes, with elders and chiefs forming some type of counsel. When disputes arose within a tribe, this counsel would deal with the individuals involved, and work towards creating some type of settlement. Even in situations where disputes between tribes arose, the chiefs involved took leadership positions in resolving differences. Only in instances where chiefs were unable to resolve differences did they resort to war.

The general practice of justice among Aboriginal people was in the form of a judge and jury system; the chief served as the judge and the elders formed the jury. Prisons and other forms of penal systems did not exist. Punishment was usually in the form of restitution, although in some cases executions may have taken place. This system of justice, however, was tested to its limits when Aboriginal people encountered Europeans, who brought with them different ideas of government, justice, and societal values.

Time Line

Ideas About Justice

KING HAMMURABI OF BABYLON
(1792 BCE–1750 BCE)
develops Code of Hammurabi

JESUS CHRIST
(C. 4 BCE–29 CE)
preaches a different type of justice

ABORIGINAL PEOPLE
(PREHISTORY–20TH CENTURY)
develop a form of justice involving a judge and jury system

Dalai Lama

Turning Injustice into Compassion

His Holiness the Fourteenth Dalai Lama Tenzin Gyatso (1935–) is the head of state and spiritual leader of the Tibetan people. His original name was Lhamo Dhondrub, and he was born to a peasant family in a small village in northeastern Tibet. At the age of two, he was recognized as the reincarnation of his predecessor, the Thirteenth Dalai Lama, and at age six, he was taken to Lhasa, the Tibetan capital, to undergo rigorous spiritual training according to Tibetan Buddhist custom.

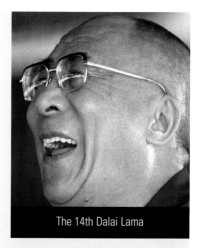

The 14th Dalai Lama

In 1950, when he assumed full political leadership of Tibet, the communist Chinese army brutally invaded Tibet. After his efforts to negotiate peace resulted in China implementing ruthless policies in Tibet, the largest demonstration in Tibetan history took place. On March 10, 1959, Tibetans called on China to leave Tibet, reaffirming their independence. This Tibetan National Uprising was brutally crushed by the Chinese army and the Dalai Lama was forced to flee to India. Today, more than 120 000 Tibetans live in exile.

In Tibet, spirituality and culture have long been intertwined. Ever since 1950, China has been adopting a policy intended to destroy the Tibetan people still in Tibet and their culture. Some of these violations of human rights include torture, imprisonment, the violation of Tibetan monks and nuns, and the massive influx of Chinese in Tibet bringing with them their social problems such as prostitution and gambling.

The Dalai Lama has worked tirelessly for over forty years to preserve Tibetan language, history, religion, and culture establishing monasteries, nunneries, and schools in India and other countries. He publicly declared a democratic constitution based on Buddhist principles and the Universal Declaration of Human Rights as a model of government for a future free Tibet. Since 1967, the Dalai Lama has travelled to many countries around the world, meeting political and spiritual leaders, always advocating a nonviolent resolution to the freedom of Tibet. In 1989, he was awarded the Nobel Peace Prize.

Understand Concepts

1. Identify the principle of justice put forward by Thrasymachus.
2. Summarize the argument made by Socrates in reply.
3. What principle of justice does Socrates use in reference to how a society is ruled?
4. What type of justice was practised by Aboriginal people?

Think Critically

5. Is justice or injustice taking place in the cases below? What do you think should be done? What principle of justice would you use to support your suggested actions?
   (a) There is a growing gap between the rich and poor in society.
   (b) Women have traditionally been paid less than men for the same work.
   (c) A criminal who has committed serious crimes all his life is finally caught for a petty theft.
   (d) A criminal argues that he committed crimes because he was unskilled and had to support a large family.
   (e) A person who has made a fortune argues that she should not have to pay taxes to support the health and education of those who have not worked as hard.
   (f) A ruler or government says that it must take away some rights of its citizens for the good of all in a national emergency.
6. Using a chart, compare and contrast the justice systems of Babylon, Aboriginal people, and our society. You may use headings: type of justice practised, forms of punishment, underlying ethical ideas, and possibility for modifying type of justice within that society.
7. How was the justice used by Jesus Christ different from previous forms? Why was this significant for lawmakers in the future?

Communicate Ideas

8. What do most people think justice is? Interview several people you know. Ask them how they would define justice, examples they would give of justice, and how they would know if justice was being served in specific instances that you suggest.
9. How can one judge if the distribution of goods is just in a society? For example, in Canadian society there is a wide variation in wealth and poverty from one group to another. Is this unjust or just? What principle of justice can be used in this case? Discuss this with several people involved in politics, and others you know who concern themselves with this. What principles would they suggest are important in this discussion?
10. Does justice vary with the individual society, or does it depend on the definition of it put forward by influential people as Thrasymachus thought? Are there principles of justice that are right for all times and places?

Inquire and Research

11. What principles of justice govern our legal and judicial system? Research this in law texts and interview someone involved in law to find out what these are.

Three Aspects of Justice

Philosophers define three aspects of justice: distributive, retributive, and corrective. Each of these aspects can be examined more closely by considering one of these questions: How should the traditional goals of the "good life" such as wealth, rank, freedom, or privilege be shared within a society? How can society punish wrongdoers in a manner that is just for both wrongdoers and victims? How should society make restitution to people who have experienced injustice?

Distributive Justice:
Who Gets What and How Much?

Distributive justice refers to the manner in which valued material and non-material items are distributed among people within a society. How should Canadians share material goods within this country? Some philosophers argue that valued goods should be awarded to those members of society who have made the greatest effort to secure those goods; others believe that those persons within a society who have made the greatest contribution to that society as a whole should receive the largest portion of the valued goods. Some people believe that material goods should be divided equally among all members of society. Still others suggest that rewards should be distributed based on need, varying from one person to another. What principle of justice do you think societies should use when distributing valued material and non-material items?

The disparity between the rich and the poor even in our society continues to be a serious social problem. What are some just ways to deal with this problem?

Retributive Justice: What Punishment Should Be Given to Wrongdoers?

How should society deal with wrongdoers and individuals who break the law? Most of us are introduced to this question early in life when, as children, we may feel it is unfair if one of us is punished severely for misbehaving while another is merely scolded. As we grow older, we may take a critical look at the sentences handed out to people convicted of various crimes.

The idea of retribution stems from the concept of vengeance, the belief in punishing a wrongdoer for his or her actions. We have already encountered the principle of "an eye for an eye," used in earlier times, and even today. An example of retributive justice from the Code of Hammurabi says: "If a surgeon has removed a cataract from a patrician [upper class person] and has made him lose his eye, his [the surgeon's] hands shall be cut off." In other cases, the retribution meant providing restitution to the injured party, a concept that has a long tradition everywhere.

Philosophers examining the concept of retributive justice consider alternative courses of action and principles of justice. For example, one goal of a legal justice system might be to rehabilitate and reform individuals who have broken the law, so that they can contribute in a positive way to society. This idea of justice stems from the understanding that people can change, and that it is socially useful to accept people back into the group, or the community. Many Aboriginal cultures traditionally supported this concept. Modern penal systems and reformatories often have this policy as part of their mission statement.

Sometimes the primary goal of retributive justice is to protect society from wrongdoers, reducing the incidence of crime by isolating the perpetrators. Banishment from society has a long history; in modern times European criminals were exiled to colonies to live out their lives. Imprisonment as we know it today originated in the nineteenth century. In Canada, the imprisonment of criminals is a common practice. In other countries, such as the United States, a death penalty is used as punishment for more serious crimes.

What principles of justice do you believe should operate in dealing with wrongdoers? Will these principles vary according to the circumstance, or according to the crime?

> The doer of injustice is unhappier than the sufferer.
>
> *Democritus*

Corrective Justice: How Does Society Correct Past Wrongs?

Corrective justice refers to the compensation that is, or should be, received by those who have been treated unjustly. Sometimes this injustice occurs to individuals. Guy Paul Morin, David Milgaard, and Donald Marshall are three people who have been wrongfully imprisoned. How should these people be compensated?

Sometimes injustice affects groups of people in society who share a common characteristic, such as ethnic origin or religion. During World War II, Canadians of Japanese origin living in British Columbia had their property seized by the government and were confined to internment camps in the B.C. interior, or farms in Alberta and Manitoba.

In 1946, the Canadian government even went as far as attempting to deport 10 000 Japanese Canadians to Japan, but was stopped due to a massive public protest. How should these people be compensated?

Another example of social injustice affected Native Canadians. From the 1830s, the Catholic and Anglican churches in cooperation with the Canadian government began to establish residential boarding schools as a means to educate and assimilate young Native Canadians in the ways of the dominant colonial culture in Canada at that time. Young children were separated from their families and sent to live in non-Native run schools, where they were taught to renounce their ancestral heritage. More than five generations of Native Canadians lost their history, their pride, and their family ties. How should these people be compensated?

An ongoing injustice in our modern society involves women and visible minorities. These individuals continue to be discriminated against in terms of types of jobs, pay, housing, education, and the cost for consumer goods and services. In particular, many women continue to be violated in domestic relationships. Incest, date rape, physical and emotional violence, and murders pose serious problems for women in our society. What corrective justice do you believe should be provided? How should these groups be compensated for these injustices, if at all? What can society do to minimize or prevent these injustices from continuing?

Guy Paul Morin was wrongfully imprisoned for many years before he was proved to be innocent. What compensation has he received? What compensation do you think is appropriate?

Understand Concepts

1. Identify and briefly define three aspects of justice indicated in this section.
2. State and explain at least one principle that might be used to guide action in each of the three aspects of justice.

Apply and Develop

3. For each of the three aspects of justice, provide one or more examples from contemporary events, not mentioned in the text.

Think Critically

4. What arguments were given for the internment of Japanese Canadians during World War II? Discuss the validity of these arguments.
5. The tense foreign relations between the United States and the countries near the Persian Gulf have led to many FBI investigations of Americans of Arab descent. Discuss the effect that this has had on the Arab American community. Do you think that the United States government is prepared to make any reparations to these individuals? Why or why not? What type of restitution do you think would be fair?

Communicate Ideas

6. Debate this issue: It is not possible to provide corrective justice for all past wrongs.

Inquire and Research

7. Find out more about the residential schools in Canada. How did that experience affect Native children? Did the schools produce the intended results? Is a policy of assimilation ever acceptable? Present your findings and ideas in a four to five page paper.
8. Read Ralph Nader's book *Women Pay More*. Discuss the accepted beliefs that society holds regarding women and the cost for goods and services. Are there strategies that women can use to establish corrective justice themselves?
9. The experience of Japanese Canadians during World War II was not unique. In many Allied countries, people of Germanic, Austro-Hungarian, and Italian backgrounds were also interned in prison camps during one or both World Wars. Find out more about the policies and societal attitudes that led to internment. Was any restitution made to these individuals by governments such as the American, British, or Canadian? Do you consider the restitution to be fair compensation?

Distributive Justice: Principles and Ideologies

All of us as small children are exposed to distributive justice, although we may have no idea of what the concept actually means. What ideas do we hold when we believe our sibling receives a larger portion of dessert than we do, or when we believe someone in our class is a "teacher's pet"? Generally we think such situations are unfair or unjust. As we grow older, we often observe many examples of apparent injustice in the distribution of important and desirable goods among individuals within our society and in other countries around the world. We develop opinions as to why this happens, and what, if anything, should be done about it.

In our modern society, distributive justice comes into play when we consider the effect of family income on the proper development of children. For many Canadians, the average household income is less than it was a generation ago. With the increase in the number of single parents, the issue of child development becomes more crucial than ever. What view of distributive justice do you hold? Are there any views of distributive justice that would benefit all individuals?

Principles of Distribution

Today, there are many divergent views about how valued goods of this world should be distributed. Each of these views is supported by one or more specific principles of distribution. As you read the principles below, ask yourself: Which of the following views do I find most or least agreeable?

- Each person should receive according to his or her abilities. If I am tall, agile, and skillful at basketball, for example, I should be paid extremely well.
- Each person should receive according to his or her needs. If, for example, I need expensive medication in order to survive, or if I have a large family to support, I should be paid more than my co-worker who is healthy or single.
- Each person should receive the benefits of his or her country, social class, or family. If my family can afford to set me up in business, or send me to university, I have every right to a better standard of living.
- Each person should receive according to the effort he or she expends. When I work longer hours, and expend more energy to produce goods, I should be paid more than someone who does not.

Ideologies of Distribution

There are many points of view, or ideologies, about distributive justice. Some of the most popular of these are libertarian, liberal, and socialist. Each of these ideologies uses different principles to justify its concept of what distributive justice means.

Libertarian

Libertarians place great value on individual political and economic rights, vigorously resisting any interference with these liberties. Libertarians believe that property rightfully acquired and possessed should be protected. Libertarians also accept the fact that social and economic inequalities may result from an emphasis on individual rights, although they argue that protection of individual rights will ultimately benefit everyone in the long run.

Liberal

Modern liberal views of justice combine political liberty with economic equality. A believer in liberal justice supports the protection of individual political liberties, and the political intervention of society to prevent serious economic inequalities from occurring. Liberals believe that all members of society should have equal opportunities to succeed in life.

Socialist

Socialists believe that economic inequalities should be minimized or eliminated. To socialists, all members of a society have an obligation to contribute to the welfare of others in that society. Socialists also believe that since equality is the primary goal of society, all goods produced by or imported into, a society should be distributed as equally as possible. Karl Marx described distributive justice this way: "From each according to his ability; to each according to his needs."

Distributive Justice
Applied to War-Torn Countries

During the previous century, the issue of distributive justice among nations became very important when many war-torn nations attempted to rebuild their countries and political systems. After World War II, parts of Asia and most of Europe were devastated and lay in ruins. The heavy Allied bombing in Germany and the atomic bombs dropped in Japan left both Germany and Japan particularly vulnerable to social unrest. In 1947, American General George Marshall proposed a plan, called the Marshall Plan, whereby the United States would supply material and financial aid to help rebuild Europe after the war. The plan allowed countries such as Germany to establish democratic governments and build their economies. A similar approach was used in Japan and was organized by General Douglas MacArthur.

Many wars followed World War II, and many countries were left in ruins. Even today, many nations such as Vietnam are still struggling to establish themselves economically after years of war. The excerpt below discusses issues related to the war in Afghanistan. What do you think about the type of distributive justice described in the excerpt?

Cost of Rebuilding After War
$4.9 Billion, Bank Says

Stephanie Nolen

What could you do with a billion U.S. dollars?

That's what the war in Afghanistan has cost the United States per month—an estimated $6 billion so far.

The World Bank, meanwhile, has told international donors that it will take $4.9 billion over five years to rebuild Afghanistan, an effort that has begun even while the bombs are still falling....

What else could the world do with a few billion dollars?

The World Bank says that everybody in the world who currently doesn't have safe water could have access to clean drinking water and basic sanitation for a total of $90 billion.

Every deprived child in the world could have primary education for $13 billion—while the United Nations says basic education for all would cost $9 billion, the World Bank builds in an extra $4 billion in economic incentives to persuade poor families to educate their daughters, an initiative that has been tried with considerable success in other countries such as Pakistan.

The World Health Organization [WHO] says that with $32 billion it could reduce child mortality, maternal mortality and infectious diseases [by] two-thirds. The WHO has put the price of getting AIDS, tuberculosis and malaria under control at between $7 billion and $10 billion. That would include spending on health-care infrastructure, education and prevention.

The Pentagon has spent money on more than just bombs, of course.

In October, for example, the U.S. military spent $27 million air-dropping food to rural areas of Afghanistan, a total of 130 000 meals. The aid agencies Oxfam and the World Food Program estimated that they delivered an equivalent number of meals to similar areas, by land, for $4800.

[Stephanie Nolen, "Cost of Rebuilding After War $4.9 Billion, Bank Says," *Globe and Mail*, 23 March, 2002.]

Understand Concepts

1. What central questions must be dealt with in distributive justice?
2. Define and briefly explain three views of distributive justice.
3. What values are in conflict between these views of distributive justice?

Apply and Develop

4. Describe what would be the result of a society governed by each view of distributive justice, that is, libertarian, liberal, and socialist. What might be the effect upon individual initiative, division of wealth, happiness, political systems, and other aspects of society?
5. What issues are raised in the excerpt?
6. (a) What do you believe should be done about child poverty in Canada?
   (b) What reasons would you give to support your proposed policies?

Think Critically

7. How should the issues in the excerpt be dealt with?
8. How would each ideology discussed in this section view the issue of child development? Explain your answer.
9. Set up principles to guide your own "fair" society. Consider the distribution of goods from both a political and an economic point of view. What political rights will people have in your "fair" society, and will all people have them? What principle will govern the distribution of goods? Will it be equality, property rights, need, individual effort, or some other principle?

Communicate Ideas

10. What principles govern the distribution of goods in Canadian society? Write a position paper that argues for or against the type of distribution that takes place.

Two Different Principles Used in Establishing Distributive Justice

Like Plato working 2500 years earlier, philosophers today have developed differ-ent ideas about how to establish a just society, and the characteristics that would exist for individuals living within that society. Two opposing points of view involve the idea of fairness and liberty. Is a just society established on the prin-ciple of fairness, or is it based on liberty for individuals?

John Rawls (1921–) is a major philosopher in the search to identify the basic principles of social justice, and is a proponent of the fairness principle. Philosopher Robert Nozick (1939–), on the other hand, argues that liberty for individuals, not fairness, is the basis of a just society. Which position do you support? Do you think other principles may be used in establishing distributive justice?

The Idea of Fairness
Applied to Justice

Rawls searches for principles that would help us to define a "just soc-iety." In doing so, he starts from the recognition that each of us is interested in pursuing goals for ourselves. In other words, self-interest is an important part of human nature. He also believes that most people are rational and reasonable, and would use that reason to shape society. How, then, can a society be developed or even thought of which provides justice for all under such circumstances?

Rawls uses an interesting "thought experiment" to develop the idea of a just society. He imagines people developing a new society in which they will live. He also recognizes that since in real life people know their own personal identity and how this will affect their position in the new society, they will likely set up a society that will benefit themselves personally. Thrasy-machus would have agreed with this view. Therefore, in Rawls' thought experiment, he supposes that these imaginary planners will not know their identities and their positions in this new and just society. They will operate, as he puts it, behind a "veil of ignorance" in which they will be unaware of their new identities in such things as: abilities, age, gender, social status, or any other personal characteristic. How will this affect the rules they will make for the new society? In what ways will it be a "just" society?

Rawls says that the planners would be fully aware that they might emerge from behind this "veil of ignorance" with any number of abilities, benefits, advantages, or with very few of these. Under such cir-cumstances, he argues, rational people, out of pure self-interest, will shape a society that is fair to all. No planner would want to risk emerging into a society in which he or she already was at a disadvantage, or in which he or she would get less than a fair share of valued goods.

Rawls believes that several additional principles of justice would be adopted from behind this "veil of ignorance":

- Since most people are reasonable and recognize that human beings are diverse in nature, the new society would allow and encourage individuals from diverse intellectual and geographic backgrounds to work together.
- Awareness of diversity in society and of different ideas would encourage the planners to ensure that different groups and cultures would have input into government and law-making.

- Since all citizens are, therefore, actively involved in determining the laws of government, each citizen would possess all political liberties, equal to all liberties possessed by any other member of society.
- Citizens would possess equal access to economic and social benefits. Inequalities would only be allowed if these inequalities resulted in advantages for all members of society as a whole, in particular to the most disadvantaged members of that society.

A Theory of Justice

John Rawls

My aim is to present a conception of justice which … carries to a higher level of abstraction the familiar theory of the social contract.… [T]he guiding idea is that the principles of justice for the basic structure of society are the object of the original agreement … the principles that free and rational persons concerned to further their own interests would accept.… I shall call [this] justice as fairness.

Thus we are to imagine that those who engage in social cooperation choose … principles which are to assign basic rights and duties and to determine the division of social benefits.… [A] group of persons must decide once and for all what is to count among them as just and unjust.…

The Veil of Ignorance

The idea of the original position is to set up a fair procedure so that any principles agreed to will be just.… Now in order to do this I assume that the parties are situated behind a veil of ignorance. They do not know how the various alternatives will affect their own particular case.…

… [N]o one knows his place in society, his class position or social status; nor does he know his fortune in the distribution of natural assets and abilities, his intelligence and strength, … his conception of the good, the particulars of his rational plan of life, or even the special features of his psychology such as his aversion to risk or liability to optimism or pessimism.… [N]o one is in a position to tailor principles to his advantage.…

Two Principles of Justice

I shall now state ... the two principles of justice that I believe would be chosen in the original position.... First: each person is to have an equal right to the most extensive basic liberty compatible with a similar liberty for others. Second: social and economic inequalities are to be arranged ... to everyone's advantage, and ... open to all....

The basic liberties of citizens are ... political liberty (the right to vote and to be eligible for public office) together with freedom of speech and assembly; liberty of conscience and freedom of thought; freedom of the person along with the right to hold (personal) property; and freedom from arbitrary arrest and seizure as defined by the concept of the rule of law. These liberties are all required to be equal by the first principle, since citizens of a just society are to have the same basic rights.

The second principle applies ... to the distribution of income and wealth.... [T]he distribution of wealth and income need not be equal, it must be to everyone's advantage, and at the same time, positions of authority and offices of command must be accessible to all.

These principles are to be arranged ... with the first principle prior to the second. This ordering means that a departure from ... equal liberty required by the first principle cannot be justified by ... greater social and economic advantages....

All social values—liberty and opportunity, income and wealth, and the bases of self-respect—are to be distributed equally unless an unequal distribution ... is to everyone's advantage.... If certain inequalities of wealth and organizational powers would make everyone better off ... then they accord with the general conception. Injustice, then, is simply inequalities that are not to the benefit of all.

[John Rawls, *A Theory of Justice*. Cambridge: Harvard University Press, 1971, 11, 12, 60–3, 136, 137, 139, 140, 145.]

The Idea of Liberty Applied to Justice

Freedom stretches only as far as the limits of our consciousness.
Carl Jung

Not everyone accepts the principles of distributive justice put forward by Rawls. Robert Nozick, for example, argues that individual liberty is the most perfect value, and should be used as the major principle to guide just distribution of goods within any society.

According to Nozick, the state has no right to interfere with the social and economic position of individuals. What you possess, what you have gained throughout your lifetime through legal means, should be yours to keep and use as you wish in the future. Nozick denies that justice is applied when individuals attempt to redistribute material wealth within a society. In the following excerpt he presents a position and an argument, markedly different from that of Rawls.

Liberty and the State

Robert Nozick

The Minimal State

The minimal state [limited to … protection against force, theft, fraud, enforcement of contracts, and so on] is the most extensive state that can be justified. Any state more extensive violates people's rights.…

Hearing the term "distribution," most people presume that some thing or mechanism uses some principle or criterion to give out a supply of things. Into this process of distributing shares some error may have crept.…

However, we are not in the position of children who have been given portions of pie by someone who now makes last minute adjustments to rectify careless cutting. There is no *central* distribution, no person or group entitled to control all the resources, jointly deciding how they are to be doled out.… There is no more a distributing … of shares than there is a distributing of mates in a society in which persons choose whom they shall marry. The total result is the product of many individual decisions which the different individuals involved are entitled to make.…

The Entitlement Theory

… The entitlement theory of justice in distribution is *historical*; whether a distribution is just depends on how it came about. In contrast, *current time-slice principles* of justice hold that the justice of a distribution is judged by how things are distributed (who has what) as judged by some … principle(s) of just distribution.…

Most persons do not accept current time-slice principles as constituting the whole story about distributive shares. They think it relevant in assessing the justice of a situation to consider … how that distribution came about. If some persons are in prison for murder or war crimes, we do not say that to assess the justice of the distribution in the society we must look only at what this person has … at the current time. We think it relevant to ask whether someone did something so that he *deserved* to … have a lower share.…

Patterning

… Almost every suggested principle of distributive justice is patterned: to each according to his moral merit, or needs … or how hard he tries … and so on. The principle of entitlement we have sketched is *not* patterned.… The set of holdings that results when some persons … win at gambling, others receive a share of their mate's income, others receive gifts from foundations, others receive interest on loans, others receive gifts from admirers, others receive returns on investment, others make for themselves much of what they have, others find things, and so on, will not be patterned....

Whoever makes something ... is entitled to it. The situation is *not* one of something's getting made, and there being an open question of who is to get it. Things come into the world already attached to people having entitlements over them....

How Liberty Upsets Patterns

... Now suppose Wilt Chamberlain [or Vince Carter] is greatly in demand by basketball teams, being a great gate attraction.... He signs the following sort of contract with a team: In each home game, twenty-five cents from the price of each ticket of admission goes to him.... The season starts, and people cheerfully attend his team's games; they buy their tickets, each time dropping a separate twenty-five cents of their admission price into a special box with Chamberlain's name on it. They are excited about seeing him play; it is worth the total admission price to them. Let us suppose that in one season one million persons attend his home games, and Wilt Chamberlain winds up with $250 000.... Is he entitled to this income? Is this new distribution ... unjust? If so, why?... Each of these persons *chose* to give twenty-five cents of their money to Chamberlain. They could have spent it on going to the movies, or on candy bars.... But they all ... converged on giving it to Wilt Chamberlain in exchange for watching him play basketball....

The general point ... is that no ... distributional patterned principle of justice can be ... realized without continuous interference with people's lives.... To maintain a pattern one must either continually interfere to stop people from transferring resources as they wish to, or continually ... interfere to take from some person resources that others for some reason chose to transfer to them.

[Robert Nozick, *Anarchy, State, and Utopia*. New York: Basic Books, 1974.]

Understand Concepts

1. Why does Rawls set up a "veil of ignorance"?
2. Identify Rawls' principles of justice.
3. Indicate the main elements of Nozick's theory of justice. How does he feel about the role of the state, the rights of property, and the distribution of goods and services in a state?

Apply and Develop

4. How would Rawls deal with each of the following situations? How would you?
   (a) A group of people in society argue that since they have earned their money through their own efforts, they have no obligation to contribute to the general social good through taxation.
   (b) A charismatic political leader promises economic wealth to all if he is granted complete power for a year.
5. The cases below illustrate principles of distributive justice. Identify the principle in each case. Argue for or against one or another principle that applies to each case.
   (a) An individual works over a lifetime to develop a buisiness. She makes a great deal of money, through good ideas, good management, and prudence. The government say that she should contribute, through taxes, to the welfare of others who have not had her benefits and good fortune. She believes that what she earned she should keep.
   (b) An individual believes that the riches of the world should be equally available to all. Therefore all people benefit equally from the efforts of society, and wealth should be distributed equally to all.
   (c) It is clear that without some redistribution of wealth in modern post-industrial societies, there would be a growing polarization of wealth: more rich, more poor, and fewer people in between.

Think Critically

6. Compare the views of Rawls and Nozick. Consider their major values, how they would define justice, how they describe existing society, how their ideal society would look, the social and economic consequences of their society, and their ideology (libertarian, liberal, or socialist).
7. Should valued goods be distributed according to who contributes most, works hardest, needs the most, or deserves more? Each of these criteria have been used to justify methods of distributing goods. What criteria would you use to determine what distributive justice should be? At some point, each of equality, liberty, effort, contribution, and need have been suggested as criteria. Which do you most agree with? Why?

Communicate Ideas

8. Debate this issue: It is up to the individual and to the family to provide for his or her own. The state has no business interfering in economic conditions.

Retributive Justice: Ideologies and Forms

How does society deal with individuals who do not conform to accepted codes of behaviour? What principles of justice apply? The answers to these questions involve some ideas about retributive justice.

If the transgression is minor, and does not infringe upon the basic values on which a society is based, society's response does not fall within the area of retributive justice. Irresponsible behaviours, such as intoxication, or unpleasant behaviours, such as rudeness, usually result in negative social reactions such as gossip, social exclusion, or ridicule. In this way, society and its members informally control minor forms of nonconformity.

However, gross violations of accepted behaviour that ignore important social values elicit much more stringent responses. All societies have legal responses to serious transgressions such as arson, pedophilia, theft, kidnapping, murder, genocide, or treason. What kinds of retribution do you believe should occur in these cases? How can justice best be served?

Different Forms of Retributive Justice

There are several types of retributive justice available to a society: deterrence, retribution, rehabilitation, and restitution. Courts make many decisions regarding retributive justice everyday, and the type that they choose depends on the specific situation, the nature of the crime,

How can punishment, or retributive justice, be justified in your opinion?

the background of the defendant, the philosophy of justice held by the society and those directly involved, and other factors.

Deterrence

A society can inflict punishment on a criminal that is intended to prevent future wrongdoing. The purpose of deterrence is to force the transgressor to cease his or her actions against the social order. The goal of deterrence is to protect society from future harm and crime.

Capital punishment is believed by some people to be a deterrent for violent crime, which is why some countries such as the United States still have it as a form of punishment. However, there is controversy about whether such forms of punishment are truly deterrents. Another type of deterrence involves the state levying heavy fines for crimes such as tax evasion.

Retribution

Another societal response to criminal activity is retribution; society claims the right to punish wrongdoing through an appropriate penalty, one equal to the level of crime committed. Society has the right and the necessity to respond to such crimes with equal force. If an individual has done wrong, justice requires that that person be penalized,

Helen Prejean

Fight Against Capital Punishment

Sister Helen Prejean (1938–) is a modern crusader against the death penalty in the United States. Prejean was born in Baton Rouge, Louisiana, and joined the Sisters of St. Joseph of Medaille in 1957. After teaching junior and senior high school students, she decided to dedicate her life to the poor of New Orleans.

In 1982, after being asked by someone from the Prison Coalition to become a pen pal to Patrick Sonnier, a death-row inmate, Prejean accepted the challenge not knowing what the experience would entail. After establishing some type of trust relationship with Sonnier, she began to question many aspects of the death penalty. Prejean became disturbed by Sonnier's inhumane confinement as well as the mental anguish he endured during the countdown leading towards his execution. She began to see the moral dilemmas encountered by the public officials responsible for carrying out the executions, even though in some cases they did not agree with the death penalty.

It became apparent to Prejean that capital punishment was not an effective form of justice in terms of cost and resources. Furthermore, the justice system can be chaotic at times, and is not immune to bias and incompetency. Prejean began to ask: How can a society benefit if it repeats the very injustice it condemns?

Prejean writes and speaks extensively against capital punishment. However, her arguments are not without strong opposition from those who uphold the validity of the death penalty.

> I realize that I cannot stand by silently as my government executes its citizens. If I do not speak out and resist, I am an accomplice.
> *Helen Prejean*

or disciplined—through fining, imprisonment, or death.

When retribution is the principle involved, it is often based on some ethical or moral concept that wrong behaviour by an individual deserves and requires a painful or onerous penalty. The Old Testament idea of "an eye for an eye" expresses this view. When prisons are used as the primary form of punishment, rather than rehabilitation for example, retribution is generally the principle of justice underlying the punishment.

Rehabilitation

The rehabilitative response to crime is based on the belief that all human beings grow and change every day. How can individuals who have offended change so that they can contribute to society in meaningful and positive ways? Supporters of rehabilitation often believe that social forces influence the characters of individuals within a society, and that if a person is prone to criminal behaviour, society is obligated to reform the behaviour of that individual. Rehabilitation has other practical advantages associated with it. It reduces the cost of keeping wrongdoers in prison for lengthy periods of time, or as unproductive members of society, and it reduces the risk of repeat offenders.

In our society, rehabilitation can take the form of counselling, therapy, community work, or remaining in the custody of a particular group or individual, among other possibilities. Depending on the severity of the wrongdoing and a judge's sentence in a court of law, an accused individual can obtain parole as an alternative to serving time in a correctional institution. Parole involves reporting regularly to a parole officer, who requires updates on the accused's patterns of behaviour.

Restitution

Restitution is an ancient, and possibly the original, concept of retributive justice. Restitution requires that a criminal pay back those individuals most seriously affected by his or her crime, with an equality appropriate for the crime committed. Some societies require murderers to pay relatives of the murdered person. Germanic societies referred to this payment as *wergeld*. A criminal making proper restitution is often absolved of the crime. In our own modern society, civil courts assess damages that a guilty individual must pay to his or her victim(s). Restitution is also important when a group of people, a business or corporation, or even government have committed crimes.

Deterrence and the Argument for Capital Punishment

The death penalty is an issue that arouses strong feelings in many individuals about the nature of retributive justice. Is capital punishment the best form of justice to use in certain cases? Is it really a deterrent? Are there other forms of justice or behaviour that are more effective at deterring crimes?

PHILOSOPHERS' FORUM

A Life for a Life

Igor Primoratz

According to the retributive theory, consequences of punishment … are irrelevant…. Punishment is morally justified … as retribution for the offense committed. When someone has committed an offense, he deserves to be punished: it is just…. So the issue of capital punishment within the retributive approach comes down to the question, Is this punishment ever proportionate retribution for the offense committed, and thus deserved, just, and justified?

The classic representatives of retributivism believed that it was ... the only proportionate and hence appropriate punishment, if the offense was *murder*.... We come across this idea as early as the ... biblical teaching on punishment: "You shall accept no ransom for the life of a murderer who is guilty of death; but he shall be put to death." ...

This view [holds] that the value of human life is not commensurable with other values, and that consequently there is only one truly equivalent punishment for murder, namely death.... Any other retribution, no matter how severe, would still be less than what is proportionate, deserved, and just....

... Accordingly, capital punishment ought to be retained ... although we have no reason to believe that, as a means of deterrence, it is any better than a very long prison term. It ought to be retained ... for one simple reason: that justice be done in cases of murder....

There are a number of arguments that have been advanced against this rationale of capital punishment....

...[One] abolitionist argument ... says that capital punishment is illegitimate because it violates the right to life, which is a fundamental, absolute, sacred right belonging to each and every human being, and therefore ought to be respected even in a murderer.

If any rights are fundamental, the right to life is certainly one of them; but to claim that it is absolute, inviolable under any circumstances and for any reason, is a different matter. If an abolitionist wants to argue his case by asserting an absolute right to life, he will also have to deny moral legitimacy to taking human life in war, revolution, and self-defense. This kind of pacifism is a consistent but farfetched and hence implausible position....

Some opponents of capital punishment claim that a criminal law system which includes this punishment is contradictory, in that it prohibits murder and at the same time provides for its perpetration.... This seems to be one of the more popular arguments against the death penalty, but it is not a good one.... Exactly the same might be claimed of other kinds of punishment: of prison terms, that they are "contradictory" to the legal protection of liberty; of fines, that they are "contradictory" to the legal protection of property.... [I]t is not valid, for it begs the question at issue. In order to be able to talk of the state as "murdering" the person it executes ... one has to use the word "murder" in the very same sense, ... which implies the idea of the *wrongful* taking the life of another—both when speaking of what the murderer has done to the victim and of what the state is doing to him by way of punishment. But this is precisely the question at issue: whether capital punishment *is* "murder," whether it is wrongful or morally justified and right....

... Thus we come to the argument against capital punishment which, historically, has been the most effective of all: ... cases of judicial errors. Judges and jurors are only human, and consequently some of their beliefs and decisions are bound to be mistaken. Some of their mistakes can be corrected upon discovery; but ... those which result in innocent people being executed—can never be rectified....

Actually, this argument ... does not speak out against capital punishment itself, but against the existing procedures for trying capital cases. Miscarriages of justice result in innocent people being sentenced to death and executed.... But this ... results from deficiencies, limitations, and imperfections of the criminal law procedures in which this punishment is meted out. Errors of justice do not demonstrate the need to do away with capital punishment; they simply make it incumbent on us to do everything possible to improve even further procedures of meting it out....

There is still another abolitionist argument that actually does not hit out against capital punishment itself, but against something else. Figures are sometimes quoted which show that this punishment is much more often meted out to the uneducated and poor than to the educated, rich, and influential ... as a proof of the inherent injustice of this kind of punishment....

I shall not question these findings, which are quite convincing, and anyway, there is no need to do that in order to defend the institution of capital punishment. For there seems to be a certain amount of discrimination and injustice not only in sentencing people to death and executing them, but also in meting out other penalties.... If this argument were valid, it would call not only for abolition of the penalty of death, but for doing away with other penalties as well. But it is not valid.

[Igor Primoratz, *Justifying Legal Punishment*. Atlantic Highlands: Humanities Press International, 1989, 158, 159, 161–6.]

Arguments Against Capital Punishment

The death penalty has been abolished in Canada for more than thirty years, although it is still used in many American states.

There are many arguments against capital punishment, the most prominent being the question of deterrence. Although many people argue that capital punishment is a deterrent for crime, the statistics do not reflect this. For example, the United States has one of the highest rates of murder involving guns even though many states enforce the death penalty.

Another argument against capital punishment involves killing an innocent individual. Recent advances in DNA technology have revealed that many people who have been convicted of serious crimes including

Public executions did not stop pickpockets at the hanging, even though the crime was punishable by death. Modern research indicates that the death penalty is not an effective deterrent. Why does it still exist in a number of places?

murder, some of whom have spent many years in prison, have been found to be innocent of the crime. If they had been executed, the search for the truth would have been useless. This also points to problems with the judicial system.

Allan Fotheringham is a well-known Canadian journalist who has strong opinions on the death penalty issue. Journalistic style has distinct characteristics, as do other forms of writing. Here is how Fotheringham argues his case.

Death Penalty Insanity

Allan Fotheringham

There is something, essentially, insane about our society. The philosopher said long ago that to those who feel, the world is a tragedy; to those who think, it is a comedy.

There is a great fuss, among North American do-gooders, about a young woman in Africa who is publicly flogged—to great applause there—for "provoking" some louts into raping her. We regard as savages those in the ... world who chop off hands and still stage public executions. We denounce China ... because it still does state murder on dissidents and other troublesome people. And in the United States, there is a major debate over whether ... Oklahoma City bomber Timothy McVeigh will have his death sentence carried out on national television, as he has demanded. The world is nuts.

Not too long ago, as the Earth turns, they still held public hangings in England—for such minor offences as pickpocketing. As the slavering crowds gathered round the gallows, hooting in glee, pickpockets worked the crowd, as was their profession. As the last two men ever executed by state murder in Canada hanged back-to-back in the Don Jail in Toronto, John Diefenbaker said quietly that there never again will be capital punishment in Canada....

The new president of [the United States] ... has been elected ... on a platform that included the death penalty. In his six years as governor, Texas not only led the nation but, considering its population, the world—beating out China and Russia— even South Africa having abolished the sport.

The Texas prison population leaped from 92 669 to 149 684 while Dubya [George W. Bush] was governor. Some 4511 of the guys in state jails in 1998 were drug offenders. And 2800 of them were jailed for possession of a gram or less of cocaine or heroin. Of those guys in jail, 28% were black, 29% were Hispanic, 43% were white....

Dubya ... has said he strongly believes that no innocent person has been executed in his state. Well. Last year Illinois Governor George Ryan, a Republican who happened to be pro-death penalty, found to his astonishment that 13 convicted murderers had been exonerated [freed from blame] by new evidence—after they had been sent to death row.

The death penalty is an act of despair by society. It says that ... there is absolutely nothing redeemable about them [the prisoners]. And to those people and their families, it signals that they are nothing but human waste.

Helen Prejean

Last year, a national survey in the United States found support for the death penalty was down to 66%, its lowest level in 19 years. Since the Supreme Court allowed executions to resume 24 years ago, 38 states have made the death penalty legal, while 12 have not.

An investigation by the *Chicago Tribune* found that of the 131 inmates executed under Governor Dubya ... 43 had defence attorneys who were disbarred, suspended or otherwise sanctioned for misconduct by the state bar of Texas either before or after their work on these cases. Forty cases involved trials where the defence attorneys presented no evidence or only one witness during the sentencing process, 29 included a psychiatrist who gave testimony that the American Psychiatric Association condemned as unethical and untrustworthy—and just to finish off, 23 included jailhouse informants, considered to be the least credible of witnesses.

Not to mention the Southern Center for Human Rights, an Atlanta-based body, that found "in recent years the Texas Court of Criminal Appeals has upheld death sentences in at least three cases in which the defence lawyers *slept* during trial." The justice system in Texas is a joke. In its Republican-controlled legislature, a bill was introduced that indigent [poor] defendants be assigned a lawyer within 20 days after arrest. (In most of the U.S., a lawyer is provided within 72 hours.) ... [Bush], as governor, vetoed the bill.

Canadians now know, thanks to Donald Marshall and David Milgaard and others, how many innocent people have been sent to prison. Ninety-five people on death row in the United States have been freed with proof of innocence since 1973. State murder is insane. The world is crazy.

[Allan Fotheringham, "Death Penalty Insanity," *Maclean's* Magazine, 19 March 2001, 56.]

Apply and Develop

1. Social protection, retribution, deterrence, and rehabilitation are several alternative goals in legal philosophy. In the cases below, which goals would you choose?
   (a) A teenager steals a car and goes for a "joyride." He is caught after several blocks of being chased by the police.
   (b) A business person uses her position to illegally manipulate stock prices. Many investors receive false information about their investments.
   (c) A middle-age man is caught breaking into a home. He is looking for jewellery and electronic equipment. He has a criminal record that goes back 25 years.
   (d) A man murders his wife and two children. It is revealed that he has recently been under stress from the loss of his job and the threat that his home will be repossessed.
   (e) Driving at excessive speed, a young woman hits a cyclist. The victim will never walk again.
   (f) A hit man for organized crime is caught. He is found guilty of assassinating many people.

Think Critically

2. (a) What arguments does Fotheringham use to support his position?
   (b) What rhetorical devices does he use? A rhetorical device is used to convince beyond strictly rational argument. It may involve the use of language, emotional appeals, organization, and selection of examples.
3. Why are consequences not important to Primoratz' retribution argument?
4. Write out a summary of the arguments, and counterarguments, discussed in Primoratz' excerpt. You may wish to use two halves of a page divided by a line down the middle to organize the arguments.
5. Primoratz uses retribution as a major position. Are there other values, mentioned or not mentioned in his excerpt, that you hold as important?

Communicate Ideas

6. Watch the documentary film "Packing Heat" by the National Film Board. How effective are the types of justice presented in dealing with violence against women? Provide reasons for your answer.
7. Often, more citizens support the death penalty than do members of parliament. What reasons can you give for this? Do you believe that majority rule should reign, that is, if most Canadians believe in the death penalty it should be reinstated?

Inquire and Research

8. Read Sister Prejean's book *Dead Man Walking*. What arguments does she give for abolishing capital punishment? Does she offer any other forms of justice that can be used for lawbreakers? What is your evaluation of her arguments?

Corrective Justice: Justice Provided for Past Inequities

People in Canada and many other parts of the world have experienced discrimination, either as individuals or as groups. Discrimination is the denial of goods, services, or opportunities on the basis of social status, class, sex, age, sexual orientation, or ethnicity. Such discrimination is not only unfair and limiting to the recipient, it also harms the social and economic well-being of society as a whole. Discrimination limits the number of contributors to the common good and hampers the success of that society in which it is present.

Countering Discrimination with Affirmative Action

Do you believe society should compensate for past injustices such as discrimination? Affirmative action and equal opportunity programs are designed to compensate specific groups within society for past injustices and inequalities. These programs set rules for future opportunities. Institutions which in the past failed to accept students or hire faculty on a fair basis are now required under affirmative action programs to accept students and faculty based on a system or rule designed to rectify that situation. Businesses that have failed to hire or promote fairly are required to compensate for such discrimination by hiring or promoting future prospects in a ratio designed to correct the imbalance.

Should affirmative action programs encourage groups who have experienced discrimination to have more opportunities?

The issue of pay inequity between men and women has been, and continues to be, an area of injustice. Although "equal pay for equal work" is in place for some jobs, such as in the government, this type of corrective justice is not enforced in many businesses.

Equal opportunity programs are important to consider in any discussion of corrective justice. Such programs are often controversial because they raise the question of group rights versus individual rights, as well as intergenerational rights—past, present, and future.

Suppose you are female and a member of a visible minority. In the past, you might well have been discriminated against when applying for a job or to a university because of your sex and/or your race. Do you believe that in future you and others who share your social position should be compensated for such discrimination? Should you be given extra consideration when applying for a job or to a university?

How Should Past Injustices Be Corrected?

Discrimination is a matter of historical record. We know that not everyone has always been treated with equal consideration. Sexism, racism, ageism, and homophobia are common forms of discrimination even today. Physically and mentally challenged individuals have been, and continue to be, targets of discrimination. Even a person's religious affiliation can subject that individual to unfair treatment within a society. How can we correct these problems? Should special efforts be made to correct past injustices by providing future compensation?

Some people argue that past injustices require correction. This point of view can be supported with this analogy: Your parent stole property from his neighbour, passed the property on to you, and you derived great benefit. Now your neighbour's son says you owe him compensation for that benefit. Using this analogy, present generations have a moral obligation to compensate others whose ancestors have suffered through discrimination and injustice. This argument might also suggest that women, minorities, Aboriginal peoples, and others who have suffered should receive preferential treatment when they apply to universities or occupations from which they were restricted in the past.

In 1990, Elijah Harper, member of the Manitoba Legislature, openly opposed the Meech Lake Accord. Many Native Canadians, women, and other groups felt that the Accord, if accepted by all provinces, would minimize the likelihood of these groups gaining government support for corrective justice.

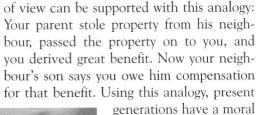

Time Line

Examples of Corrective Justice

WAR MEASURES ACT *(JULY 1988)* is repealed

"REDRESS SETTLEMENT" *(SEPTEMBER 22, 1988)* presents Japanese Canadians with restitution for discrimination during and after World War II

MOHAWKS IN OKA *(1990)* oppose government over unsettled land claims

"GATHERING STRENGTH" *(JANUARY 7, 1998)* presents the federal government's apology and compensation to Native Canadians for the impact of residential schools

INUIT IN NUNAVUT *(APRIL 1, 1999)* successfully settle land claims creating the first majority Native controlled territory in Canada

Arguments For and Against Affirmative Action

An argument that supports equal opportunity or affirmative action looks to the future. This view suggests we must move actively to ensure that people and groups who have experienced discrimination in the past are guaranteed present-day and future access to equal opportunities within the social institutions of society, and those schools and jobs which might have been previously out of reach. Thus, if in the past only twenty-five percent of working women were promoted to management, a minimum of fifty percent should be promoted in the future.

Those persons who have not experienced discrimination in the past may feel that their rights are being trampled on in the present, and that they are subject to "reverse discrimination." Philosopher Lisa H. Newton draws the following distinction with regard to such an argument, by suggesting that if a discriminatory action was against the law at the time it occurred,

compensation should be made. Newton also suggests, however, that if such an action was not against the law when it occurred, it becomes impossible to determine who should receive compensation, or even how much compensation should be awarded.

Some people have argued that the most deserving, or able, candidate should receive positions in higher education or in desired jobs. This position holds that setting quotas or implementing hiring preferences ensures that those applicants most suited to specific jobs will not get them. One counter to this position is the argument that there really is no level playing field at all in life, and that those individuals who do acquire prestigious or financially rewarding educational or occupational positions are not necessarily the best qualified people, but only the most socially privileged. Philosopher Richard Wasserstrom critiques such a comment in the following excerpt.

PHILOSOPHERS' FORUM

A Defense of Programs of Preferential Treatment

Richard Wasserstrom

There are several problems with this argument. The most substantial of them is that it is an empirically implausible picture of our social world. Most of what are regarded as the decisive characteristics for higher education have a great deal to do with things over which the individual has neither control nor responsibility: such things as home environment, socioeconomic class of parents, and, of course, the quality of the primary and secondary schools attended. Since individuals do not deserve having had any of these things … they do not, for the most part, deserve their qualifications. And since they do not deserve their abilities they do not in any strong sense deserve to be admitted because of their abilities.

[Richard Wasserstrom, "A Defense of Programs of Preferential Treatment," *National Forum* 58, no. 1, Winter 1978.]

How Can We Prevent Injustices from Occurring in the Future?

In his article "Message of Affirmative Action" (*Social Philosophy and Policy* 8 (1991): 108–129) philosopher Thomas E. Hill, Jr. suggests yet another argument. He believes that neither backward-looking nor forward-looking arguments in themselves are sufficient. Hill defines backward-looking arguments as those that look to compensate for past injustices; while forward-looking arguments are those that seek to equalize opportunities in the future. Some people argue that past injustice should not be the responsibility of those who live in the present. Future attempts at creating equal opportunity come with problems, as certain groups or individuals living in the future will undoubtedly claim "reverse discrimination."

Hill writes that society must have a sense of history and of community values, that its people must care about how our past, present, and future fit together, and not just in isolation. According to Hill, a society and its individuals will be more functional when they acknowledge wrongs that have been done in the past, and make efforts to restore the damage in the future.

Hill's crucial question is: Given past injustices, how can we express mutual respect and trust? We cannot change a past filled with racism or sexism, but neither should we ignore it if we want to express respect for present individuals who live in its aftermath. It is not only a repayment of debts from past injuries. We must also send a message to counter the insult that is inherent in racism and sexism. Public institutions should be arranged so that, over time, each person is provided with equal opportunities to develop and make use of natural talents, and contribute to society.

Hill believes affirmative action communicates a much-needed message, a message that not only represents payment for past wrongs, but also facilitates harmonious future relations. Hill believes affirmative action is also a part of being related to other human beings over time. It reflects the responses of those who care about fair opportunity, mutual trust, and respect for all.

By using affirmative action, social institutions acknowledge and denounce wrongs that have been done. Affirmative action acknowledges that many have had their opportunities diminished and that this practice should not continue. Special opportunities provide recognition of past disadvantages, while showing respect for talents.

Bigotry tries to keep truth safe in its hand With a grip that kills it.
Rabindranath Tagore

Land Claims: Native Canadians Fight Against Past Injustice

Over the last several years, many Native Canadian groups have contested the federal government over hundreds of unresolved land claims. In the past, the government tended to adopt a pattern of putting things aside, perhaps hoping that the push for the claims would fall by the wayside. However, Native people are starting to raise their voices against injustice after decades of silence. According to one government estimate, the process of settling land claims could potentially cost $140 billion dollars over the next several decades. Once completed, Native Canadians will gain control of approximately ten percent of the land in Canada's ten provinces; the figure is currently about 0.3%. In the United States, Native Americans control approximately two percent of the land.

A recent example of Native Canadians fighting for land rights occurred during the summer of 1990. The Mohawk community near Oka opposed the mayor's plans to expand a nearby golf course. The expansion involved the desecration of an area that the Mohawks declared was sacred ground. Ten-

Paul Okalik, premier of Nunavut, is the first Native Canadian to head a provincial or territorial government.

sions mounted between the Mohawks and the Oka police. Things escalated to a point where other Native groups came to support the Mohawk cause. Violence and rioting followed. In the end, the Canadian military stepped in. Talks between the Mohawks and the army proceeded, and eventually led to both sides tearing down the barricade that the Mohawks had initially set up. The Mohawk standoff lasted 78 days, and both the police and the military withdrew. In 1997, the federal government purchased the land under dispute and allowed the Mohawks to expand their existing cemetery.

Another example of Aboriginals successfully gaining land rights occurred on April 1, 1999. The Inuit communities in an area equal to approximately one-fifth the size of Canada joined forces to create Nunavut, Canada's third territory. The government of Nunavut is the first in Canada and the United States to be dominated by Native people. The creation of Nunavut, which means "our land," was a breakthrough for Native Canadians, putting to rest many unresolved land claims.

The Dark Past of Residential Schools in Canada

The implementation of residential schools in Canada for over a hundred years is a dark example of discrimination against Native Canadians, and how far racism can go in our society. The purpose of the schools was assimilation, and the obliteration of Native culture and language. The effect of the residential schools has been very far-reaching, even today, as Native Canadians struggle to piece together their fragmented sense of identity and history. What is even more tragic is that many Native students at the schools endured physical and sexual abuse, the scars of which have contributed to many emotional and addiction problems among Native Canadians.

And yet where in your history books is the tale
of the genocide basic to this country's birth?
of the preachers who lied?
how the Bill of Rights failed.

Buffy Sainte-Marie,
"My Country 'Tis of Thy People You're Dying"

Residential schools are just one part of a long tradition of racism and discrimination faced by Aboriginal Canadians.

On January 7, 1998, Jane Stewart, then Minister of Indian Affairs and Northern Development, made a public address where she, on behalf of the federal government, offered some type of corrective justice for the long history of discrimination against Native Canadians in Canada. For many people, including Native Canadians, Stewart's proposal was not just long overdue, but a poor attempt at making peace with Native Canadians. What is your evaluation of the type of corrective justice Stewart is proposing? What do you think would constitute fair compensation for the harm caused by Canada's long history of discrimination against Native Canadians?

Statement of Reconciliation

Jane Stewart

One aspect of our relationship with Aboriginal people over this period that requires particular attention is the Residential School system. This system separated many children from their families and communities and prevented them from speaking their own languages and from learning about their heritage and cultures. In the worst cases, it left legacies of personal pain and distress that continue to reverberate in Aboriginal communities to this day. Tragically, some children were the victims of physical and sexual abuse.

The Government of Canada acknowledges the role it played in the development and administration of these schools. Particularly to those individuals who experienced the tragedy of sexual and physical abuse at residential schools, and who have carried this burden believing that in some way they must be responsible, we wish to emphasize that what you experienced was not your fault and should never have happened. To those of you who suffered this tragedy at residential schools, we are deeply sorry.

In dealing with the legacies of the Residential School system, the Government of Canada proposes to work with First Nations, Inuit and Métis people, the Churches and other interested parties to resolve the longstanding issues that must be addressed.... No attempt at reconciliation with Aboriginal people can be complete without reference to the sad events culminating in the death of Métis leader Louis Riel. These events cannot be undone; however, we can and will continue to look for ways of affirming the contributions of Métis people in Canada and of reflecting Louis Riel's proper place in Canada's history.

Our words must be supported by concrete actions. We must work together to help Aboriginal individuals, families and communities to heal the wounds caused by physical and sexual abuse in the Residential School system. Today, the federal government commits $350 million for community-based healing as a first step to deal with the legacy of physical and sexual abuse at residential schools. It will be First Nations, Inuit and Métis people themselves, along with health and social professionals, who will help us in shaping support that is culturally sensitive and reflects the experiences of different communities....

[Jane Stewart, "Gathering Strength—Canada's Aboriginal Action Plan," 7 January 1998. Posted on http://sisis.nativeweb.org/resschool/main.html.]

Discrimination Against Japanese Canadians

Japanese Canadians are a cultural group within our society that has long endured massive discrimination starting from the first Japanese immigrants to Canada in the late 1800s. Before World War II, immigration restrictions coupled with job discrimination led to the Japanese community in Canada forming their own enclaves with their own social, religious, and economic institutions. Japanese Canadians educated in Canadian universities were unable to work outside the enclaves except as labourers.

After the Japanese attack on Pearl Harbour in 1941, the *War Measures Act* required all Japanese Canadians to register as "enemy aliens." During the internment of Japanese Canadians during World War II, the Canadian government sold all Japanese-Canadian owned property, deducting from the proceeds any welfare received by the owner while confined unemployed in the detention camp. In 1945, Japanese Canadians were forced to choose between dispersal east of the Rocky Mountains or deportation to war-ravaged Japan. Before public protests occurred, the federal government deported more than 4000 Japanese Canadians to Japan in 1946. It was not until 1949 that the restrictions imposed under the *War Measures Act* were lifted allowing Japanese Canadians to gain full rights of Canadian citizenship. Later in 1950, the Canadian government allowed some of those Japanese Canadians to return to Canada; about 1000 ended up re-immigrating.

Beginning in 1984, the National Association of Japanese Canadians (NAJC) began a concerted campaign seeking retribution for the internment of Japanese Canadians during World War II. The first step was the repeal of the *War Measures Act* in July 1988.

> A nightmare is terrifying because it can never be undone....
> *Judith Rossner*

During the Second World War Japanese Canadians were considered enemy aliens, and were forced into concentration camps.

On September 22, 1988, then Prime Minister Brian Mulroney announced a Redress Settlement for the injustices caused by the Canadian government against Canadians of Japanese origin during and after World War II. The settlement involved:

- payment of $21 000 to each Japanese Canadian directly wronged by the *War Measures Act*
- the removal of criminal records of those charged with offenses arising from violations of the *War Measures Act*
- the re-instatement of Canadian citizenship to those deported to Japan
- the establishment of a $12 million community fund to build community centres across Canada
- $24 million half in the name of the NAJC and half in the name of the federal government to establish the Canadian Race Relations Foundation

One study revealed that the economic losses sustained by Japanese Canadians during the confiscation of their property amounted to $443 million in 1986 dollars. Do you think that this settlement is fair compensation for the injustices that Japanese Canadians have endured? What can we do as individuals to prevent discrimination from occurring?

Hell is when you don't have justice.

Malcolm X

IDEAS AND ISSUES

Understand Concepts
1. Define corrective justice, affirmative action, and equal opportunity.
2. What is the primary issue discussed in the excerpt from Wasserstrom?

Think Critically
3. (a) Why do many women still continue to earn less than men in many jobs?
   (b) What can be done to change this situation?
4. (a) What criticisms does Hill make of both forward-looking and backward-looking arguments in support of affirmative action?
   (b) Does he discount these arguments altogether?
5. (a) What alternative does Hill put forward to these types of arguments?
   (b) How strong do you think Hill's arguments are for a historical approach to the issue?

Communicate Ideas
6. What laws govern equality in the workplace in Canada?
7. Debate this issue: Colleges and universities should use equal opportunity rules in evaluating potential candidates.
8. Comment on the effectiveness of the Canadian government's response to Native Canadians and Japanese Canadians to make right for its past wrongs.

Inquire and Research
9. Research five events in Canadian history, other than those mentioned in this section, that deal with corrective justice provided by government or corporations. How was corrective justice achieved? What methods do you think are effective in achieving corrective justice? Why?

Review and Reflect

The concept of social justice has been with us since the beginnings of organized governments. In ancient times, rulers such as King Hammurabi set out rules that they felt reflected just actions. These early laws dealt with things ranging from disputes between individual citizens to actions against the state.

Ideas about what constituted right or just action changed over time and varied from place to place. The early principle of "an eye for an eye" was not the form of justice that Aboriginal people around the world used. Furthermore, Jesus Christ advocated a form of justice that was tempered by forgiveness on the part of the person exacting justice and behaviour changes on the part of the accused.

Three major categories of social justice include: distributive justice (how goods and services should be distributed in a just manner), retributive justice (how wrongdoing should be dealt with in a society), and corrective justice (how past inequities and injustices should be dealt with in the future).

Social justice affects us all, and developing a sense of just actions allows ordinary citizens to be pro-active in seeking positive changes in our society.

ART AND AESTHETICS

Before language and writing systems evolved, prehistoric humans developed various forms of art. Cave paintings and prehistoric sculptures are some of the few remaining artifacts that exist from that early time period. Throughout the ages, art served many purposes, including allowing humans to transcend the physical world and enter the realm of spirits and deities. But what exactly is art? How do we know that something is beautiful? Does art have to be beautiful? Is a judgement about a work of art relative to the time period and the culture involved? Who is best able to judge art?

These questions and others have been asked by philosophers and non-philosophers alike. Some developed theories about what makes something a work of art. Others put forward ideas about what makes something beautiful and our human appreciation of it. Still others believed that art was harmful to society and felt that it should be censored. Despite all this, artists continue to amaze, shock, entertain, and excite us.

Just as works of art involve some type of personal interaction between the artist and the spectator, so too does applying philosophy in everyday life. What is the meaning of life? How can philosophy be applied in modern life? Perhaps we asked these questions as we tried to make sense of events around us or to better understand ourselves.

In this unit, we will explore questions about art and aesthetics, and about applying philosophy in everyday life. We will look at classical ideas about art and aesthetics, and then we will investigate several modern theories. Throughout this unit, we will apply the process of philosophic inquiry to examine these questions.

Art is a universal language. No matter where we came from, art allows us to express thoughts and emotions that are deep inside us.

Introducing Art and Aesthetics

What is art? Is it necessary for humans to express themselves through art? What purpose does art serve? Art can be defined as any human skill or activity that is creative in nature. These skills and activities include dances, sculptures, paintings, clothing, culinary arts, architecture, literature, and even engineering designs such as ships or precision metalwork.

But what exactly makes something a work of art? Many philosophers, art critics, and even artists themselves have different criteria for judging a work of art. Some believe that a work of art should provoke ideas and emotions in the spectator. Others believe that our ideas about art vary from culture to culture and from time period to time period.

What is aesthetics? In philosophy, aesthetics deals with the human perception of beauty as distinguished from the useful or moral. Humans since ancient times were very concerned about aesthetics. Greek mathematician Euclid (3rd century BCE) and Roman architect Marcus Vitruvius Pollio (1st century BCE) discussed the golden ratio or golden section, a proportion that was believed to possess aesthetic value because it allegedly corresponds with the laws of nature and objects within the universe. Although most artists are intuitively aware of aesthetically pleasing proportions, they do not necessarily use the golden ratio intentionally in their works of art. However, when their works are analyzed by art critics and others, the proportions that are used approximate the golden ratio.

Both art and aesthetics have played important roles in cultures around the world, and the two are inseparable. Art refers to a process and an end product, while aesthetics are judgements made about art. When we study the philosophy of art, we are seeking to understand what art is, what beauty is, and how both can be judged.

What motivates artists to create something artistic? What value does art have?

Birth of "The Arts"

What is a work of art? Perhaps you think of a painting, a poem, a sculpture, or a dance as a work of art. On the surface, each of these items appears to be quite different from the other. A painting bears little resemblance to a poem, and a sculpture is different from a dance. Yet each of these items represents a work of art, although the form the art takes is quite different. In earlier times, any object or activity that developed as a result of creative thought on the part of the creator was regarded as "art." However, over time the term "art" acquired a slightly different meaning.

How have ideas about art and crafts changed throughout the age?

The Distinction Between Arts and Crafts

What characteristics do works of art share? For much of human history, the term "art" was used to describe any object created by human beings. This might include a picture, a piece of furniture, a play, a wall hanging, a building, a basket, or even a pair of shoes. During the eighteenth century, however, the "arts" and in particular the "fine arts" such as painting, sculpture, music, and dance came to be regarded as being distinct from other human creative activities.

The arts were increasingly viewed as being different from crafts such as building a house, planting a garden, or knitting a sweater. This belief continued well into the twentieth century as crafts were viewed as having a more practical nature. Even though crafts were recognized as possessing artistic and aesthetic components, many people felt that the utilitarianism underlying their development placed crafts in a separate category.

The "fine arts," on the other hand, were seen as being created primarily for the sake of the art itself, and not generally for practical purposes. Such a distinction between arts and crafts can still be found today, but the division between these two areas is in a state of constant flux.

> Every work of art is a permanent possibility of metamorphosis offered to all human beings.
>
> *Octavio Paz*

Why the Arts Are in a Separate Category

One of the early reasons for the popular belief that the arts are a separate category was the increase in knowledge and its acquisition in various fields, particularly during the seventeenth century. Leonardo da Vinci (1452–1519) has often been called a "Rennaissance man" because of his vast intellect and far-reaching achievements during the fifteenth and sixteenth centuries. He was an artist, an architect, an inventor, a scientist, and an engineer. At that time, it was possible to achieve significantly in each of those fields.

However, as an ever increasing base of knowledge accumulated in more and more subject areas, it became apparent that individuals should increase their area of specialization in order to keep up to date with the constantly expanding knowledge base that characterized a particular field. Each subject of inquiry developed a unique method of finding truths and new knowledge, and these methods led to a distinct way in which new products could be created. The fine arts, sciences, trades, and many other areas of life were viewed as distinct and separate from each other both in knowledge and methodology. The arts were specifically identified as a separate and unique form of activity.

Another reason for separating the fine arts into a distinct category was the result of the unique interests of certain social classes. The wealthy and socially privileged individuals of society became increasingly interested in music, dance, and paintings. These areas of art were often different from the creative impulses enjoyed by the other social groups, who tended to support folk arts and traditions. As a result, the fine arts gained a reputation as a discipline that only wealthy and educated members of society could appreciate and enjoy.

> Fine art is that in which the hand, the head, and heart of man go together.
>
> *John Ruskin*

The Process of Artistic Inquiry

Artists, much like philosophers, have developed unique methods of inquiry. Throughout human history, artists have asked the same questions as philosophers, questions such as "Who are we?"; "What is reality?"; "What is evil and how does it affect us?"; "What is our essential nature as humans?"; and "How do governments and wars affect citizens?" Instead of using a process of discourse and reasoning, artists use colour, line, form, movement, and sometimes sound to convey their ideas. These elements provide us with a window through which we can enter the artist's mind and try to understand their thoughts and perceptions of philosophic questions.

Artists use their emotions and creativity to make statements about the world and reality. Sometimes artists mirror the world around them, as in portraits or landscapes. Others alter the appearances in the world, as in many twentieth-century paintings such as those by Pablo Picasso. Still others invent new ways of looking at the world, as in music, dance, and architecture.

Proportion, texture, light, space, tone, theme, balance, and technique are some of the major building blocks that artists use to create a work of art. Understanding how to work with these building blocks distinguishes a masterpiece from just an image, for example. Some artists are so skillful with these building blocks that they can trick us by creating illusions.

Art and beauty are closely related; however, they are not the same. Some artists are inspired to create masterpieces that mirror their idea of beauty. This was particularly true of artists such as Michelangelo Buonarroti (1475–1564) who strove to depict human forms that were realistic, strong, virtuous, and often mythical in appearance. On the other hand, other artists are not concerned with beauty. Pablo Picasso (1881–1973) was an artist who skillfully depicted the turmoil and social horrors that occurred during the Spanish Civil War and World War II.

Pablo Picasso

It is important to note that, like the ideas presented by some philosophers, many of the masterpieces of art that we know about and cherish today were not considered worthy of praise or recognition at the time they were created. Many musicians, sculptors, painters, and designers had ideas that conflicted with the commonly held values in society at the time. As the attitudes in society changed, these artists' works of art became appreciated and highly valued, though many times this change occurred after the artists died.

In the following excerpt, noted Canadian literary critic and English professor Northrop Frye (1912–1991) presents his distinction between art and science. Frye believed that art begins with imagination; however, the mental processes that scientists and artists use are not vastly different after all. What do you think of Frye's distinction between art and science?

The Educated Imagination

Northrop Frye

We have three levels of the mind now, and a language for each of them, which in English-speaking societies means an English for each of them. There's the level of consciousness and awareness, where the most important thing is the difference between me and everything else. The English of this level is the English of ordinary conversation, which is mostly monologue, as you'll soon realize if you do a bit of eavesdropping or listening to yourself. We can call it the language of self-expression. Then there's the level of social participation, the working or technological language of teachers and preachers and politicians and advertisers and lawyers and journalists and scientists. We've … called this the language of practical sense. Then there's the level of imagination which produces the literary language of poems and plays and novels. They're not really different languages, of course, but three different reasons for using words.…

On this basis, perhaps, we can distinguish the arts from the sciences. Science begins with the world we have to live in, accepting its data and trying to explain its laws. From there, it moves towards the imagination: it becomes a mental construct, a model of a possible way of interpreting experience. The further it goes in this direction, the more it tends to speak the language of mathematics, which is really one of the languages of the imagination, along with literature and music. Art, on the other hand, begins with the world we construct, not with the world we see. It starts with the imagination, and then works toward ordinary experience: that is, it tries to make itself as convincing and recognizable as it can. You can see why we tend to think of the sciences as intellectual and the arts as emotional: one starts with the world as it is, the other with the world we want to have. Up to a point it is true that science gives an intellectual view of reality, and that the arts try to make the emotions as precise and disciplined as sciences do the intellect. But of course it's nonsense to think of the scientist as a cold unemotional reasoner and the artist as somebody who's in a perpetual emotional tizzy. You can't distinguish the arts from the sciences by the mental processes the people in them use: they both operate on a mixture of hunch and common sense. A highly developed science and a highly developed art are very close together, psychologically and otherwise.

[Northrop Frye, *The Educated Imagination*. In *The Massey Lectures*, Toronto: CBC Merchandising, 1963, 6, 7.]

What Types of Truths Can We Learn From the Arts?

What types of truths can we learn from poetry, literature, music, sculpture, design, or painting? Aristotle believed that all types of art provide pathways from which we learn important philosophic and social truths. Is the knowledge we gain from the arts as important as the knowledge we acquire from science, observation, or logic?

In modern times, scientific knowledge has gained wide acceptance, largely as a result of its technological advances and practical benefits. Scientists, computer programmers, and mathematicians are modern-day symbols of knowledge and truth. Yet perhaps there are truths that go beyond the analytic and logical parts of our thinking. Austrian psychiatrist Sigmund Freud (1856–1939) noted that we possess many important ideas that are not in our conscious and logical mind. Many of these ideas originate from our emotional, subconcious, and unconscious mind.

Early philosophers such as Plato and Aristotle believed that reason is the ultimate way to find truth. Plato denied that art enabled one to use reason, and he distrusted art as a source of truth. Aristotle, on the other hand, believed that artists use reason to determine general principles or universal truths about existence.

Not all philosophers have supported the importance of reason in our human search for the truth. Nineteenth-century Romantic philosophers were convinced that our imagination and creative use of emotions were the primary route to knowledge and truth. The Romantics believed that artists revealed the deepest insights into human nature and knowledge.

The Romantic Movement developed in reaction to the European eighteenth-century Enlightenment. Enlightenment thinkers, much like Plato before them, had little faith in art as a useful form of understanding. Most of these people were rationalists, and they regarded science as the pathway to truth. As a result, art during the Enlightenment tended to be formal, cool, and structured, and was judged by its conformity to balance, structure, and the rules of that particular art form.

IDEAS AND ISSUES

Understand Concepts

1. Why were the arts viewed as being distinct from other disciplines?
2. Distinguish between "arts" and "fine arts." How are they the same? How are they different?
3. How does artistic knowledge compare to scientific knowledge, according to Wordsworth? How would he justify this position?

Think Critically

4. Compare and contrast the methods used by artists and philosophers in seeking truths and new knowledge.
5. Is it possible for art to be better suited to reach new truths and new knowledge, compared to other forms of inquiry? Explain your answer.
6. How does Northrop Frye distinguish between the language of art and the language of science.

Communicate Ideas

7. Debate this issue: Artistic inquiry into the truth is necessary for philosophers and non-philosophers alike.
8. Discuss this issue: Art can access knowledge that cannot be gained any other way.

Early Ideas About Art:
Art as a Reproduction of Our World

One of the early definitions of art suggests that it is the reproduction of our world. Plato supported this view, although he considered art to be a poor copy of true existence. This view defines a work of art, such as a painting or a sculpture, as a realistic representation of the world around us. According to this view, a story or poem is also a description of our world as we know it, as is a play or a photograph.

The problem with this definition is that while some art represents or reproduces images of our world, many other works of art do not. All of us are familiar with paintings, photographs, and sculptures that do not represent copies of images in the world as we view it. The definition of art as a reproduction of our world also ignores many art forms, such as music, architecture, and dance, which do not fit this definition.

Katsushika Hokusai (1760–1849) was a Japanese artist who made numerous paintings depicting the sacred mountain Fuji. Do you consider this painting to be a mere reproduction of Fuji? Why or why not?

A Shift in Art
Representing the "Real" World

Nineteenth- and twentieth-century artists, audiences, and philosophers began to increasingly accept different and more broad definitions of art, going beyond a representation of reality. The mid-nineteenth century invention of photography probably hastened this broader view of art, as photographs could reproduce more realistic images of the world around us. Even eighteenth-century painters produced works of art that portrayed emotional images and/or abstract ideas rather than true-to-life visual recreations.

Several differing views of art became popular during the late nineteenth and twentieth centuries. The Impressionists, for example, created a visual representation of contemporary life in all its aspects. Expressionism, which emerged during the early twentieth century, sought to portray the inner psychological world, and by the mid-twentieth century, abstract expressionism had won the day. Jackson Pollack and his fellow Expressionists created masterpieces of art that bore no relation at all to real objects as we know them; their works represented a total rejection of representational art.

PHILOSOPHERS' FORUM

The Painter

Leonardo da Vinci

The painter is lord of all types of people and of all things. If the painter wishes to see beauties that charm him it lies in his power to create them, and if he wishes to see monstrosities that are frightful, buffoonish or ridiculous, or pitiable he can be lord and god thereof; if he wants to produce inhabited regions or deserts or dark and shady retreats from the heat, or warm places in cold weather, he can do so. If he wants valleys, if he wants from high mountain tops to unfold a great plain extending down to the sea's horizon, he is lord to do so; and likewise if from low plains he wishes to see high mountains.... In fact whatever exists in the universe, in essence, in appearance, in the imagination, the painter has first in his mind and then in his hand; and these are of such excellence that they can present a proportioned and harmonious view of the whole, that can be seen simultaneously, at one glance, just as things in nature.

[Leonardo da Vinci, *The Notebooks of Leonardo da Vinci*. Ed. by Irma A. Richter. London, UK: Oxford University Press, 1952, 195.]

Genius

Susan Bush and Hsio-yen Shih

If anyone discusses painting in terms of formal likeness,
His understanding is close to that of a child.
If someone composing a poem must have a certain poem,
Then he is definitely not a man who knows poetry.
There is one basic rule in poetry and painting;
Natural genius and originality....

[Susan Bush, ed. and Hsio-yen Shih, ed. *Early Chinese Texts on Painting*. Cambridge: Harvard University Press, 1985, 224.]

Pablo Picasso's painting Guernica *vividly depicts the horror and brutality of war. What role should art play in dealing with such issues?*

Understand Concepts

1. (a) How did Plato view art?
   (b) Why did he hold this view?

Think Critically

2. How would Plato react if he saw paintings representing impressionism, cubism, and expressionism?
3. Why might an artist want to reproduce something in the real world? Why might an artist not want to?

Communicate Ideas

4. Many computer technologies exist today that can alter and distort realistic photographs. Discuss the usefulness of using such technologies and how they affect our view of the world.

5. Research the major trends in the history of Western art. In what ways were artists during those periods imitating realistic forms? In what ways were they deviating from representing the physical world? What were the motivations behind the artists during those periods?

What Makes Something a Work of Art?

How can a work of art be judged, other than by its resemblance to the visible world? Many philosophers and art critics have debated how to judge a work of art, and some have put forward a number of theories to address this question.

What characteristics make an object a work of art? Can useful objects be works of art?

Some critics believe that a work of art is characterized by the artist's original idea or emotion being conveyed effectively to the spectator. Other critics maintain that judging art is relative and depends on the culture that produced it and the culture of the intended audience.

Regardless of the theories put forward, there is no doubt that judging art is both very personal and subjective. Art in all its forms is a universal language and great works of art have the ability to transcend time and space.

Significant Form Theory: Art Produces an Aesthetic Emotion in the Spectator

Art critic Clive Bell (1881–1964) developed the idea of art as significant form. His significant form theory involved judging a work of art using two criteria: how elements within a work of art are combined, and how the work produces an aesthetic emotional reaction in the spectator.

This theory suggests that art exists when the elements of an art genre are contained and correctly combined within a work of art. The combination of correct elements within a piece of music or dance produces a work of art. Paintings by Van Gogh contain the correct elements for a painting; a play by Shakespeare contains the proper elements for a drama. Moreover, the painter or playwright has com-

bined these elements within each work, so that they relate to each other as they should, according to the principles of that specific art form. According to this view, a blues refrain by Eric Clapton or a symphony by Wolfgang Amadeus Mozart can equally be considered works of art, because the elements within each art form combine in a way that a trained critic would recognize.

Bell also believed that true works of art produce an aesthetic emotion in the spectator, listener, or reader. This aesthetic emotion is markedly different from our everyday emotions. Bell believed that aesthetic emotion has nothing to do with practical concerns, and is purely a feeling of appreciation for a piece of art.

Critics of significant form theory argue that two people may view the same work of art and agree that it is a work of art, while disagreeing on the aesthetic emotion produced. One viewer may experience an aesthetic emotion, while the other does not. Bell countered this criticism by suggesting that either observer may not have fully experienced the work of art, or that one of the observers was not a sensitive critic.

Art as Significant Form
Clive Bell

The starting-point for all systems of aesthetics must be the personal experience of a peculiar emotion. The objects that provoke this emotion we call works of art.... That there is a particular kind of emotion provoked by works of visual art, and that this emotion is provoked by every kind of visual art, by pictures, sculptures, buildings, pots, carvings, textiles, etc., etc., is not disputed … by anyone capable of feeling it. This emotion is called the aesthetic emotion; and if we can discover some quality common and peculiar to all the objects that provoke it, we shall have solved what I take to be the central problem of aesthetics. We shall have discovered the essential quality in a work of art, the quality that distinguishes works of art from all other classes of objects.

… There must be some one quality without which a work of art cannot exist.... What quality is common to Sta Sophia and the windows at Chartres, Mexican sculpture, a Persian bowl, Chinese carpets, Giotto's frescoes at Padua, and the masterpieces of Poussin, Piero della Francesca, and Cézanne? Only one answer seems possible—significant form. In each, lines and colours combined in a particular way, certain forms and relations of forms, stir our aesthetic emotions. These relations and combinations of lines and colours, these aesthetically moving forms, I call "Significant Form"; and "Significant Form" is the one quality common to all works of visual art.

… We have no other means of recognising a work of art than our feeling for it. The objects that provoke aesthetic emotion vary with each individual. Aesthetic judgments are, as the saying goes, matters of taste; and about tastes, as everyone is proud to admit, there is no disputing. A good critic may be able to make me see in a picture that had left me cold things that I had overlooked, till at last, receiving the aesthetic emotion, I recognise it as a work of art.... But it is useless for a critic to tell me that something is a work of art; he must make me feel it for myself. This he can do only by making me see; he must get at my emotions through my eyes. Unless he can make me see something that moves me, he cannot force my emotions.... All systems of aesthetics must be based on personal experience—that is to say they must be subjective....

Some people may be surprised at my not having called this "beauty." Of course, to those who define beauty as "combinations of lines and colours that provoke aesthetic emotion," I willingly concede the right of substituting their word for mine. But most of us, however strict we may be, are apt to apply the epithet "beautiful" to objects that do not provoke that peculiar emotion produced by works of art. Everyone … has called a butterfly or a flower beautiful. Does anyone feel the same kind of emotion for a butterfly or a flower that he feels for a cathedral or a picture? Surely, it is not what I call an aesthetic emotion that most of us feel, generally for natural beauty.… [S]ome people may occasionally see in nature what we see in art, and feel for her an aesthetic emotion; but … most people feel a very different kind of emotion for birds and flowers and the wings of butterflies from that which they feel for pictures, pots, temples and statues.…

… We are all familiar with pictures that interest us and excite our admiration, but do not move us as works of art. To this class belongs what I call "Descriptive Painting"— that is, painting in which forms are used not as objects of emotion, but as means of suggesting emotion or conveying information. Portraits of psychological and historical value, topographical works, pictures that tell stories and suggest situations, illustrations of all sorts, belong to this class. That we all recognise the distinction is clear, for who has not said that such and such a drawing was excellent as illustration, but as a work of art worthless? Of course many descriptive pictures possess, amongst other qualities, formal significance, and are therefore works of art: but many more do not. They interest us; they may move us too in a hundred different ways, but they do not move us aesthetically. According to my hypothesis they are not works of art. They leave untouched our aesthetic emotions because it is not their forms but the ideas or information suggested or conveyed by their forms that affect us.…

[Clive Bell, *Art* (1914). New York: G.P. Putnam's Sons, 1958, 15–34.]

How does Bell's theory of aesthetic emotion apply to this Emily Carr painting?

Idealist Theory: Artist's Idea or Emotion Is Communicated to the Spectator

The idealist theory proposes the idea that a work of art is not something physical, but rather is the result of an idea or emotion in the artist's mind. This theory was first suggested by R.G. Collingwood (1889–1943) in his book *Principles of Art*. According to Collingwood, the artist uses physical means and a particular artistic medium to express a specific idea or emotion. The work of art can then be judged by the degree to which the artist's emotion or idea is communicated to the viewer, or listener in the case of music, in the manner intended by the artist.

The idealist theory separates art from craft: works of art serve no practical purpose while craft objects have a utilitarian function. Based on this view, we conclude

Idealist theory separates art from craft: art has no purpose while craft serves a utilitarian purpose, but art on the other hand has no functional reason of existing—it serves no practical purpose.

that a work of art is also not a form of entertainment, because entertainment is created to entertain people. Some critics disagree with such a rigid distinction between art and craft. They argue that many arts, such as portraits and architecture, are created with a purpose in mind.

Some critics also object to the theory of art as ideas within the mind of the artist, because the viewer must see or experience something physical before his or her emotions can be aroused. Idealists respond by saying that any physical object is but a pale imitation of the artist's idea.

The Artist and the Community

R.G. Collingwood

What is meant by saying that the painter "records" in his picture the experience which he had in painting it?… It means that the picture, when seen by someone else … produces in him … a total imaginative experience identical with that of the painter. This experience of the spectator's does not repeat the comparatively poor experience of a person who merely looks at the subject; it repeats the richer and more highly organized experience of a person who has not only looked at it but has painted it as well.

That is why, as so many people have observed, we "see more in" a really good picture of a given subject than we do in the subject itself.… A great portrait painter … , intensely active in absorbing impressions and converting them into an imaginative vision … may easily see through the mask that is good enough to deceive a less active and less pertinacious observer, and detect in a mouth or an eye or the turn of the head things that have long been concealed.…

How is any one to know that the imaginative experience which the spectator … receives from a painting "repeats," or is "identical" with, the experience which the artist had in painting it?… We can never absolutely know that the imaginative experience we obtain from a work of art is identical with that of the artist. In proportion as the artist is a great one, we can be pretty certain that we have only caught his meaning partially and imperfectly. But the same applies to any case in which we hear what a man says or read what he writes. And a partial and imperfect understanding is not the same thing as a complete failure to understand.

[R.G. Collingwood, *The Principles of Art*. Oxford: Clarendon Press, 1945, 308–24.]

Most artists would agree with Collingwood in that artists do indeed have ideas and emotions which are in turn conveyed through the medium of their work. This is especially true when you consider the art of music. Most musicians, from classical to rock to reggae, express profound ideas and emotions that are conveyed to the listener.

The Sense of Zen

D.T. Suzuki

Zen in its essence is the art of seeing into the nature of one's own being, and it points the way from bondage to freedom. By making us drink right from the fountain of life, it liberates us from all the yokes under which we finite beings are usually suffering in this world. We can say that Zen liberates all the energies properly and naturally stored in each of us, which are in ordinary circumstances cramped and distorted so that they find no adequate channel for activity.

The ancient Japanese tea ceremony brings aesthetic pleasure to the act of drinking tea.

This body of ours is something like an electric battery in which a mysterious power latently lies. When this power is not properly brought into operation, it either … withers away or is warped and expresses itself abnormally. It is the object of Zen, therefore, to save us from going crazy or being crippled. This is what I mean by freedom, giving free play to all the creative and benevolent impulses inherently lying in our hearts. Generally, we are blind to this fact, that we are in possession of all the necessary faculties that will make us happy and loving towards one another. All the struggles that we see around us come from ignorance. Zen, therefore, wants us to open a "third eye," as Buddhists call it, to the hitherto undreamed-of region shut away from us through our own ignorance. When the cloud of ignorance disappears, the infinity of the heavens is manifested, where we see for the first time into the nature of our being. We now know the signification of life, we know that it is not blind striving, nor is it a mere display of brutal forces, but that while we know not definitely what the ultimate purport [meaning] of life is, there is something in it that makes us feel infinitely blessed in the living of it and remain quite connected with it in all its evolution, without raising questions or entertaining pessimistic doubts.

[D.T. Suzuki, *Essays in Zen Buddhism: First Series*, London: Luzac and Co., 1927. Found in *The World of Zen*, ed. by Nancy Wilson Ross, New York: Random House, 1960, 39, 40.]

Institutional Theory:
Art Is Defined by Its Culture

Institutional theory suggests that art is defined by its culture, and that what is considered art in one culture may, or may not, be considered art in another. According to this theory, experts within a particular culture have the authority to define an object or creation as a work of art. In North America, for example, movie and television critics rate movies providing the public with information as to which movies are worth watching.

Critics who object to this institutional or cultural definition of art want to know why some objects are considered works of art and others are not. They also ask what criteria are used to determine if something is a work of art.

Is it possible for any object in the world to become a possible art subject? Philosopher Paul Ziff discusses this question in the following excerpt. How does he make his argument? Do you agree with him?

Notice that Ziff has an unconventional way of punctuating his writing. Do you think this helps or hinders him as he expresses his ideas?

Anything Viewed

Paul Ziff

Look at the dried dung!

What for?

If I had said "Look at the sunset!" would you have asked "What for?"?

People view sunsets aesthetically. Sunsets are customary objects of aesthetic attention, So are trees rocks wildflowers clouds women leaping gazelles prancing horses: all these are sometime objects of aesthetic attention. But not everything is: not soiled linen greasy dishes bleary eyes false teeth not excrement.

Why not? It's not because they're unbeautiful or even ugly. Beautiful things are no problem for a rambling aesthetic eye but not all objects of aesthetic attention are beautiful: Grunewald's *Crucifixion* isn't neither is Picasso's *Guernica*. Brueghel's rustics aren't lovely. The stark morning light in a Hopper is powerful but it is not beautiful. Not being beautiful needn't matter.

These unbeautiful objects are works of art. By chance some objects of aesthetic attention have been naturally produced. For the rest: they are products of art.

What is a work of art? Something fit to be an object of aesthetic attention.... What does a work of art have or lack that dung doesn't?

What is a work of art? Not everything. Leonardo's portrait of Ginevra de' Benci is. A mound of dried dung isn't. Nor is an alligator at least a living gator basking in the sun on a mud bank in a swamp isn't. A reason they are not is plain, nothing is a work of art if it is not an artefact something made by man. A gator basking a mound of dried dung are products of nature made or produced by natural forces. Not being made or produced by men they are not classed artefacts. Not being artefacts they are not classed works of art....

What's a fit subject to photograph? Anything that can be seen. Or is it not what the photographer photographs but what he makes of it? With his camera and darkroom and skills? What he does with art I can do with my ... eyes. One can look at anything and within limits and depending on one's powers create an appropriate frame and environing conditions for what one sees....

But isn't one painting better than another? In some ways and not in others. Rubens' paintings were superior to those of many of his contemporaries with respect to technique and pigmentation. Ingres' work displays finer draftsmanship than that of David. Vuillard's works have finer color than Manet's. But this isn't to say that Vuillard's works are more fit than those of Manet for aesthetic attention.... But there are other things to attend to in viewing Manet's works. There are always other things to attend to.

In looking at *Ginevra* one can attend to the display of craftsmanship and the beauty of form and shape: in looking at the gator basking one can attend to the beautiful grinning display of life. Anything that can be viewed can fill the bill of an object fit for aesthetic attention and none does it better than any other....

[Paul Ziff, "Anything Viewed," *Antiaesthetics: An Appreciation of the Cow with the Subtile Nose.* Dordrecht: Reidel, Kluwer Academic Publishers, 1984, 129–39.]

What is the relationship between art and beauty? Does art have to be beautiful from Ziff's point of view? What is your point of view?

Understand Concepts

1. What questions can be asked about art, beauty, and aesthetics?
2. Identify the various theories of art and their views of art.
3. Summarize Ziff's arguments about art, aesthetics, and beauty.
4. What questions arise from Ziff's excerpt?

Apply and Develop

5. Apply Ziff's view of art and aesthetics to any of the pictures in this chapter. To what degree do you agree with his points of view?
6. Choose a painting or other work of art that you consider beautiful. Defend your choice by pointing to elements of beauty in the work of art.
7. Support the view that art and beauty is important in life. Choose some work of art and beauty that illustrates this.

Think Critically

8. How would you define art?
9. How would you identify something as beautiful?
10. How important is it for us as spectators and/or art critics to understand a particular art form before judging its worth?
11. (a) What characteristics would enable an individual to be better able to judge art?
    (b) How would artists respond to part (a)?
12. What are the similarities and differences between Frye's view of art and Collingwood's?
13. Present your own opinion about judging art. With which theory, if any, do you most agree?

What Value Does Art Have?

Does art have any value at all? What would the world be without art? Some philosophers such as Plato believed that art corrupted society. This view was held many times during the course of human history. During various political regimes, the works of various artists were censored or destroyed, for example, the burning of Thomas Mann's books during Nazi Germany and the imprisonment of Russian composer Dmitri Shostakovich during the communist regime. Even during the Vietnam War, many American film producers and entertainers had their careers end abruptly because of their views on the war.

Bob Marley played a significant role in addressing injustices in Jamaican society, should any restrictions be placed on artistic expression?

In some cases, the work of artists has been considered a threat to society; Bob Marley was regarded by Jamaican political leaders at the time as an individual who incited the Jamaican people to rebel against the status quo. Bob Marley's music caused a noticeable disturbance in Jamaican society that his life was threatened on several occasions. To a much less degree, noted haute couture designer Yves Saint Laurent's "Beat Look" collection in 1960 caused such a commotion in the fashion world that he was asked to leave the House of Dior, where he worked.

In our society, many artists are free to pursue their work without interference although from time to time the established values of society are put to the test. In most cases, artists are a barometer of where society is at emotionally and intellectually, and they challenge us to confront issues that we may otherwise ignore. Do you think that art has value in society? If so, what value does it have?

Plato's View:
Art Corrupts Society

Plato believed art was harmful because of its corrupting influence on society. Plato was convinced that art encouraged human emotions to intensify and spread in socially harmful ways. As a result, Plato argued for the strict censorship of music and poetry.

Many people today disagree with Plato's views about art, and argue that art has a number of important social values. Some critics believe that art reveals important elements of social reality, communicating ideas in a way that could not be done otherwise.

PHILOSOPHERS' FORUM

Art As Imitation

Plato

… [A]ll poetical imitations are ruinous to the understanding of the hearers, and that the knowledge of their true nature is the only antidote to them…. [T]he imitator has no knowledge worth mentioning of what he imitates….

And now we may fairly take [the poet] and place him by the side of the painter, for he is like him in two ways: first, inasmuch as his creations have an inferior degree of truth … we shall be right in refusing to admit him into a well-ordered State, because he awakens and nourishes and strengthens the feelings and impairs the reason….

But we have not yet brought forward the heaviest count in our accusation … the power which poetry has of harming even the good…. [W]hen we listen to a passage of Homer … in which he represents some pitiful hero who is drawling out his sorrows in a long oration, or weeping, and smiting his breast … [w]e delight in giving way to sympathy, and are in raptures at the excellence of the poet who stirs our feelings most….

But when any sorrow of our own happens to us, then you may observe that we pride ourselves on the opposite quality—we would fain be quiet and patient…. Now can we be right in praising and admiring another who is doing that which any one of us would abominate and be ashamed of in his own person?… And the same may be said of lust and anger and all the other affections, of desire and pain and pleasure, … poetry feeds and waters the passions instead of drying them up; she lets them rule, although they ought to be controlled, if mankind are ever to increase in happiness and virtue.

… [W]e are well aware that poetry being such as we have described is not to be regarded seriously as attaining to the truth; and he who listens to her, fearing for the safety of the city which is within him, should be on his guard against her seductions….

[Plato, *The Republic*, Book 10. In *The Dialogues of Plato* (3rd ed.), trans. by Benjamin Jowett. London: Oxford University Press, 1892, 852–66.]

Plato criticized art for being a poor imitation of reality. Painters such as Renoir and Riopelle would argue that they each capture some aspect of reality that a photograph does not, despite their different techniques. Do you agree?

Aristotle's View: Art Allows Us to Understand and Appreciate Human Existence

Plato criticized art because he believed it did not provide a means to find the truth. Instead, Plato argued, art only presented a pale imitation of real objects. Plato urged his students to find truth by searching for the universal idea of an object. He believed art was a negative and dangerous element in society, because it encouraged emotions and actions that were socially harmful.

Aristotle disagreed with these views. Aristotle believed the universal form, or truth, of an object was within the object itself, and that the only way human beings could understand these universal, or true, forms was to analyze those objects which contained them. According to Aristotle, artists were particularly well equipped to comprehend universal forms because artists were trained to observe objects, people, and actions in the world around them. Aristotle believed a well-written story about people and their relationships could provide invaluable insights into the universal idea of human relationships and social life. Aristotle was convinced that art could provide an important medium for understanding and appreciating human existence.

Today, philosophers engage in a similar debate. Some thinkers believe that the violence portrayed on television and other media has a harmful influence on viewers, encouraging them to repeat the antisocial acts portrayed. Such critics argue for controls or censorship over art. Other philosophers agree with Aristotle that since art explores all aspects of human thought and existence, it helps us to control and or remove our negative emotions and actions. Aristotelians would probably not be in favour of censorship because they believe artistic expression is usually insightful and helpful in gaining understanding.

> The scholar seeks, the artist finds.
> *Andre Gide*

Poetics

Aristotle

... Imitation is natural to man.... [Humanity] is the most imitative creature in the world, and learns at first by imitation. And it is also natural for all to delight in works of imitation.... The explanation is to be found in a further fact: to be learning something is the greatest of pleasure not only to the philosopher, but also the rest of mankind.... [T]he reason of the delight in seeing the picture is that one is at the same time learning....

... [T]he poet's function is to describe, not the thing that has happened, but a kind of thing that might happen.... Hence poetry is something more philosophic and of graver import than history, since its statements are of the nature rather of universals, whereas those of history are singulars.... The poet being an imitator, just like the painter or other maker of likenesses, ... represent[s] things ... either as they were or are, or as they are said or thought to be or to have been, or as they ought to be....

[Aristotle, *Poetics*. In *The Works of Aristotle*, ed. by W.D. Ross, trans. by Ingram Bywater. Oxford: Clarendon Press, 1924.]

> There can be no transforming of darkness into light and of apathy into movement without emotion.
> *Carl Jung*

Rabindranath Tagore (1861–1941) was an Indian philosopher and poet. His mystical poetry reveals his keen awareness of our human connection with the eternal.

Apply and Develop

1. How would Plato and Aristotle consider the question of censorship of art, movies, and other media?

Think Critically

2. Compare the views of Plato and Aristotle on the social value of art.
3. What conclusions do you draw from these two positions?
4. What would be the social costs of eliminating art from a society?

Inquire and Research

5. Research the effects of television violence on viewers. Is such violence harmful or is it a release for antisocial ideas and behaviour?
6. View a number of music videos. What would Plato and Aristotle have to say about the social messages of each?

The Many Purposes of Art

Does art have important purposes? How does art influence an individual or society? Some people believe that art reveals important elements of human existence; others have dismissed art as insignificant.

It has been suggested that art began as a means to transcend the physical world.

Can art teach in ways that words cannot? What does this painting illustrate that cannot be revealed through the written word?

Artists in Africa and the Pacific islands still use art for magical and religious purposes. Art eventually began to include utilitarian objects, such as making textiles, furniture, and buildings. In some cultures and during various time periods, art has been viewed as a method to communicate ideas, from religious ideas to recording historical events to propaganda. However, art as a means to satisfy our desire for beauty is probably the most common purpose that most of us can identify.

In modern times, we are presented with a variety of views about art and its purpose. Some philosophers and art critics argue that art only satisfies an aesthetic purpose. Others believe that the social value of art transcends aesthetics, providing us with a means to understand ourselves, others, society, and/or nature. This interpretation was also held by nineteenth century Romantics, and suggests that art provides us with knowledge and understanding that cannot be acquired in other ways. Still other thinkers believe that art requires no practical, useful, or social justification at all; art is to be appreciated and accepted on its own merits.

Art as a Means to Transcend the Physical World

The earliest known sculpture (c. 20 000 BCE) from Grimaldi Cave in Italy depicts a woman with an imposing form suggesting the presence of divine powers. A great deal of art since that time was created primarily as a means to reach the world of spirits and the divine.

The rich tribal cultures in Africa and on the many Pacific islands to this day produce works of art that are mainly used for magical and religious rituals. Objects such as masks and sculptures of human figures are believed to possess magical powers and can heal the sick, punish an enemy, promote fertility, or bring rain. Other forms of art such as music and dance are equally important in Aboriginal cultures; these forms of art are used to allow both the spectators and participants to transcend the physical world and enter the realm of powerful spirits and deities.

The ancient Egyptian pharaohs built colossal pyramids, and erected obelisks and temples in an attempt to reach the world that they believed existed beyond death. These forms of art were not unique to Egypt. The Maya (300 BCE–10th century CE) in what is now Central America, the Incas (c. 1100–1532) in Peru, and the Aztecs (13th century–1519) in what is now Mexico City all developed elaborate forms of art for religious purposes; they built temples, such as the Mayan pyramids and the Inca temples on Machu Picchu, and monumental sculptures depicting various deities.

During the establishment of the world's great religions, art played an important role in the building of ornate and magnificent temples, mosques, churches, and cathedrals. These buildings were intended to be architectural wonders with their massive domes, intricate mosaics, elaborate paintings, or imposing statues. These places of worship were to transcend time and space, and move worshippers beyond the world of physical experiences.

Time Line

Examples of Art Transcending the Physical
- - - - - - - - - - -

FEMALE STATUETTE (C. 20 000 BCE) is found in Grimaldi Cave, Italy

PYRAMID OF KHUFU (2650 BCE) is largest pyramid in Giza, Egypt

PYRAMID OF JAGUAR TEMPLE (8TH CENTURY CE) is constructed in Tikal, Guatemala

ISLAMIC ART (670 CE–1300 CE) flourishes in the Middle East

GOTHIC ART (1135 CE–1450 CE) is found in Western cathedrals and churches

INCA TEMPLES (C. 1450 CE) three temples are built on Machu Picchu, Peru

KONDO OF HORYU-JI (LATE 17TH CENTURY–EARLY 18TH CENTURY CE) is oldest surviving wooden building (Nara, Japan)

The Mayan pyramids were temples of precisely cut stone that were used to honour their gods.

Art as a Form of Communication

Time Line

Examples of Art as Communication

LASCAUX CAVE PAINTINGS

(15 000 BCE)

show scenes from prehistoric human life

HAN DYNASTY PAINTINGS

(206 BCE–220 CE)

encourage emperors and their subjects to lead ethical lives

MOGHUL SCHOOL

(LATE 16TH CENTURY CE –18TH CENTURY CE)

produces paintings illustrating memoirs of emperors of India

HARUNOBU

(1760 CE)

introduces the colour print (Japan)

IMPRESSIONIST PAINTERS

(1874 CE–1886 CE)

depict scenes from everyday life

The oldest record of art as a means of communication is found in cave paintings and paintings on rocks in sheltered places, notably those in northern Spain, France, and India. Although it is still not clear whether or not there was any religious ritual associated with these paintings, we do know that these paintings communicated ideas about the world at that time (c. 20 000 BCE). These ideas could not have been communicated in any other way because the invention of writing did not occur until about 3000 BCE.

In the Far East, the main inspiration for art came from the great religions and philosophies of Chinese culture: Confucianism, Taoism, and Buddhism. Unlike Western paintings, Chinese artists did not attempt to depict forms as they appear in the world around us or to convey the illusion of space. During the Han dynasty (206 BCE–220 CE), Chinese artists used art as a way to teach emperors and their subjects to lead ethical lives. During the eighth and nineteenth centuries CE, landscapes, which became the major theme of Chinese painting, portrayed harmony between humans and nature, a key element in Taoist philosophy.

Beginning in the second century CE, the Chinese art of paper manufacture in conjunction with their unique writing system led to the development of calligraphy as an art form. Chinese symbols by their very nature are both artistic and functional at the same time, a characteristic that Arabs can also appreciate although Arabic lettering

In the Far East, art was used as a means to spread philosophy and religion.

lacks the same scope for artistic potential.

Throughout Asia, the artistic form of writing became in-creasingly used to spread religious ideas and philosophies. In the Far East, Buddhism spread to Korea and Japan, while Islam spread throughout the Middle East and later North Africa. In Europe, the art of calligraphy was restricted to scribes within the Christian Church because it was time consuming and paper manufacture had not yet fully developed. However, with the advent of the Chinese invention of printing with movable type, followed centuries later by the Europeans, the prominence of calligraphy as an art form in the Western world waned.

Various forms of art have been used as a way to transmit information to people. Writing, painting, sculptures, music, and even tapestries have been used to convey historical information or ideas about human nature, ethics, and metaphysics, among others. Aboriginal cultures also used art as a way to communicate ideas about the way they viewed the world.

During the twentieth century, art was used as a means of spreading propaganda by various political regimes. In Nazi Germany, art was used to encourage the populace to think and act in certain ways. Art produced for political propaganda is generally considered inferior to art that is not shaped by political ideas. Many artists fled from totalitarian regimes once they realized they would not be able to do their best work.

Art is also used for commercial purposes, to sell products and services. Television commercials, magazine advertisements, and other media use music, pictures, and speech in creative and persuasive ways.

Nineteenth century Russian author and philosopher Leo Tolstoy (1828–1910) believed that art is a form of interpersonal communication. If someone sends a message and another person receives it, then art is successful, particularly if the message is an emotional one.

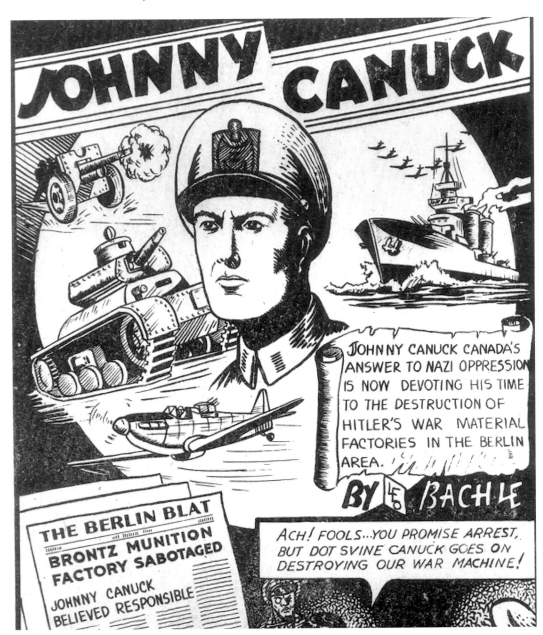

Can a commercial message be considered a work of art?

Emily Carr:

Artist of Native Canadians on the West Coast

One of Canada's most prominent painters is Emily Carr (1871–1945). Carr, the youngest daughter of a successful businessman, was born in Victoria, British Columbia. Although the only child in the family to have a good relationship with her father, her life became difficult when she was orphaned in her teens.

Women at that time had to overcome many obstacles if they wanted to become artists. Despite all this, in 1891, Carr went to the California School of Design to study art. When she returned to Victoria, she began teaching art to children. Eventually, she grew restless and went to England in 1899 and then France in 1910 to continue her art studies. It was at this point that her work took a different turn, and in 1911 her paintings reflected a strong post-impressionist style.

Emily Carr

Beginning in 1908, Carr had set out to visit and paint remote Aboriginal sites in British Columbia. She wanted to paint a record of the vanishing villages, houses, and totem poles that once represented a vibrant West Coast culture. By 1913, she had completed a significant body of work, but she was unable to generate an income from her art.

Interestingly, her reputation as an artist is based on work that began when she was fifty-seven. She took a trip to Eastern Canada, where she met several members of the Group of Seven. Their innovative work and encouragement inspired her to pursue a new direction in her art. As a result, Carr's art started receiving critical recognition.

Due to ailing health, Carr spent the last eight years of her life devoting more time to writing books.

What Is Art?

Leo Tolstoy

Every work of art causes the receiver to enter into a certain kind of relationship both with him who produced ... the art.... Speech, transmitting the thoughts and experiences of men, serves as a means of union among them, and art acts in a similar manner.... [W]hereas by words a man transmits his thoughts to another, by means of art he transmits his feelings.

The activity of art is based on the fact that a man, receiving through his sense of hearing or sight another man's expression of feeling, is capable of experiencing the emotion which moved the man who expressed it....

And it is upon this capacity of man to receive another man's expression of feeling and experience those feelings himself, that the activity of art is based. Art begins when one person, with the object of joining another or others to himself in one and the same feeling, expresses that feeling by certain external indications. ... [For] example: a boy, having experienced... fear on encountering a wolf, relates that encounter; and, in order to evoke in others the feeling he has experienced, describes himself, his condition before the encounter, the surroundings, the wood, his own lightheartedness, and then the wolf's appearance, its movements, the distance between himself and the wolf, etc. ... [If] ... the boy, ... again experiences the feelings he had lived through and infects the hearers and compels them to feel what [he] had experienced, is art. If even the boy had not seen a wolf but had frequently been afraid of one, and if, wishing to evoke in others the fear he had felt, he invented an encounter with a wolf and recounted it so as to make his hearers share the feelings he experienced when he feared the wolf, that also would be art. And just in the same way it is art if a man, having experienced either the fear of suffering or the attraction of enjoyment (whether in reality or in imagination), expresses these feelings on canvas or in marble so that others are infected by them. And it is also art if a man feels or imagines to himself feelings of delight, gladness, sorrow, despair, courage, or despondency and the transition from one to another of these feelings, and expresses these feelings by sounds so that the hearers are infected by them and experience them as they were experienced by the composer....

To evoke in oneself a feeling one has once experienced, and having evoked it in oneself then, by means of movements, lines, colors, sounds, or forms expressed in words, so to transmit that feeling that others may experience the same feeling—this is the activity of art.

Art is a human activity consisting in this, that one man consciously, by means of certain external signs, hands on to others feelings he has lived through, and that other people are infected by these feelings and also experience them....

[Leo Tolstoy, *What Is Art?* (1898). Trans. by Aylmer Maude. Indianapolis: Bobbs-Merrill Co., Inc., 1960, 42–53.]

Art for Art's Sake

Poetry is the wine of love....

Rumi

Aristotle, the Romantic philosophers, Freud, and other thinkers believed that art should have some external effect, or some extrinsic value. They believed that art led to something else such as understanding, emotional well-being, or social benefit.

When something has value within itself, we say it has intrinsic value. What events in life have intrinsic value? Many philosophers argued that different aspects of ourselves are intrinsically valuable: for Immanuel Kant it is human life, for Aristotle and Jeremy Bentham it is happiness or pleasure. Irish author and playwright Oscar Wilde (1856–1900) argued that art has intrinsic value, and does not need to be explained or justified beyond itself.

Wilde saw the importance of art in shaping how we view all things. While Plato said that art is a poor reproduction of what we understand as reality, Wilde turned this view on its head. He argued that how we see the world and anything at all is shaped by art. How we view a scene in nature or how we view other people and society is shaped by the art that exists within that society and culture. Think about the movies and television programs you watch that portray human relationships. To what extent do these dramas or comedies shape how we view our own relationships in life?

Oscar Wilde

Every child is an artist. The problem is how to remain an artist once he grows up.

Pablo Picasso

IDEAS AND ISSUES

Understand Concepts

1. What are the main ideas of art put forward by Wilde and Tolstoy?
2. In what way, if at all, are Wilde's ideas similar to those of Wordsworth?
3. Summarize the argument made by Wilde.

Apply and Develop

4. Choose any three poems, or any three paintings, with which you are familiar. Show how, in each case, the poet or artist shapes how we view the world through the use of language or visual techniques.

Think Critically

5. In what way is Wilde's view of the relationship between life and art different from all those who preceded him?
6. How did both Wordsworth and Wilde disagree with the views of Plato and Aristotle?
7. What makes art a universal language? Are the messages that art conveys timeless? Why or why not?

Communicate Ideas

8. Debate this issue: Oscar Wilde's idea that life imitates art is incorrect and misleading.
9. Review the ideas in this chapter on the purposes of art. Write a position paper in which you argue for or against the idea: Art should have a social purpose in order to exist.

Inquire and Research

10. Find out more about the history of women artists in Canada. What contributions to society did they make? What obstacles did they have to overcome? What challenges still face women today?

Two Other Views of the Purpose of Art

With the advent of new technologies and new knowledge during the twentieth century different views about the purpose of art emerged. The invention of movies allowed many people to view the world in ways that were unheard of a generation earlier. In fact, movies allowed people to learn about parts of the world that they previously knew nothing about. Furthermore, Freud's work in understanding the role of the unconscious in shaping our personal identities provided us with a new way to view ourselves and our world. Movies and our understanding of the unconscious opened up a new set of possibilities for us to express ourselves artistically and to appreciate art.

Art and the Imagination

English artist and art critic Roger Fry (1866–1934) believed that art allows us to think about and imagine life situations without having to act or react to them. In this way, we can perceive these hypothetical situations differently from the way we normally do. Fry used the example of film, wherein we can view and experience situations as spectators but are not required to be personally active on the set. Art allows our imaginations, rather than our physical selves, to deal with such situations.

Is there value in imagining life situations that are removed from our reality? What argument does Roger Fry put forward regarding this question?

An Essay in Aesthetics

Roger Fry

"The art of painting," says [a certain painter] … "is the art of imitating solid objects upon a flat surface by means of pigments." It is delightfully simple, but prompts the question—is that all?… Plato, indeed, gave a very similar account of the affair, and himself put the question—is it then worth while? And, being scrupulously and relentlessly logical, he decided that it was not worth while, and proceeded to turn the artists out of his ideal republic. For all that, the world has continued obstinately to consider that painting was worth while, and though, indeed, it has never quite made up its mind as to what, exactly, the graphic arts did for it, it has persisted in honouring and admiring its painters.

Can we arrive at any conclusions as to the nature of the graphic arts, which will at all explain our feelings about them?…

A great many objects in the world, when presented to our senses, put in motion a complex nervous machinery, which ends in some instinctive appropriate action. We see a wild bull in a field; quite without our conscious interference a nervous process goes on, which … ends in the appropriate reaction of flight.… The whole of animal life, and a great part of human life, is made up of these instinctive reactions.… But man has the peculiar faculty of calling up again in his mind the echo of past experiences of this kind, of going over it again, "in imagination" as we say. He has, therefore, the possibility of a double life; one the actual life, the other the imaginative life. Between these two lives there is this great distinction, that in the actual life the processes of natural selection have brought it about that the instinctive reaction, such, for instance, as flight from danger, shall be the important part of the whole process.… But in the imaginative life no such action is necessary, and, therefore, the whole consciousness may be focussed upon the perceptive and the emotional aspects of the experience. In this way we get, in the imaginative life, a different set of values, and a different kind of perception.

We can get a curious side glimpse of the nature of this imaginative life from [films].… This resembles actual life in almost every respect, except that … the appropriate resultant action is cut off. If, in a [film] … , [w]e see a runaway horse and cart, we do not have to think … of getting out of the way.… The result is that in the first place we see the event much more clearly; see a number of quite interesting but irrelevant things, which in real life could not struggle into our consciousness, bent, as it would be, entirely upon the problem of our appropriate reaction.…

In the second place … , [o]ne notices that whatever emotions are aroused by … [films], though they are likely to be weaker than those of ordinary life, are presented more clearly to the consciousness. If the scene presented be one of an accident, our pity and horror, though weak, since we know that no one is really hurt, are felt quite purely, since they cannot, as they would in life, pass at once into actions of assistance....

That the graphic arts are the expression of the imaginative life rather than a copy of actual life might be guessed from observing children. Children, if left to themselves, never, I believe, copy what they see, never, as we say, "draw from nature," but express, with a delightful freedom and sincerity, the mental images which make up their own imaginative lives.

Art, then, is an expression and a stimulus of this imaginative life, which is separated from actual life by the absence of responsive action. Now this responsive action implies in actual life moral responsibility. In art we have no such moral responsibility—it presents a life freed from the binding necessities of our actual existence.

[Roger Fry, "An Essay in Aesthetics," *Vision and Design*. Ed. by J.B. Bullen. London, UK: Oxford University Press, 1920.]

Art as a Form of Play

When Sigmund Freud was asked what psychological purposes art might have, he suggested yet another view of art, one that originated from his study of how the mind works. To Freud, daydreams and fantasies in adults had the same function as play for a child.

The Relation of the Poet to Daydreaming

Sigmund Freud

We laymen have always wondered ... how ... the poet, comes by his material. What makes him able to carry us with him in such a way and to arouse emotions in us of which we thought ourselves perhaps not even capable?...

If we could only find some activity in ourselves, or in people like ourselves, which was in any way akin to the writing of imaginative works! If we could ... it would give us a hope of obtaining some insight into the creative powers of imaginative writers. And indeed, there is some prospect of achieving this—writers themselves ... so often assure us that every man is at heart a poet, and that the last poet will not die until the last human being does.

We ought surely to look in the child for the first traces of imaginative activity. The child's best-loved and most absorbing occupation is play. Perhaps we may say that every child at play behaves like an imaginative writer, in that he creates a world of his own or, more truly, he rearranges the things of his world ... in a new way that pleases him better. It would be incorrect to think that he does not take this world seriously; on the contrary, he takes his play very seriously and expends a great deal of emotion on it....

Now the writer does the same as the child at play; he creates a world of phantasy which he takes very seriously ... while separating it sharply from reality. Language has preserved this relationship between children's play and poetic creation. It designates certain kinds of imaginative creation ... as "plays"; the people who present them are called "players." ...

As they grow up, people cease to play, and appear to give up the pleasure they derived from play. But anyone who knows anything of the mental life of human beings is aware that hardly anything is more difficult to them than to give up a pleasure they have once tasted.... When we appear to give something up, all we really do is to adopt a substitute. So when the human being grows up and ceases to play he only gives up the connection with real objects; instead of playing he then begins to create phantasy. He builds castles in the air and creates what are called daydreams. I believe that the greater number of human beings create phantasies at times as long as they live....

The phantasies of human beings are less easy to observe than the play of children.... [A] child does not conceal his play from adults.... The adult, on the other hand, is ashamed of daydreams and conceals them from other people; he cherishes them as most intimate possessions and as a rule he would rather confess all his misdeeds than tell his daydreams.... Daydreaming is a continuation of play, nevertheless, and the motives which lie behind these two activities contain a very good reason for this different behaviour in the child at play and in the daydreaming adult....

You will remember that we said the daydreamer hid his phantasies carefully from other people because he had reason to be ashamed of them. I may now add that even if he were to communicate them to us, he would give us no pleasure by his disclosures.... But when a man of literary talent presents his plays, or relates what we take to be his personal daydreams, we experience great pleasure.... Perhaps much that brings about this result consists in the writer's putting us into a position in which we can enjoy our own daydreams without reproach or shame.

[Sigmund Freud, "The Relation of the Poet to Day-Dreaming." In *On Creativity and the Unconscious*, trans. by Jan Riviere. New York: Harper & Row Publishers, 1958.]

What connections did Freud make between art and childhood play? Do you agree with him?

Understand Concepts

1. (a) What is Roger Fry's definition of art?
   (b) What is Sigmund Freud's definition of art?
2. (a) Compare the ideas of art put forward by Fry and Freud using these categories: what art is and the purposes art serves.
   (b) Describe the way Fry and Freud put forward their arguments.
3. In what ways are Fry and Freud agreeing or disagreeing with each other? Are they talking about different things?

Apply and Develop

4. Apply Fry's and Freud's views to a recent movie you have seen. Analyze the plot, characters, setting, and other elements of importance. Do the ideas of Fry or Freud help you to understand the movie more fully? Explain your answer.

Inquire and Research

5. (a) Look at and analyze Michelangelo's statue of Moses. What elements do you see? How would you judge this sculpture?
   (b) Read Freud's article "The Moses of Michelangelo" (1914). How does he analyze it? How useful do you think his analysis is?
6. Find out more about Freud's ideas about instincts, especially the id and its instincts of aggression and sexuality. Consider a movie you have recently watched. How would Freud analyze the characters using psychoanalytic theory?

Aesthetics: Appreciating Beauty in Art

Can one appreciate art or beauty without knowing anything about it? Is it enough to say of a painting or of a piece of music "I like it" without knowing why? If you listen to a song on the radio, or see a play, do you have an immediate response for or against it? Several thinkers put forward ideas about how works of art should be judged and who is best qualified to do the judging.

What response do you have to this work of art? What are your reasons?

David Hume: Aesthetics is Most Credible by Connoisseurs

What makes one person's judgement of a work of art, or a beautiful object, more acceptable than another's? As you leave a theatre with a friend, discussing the merits of a movie you have both just seen, what standards are you applying to your judgement? When you visit an art gallery or listen to a lecture on the merits of a great master, why is the opinion of that artist or teacher valuable? Should art be judged solely by personal taste, since "beauty is in the eye of the beholder," or are there recognized and shared standards that can be applied to judging art?

Empiricist philosopher David Hume was highly interested in our perceptions of the world around us. Hume asked questions about the judgement of art; he also defined standards he thought could be used in judging art. Hume believed that some people have a greater aptitude for, or sensitivity to, certain kinds of art whether it is music, dance, painting, or drama. Today, we might call these people connoisseurs. Hume believed that critical analysis of works of art by connoisseurs should be given more credibility than such an analysis by people less familiar with the discipline. He also believed that training and culture can also increase a person's ability to judge art and beauty.

What are the merits of each of these works of art, in your opinion? What makes them beautiful if at all?

Of the Standard of Taste

David Hume

There is a species of philosophy, which cuts off all hopes of … ever attaining any standard of taste…. [This position holds that beauty] is no quality in things themselves: it exists merely in the mind which contemplates them; and each mind perceives a different beauty…. But though this … seems to have attained the sanction of common sense, there is certainly a species of common sense, which opposes it….

The same Homer who pleased at Athens and Rome two thousand years ago, is still admired at Paris and at London. All the changes of climate, government, religion, and language, have not been able to obscure his glory. Authority or prejudice may give a temporary vogue to a bad poet or orator; but his reputation will never be durable or general…. On the contrary, a real genius, the longer his works endure, and the more wide they are spread, the more sincere is the admiration which he meets with….

It appears, then, that … there are certain general principles of … [approval] or blame…. Some particular forms or qualities … are calculated to please, and others to displease; and if they fail … , it is from some apparent defect or imperfection in the organ. A man in a fever would not insist on his palate as able to decide concerning flavours; nor would one affected with the jaundice pretend to give a verdict with regard to colours. In each creature there is a sound and a defective state; and the former alone can be supposed to afford us a true standard of taste and sentiment….

One obvious cause why many feel not the proper sentiment of beauty, is the want of that delicacy of imagination which is requisite to convey a sensibility of those finer emotions. This delicacy everyone pretends to: everyone talks of it; and would reduce every kind of taste or sentiment to its standard. But … it will be proper to give a more accurate definition of delicacy…. And not to draw our philosophy from too profound a source, we shall have recourse to a noted story in Don Quixote.

It is with good reason, says Sancho … that I pretend to have a judgement in wine: this is a quality hereditary in our family. Two of my kinsmen were once called to give their opinion of a hogshead [barrel of wine], which was supposed to be excellent, being old and of a good vintage. One of them tastes it, considers it; and … pronounces the wine to be good, were it not for a small taste of leather which he perceived in it. The other after using the same precautions, gives also his verdict in favour of the wine; but with the reserve of a taste of iron which he could easily distinguish. You cannot imagine how much they were both ridiculed for their judgement. But who laughed in the end? On emptying the hogshead, there was found at the bottom an old key with a leathern thong tied to it….

But though there be naturally a wide difference … between one person and another, nothing tends further to increase and improve this talent than practice in a particular art…. When objects of any kind are first presented to the eye … the mind is …

incapable of pronouncing concerning their merits or defects.... But allow him to acquire experience in those objects, his feeling becomes more exact and nice: he not only perceives the beauties and defects of each part, but marks the distinguishing species of each quality, and assigns it suitable praise or blame....

It is impossible to continue ... contemplating any order of beauty, without being frequently obliged to form comparisons.... One accustomed to see, and examine, and weigh the several performances admired in different ages and nations, can alone rate the merits of a work....

Thus, though the principles of taste be universal, and nearly ... the same in all men; yet few are qualified to give judgement on any work of art.... The organs of internal sensation are seldom so perfect as to allow the general principles their full play.... When the critic has no delicacy, he judges without any distinction, and is only affected by the grosser and more palpable qualities of the object: the finer touches pass unnoticed and disregarded. Where he is not aided by practice, his verdict is attended with confusion and hesitation. Where no comparison has been employed, the most frivolous beauties ... are the object of his admiration. Where he lies under the influence of prejudice, all his natural sentiments are perverted. Where good sense is wanting, he is not qualified to discern the beauties of design and reasoning.... Under some or other of these imperfections the generality of men labour, and hence a true judge in the finer arts is ... rare....

But where are such critics to be found?...

... Where these doubts occur, men can do no more than in other disputable questions ... they must produce the best arguments that their invention suggests to them; they must acknowledge a true and decisive standard to exist somewhere....

But notwithstanding all our endeavours to fix a standard of taste ... there still remain two sources of variation, which ... will often serve to produce a difference in the degrees of our approbation [approval] or blame. The one is the different humours [characters] of particular men; the other, the particular manners and opinions of our age and country....

A young man, whose passions are warm, will be more ... touched with amorous and tender images, than a man more advanced in years, who takes pleasure in wise, philosophical reflections, concerning the conduct of life.... We choose our favourite author as we do our friend, from a conformity of humour and disposition....

For a like reason, we are more pleased ... with pictures and characters that resemble objects which are found in our own age and country than with those which describe a different set of customs. It is not without some effort that we reconcile ourselves to the simplicity of ancient manners, and behold princesses carrying water from the spring, and kings and heroes dressing their own victuals [provisions]. We may allow in general that the representation of such manners is no fault in the author, nor deformity in the piece; but we are not so sensibly touched with them.

[David Hume, "Of the Standard of Taste," *Four Dissertations* (1757). In *Essays Moral, Political and Literary*, ed. by T .H. Green and T .H. Grose. London: Longmans Green, 1875, Vol. 1, 266–84.]

Immanuel Kant:
Beauty Is Universal

Philosopher Immanuel Kant had firm opinions about aesthetics and the judgement of beauty. Kant believed that any judgement of beauty could not be a rational judgement, because it is based on feelings of pleasure aroused in the viewer. Things beautiful, he wrote, produce a particular form of delight.

To make his argument, Kant contrasted three types of pleasure: the agreeable, the good, and the beautiful. He suggested that the delight we feel in response to each of these pleasures is different. Things that are agreeable, such as food and drink, please us in a sensory way. Kant noted that this pleasure is also experienced by other non-human species. Our pleasure in what is good, such as a well-made machine or an effective social organization, is shaped by what has worth and what is useful. In both cases, this pleasure is based on self-interest. Kant argued that our delight in the beautiful is different from the delight that we derive from either the agreeable or the good.

Kant suggested that one reason why the beautiful differs from both the agreeable and the good is that something can be beautiful without possessing a use or purpose; we may call something beautiful without having any personal interest in it.

Kant also reasoned that although our idea of beauty is a subjective and personal judgement, we make this judgement in a manner that resembles the way others would also make it. This consensus makes the beautiful different from the agreeable and the good, Kant argues, because we expect that others will have different judgements from ours when determining these two concepts. Judgements of what is agreeable, such as good food, vary from one person to another; judgements of what is good, such as a well-made car, will vary as well. Kant believed that when we judge something as beautiful we are proclaiming it beautiful for all. Kant believed that although aesthetic judgements are a subjective process, they also have universal value.

PHILOSOPHERS' FORUM

Critique of Judgement
Immanuel Kant

If we wish to discern whether anything is beautiful or not, we do not [use] … understanding … but … imagination…. The judgement of taste, therefore, is not a cognitive judgement, and so not logical, but is aesthetic—which means that it … cannot be other than subjective…. This denotes nothing in the object, but is a feeling which the subject has of itself and of the manner in which it is affected by the representation….

… Now, where the question is whether something is beautiful, we do not want to know [about] … the real existence of the thing…. All one wants to know is whether the mere representation of the object is to my liking, no matter how indifferent I may be to the real existence of the object of this representation….

[Kant compares the beautiful with the agreeable and the good.]

That is agreeable which the senses find pleasing in sensation…. [It] provokes a desire for similar objects…. Hence we do not merely say of the agreeable that it pleases, but that it gratifies…. Delight in the good is coupled with interest…. To deem something good, I must always know what sort of a thing the object is intended to be, i.e. I must have a concept of it. That is not necessary to enable me to see beauty in a thing. Flowers, free patterns, lines aimlessly intertwining … have no signification … and yet please…. The agreeable, the beautiful and the good thus denote three different relations of representations to the feeling of pleasure and displeasure…. The agreeable is what gratifies a man; the beautiful what simply pleases him; the good what is esteemed (approved)….

As regards the agreeable, everyone concedes that his judgement … is restricted merely to himself personally. Thus he does not take it amiss if, when he says that Canary-wine is agreeable, another corrects the expression and reminds him that he ought to say: It is agreeable to me…. With the agreeable, therefore, the axiom holds good: Every one has his own taste….

The beautiful stands on quite a different footing. It would, on the contrary, be ridiculous if any one who plumed himself on his taste were to think of justifying himself by saying: This object (the building we see, the dress that person has on, the concert we hear, the poem submitted to our criticism) is beautiful for me. For if it merely pleases him, he must not call it beautiful…. [W]hen he puts a thing on a pedestal and calls it beautiful, he demands the same delight from others. He judges not merely for himself, but for all men….

[Immanuel Kant, *Kritik der Urteilskraft* (*Critique of Judgement*, 1790). Trans. by J.C. Meredith. Oxford, UK: Clarendon, 1928, Book 1, Part 1, sect. 1–7, 41–53.]

Ludwig Wittgenstein: Aesthetics Requires Knowledge of the Art and Culture Involved

Twentieth century Austrian philosopher Ludwig Wittgenstein (1889–1951) examined the language we use when we discuss art and the culture with which it is associated. Wittgenstein did not believe it was possible to understand the characteristics and the quality of a work of art without being familiar with its language and associated culture. He wondered how anyone could appreciate and understand prehistoric cave paintings in France, Spain, and India; or classical Greek sculptures; or baroque masterpieces of the eighteenth century without knowing something about how the people during those periods in human history thought, spoke, and behaved.

Wittgenstein also believed that any critical assessment of art is based on a feeling of discomfort and on an individual's personal knowledge of why he or she is feeling that way. According to Wittgenstein, judging or appreciating a work of art, like judging any other product, depends on knowing the criteria upon which such a judgement is made. It is not enough simply to say that one likes or does not like the creation or object; it is necessary to know why. Knowing why involves understanding the culture and knowing what that culture considers to be art.

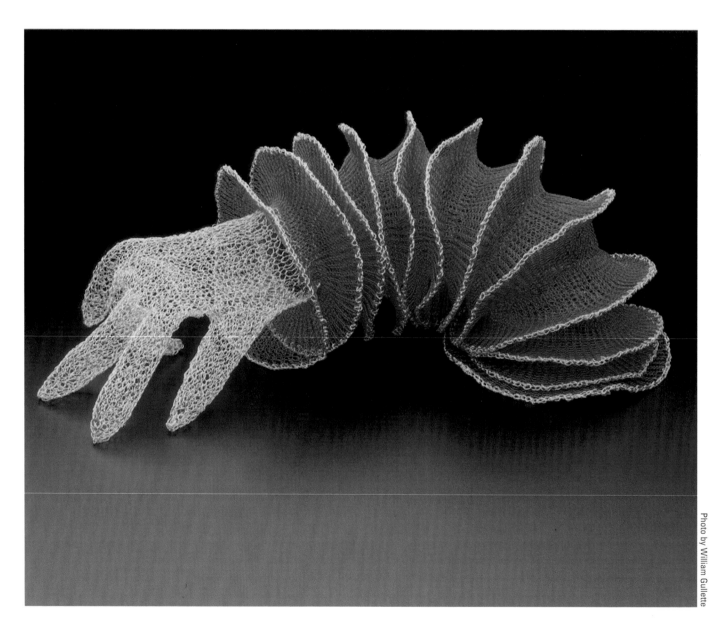

What factors influence our judgement of art, according to Hume, Kant and Wittgenstein? How likely is it to reach an agreement as to what is beautiful? What criteria would you use to judge these pieces of art?

Ludwig Wittgenstein:

The Relationship Between Philosophy and Language

Ludwig Joseph Wittgenstein was one of the most influential philosophers of the twentieth century. Wittgenstein was born in Vienna but went to Cambridge in 1912 to study philosophy with Bertrand Russell. He fought in the Austrian army during World War I. After abandoning philosophy for a decade, he returned to Cambridge where he became Professor of Philosophy in 1939.

Wittgenstein's famous early work *Tractatus Logico-Philosophicus* (1921) discussed the relationship between language and the world. Propositions, statements that describe the world, he wrote, are "pictures" of states of affairs. The truth of more complex propositions depends on how they are constructed out of more elementary propositions. He believed that philosophy can reach no conclusions without such statements.

In his later works, such as *Philosophical Investigations* (1953), Wittgenstein developed a more flexible view of the possible functions of language. He argued that meaning must be understood within the context of social life, and that many philosophic problems are due to conceptual confusions. The role of true philosophy, wrote Wittgenstein, is to free us from the "bewitchment of the intellect by means of language."

Wittgenstein and other analytic philosophers focussed on the analysis of language, turning away from inquiries into metaphysics and other less concrete topics. More recently, however, the trend in philosophy has been to move into wider areas of inquiry, returning to some of the major questions that have puzzled people for centuries.

Lectures on Aesthetics

Ludwig Wittgenstein

… When we make an aesthetic judgement about a thing, we do not just gape at it and say: "Oh! How marvellous!" We distinguish between a person who knows what he is talking about and a person who doesn't. If a person is to admire English poetry, he must know English. Suppose that a Russian who doesn't know English is overwhelmed by a sonnet admitted to be good. We would say that he does not know what is in it at all.… In music this is more pronounced. Suppose there is a person who admires and enjoys what is admitted to be good but can't remember the simplest tunes, doesn't know when the bass comes in, etc. We say he hasn't seen what's in it. We … [do] not … call a man musical if he says "Ah!" when a piece of music is played, any more than we call a dog musical if it wags its tail when music is played.

The word we ought to talk about is "appreciated." What does appreciation consist in? If a man goes through an endless number of patterns in a tailor's and says: "No. This is slightly too dark. This is slightly too loud," etc., he is what we call an appreciator of material. That he is an appreciator is not shown by the interjections he uses, but by the way he chooses, selects, etc. Similarly in music: "Does this harmonize? No. The bass is not quite loud enough. Here I just want something different." …

The words we call expressions of aesthetic judgement play a very complicated role, but a very definite role, in what we call a culture of a period. To describe their use or to describe what you mean by a cultured taste, you have to describe a culture.… An entirely different game is played in different ages.… In describing musical taste you have to describe whether children give concerts, whether women do or whether men only give them.… This is an example of a tradition in music.…

Perhaps the most important thing in connection with aesthetics is what may be called aesthetic reactions, e.g., discontent, disgust, discomfort. The expression of discontent is not the same as the expression of discomfort.… I call an expression of discontent something like an expression of discomfort *plus* knowing the cause of the discomfort and asking for it to be removed.… If I say: "This door is too low. Make it higher," should we say I know the cause of my discomfort?…

There is a "Why?" to aesthetic discomfort, not a "cause" to it. The expression of discomfort takes the form of a criticism and not "My mind is not at rest" or something. It might take the form of looking at a picture and saying "What's wrong with it?"

[Ludwig Wittgenstein, "Lectures on Aesthetics." In *Lectures and Conversations on Aesthetics, Psychology and Religious Belief,* ed. by C. Barrett. Oxford: Blackwell Publishers Ltd., 1978, 6–8, 11–15, 17, 18, 28–30.]

IDEAS AND ISSUES

Understand Concepts

1. What factors influence our judgement of art, according to Hume?
2. (a) How does Kant categorize all things in the world?
   (b) What characteristics does each of these categories of the world have?
3. What is Wittgenstein's central idea in his excerpt?
4. What is central to making a judgement about a work of art, according to Wittgenstein?

Apply and Develop

5. Apply Hume's criteria for making a judgement to an artistic activity with which you are involved, or a field you know something about. For example, how would you and Hume determine whether someone was a good judge of music, dance, fashion, or photography?

Think Critically

6. How does Wittgenstein's theory differ from Bell's concept of art and its appreciation? With which philosopher do you agree?
7. Hume used the example of those works of art that have stood the test of time to indicate that there are standards of taste and beauty that go beyond the individual or culture. What argument can be made against this point?
8. Respond to Kant's view of the beautiful. Are there elements of his position with which you disagree?
9. Compare ideas of the beautiful put forward by both Kant and Hume. With which do you agree? Why?
10. Does aesthetic judgement have constant standards over time? What would Hume and Wittgenstein say?
11. Do you believe that good art, in whatever form, will always be respected, or do you think it depends on the time period and culture?

Communicate Ideas

12. Choose what you consider to be the best examples of your favourite music. Play these to the rest of the class. Explain why you think these are good pieces of music. How do others judge these examples?
13. Debate this issue: One can appreciate and judge a work of art without knowing anything about the culture within which it was produced.
14. Use a panel discussion to present and defend the aesthetic views of Tolstoy, Bell, and Wittgenstein. Use paintings and other illustrations to support your position. Have the class judge, through private ballot, which position is most convincing. Discuss why.

Inquire and Research

15. Choose several examples of recognized art from an art history book. Can the same standards be used to judge each of these works of art? To what degree is it necessary to understand the time and culture to truly appreciate the particular works of art?

Review and Reflect

Questions about art and aesthetics have fascinated humans since the beginning of our history. Artists have used various media to communicate their ideas, emotions, and perceptions about themselves and the world around them. Though representing beauty was, and continues to be, important for many artists, art does not need to be beautiful in order to be a masterpiece.

Many philosophers, art critics, and others have put forward several ideas about art, such as what makes something a work of art, and how art should be judged. The significance and impact of art can be felt all around us even today. However, mass media commercials and ads and the overwhelming number of cheap imitation goods have made us reconsider our ideas about what makes something truly a work of art, how art should be judged, and the purpose that art serves.

All of us encounter art and aesthetics regularly in our everyday lives. We look at a painting or watch a movie, and find the experience interesting, boring, creative, or predictable. We listen to music or evaluate an article of clothing, and decide if we like it and want to include it in our lives. We are constantly making judgements about beauty and aesthetics, though sometimes we do not agree with the opinions of others. There is no doubt that art makes the world a much more interesting place for all of us.

C H A P T E R   1 6

Philosophies of Life

At one time or another, most of us have asked ourselves these two important questions: How should I live my life and what is my life's meaning or purpose? Philosophers both ancient and modern have also wondered about these two

issues. Friedrich Nietzsche believed that once we figured out the purpose of our lives, we could endure almost anything: "He who has a why to live can bear almost any how." Viktor Frankl believed that "man's concern about a meaning of life is the truest expression of the state of being human." And, of course, Socrates felt that an "unexamined life was not worth living."

Each of us must develop our own unique view of life and its meaning. It is, after all, our life. No one can live it for us. Nonetheless, it is often helpful to consider the life philosophies of others when pondering such immense issues. These alternative perspectives may provide us with new ideas to consider and avenues to explore. At the very least, they can show us paths we definitely do not want to pursue.

As you read the material, try to keep an open mind about the various views being presented. Try to determine the starting point of each of these philosophies. Which ones see the individual as the central piece in the quest for meaning and fulfillment? Which see society as playing a crucial role in determining life's meaning, and which look to a higher consciousness in order to find meaning and purpose in life? Which of the views presented most closely resembles your own? Which would you argue has the least significance to you as you embark on your own exploration of the meaning of life?

Each of us must determine our own view of the meaning of life, although it never hurts to find out what others have said about the issue before we embark on such an onerus quest.

Starting Points
For a Philosophy of Life

How should we live life in the best possible way? All of us must deal with this question. How should we behave during our lives? How should we act towards others? How should we expect others to act towards us? Do we live life for maximum personal enjoyment, do we live life because we want to do good for others, or do we live life for some other purpose? Do we participate seriously in the events of our lives, do we try to change things, or do we view what happens in the world around us with acceptance or resignation? Along with the "how" of life's meaning, we must also address the "why." *Why* do I live my life in one way or another? *Why* should I choose one option and not another?

There are several starting points for this inquiry. Some people begin by examining human nature. Others believe that an awareness and understanding of human society is the crucial place to start. Still others begin their inquiry by moving beyond human experience to study the universe as a whole. When we study human behaviour, we turn our attention inward, to those mental or physical traits that shape our human capacities and, ultimately, our lifestyles. If, for example, we believe humans are intrinsically selfish and will always act in their own best interests, that outlook will affect our approach to life. If we believe that humans are capable of making important decisions, of directing their destinies, and of adapting to a wide variety of situations, we will hold a different view of the meaning of life.

Life philosophies can also be determined by examining the kinds of society in which we live. Society provides us all with opportunities and restrictions, both of which can determine how we answer the question of life's meaning. If we are born into slavery or dire poverty the meaning we give our lives will be quite different than the meaning given by those born to wealth and privilege. Furthermore, some people view social or economic success as life's ultimate goal; others believe that cooperation and community are the most rewarding aspects of human existence, while still others see personal fulfillment of one kind or another as the meaning of life.

Some people search for the meaning of life on a broader, more cosmic scale—one well beyond the here and now of our present existence. People who begin their inquiries using this frame of reference ask if there is some purpose to the universe as a whole, some grand design which transcends human existence. Is there meaning beyond our limited understanding of the universe, they ask; beyond the time and space that shape our lives? If, however, a person believes that events in the universe occur at random, he or she is more apt to live by a different set of rules.

Are we, as human beings, able to develop answers to the question of life's meaning by examining our own human experiences, and the experiences of human society? Are we able to establish a higher purpose to life than our mortal term on earth? What does each of these starting points for discovering life's purpose suggest about how life should be lived? As you read about how other philosophers and teachers have addressed this question, try to determine the starting point for each viewpoint, whether it be human nature, society or the universe as a whole. Ask yourself how each thinker proposes that life should be lived, and why.

There are several ways to begin the process of inquiry regarding what is the meaning of life. Some people look to human nature, others believe that society determines destiny and still others look beyond human experience for the answer.

Meaning and Virtue

Many philosophers have suggested that practising personal virtue is the only way to create meaning and order in our lives. These philosophers believe that the universe is split between a natural or material world and a spiritual or cosmic one. Humans are the only beings who are connected to both worlds. Our senses and instincts connect us to the material or natural world. Our ability to reason, to think analytically and rationally about the world around us, connects us to the divine.

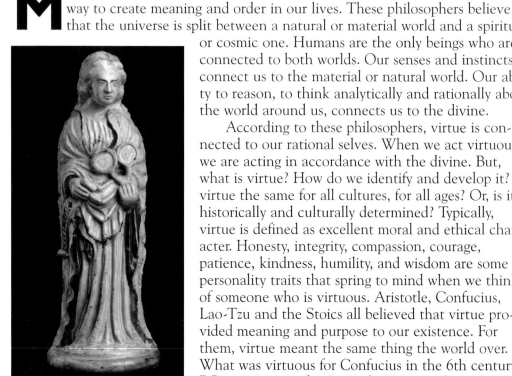

Some philosophers, like the Stoics, argued that we must accept life's vicissitudes with resignation and grace, since we were incapable of altering them.

According to these philosophers, virtue is connected to our rational selves. When we act virtuously we are acting in accordance with the divine. But, what is virtue? How do we identify and develop it? Is virtue the same for all cultures, for all ages? Or, is it historically and culturally determined? Typically, virtue is defined as excellent moral and ethical character. Honesty, integrity, compassion, courage, patience, kindness, humility, and wisdom are some personality traits that spring to mind when we think of someone who is virtuous. Aristotle, Confucius, Lao-Tzu and the Stoics all believed that virtue provided meaning and purpose to our existence. For them, virtue meant the same thing the world over. What was virtuous for Confucius in the 6th century BC was virtuous for Aristotle 300 years later. It wasn't until the twentieth century that the concept of virtue became something that was questioned by thinkers and philosophers. The radical nineteenth-century genius, Friedrich Nietzsche, for example, turned the definition of virtue on its head. Nietzsche redefined virtue to fit his own philosophic position. For him, a virtuous person was one who possessed character traits hitherto regarded as negative and undesirable. Instead of humility, patience, temperance and modesty, Nietzsche celebrated courage, power, arrogance and determination.

Confucius and Lao-Tzu

Confucius and Lao-Tzu were two early champions of the idea that a virtuous life was a meaningful one. These two acclaimed Chinese philosophers lived during a period of Chinese history called the Spring and Autumn Age (871-473BC). During this time, the principalities that made up China rose up against one another and refused to pay homage to the Chou King. These rulers proclaimed their states independent nations and themselves independent sovereigns. They each wanted to unify China and become its new leader. During the strife and chaos that followed, the social, political, moral and spiritual orders of China were destroyed. There seemed to be little hope that the fighting and confusion would ever end. But, out of the darkness and despair of this period grew a class of educated men. Confucius and Lao-Tzu were two such scholars. Both these brilliant philosophers offered a way out of the despair and madness of war-torn China. Both argued that virtuous behaviour was what was needed to provide order and meaning to existence.

Confucius prescribed a return to the traditional way of life—a life based on ritual and decorum. He created a practical system of behaviour from what had previously been religious codes of conduct. For Confucius, the way to make meaning out of life was to strive for perfection of character. Confucius believed that we should all strive to become *chun tzu*, noble or virtuous people. To do so, we must adhere to strict moral guidelines. For one, we must practice *jen*, the love of our fellow beings, benevolence. For Confucius, *jen* and *ching*, reverence for those in positions above you, are the most important qualities or virtues. They are achieved by following the middle way of balance and harmony and by applying the Golden Rule: "Do not impose on others what you yourself do not desire." We must also practice *chih*, wisdom, which is the ability to recognize right from wrong. Confucius thought we were born with some natural wisdom, but that we could gain greater wisdom through study. He believed that knowing right from wrong meant having the ability to judge the character of others. It also meant having curiosity about the world around you. And, more importantly, wisdom meant humility—a central characteristic of a virtuous person.

Lao-Tzu's approach to living virtuously was very different than Confucius's. Confu-

Confucius and Lao-Tzu offered differing philosophies of life to their respective adherents. Confucius called for a return to the traditional rituals and customs, while Lao-Tzu asked that we live in complete harmony with the natural world and that we simply follow the path of Tao

cius's ideal character displayed high moral qualities in all his or her social interactions, Lao-Tzu's, on the other hand, was spontaneous and childlike. While Confucius described a hierarchical world where the virtuous must adhere to the social etiquette prescribed by his or her social position, the world for Lao-Tzu is cyclical and interconnected. His ideal person possesses a different kind of virtue. This person lives in complete harmony with the natural world, effortlessly and spontaneously following the way of the Tao.

As the ultimate principle guiding Lao-Tzu's philosophy, "Tao" is not simply a path that one can follow, it is also the fundamental principle of the universe. It has sometimes been called the way of Heaven. As the ultimate reality, the Tao is impossible to define.

As a thing the way is
Shadowy, indistinct.

Indistinct and shadowy,
Yet within it is an image;
Shadowy and indistinct,
Yet within it is a substance.
Dim and dark,
Yet within it is an essence.
This essence is quite genuine
And within it is something that can be tested.
(XXI.49)

Although it is impossible to fully grasp the complete meaning and importance of the Tao, we can find it in the form of '*te,*' virtue and moral purity, as well as the power that attends such excellence. For Lao-Tzu, moral and virtuous purity can only be achieved when a person gives up or abandons any preconceived notions of selfhood. A true person of Tao is not even conscious of living and acting morally. Rather, the principles of right and wrong, goodness and evil, have become part of his or her nature.

Stoicism

Virtue is also a central part of the philosophy of Stoicism. For the Stoics, a fulfilled, meaningful life is one in which its inhabitants accept what happens to them with humility and grace. The Stoics believed that living according to Nature was the way to find meaning and happiness in life. All reality was governed and ordered by a divine force, which they called Nature. Since we cannot begin to know the intricate workings of this force, the Stoics argued, we must accept that many things will happen in life that we cannot understand or change. For the Stoics, to be free was to accept these external forces—to accept, in other words, Fate. Trying to change what we cannot control only leads to strife and frus-tration. Acceptance and surrender, by contrast, lead to a life of tranquility and peace. Seneca, a peer of the philosopher Cicero, describes it this way: "The one alleviation for overwhelming evils is to endure and bow to necessity."

Reason plays an important role in the Stoic's worldview. For them, the universe is a rational whole. Humans are connected to this natural force because we have the ability to reason. Each of us must follow the rational will of the universe and live in conformity with it. It is through reason, moreover, that we are able to know these universal laws.

The Stoics believed in four cardinal virtues: reason, courage, justice and self-

Although the Stoics advocated an acceptance of life's circumstances, they did not believe that one could withdraw from the world and refuse to take action and make decisions

discipline. Another important virtue was moral duty. This meant doing the most rational thing possible in accordance with the laws of nature. The Stoics advocated indifference to our material successes and failures. Instead, we must practice *apatheia*, immunity from feeling. We must, in other words, be indifferent to health, wealth, status and power. When we become ill, for example, we must recognize the necessary part of this illness in the larger scheme of things, even if we do not understand it.

This acceptance of life's circumstances did not mean that the Stoics could withdraw from the world and refuse to take action or make decisions. On the contrary, the Stoics believed that wise individuals would expend every effort to do what is right in any given situation. They preferred health and wealth to sickness and poverty and believed such positive goals should be actively pursued as long as this pursuit did not harm others. The actual achievement of health and wealth as a result of human effort was, according to Stoic philosophy, beyond human control.

Epictetus, in his *Discourses and Manual*, sums up the philosophy of Stoicism when he writes:

"....When we are hindered, or disturbed, or distressed, let us never lay the blame on others, but on...our own judgements. To accuse others for one's own misfortune is a sign of want of education, to accuse oneself shows that one's education has begun; to accuse neither oneself nor other's shows that one's education is complete." (reprinted with permission from Epictetus. *The Discourses and Manual*. Translated by P.E. Matheson (1916). Oxford: Oxford University Press.)

Unlike the Epicureans, the Stoics did not teach withdrawal and inaction. Their schooling did not occur in a quiet garden, but front and centre, on the front porch, or *stoa*, in the Athenian city centre. The Stoics', involvement in society was one reason why this philosophy was widely accepted by the governing classes of Rome.

Relationships and the Meaning of Life

Not everyone believes that practising virtue is the only way to find meaning and fulfillment in life. Some people have argued that we also need social interaction to find satisfaction and purpose. "No man is an island," as John Donne, seventeenth-century metaphysical poet, so eloquently put it. Rather, we are all interconnected in an intricate web of life. Some philosophers have argued that building relationships with others is essential for personal fulfillment and for a meaningful life. Without this feeling of connection afforded by social interaction, we would all be lost and unfulfilled, isolated and alone. Our relationships with others show that we are part of a bigger world—part of a wider community. Other philosophers, however, have argued just the opposite. Some, like Soren Kierkegaard and Carl Rogers believe that it is our relationship with ourselves that determines our ultimate fulfillment. For Kierkegaard, the challenge of life is to live consciously as an individual. "To thine own self be true," is one of Kierkegaard's most often used quotation.

Martin Buber

Martin Buber, a twentieth-century metaphysical philosopher, believed that it is only through authentic relationships with others that we are able to give meaning and purpose to our existence. There are two ways of looking at the world, according to Buber. Some people have a completely objective view of their environment. They see the world as events, circumstances and people that exist outside and apart from themselves. These people see themselves as fully independent and autonomous beings. Philosophers like Soren Kierkegaard and Carl Rogers share this view of the separate and detached individual. They base their philosophic arguments on the assumption that we are all individual and unique. Buber believes that this type of thinking, though common, leads to a life devoid of meaning— a life of isolation and emptiness. He offers an alternative way of perceiving the world around us as well as our relationship to it.

Martin Buber argued that genuine conversations with others are what will ultimately provided our lives with meaning.

Buber argues that true relationships with others will lead to a greater understanding of ourselves, each other and the divine. Rather than watching others like they are characters in a television show, we must feel what others feel, experience what others experience, live how others live, albeit only in our imaginations. This type of perception calls for a deep identification and connection to the people and events around us. To achieve this type of deep connection with the world and others around us, we must engage in what Buber calls "human effective dialogue," a listening and responding to each other at a level deeper than just words: "Meaning by dialogue is not just talking. Dialogue can be silence…we could sit together, or rather walk together in silence and that could be a dialogue." This type of communication requires an openness from everyone involved. It also requires complete acceptance of the other person.

In the following excerpt from his classic work *I and Thou*, Buber explores how our relationships with others provide us with a sense of community and purpose in life. As you read the selection, ask yourself why open dialogue with others is so important to Buber? What are some of the consequences of open dialogue? What are some of the ways we block open dialogue with others?

I and Thou

Martin Buber

To man the world is twofold, in accordance with his twofold attitude. He perceives what exists round about him —simply things, and beings as things; and what happens round about him—simply events, and actions as events; things consisting of qualities, events of moments; things entered in the graph of place, events in that of time; things and events bounded by other things and events, measured by them, comparable with them: he perceives an ordered and detached world. It is to some extent a reliable world, having density and duration. Its organization can be surveyed and brought out again and again; gone over with closed eyes, and verified with open eyes. It is always there, next to your skin, if you look at it that way, cowering in your soul, if you prefer it so. It is your object, remains it as long as you wish, and remains a total stranger, within you and without. You perceive it, take it to yourself as the "truth," and it lets itself be taken; but it does not give itself to you. Only concerning it may you make yourself "understood" with others; it is ready, though attached to everyone in a different way, to be an object common to you all. But you cannot meet others in it. You cannot hold on to life without it, its reliability sustains you; but should you die in it, your grave would be in nothingness.

Or, on the other hand, man meets what exists and becomes as what is over against him, always simply a single being and each thing simply as being. What exists is opened to him in happenings, and what happens affects him as what is. Nothing is present for him except this one being, but it implicates the whole world. Measure and comparison have disappeared; it lies with yourself how much of the immeasurable becomes reality for you. These meetings are not organized to make the world, but each is a sign of the world-order. They are not linked up with one another, but each assures you of your solidarity with the world. The world which appears to you in this way is unreliable, for it takes on a continually new appearance; you cannot hold it to its word. It has no density, for everything in it penetrates everything else; no duration, for it comes even when it is not summoned, and vanishes even when it is tightly held. It cannot be surveyed, and if you wish to make it capable of survey you lose it. It comes, and comes to bring you out; if it does not reach you, meet you, then it vanishes; but it comes back in another form. It is not outside you, it stirs the depths of you; if you say "Soul of my soul" you have not said too much. But guard against wishing to remove it into your soul—for then you annihilate it. It is your present; only while you have it do you have the present. You can make it into an object for yourself, to experience and to use; you must continually do this—and as you do it you have no more present. Between you and it there is mutual giving: you say Thou to it and give yourself to it, it says Thou to you and gives itself to you. You cannot make yourself understood with others concerning it, you are alone with it. But is teaches you to meet others, and to hold your ground when you meet them. Through the graciousness of its coming and the solemn sadness of its goings it leads you away to the Thou in which the parallel lines of relations meet. It does not help to sustain you in life, it only helps you to glimpse eternity.

(reprinted from Martin Buber, *I and Thou* (New York: Charles Scribner's Sons, 1970) 31-33)

Soren Kierkegaard and the Authentic Self

Soren Kierkegaard offers a different answer to the question "what is the meaning of life?". Unlike Buber, Kierkegaard believes that the answer lies not in our external relationships, but rather in our internal ones. For Kierkegaard, society and community—though necessary human endeavours—will ultimately lead an individual away from his or her true purpose in life. Instead of looking outward to our communities in order to find fulfillment, we must look within the individual to find that meaning or order so necessary to a happy and productive life.

For Kierkegaard, the challenge of life is to exist consciously as an individual—to be, in other words, aware of the choices we make and to take responsibility for the actions we take. Every person must make decisions and take action in a way that is *authentic* to that individual alone. Our families, friends, communities and churches are not responsible for who we are or for how we live our lives. We must accept that responsibility for ourselves. Living a meaningful life means being conscious of one's unique existence, and accepting as truth one's own set of values and beliefs.

Kierkegaard believed that there are two ways of existing in the world. We can either forget that we are, what he called, "existing" individuals, by which he meant aware and responsible for our choices and actions. Or, we can fully accept that we alone are responsible for our destinies. When we accept complete responsibility for our actions and choices, we become completely independent. Such freedom, however, can be terrifying. Very few people can achieve it. Kierkegaard calls those who do "knights of faith." Most of us are filled with dread and despair when faced with a life of conscious existing, when faced with the challenge of accepting responsibility for all our actions. But why is freedom frightening rather than liberating? Why are we filled with dread at the prospect of a life based on total independence of thought and action?

According to Kierkegaard, when we consciously choose one alternative over another, we must, by the very nature of being self-conscious, also be aware of other choices and the possibilities associated with those alternatives. As a result, we can always doubt that what we chose was best. Furthermore, since we alone define our existence—since truth is subjective—we have no one to depend on for guidance. We must make decisions and choices completely on our own. No one else can help us choose what is best for us. It is precisely this doubt and vulnerabil-ity that Kierkegaard says fill us with dread.

According to Kierkegaard there are three ways we can choose to live our lives— three stages of conscious living. The first, which he calls the aesthetic life, consists of a life dominated by worldly concerns. This is an absent-minded existence. Next comes the ethical life. Here a person is committed to duty, to getting married, taking care of children, charitable work. An ethical life is a responsible life. Finally, for Kierkegaard, comes the religious life—the highest stage of self-consciousness. It is here that a person accepts the absurdity of life and takes what Kierkegaard calls a "leap of faith" to acknowledge a belief in God. Without God, life would ultimately be meaningless. Even though Kierkegaard believes that we must all follow our own paths and live a life in accordance with our authentic selves, he also believes that we must ultimately find fulfillment and purpose in a direct relationship with God.

Kierkegaard believed that we are each responsible for finding our own paths and for being true to our authentic desires and wishes.

Carl Rogers and Self-Actualization

Carl Rogers offers a slightly different perspective than either Martin Buber or Soren Kierkegaard. Like Kierkegaard, Rogers is an existentialist. He believes that each person must determine for his or herself the purpose and meaning of life. Rogers, however, does not depend on a religious or spiritual relationship with God to find meaning and a purpose to life. Rather, Rogers believes that being alone is the only way to fulfill our unique destinies. Rogers argues that we all have a built-in drive to develop our potential to its fullest. Called the "actualizing tendency," this drive is the force behind our need for air, water and food, as well as our desire for love, safety and respect. It is also the motivation behind our drive to cure the world of disease, solve today's scientific mysteries or create a modern masterpiece. For Rogers, all living creatures share this biological imperative to be the best that they can be. A meaningful life, for Rogers, is one in which we are each able to cultivate ourselves to our full potentials.

Rogers believes that every organism instinctively knows what is good and necessary for it to reach its actualizing potential. According to Rogers, we all instinctively value such things as love, affection, nurturance, and attention. Recent psychological studies have demonstrated that babies who are not given the love, caring and attention they need, fail to thrive and to develop at a normal rate. Often, this developmental lag can never be overcome. Rogers calls this instinctive desire for love and attention, "positive regard." As a species, we also naturally value self-esteem, self-worth and a positive self-image. Called "positive self regard," we achieve this healthy psychological state by growing up in an environment that is happy, nurturing, and lavish in love and affection.

Sometimes, however, as we are growing up, parents, teachers, friends and acquaintances—not to mention the media—give us love and attention only when we behave in

Carl Rogers believes that we experience positive self regard if we are shown love, caring, nurturance and attention as infants. Recent studies have shown that babies who are denied this basic human interaction suffer developmental delays and fail to thrive at a normal rate.

a way in which they want us to behave. We are given dessert after we have eaten all our vegetables, for example, given permission to play outside after our homework is done or, more importantly, receive love and affection after we behave in an appropriate manner. Rogers calls these conditions, "conditions of worth." When we receive attention because we have behaved in a way our parents or our society deem worthy of positive feedback, we eventually bend our shape to fit what society wants us to be, rather than allow our instincts and drives—our own actualizing tendencies—

to shape our personalities and our lives. A meaningful life, according to Rogers, is one in which we can ignore or overcome the conditions that society puts upon us and follow the drives and desires of our hearts.

In the following selection Carl Rogers discusses his view of the purpose and meaning of life. As you read along, try to identify some of the limitations and restrictions you have experienced that might have thwarted your efforts toward self-actualization? What are some future restrictions you might envision?

To Be The Self Which One Truly Is

Carl Rogers

Another View

… As I watch person after person struggle in his therapy hours to find a way of life for himself, there seems to be a general pattern emerging … . The best way I can state this aim of life … is to use the words of Soren Kierkegaard— "to be that self which one truly is." … What does it mean? …

Away from Facades

… [C]haracteristically the client shows a tendency to move away…from a self that he is *not* … . And of course in so doing he is beginning to define, however negatively, what he is.

At first this may be expressed simply as a fear of exposing what he is. Thus one eighteen-year-old boy says … "I know I'm not so hot, and I'm afraid they'll find it out … . I'm not going to tell you the person I really think I am … ."

It will be clear that the very expression of this fear is a part of becoming what he is. Instead of simply being a facade, [false front] … he is coming closer to being himself, namely a frightened person hiding behind a facade because he regards himself as too awful to be seen.

Away from Meeting Expectations

Other clients find themselves moving away from what the culture expects them to be … . [T]here are enormous pressures to … be fully a member of the group, … to fit into the group needs … .

… I find that when clients are free to be any way they wish, they tend to resent and to question the tendency of the organization, the college or the culture to mould them to any given form. One of my clients says with considerable heat: "I've been so long trying to live according to what was meaningful to other people, and what made no sense at *all* to me … ."

I find that many individuals have formed themselves by trying to please others, but again, when they are free, they move away from being this person. So one … writes, toward the end of therapy: "I finally felt that I simply *had* to begin doing what I *wanted* to do, not what I thought I *should* do, and regardless of what other people feel I *should* do … .

Toward Openness to Experience

"To be that self which one truly is" … the individual moves toward living in an open, friendly, close relationship to his own experience … . As one client says with some shock after experiencing the dependent, small boy aspect of himself, 'That's an emotion I've never felt clearly—one that I've never been!" … .

Toward Trust of Self

Still another way of describing this pattern which I see in each client is to say that increasingly he trusts and values the process which is himself. Watching my clients, I have come to a much better understanding of creative people. El Greco, for example, must have realized as he looked at some of his early work, that "good artists do not paint like that." But somehow he trusted his own experiencing of life … sufficiently that he could go on expressing his own unique perceptions. It was as though he could say, "Good artists do not paint like this, but I paint like this." … Time and again in my clients, I have seen simple people become significant and creative in their own spheres, as they have developed more trust of the processes going on within themselves, and have dared to feel their own feelings, live by values which they discover within, and express themselves in their own unique ways.

The General Direction

… One client … asks himself: "You mean if I'd really be what I feel like being, that that would be all right?" … . To be what he truly is, this is the path of life which he appears to value most highly, when he is free to move in any direction. It is not simply an intellectual value choice, but seems to be the best description of the groping, tentative, uncertain behaviours by which he moves exploringly toward what he wants to be.

Reprinted from Carl Rogers, "To Be the Self Which One Truly Is." from *The Philosophical Quest: A Cross-Cultural Reader*, 2nd Ed., Gail M Presbey, Karsten J. Struhl and Richard Olsen. New York: McGraw Hill, 2000.

Understand Concepts

1. (a) What two important questions are involved in the topic "philosophies of life"?
    (b) How do these questions refer to distinct, yet related, aspects of developing a philosophy of life?
2. (a) Identify the essential characteristics of a meaningful life, according to Confucius and Lao-Tzu.
    (b) In what ways are these two views similar; in what ways are they different?
3. Identify the attitudes and actions that a Stoic would advocate for living life well. What reasons did Stoicism give for living life this way?
4. Martin Buber describes two ways of dealing with the people and events in our lives. Identify and briefly describe these two ways.
5. Summarize Soren Kierkegaard's views on how to live one's life. Identify his main idea and the major elements of his philosophy.

Apply and Develop

6. How would you answer the two questions that are involved in developing a "philosophy of life"?
7. In practical terms, what attitudes does Buber believe we should have in our relationships with others?

Think Critically

8. (Respond to the following statements by agreeing or disagreeing, and giving your reasons.
    (a) "Man's concern about a meaning of life is the truest expression of being human" (Viktor Frankl).
    (b) "The unexamined life is not worth living" (Socrates).
9. Compare the forms of existentialism held by Kierkegaard and Rogers. Indicate ways in which they agree, and ways in which they disagree.

Inquire and Research

10. Find out more about one of these philosophers by reading a brief biography, and reading selections from one of their books, for example Martin Buber, *I and Thou*; Soren Kierkegaard *Either/Or*; or Carl Rogers, *On Becoming a Person*.

Man's Search For Meaning

Life is scary. That's no excuse for not living.

Lori Villamil

Many twentieth-century philosophers have used Kierkegaard's existential theories as a starting point for their own philosophical reflections. Two such philosophers are Viktor Frankl and Thomas Nagel. Both Nagel and Frankl depend heavily on Kierkegaard, yet both diverge at different points of Kierkegaard's claims. As you read further, see if you can determine which of Frankl's and Nagel's points are most similar to Kierkegaard's and which are clearly unrelated or opposed.

Logotherapy: The Search for Meaning As Therapy

Viktor Frankl shares Rogers's psychological approach to determining what gives life meaning and purpose. Unlike Rogers, however, who believes that self-actualization is the primary motivational force behind all human activity, Frankl argues that it is a need to find meaning and purpose in our lives that drives all our actions. Imprisoned in Nazi concentration camps during the Second World War, Frankl witnessed firsthand just how destructive and brutal life can be at times. His mother, father, brother and wife were all killed by the Nazis in these death camps. Frankl, however, survived.

A practising psychologist in Germany during the 1930's, Frankl had been working on a theory of man's search for meaning before being imprisoned by the Nazis. His experiences in the concentration camps helped solidify his earlier philosophical position. In the concentration camp, Frankl writes, "it seemed to me that I would die in the near future. In this critical situation, however, my concern was different from that of most of my comrades. Their question was, 'Will we survive the camp? For, if not, all this suffering has no meaning.' The question which beset me was, 'Has all this suffering, this dying around us, a meaning?' For, if not, then ultimately there is no meaning to survival; for a life whose meaning depends upon such a happenstance—as whether one escapes or not—ultimately would not be worth living at all."

Frankl discovered that the suffering and despair he saw around him hour after hour, day after day, did indeed have a meaning. He realized that those prisoners who had a will to live—who had a reason to get up in the morning—were the ones who could

Is there meaning even in hopeless situations, according to Frankl? How can that be?

Life begins on the other side of despair.

Jean-Paul Sartre

keep going despite the horror and despair around them. "We who lived in the concentration camps," he said, "can remember the men who walked through the huts comforting others, giving away their last piece of bread. They may have been few in number, but they offer sufficient proof that anything can be taken from a man but one thing: the last of the human freedoms—to choose one's attitude in any given set of circumstances, to choose one's own way."

From these observations and experiences, Frankl developed a revolutionary approach to psychotherapy. Called logotherapy, Frankl's therapy helps people uncover the meaning in life, regardless of how dismal or depressing their circumstances may be. As Frankl explains, "a man who becomes conscious of the responsibility he bears toward a human being who affectionately waits for him, or to an unfinished work, will never be able to throw away his life. He knows the 'why' for his existence, and will be able to bear almost any 'how'."

In the following selection from his book, *Man's Search for Meaning*, Frankl discusses our limitless ability to find meaning in life despite the frequency with which we experience both tragedy and grief. Like both the Stoics and the existentialists, Frankl ultimately argues that although we must live in a world that is often tragic and distressing, we must all learn from the suffering we experience and observe around us. As Friedrich Nietzsche once put it "that which does not kill us makes us stronger."

> People in the West are always getting ready to live.
> *Chinese Proverb*

Man's Search For Meaning

Viktor Frankl

Let us first ask ourselves what should be understood by ' a Tragic Optimism.' In brief it means that one is, and remains, optimistic in spite of the 'tragic triad,' as it is called in logotherapy, a triad which consists of those aspects of human existence which may be circumscribed by: 1) pain; 2) guilt; and 3) death. This chapter in fact raises the question, How is it possible to say yes to life in spite of all that? How, to pose the question differently, can life retain its potential meaning in spite of its tragic aspects? After all, 'saying yes to life in spite of everything' … .presupposes that life is potentially meaningful under any conditions, even those which are most miserable. And this in turn presupposes the human capacity to creatively turn life's negative aspects into something more positive or constructive. In other words, what matters is to make the best of any given situation. "The best," however, is that which in Latin is called optimism—hence the reason I speak of tragic optimism, that is, an optimism in the face of tragedy and in view of the human potential which at its best always allows for: (1) turning suffering into human achievement and accomplishment; (2) deriving from guilt the opportunity to change oneself for the better; and (3) deriving from life's transitoriness an incentive to take responsible action.

Viktor Frankl. *Man's Search for Meaning*. Boston: Beacon Press, 1992. p139-40)

> Life is ours to be spent not saved.
> *D.H. Lawrence*

Is Human Existence Absurd?

Most of us take our lives quite seriously. We plot and plan what we will do in any given circumstance; we experience intense joy and pain over life's victories and defeats; we look back at our lives with a mixture of pleasure and regret. We generally think and act with the conviction that our own lives, and the lives of the people around us, have importance and significance in the larger scheme of things. For most of us, living is serious business—a labour of love, if you will.

There are times, however, when we look at the scope of the universe, its eternal and infinite structure, and see the limitations of our own lives in comparison. Sometimes we may even look at the effort and energy we put into things and recognize that they might have been pointless, that in the end our efforts might have little or no impact. Some have taken this gap between what we strive to achieve and what these achievements actually mean in the larger scheme of things as proof that life is absurd.

Thomas Nagel, for example, investigates the question of life's absurdity. He defines absurdity as the discrepancy between what we want to achieve and the reality of any given situation: "In ordinary life a situation is absurd when it includes a conspicuous discrepancy between pretension or aspiration and reality....you declare your love over the telephone to a recorded message; as you are being knighted, your pants fall down."

The essence of absurdity, says Nagel, is our human ability to step outside our own selves, and to see ourselves from the point of view of someone outside our own skins. This self-consciousness is what makes us able to see the gap between our life struggle and the universal picture. Contrary to what you may expect, Nagel offers a positive take on the absurdity of life

In the following selection from his book, *Mortal Questions*, Thomas Nagel discusses his views on the absurdity of life. When you read the excerpt ask yourself about your own life. Do your expectations about what is going to happen always coincide with the reality of a given situation?

PHILOSOPHERS' FORUM

The Absurd

Thomas Nagel

We cannot live human lives without energy and attention, nor without making choices which show that we take some things more seriously than others. Yet we have always available a point of view outside the particular form of our lives, from which the seriousness appears gratuitous. These two inescapable viewpoints collide in us, and that is what makes life absurd ... .

We take ourselves seriously whether we lead serious lives or not and whether we are concerned primarily with fame, pleasure, virtues, luxury, triumph, beauty, justice, knowledge, salvation, or mere survival … . Think of how an ordinary individual sweats over his appearance, his health, his sex life, his emotional honesty, his social utility, his self-knowledge, the quality of his ties with family, colleagues, and friends, how well he does his job … . Leading a human life is a full-time occupation, to which everyone devotes decades of intense concern.

… Yet humans have the special capacity to step back and survey themselves, and their lives to which they are committed, with that detached amazement which comes from watching an ant struggle up a heap of sand … . [T]he view is at once sobering and comical.

… We see ourselves from outside … . Yet when we take this view and recognize what we do as arbitrary, it does not disengage us from life, and there lies our absurdity, not in the fact that such an external view can be taken of us, but in the fact that we ourselves can take it … .

One may try to escape the position by seeking broader ultimate concerns, … the idea being that absurdity results because what we take seriously is something small and insignificant and individual. Those seeking to supply their lives with meaning usually envision a role or function in something larger than themselves. They therefore seek fulfillment in service to society, the state, the revolution, the progress of history, the advance of science, or religion and the glory of God … .

Why is the life of a mouse not absurd? The orbit of the moon is not absurd either, but that involves no strivings or aims at all. A mouse, however, has to work to stay alive. Yet he is not absurd, because he lacks the capacities for self-consciousness and self-transcendence that would enable him to see that he is only a mouse. If that did happen, his life would become absurd, since self-awareness would not make him cease to be a mouse and would not enable him to rise above his mousely strivings. Bringing his new-found self-consciousness with him, he would have to return to his meager yet frantic life, full of doubts that he was unable to answer, but also full of purposes that he was unable to abandon … .

… [I]t would be wise to consider carefully whether the absurdity of our existence truly presents us with a problem, to which some solution must be found….I would argue that absurdity is one of the most human things about us: a manifestation of our most advanced and interesting characteristics … . [I]t is possible only because we possess a certain kind of insight— the capacity to transcend ourselves in thought.

If a sense of the absurd is a way of perceiving our true situation … then what reason can we have to resent or escape it? … [I]t results from the ability to understand our human limitations. It need not be a matter for agony unless we make it so. Nor need it evoke a defiant contempt of fate that allows us to feel brave or proud. Such dramatics … betray a failure to appreciate the cosmic unimportance of the situation. If … there is no reason to believe that anything matters, then that does not matter either, and we can approach our absurd lives with irony instead of heroism or despair.

[From Thomas Nagel, *Mortal Questions* (Cambridge: Cambridge University Press, 1979), pp. 11—23.]

Understand Concepts

1. Explain how the circumstances of Viktor Frankl's life helped to shape his philosophy of life.
2. What is the central important factor, according to Frankl, in developing one's philosophy of life?
3. Read the selection "The Absurd" by Thomas Nagel. What is his idea of "the absurd"?

Think Critically

4. Is it possible for a life that has pain and suffering in it still to have meaning, according to Frankl? How can this be?
5. Summarize Nagel's argument in the selection "The Absurd." What main conclusion does he reach?

Review and Reflect

As we have seen, philosophy deals with many important topics. One such subject is that of determining a "philosophy of life." Each one of us asks ourselves, at one time or another—and sometimes quite often—the two questions that are involved in developing a philosophy of life: How should I live my life and what is my life's meaning or purpose? Philosophers and non-philosophers alike have pondered these weighty issues.

This chapter presented some potential answers to these questions. Like many other important topics these ready-made answers are only meant to be guidelines. In the long run we must come up with our own answers to these questions and, in fact, develop our own philosophy of life. As many have said, this search—this self-examination— is both challenging and necessary if we are to live our lives to the fullest.

Perhaps this is true of many of the philosophical questions we have been addressing in this book. It is the journey, the questions asked and the search for answers, that is important. The study of philosophy can help us on this journey and this quest for truth, and provide us with interesting avenues to explore. In the long run, however, we travel our own path, and search for our own destination. This is both the challenge, and the excitement, of philosophy.

and power, 468-69

Lao-Tzu, on the meaning of life, 638-40

Laplace, Pierre
on natural determinism, 395, 397
"Philosophical Essay on Probability," 396

Lenin, Vladimir, 527

Leonardo da Vinci, 8, 585
"The Painter," 591

liberalism, 506-10
and distributive justice, 553

libertarianism, 397, 535
and distributive justice, 552-53

liberty, 558-60
see also freedom

Locke, John, 114
"Civil Government," 452
Essay Concerning Human Understanding, 115, 117-18, 325-28, 359-60
on government, 451-52
on personal identity, 324-25
"Political Power and the Family," 268
on reality, 358-60
"The Self," 325-28
theory of knowledge, 115-16

logic, 9, 29, 58
formal, 29, 30-32
informal, 29, 48-51

logical fallacies, types of, 54-56

logotherapy, 650-51

M

Machiavelli, Niccolò, 474-75
The Prince, 475-76

Mackie, J.L., 392
"Evil and Omnipotence," 439-40

Man's Search For Meaning (Frankl), 651

Marcel, Gabriel, 196

Marx, Karl, 430, 515-17, 527
"The Communist Manifesto," 517-19

material objects, 355
see also matter

materialism
on mind and body, 314, 318
and reality, 346, 368-70

mathematics, 65-66, 71-72, 110

matriarchal society, 266

matter, 358-59
primary and secondary qualities of (Locke), 115-16, 359-60
see also materialism

McClelland, Susan, "A Return to Earth," 414-15

The McMullin Plumbing Case, 207-08

meaning of life, 635, 636, 656
and the absurd, 652-53
and logotherapy, 650-51
and relationships, 642-44
and the self, 644-48
and Stoicism, 640-41
and virtue, 638-40

medical ethics, 208-10

Meier, Chana, 412

memory, and personal identity, 324-28

Mencius, 226, 227

men's movement, 298-99

metaphysics, 9, 11, 64, 305, 345
views of reality, 346

Middle Ages, 95

Mill, James, 506
"An Essay on Government," 508

Mill, John Stuart, 178-79
on ethics, 180
on freedom, 480
on minority rights, 509
On Liberty, 481-83
"Representative Government," 510
The Subjection of Women, 179, 277-78
Utilitarianism, 180-81

mind and body
and behaviourism, 318
in Buddhism, 335-36
Descartes on material objects, 355
the Ghost in the Machine, 320-21
and materialism, 318
and personal identity, 308-16

Mohammed, 166-67

monotheism, 163, 410

moral philosophy *see* ethics

Mother Teresa, 229

Mussolini, Benito, 483-84, 527-28

mystic theology, 416

mysticism, and reality, 346

N

Nagarjuna, 105

Nagel, Thomas, 652
"The Absurd," 652-53

natural philosophy, 5, 64-69
and reality, 348-49

natural theology, 415-16

nature-nurture debate, 223, 250

Nazism, 527-29, 532

Newton, Isaac, 368

and concept of God, 409

Newton, Lisa H., 572

Ng, Roxana, 294-95
"Racism, Sexism and Immigrant Women," 295-96

Nietzsche, Friedrich, 185
Beyond Good and Evil, 186

Nirvana, 158

Nolen, Stephanie, "Cost of Rebuilding After War $4.9 Billion, Bank Says," 554

Nozick, Robert, 558
"Liberty and the State," 559-60

numbers, 65-66, 71-72

O

observation, 40-42, 44-45
Bacon's scientific methodology, 104
and science, 128

ontological argument
on the existence of God, 421-22
St. Anselm's argument, 422-23

original sin, 229, 230

P

pantheism, 408

Parks, Rosa, 488-89

Parmenides, 67, 68, 349

patriarchal society, 266

Peacocke, Dr. Arthur, 412

personal attack, 54

personal identity, 305, 307, 344
Carl Jung on, 340-41, 342
David Hume on, 330-32
Descartes on mind and body, 310-13
John Locke on memory, 325-28
and memory, 324-25
and the mind, 308-09
and psychology, 340-42
Sigmund Freud on, 340-41
views on mind and body, 314-16

Phaedo (Plato), 221, 222

philosophers, 4, 8

philosophic inquiry
in everyday life, 19-20
on the existence of God, 420-25
process of, 16-19

philosophy, 28
and aesthetics, 583
and art, 581, 583-88
branches of, 9, 11-14
definition, 3
Eastern, 67-68

pg 2 ©John Mardon, pg 3 ©Bettmann/CORBIS/MAGMA, pg 4 ©Arte & Immagini srl/CORBIS/MAGMA, pg 5 ©Bettmann/CORBIS/MAGMA, pg 7 ©Francis G. Mayer/CORBIS/MAGMA, pg 8 ©Bettmann/CORBIS/MAGMA, pg 9 ©Michael S. Yamashita/CORBIS/MAGMA, pg 11 ©Craig Aurness/CORBIS/MAGMA, pg 12 ©Bettmann/CORBIS/MAGMA, pg 13 ©Reuters NewMedia Inc./CORBIS/MAGMA, pg 14 ©CP, pg 18 ©Archivo Iconografico, S.A./ CORBIS/MAGMA, pg 22 ©Digital Art/CORBIS/MAGMA, pg 29 ©Matt Tweed, reprinted with permission by Walker & Company, pg 30 ©CP, pg 36 ©Bettmann/CORBIS/MAGMA, pg 38 ©Lester Lefkowitz/CORBIS/MAGMA, pg 42 ©JulieHouck/CORBIS/MAGMA, ©Digital ART/CORBIS/MAGMA, ©Steve McDonough/CORBIS/MAGMA, ©Robert Semeniuk/CORBIA/MAGMA, ©Philip Marazzi/CORBIS/MAGMA, pg 46 ©Bettmann/CORBIS/MAGMA, pg 49 ©Ariel Skelley/CORBIS/MAGMA, pg 51 ©CP, pg 55 ©H.Prinz/CORBIS/MAGMA, pg 59 ©Bojan Brecelj/CORBIS/MAGMA, pg 60 ©Bettmann/CORBIS/MAGMA, pg 64 ©John Mardon, pg 66 ©Zach Gold/CORBIS/MAGMA, pg 68 ©CORBIS/MAGMA, pg 70 ©Freeman Patterson, pg 71 ©Archivo Icongraphico S.A./COR-BIS/MAGMA, pg 74 ©Bettmann/CORBIS/MAGMA, pg 78 ©Richard Hamilton Smith/CORBIS OUTLINE/MAGMA, pg 79 ©Bettmann/CORBIS/MAGMA, ©Bettmann/CORBIS/MAGMA, pg 80 ©Jeffrey L. Rotman/CORBIS/MAGMA, pg 82 ©CORBIS/MAGMA, pg 85 ©Bettmann/CORBIS/MAGMA, pg 88 ©Archivo Iconografico, S.A./CORBIS/MAGMA, pg 93 ©Richard T. Nowitz, pg 94 ©Japack Company/CORBIS/MAGMA, pg 96 ©Bettmann/CORBIS/MAGMA, ©Christie's Images/CORBIS/MAGMA, pg 99 ©AFP/CORBIS/MAGMA, pg 100 ©Leonard de Selva/CORBIS/MAGMA, pg 102 ©Michael Nicholson/CORBIS/MAGMA, pg 104 ©Art Becker Photo/CORBIS/MAGMA, pg 108 ©Bettmann/CORBIS/MAGMA, pg 110 ©Bettmann/CORBIS/MAGMA, pg 114 ©Bettmann/CORBIS/MAGMA, pg 116 ©Richard Hamilton Smith/CORBIS/MAGMA, pg 118 ©Bettmann/CORBIS/MAGMA, pg 122 ©Christie's Images/CORBIS/MAGMA, pg 124 ©Chris Simpson; Cordaiy Photo Library Ltd./CORBIS/MAGMA, pg 126 ©William White-hurst/CORBIS/MAGMA, pg 127 ©Hulton-Deutsch Collection/CORBIS/MAGMA, ©Steve CHEN/CORBIS/MAGMA, ©Roger Ressmey-er/CORBIS/MAGMA, pg 128 ©Paul Hardy/CORBIS/MAGMA, pg 132 © Stanley Rowin, pg 134 ©Bettmann/CORBIS/MAGMA, pg 138 ©Bruce Burkhardt/CORBIS/MAGMA, pg 139 ©Bettmann/CORBIS/MAGMA, pg 141 ©Tim Wright/CORBIS/MAGMA, pg 145 ©Michael St. Maur Sheil/CORBIS/Magma, pg 146 ©Araldo de Luca/CORBIS/MAGMA, pg 150 ©Julie Dennis Brothers/CORBIS/MAGMA, pg 152 ©MAPS.com/CORBIS/MAGMA, pg 153 ©Bettmann/CORBIS/MAGMA, pg 154 ©Araldo de Luca/CORBIS/MAGMA, pg 156 ©Sheldon Collins/CORBIS/MAGMA, pg 157 ©David Samuel Robbins/CORBIS/MAGMA, pg 160 ©Historical Picture Archive/CORBIS/MAGMAN, pg 162 ©Chris Hellier/CORBIS/MAGMA, pg 163 Christie's Images/CORBIS/MAGMA, pg 165 ©Massimo Listri/CORBIS/MAGMA, pg 168 ©Bettmann/CORBIS/MAGMA, pg 171 ©Araldo de Luca/CORBIS/MagMA, pg 172 ©Archivo Iconografico, S.A./CORBIS/MAGMA, pg 176 ©Bettmann/CORBIS/MAGMA, pg 178 ©COR-BIS/MAGMA, pg 179 ©Hulton-Deutsch Collection/CORBIS/MAGMA, pg 181 ©Yann Arthus-Bertrand/CORBIS/MAGMA, pg 184 ©Laura Dwight/CORBIS/MAGMA, pg 185 ©Bettmann/CORBIS/MAGMA, pg 188 © Bettmann/CORBIS/MAGMA, pg 189 © Bettmann/CORBIS/MAGMA, pg 190 ©Arne Hodalic/CORBIS/MAGMA, pg 192 ©Bettmann/CORBIS/MAGMA, pg 195 ©Peter Turn-ley/CORBIS/MAGMA, pg 198 ©Stephen Frink/CORBIS/MAGMA, pg 199 ©Reuters MewMedia Inc./CORBIS/MAGMA, pg 200 ©COR-BIS/MAGMA, ©Bart Harris/CORBIS/MAGMA, ©Wolfgang Kaehler/CORBIS/MAGMA, pg 202 ©Laura Dwight/CORBIS/MAGMA, pg 204 ©Jerry Cooke/CORBIS/MAGMA, pg 209 ©Bettmann/CORBIS/MAGMA, pg 214 ©Bettmann/CORBIS/MAGMA, pg 215 ©Paul A. Souders/CORBIS/MAGMA, pg 218 ©Bettmann/CORBIS/MAGMA, pg 220 ©David H. Wells/CORBIS/MAGMA, pg 223 ©Hulton-Deutsch Collection/CORBIS/MAGMA, pg 228 ©Burstein Collection/CORBIS/MAGMA, pg 234 ©Leonard del Selva/CORBIS/MAGMA, pg 235 ©Hulton-Deutsch Collection/CORBIS/MAGMA, pg pg 237 ©Bettmann/CORBIS/MAGMA, ©242 ©Hulton-Deutsch Collec-tion/CORBIS/MAGMA, pg 243 ©Hulton-Deutsch/COBIS/MAGMA, pg 244 ©John Drysdale/CORBIS/MAGMA, pg 246 ©Bettmann/CORBIS/MAGMA, pg 247 ©Bohemian Nomad Picturemakers/CORBIS/MAGMA, pg 250 ©Digital Art/CORBIS/MAGMA, pg 252 ©Bettmann/CORBIS/MAGMA, pg 254-255 ©E.O. Hoppé/CORBIS/MAGMA, ©Wolfgang Kaehler/CORBIS/MAGMA, ©Lindsay Hebbetd/CORBIS/MAGMA, ©Reuters NewMedia Inc./CORBIS/MAGMA, pg 259 ©Bettmann/CORBIS/MAGMA, pg 260 ©Gianni Dagli Orti/CORBIS/MAGMA, pg 266 ©Bettmann/CORBIS/MAGMA, pg 267 ©Michael Nicholson/CORBIS/MAGMA, pg 269 ©Carl & Ann Purcell/CORBIS/MAGMA, pg 270 ©Bettmann/COBIS/MAGMA, pg 272 ©Hulton-Deutsch Collection/CORBIS/MAGMA, pg 273 ©Archivo Iconografico, S.A./CORBIS/MAGMA, pg 275 ©Swim Ink/CORBIS/MAGMA, pg 278 ©Hulton-Deutsch Collection/COR-BOS/MAGMA, pg 280 © Hulton-Deutsch Collection/CORBOS/MAGMA, pg 281 ©Northern Indiana Center for History, pg 282 ©Roger Ressmeyer/CORBIS/MAGMA, pg 283 ©Hulton-Deutsch Collection/CORBIS/MAGMA, pg 285 National Archives of Canada, pg 286 ©Bettmann/CORBIS /MAGMA, pg 288 CP, pg 290 ©Natalie Fobes/CORBIS/MAGMA, pg 294 ©AFP/CORBIS/MAGMA, pg 296 ©Ariel Skelley/CORBIS/MAGMA, pg 299 ©Hulton-Deutsch Collection/CORBIS/MAGMA, pg 306 ©ACS Science and Engineering Team, NASA, pg 307 ©Janet Skok/CORBIS/MAGMA, pg 309 ©Najlah Feanny/CORBIS/MAGMA, pg 319 ©Otto Rogers, reprinted with per-